Models
of Man

edited by

Antony J. Chapman and Dylan M. Jones

The British
Psychological Society

Published by The British Psychological Society
St Andrews House, 48 Princess Road East, Leicester LE1 7DR

© 1980 The British Psychological Society

Reprinted 1981, 1984

ISBN 0 901715 12 3 Cased
0 901715 11 5 Paper

Printed in Great Britain by Clark Constable (1982) Ltd.

Preface

As psychological conferences become more numerous so a greater proportion of them seem to adopt a narrow focus. Whether this is a symptom of a general fragmentation and isolation within the discipline of psychology is a matter for conjecture. In any case a narrowing of scope may not in itself be a bad thing, but it does have at least one undesirable side-effect: it leaves little room for discussion of broad issues, for taking stock, for charting progress, for statements about one's theoretical or empirical stance. Conferences have increasingly become meetings of like minds rather than forums for debate and argument. It was partly out of this observation that the Conference on 'Models of Man' was conceived, and this book is based upon that Conference.

The Conference took place in Cardiff, under the auspices of the Welsh Branch of The British Psychological Society between 2 and 6 July 1979. Its aim was to identify 'ways of working', research strategies and tacit assumptions employed by leading figures drawn from the spectrum of British psychology. The emphasis was on illuminating the similarities and differences between the various approaches with an eye to both practical and theoretical constraints. The aim was not to attempt a synthesis of a single unitary model: our own view is that such an ambition would be absurd. Indeed, by design, some of our participants were invited because they were known even to be opposed to the adoption of any model. In the pages that follow, therefore, the reader can find many fundamental notes of disagreement, some less muted than others. As a published account of the Conference proceedings we believe that this volume offers a reasonable representation of present-day opinion in psychology.

Given the aims of the Conference it became plain at a very preliminary stage of planning that as much time as possible should be spent in discussion. So, in 1977, we began to plan 'Models of Man' in the form of an extended symposium. In the end there were 20 papers in the programme, each of 40 minutes duration, presented over a period of 5 days, with considerably more time given to discussion than to the oral presentation of papers. On the middle 3 days of the Conference, the debates began at nine in the morning and ended at ten in the evening. The number of participants was restricted to 100, and they sustained that regime without any signs of rebellion. No doubt this was partly because of the briefing given to everyone in advance of the Conference itself. Extended abstracts and reading lists were issued beforehand and these were effective in priming the discussion. Chairmen, discussants and speakers were circulated with extended versions of papers (each approximately 10,000 words) over a period of several months before the Conference. Aside from the speakers those participants with the most exacting roles were the chairmen and discussants. Their chief duty was to guide discussion in review sessions during the evenings. The breadth and diversity of the discussion which took place is a tribute to their hard work in preparing for the Conference. We are especially grateful to our Conference Chairmen, Harry Kay and Kevin Connolly, and to our Overseas Discussant, Georges Thinès.

Much of our work after the Conference was in transcribing and editing the tape-recordings of discussion. In this volume the discussions do not always appear in their original order, and nor does the order of chapters correspond exactly to the Conference schedule. One reason for the new arrangements is that some themes which were developed early were later revived and in arranging the chapters and items of discussion we have sought maximum coherence and minimum repetition. To the same ends, discussion sections have undergone considerable truncation: a full, verbatim account would have extended to about three volumes. Some of the speakers' 'chapters' (Section I) have undergone minor revision since they were circulated, in advance of the Conference. The shorter 'papers' (Section II) were contributed by chairmen and discussants after the Conference. In some cases their principal value is that they elaborate upon issues which were not fully vented in the discussions. Some of them underline themes, and some present perspectives which were not exposed sufficiently during the Conference. A general review of the Conference is provided by Georges Thinès at the end of the volume, and some 'reflections and recollections' are provided by Harry Kay and Kevin Connolly in the Foreword.

No conference, particularly one of this sort, can be initiated or sustained without the goodwill and active support of organizations and individuals. In the first instance the Committee of the BPS Welsh Branch was a reliable source of goodwill and encouragement. The Conference was mounted against a backdrop of several successful Welsh Branch conferences, beginning in 1976, and consequently there was a fund of experience and expertise to draw upon. We have already implied that the depth of discussion, and hence the quality of the Conference generally, was enhanced by its relatively small size (100 participants) and by the precirculation of literature. The Social Science Research Council, in awarding a conference grant, helped to accomplish those objectives. The grant also assisted the attendance of 24 new/young research workers. The UWIST Department of Applied Psychology provided a convivial setting for the Conference, and we were able to call upon its excellent technical and clerical staff.

Several individuals contributed in major ways to the shaping of the programme and, in this regard, Donald Broadbent, Anthony Gale, John Shotter and Peter Warr deserve special mention. There is one person who we would dare to say was indispensable to the Conference, and he is Eric Hellerman. He undertook all the printing and photocopying work, and he always did so with good humour and diligence. Liz Clarke, Jane Francis, Cynthia Couch and Joan Joshua bore the brunt of the typing, and to them we offer much thanks. At the Conference many of the day-to-day arrangements, to do with accommodation, registration and tape-recording, were undertaken by colleagues and students. They provided an essential infrastructure for the smooth running of the Conference: crises were averted, queries answered and tempers placated. We are indebted to Tim Auburn, Noel Sheehy and Russell Thomas, and to Jean Chapman, Siriol David, John Gallacher, Alec Gill, Juliet Gordon, Corky Gormly, Catherine Khorshidian, Shirley Reynolds, and Marina Tilic. In preparing the indexes and bibliography for the book we were assisted enormously by Margaret Jones and Siriol David.

Our enduring memory of the Conference is of the vigour and good humour in the presentations and discussions. Our hope is that the record in these pages stands as adequate testimony to that week in July 1979.

TONY CHAPMAN
DYLAN JONES
December 1979, UWIST, Cardiff

Contents

SECTION I: SPEAKERS' CONTRIBUTIONS

DISCUSSANTS' AND CHAIRMEN'S COMMENTARIES

Contributors

H. BELOFF: Department of Psychology, University of Edinburgh, 7 George Square, Edinburgh EH8 9JZ.

D. E. BLACKMAN: Department of Psychology, University College Cardiff, PO Box 78, Cardiff CF1 1XL.

M. A. BODEN: School of Social Sciences, Arts Building, University of Sussex, Falmer, Brighton BN1 9QN.

J. M. BRENER: Department of Psychology, The University, Hull HU6 7RX.

D. E. BROADBENT: Department of Experimental Psychology, University of Oxford, South Parks Road, Oxford OX1 3UD.

A. J. CHAPMAN: Department of Applied Psychology, University of Wales Institute of Science and Technology, Llwyn-y-Grant Road, Cardiff CF3 7UX.

N. M. CHESHIRE: Department of Psychology, University College of North Wales, Bangor, Gwynnedd LL57 2DG.

K. J. CONNOLLY: Department of Psychology, University of Sheffield, Sheffield S10 2TN.

K. D. DUNCAN: Department of Applied Psychology, University of Wales Institute of Science and Technology, Llwyn-y-Grant Road, Cardiff CF3 7UX.

H. J. EYSENCK: Department of Psychology, University of London Institute of Psychiatry, De Crespigny Park, Denmark Hill, London SE5 8AF.

R. M. FARR: Department of Psychology, Adam Smith Building, University of Glasgow, Glasgow G12 8RT.

F. FRANSELLA: Academic Department of Psychiatry, University of London, Royal Free Hospital School of Medicine, Pond Street, London NW3 2QG.

A. GALE: Department of Psychology, University of Southampton, Southampton SO9 5NH.

J. A. GRAY: Department of Experimental Psychology, University of Oxford, South Parks Road, Oxford OX1 3UD.

D. H. HARGREAVES: Department of Educational Studies, University of Oxford, 15 Norham Gardens, Oxford OX2 6PY.

R. HARRE: Sub-Faculty of Philosophy, University of Oxford, 10 Merton Street, Oxford OX1 4JJ.

C. I. HOWARTH: Department of Psychology, University of Nottingham, University Park, Nottingham NG7 2RD.

G. JAHODA: Department of Psychology, University of Strathclyde, Turnbull Building, 155 George Street, Glasgow G1 1RD.

M. JAHODA: Science Policy Research Unit, University of Sussex, Mantell Building, Falmer, Brighton BN1 9RF.

D. M. JONES: Department of Applied Psychology, University of Wales Institute of Science and Technology, Llwyn-y-Grant Road, Cardiff CF3 7UX.

R. B. JOYNSON: Department of Psychology, University of Nottingham, University Park, Nottingham NG7 2RD.

H. KAY: University of Exeter, Northcote House, The Queen's Drive, Exeter EX4 4QJ.

R. P. KELVIN: Department of Psychology, University College London, Gower Street, London WC1E 6BT.

P. KLINE: Department of Psychology, Washington Singer Laboratories, University of Exeter, Exeter EX4 4QC.

A. J. LOCK: Department of Psychology, University of Lancaster, Fylde College, Bailrigg, Lancaster LA1 4YF.

E. MILLER: Department of Clinical Psychology, Addenbrooke's Hospital, 2 Bene't Place, Lensfield Road, Cambridge CB2 1EL.

R. L. REID: Department of Psychology, Washington Singer Laboratories, University of Exeter, Exeter EX4 4QG.

V. REYNOLDS: Department of Biological Anthropology, University of Oxford, 58 Banbury Road, Oxford OX2 6QS.

J. SHOTTER: Department of Psychology, University of Nottingham, University Park, Nottingham NG7 2RD.

A. STILL: Department of Psychology, University of Durham, Science Laboratories, South Road, Durham DH1 3LE.

G. THINES: Centre de Psychologie Expérimentale et Comparée, Université de Louvain, B-3041 Pellenberg, Belgium.

D. WALLIS: Department of Applied Psychology, University of Wales Institute of Science and Technology, Llwyn-y-Grant Road, Cardiff CF3 7UX.

P. B. WARR: MRC Social and Applied Psychology Unit, Department of Psychology, The University, Sheffield S10 2TN.

N. E. WETHERICK: Department of Psychology, King's College, University of
Aberdeen, Old Aberdeen AB9 2UB.

D. J. WOOD: Department of Psychology, University of Nottingham, University
Park, Nottingham NG7 2RD.

D. S. WRIGHT: School of Education, University of Leicester, 21 University
Road, Leicester LE1 7RF.

Contributors to edited discussion (additional to those listed above)

A. P. BAILLIE: London School of Economics

D. B. BROMLEY: University of Liverpool

J. H. CLARK: University of Manchester

H. COWIE: Whitelands College, London.

G. DELAFIELD: University College Cork, Eire

B. FLETCHER: Hatfield Polytechnic

N. FRUDE: University College Cardiff

K. J. GERGEN: Swarthmore College, USA

J. GREENE: Open University

M. M. GRUNEBERG: University College Swansea

P. HERRIOT: City University, London

M. J. MORGAN: University of Durham

H. PRICE: University College Cardiff

I. ROTH: Open University

L. SMITH: University of Leicester

S. G. STRADLING: University of Salford

J. TURNER: University of Bristol

I. VINE: University of Bradford

H. WEINREICH-HASTE: University of Bath

that all dichotomies are misleading.   But then, 'the middle of the road is a dangerous place' and our practice is to test ideas to destruction.   Perhaps different standpoints have to be exaggerated in order that their strengths and limitations may become evident.   What we should beware of are those dichotomies that have had a long innings in psychology and have often been harmful, for example, the great nature versus nurture debate.

In the physical sciences, in much of biology and in the greater part of experimental psychology for the past 100 years the kind of explanation sought has been reductive in character.   The scientist has looked for antecedent causes.   So evident is this in psychology that many students believe that here lies 'the' explanation.   On the other hand, the social sciences have developed different models from those in the physical sciences where often they have become laws or high-level generalizations which can be used in applied science, in engineering design and technology.   In the social sciences, models are often mathematically naive and not always open to experimental verification.   These abstract types of model are open to the dangers of extreme simplification and the consequent distortion of reality.   It is well to bear in mind that models are rarely abandoned when found to be inadequate; they are patched up and adapted in an ad hoc way. Generally we cling to them until some better model comes along.   Only then are they consigned to the graveyard of the conceptual history of a discipline.

It follows that we must not expect every model, irrespective of the phenomena with which it is concerned, to conform to some idealized theoretical standard. Some of the models available in psychology, often in highly circumscribed areas, are powerful tools for thought and valuable predictive instruments.   In other areas our models are frankly poor but, for the present, they are all we have.   Prudence and shrewdness would indicate that we do not blithely abandon them because we know that they are wanting, rather we should attempt to refine or replace them with something distinctly better.

But much of what was discussed at the conference went beyond a formal examination of models.   Rather, it was concerned with the proper study of psychology.   What is it that psychology and psychologists should be doing?   Most of us have our own views about this and usually they accord only too well with what we ourselves are engaged in.   Functional autonomy is a powerful agent.   Looking back on the discussions it would seem that the major divide between us was indeed the mechanist/humanist issue.   Is psychology the study of behaviour or the study of mind, the search for antecedent causes or for purposes, the effort to understand brain-behaviour relationships or personal motives?   But at the risk of seeming trite, it became ever clearer that all of these studies were legitimate and were ably defended by their protagonists.   The behaviourist was not prepared to let himself be labelled as a muscle-twitch specialist; he was concerned with acts and could engage in dialogue with the humanist, who for his part was content to point out that there was no proof that behaviour could, or could not, be explained in terms of physical events.   As the conference neared its end our abiding impression was that the exchanges had brought considerable understanding of quite different approaches to the study of man; that in spite of the theoretical orientation of the conference, there was strong support for the empirical method and for beginning the study of problems in real-life situations.   It was clear that the conference accepted that if there is a right answer it is very likely there is more than one right way of finding out.   On that note the participants folded their tents - but it is no prediction to say they will be back.

Section I

Speakers' contributions

Chapter 1

Models of man: 1879–1979

R. B. Joynson

PSYCHOLOGY FROM TWO STANDPOINTS

It may be said that at present the psychological world is divided into two camps; on the one side are the champions of mechanism, on the other side the champions of the person. The first camp makes its headquarters in biological psychology; animal behaviour provides the key to man's more complex functions, and objective experiment is the preferred method. The second camp is more loosely organized and more varied in its opinions; its adherents are more likely to be found in clinical, differential and social psychology; they employ self-report and conceptual analysis, and prefer purposive to mechanistic explanation.

Any such division is certainly a great over-simplification. There are many shades of opinion in each camp; some theorists combine aspects of both; yet others are hard to place in these terms at all. But it provides a useful first approximation to the different kinds of 'models of man' that we are likely to encounter in psychology today, and reminds us that this division in psychology is part of a much wider debate in philosophy and the social sciences generally, which Hollis, in 'Models of Man' (1977), terms the rivalry between 'plastic' and 'autonomous' man.

This chapter is concerned with the historical background of the division in psychology. Neither camp has sprung up overnight; each has a long and chequered past. Indeed, the argument between them forms a central theme in the history of psychology. Often the argument is merely repetitive and rancorous, but it may also be seen more hopefully as a necessary dialogue between positions which may prove to be complementary rather than mutually exclusive. Each stimulates the other to formulate its views more exactly, and the tension between them drives psychology forward. The relation between them, at least in its more productive phases, recalls the analogy which William James used to describe the cooperation between analysis and synthesis in the development of mental life; they are 'the incessantly alternating mental activities, a stroke of the one preparing the way for a stroke of the other, much as, in walking, a man's two legs are alternately brought into use, both being necessary for any orderly advance' (James, 1890, I, p. 550).

Some observations in Howarth's chapter on 'The structure of effective psychology' (11) are relevant here. He too begins by remarking that psychologists fall into two camps, and the distinction which he draws, between 'mechanists' and 'humanists', is very similar to that made here. Howarth argues that the theoretical differences between the camps tend to obscure the remarkable extent to which applied psychologists borrow their techniques from both. Effective practice often demands this more catholic approach; in his words, 'To be effective, psychologists must be both humanists and mechanists' (p. 145). A satisfactory account of psychological history requires, I believe, a similar willingness to find room for the contribution of each.

This is an opportune time to consider the history of psychology, for the year 1979 marks the centenary of the foundation by Wundt of the first psychological laboratory. It was Wundt, perhaps more than anyone else, who gave impetus to the belief that the competing philosophies of human nature were destined to give place to a system of scientific law, and this is accordingly a great event in the calendar of the mechanist. The humanist, on the other hand, will regard it with a more quizzical eye. If we ask what progress psychology has made during the past 100 years towards the status of a natural science, the question is not only topical, it is also central to the long debate between the rival camps.

In considering this question, I want to begin by asking the reader to look again at that famous passage with which James concluded his 'Briefer Course', written in 1892 when psychology stood upon the threshold of its modern development. This passage is remarkable not only for the vivid description which James gives of the position from which psychology was starting, and the goal at which it should aim, but also because, in his concluding sentences, James made a very important qualification, which is rarely quoted yet contains the most essential part of what he wanted to convey.

The earlier part of this concluding section gives James's well-known description of psychology in the 1890s:

A string of raw facts; a little gossip and wrangle about opinion; a little classification and generalization on the mere descriptive level ... but not a single law in the sense in which physics shows us laws, not a single proposition from which any consequence can causally be deduced ... This is no science, it is only the hope of a science ... At present psychology is in the condition of physics before Galileo and the laws of motion, of chemistry before Lavoisier and the notion that mass is preserved in all reactions.

But then came his qualification:

The Galileo and the Lavoisier of psychology will be famous men indeed when they come, as come they some day surely will, or past successes are no index to the future. When they do come, however, the necessities of the case will make them 'metaphysical'. Meanwhile the best way in which we can facilitate their advent is to understand how great is the darkness in which we grope, and never to forget that the natural-science assumptions with which we started are provisional and revisable things. (James, 1892, p. 335)

The emphasis which James gives to the discovery of laws analogous to those of physics, and the strength of his conviction that the Galileo of psychology will one day come, are enough to satisfy the most tough-minded of mechanists. But the suggestion that psychology's Galileo will also be 'metaphysical', and that natural-science assumptions are provisional, strikes a much less welcome note. In saying that he will be 'metaphysical' James is harking back to his comments, earlier in his book, upon the difficulties of applying the conventional scientific modes of thinking to the subject matter of psychology. Psychologists, he there said, tend to adopt as a working hypothesis the notion that states of mind correspond to states of the brain; but this becomes obscure in the extreme as soon as we try to determine precisely what 'corresponds' means, and what in fact are the elements which 'correspond'. Psychology is concerned with the relations between the knower and the known, which physics leaves aside, and 'a genial, whole-hearted, popular-science way of formulating them will not suffice' (James, 1892, p. 333). In short, James is warning that psychology's philosophical connections cannot simply be swept aside as 'pre-scientific', but demand a special caution and flexibility.

Psychologists in general, however, have brushed such warnings aside, or accepted only those philosophical assumptions which supported their scientific preconceptions. In consequence, the contribution of the traditional philosophical psychology has too often been underrated. It played a crucial role in the foundation of psychology as an independent discipline in the late 19th century, which extended far beyond the narrow confines of Wundt's 'new psychology' of experiment. It is in this tradition that we find the origins of our two camps, and this must be our starting-point in any attempt to understand where they came from, and hence how far they have now travelled.

THE ACHIEVEMENT OF THE FOUNDERS

James began his 'Principles of Psychology' (1890) by observing that psychology had traditionally contained two contrasting ways of attempting to bring order into the chaos of mental life. These were the theory of faculties and the theory of association, and they are the prototypes of 'autonomous' and 'plastic' man. The 'theory of faculties' was described by James as the most natural way of unifying the material, and as the theory of common sense. Our ordinary language refers to people carrying out various activities: I remembered ... you believed ... he decided. Faculty theory is fundamentally in sympathy with this way of talking. It attempts to explore the implications of our common-sense understanding, and make it more reasonable and comprehensive. Thus it postulates a simple entity, the personal soul, which manifests its nature in various natural powers or abilities. Numerous lists of supposed faculties were drawn up by different writers, but they were eventually superseded by the Kantian analysis, according to which any mental activity displayed at once a knowing, a willing and a feeling aspect.

The 'theory of association' adopted a much finer analysis. It sought for 'common elements in the diverse mental facts rather than a common agent behind them' (James, 1890, I, p. 1). The elements were found in the sensory units, with their imaginal copies, which impinged upon the mind through the senses. The gradual growth and elaboration of mental life was then pictured as the forging of links among these elements through the mechanical principle of habit or association, which established trains of ideas corresponding to the sequence of events in experience. Thus the 'agent' and its 'faculties' cease to be principles of explanation, but are themselves explained in other terms. This was the 'psychology without a soul' which challenged the notions of common sense at every turn.

Allport, in 'Becoming' (1955), has labelled these two traditions the Leibnitzian and the Lockean respectively, from their philosophical forbears. For the Leibnitzian, the person is the source of acts; for the Lockean, man is passive until roused by stimulation from without. In the late 19th century they still provided the major theoretical alternatives, and exerted a strong influence on the new movements which were then taking shape. In this period their leading exponents were Brentano and Wundt, each offering a distinctive conception of the way ahead. For Brentano, the essence of mental life lay in intentional activity, and he stressed the variety of different empirical approaches that were required. For Wundt, the analysis of the sensory content of mind took priority, and this was to be achieved in the context of the laboratory. This contrast between the 'spiritualist' and the 'associationist' positions, a century ago, forms an intriguing parallel to the contemporary debate between 'humanists' and 'mechanists'.

The traditional psychology was transformed during the second half of the 19th century by a remarkable series of new explorations. They may be grouped roughly under the heads of physiological, experimental, pathological and differential psychology, and depended closely upon the growth of other sciences with obvious implications for psychology. They introduced fresh data and methods which dramatically increased the scope of the subject. Previously restricted to the self-reports of the normal adult, it now embraced the child, the animal, the abnormal and the primitive, and began to include experimental and statistical methods. These new approaches were initially seen, not as replacing, but as extending and perfecting the traditional modes of investigation. Wundt conceived the laboratory as permitting more accurate introspection, while the French psychologist Ribot, in his opening address to the first International Congress of Psychology (held at Paris in 1889), declared that 'psychology advances by combining physiological and pathological observation and experiment with the older introspective method' (James, 1889). Much of the perennial fascination of James's 'Principles' must be attributed to his remarkable capacity to weave together the traditional philosophical material and the newer empirical findings.

It was natural, then, that these new explorations were often profoundly influenced by traditional ideas. Psychology was generally regarded as the study of mind, depending primarily on self-observation. Hence even new fields such as animal psychology, where direct introspection was obviously out of the question, were nevertheless cast in this mould. For Lloyd Morgan, the task of the animal psychologist was to 'impute' the appropriate mental process to the animal, in the light of analogies between its behaviour and that of human beings in comparable circumstances. Again, in early physiological psychology discussion often centred round the question of where, if anywhere, 'consciousness' might interact with nervous mechanisms.

It is important to note, however, that the kind of psychology which was utilized depended very much upon the particular problem under investigation. The early experimentalists were mainly concerned to discover the precise relationship between the simplest sensory experiences and the physical and physiological events with which they were connected, as in the psychophysical laws of Weber and Fechner. This interest in the simpler and more automatic forms of mental life, and their determination by environmental events, lent itself readily to an associationist framework. Similarly Ebbinghaus, in his pioneering experiments on memory, conceived his task as that of elucidating the precise conditions under which the elementary forms of association were established. Again, Janet's pathological studies centred round the concept of 'dissociation', a dismembering of mind, the reverse of association. It is probably safe to assert that, in general, those who were most desirous of treating psychology as a natural science thought it best to begin by studying the more elementary forms of mental life, and found associationism congenial. This is especially striking in the most influential of these new approaches, Wundt's 'new psychology' of experiment.

But even in these areas there was a reaction against associationist ideas as research progressed. Von Ehrenfels (1890) drew attention to certain forms of perceptual combination, such as shapes and tunes, which resisted analysis into sensory elements, and foreshadowed the Gestalt contribution. Muller repeated some of the experiments of Ebbinghaus and stressed the importance of actively grouping the material in contrast to sheer passive contiguity. The Wurzburg studies of thinking pointed to non-sensory components, and to 'determining tendencies' which were hard to explain in associationist terms. In general, there was a marked reaction against Wundt, and in favour of Brentano, as the century drew to its close. This was especially pronounced in British theoretical psychology where Ward (1886), and later Stout (1896), mounted a powerful critique of associationist views. Ward, in particular, developed a 'Leibnitzian' point of view which was out of sympathy with many of the contemporary scientific developments (Hearnshaw, 1964, p. 136). Those who were interested in the complexities of personality or social psychology were also sometimes inclined to suggest that psychology must be regarded as a cultural rather than a natural science.

The events of the later 19th century ensured that, in future, psychology would be far more extensive, and far more varied in its methods, than it had ever been in its traditional form, whether of the Lockean or the Leibnitzian variety. Indeed, when we now look back on the men who launched psychology upon its modern path, as shown for example in the membership of the early International Congresses (Paris, 1889; London, 1892; Munich, 1896), we are struck by the immense variety of points of view and background which they represented, ranging from physiology to sociology, and from philosophy to pathology. This was at once the strength and weakness of psychology. Its vast subject matter required the cooperation of numerous experts in different fields; yet this very variety posed immense problems in maintaining even the roughest unity, as was to be dramatically illustrated over the next 50 years. If these problems sometimes seem insuperable, one can nevertheless say that psychology seems well endowed with the contrasting forces that are needed to breed a 'metaphysical Galileo'.

One writer who did much to reconcile these conflicting forces was G.F. Stout, whose 'Analytic Psychology' (1896) marked the culmination of the traditional psychology. In his view, that 'time-honoured procedure' could in future be no more than a fragment of the whole, but he thought that its value was nevertheless immensely enhanced. It provided a general analysis of ordinary experience which was not only useful in itself but could also furnish a guide to those 'inland explorers' who were following more specialized lines of investigation, such as the physiological, the experimental, or the pathological. Such a conception offered a bridge between the old and the new, and also a means of reconciling differences among the newer investigations should they arise. Stout also did much to heal the breach between the associationists and their critics. 'It may be said that at present the psychological world is divided into two camps; on the one side are the champions of Association, on the other the champions of Apperception' (Stout, 1896, II, p. 41). Stout sided with the second party, but he found a place for association in his system. It was prominent in the simpler and more automatic forms of mental life, but gradually became less conspicuous in the more intelligent, highly developed, and attentive processes. The history of the next half-century might have been very different if Stout's uncombative temperament had been more widely distributed.

THE ACHIEVEMENT OF THE SCHOOLS

By the time James died in 1910, it was clear that there was to be no shortage of Galileos. In the first decade of the new century, they came thick and fast: behaviourists, Gestaltists, psychoanalysts, factor analysts - and a plentiful supply of lesser luminaries. Psychology was launched upon the period of the 'schools'. Each was convinced that it alone possessed the key to the scientific psychology of the future, but since each key was different it was clear that a long and difficult struggle lay ahead.

The schools typically arose in reaction against Wundt's 'new psychology' of experiment, itself the dominant scientific movement of the previous generation. But the temporary character of that once popular solution inevitably suggested that the schools themselves might prove ephemeral in their turn. Meanwhile, they dominated psychology with their divisions for the first half of the century, providing an unwelcome advertisement of the difficulty of creating a mental science. As Woodworth wrote in his 'Contemporary Schools' (1931, p. 3), a school 'is a group of psychologists who ... point the way that all must follow if psychology is ever to be made a genuine, productive science ... '. And as he added, rather wistfully, 'We have several such schools pointing in different directions'.

The major schools might be described as 20th century psychology's great 'models of man'. Each in effect claimed to have hit upon the system of generalizations which furnished 'laws as physics shows us laws'. But there seemed no satisfactory way of deciding among them. Each seemed to embody different modes of explanation, calling for different forms of verification. This makes it difficult, if not impossible, to trace in the first half of the century any single central tradition which could properly be regarded as constituting 'the' scientific psychology. Each school, of course, claimed to represent this central tradition, and deprecated the attempts of others to offer an alternative. But at least down to mid-century none could claim to have established its priority. The schools have become the skeletons in our scientific cupboard, all the more disturbing because they plainly belong to diverse species. The problem which the second half of the century has inherited from the first is that of coming to terms with their unresolved rivalries.

The rise of the schools was a disappointment to those who were hoping for the rapid emergence of a unified science, and there has sometimes been a tendency to play down their importance. But they represent a prodigious outburst of creative energy, and the task of the historian is to provide a perspective in which the permanent achievement of each can be given full weight. In pursuit of this aim, we may first note that, despite their revolutionary claims, the schools were a very natural outcome of late 19th century psychology. Each of the major schools tends to be especially closely related to one of those new fields of exploration which grew up in the 19th century. Thus behaviourism is a development within the field of physiological and animal psychology; Gestalt theory within human laboratory studies; psychoanalysis within pathological, and factor analysis within differential, psychology. The leaders of the schools might be described as the 'second generation' of 'inland explorers', each offering, in a particular research area, the methods and theories which were needed to exploit the new ground which the 'first generation' had opened up. These historical connections are further strengthened by the extent to which the founders of the schools derived some at least of their key ideas from their predecessors in these research areas. Thus Watson learned much from Loeb, Wertheimer from von Ehrenfels, Freud from Charcot, and Spearman from Galton. Their function was often to crystallize and apply what was already in the air, rather than invent an entirely novel approach.

Each school was of great value in providing the framework and inspiration needed within its particular field at that particular time. In a period of explosive growth, psychology needed all the schools, and if any had been missing the whole would have been poorer. But each school made the mistake of supposing that the standpoint which was appropriate in dealing with its own specialized problems was equally appropriate for psychology as a whole. Everything must be seen from this point of view, and from this point of view alone. The traditional psychology, with its preliminary outline of the whole, was brushed aside as outdated, and the rough unity of the 90s was replaced by a set of warring factions, incapable of reconciling their differences, and unwilling to concede their limitations.

But as the schools recede into the past, a more detached view becomes possible. We may now be able to discern a recognizable pattern in their divergent doctrines. As a first step, the major schools may be arranged roughly in order of the complexity of the functions with which each was typically concerned. Behaviourism originated in the study of the simplest animal functions, the reflex and the conditioned reflex; Gestalt theory in the rather more complex functions of human perception and cognition; psychoanalysis, in dealing with neurotic conflict, began to concern itself with human personality as a whole; and factor analysis dealt with the most complex functions of human intellect and character. Each school began by developing those theories and methods which seemed most apt for the level of behaviour in question.

We have already seen that the lower and simpler levels of behaviour lend themselves better to understanding in terms of the mechanical linkage of elements, whereas the higher and more complex levels are more prone to suggest the active expression of natural powers. To place the schools in this order, then, is to ask whether they can also be considered, at least in some important respects, in terms of the Lockean-Leibnitzian dimension. In fact, it has often been remarked that behaviourism renews the associationist scheme in objective form, and that Watson rejected the content rather than the form of Wundtian theory. The external stimulus evokes the reflex response in place of the sensation, and the conditioned response is the objective substitute for association by contiguity. There is the same emphasis on environment, and on the passivity of the organism until aroused from without. So far as the Lockean pole of the dimension is concerned, behaviourism illustrates the continuity of the mechanist tradition.

The remaining schools, following Allport (1955), may be seen as moving away from the mechanist position and approaching, in varying degrees, the Leibnitzian pole. Gestalt theory, in rejecting atomistic analysis, was opposed to both historical associationism and contemporary behaviourism; and its emphasis on such inherent organizing activities as 'closure' and 'insight' marks the continuation of the continental tradition of active intellect. Psychoanalysis is probably best regarded as a hybrid theory, but its purposive explanations and its id, ego and super-ego belong to the tradition of faculties, like the inborn traits of the factor analyst. We should have to go over to the personalistic and existentialist movements, however, to find the purest representatives of the Leibnitzian position, and these have been too far removed from the spirit of natural science to find much favour in Anglo-Saxon psychology.

It is often possible to discover more detailed similarities among the doctrines of the schools, but it may be safely asserted that it will never be possible to effect a final integration. This is because a school is not a fixed set of principles, though it may often be depicted as such for ease of exposition, but a continuously evolving tradition. In general, this evolution has tended to erode the more extreme features of the theory, either through internal reform or external pressure. Thus behaviourism has moved from pure stimulus-determination towards the admission of intervening variables; Gestalt theory has allowed greater weight to experience; psychoanalysis has allotted a larger role to the conscious ego; and factor analysis has accepted that no one statistical method is paramount. In abandoning extremes, the differences among the schools are reduced. But this does not mean that the original doctrines are being reconciled. The more extreme aspects of a school tend also to be its more distinctive features. Thus their differences are disappearing, not because they are being successfully combined, but because they are tending to dissolve. The original doctrine then remains as a classic exemplar of a particular standpoint, significant and useful in its day, and still a source of insight, but no longer the indispensable guide in contemporary research.

On the credit side, the schools can claim to have consolidated and extended those major new explorations which originated in the 19th century, and to have elaborated further psychology's two great forms of order, the Lockean and the Leibnitzian. On the debit side, however, they had failed to realize the limitations of their respective points of view, and had left to the future the task of reuniting the subject. Above all, their generalizations were too restricted and uncertain to qualify as 'laws as physics shows us laws'. By mid-century, psychology was still in the condition of physics before Galileo and chemistry before Lavoisier.

CONTEMPORARY INTEGRATIONS

The closer one comes to the present day, the harder it is to say what trends will prove significant. Moreover this is particularly difficult in relation to recent psychology, because of the rapid expansion of the subject and the emergence of numerous fresh movements and points of view. All this has made for even greater diversity than existed before. At the same time, and perhaps partly in reaction against these centrifugal tendencies, there have also been movements towards greater integration. Around 1950, it seems to me, there was a change of mood. Psychologists were becoming increasingly weary of the warring schools, and the schools themselves were losing impetus as their original leaders passed from the scene. The psychologists of the 1950s wanted to be rid of the schools, and their desire for greater unity and progress found expression in the conception of psychology as a biological science. This was the immediate origin of the camp of mechanism to which I referred at the outset, and the camp of the person arose later in reaction to it.

Those who regard psychology as a biological science do not form a school in the old sense. This integrating movement did not derive from one man, working in one place, with a single model. Rather it arose from a widespread desire to order the chaos which the schools had left, and it emerged in the textbooks of the 1950s and 1960s in the form which has become so familiar to students in the recent past. First, psychology studies its biological foundations - the nervous system, animal behaviour, and human experimental psychology; then it goes on to the social superstructure - differential, clinical and social psychology.

In its early stages, this movement was often cautious and hesitant. 'Small-scale' models were usually preferred to the ambitious structures of the schools. The spirit in which many of its adherents worked is well caught in the following passage from one of its leading exponents:

> The optimist may surmise that as the confused speculation and ill-directed experiment of the present day steadily gives place to precise hypothesis, amenable to experimental verification, a coherent science of behaviour will gradually evolve. If - and only if - this should occur James's hope will be translated into fact. (Zangwill, 1950, p. 2)

But the growth of the movement brought a rapid increase in confidence. The experimental method was extended even to the complex problems of personality and social interaction, and it came to be accepted that significant generalizations were indeed being discovered over a wide area. The idea took root that it was no longer a question of whether a coherent science of behaviour would evolve in the future. It was emerging now.

In many respects, this movement has done a great deal to give psychology a greater coherence. Its theoretical framework lacks precision, but perhaps for this very reason it can encompass a wide variety of studies. It can find a home for almost any investigation, provided it attempts to determine the conditions of behaviour in a broadly experimental context, and provided its explanatory terms conform to the general mechanistic model. It has become plausible to regard this as the 'mainstream' of psychology, and to suppose that competing schools are now things of the past. The chapters in this volume by Blackman, Broadbent and Eysenck illustrate the continuing influence of this powerful movement.

But other psychologists have been more impressed by the limitations than by the achievements of this attempt at integration. A science demands something more than the indefinite accumulation of miniature generalizations, each tied closely to some restricted experimental situation. It requires that these should contribute to some far-reaching explanatory structure, such as would deserve the name of 'laws as physics shows us laws'. In so far as this has been attempted, there seems to have been little advance beyond the schools and their conflicts. In 1950, Zangwill had remarked that 'Behaviourism still exercises a lingering influence' (p. 10). But news travels slowly in Cambridge. Eleven years later this intelligence had not yet reached the APU in Chaucer Road, where in 1961 Broadbent published his 'Behaviour' in which psychology was virtually equated with the behaviourist movement. Even Zangwill was unable wholly to avoid discussion of the schools: thus the effect of Freud's researches was 'so fundamental as to justify the comparison with biology before and after Darwin' (1950, p. 166); whereas factorial analysis was 'a brilliant but misguided departure from the central path of empirical psychology' (1950, p. 160). But these judgements are reversed by Eysenck, whose system is based upon factorial analysis, and who compares psychoanalysis to 'ordeal by quackery' (Eysenck, 1965, p. 130). It may be doubted, therefore, whether the mainstream has managed to find a solution to the problem of the schools. It is an integration which in practice leans heavily upon the mechanistic model of behaviourism, while the contribution of the other schools - of psychoanalysis, factor analysis, even Gestalt theory - has never been fully accepted. Alternatively expressed, this means that those areas of psychology which are most directly concerned with the complexities of human behaviour - clinical, differential, and social psychology - have either been viewed with scepticism, or required to adopt the concepts and methods appropriate to the simpler levels of behaviour as a badge of respectability.

In short, it is not unreasonable to suggest that the biological integration, while admirable in its general intention, has proved partial and ineffective in its execution. It has been grounded too exclusively in the Lockean tradition. To anyone with a sense of history, a revival of that other mainstream, the Leibnitzian tradition, was highly predictable. That a change was in the offing was strongly suggested by J.J. Gibson in 1967 when he remarked that psychologists:

> seem to feel, many of them, that all we need to do is consolidate our scientific gains. Their self-confidence astonishes me. For these gains seem to me puny, and scientific psychology seems to me ill-founded. At any time the whole psychological applecart might be upset. Let them beware! (Gibson, 1967, p. 142)

A leading figure in the reaction has been Sigmund Koch, who in a series of publications (1959, 1961, 1964, 1974) has mounted an attack of increasing ferocity upon the mechanistic standpoint, an attack which has been all the more influential in that he himself had been for long a 'virile rat-runner'. Koch has been called the 'rogue elephant' of American behaviourism, and it has become a matter of some interest to know what happens to the applecart when the elephant sits on it. Koch has been followed by many others, notably by Deese (1972) in America, and in Britain by a numerous band of writers among whom may be mentioned Bannister & Fransella (1971), Harre & Secord (1972), Hudson (1972), Joynson (1974), Gauld & Shotter (1977) and Shotter (1977). The chapters by Beloff, Fransella, Harre and Shotter illustrate this mode of thinking.

This reaction also is not a school in the old sense. One of its most striking features has been the relative independence with which different critics have come forward from diverse areas to express similar objections to the dominant integration. They seem to have two things in common. First, they are impressed by the limitations of the mechanist standpoint. They argue that it has not achieved that system of reliable generalizations which it promised, not in its preferred fields such as cognition or learning, still less in more complex areas such as personality or social interaction; and they doubt whether its conventional principles and methods will ever enable it to do so. Second, they believe that fresh concepts and methods must be introduced if psychology is ever to attain its historic aims. Their emphasis is on the personal, the adult, the openness of human development, the rationality of human behaviour, the value of philosophical analysis and the need for rethinking fundamental problems. It marks, one might say, the beginnings of an integration from the Leibnitzian pole.

And so we come, very briefly and incompletely, to the two camps with which we began. Both can claim an extensive historical background. The camp of mechanism reaches back through the behaviourist movement, and much related empirical investigation, to the associationist tradition of philosophical psychology. The camp of the person, in the broad sense taken here, has an equally lengthy pedigree. It includes all the anti-mechanist schools of the 20th century, from the Gestalt to the personalistic, and has its roots in the old psychology of faculties. But neither can properly claim to be the mainstream of psychological thought; both have always existed side by side. It is no doubt a great over-simplification to present the history of psychology as the interaction of two major traditions, but it is far less misleading than to present it as the record of one alone.

PROGRESS IN PSYCHOLOGY

In conclusion, we may ask what progress psychology has made towards its scientific goal over the past century. The whole enterprise has undoubtedly proved far harder than many psychologists originally expected, and the persistence of competing schools of thought may seem discouraging. It becomes tempting, when the journey seems endless, either to claim that we have already arrived, or to suggest that we never shall. Can an historical perspective help?

In a recent paper entitled 'The progress of psychology', Farrell (1978) discusses these questions in terms of Kuhn's distinction (1962) between paradigmatic and preparadigmatic science. A paradigmatic science is one which has achieved a system of 'invulnerable lawlike generalizations' or 'an edifice of hard knowledge' (Farrell's phrases) like that of Newton or Lavoisier. This is clearly what James had in mind when he asked for laws 'in the sense in which physics shows us laws', and what others mean when they ask whether psychology is yet a 'mature science'. Like Kuhn, Farrell believes that psychology has not yet reached the paradigmatic stage; thus he refers to 'the notorious fact that psychologists have not unearthed many satisfactory or invulnerable lawlike generalizations' (Farrell, 1978, p. 6). In short, psychology still awaits its Galileo.

This negative conclusion endorses what Koch and many other critics of contemporary psychology have long been saying. Thus in a passage quoted by Farrell, Koch (1974) writes that 'its larger generalizations are not specified over time and effort; they are merely replaced' (Farrell, 1978, p. 1). Farrell accepts that the critics are correct in this respect when he concludes that 'it is quite wrong to think of contemporary psychology as being like physics, or any other post-paradigmatic natural science. Here the sceptics are right; this traditional picture of psychology has indeed broken down' (Farrell, p. 8; cf. Joynson, 1970). But if psychology has not yet reached the paradigmatic stage, are there grounds for believing that it has nevertheless made progress in that direction?

Farrell believes that there are such grounds. He suggests that psychology is 'still in its exploratory stages' (p. 8), and that we can detect what he calls the progress 'characteristic of the preparadigmatic stage of science' (p. 6). I have already tried to indicate that much of psychology - for example, the work of the 19th century pioneers, and that of their successors in the schools - can be seen as valuable exploration. But it is not easy to go beyond such general statements, and provide evidence of detailed and concrete progress. The attempt which Farrell makes rather bears out this observation. He refers particularly to work on learning, of which Koch had been especially sceptical, but his arguments are hardly likely to carry conviction. Much of what he says is remarkably vague: 'we came to appreciate all sorts of things we did not know before' and 'in some sense there has been a significant development of knowledge' (p. 3). And some of what he says is difficult to take seriously: the failure of learning theories becomes a discovery that 'the subtleties of organismic reactivity were very much greater than had been supposed' (p. 3). With arguments such as this, there will be little difficulty in depicting the whole history of psychology as a triumphal march.

But perhaps we ought not to expect to find much evidence of progress. It seems that Farrell, in looking for progress 'characteristic of the preparadigmatic stage', misinterprets Kuhn's views in this respect. For Kuhn, the preparadigmatic stage is defined precisely by the fact that its practitioners have not yet discovered how to make the progress characteristic of science. That progress comes only with the paradigm, which makes it possible. We may be able, after the discovery of the paradigm, to look back and, with the advantage of hindsight, see what factors helped to bring it to birth. But even so, the function of the paradigm, and the reason for attaching so much significance to it, is that it introduces scientific progress where little or none existed before. Koch and other critics are therefore correct in attaching crucial importance to the question of reliable generalizations, for it is their advent which signals the beginning of the progress characteristic of science. It is no doubt natural for those who think we need encouragement, to try to find evidence of progress. But, if Kuhn is right, a preparadigmatic inquiry is characterized by the absence rather than the presence of progress, particularly progress in the discovery of significant generalizations. The path of preparadigmatic inquiry, as Kuhn describes it, is unenviable. It is 'something less than science'; 'the road to a firm research consensus is extraordinarily arduous'; it has not yet 'crossed the divide between what the historian might call its prehistory as a science and its history proper' (Kuhn, 1962, pp. 13, 15, 21). These phrases are applicable to much of the psychology of the past 100 years, and recall the warnings which James gave at the outset. There can be no guarantee that we shall reach the paradigmatic stage; but at least we know that others have passed this way before, and achieved success in the end.

Meanwhile, there are two lessons which I think we can learn from our experience. The first is that we cannot afford to deride the sceptic. With regard to cognitive psychology, Allport (1975) writes 'In the areas of psychology I happen to be acquainted with, I cannot point to one laboratory phenomenon whose interpretation is secure enough for one to build confidently on it'. The advent of a paradigm can only be delayed if we fail to recognize - in James's phrase - 'how great is the darkness in which we grope'. The second is that we cannot afford to dismiss entire traditions of thought - whether mechanistic or personal - because they do not happen to fit our preconceptions of what a 'scientific' psychology should be. If our Galileo is to be 'metaphysical', he may well reconcile these ancient rivals. If we could all get a foot in both camps, we might begin to walk more steadily.

EDITED DISCUSSION

J. H. CLARK: If the division that you have put forward between the two camps is based upon the philosophical mind-body problem, and if that is a true philosophical problem, and if we define philosophy as the collection and study of insoluble problems, then it could be that the paradigm that we await may never come because it would have to be a philosophical paradigm solving the mind-body problem.

R. B. JOYNSON: That might be the case. I am not trying to say with any certainty what the future will be.

R. L. REID: I am rather worried by your war-like metaphors - 'warring factions' and so on. Most psychologists do not exist in warring camps at all. But if we must use such metaphors then it occurs to me that the missiles tend to come from one direction - from the humanist camp.

R. B. JOYNSON: I cannot agree with you that the missiles fly from one side: that is a piece of propaganda. The metaphors merely offer a convenient way of making my case rather vivid, and actually one hopes thereby to persuade people not to take the disputes too seriously.

J. TURNER: Referring to the optimism in your message, I wonder whether you can give me one concrete example from the long pasts of these two movements in which there has been a productive cross-fertilization between them? I find it difficult to think of one unless 'humanist' is used in a very broad sense indeed.

R. B. JOYNSON: Well, I do indeed use that term in a very broad sense, and I do actually believe that there have been many successful attempts to bridge the gap. Tolman, for instance, combined, on the one hand, Watsonian behaviourism and, on the other hand, McDougall's purposive psychology and Gestalt anti-associationism. Tinbergen tried to produce a synthesis, as he called it, between the reflex account of instinct and the purposive account of McDougall ... Whether you think links such as these have been productive is another matter, and one might well wonder why the attempts have not been more successful or more numerous. Attempts at reconciliation are extremely difficult and, at any given time, you only get partial reconciliation.

J. A. GRAY: I find extraordinary your premise that, since William James, there has been no advance in the experimental investigation of psychology from what you call the mechanistic camp. I can think of work that has been refined over the years, and certainly not cast aside - Pavlov's work on the conditioned reflex (see p. 319) for instance, and there are enormous numbers of examples in learning and personality. Many generalizations have stood the test of time.

M. J. MORGAN: May I back that up by saying that in perception we have Helmholtz? It seems absurd to ignore people of this stature when discussing contributions that have been made to psychology.

R. B. JOYNSON: I think it is inevitable that someone would make this form of comment, but I am convinced by Brian Farrell's views on generalization in his recent analysis of the progress of psychology (Farrell, 1978).

K. J. GERGEN: I want to make a comment about what constitutes progress. I would strike your distinction a little differently, perhaps in terms of empiricist versus rationalist metatheory in epistemology: we are talking about two differing philosophic traditions, which have fundamentally different notions of human workings. To put those traditions together is problematic. From a rationalist standpoint, one might have different conceptions of the notion of progress. It might be seen as increasing the capacity of the individual to make rich conceptual distinctions about his or her life, to alter the course of one's life, to gain awareness of one's conditions, and so on: that is quite different from the empiricist's 'progress' which emphasizes the accumulation of predictive laws.

N. FRUDE: If anyone thinks we have different models warring over the same territory then he or she is absolutely missing the point. We need a different model of man to look at different problems, or we need something that is going to attempt an integration - but there are very few models that actually integrate. As it is, the sorts of problems tackled by humanists and empiricists are rather different. It would be absurd, for example, to imagine that there is a warring faction over colour perception, and I doubt whether Pavlov had very much to say about human reactions to bereavement. If there is a war, or a need for war, it is because our various models of man are locked into our political endeavours.

H. WEINREICH-HASTE: There is a hidden curriculum in the discussion so far which has me worried. We are supposed to be talking about models of man (which I would rather call 'models of person') but we are actually talking about models of experimentation and models of science. The discussion is about 'how should we study the person?', rather than about 'what is the person?' and 'how should we approach the person?'

Chapter 2

Men the magicians: The duality of social being and the structure of moral worlds

J. Shotter

ESTRAGON: We always find something, eh Didi, to give us the impression we exist?
VLADIMIR: (impatiently) Yes, yes, we're magicians. But let us persevere in what we have resolved to do, before we forget.
(Samuel Beckett: 'Waiting for Godot')

Merely to mention magic and mystery - never mind proposing as I shall do their reinstatement as real properties central to the world in which we live - is perhaps to court total obloquy in such an avowedly scientific gathering as this. Nevertheless, that is what I shall do. If, as is clearly the case, we have not yet managed to substitute a clear order for the vagueness and mystery, uncertainty and conflict apparent in our current forms of everyday social life; if our experts in social engineering have not yet managed to replace the arenas of moral, legal, political, economic, and academic conflict in our society with various scientifically designed 'procedures of behavioural management', then I take it such vagueness and mystery still remains. We live with them continually in the living of our daily lives. If vagueness and mystery are really there in the actual structure of our social lives together, then if we are to construct a realistic account of our actual social being, they cannot be ignored; account has to be taken of them too.

I shall take them to be a central feature of the world - the moral world of our social being - that I wish to investigate. In such an uncertain world, if there is to be any order and reliability in it, then it is crucial whether people can and do take responsibility for their actions. If they do, then in Arendt's (1959) words: 'even if there is no truth, men can be truthful, and even if there is no reliable certainty, men can be reliable' (p. 254). Thus vagueness and mystery at the heart of a moral world do not preclude the possibility of orderliness in social life. Indeed, their presence motivates the effort to achieve it, and makes the living of our lives the task it is.

SOCIAL BEING, MAGICAL ACTION AND OUR SELF-IMAGES

In the second part of this chapter, I want to discuss in detail the nature of a moral world and the structure of our normal being within it. To set the scene, however, discussion of a number of ancillary issues will take up its first part.

The duality of social being

My title is as ambiguous as many of the things I want to talk about; its appropriateness will hopefully emerge as I proceed.   Essentially, I want to distinguish between what I take to be our two major modes of being in social life; either living immersed in it as, to use Macmurray's (1961) expression, 'one term in a personal relationship' - a mode in which people come to coordinate their actions with one another effortlessly, almost magically; or living somewhat outside such a relationship, detached from it rather than immersed in everyday social life - a mode in which we can live as wilful, contemplative individuals, able to achieve our own ends, a mode in which we must plan and deliberate before we act, and then work and make 'efforts' to achieve what we have resolved to do.

I want to argue that this first mode of existence, this almost magical, unselfconscious, effortless mode is for us primary, and that our other more cognitive mode is secondary and derived from it - even though many of us may seem to spend most of our waking lives within it.   Our socially immersed mode still remains primary, I want to argue, as it is from its realm that we draw the ultimate guidelines for all of what we are pleased to call our normal conduct.   Whatever mode of being we may be in, we cannot escape the fact that in a moral world, as a member of a community, our conduct must at some point (a) be evaluated, and (b) be evaluated in normative terms.   Psychology, in taking mere behaviour as its subject matter, has tried to ignore this fact: that the language in terms of which human action is described as such is evaluative and normative - it only qualifying as 'human action' if it can be so described (Abelson, 1977).   In taking our more cognitive mode of being as its primary focus and in ignoring our other more socially immersed mode almost completely, psychology has rendered invisible the processes of social interaction within which social norms are constructed, reconstructed, established and transmitted.   Men have been treated as rule-followers (Peters, 1958; Winch,1958; Harré & Secord, 1972) and program-users (Neisser, 1967; Boden, 1977), but not as rule- or program-makers.   Rather than a human 'achievement', social order has been seen as intrinsic to human nature.   Why this should be - why social orders are not seen as human achievements, why the processes in which they are produced remain invisible to those involved in them - is something I shall discuss later.

Let me continue here by trying to put my distinction between our two modes of social being in more concrete terms.   As our more wilful and cognitive mode of existence is so familiar, especially to intellectuals as it is their stock in trade, little more of a general nature need be said about it here: it is that mode in which we do-this-in-order-to-achieve-that, and while doing so insulate ourselves against (distracting) events in our surroundings to which, in our other mode, we would otherwise be sensitive.   The nature of our primary mode of being, though, being not so visible to us, is more unfamiliar; let me therefore give a fuller example of it here.   Fingarette (1967) in illustrating its 'magical' quality describes the following episode of everyday behaviour:

> I see you on the street; I smile, walk toward you, put out my hand to shake yours.   And behold! - without any command, stratagem, force, special tricks or tools, without any effort on my part to make you do so, you spontaneously turn towards me, return my smile, raise your hand toward mine.   We shake hands - not by my pulling your hand up and down or your pulling mine, but by spontaneous and perfect cooperative action.   Normally we do not notice the subtlety and amazing complexity of this co-ordinated 'ritual' act.   This subtlety and complexity become evident, however, if one has to learn the ceremony only from a book of instructions, or if one is a foreigner from a non-handshaking culture. (p. 168)

And this spontaneous coordination is typical of all the so many other normal aspects of daily life we continually take for granted: for instance, people around us - those with whom we have grown up - flap their mouths about and make noises, and we, whether we like it or not, directly and immediately hear what they say, not just their words but what they mean; no mental effort seems to be involved in the process. Similarly, they talk not by first planning their talk and laboriously executing their plan, impervious to the reactions of their audience: they in fact just talk, modifying what they say to accord with the nods of comprehension and grimaces of bafflement they receive. They act, and some activity in us coordinates itself with what they do; we have little choice in how people's meaning presents itself to us. Not that we are coerced into our comprehension of them: the vast forces at work in producing this spontaneous coordination of the everyday social processes involved here are quite intangible and invisible to us, quite unlike those apparent in the attempts one person may make to coerce another. This uniquely human way of doing things, of people exerting influences of a precise kind directly upon others in their community, though very like instinct, is not inborn; it must be learned, acquired, as one grows up in the community as 'one term in a personal relationship'; then and only then can one be a beneficiary of that community's conventions and institutions, its traditional ways of people relating themselves to one another.

Logically, this mode of direct social action is possible only between members of a community. But it is worth mentioning at this stage that we may, of course, exist in this mode of direct relation with non-personal things also. Buber (1970) asks us to consider a tree: we may contemplate it in many different ways - as a picture, as a movement, as an instance of a species, as an example of a law, as a pure relation between numbers, and so on. In all such instances we ignore its uniqueness and view it generally, as an object having certain features located in space and time. But how in all this can we see it simply as being the tree it is, a tree which we will recognize later as one already known to us? Because, Buber says, besides being able to contemplate as an external observer the tree, using one or another analytic schema (Neisser, 1976) to direct our way of looking at it and to evaluate the sensory input we receive as a result, we may also know it by entering into a direct relation with it. Then our experience of it is not limited to just this or that dimension, but it becomes known to us in the totality of ways in which it affects us. Thus, in such a relation, a tree may be known to us for the tree it is independently of and prior to any of the analytic schemes discovered to be applicable to it in contemplation; known in terms just of the particular totality of affect it arouses in us when we do not actively contemplate it but merely stand unselfconsciously before it open to its presence.

Each mortal thing does one thing and the same:
Deals out that being indoors each one dwells:
Selves - goes itself; myself it speaks and spells;
Crying what I do is me: for that I came.
(Gerard Manley Hopkins)

Because the only rationally accountable - and thus recognizable - form of social being available to us currently is that of living life as self-conscious individuals, we hardly appreciate now the reality of such a relational mode of being as this. But its nature is readily apparent in the magical 'world-image' of primitive peoples; to anything which stirs activity within them they are prepared to attribute existence and power: to the moon and the 'dead' who haunt them at night, to the sun that burns them, to the beast that howls, to the chief whose glance compels them, and to the Shaman whose song fills them with strength for the hunt (Buber, 1970). Instead of their being disturbed by what we would call 'memories', the Dinka (Lienhardt, 1961) think that the powerful spirits of events and places have returned to haunt them and that they can be placated with ritual acts. But we are not as free from the influences of similar such powers working in us as we might believe: of looks that may turn us to stone, of experiences which haunt us, of untouchable objects of awe and veneration. The point here is that when immersed in our primary mode of being, rather than we ourselves directing the nature of our experience, we literally find ourselves with experiences not of our own immediate making: as Farber (1976, p. 7) points out, we can will commiseration, but not sympathy; congratulations, but not admiration; lust, but not love; reading, but not understanding - or in relation to ourselves: one may will going to bed, but not sleeping; eating, but not hunger; knowledge, but not wisdom; and so on. It is as if 'I' were two selves in one, an impersonal self which, as Merleau-Ponty (1962) puts it, is as if it has 'already sided with the world' (p. 216) and which constructs the 'situation' in which I as a personal being find myself placed. As such, that situation, although it is peculiarly mine and no one else's and is powerful enough to demand attention as 'my' situation, is not open to my choice to change: I can look, but it is not up to me exactly what I see, even though I may see what others do not and can not; I can listen, but again what I hear as a result is not a matter of my volition. '... I am, as a sentient subject' says Merleau-Ponty (1962, p. 215), 'a repository stocked with natural powers at which I am the first to be filled with wonder' (my emphasis, see Shotter, 1973).

The dream of wilful magical action

In our primary mode of being, there is thus a hint of magical power: when immersed in a certain special relation to one's situation, one can attain ends appropriate to it without thought or effort, spontaneously - as in the hand-shaking example, or as we know from when our game 'just flows out of us' as in tennis, say. When that happens, it happens in a way utterly mysterious to us at present, for it happens without our intending it, without our intending any specific goals: indeed, it only happens in the subtly coordinated manner Fingarette describes, if we intend no specific goals; if we do, its spontaneity is disrupted

Hints as to the existence of an effortless, 'magical' form of action thus abound. But could we ever really be magicians, attempting to control such power, to attain all our own particular goals in the same effortless way - perhaps by the mere incantation of the 'right' ritual gesture?

To the wise men of old, the answer was a qualified 'yes'. The solution was to work at conforming one's being to reality in some way; usually by efforts after self-knowledge, self-discipline, and virtuous living. 'Correct living' was what was required, and if one's efforts were successful and the 'right way' (the Tao) found then one was rewarded by being able to attain one's ends effortlessly, as if by magic. 'Do that which consists in taking no action', says the Lao tzu mysteriously, 'and order will prevail'. But the 'right way' (Tao) was not so easy to teach, especially as, 'The way that can be told', begins the Lao tzu, 'is not the constant way. The name that can be named is not the constant name ... The way is forever nameless.'

> In order to arrive at what you do not know
> You must go by a way which is the way of ignorance
> In order to possess what you do not possess
> You must go by the way of dispossession.
> In order to arrive at what you are not
> You must go through the way in which you are not.
> And what you do not know is the only thing you know
> And what you own is what you do not own
> And where you are is where you are not.
> (T. S. Eliot: 'East Coker')

But it is not the easiest thing in the world to grasp what something is by only being told what it is not, even if what one is told is true.

Beginning in the 16th century, a radically new approach to the acquisition of magical powers was conceived: rather than man attempting to conform himself to reality, the dream was to conform reality to man, to subdue reality, in its guise as nature, to men's wishes. Somewhere, it was thought, the right technique or formula must exist, and the search to find it began upon two fronts at once. Both alchemy and science were born of that same impulse. Ritual gesture and incantation, however, did not work to subdue nature and alchemy died; it did not give men the gold, guns and girls (Faustus) they desired. Science, however, was more successful. It achieved its goal, not by magic but by methodical reasoning and observation, and by planned effort. But what was its goal? The same magician's goal as that of the alchemists in fact. It worked, as Descartes had hoped it would, to 'make ourselves, as it were, masters and possessors of Nature'.

But in what sense does it work to give man power over nature? Does it work to increase what we might call people's personal powers (Shotter, 1973, 1974), to increase their individual ability to control and use the natural powers available to them from within their own individual beings? Or: does what we call man's power over nature mean something quite different? There is in fact an unfortunate ambiguity in the word 'power' here: power as an ability in oneself to do something is not the same as the possession of control or command over others. And there is reason to suspect that it is only man's power in its second sense - his possession of control or command over other things - that is increased by scientific research. For, to the extent that science deals only with generalities, that which is unique and individual inevitably gets something of a bad deal; and doubly so of course in the psychological sciences, for there one is concerned not only with what is general but also with what is impersonal as well: science attempts to describe the order in natural phenomena without any reference to their authorship; men cannot be treated as being in any way personally responsible for any of their actions. Hence the idea of unique and individual human beings and their special personal powers and talents is ruled out in such a view.

Some comments of C. S. Lewis (1943) reinforce the conclusion that it is only power in the second sense that is enhanced by scientific research. He points out that all current products of such research - such as new sources of energy, communication, travel, population control, etc. - are all things which can be withheld from some people by others. Thus, what we call man's power over nature is, in reality, a power possessed by some people which they may, or may not, allow other people to profit by. Man is as much the patient or subject of such powers as possessor of them, as nature as such can be used just as much against him as for him. Not only are people's personal powers not enhanced by such research, in the longer term they may even be reduced by it.

Lewis' argument here is as follows: all long-term exercises of power in the second sense must mean, in the end, the power of earlier generations over later ones. Each generation exercises that power over its successors to the extent that it rebels against tradition and modifies the environment bequeathed to it; it controls the future within which those who come after it must live. There is therefore no question, Lewis suggests, of a power in the first sense vested in the community as a whole steadily growing as long as that community survives. The last men, far from being the heirs of such power, will be of all men most subject to the dead hand of the great planners and conditioners and will themselves exercise least power upon the future. 'The final stage is come', Lewis suggests,

> when Man by eugenics, by pre-natal conditioning, and by an education and propaganda based on a perfect applied psychology, has obtained full control over himself. Human nature will be the last part of Nature to surrender to Man ... The battle will indeed be won. But who, precisely, will have won it? (p. 37)

For, as we have seen, man's power over nature means the power of some men over others with nature as their instrument, and this, with human nature substituted for nature, means the power of some men to make other men what they please. But: Quis custodies ipsos custodies?

The progressive emancipation of people from the traditions of a community - the decision of one generation not to hand on to its successors what it has received from its predecessors - in pursuit of the magician's goal of effortless power, leads in fact, Lewis suggests, to the exact opposite of what is sought; only from a position of prior immersion within the traditions and institutions of community life can such an effortless power be discovered. The dilemma for the progressive intellectual confronted with such a deeply conservative conclusion as this is plain, but no effort to resolve that dilemma will be made here; both progressive and conservative attitudes will have a part to play in the views put forward below.

Self-images in a moral world

I will return to the theme of spontaneous, effortless social action, and factors influencing its structure later. For the moment let me turn to the 'models of man' issue to put it into the context of a moral world, into a context of human concerns, values and interests; the relation of people, one to another as well as their relations to themselves.

Straight away, let me say why I prefer the expression 'images of man' to that of 'models of man'. My concern is not just with what in general man currently is, but with what in the everyday living of their social lives people may and can become. Hence, to reiterate, I am not concerned (except negatively) with that type of scientific thought about ourselves in which - in order to help gain power over 'human nature' - we model it in one or another of its current forms. My concern is with that task each of us as unique individuals faces every day afresh, the task of deciding the best thing we should do for ourselves - a question we cannot even begin to answer without at least a vague idea of who or what we are. An 'image of man', as I shall use that term, is an integral part of people's attempts in the living of their daily lives to understand themselves in order to become themselves, a part of their search for authentic personal existence. And I follow Friedman (1967) in what I mean by 'authentic personal existence':

> (It) does not mean some moral standard imposed from without, or some universal 'ought' that need only be applied. It implies a meaningful, personal direction, a response from within to what one meets in each new situation, standing one's ground and meeting the world with the attitude that is rooted in this ground. (p. 17)

People need 'an exemplary image of man', Friedman suggests (1967), which helps them discover, in each age anew, their 'true selves' ... whatever that may mean! But perhaps that comment itself is an indication of 'the crisis in man's knowledge of himself' (Cassirer, 1944) which characterizes our age: it is that about which we surely should be most certain - ourselves - which puzzles us most; the idea of our having 'true selves' thus being somewhat incomprehensible to us, hence our difficulties often in deciding what to do for the best for ourselves.

Our images of ourselves thus matter; they are not just curios to toy with and contemplate. Every self-conscious choice we make - in its very nature - implicitly refers to one or another image of ourselves. 'Are we the kind of person who flourishes best in conflict or cooperation?' 'Is writing about psychological theory my true work or are my talents of a different kind?' 'Are we divided into different parts - spiritual, intellectual and physical, say - all needing balanced satisfaction if we are to find ourselves?' 'Would my children be best educated formally rather than informally in "the great university of life"?', and so on. Without some notion of our own natures, these questions remain unanswerable and our future action thus unclear.

But what might be our 'exemplary image' at the moment? Currently, when we speak of 'human nature' we tend to think of it as something fixed, as something already there, external to us, existing independently of our thoughts about it. Hence we believe it possible by conducting research to accumulate 'facts' about it, thus to increase our power over whatever that nature is. Most of these features are present, for instance, in Skinner's (1971) views about human nature: 'no theory changes what it is a theory about' he suggests,

> man remains what he has always been. And a new theory may change what can be done with its subject matter. A scientific view of man offers exciting possibilities.   We have not yet seen what man can make of man. (p. 210)

If human nature is fixed, what else is there we can do except to investigate the different uses to which it may be put?

But what if the opposite were the case and we construct a quite different exemplary image for ourselves? What if human nature is not independent of our thoughts about it, and theories can in some instances change the things they are theories about; what if human nature is a continuously changing and developing artifact, a product of the processes of exchange and contact between people as they live their daily lives? If that were the case (and I think it is), then what men are and what they may become is very much a function of how they treat themselves and one another; in this sense, if in no other, beings in a moral world may have quite a different quality to them than entities in a physical world with a fixed nature. Thus, in a moral world, we must treat the existence of our objects of study in a way quite different from the way in which natural scientists treat theirs. Rather than assuming that what we want to investigate already exists, fully formed, quite independent of any mode of investigation used to study it, our 'objects' of study will be of an intentional kind, that is, they need not be taken as existing in a fully formed state at all: an object of investigation - for instance, our social being or our rationality - may be brought more fully into existence as investigation into it proceeds; the direction of its investigation and thus the form of its new existence being shaped and influenced by whatever thoughts, beliefs or theories are held at that time.

The general nature of intentionality and intentional objects is considered more fully elsewhere (Shotter, in press b). Here I would like to continue to explore in more concrete terms the possible consequences of our being influenced by how we depict ourselves in our theories; how the way in which we treat one another and ourselves in their terms may influence our social being in fundamental ways. With that possibility in mind, let me briefly review how we think, and have thought, about ourselves; examining the associated modes of consciousness and moral commitments.

At the moment, we certainly tend to assimilate man to the modern mechanical view of the cosmos (the view inaugurated by Descartes and developed by Newton). Rather than viewing ourselves as in ancient Greek or Mediaeval times as distinctly individual but necessarily related parts of an organic whole (perceptually distinguishable but not physically separable), we now view ourselves as separately existing, intrinsically indistinguishable human atoms - our relations to one another, not being intrinsic to our nature in such a view, thus becoming something of a problem to us. Rather than valuing our activities as being worth pursuing for their own sake, as legitimate contributions to a 'whole life', we now evaluate them in instrumental terms for their efficiency, productivity, or general effectiveness (all terms essentially applicable to machines - the vocabulary extends now, of course, to being 'turned on' and 'turned off', and so on). If we value only the instrumental function of our actions, we tend to ignore the expressive dimension of our lives, the activities within which we express, develop and reconstruct our selves (Sennett, 1974). Our exemplary image of man becomes one of the person as a generalized machine, as something which in fact men use as a means to an end. Thus it is that we think of ourselves and our activities as well paralleled at the moment by computers and their programs, as reduced to one of the tools of our own intelligence, with individuals being distinguished by the different programs they have available to employ - the different uses to which they may efficiently be put (some men by others).

I think we can now begin to see how a way of thinking about ourselves - the model of men-as-a-generalized-machine - can tend to create the very reality of which it is only supposed to be the model: we can become what we pretend to be (Kurt Vonnegut, Jr).

To appreciate the depth of the 'reality' being created here (if 'reality' is the right word) let me consider the moral and experiential consequences of centring ourselves in such an 'objective consciousness' in our daily lives. Let me first mention its consequences for how we treat others, and then for how we treat ourselves.

Treating others amorally If we treat other people as objects this does not mean necessarily that we do them harm; people do not usually go about damaging all objects in sight. But it does mean treating them amorally and ameaningfully: treating them in a manner which ignores their ability to judge and control their own behaviour in relation to their own standards and ideals, their ability to express themselves and their personal truths. We cannot legitimately see them as wrestling with moral dilemmas, as suffering disappointments, as trying to achieve (but not always succeeding) their goals, as being sincere, dishonest, as acting to put right wrongs, to achieve fame or another kind of reputation, and so on; to be, in short, the kind of person they think they want to be. Not to take a moral attitude to others is to risk becoming incapable of spontaneous identification or empathy with them, of becoming bemused and mystified by their behaviour - the authenticity of mutual identification not being a task requiring self-conscious effort, but, like hand-shaking, a matter of membership in a moral community. Lacking such a spontaneous identification, one has then to try to learn explicitly the function of facial expressions, the function of pauses in conversation, etc., as if there are clear rules for the use of such things - which is not the case (Birdwhistell, 1970); a facial expression is only a smile in a certain context, to members of a community. Treating others as objects, as different kinds of being from ourselves, we think they merely act as external circumstances demand - smoothly, automatically, without feeling or fuss; it is we alone who suffer from self-doubt and irresolvable moral confusion.

On the social and political level too, there are consequences: it means that we attempt to replace politics by 'social engineering', that we think in terms of Skinner's (1972) 'technology of behaviour', or Eysenck's (1969) 'technology of consent'. We see people's problems as being solved by them (the people) being channelled, using neutral administrative methods, into situations which others (we?) 'calculate' will 'do them good'. Claiming to know the causes of their behaviour and the nature of their social conditions, we feel we no longer need listen to their views; thinking we can determine their needs scientifically, what they themselves might want is ignored. Instead of treating them as moved by their experience - their experiences of fear and conflict, of anxiety, and despair, their terror at being attacked by an in-group for being a member of an out-group - we talk of them simply as existing in morally and politically neutral 'fields of force', and 'undergoing energy transformations' or as 'processing information', as if they were indistinguishable from the blind, unfeeling entities making up merely physical systems.

To deny people the opportunity to describe their experience, to explain and justify themselves, or at least to participate in the effort to illuminate the reasons for their conduct in their own terms, is, as I argue later, to refuse to confer upon them their status as persons in their own moral world. It is to deny them their access to self-expression, and to confer upon them a merely instrumental status - to treat them not as ends in themselves (both 'from which' and 'to which' action is directed), but merely as the means to presumably, the ends of other people (Lewis, 1943). In a moral world, people must normally be listened to and treated as meaning what they say; if they cannot be treated as knowing what something is and is not, as knowing what can properly be said and what cannot, then there is no way of discovering what counts in their world (Cavell, 1969). And furthermore (it is worth adding here as it will be of central importance later): it is not a question of whether in their judgements they have evidence in support of them; members of a moral community do not normally need evidence for what may be said or done legitimately in their community; as competent members of that community, they are the source of such evidence (Cavell, 1969) - if what happens is apparently abnormal or unusual then, of course, the matter is different. How that evidence is gathered, evidence of a moral world's 'structure of normality', I shall discuss in a moment; here let me turn to what happens if we treat ourselves amorally.

Treating ourselves amorally Personally too, in ourselves, there are consequences of taking inappropriately an amoral attitude, ones perhaps of a surprising kind. In becoming increasingly objective and detached in relation to ourselves we may become unable, as it were, to treat even ourselves morally. We may cease to think even of ourselves as beings who act in relation to interests and values of our own, who have both the ability and the right to monitor and evaluate our actions as we perform them in relation to our own personal ends. Viewing ourselves as merely the product of external causes, we may mistrust and debunk even our own judgements; we become afraid to say what we think, what we feel, what we want; perhaps we do not even bother to think certain things through to their end for ourselves - for who are we when there are 'experts' for so many of life's really important problems. Unable to commit ourselves to a position, to something in which we really believe, we lose the capacity for sustained, self-directed, purposeful action (heteronomy rather than autonomy becomes our prevalent mode of being). Further: just as we are cast in the role of observers of others (rather than as co-participants in life with them), so we find a part of ourselves always seems to be standing to one side and to be observing, 'objectively', what we ourselves are doing; such self-consciousness not only prevents that effortless, spontaneous coordination possible in more unselfconscious interchanges, it also prevents us from making ourselves truly responsible for ourselves. For even as we take a stand we are aware of the 'social influences' upon us, the possibility of our having 'unconscious motives', an 'ideologically distorted' or 'false consciousness'. We are not sure whether our views are really ours.   There seems to be an absence of any clear points of reference to guarantee the validity of what we have to say.

We forget - when treating people objectively - that in an uncertain world, what matters most is that people learn what it is to take responsibility for their actions, then if they do learn what it is and how to do it, it means that they will do (or at least try to do) what they say they will do, or what their momentary position in the community commits them to doing. Without that determination of people to be responsible for themselves and their actions, without that kind of self-control, there can be no guarantee of order in the community at all. In becoming detached from ourselves we risk losing exactly what it was we had hoped to gain: our own greater autonomy and self-control over our own lives. We risk losing it because we confuse becoming a free, autonomous individual in relation to all those with whom we share our lives, with living a life of impulse, doing what we like whenever we like. In such an impulsive form of life we might be acting as we (who?) please, but we would be in a social void, robbed of all our moral purchase upon human affairs. It is not by ignoring our society's ways and means that we set ourselves free, but by increasing our practical knowledge of them thus to use them all the more in the reasonable and legitimate expression of our purposes.

In using our capacities to reflect upon and change the way we live to new forms - forms in which not only the human capacity to judge and reflect is ignored, but the way in which the evaluative basis of moral action is used, developed, changed and transmitted in a community is also ignored - we are dismantling just that aspect of our being in the world that distinguishes us from all else that there is: the peculiarly human way of doing things we have as members of a community, ways which have been long in construction throughout the history of our culture.

NORMALITY: ACTION AND JOINT ACTION IN A MORAL WORLD

I want to discuss in this part of my chapter the nature of a moral world and the proper focus of research in it. I want to show that although the 'workings' of such worlds are just as 'invisible' to us - that is, outside our experience - as the worlds of modern physics, they are no less full of charm and strangeness. Their peculiar charm and strangeness resides in the paradox that while people quite clearly do construct and reconstruct their own ways of life for themselves, their own 'worlds', they nonetheless experience them as 'given', as 'realities' existing externally to them and independently of them, and as containing entities which, even before they actually discover them or become conscious of them, are thought of as already existing 'somewhere' in that world; in failing to experience the part we play in producing such a world, we have failed to grasp that the world so produced is a world of a peculiarly human kind.

The language of action

Although quite invisible and intangible and only grasped through an active involvement in a community's activities, a community's culture and the set of legitimations or structure of normality it provides, is not experienced as a subjective matter, as merely a matter of interpretation: it is experienced as something given, external, and objective; it is not something which can be discovered by introspection (Berger & Luckman, 1967). Thus, not surprisingly, we have remained somewhat ignorant of quite what it was we had acquired in growing up when it was said that we had acquired 'common sense', for how could the nature of something invisible and intangible, apparently locked in people's heads but unavailable to introspection, be discovered? Ignorant of its true nature but aware that our common-sense accounts of things were full of fantasies, fallacies, and falsehoods, we did not take much convincing that it should be replaced by something better.   Positivists dreamed of replacing it by a scientific account, and of replacing the concepts enshrined in our ordinary everyday language by scientific ones.

The 'ordinary language' movement in philosophy - led by Wittgenstein, Ryle and Austin - has, by demonstrating the extraordinarily subtle and rich logic of ordinary language thwarted this positivist dream. By closely examining exactly how we do things with words in everyday life, it has helped to clarify both the nature of human agency in human affairs, and to dispel, as Ryle (1949) called it, 'Descartes' myth: the dogma of the Ghost in the Machine' - the polar opposition between mind and matter in our currently 'official doctrine'.   If it seems surprising that so much can be discovered about the nature of our social world by investigating the language in terms of which we talk about it - instead of investigating that world itself in some way - then we should remember that we learn about what counts as belonging to our worlds through learning our community's language; language and world are learnt together.   Thus, 'in discussing language philosophically', says Winch (1958), 'we are in fact discussing what counts as belonging to the world'.

Now the fact which impresses ordinary language philosophers - and should impress us too with our interest in spontaneous, unreflective, and nonetheless appropriate action - is that we use all kinds of philosophically and psychologically puzzling words in everyday life affairs without it being necessary normally to pause for reflection at all when we do. We say 'Oh, that was a thoughtful, intelligent, thoughtless, kind, mean, jealous, etc., ... act'; normally, we use all these words quite precisely, without causing any puzzlement at the time of their use; indeed, quite the opposite is the case, for their use is usually highly informative. Yet, of course, as soon as we stop to reflect and to ask 'what actually is it to be intelligent, etc.', then we run into trouble. As Ryle (1949) says,

> Many people can talk sense with concepts, but cannot talk sense about them; they know by practice how to operate with concepts, anyhow inside familiar fields, but they cannot state the logical regulations governing their use. (p. 9)

Thus what ordinary language philosophers do is to study those familiar fields inside which people's actions seem to be regulated by reference to, apparently, a conceptual framework implicit in the structure of their common sense, and they bring its logic to light by asking 'what should, or what normally do we say or do here?' - taking it to be the case that, although they may need to remind themselves, competent members of a moral community do not normally need evidence to reveal to them what may legitimately be said or done in their community; knowing it already is a part of what it is to be a competent member.

It is worth adding here that in achieving one's status (and mode of social being) as a competent member - as an 'autonomous' person - means functioning within an enormous amount of constraint. Being acquired during our socialization into the community, such conceptual frameworks are prior to any observation and theorizing that we may intelligibly do within it. There are thus severe limitations on what are communally acceptable ways of perceiving, acting, speaking, thinking and valuing. But furthermore, and most importantly, as Smedslund (1978) points out,

> these shared constraints form a highly organized system, such that, given one set of percepts, acts, sentences, thoughts or values, others follow necessarily or are necessarily excluded. Becoming socialized as a human being, therefore, involves acquiring an implicit psychology which one cannot, as an individual, transcend. Psychologists are also persons, and consequently, their observations, descriptions, and explanations must also conform with the common sense conceptual network. (p. 11)

In other words, although as an individual one may discover by implication something about one's moral world which one has never directly learned (which is, of course, an important point in itself), what one discovers is in a sense 'already there' (Merleau-Ponty); one cannot go beyond the terms of that system, it is reflexive, or as Piaget (1971) calls it, 'self-regulating' - no matter what happens it will be dealt with and understood in terms already provided by the system. And Smedslund (1978) demonstrates this brilliantly in a most detailed way: he shows how in a selected area - namely, Bandura's (1977) theory of self-efficacy, a theory to do with the way in which people's beliefs about themselves, and thus their behaviour, changes as a result of how they are treated by others - a system of theorems may be extracted from one's common-sense knowledge of what certain terms already mean to us in our ordinary language, and that Bandura's theory is thus not an 'empirical' theory in the sense that facts could prove it wrong; it merely states in fact what is logically necessary given the ways we currently use to relate ourselves to one another linguistically.

As already mentioned, the guiding principle of the conceptual revolution brought about by the 'ordinary language' movement is the recognition that the language in terms of which human conduct must be described (if it is to be treated as human conduct) is normative and evaluative: that what people do is judged, both by others and by them, as right or wrong, correct or incorrect, successful, skilful, stupid, etc.; that it is performed in some way in relation to a 'structure of normality'.

Now one approach as to how such a structure of normality enters into and informs people's actions is Ryle's (1949). He says,

The well-regulated clock keeps good time and the well-drilled circus seal perfoms its tricks flawlessly, yet we do not call them 'intelligent'. We reserve this title for the persons responsible for their performances. To be intelligent is not merely to satisfy criteria, but to apply them; to regulate one's actions and not merely be well-regulated. A person's performance is described as careful or skilful, if in his operations he is ready to detect and correct lapses, to repeat and improve upon success, to profit from the examples of others and so forth. He applies criteria in performing critically, that is, in trying to get things right. (p. 29)

Not only as observers of other people's actions, but as agents too, we seem to monitor and modulate our actions in the course of their execution by reference to certain considerations: not just our circumstances, but our goals, knowledge and beliefs. We do not just satisfy criteria in our actions, but as Ryle says, we try to apply them. At least, in our secondary, more cognitive mode we do, the mode in which trying is necessary if we are to get things right.

On Ryle's account, only beings who actually do apply criteria in their actions can be said to be responsible for their actions, and to be aware of what they are doing - or trying to do. And what follows from his account is that when we treat someone as-responsible-for-his-action, and think of 'him' as being its source (rather than of him as being caused to do it by external forces), it does not mean that we think of his action as necessarily occurring 'out of the blue', with no rational connection with what has gone on before. On the contrary: it means that we expect him to know both what he did and why he did it, what his reasons for doing that rather than all the other things he might have done, but did not; in short, we expect him to give an account of his action, to be able to justify it to us in terms of certain goals, interests, and values describable within the 'vocabulary of motives' (Mills, 1940) that we share with him. Even if we cannot account for his action, we expect him to be able to - if, that is, he is to count as an autonomous person for us in our community.

So far so good: Ryle has marked out here a sphere of autonomous, skilful conduct in which men are seen as the originators of their own actions, and in this sphere, as Hollis (1977) has remarked, 'rational action is its own explanation': that is, Smith or Jones is _there_ as an agent in his own action, and 'he' is executing it in terms of certain grounds and other rational considerations. And his actions are explained when, roughly speaking, those grounds are as plain to us as they are to him. The considerations in terms of which he acts, explain his action. The particular understanding achieved here may be used as an explanation, that is, as a generalization, when it is offered in the context of the assumption that in such circumstances as Smith's or Jones' all other rational agents in the community would have done the same.

Within this limited sphere at least - the sphere of wilful, deliberate action - it is possible to oppose an image of man-the-autonomous-rational-agent to that of man-the-mechanism, and to show that there is a mode of rational explanation which can be applied legitimately to his conduct. The most well-known approach of this kind in social psychology at present is Harré & Secord's ethogenics: in which they attempt to explain social behaviour very much in terms derived, at least initially, from the 'accounts' people themselves give of their own reasons for their actions (e.g. Marsh et al., 1978).

But there is something very wrong, I think, with this Ryle/Harré & Secord account of social being, in which its dual nature is not acknowledged. Not only do they take deliberate activity - activity in which people 'apply criteria', or 'refer to theories', 'ideas', 'grammars', or some other 'cognitive structures' somewhere in their heads in structuring their activity - as a model for all that people do, they also see people's activity as determined in some way by factors external to it, by pre-established 'grammars of the social order' (Harré & Secord, 1972, p. 123). But as Hollis (1977) shows, actors who are creatures of rules are still passive in the sense that the actions they perform are not necessarily 'their' actions. Why they put themselves under the guidance of such rules, and what their intention was in following them, is still open to question. If there is nothing more to bring to light in ethogeny than, as Harré & Secord term it, 'the "generative mechanisms" that give rise to behaviour,' then once again, as in the behaviourist's paradigm, the idea of people themselves, as individual personalities, being the authors of their own actions disappears; the threat to self and genuine individuality still remains.

Joint action and the construction of a moral world

Besides those activities in which we feel clear as to what it is that we are doing - activities which, for the bureaucrat and intellectual, may be the only kind of activities visible to them - there are also, I feel, many other activities in daily life in which we remain deeply ignorant as to what exactly it is that we are doing. This is so, not because the 'ideas' or whatever supposedly in us somewhere informing them are too deeply buried to bring out into the light of day, but because the formative influences shaping our conduct are not wholly there in our individual heads to be brought out; our activities are such that they cannot occur except when interlaced with the actions of others, and their actions are just as much a formative influence determining what we do as anything within ourselves. Within such circumstances the overall outcome of the exchange is not simply up to us. Such is the case in playing tennis, for instance, or in general conversation, or in a mother just playing with her child, etc.; whether the situation is highly constrained or not - whether in industrial negotiations, football matches, tutorials, greetings, insults, promises, or listening to academic papers - there is a sense in which what happens is simply not up to the individual: the meaning of what is given out is a matter of how it is taken in. Only those who have become competent members of a community and know how an action is taken in that community, know what they are meaning in giving it, and can thus autonomously express a meaning. In joint action, such autonomy is limited; what later we may individually internalize as the meaning of an act seems only to exist initially shared between us. Or to put the matter in Mead's (1934) words:

> The mechanism of meaning is ... present in the social act before the emergence of consciousness or awareness of meaning occurs. The act or adjustive response of the second organism gives to the gestures of the first organism the meaning which it has. (pp. 77-78)

Thus the child, while learning to be a competent member of his moral community, need not at first be at all self-consciously aware of what he is actually doing, he need only learn at a practical level to do that which will satisfy the demands of his social situation. And he can do that by relying upon other more competent members to complete and give meaning to his acts, reflecting back to him the particular social consequences to which his particular movements may lead in their community (Shotter, 1976, 1978) - showing him, for instance, that pointing may be used, according to context, to direct people's attention, to request an object, or to request an object's name.

Besides the lack of self-conscious awareness of the meaning of one's action, another interesting feature of joint action is this: that while it cannot be performed wholly by following rules or by referring to pre-established plans, it is nonetheless action with one or another particular style to it - friendly conversation clearly differing from philosophical debate, which differs from psychotherapy, which differs from formal interviews - and people can discriminate things appropriate from things inappropriate to that style. How? Because, I suggest, in joint action people exercise a power, a 'social power' (Hollis, 1977), to create and sustain between them a 'social or moral world', and it is having to make one's actions appropriate to that 'world' which gives them the style they have.

Thus what interests me here is that particular kind of human activity in which people are allowed to retain their existence as unique individuals while relating themselves together into a social whole, into a unity of a distinct kind, with a style or order to it. Indeed, such an order does not just allow individual existence, it demands it: for, if a social order is to endure, then of necessity it must be possible for the entities within it to identify transgressions of it, and for the transgressors to make restitution and help to reinstitute the order. Without persons, without individually accountable elements, a social order would fall apart; human beings are not born with, as far as we can tell, any particular species-specific way of life. Other social unities will not do in constituting the basic elements in such an order: interactive unities - for example, mother/child, husband/wife, boss/worker, teacher/pupil - which in theory might constitute such unities would in practice, in their activities, produce actions for which they cannot be held accountable (see below); and it would be their general lack of accountability which would disqualify them as suitable units out of which to construct a social order. Persons are the only entities able to account for their actions, to justify, acquit, and redeem themselves, to be able to be responsible and to 'answer for' what they do. In organizing themselves into a social world with a moral order to it, human beings also constitute themselves as persons, discover and learn how to act rationally and accountably (Shotter, in press a).

It is in terms of the nature of that 'world' - the entities it contains and the structure of the relations between them - that people, if pressed, can justify their actions and render them 'visibly-rational-and-reportable-for-all-practical-purposes' (Garfinkel, 1967, p. vii); their justifications only being understood though by those who can inhabit that same world of meaning with them. Nonetheless, although thus limited, it is a way in which people can give reasons for their actions, giving an account of them in a way quite different from those couched in terms of rule-plan or script-following. Some of Laing's (1971, p. 21) 'knots' illustrate in quintessential form the creation of such 'worlds' and people's accounting for their actions by reference to the 'entities' they contain:

JILL: You put me in the wrong.
JACK: I am not putting you in the wrong.
JILL: You put me in the wrong for thinking you put me in the wrong.

The 'objective entity' being created between Jack and Jill here being 'the wrong' in which Jill is - but did she jump or was she pushed?

JACK: Forgive me.
JILL: No.
JACK: I'll never forgive you for not forgiving me.

Here, 'Jill not forgiving Jack' has been brought into 'objective' existence between the two of them.

Illustrated in Laing's examples are two features in the process of constructing 'moral worlds' I would like to examine in a little more detail. The first follows simply from the fact that, as people must often interlace their actions in daily affairs in with those of others, what they as individuals desire and what actually happens, are often two quite different things; a result intended apparently by nobody is produced.

Men mean to gratify their bestial lust and abandon their offspring and they inaugurate the chastity of marriage from which the families arise. The fathers mean to exercise without restraint their paternal power over their clients and they subject them to the civil powers from which the cities arise. The reigning orders of nobles mean to abuse their lordly powers over the plebians and they are obliged to submit to the laws which establish popular liberty ... Unable to attain all the utilities he wishes, he (a man) is constrained to seek those which are his due; and this is called 'just'. (Vico, 1744, quoted in Pompa, 1975, pp. 24-25)

The results of joint action, appearing to be independent of any particular individual's wishes or intentions, appear to be nobody's; they cannot be attributed (Heider, 1958; Jones & Davis, 1965) to an author. Thus they may have attributed to them an 'external' or 'objective' quality, the quality of things which 'just happen' rather than things which 'someone does'. Rather than their reasons, one seeks their external causes, just as one does for all other 'just-happening' events in the world. The outcome of joint action, rather than being experienced as a product of the participants in the action is thus attributed to something external to them, beyond their control - their genes, their environment, their social class, the rules they follow, or to any other external force or energy acting upon them and structuring their action, willy-nilly. A paradigm example here is the movement of the wineglass on the Ouija board. Clearly it does not move unless people's fingers are on it. But so strong is the conviction that its movements cannot be traced back to any intentions of the people there present - while its movements nonetheless display intelligence - that they are attributed often to an external 'spirit', acting through the medium of the people involved. The 'workings' of such social processes as these, by their very nature, are not subjectively experienced by the individuals involved in them, for the workings are not wholly there within them, but are spread out in the processes going on between them - hence their 'invisibility', and the possibility of people tying themselves up in knots of their own devising.

The second feature I want to mention may seem to be one totally at odds with the first; that, however, is not so. It is that all human action, whether autonomous or joint action, has an intentional quality to it; that is, in some fundamental sense it always seems 'to refer to something', ' to be directed upon an object', 'to contain something other than itself', 'to point to or mean something' - even if that something, like a unicorn, does not exist. It was Brentano (1973) who was essentially responsible for introducing this conception of intentionality into modern philosophy and psychology in an attempt to clarify the distinction between physical and mental phenomena. 'Every mental phenomenon contains within itself' said Brentano (1973),

something as an object. In a presentation something is presented, in a judgement something is affirmed or denied, in love something is loved, in hate something is hated, in desire something is desired, etc. (p. 124)

In their very occurrence, people's actions 'point to', 'indicate', or 'contain' something beyond themselves; physical phenomena cannot be said to contain something other than themselves in this way. What I take Brentano's doctrine to mean is this: action in progress, before it is complete (or abandoned) and its end attained (or not, as the case may be), contains at any one moment aspects of what so far has been done towards that end as well as specifying the style of what further may be done (Shotter, in press a,b). Thus 'intentional objects' are entities whose nature, while specified to a degree, is open to yet further specification. 'The wrong' into which Jack is supposed to have put Jill is open to argument. That it is something to argue about, an existent thing for them, follows from the first feature of joint action above; that its nature is still not settled follows from the intentional quality of the joint action within which it has been produced.

Taking these two features of joint action together suggests something of what is involved when people, without being aware even that they are doing it (never mind how they do it), create and sustain between themselves 'moral worlds' with their associated 'realities'. While in one sense 'objective' to the extent that their nature is independent of the wishes of individuals, in another sense they are not; they lack the completeness of truly objective entities. In their incompleteness they are 'intentional' in so much as what is so far rationally 'visible' in them dictates the style of that which is as yet to be discovered. So although they are purely mental constructions, the nature of such 'socially constructed realities' is quite different from that of scientific theories (constructed and proposed by individuals): as Popper (1963) points out, scientific theories should be falsifiable, but the nature of the 'reality' associated with a moral world cannot be falsified for it is both coercive and reflexive. That is, it provides a reality in terms of which the people who inhabit it must determine their actions; and this is the case not just for everyday realities, but for scientific ones too: for example, rational Skinnerians, if they want to remain living in a Skinnerian world, must see the human world in terms of stimuli and responses, and must, even if they disagree upon their precise form, structure their explanations in terms of schedules of reinforcement, and so on. In determining to live in such a world, its structure exerts a coercive force upon them, a morally coercive force in fact: that is what they have to do if they want to be good Skinnerians. But in so determining their actions, there is no way in which their actions can lead to results beyond that reality: that is the sense in which it is reflexive: no matter what happens, it is understood and dealt with in terms that the 'reality' provides. Lakatos (1970) has shown how a similar 'irrefutability' is also a property of all great scientific research programmes - such programmes revolving around a 'hard core' of irrefutable principles and progressing by rendering more and more things rationally visible by means of secondary elaborations ('auxiliary hypotheses') in terms of those hard core principles (see Shotter, in press b).

CONCLUDING REMARKS

I began this chapter by suggesting that rather than a fixed order of which we were merely ignorant, ambiguity and vagueness, uncertainty and conflict were real features of the world in which we lived. Thus if there were to be any truth or reliability in our social lives in such a world, it could only be because men took responsibility for being truthful and reliable; and I set out to construct an account of a world, a 'moral world', in which this was possible. It entailed the setting out of a quite new 'image of man' as the current 'model of man' - of man-the-mechanism - allowed discussion of human action only in non-evaluative terms, only as 'behaviour' in fact, and excluded the normative and evaluative terms essential to any account of human action, and people's responsibility for it. My first step was to distinguish between what I suggested were our two major modes of social being, our primary mode having an immersed, unselfconscious character, while our secondary mode, derived from it, was of a detached, self-conscious kind. I then suggested that it was in our more primary mode of being that we not only acquired the basic guidelines for all our subsequent conduct, but that it was within that mode that we were able, effortlessly, almost 'magically', to coordinate spontaneously our activities with others socialized into the same community as ourselves - this form of exchange, not being inborn, but humanly produced and inherited by us from our predecessors after birth, being the most truly human aspect of our human nature. And in the second part of the chapter I tried to illustrate in more detail the nature of activity in that mode: how a 'moral world' constructed unselfconsciously by its members in their exchanges with one another and experienced by them as an 'external' world, exerts a coercive force upon them to think, perceive, act and communicate in its terms. Given that the nature of its structure, and that of the entities it contains is determined by the patterns of exchange between the people producing it, it is possible for us to become what we treat ourselves as being.   And I illustrated the possible consequences for ourselves if we continue to treat ourselves merely as one of our own instruments or mechanisms, and ignore our ability to be responsible for ourselves, and the expressive dimension of our social lives in which we make, sustain and transform ourselves - not just in our concepts but in our very human being.

These consequences are, I think, real possibilities for us at the present time, for as we press ahead only with a form of psychological research apparently aimed at people increasing their powers of control or command over others, we misunderstand or ignore that aim of people themselves seeking to control and use powers from within their own being; it is not a 'visibly-rational-and-reportable' aim within our current modes of scientific thought and expression.   We must be careful that in our current attempts to survive our circustances, applying 'technologies of behaviour' (Skinner), we do not 'renounce or cripple our own form-shaping powers, which in the last analysis are to be brought out of ourselves' (Cassirer, 1953) - for if we do, we will lose rather than gain the ability to survive in our peculiarly human form, that is, our ability to construct and reconstruct for ourselves forms of life in which, as members of a community, we may spontaneously both coordinate our behaviour and understand one another (and perhaps ourselves) almost 'magically', without effort.   Rather than offering here, then, yet another generalized 'model of man' which attempts, as an object of contemplation to parallel in its structure some essential feature of human nature, I have tried instead to present an 'exemplary image', one which indicates what each of us as individuals might do, if we together want to retain our humanity, not what we must be.

APPENDIX:

PSYCHOLOGY AND OURSELVES: THE CASE FOR NON-EMPIRICAL RESEARCH

But how is the account of the 'exemplary image of man' proposed above to be validated?   What legitimates its claims to be taken seriously?   What is its status?   If it were being presented as a scientific theory, then one would, of course, ask straight away for evidence in support of it.   But none apparently is presented; it clearly lacks that kind of support.   The account seems to consist in merely the continual drawing of distinctions, in the describing of contrasts and relations, and in the appeal merely to self-evident facts in support of their reality - with the claim that such a form of description is a revealing one in some way, and that we have misled ourselves in the past by ignoring some of the distinctions it exemplifies.   But whether that is true or not, it, nonetheless, seems to have a 'take-it-or-leave-it' quality: either you find it useful or you do not; either you recognize its truth or find it meaningless; either you find it the 'exemplary image' claimed or a vapour of words with no substance.   'What is its source?' 'Can it be proved?' 'Could a research team be set up to investigate it?' 'Does it have any empirical consequences?'

In fact, it is an account of a non-empirical kind, not only one that 'fact' could not show to be wrong, but one which is prior to any empirical observation or theorizing, and which determines what are to count as 'facts' in subsequent empirical investigations.   Rather than aimed at answering questions like 'Are there any responsible people left at all in our society at the present moment?', it is directed at questions like 'What is it to be a responsible person?' Once we know the latter, we may set out to investigate empirically the former.   But the question as to what responsibility is is not settled by evidence; it is settled by asking those who already know, namely ourselves.   As more or less competent members of a moral community we know (or else we are not competent members, by definition) what in this or that, or some other circumstances is entailed in acting responsibly. But what we know cannot, in itself, easily be said, as it has an 'intentional' quality: although it is already specified to a degree it is open to yet further specification (but only of a specified kind). What we know cannot thus be rendered simply into rational principles, complete; there is always more about it which could be said. We remind ourselves of what we can legitimately do or say by continually confronting ourselves, in actuality or imagination, with this or that or some other particular situation, and simply asking ourselves 'What normally should be done or said here, and why (that is, what are my grounds for so doing or saying)?' What we know seems to have at any one moment the character of a landscape, one which can be characterized in terms of its landmarks and the relations between them, its regions and their boundaries, and in so describing it one may construct its 'map', its 'logical geography', as Ryle (1949) called it. As such, like any other map of a landscape, others can investigate it; such a map can be subjected to critical scrutiny and be checked out by other competent members of one's society - one is, after all, not offering it as an isolated individual but as such a member. Hence the account one offers, although not empirical, is not metaphysical either; to the extent that one is not proposing possible principles of natural or social order out of the blue, we may say that it is quasi-empirical - others may ask themselves the same questions and cross-check their answers with one's own.

The 'crisis' in social psychology   This non-empirical activity, although quite scandalous in a discipline proud of its empirical nature - its ability to support all its claims with 'facts' - is not uncommon. It has been creeping in, in one disguise or another, for some time now. McGuire (1973), for instance, in criticizing the hypothesis-testing paradigm in social psychological research, points out:

> Experiments on such hypotheses (as those in the area of interpersonal attraction, say) naturally turn out to be more like demonstrations than tests. If the experiment does not come out 'right', then the researcher does not say that the hypothesis is wrong but rather that something was wrong with the experiment, and he corrects and revises it ... (p. 449)

We know already that, at least in some circumstances, our hypotheses are obviously true, and our skill as experimenters is whether we can as 'ingenious stage managers' (McGuire, 1973) produce in the laboratory conditions which demonstrate that obviously true hypotheses are in fact correct. We rely in trying to do this, of course, upon being members of the same community into which our subjects have also been socialized.

Bem's self-perception theory   Bem (1967) has demonstrated that results produced in people by experimental manipulations (of a 'cognitive dissonance' kind - Festinger, 1957), could be accurately inferred by people not actually experiencing the manipulation, merely on the basis of their externally observing those people (tape-recordings of them) executing the experimental task. Leaving on one side here argument about Bem's own self-perception theory - that is, that we evaluate our own attitudes and beliefs as an external observer, by inference from our own behaviour; a hypothesis that I think is 'obviously true', but only in some circumstances - Bem claims validity for his simulation or 'interpersonal replication' approach because, not only may,

> The original Ss (actually involved in Festinger et al.'s experiments) ... be viewed as making self-judgements based on the same kinds of public evidence that the community originally employed in training them to infer the attitudes of any communicator, themselves included. (p. 187)

but 'dissonance theorists' themselves may also be viewed as having no difficulty in inferring that 'dissonance phenomena' will result from their experimental manipulations, because,

... in that inference they implicitly make use of the fact that they have been raised by the same socializing community as their Ss. (p. 198)

So here again we encounter a conceptual framework of a non-empirical kind, for, as Bem shows, rather than fact being able to prove it wrong, it functions to determine what are normally to count as 'the facts'.

I will not attempt a full-scale review of the non-empirical nature of much so-called empirical research here, but as McGuire (1973) indicates, if one were to, one would not have much difficulty in finding many more examples to illustrate his point that experiments are used more to illustrate or demonstrate the nature of a hypothesis rather than to test it. Indeed Tajfel & Fraser (1978) cite it as one of the main functions of experiments, to 'provide new hints about the texture of our social life' (p. 12).

The surprising and scandalous thing about such research, though, is this: it has no truth-value. It is neither true nor false. To repeat, such non-empirical (but quasi-empirical, rather than metaphysical) frameworks are prior to and determine what are normally to count as facts; they provide a system of necessarily interrelated categories (cf. Shotter, 1975, pp. 116-118) which serve to order empirical phenomena - only when one knows how to distinguish, for example, ' a promise' from all the other forms of human commitment like it but different from it, can one set out to answer empirical questions as to how many were actually honoured last year, for instance, or whether it is true that those sworn in blood are more likely to be kept than those not, and so on. Psychologists propose 'theories' with all the trappings of their having been tested for their truth; but in truth, if the experimenter is sufficiently competent and clever, his 'theories' are irrefutable in principle.

How, then, are they to be judged? How are accounts which reorder, disorder, or otherwise distort the normal order implicit in everyday life to be detected and replaced? Hints as to what is involved here have already been provided above, but I will try to draw them together here. First, rather obviously, if the account has not been produced by competent members of one's society asking themselves or others 'What here normally should be said or done?', but have merely asked themselves 'What theory might fit the facts here?', the normal order has been ignored, and its distortion is clearly a risk. Second, as Cavell (1969) points out, in general we do not require evidence for what normally should be said or done because, as competent members of a moral community, by definition we know it. In other words, we ought usually to be right: the extent of our ability to articulate that knowledge being, however, a matter of our skill at inventing and organizing the appropriate pattern of questions with which to confront ourselves, bearing in mind the massive richness of the landscape to be mapped. Thus, as Cavell (1969) adds, the claim that in general we do not require evidence does not rest upon a claim that we cannot be wrong about what we should do or say, but only that it would be extraordinary (i.e. not normal) if we were (often). The point about all actions in a moral world is that they are only sensibly questioned if there is some special reason for suspicion (Mills, 1940; Peters, 1958; Scott & Lyman, 1968; Cavell, 1969). And even questioned actions may still be justified; a successful justificatory account linking the action in question to other normally unquestioned acts, thus illustrating its normality. Thirdly, although we ought not (often) to be wrong, we sometimes most certainly are, and there is thus a clear advantage in others in our community proposing alternative accounts to ours, and our cross-checking with one another.

None of all this, however, can guarantee the truth of the accounts offered; it is a question of whether in their explicit order they parallel or distort the implicit forms of order already existing in our social life together. Furthermore, such accounts being 'intentional', there may be a number of alternatives, each specifying different 'directions' into the future, and so on. There is not space to go into such difficulties here. Suffice it here to say that, as Gergen (1978) suggests, there is now a strong case to be made out for what he calls 'generative theory', theory of a non-empirical kind which has the capacity to challenge our current accounts of the order in social life, and to offer accounts of fresh modes of social being. Such theory, liberated both from the press of immediate fact and the necessity for verification, while still open, of course, to critical scrutiny, could result from many other kinds of investigation other than just experimentation, as at present - literary, dramatic, poetic, organized patterns of questions, ritual exercises, plus whatever other 'aids to a sluggish imagination' (Garfinkel) one might invent, could all be used. Their point, to recall a point made earlier, would be to remind us of what (as members of a community) we must do to sustain and enhance our peculiarly human mode of existence (in which direct and spontaneous understanding is possible); something that we already know, but which have some difficulty in articulating. For us, our theories about ourselves can change us. Investigation of how such processes work though, is hardly as yet begun.

EDITED DISCUSSION

B. FLETCHER: Given the unaccountability and uncertainty of the results of joint action, and the distortion of individual intentions occurring as a result of that joint action, how can individuals be held to be morally responsible for any interactions they have with others?

J. SHOTTER: I would like to make a clear distinction between a social world and a moral world. While in a social world there can be unaccountable joint action, in a moral world - with its associated social order - there is a tendency to minimize it. A social order, besides working to produce a division of labour, seems to work also to 'manufacture' (socialize) individuals who know how to take responsibility for their actions; a kind of self-organizing process is at work to minimize accountability. For without accountability a social order cannot endure. People in a society, without any self-conscious planning, seem to take decisions and arrange themselves in relation to one another so that accountability and individual responsibility are not only brought into being but are maximized.

M. J. MORGAN: A great deal of what you say about the nature of social experience could be applied just as readily to many other aspects of experience (e.g. perceptual experience - seeing, smelling and so on). So, I wonder how many different worlds you want to invent. What criteria have to be satisfied for qualification as a separate world?

J. SHOTTER: I want to distinguish everyday 'physical activities' (like breathing) which one does without thinking from 'social activities' (e.g. I raise my eyebrows, say a word, move my hand) which in my community have particular functions which bring about particular types of results when directed towards particular people. I am interested in the latter types of activity. As for inventing worlds, it seems to me that all the time people are inventing worlds between themselves. It is the actual process of invention that I want to understand.

J. A. GRAY: I am going to sound a note of warfare, because I think that what you talk of is something very different from scientific explanation and something actually not as important or valuable as scientific explanation. You offer us description and, as description, it is very good. But does it offer anything that we could not have got from a good novelist a hundred years ago? Secondly, if explanation is offered, you do not offer any means of testing your explanation.   Of course, testing is the cardinal feature of scientific work through which we can discard theories which are proved useless; and so we can make progress.   The danger in your approach is that we may go round in circles.   Thirdly, you are taking social interaction as given, rather than as something requiring explanation.   I want to know why people do interact the way they do, why they form the social constructions they do; and I have no doubt whatsoever that in any ultimate explanation of that we are going to have to take into account those features of our social interaction which derive from our status as biological organisms.   Fourthly, I find in your chapter a 'magical incantation' which goes: intentions/intentionality.   What is that incantation saying?   You have tried to explain that there is always an object to an intentional action.   You have said that, in loving, someone is loved; and, in thinking, a thought is thought.   Would you say that, in defecation, something is excreted?   And does that make defecation an intentional action? You have said that intentional objects are always open to further specification.   But is not the same true of an atom?   I regard that as a scientific concept.   Is there a difference?   I am not sure that the language of intentionality is meant to give explanations.

J. SHOTTER: Let me say first that I offer a specific theory of what constitutes important aspects of personhood in a social order.   You may very well be right, ultimately, that what I have offered is mere description and does not do any kind of work.   My efforts are towards describing activities in a human world in such a way that one can see the functions they serve.   So, in childhood socialization, one points to some mother-child behaviours as being relevant, say, to language learning and others not being relevant.   This may not be explanation but it is description which aids understanding and is more revealing than reading a novel.   Now let me take the point about testability. Well, testability can come in various forms.   If by studying everyday mother-child interactions one successfully partials out the important behaviours, one can then put into operation a planned form of interaction, say for deaf, blind or autistic children.   One can test in practical situations.   Then there is the type of testability in which, through a formal account, the people involved in an affair actually come to recognize their actions, and this has direct repercussions for subsequent interactions.   On your point about social interaction being taken as given, I would want to agree with you.   But I would add that one has got to start somewhere.   It seems to me that any attempts that you personally might want to make to explain social interaction biologically cannot take place until you know precisely what it is that needs explanation. I have actually said that we are something more than just persons, but this personal mode of being is one that we have access to.   And now let me answer your point concerning incantations about intentionality.   I understand your complaint, but I claim that, because of this peculiar position we have inside our own being, so to speak, we know about intentionality because it is part and parcel of everything we are and everything we do.   We may not understand it but we are in a good position to investigate it.

M. J. MORGAN: You refer to non-empirical research which, as far as I can understand it, refers to the study of that body of knowledge that we already possess.   In what sense, therefore, can that be called 'research'?

J. SHOTTER: Once you have accepted as a starting-point an ability to discriminate things you do from things that happen (that is, to discriminate actions), then other types of distinctions are possible.   For example, you are aware of the relation between believing something and trying to put beliefs into practice. To tease out that sort of relationship requires orderly investigation.

J. A. GRAY: I am not sure that is an answer.   So let me take an example.   Vygotsky says that consciousness and control appear only at a late stage in the development of a function, after it has been used and practised unconsciously and spontaneously.   But there is also an opposite view of consciousness: that it is present at that very time when you are first learning and practising a form of behaviour. You admit that there is no point in proposing a theory that you cannot test. How would you defend one of these views against another? They are diametrically opposed. How do you rule one out?

M. J. MORGAN: Well, let us note that the theory of natural selection has been cited as the sort of scientific theory to which we ought to aspire. Yet we have there a clear example of where direct experimentation is not feasible.

J. A. GRAY: That is perfectly true but, since Darwin, there has been a large number of experimental tests of theories constructed with the axioms of natural selection in the background. If findings were negative then the theory of natural selection would be accorded less respect. If there are axioms in the humanist approach, let us hear what they are, and how on the basis of those axioms you can construct testable theories.

B. FLETCHER: I should like to ask Jeffrey Gray whether, in his view, the range of phenomena to which people like John Shotter refer are actually worth studying? Secondly, if so, does he think that they are outside the scope of psychology? Does he think that they are not amenable to investigation, or is it that our scientific methods are inadequate?

J. A. GRAY: Yes, those phenomena are extremely important; of course they are. There is absolutely no reason why they should not come within the normal compass of scientific investigation and explanation. The four points which Peter Warr raised in discussion (see p. 305) are in my view unnecessary: the key issue is that of testability. It is possible, for example, to place experience under laboratory scrutiny. If somebody could propose a way of testing John Shotter's views about social behaviour, we should have a useful theory. Until that is done, his proposals are not useful. I can think of no good reason in principle why that should not be done.

B. FLETCHER: But perhaps there are some phenomena that can be studied only in the natural setting: otherwise, you will distort the reality.

J. SHOTTER: And I would add that the question of testability is not simply a question of scientific experiment in itself, but a question of the precise way in which a theory is formulated.

N. M. CHESHIRE: It seems to me that there is a considerable body of informed opinion which would argue that there are a great many ways that scientific theories and understanding develop, other than .by falsifying particular hypotheses.

L. SMITH: I agree. You cannot expect the testability criterion to settle a conceptual issue.

R. L. REID: To me, as a 'radical behaviourist', an explanation is something that answers a question. Depending on the kind of question you ask, say about behaviour, you might draw upon a vast range of sources for the answer. You might refer to a historical context or a cultural context; you might even refer to literature; you might refer to evolutionary theory; you might refer to Pavlovian conditioning or to information-processing.

M. J. MORGAN: But let us not pretend that there are not fundamental disagreements. We cannot do any harm by thrashing out these issues: to suggest otherwise is destructive.

R. L. REID: Well, I would just say that the technique of exaggerating a point of view is perhaps used rather too much in psychology.

Chapter 3

The rise and fall of human nature

V. Reynolds

The title of this chapter sounds rather grand so perhaps I had better start by clarifying what it means. By the 'rise' of human nature is meant the coming into existence of man as a natural phenomenon. By the 'fall' of human nature is meant the disappearance of man as a form of life which can be comprehended in naturalistic terms.

The title of this volume, 'Models of Man', leaves the door wide open to contributors to say whatever they want about how they envisage man, or how they think man ought to be envisaged. There are at least four types of approach to this challenge. First, one could present the basis for a general model. As I see it this is the approach of (among others) Harre, Eysenck, Fransella, Joynson and Shotter. Second, one could discuss questions of method mainly, for example whether to have one model or a more pluralist approach, and what types of conceptual framework and theory to use. This seems to be more the approach of people like Jahoda and perhaps Warr. Third, one could try to avoid model construction altogether as being premature and do something else, as Gray appears to have done. And fourth, one could take on a part of the field of action and discuss it, but be explicit that other fields or approaches exist, so one would see oneself as presenting a model among many possible models without any claim to superiority of one's own. This seems to be the approach of Beloff, Boden and Miller.

The kind of model presented here is of the first kind - in other words, a general model. General models tend to be quite different from each other, and the present one is no exception. This, however, seems to be an inevitable outcome of throwing the net so wide in the first place, and need not worry us in the least; indeed it tells us something significant about our object of study.

The major feature of the model presented here is an emphasis on the time dimension. This seems often to be lacking from the models presented by psychologists. Two features of this time-based model are as follows: first, a pre-occupation with evolutionary time, which throws the entire model into a very long-term perspective by normal psychological standards, although not by the standards of people who are normally concerned with the evolution of life as a whole, let alone the evolution of the planets, or the solar systems of the universe. Second, the present model emphasizes the time dimension of individual lives. Indeed evolution cannot be understood without thinking in terms of the birth, life-span and death of the individuals concerned. The past, therefore, whether of the species or of the individual is very important in an anthropologist's model, and in so far as he is a physical anthropologist· he means the organic past of the species. Of course, if he were a historian, he would be much more concerned with the immediate cultural past and indeed we do need to consider this past and shall consider it in the present model. However, anthropologists do often acknowledge their relative ignorance of this aspect. In the case of pre-literate societies there is no written history and the only history available to field workers is an orally transmitted tradition which goes back a few generations and then becomes mythological. In other societies this is not the case. For instance, in the case of the Mayas of Yucatan we have quite extensive sources of data for the historical past and these can be brought into play in presenting models of Mayan activity in bygone times.

Second, there is the matter of what happens in the here and now as we currently conceive of it. We should not fool ourselves into thinking that our conception of the here and now is not very much conditioned by our historically derived view of things as well as by the accepted paradigms of thought and concepts available to us at the moment of thinking. However, we can try to produce models of man as he now is.

Third, a model of man which has any claim to universality should concern itself with the future, both at the organic level and at the historical level.

Thus in the model presented here, time is not just a bit extra added on, it actually is the basis of the model from which the other dimensions and ideas follow. It has in fact such significance that it changes the rules of method as it proceeds. The model thus becomes a dynamic or diachronic model which itself is subject to variation as time proceeds.

As life proceeded it brought into existence the class of mammals. The early mammals, which appear to have been insectivorous, threw off a branch which became arboreal, frugivorous and herbivorous and this group included the earliest primates which date back some 60 million years. From the early lower primates there evolved a number of different types: the extant lower primates, the monkeys (New World and Old World) and the Dryopithecinae, a variety of ape-like creatures living in the Miocene some 15-20 million years ago. These ape-like creatures gave rise to Australopithecus in the Pliocene some five million years or so ago and we have finds of early Homo something like two or three million years ago, well established by a million years ago (Pilbeam, 1972; Simons, 1972). Looking ahead we are faced with the question whether the evolution of our species will last another one million, five million, 50 million, 100 million years, etc., or whether it is doomed to cease after another 50 years or so when mankind blows itself to bits. This is a speculative question though scarcely an idle one. From the perspective of studies of the length of species in evolution (e.g. Simpson, 1949), we can derive figures that relate to the average life expectancy of species and apply them to ourselves. However, this does not seem a particularly useful procedure since in the case of all other species the processes have been limited to wholly naturalistic organic evolution, whereas in the case of man, this is not so. Culture and technology have brought about radical changes. Mankind may well have to leave this planet and go in search of other habitable planets, in which case it is an almost inevitable outcome that he will speciate since the groups so formed will be effectively isolated from each other probably for several thousands, if not millions of years. Thus, if we can survive this coming century or two, there may be a great future ahead.

PHYLOGENY

Life in the early hominid past has to be construed very largely as the last phase of man as a natural phenomenon, that is, one who is subject entirely to the processes of animal evolution generally. Here one is thinking of Australopithecus, a rather small, upright creature with a brain size that was proportionate to overall body size. The overall context in which the behaviour of this early hominid has to be understood is primarily ecological and evolutionary. We can speak confidently about the 'behaviour' of hominids and deal with them as animal species. We can describe their way of life in terms of adaptation to the environment. We can be very certain that they were subject to all the normal rules of natural selection in regard to the evolution of their physical form and their behaviour. Being primates of an advanced kind we can assume they had fairly complex signalling techniques, that they expressed fairly complex emotions and that they were capable of a sophisticated degree of manipulating the objects in their environment, of learning how to use objects to increase their food supplies, and it would certainly be quite wrong to think of them as 'creatures of instinct'. Regarding their social structures and the extent of social relationships in early hominids we can almost certainly expect these to have been exceedingly complex. The social organization and social relationships of apes at the present time have only recently been subject to scientific scrutiny but have already yielded many surprises and show promise of giving us a lot more information in the years to come. Man was, at the Australopithecine stage, part of nature and any characteristics of the early hominids would be characteristics that one could compare on a one-to-one basis with those of closely related species, especially chimpanzees and gorillas.

THE RECENT PAST: HISTORICAL FACTORS

From the consideration of the early hominids, we next move on to a consideration of the more immediate past, that is man in historical times. We can perhaps, for simplicity's sake, consider three main regions, Africa and South America, Asia, and Europe and the Near East, with a view to isolating cultural differences which are going to affect the model of man that we wish to present.

In African and South American societies we have mostly to deal with small-scale societies of a kind beloved by social anthropologists, though there are exceptions such as at Benin, at Ife, and at Zimbabwe, to name but a few of the ancient kingdoms of Africa. Although it is hard to generalize, we are mostly dealing with pre-literate cultures with relatively short-depth oral traditions, relatively clear cut social rules and social structures, and relatively unequivocal prescriptions about how individuals ought to act and ought not to act. These very general features affect the model of man appropriate for pre-literate peoples in areas that have not been subject to modernization to any great extent at the present time. The same applies to parts of the world which continue to be inhabited by peoples who have not so far fallen into Western or Asiatic frames of reference. We should be careful to avoid drawing any conclusions about 'man' in general without including man as he exists in these societies, unless we specifically wish to exclude them. An example of the latter, for instance, is Morris's (1967) model of man in 'The Naked Ape' in which he initially states quite clearly at the outset that he is concerned with man as he exists in modern industrialized society, rather than peoples living in primitive tribes. His argument for making this decision is that the more industrialized nations are the successful ones and that these, therefore, provide the best basis for drawing up the model of man which he wants to present, which is, in his case, a biological model. This exclusion of pre-literate tribes has seemed unjustifiable to most anthropologists who, by definition, are more pre-occupied with small-scale societies in parts of the world relatively free of the very constraints of modern civilizations that Morris wants to emphasize.

The second region we want to look at is the Asian region. Here we have seen the growth of major civilizations in bygone times, for example at Mohenjo-Daro in India. In India too we have the rise of Hinduism and the caste system. The ancient civilizations of China developed complex and ramified bureaucracies, religions such as Tao, Confucianism, and Buddhism and science some 2000 years ago, documented in detail by Needham (1954). The civilization of Japan has produced the Shinto religion and philosophies such as Zen Buddhism, which though originating in

China has subsequently found expression in other parts of the world.   All such developments have been responsible for producing models of man in which he has been mostly construed as a spiritual entity, or as an entity which can enter into some relationship with spiritual forces in the inanimate world.   The major difference between them and the third group, to which I refer next, is the extent to which a scientific approach based on the notion of 'objectivity' has been considered relevant to the understanding of man himself.

The third region includes the societies of Europe and the Near East and deriving from them those of modern USA, Russia, Australia, etc.   Here we can see the growth of medium-sized states in ancient times, especially those of Greece and Rome with their associated religions.   The post-Greco-Roman religions are for the most part Islam, Judaism and Christianity.   In the case of the vast societies that have arisen in the Western world, we have to consider man as very much a part of, not to say a product of, enormous bureaucratic structures whose existence is an outcome of a number of forces, perhaps the most important of which is the existence of continuous conflict over the rich resources of the European and Middle Eastern area during the last few millennia.   Ever since the Egyptians cultivated the fertile land along the River Nile and their society brought into existence the Pharaohs and the succession of dynasties in the old and new kingdoms, the problem of whether or not there is one god or many has existed.   Religions which have promoted the existence of one god have tended to be outward-looking and have often become quite aggressive in their efforts to convert the so-called unbelievers or heathens to their ways of thinking.   This aggression has seemed to some to point to an inherent aggressiveness of man; however, this seems an unwarranted conclusion and one can more easily understand human aggression in terms of rational efforts (i.e. rational in terms of the people making the efforts, not necessarily in terms of others outside the situation such as biologists, sociologists, students of politics, etc.) to obtain more of scarce resources, backed by religions that give people motivational reasons for accepting the need to fight other human beings.

THE PRESENT: ONTOGENETIC CONSIDERATIONS

We come now to ourselves as we are at the present time. Today we can see ourselves as the creatures of those cultures that went before us in our particular part of the world which is a very pluralist one. We can note convergences, for instance in the field of economics and in the nature of the organization of bureaucratic states, a subject which has been extensively investigated by Weber (1947). We can see the growth of science as we understand it and relate this to the processes of states in winning wars. It is impossible to see the growth of science without appreciating the impact of scientific thinking, with its ability to improve technology, as one of the great forces underlying the political achievements of some countries against others.   Those nations and states that developed the greatest force, coupled with the most sustained effort, were able to survive intact while those that were beaten had to change and their versions of 'reality' and the kind of people that they promoted or regarded as acceptable, had to change. Scientific war and rational bureaucracy have come to treat man as a unit, an object to be manipulated for purposes of obtaining the maximum concerted effort in times of national crisis and peace-time productivity.

The individual lifespan has to be understood as part of an ongoing, socio-economic, political process. Theories which emphasize personal freedom from the immediate here and now, such as existentialist theories which hold that there are no constraints on human action, can be seen to have their significance against a background view of man as a very much constrained creature, and without that background they lose their force. If we all agreed that there were no constraints on human action and that there was no such thing as human nature, the contentiousness of such arguments would cease to exist. It is because the opposite is thought to be the case that such arguments tend to be relegated to an intellectualist fringe or to be considered as wholly inappropriate or wrong.

Let us come down from this rather abstract level of discussion to a more tangible level and ask some questions about the individual lifespan as it now occurs. For a start, we can ask whether there are any very early differences or similarities in the human lifespan which might be worthy of note. For example, given our ideas about human nature, its rise and fall, and given that with the advent of cultural life man was no longer subject primarily to the forces of natural selection in the way in which other species are, could it not perhaps still be the case that in early infancy man shows certain characteristics the world over that indicate he is in fact very much an animal in the true sense of the word, that is a creature lacking cultural inputs and outputs? If there is any point in the life cycle at which man can be considered to be free of culture then certainly early infancy is that time. The question is whether there is any such time at all. Writers such as Eibl-Eibesfeldt (1970) and some other ethologists have claimed that there is such a time in early infancy, and have focused on such things as the infant's early cries, the 'rooting' response by which the infant comes to find the mother's milk, the sucking response and so on, as evidence that man the world over is acting in a purely mammalian, or animal-like way, at the very early stages of the life cycle. Indeed it would be rather difficult to imagine man entering the world a fully fledged cultural being, although it must be remembered that much of his antenatal life has existed in a cultural context. As against the more ethologically oriented school, are those who while embracing ethological concepts wish to emphasize that the mother with whom the infant interacts, to whom it cries and so on, is a highly cultural creature and her responses from the very outset during pregnancy and the birth process are cultural responses. There is thus a conditioning process which has been in existence both before birth, during birth, and is present after birth, and as with all natural phenomena, this conditioning process must be considered as part of the causation of what the infant does. This is not to deny that a conditioning process is present in the ongoing behaviour, early or late, of all animal species. To deny this would be to deny one of the basic tenets of ethology itself. No animal at any point in its lifespan acts without responding to the environment which serves as a conditioning agent. In insects, for example, it has been shown that what appear to be very largely innate processes are subject to changes in their form and timing and function, depending on environmental circumstances (Von Frisch, 1954). What is at issue in the human case is whether the conditioning is cultural conditioning, that is the result of ideas of appropriateness and inappropriateness, or is conditioning of a more tangible physical kind, for example dietary, prevailing temperature, etc. Authors such as Richards (1974) have argued that the early infantile stage has to be seen as a stage during which many of the inputs into the infant's world are indeed cultural inputs and with this I wholly agree.

This raises the question of whether the distinction between cultural and natural inputs is a valid one and here I think it is most important to be clear that it is both valid and very significant. Nevertheless, having said that we must bear in mind that cultural inputs do serve to produce differences which may well have significance for survival and thus for the process of natural selection. To say this is not to deny that they are cultural inputs, but to show how cultural inputs are related to natural inputs. To give an example, it has been shown that very shortly after birth there are differences between peoples from different societies in regard to such things as head and body movement. A series of tests was performed on North American Indians of the Navaho tribe, European babies and Australian Aborigine ones (Freedman, 1974, and film). These three groups were shown to differ in regard to some behaviours which had hitherto been regarded as having 'reflexive status' by clinical paediatricians. The Navaho Indian baby lies very still after birth, it rarely cries and appears very relaxed and lacking in muscle tone and general vitality. If its head is placed face down on the pillow, instead of moving it rapidly to one side to enable itself to breathe it tends to suffocate and has to be moved. By contrast the European infant has a quite clear head response which moves its head to the side so that it can obtain an unobstructed air supply, on top of which it is quite active at birth crying noisily and moving its arms and legs in all sorts of directions. By contrast again the Australian Aborigine not only does the actions of the European baby but can also produce aspects of coordinated behaviour not seen in European babies until later in the life cycle. It can lift its head well off the pillow, it can grasp in a directed fashion rather than in the undirected fashion of the newborn European infant, it has better eye control and generally has more advanced features. How should we interpret these neonatal differences? A possible answer could be that in the three systems of infant care adopted by these societies, three different kinds of infant have been selected for, namely, late developers (Navaho); standard developers (ourselves) and early developers (Australian Aborigine). The Navaho child is traditionally wrapped rather tightly in a series of long cloth strips and then placed in a cradle basket which is, at any rate traditionally, carried on the back, propped up on the ground, or hung from a horse's saddle (Leighton & Kluckhohn, 1947). In the case of the European child, it is wrapped and placed in a cot which gives it some freedom of movement. In the case of the Aborigine child, it is placed more or less naked on the mother's shallow cradle board which is slung from her shoulder and balances on her hip bone as she moves around on the walkabout. Owing to the way of life she is forced to move around frequently and cannot put the baby in a fixed position.

These three sets of circumstances, which are cultural differences based on economic and other factors can be seen to have provided the matrix for selection of different kinds of individuals at birth. In such ways culture and nature can act on each other and produce different levels of viability of different kinds of behaviour and thus we can see in early infancy that what we might take to be wholly natural behaviour may have been subject to the force of cultural selection as part of natural selection. It will not have escaped notice that in the above example, our own infant was regarded as a sort of standard, while American Indian and Australian Aborigine children were seen as extremes. This presumably is a form of sociocentrism which should have been avoided. Although this may not be an important point in that discussion, it certainly becomes a most important point in the evaluation of, for instance, our own science as opposed to other sciences; that is, we should not regard our own way of thinking or doing things as in some sense a standard, but should be prepared to see ourselves as a bizarre or extreme form of solution to the possibilities open to us.

It remains the case that there is one strong element of human life that can be seen to follow the normal pattern of causation found in animal life generally, namely physical development, and to the extent that our development can be understood as physical development, we can ally ourselves for purposes of comparison, and in respect of the ideas we use in the analysis, to the field of animal psychology and mammalian physiology in general. Thus the development of the body and the brain proceeds along programmed lines, that is, lines programmed both by the genes and by the physical environment in which those genes function. For present purposes, behavioural development can be construed as that aspect of the development of action which refers to the organic side. Action itself is reserved as a term for behaviour plus meaning, where meaning is taken to include those aspects of the cultural input which have a non-tangible existence, namely the exhortations to do things in particular ways and the taboos on doing them in other ways which give our actions communicative significance at the cultural level. These rules themselves, although they have a great impact on physical development, do not lend themselves to naturalistic observation, cannot be measured in naturalistic fashion and have no physical existence (even if they have physical equivalents). The fact that they are intangible should not lead us to think that they are not absolutely fundamental to an understanding of human action.

After infancy we move on to the period of early and middle childhood. During this time there is an ever-present development but it appears to be a long and slow one. It often seems puzzling that middle childhood in particular takes so long. It seems as if a whole period of years could be shortened; there is a reduction in the rate of physical growth between the ages of, say, 5 or 6 to 10 or 12 years, and the same is true of the rate of mental progress when we compare those years with the preceding ones, or the ones that follow immediately afterwards (the so-called 'adolescent spurt'). But in fact quite a lot is going on. There is the development of an orientation of the child toward its peers while at the same time it continues to have a dependent relationship with its natal family. It alternates between the two: there are periods of return to the home and periods when the child goes out and explores the world and in particular the world of its peers. There is a lot of play, often of very imaginative kinds, cultural dramas are enacted and there are also more physical kinds of play in which a great deal of rough and tumble romping occurs. Gender differences develop on the basis of sex differences present since infancy.

There is also development of a cultural version of appropriate action for each individual. That is to say that side by side with physical development there is a shaping of knowledge and a consequent shaping of action such that the child sees itself as an acceptable member of both the family group and the peer group. This involves a certain amount of mastery of the ongoing language and its concepts, a development of competence at self-presentation with regard to matters such as dress, and attention to those things in life that are shown to be significant by the important people, such as teachers, whom the child comes across. If we consider differences from place to place, we see differences that are often quite remarkable. Some societies seem to favour a quiet child who is encouraged to be self-effacing and not to interfere in matters concerning adults. This, for instance, is, or was, the trend among some American Indian tribes of the South Western USA. In other societies a noisy, rather aggressive, competitive way of life is encouraged and children are launched into their own little competitive spheres at school and even in the home. Such for instance seems to be the case in such countries as the USA, Canada, Britain, Australia and so on, and is clearly related to the need for a competitive nature in later life.

Besides this well-known contrast, we should think of the contrast in gender types within cultures. For instance, Beloff's contribution to the present volume (chapter 18) asks 'Are models of man models of women?', and this question is of course one which is of great current interest and we are beginning to understand how our own society has conceived of the difference between the sexes in terms of what can and cannot, should and should not be said, thought and done by members of the two sexes, what their aspirations should or should not be, and so on. We are finding that many of our hitherto unquestioned assumptions are not only questionable but have been inhibiting to the process of self-development of women. Alleviating this problem, even though it has been clearly seen, has not been easy and again here some people have turned to biology for the explanation, claiming that behavioural differences based on genetic predispositions exist between the two sexes and that these underlie the difficulty of changing the way of life and the traditional occupations and aspirations of one sex or the other. Again it is possible to dispute this claim that there are biological predispositions that underlie the difficulties encountered. It is by no means clear that the different ideas of appropriateness and so forth which are currently subject to review, are not most immediately tied up with our kind of social structure which again is tied up with the economic and political structure and basis of our own society. Thus to change conventional attitudes without changing the fundamental social structures and economic circumstances of the groups within which those attitudes exist is probably impossible. Indeed it could even be said that the whole project of changing things by bringing them into conscious thought and making them explicit may be putting the cart before the horse. It could well be that the attitudes themselves will only change after a more fundamental shake-up of social forms.

After childhood comes adolescence. The adolescent is currently thought of as a highly troublesome creature and is indeed in very many cases a highly troublesome creature to his parents and to society and its agencies. Adolescents do seem to have difficulty coming to terms with the manifold restrictions and dictates they see all around them and thus they appear, to more orthodox members who have got past this difficult transition period, to be 'revolting' and to need disciplining in various ways. This difficult adolescent period must, I think, be related to the kind of society we ask individuals to live in and also to the fact that we have not yet adjusted the timing of education and the age at which adult status is given to individuals to their increasingly rapid physical development. It is thus, to take an example, still an offence for a man to have sexual intercourse with a girl aged 15, when in actual fact girls aged 15 are often as fully mature in the physical sense and arguably as mature in the psychological sense as they ever will be. Naturally the question of 'maturity' raises further issues and it can always be argued that a person is not 'mature'. Nevertheless, it could well be that individuals aged 15 are more 'mature' than older people, since they may see more clearly for not being ensnared in the socio-cultural mesh which subsequently stultifies their vision and their possibilities for self-expression. For present purposes, however, the matter can perhaps be summed up by saying it is in adolescence particularly that there appears to be the widest gulf between the model of man experienced by the individual himself or herself and the model of man that is more universally accepted in the society as a whole. Thus the adolescent says and feels he or she is different. It may not go much further than this, or the individual may be quite explicit as to how he or she is, or feels, different. Often adults are seen as boring and, indeed, some of us recognize that by the standards being applied, we are boring. We, however, most likely take the view of the old man in Shaw's 'Back to Methuselah' that our own boringness masks a degree of wisdom and intellectual sophistication not to be found among adolescents.

Passing beyond adolescence we move on to the fully adult world. Adult status is commonly defined in terms which in any given society give such individuals full rights and expect them to behave in ways which indicate an understanding of the social rules and hold them responsible for doing so, so that they can be incriminated and if need be imprisoned for failure to abide by the rules. It is in this adult world that Rom Harré's 'Rhetoricians' talk and strut (see Harré, chapter 14). It is in this world that we find the rhetoric of science, and the world of Hans Eysenck (see chapter 4). It is also in this world that we find the 'loners' who are totally out of touch with the world as most of us know it and those who have a grudge against it. We adults can opt to emulate and follow particular schools of thought, or to reject them. In our early adult years, some of us opt for further training in the particular field of study we have chosen to make our own. This is not just the case in our own culture; for instance, in Buddhism, some young men, indeed very many of them, opt (or at any rate used to opt) for further training in the religious field and eventually some of them become monks. Such training may take considerable periods of time during the impressionable years of early adult life. There may be a long period of rebuffs during which the older masters simply reject the status of the newcomers as having any claims to true understanding of what is at issue in the sciences concerned. Long periods of study are thus called for, and finally the individual emerges as a confident 'master' of his field. He then proceeds to do two things. Firstly to teach pupils of his own and, secondly, to discover to his chagrin that the world is full of others who have developed in their own particular ways and who are not able to share his view of reality, or of what is important, or of what should and should not be done, or of what his own personal value and contribution are to his own field of science or study, or the world as a whole. It is given to very few indeed to become acknowledged masters in the general sense and, in most cases, people who emerge as having very widespread influence are more or less spiritually inclined, so that the very greatest men who have ever existed have been those who have founded new religions. Their impact is to be measured in terms of the thousands or even millions of people who have accepted the version of life, the parameters of existence, which they first put forward as being the best. In the case of science, we also have to do with the production of better theories, but here 'better' means more in harmony with the natural working of the universe and, at any rate in Western cultures, the physical rather than the non-physical or spiritual world. Thus it is only in parts of the world where physical matters have been given such pre-eminence that scientists have achieved any degree of what could be called fame. Even in such cases, however, the scientific world has seen famous scientists come and go as their theories have been shown to be incapable of explaining more than a small part of the phenomena that they initially set out to explain. This has been particularly obvious in the field of astronomy and in the physical sciences. In other sciences, such as psychology, there are currently many rival theories, and the newcomer to the field has to decide which one to adopt. His answer will depend very largely on his prior training, his general orientation and his perhaps intuitive feeling that one or other approach is likely to be more rewarding. Thus we have some who want to adopt rather rigid scientific approaches and others who want to approach man in a much more open-ended way.

MORALITY AND VALUES

A point that needs at least some discussion is the issue of morality or of evaluation as stressed by Shotter (chapter 2). Any model which does not deal properly with this cannot amount to much as a general model of man. As stated at the outset, one may not wish to engage in this kind of discussion and there is no reason why a limited model should do so. On the other hand this chapter presents a general model and therefore the issue of morality has to be included. The need to say this is altogether an indication of the place which morality currently holds in the field of scientific discourse in general. We see morality as a difficult problem in so far as we consider ourselves to be scientists or those who wish to be scientific. We see the issue of value judgements often as completely opposed to the issue of the understanding of causal processes. There is such a thing as the 'naturalistic fallacy', so-called because it is felt to be a mistake to confuse what is with what ought to be. This long-standing dichotomy in our thinking must somehow relate to the nature of our society and our view of science and our view of ourselves. Certainly in so far as we think we can see the processes of nature and 'reality' as lying outside and beyond ourselves, we almost inevitably run into this dichotomy. The problem of course is how to relate those aspects of ourselves which we feel to be important to reality itself, and this is no place to get into that interminable series of arguments about whether man is the centre of all human understanding, or whether human understanding is primarily a coming to grips with a non-human reality. That, however, is the field of argument as it historically exists within our culture and we often take rather a sceptical view, or we frankly reject the view of others in other cultures who see man as being part of a universe that, all through from the atomic level to the astronomical one, contains a spiritual and a moral dimension. Such a view would hold that there is right and wrong in the relations between, let us say, stones and plants and such ideas have, of course, found expression, for instance in the Japanese garden, the elements of the Yin and Yang in Taoism and other religions of the East, especialy some of the ancient Chinese sciences and philosophies. Thus it is not necessarily the case that man should divorce the ideas of good and bad, right, wrong, should be, etc., from the physical world.

This may be an aspect of current thinking which will have to be superseded in due course by something better. In the meantime there does not seem to be any way in which we can bring moral issues and moralistic matters of judgement into science as we now know it. This creates enormous problems for us. We have developed a science which can predict the relations between physical phenomena with greater or lesser accuracy. This science has, as already described, played a not inconsiderable part in the survival of our culture and is therefore generally held in respect. At the same time man is everywhere aware that morality has been severely neglected as an ingredient of human happiness or the success of our culture. In any case, there is this awkward opposition of moral issues and non-moral ones, or ones that are held to be non-moral.

At the present time 'westernization' is proceeding apace in many parts of the globe. Societies living in balance with nature - such as for instance the Aboriginal Malaysians, or peoples of Central India or Bushmen of the Kalahari or Australian Aborigines before most of them became urbanized or extinct - having imbued their physical worlds with morality, have also developed long-term survival strategies that enabled them to avoid over-exploiting their habitats and thereby becoming extinct. Some such thinking would appear to be necessary if the human race is to survive. It is therefore quite possibly the case that it is totally unproductive and even dangerously destructive to hold that science needs to proceed without regard to the oughts of what it is doing, the shoulds and should nots - it may well be that only by the incorporation of a value judgement all along the line can mankind hope to avoid the destruction of itself through the thinkings and machinations of scientists. If scientists choose not to consider the rights and wrongs of what they do and prefer to leave this to others, their strategy will only succeed if they are answerable to the moral elements in the community. So far this century we have not seen much impact on science of the moralists. It has been the century of the scientist, and this continues to be the case. Until or unless we can achieve some harmonious relationship between scientists, governments, industrialists and world resources the dangers will remain. It is our particular duty as responsible scientists to act as moral beings. Efforts to reduce man's moral dimension to the workings of mechanical processes or any processes other than those over which he has personal control will constitute the greater failure the more they succeed.

CAUSES AND REASONS

If this were a sermon things could be left there. But there is something more that can be done. We said at the outset that the model to be presented would be based on change, not only of the thing studied (man) but of the rules for studying it. Having looked, albeit briefly, at human evolution, the emergence of culture, historical differences in cultures, patterns of development within cultures, and finally at the need for a value system in science or in relation to it, we can finally approach the question of what is involved in the change in the rules of study referred to above.

The chief distinction to be made in progressing with the analysis is that between causes and reasons. Harré, in his notable contribution to the present volume (chapter 14) and to the Conference, has pointed out that there are many fallacies currently widespread as to the methods of scientific analysis. Science, he argues, begins with the discovery of patterns in the universe and proceeds with the business of explaining them. Explanations become more or less refined as the process continues, especially as a result of the discovery of exceptions or cases that do not fit the patterns observed. Science itself is a system of reasoning, a human process.

This process is in sharp contrast with the actual properties of the physical world. The relations between the parts of the physical world are cause-effect relationships, not reasons. Scientific reasoning, in so far as it comes close to an understanding of the cause-effect relationships of the physical world, achieves an increasingly one-to-one match between its words or units and the processes of the physical world.

The human process of reasoning itself, however, is not a system of causes and science cannot explain it. Thus science cannot explain culture because cultures are systems of explanation. Cultures, are, in a certain sense, sciences. But

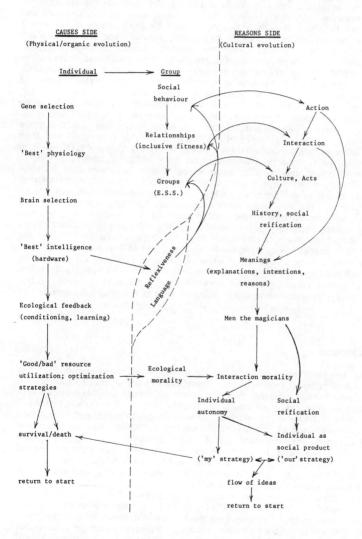

CAUSES SIDE
(Physical/organic evolution)

REASONS SIDE
(Cultural evolution)

Individual ⟶ Group

Social behaviour

Gene selection

Action

'Best' physiology

Relationships
(inclusive fitness)

Interaction

Brain selection

Groups
(E.S.S.)

Culture, Acts

'Best' intelligence
(hardware)

History, social
reification

Reflexiveness
Language

Meanings
(explanations, intentions,
reasons)

Ecological feedback
(conditioning, learning)

Men the magicians

'Good/bad' resource
utilization; optimization
strategies

Ecological
morality

Interaction morality

Individual
autonomy

Social
reification

survival/death

Individual as
social product

('my' strategy)   ('our' strategy)

return to start

flow of ideas

return to start

Figure 1. The relation of causes to reasons in human evolution (time proceeds top to bottom of page).

science as a particular branch of cultural activity, is particularly acutely concerned with the explanation of observed patterns, other branches of culture less so.

There is thus no a priori reason why our kind of science should not in the end be able to produce and perfect a model of man that would do justice to the processes of his prehuman phylogeny and all those aspects of his human existence that are of a physical, organic kind. But its efforts to explain cultural processes themselves - thoughts, ideas, words, signs, and the relationships and social structures in which they exist - are doomed to fail. Even if, as seems likely or even certain, cultures, social structures, relationships and actions are caught up in a two-way process with the physical world of genes, organic development, inclusive fitness and natural selection, their particular features are nevertheless outside the world of organic-physical cause-effect process. It is thus a methodological error to undertake to explain them in cause-effect terms, as if they were natural phenomena and could be so understood.

The change in the rules of study thus occurs between the time of the pre-cultural hominids and man-with-culture. Before the emergence of man there was a single evolving world of causes and effects. After it there was still this same world, evolving as before, but now within it were tens, then hundreds and then thousands of little worlds of explanation, coming to grips with the causal world in a vast range of ways. Social anthropologists have made it their business to describe some of these and have to some extent discovered rules that underlie social life. Some of these rules look superficially like the rules that describe cause-effect relations in the physical world. There are parallels, but they are no more than parallels. The two sets of processes remain distinct. Each has its own characteristics and appropriate methods of study. In our search for a general model of man we are obliged therefore to abandon the hope of a naturalistic causal scheme of explanation that will encompass both the organic side of man and the cultural side. Our model has to have room for both, and be based on two kinds of explanation. Figure 1 is a rough shot at some of what is involved. Something approaching this dual method has already been suggested by Durham (1978). The science of man is now faced first with comprehending this duality and then, in due course, no doubt, with abandoning it too in favour of a new and as yet undreamt of synthesis.

EDITED DISCUSSION

J. SHOTTER: Let me thank you for supplying a large background context which is one that I feel many of us may need. There are two points that I would like to raise. First, I am concerned that you speak as though language began at a single point in time, as if we could discover the day of the week. Instead, I think we need to imagine how physical elements begin to communicate and thus to develop a prototype of linguistic communication. Otherwise, we get into a metaphysical mess by searching for a single point in time when language started. My other point is one of agreement. I too argue that the logical character of a social order is such that order is not self-maintaining: it requires individuals with a moral sensibility to maintain it - individuals able to detect disturbances and repair the order.

V. REYNOLDS: Yes, I accept both your points entirely.

R. HARRE: I would like to take up one of your basic assumptions which I am not altogether happy about. You suggest that individual behaviour, social rela-tionships and social structure are cultural representations of ecological adaptations. Let's take that a step further. There is much anthropological work on the extent to which 'primitive' people actually engage in ecological work; and this proportion is very small. In my view the cultural representations to which you refer only come about with the development of self consciousness: this development is detached from ecological considerations.

Somehow the balance between ecology and 'showing off' is not quite to my taste!

V. REYNOLDS: I am very impressed with anthropological ecology as it is currently developing. Certainly a lot of what people do in cultures is ecological-type activity and has a lot to do with survival in naturalistic terms. Much of what is transmitted socially is concerned with survival. Don't you agree?

R. HARRE: I am not sure that is true, and I am left uneasy about the diagram you have presented.

V. REYNOLDS: Well, we are dealing with a current debate in the literature.

R. HARRE: Yes, and an awful lot hangs on it in regard to your analysis.

A. STILL: A lot hinges on the way language develops and I could not agree that you can divorce language from social structure. As soon as there is language there is culture: this is not a sequential process.

V. REYNOLDS: I must admit to being deeply puzzled by the onset of language in man's development. I regard it almost as 'just happening' - an epiphenomenon ...

A. STILL: Well, yes, that is how you seemed to present it. But are you happy that it is an epiphenomenon and does not arise from selection pressures?

V. REYNOLDS: Well, for example, I do not think one can see language as arising through a mutation. It is not clear to me how anything like language would be 'selected for' in the first place. It seems to me that it would be 'selected against' because no one would be able to understand what was being said. In the first instance there has to be an advantage in making utterances.

D. E. BROADBENT: Why is there any greater difficulty there than, say, in the evolutionary selection of the behaviour of the cuckoo? Maybe cuckoos could have started by throwing eggs out of their own nest: but that plainly would have been maladaptive. The cuckoo's behaviour, its structure, its rate of growth and so on, are all coordinated towards this behaviour of its eggs being laid in the nests of others. Throwing eggs out of nests does not appear to be adaptive until you can see the whole context. Now that leaves us with a major problem, but it is no different in character from the problem of the development of the structure of the eye.

V. REYNOLDS: Yes, they are similar problems. If you can have an eye - if you can have a cuckoo - then you can have a language.

D. E. BROADBENT: That's right.

J. SHOTTER: I think it is crucial to distinguish between speech and language - where speech is seen as having causal effects ...

A. STILL: But you cannot have speech without language.

G. THINES: I am surprised that you have not found time in your talk to make reference to ritualization, in the ethological sense.

V. REYNOLDS: The term 'ritualization' is one which I avoid. It tends to promote confusion: that is, between those who adopt biological meanings and those who adopt anthropological meanings.

G. THINES: But surely you have to take it into account.

C. I. HOWARTH: I find your diagram perfectly acceptable just as long as, on both sides of the dotted line, we can talk of reasons and of causes; but then perhaps there is little value in having that line.

V. REYNOLDS: I cannot accept your proviso ...

J. SHOTTER: And nor would I ...

L. SMITH: Why would we want to discuss reason in the causal section? Can Professor Howarth provide us with an answer?

C. I. HOWARTH: How can you talk of anything in the causal section except by recourse to concepts developed in that other section?

D. E. BROADBENT: Before man's emergence, there were in the causal section still system-aspects to performance. There were systematic processes going on for which it was legitimate to ask: 'what was the reason?' - for example, for the particular structure of the dinosaur. That is a different question from 'what was the cause of the dinosaur?' which is a genetic issue.

Chapter 4

The bio-social model of man and the unification of psychology

H. J. Eysenck

Many people who take up the study of psychology believe and hope that it will teach them something about man; they share with Pope the belief that 'the proper study of mankind is man'. Such hopes are usually disappointed. What they find is rather a large mass of detailed experimental findings, arranged in textbooks under unrelated chapter headings. Many psychologists have expressed the fear that this state of affairs may be endemic and that psychology will always remain what William James called 'the hope of a science', rather than a unified science in the sense that physics or chemistry can be so regarded.

However 'if hopes are dupes, fears may be liars'. I believe that psychology can be made into a unified science, and also that it can teach us something about the nature of man which will enable us to look at ourselves as we really are, rather than the angels or devils of popular mythology. I further believe that the achievement of these two objectives is impossible without the realization that they are two aspects of the same problem. Why has the past produced so much disappointment? The answer to this question too is intimately bound up with the search for a proper model of man.

There have been two major lines of research devoted to the construction of a proper discipline of psychology. On the one hand we have had what might be called the idiographic, literary type of approach, identified perhaps with psychoanalysis, with phenomenology, with existentialism and other essentially non-scientific movements. These rather different approaches have indeed looked at man as a whole, but in a disorganized, unscientific and fundamentally subjective manner. The student has a choice of either believing or disbelieving; he has no opportunity of objectively appraising experiments and proofs in the manner usual in a science. When I say that we must reject this approach I do not mean to put any restraint on people's choices; just as a student is free to believe in the truth of Christian, Moslem or Buddhist religions, so he is free to believe in the sayings of Freud, Sartre or Heidegger. Such a choice removes the students from the ranks of those who search for a scientific answer to the problem of man - naturwissenschaftlich rather than geisteswissenschaftlich. I shall not take the time to argue that in a very meaningful manner the former approach is superior to the latter; I shall simply leave the adherents of subjective and inspired truth to the contemplation of their particular navels, and concentrate on students who wish to approach the problem in a more objective frame of mind, subject to the rigours of theory-making followed by experiment and attempted disproof. Those who wish to argue the point I refer to the writings of Popper (1959), Lakatos & Musgrave (1970), Suppe (1974) and many other philosophers of science. Criticisms of science are discussed by

Passmore (1978), and an interesting discussion of 'The subjective side of science' is given by Mitroff (1974).

The major alternative to this rejected approach has been behaviourism. Here we have a movement which at least attempts to be scientific in the accepted sense, but which unfortunately has fallen foul both of philosophical and scientific precepts which are of considerable importance (Mackenzie, 1977). Behaviourists like Watson and Skinner have adopted a philosophy of naive realism which is stultifying and unnecessary, and which is probably not shared by most experimental psychologists. Thus, they have arbitrarily rejected certain aspects of man which are of vital importance for a proper understanding of what man is. Examples are the rejection of the contribution that physiology and neurology can make, as exemplified in the doctrine of what Boring called 'the empty organism' and the disregard of genetic factors, explicit in Watson, implicit in Skinner, and in the work of their followers. We may generalize this point by saying that essentially S-R psychologists of the behaviourist school have disregarded explicitly or implicitly the essential role played by the organism, which mediates between stimuli and responses, and which indeed is indispensable in defining both the concept of the stimulus, and that of the response. Simple sensations are not stimuli, and muscle twitches are not responses; the realization of the difference is the beginning of wisdom in the study of psychology along scientific lines.

The absolutely central importance of the organism in the study of human (or even animal) behaviour may be recognized in theory, but is denied in practice, by the great majority of experimental psychologists. Believing in the existence of general laws, they study quite small and usually highly selected samples of sophomores, rats or lunatics, in an attempt to unlock the secrets of memory, perception, learning, or whatever else may attract their interest, without realizing that these abstract terms hide the behaviour of organisms whose responses to identical stimuli are highly differentiated, so that any averaging becomes almost meaningless. To take but one illustrative example, after learning paired associates to a standard criterion retrieval is good for extraverts, but deteriorates over time, whereas retrieval is bad for introverts, but improves over time. Curves for introverts and extraverts in several experiments carried out by different authors have shown this distinctive crossover effect, which indeed was predicted on a theoretical basis (M.W. Eysenck, 1977). Many other examples could be given; the reader is referred to two of my books which list a fair selection of these (Eysenck, 1967, 1976c). If we want to make any meaningful predictions about behaviour, we must specify not only the stimuli and the situation, but also the nature of the organism, in the same way that a physicist would specify not only the experimental arrangement and parameters, but also the nature of the material studied, whether element, alloy or whatnot. He would find it meaningless to talk about 'material' in general, and in the same way we should regard it as meaningless to talk about 'people' in general.

In looking at this 'organism' which is the main object of our study we must come to terms with the fact that this organism combines two in many ways different and even contradictory aspects. Man is a bio-social organism; we will never understand man if we regard him merely from the biological point of view as an animal, or only from the social point of view as a social being. Man is both, and many of the difficulties of psychological research and understanding develop from this fundamental reality. Furthermore, man has to be looked at from the point of view of evolution; no understanding of man can be derived from approaches which neglect this essential qualification. As McLean (1969) has put it so well, man has a triune brain, both functionally and anatomically. There is first of all the reptile brain, wrapped around which we have the paleocortex, crowning and surrounding which we have the neocortex. These three major subdivisions of the total brain, developed one after the other through evolution, are not entirely independent, but do seem to control different aspects of our behaviour, and we must recognize their existence if we want to obtain a true measure of mankind. Man as homo sapiens recognizes the importance of the neocortex, but neglects the lower cortical centres; man as animal recognizes the existence of the limbic system, but disregards the pre-frontal lobes. Difficult as it may be, we must try and combine these various aspects into a recognizable picture of man, and not fall prey to the temptation of over-simplifying by disregarding contrary evidence.

The distinction just made between the biological and the social aspects of man is parallel although not quite identical with that between nature and nurture, heredity and environment. There has been much impassioned discussion, usually motivated by social and political ideals, on this topic; these discussions have unfortunately not always been conducted in the impartial spirit of science, nor has there been informed knowledge of the issues involved, and the appropriate method to be used in the study of nature and nurture. A widespread assumption has been made by many researchers into social psychology that environment is all important; following Watson, they have tended to disregard biological and genetic determinants. This has led, in turn, to the widespread adoption of what has been called 'the sociological fallacy', namely the habit of regarding observed correlations as evidence of causation. Because broken homes are correlated with criminality in children (although the correlation is very weak), it has been assumed that broken homes cause delinquency in children. This of course does not follow. It could be that delinquent children make such difficulty for their parents that the marriage is broken up as a consequence. It could be that the bad genes which cause parents to separate cause their children to commit crimes. The simple correlation observed is compatible with a large number of different explanations; it does not give support to any one of them, as compared with others. Yet this is precisely the assumption made by many sociologists and social psychologists; all they observe is correlation, but the interpretation is along causal lines. This gives an entirely erroneous picture of man overemphasizing the environmental, social and non-biological factors, and disregarding the strong evidence for genetic factors.

Curiously enough the approach of the geneticist, particularly the behavioural geneticist, is much less committed to a one-sided approach (Mather & Jinks, 1971). The geneticist knows that what he is observing is merely the phenotype, and that the genotype is by no means identical with the observed behaviour. Hence he is forced to construct a model which embraces all causal determinants of observed variability; he looks at additive genetic factors, as well as at epistasis, assortative mating and dominance on the hereditary side, just as he looks at additive environmental effects, dividing them into within-family and between-family effects, and at the various types of interaction between environmental and genetic causes that may exist. In this way he presents a much more realistic model of man, embracing all the genetic, environmental, and interactional causes of variations in behaviour. This, curiously enough, is foreign ground to most psychologists, and is not taught in any psychological department that I know of. This is one of the tragedies of psychology; impatient to assert its independence, influenced by ideological considerations, and desirous of changing society for the better, it disregards the only model that is scientifically acceptable in accounting for individual variation. To say that this is inexcusable is putting it mildly; the effects of this disregard have been catastrophic, in making much of what psychology has to say on social issues meaningless, unscientific and potentially dangerous. The disregard of the genetic model has led to a completely erroneous view of man; that is the sad state of the balance sheet to date.

In looking at the implications of the evolutionary, biological theory for modern psychology, we are clearly concerned with individual differences, on the one hand, and more general species characteristics, on the other. Ultimately perhaps the distinction breaks down, in that individual differences at a given moment are the raw material for selection, giving rise to species differences in the distant future. However, at any one moment of time there is a clear distinction, and I will briefly give some examples of the importance of both for the development of a proper model of man. I will begin by looking at the realm of individual differences. Here, I think, the evidence is pretty compelling that we must follow the ancient Greeks in distinguishing between cognitive or intellectual functions on the one hand, and emotional and conative ones, on the other.

On the cognitive side the evidence is strongly in favour of the view, originally put forward by Sir Francis Galton, that the quality of cognitive processes is determined very largely by a general factor of intellectual ability, which we may call intelligence or 'g', which enters into all cognitive processes to a varying degree, depending upon complexity, and which is heritable to a conspicuous degree. I have reviewed the literature in my book 'The Nature and Measurement of Intelligence' (Eysenck, 1979) and will not go into all the details again here; at the present time and in our kind of society, the heritability of this general intelligence is approximately 80 per cent, with non-additive sources of heredity like assortative mating and dominance contributing something like 10 or 12 per cent, the rest being additive variance. (It should be noted that these figures were arrived at by a survey of all the existing evidence, only leaving out the data contributed by Sir Cyril Burt, regarding the authenticity of which some doubts have recently been raised.) There is also evidence, of course, for a variety of rather less important special, group or primary factors of intelligence, like verbal, numerical, spatial, etc., intelligence, and the evidence suggests that these also are largely heritable.

If intelligence is heritable, then one must assume that there are physiological, anatomical, or neurological systems variations which are accountable for the observed variations in performance. Recent years have shown an increase of interest in this field, and in particular the role of evoked potentials as measures of cortical information-processing quality has been investigated. There are many artifacts to guard against in this field, but recent work in our laboratories by Alan and Elaine Hendrickson (1978) has shown not only that correlations between appropriate aspects of the evoked potential, such as amplitude and latency, can be shown to correlate with orthodox intelligence tests to almost the same extent to which these intercorrelate with each other, but also that the findings agree very well with theory-based predictions arrived at on the basis of certain hypotheses concerning the ultimate neurological nature of memory, and of information-processing in the brain. It would seem that we are in sight of a major breakthrough in our understanding of the nature of cognitive processes, and their measurement.

The basis of differentiation in cognitive processing, therefore, must be located largely in the neocortex; the basis of personality differences in the emotional and conative field, however, are probably located in the limbic system, the reticular formation, and other paleocortical and brain-stem formations (Eysenck, 1967). There is now much evidence that there are three major dimensions of personality which determine a good deal of our everyday behaviour, and variations therein; these occur under various names, but I shall refer to them as extraversion-introversion (E), neuroticism or emotionality as opposed to stability (N), and psychoticism or toughmindedness as opposed to tendermindedness (P). These behaviour patterns have been observed in monkeys (Chamove et al., 1972), and at least one of them (N) has also been measured and experimented with extensively in rats (Broadhurst, 1975). It seems now fairly certain that extraversion-introversion is related to differences in cortical arousal, themselves caused in some degree by differences in reticular formation activity, while differences in emotionality are presumably due to differential processes in the limbic system. Differences in P are somewhat more difficult to localize, but androgen and other hormonal secretions are likely to be involved. We thus see that the major sources of variation in human conduct are associated with biological variables which can be identified and studied.

Furthermore, it should be noted that there is now considerable evidence that variation in these dimensions is largely the product of genetic determinants (Eysenck, 1976a; Eysenck & Eysenck, 1976). The amount of additive genetic determination to the variance in these personality traits is almost identical with that observed in intelligence but there are also important differences. In personality there is no assortative mating (or very little), and there is no dominance; these are important differences. Furthermore, the environmental factors determining differences in personality are practically all of the within-family rather than the between-family kind; this is important in discounting certain types of theory, such as the Freudian and Laingian, which adduce between-family factors as accounting for the observed abnormalities of neurotic and psychotic patients (Eaves & Eysenck, 1977). I would be the last to claim that the evidence on all these points is conclusive, and that many further additions will not have to be made to make the picture more lifelike; nevertheless, I believe that we now have the beginning of a recognizable picture or model of man as far as both intellectual and personality variables are concerned.

It may be said that so far the picture seems to be exclusively biological, and that there is no involvement of social parameters. This, up to a point, is true; so far I have only spoken about normal deviations along certain dimensions, cognitive or orectic/affective, of personality. When we come to consider such human activities as criminality and antisocial conduct, or neurotic behaviour, we enter into an area where there is a clear interaction between inherited biological dispositions and social influences and determinants. Consideration of neurosis and criminality force us to consider just precisely what it is that is inherited, and the way this interacts with environment. Clearly we cannot inherit behaviour as such; all that we can inherit is a particular neurological-physiological-anatomical structure, whose functioning differentiates between people, and which interacts with various types of environmental influences to produce the phenotypic conduct which constitutes the primary source of our information.

Let us consider the field of psychopathic and criminal conduct, or antisocial conduct in general. The theory I have developed (Eysenck, 1977) suggests that such conduct is mediated by a whole series of events which start out with the low level of arousal which certain people, particularly extraverts, experience as a consequence of the inadequate functioning of the reticular formation. Low arousal leads to poor conditioning and, as my theory makes Pavlovian conditioning responsible for the acquisition of those conditioned socializing responses which we normally label 'conscience', such a person would be disadvantaged in developing appropriate socialized reactions. Equally, low arousal leads to sensation-seeking, in order to increase the cortical arousal level to acceptable degrees, and this sensation-seeking behaviour often leads to socially unacceptable activities. Thus a person with an unusually low arousal level both has greater temptations, leading him to seek arousal-increasing stimuli, and also has less resistance to temptation, because of his lack of conditionability. There is direct evidence for the lower level of arousal of psychopaths (e.g. Hare, 1970) and there is much evidence for the involvement of extraversion in antisocial activity, both in children and adults, and both in countries of the Western World and in Communist and Third World countries (Eysenck, 1977b).

So far we seem again to have sketched only a biological description of antisocial behaviour, but note the absolutely vital inclusion of the concept of 'conditioning' in this account. Such conditioning I envisage to be taking place when children who behave in an antisocial manner are castigated and punished by their parents, their teachers, their peers, and persons in authority; the antisocial activity, or its contemplation, constitutes the conditioned stimulus, and the punishment the unconditioned stimulus, with the resulting fear and pain being the unconditioned response. Thus the process of conditioning involves very powerful social influences of one kind or another, and these play an absolutely indispensable part in first identifying what is antisocial, and then in trying to internalize these rules through the conditioning process (although of course the people who are carrying out this task usually are not aware of the fact that what they are doing is in fact Pavlovian conditioning!). Thus the final product, that is the conditioned, socialized 'conscience', is the product of the interaction of biological and social factors. It is along these lines that I would account for the fact that in the last 30 years or so there has been a tremendous increase in criminality and antisocial conduct in the Western World, and also the Communist countries. The final product (socialization) is mediated by the constitution of the people involved (which cannot have changed sufficiently in the short period of time to make any difference - genetic causes work extremely slowly in order to make notable changes), as well as by the number of conditioning experiences to which the child is exposed. The general increase in permissiveness in recent years has led many parents and teachers to abjure their role as socializing agents, and has led them to allow children to misbehave without any punishment. In other words, the amount of conditioning, or the number of conditioning experiences to which children are exposed, has been drastically reduced, and consequently the product of organism x environmental pressure, has been reduced by the reduction in the number of these conditioning experiences. Note the success of this explanation in accounting for the recent increase in antisocial behaviour, as compared with the utter failure of the environmental-sociological theory which ascribes criminal conduct to environmental causes, such as gross differences in wealth, low standard of living, poor accommodation, etc. On all these environmental factors there has been immense improvement during the last 30 years, standard of living going up by something like 50 per cent, yet the predicted decline in criminality has not been observed, and in fact exactly the opposite has taken place. Such failure of a theory to predict the facts must seriously weaken one's belief in its efficacy.

What is true of criminality is also true of neurosis (Eysenck, 1977a). Here the theory states that introverts, that is people with high arousal who condition easily, are more likely to develop neurotic disturbances, which are defined as conditioned emotional responses, and the evidence strongly supports this view. However, conditioned responses can be extinguished, and the success of behaviour therapy in this field indicates that a recognition of the particular part that arousal and conditioning play in the genesis of neurosis enable us to develop methods of counteracting it, just as in the case of criminality it has been found that introducing new conditioning experiences into the life of the adolescent or adult criminal, by way of token economies, etc., may lead to successful rehabilitation. Again note that a neurosis does not develop simply on the basis of biological predisposition; what is required is either a traumatic conditioning experience, or a series of subtraumatic conditioning experiences, escalating through the mechanism of what I have called the incubation of anxiety.

We now have a model of man which shows him as driven by subcortical impulses, achieving his ends through the use of intellectual abilities located in the cortex, influenced very much by conditioning and learning experiences provided by society, and showing large individual differences in all the particular aspects involved in these functions - intellectual, emotional, arousal, etc. This may seem a very rough and ready picture, but it does account for a surprisingly large number of behaviour patterns. To demand more from it at the present stage of development would be absurd; we do not criticize Copernicus for failing to land a man on the moon, or send space probes to distant planets. We are still at the beginnings of this particular voyage into space, and to find a model which accounts for some of the behaviours of man should not be viewed in the context of a failure of finding an explanation of all the behaviours of man.

In recent years there has been some dissatisfaction with such a simple (and possibly over-simplified) concept as that presented here, and we have had the growth of what are sometimes called 'cognitive theories' of behaviour. Let me first of all quote from Allport (1975) an evaluation of cognitive psychology, as it is presently organized. He finds that the field is characterized by 'an uncritical, or selective, or frankly cavalier attitude to experimental data; a pervasive atmosphere of special pleading; a curious parochialism in acknowledging even the existence of other workers, and other approaches, to the phenomena under discussion; interpretations of data relying on multiple, arbitrary choice-points; and underlying all else the near-vacuum of theoretical structure within which to interrelate different sets of experimental results, or to direct the search for significant new phenomena' (p. 152). This, I think, is a fair picture of what poses as a new direction in psychology. The model of man presented by cognitive psychology is no model at all; it is not even a caricature. There is nothing there that could be experimentally tested, and either supported or rejected; cognitive psychology, as such, does not exist as a cohesive body of knowledge enabling any form of prediction to be made.

This does not mean, of course, that we must reject cognitive factors as taking an important part in processes of conditioning, etc. Pavlov already recognized the vital role played by the second signalling system, which is essentially what cognitive psychology is all about, and work such as that on evaluative conditioning (Martin & Levey, 1978) indicates that even cognitive processes are subject to conditioning. Equally, the early and little recognized work of Platonov (1959), 'The Word as a Physiological and Therapeutic Factor', indicated that words can and do act as conditioned stimuli, and may also act as second-order or third-order stimuli in a conditioning paradigm; this and much experimental work since underlines the relevance of cognitive factors in Pavlovian conditioning, without for a moment suggesting that cognitive factors can act independently, or that the laws of conditioning do not apply in this field as elsewhere. As Pavlov pointed out: 'owing to the entire preceding life of the human adult, a word is connected with all the external and internal stimuli coming to the cerebral hemispheres, signals all of them, replaces all of them and can, therefore, evoke all the actions and reactions of the organism which these stimuli produce.' It may be admitted that some behaviourists have grossly over-simplified the mechanism of conditioning and its application to everyday life; this does not justify the rejection of the principles so carefully established, nor the empirical application of such principles to social problems like criminality and neurosis.

Let me next turn to another area, leaving the field of individual differences, and coming over into the more general area of the effects of evolution. It is well known that men and women show differential responses, both socially and sexually, and there has been much debate about the causation of these differences. At the moment, there is a distinct tendency to attribute observed differences (other than the purely anatomical ones and their direct consequences) to social determinants (Davidson, 1979). Such a view of gender identity as being the product of social modelling is very one-sided, and leaves out a great deal of evidence which fairly conclusively demonstrates the long-term effects of evolution, and therefore of biological causes in this field (Merz, 1979). The empirical evidence shows that in many different countries which have been studied with respect to sexual behaviour, men are more impersonal, more easily excited, more pleasure orientated, less inhibited sexually, more permissive, more attracted by illicit sexual practices, less easily disgusted, more highly sexed, more interested in nudity and voyeurism, in prostitution and in pornography (Eysenck, 1976b). There is some overlap between the sexes, of course, but the general direction of the differences is unmistakable. To some degree, of course, these differences are culturally determined (Beach, 1977). However, many of the differences are also found in animal societies, and can hardly therefore be said to be due to social conditioning and, furthermore, many of them are found almost universally in all sorts of different types of human societies, so that again the social influence of a particular society has to be largely discounted. We may note, for instance, the prevalence of polygyny and the almost complete lack of polyandry in both human and animal societies. Even where monogamy is the rule, it is usually the males who indulge in extra-marital activities, whether with prostitutes or mistresses. In most societies and certainly among animals, men take the initiative and, without extended foreplay, proceed vigorously to satisfy themselves and achieve climax, without much regard for allowing the woman concerned to achieve orgasm also. These and many other differences can be better accounted for in biological than in social terms (Eysenck & Wilson, 1979).

Consider for instance the administration of androgens to female foetuses in animal experiments; the result is universally a much more masculine type of behaviour, both socially and sexually, in the grown female animal. In humans, similar experiments are impossible, but masculinization in human females has been produced by hormonal drugs given to the mother to prevent a miscarriage (Money & Ehrhardt, 1972). These hormones belong to a recently synthesized group of steroids which were related in chemical structure to androgens, but were, in biological action, substitutes for pregnancy hormones (progesterone) and hence were named progestins. When these progestins were first synthesized it was not known that certain of them would, under certain circumstances, exert a masculinizing influence on a female foetus, and thus in the 1950s a small number of girl babies showing this masculinization were born. At the age of puberty the girls' ovaries would function normally, would totally feminize the body, and induce menstruation. It is these girls, as girls, who are of interest to us, because the progestin would have indelibly affected their psychological make-up, and would have made it more masculine. Similarly there is a small number of females suffering from the adreno-genital syndrome, which is an abnormality of development occurring quite naturally in a small number of cases, where the adrenal glands functioned ineffectively, the effect already beginning in foetal life. The primary defect is a genetic one which prevents the adrenal gland from synthesizing the proper hormone, cortisol, and instead releasing an androgen, that is a male sex hormone which enters into the bloodstream of the foetus, masculinizing it to a certain extent. The babies are allowed to grow up as normal females, being given hormonal regulation from birth onwards.

The behaviour of both these groups of girls, those suffering from the adreno-genital syndrome, and those whose mothers had been treated with progestins, was compared with the behaviour of a control group of normal girls, matched on the basis of age, intelligence quotient, socio-economic background, and race; in some cases the control group consisted of the non-affected sisters of the probands. The masculinized girls, in the first place, differed from the controls in regarding themselves as tomboys. Nine of 10 girls with a progestin-induced syndrome and 11 of 15 with the adreno-genital syndrome claimed they were tomboys, and this was confirmed by the mother, and was recognized and accepted by playmates and friends. In this they differed very significantly from the control group girls. In addition to this masculine, tomboy behaviour, many of the girls would rather have been born a boy, had there been a choice, and others were ambivalent. In this, too, they differed from the normal girls.

The masculinized girls showed a high level of physical energy expenditure, demonstrated in vigorous outdoor play, games, and sports generally considered typical of boys. (In this they seem to resemble prenatally masculinized female rhesus monkeys, who also indulge in typically masculine rough-and-tumble play.) Team games with a ball such as neighbourhood football and baseball, were a favourite with the masculinized girls and many preferred boys as playmates. Money & Ehrhardt (1972), who carried out these studies, formulated the generalization that dominance, assertion, and striving for position in the dominance hierarchy of childhood was a variable which most distinguished the masculinized girls from the others. It is interesting that differences also appeared in relation to clothing and adornment. The masculinized girls preferred utilitarian and functional clothing, as compared with the chic, pretty or fashionable feminine. They preferred slacks and shorts to dresses, and also showed less interest in accessories like jewellery, perfume and hairstyling. As regards preferences for toys, the girls were indifferent to dolls, or openly neglectful of them, and preferred cars, trucks and guns, and other toys traditionally associated with boys. Later on, this lack of interest in dolls became a lack of interest in infants; they did not enjoy doing things for the care of babies and did not anticipate doing such things, even as babysitters in the future. Some girls even disliked handling little babies and believed they could not do this well. The choice between career and marriage similarly produced marked differences between the control girls and the masculinized girls, with the latter preferring careers to marriage.

Similar results were obtained in the work of Schlegel (1966) who used as a measure of antenatal androgen hormonal level in the foetus the shape of the pelvis, funnel-shaped pelvis being produced by high androgen hormonal levels, tube-shaped pelvis being produced by low levels. There are well-known differences in pelvis shape between men and women, but also a great deal of overlap; Schlegel found that within each sex, the men and women with masculinized pelvises showed social and sexual behaviour typical of the male, those with a feminine-type pelvis showed social and sexual behaviour typical of the female.

The failure of social conditioning to affect these behaviours to any marked extent is documented in research on the Israeli Kibbutz (Beit-Hallahmi & Rabin, 1977). Here for many years the children were brought up and indoctrinated in the firm belief in labour-sharing, socialism and feminine equality in work and everything else; parents were prevented from looking after their children, and these were instead brought up in groups by caretakers, called metapelets. How did these children behave when they grew up? The answer seems to be that a great majority quietly reverted to the old-fashioned practices, and disregarded the social conditioning to which they had been subjected. This is an important experiment, and the accounts given of it, and its effects, should be consulted in detail by anyone interested in the nature of man.

We have made appeal to evolution to account for the many asymmetries in male-female relations which crop up in all cultures, and also among most mammals; this appeal can be made even more precise by reference to the concept of the 'selfish gene', that is the notion that man is in effect nothing more than a carrier of a set of genes, the preservation of which determines all his major activities (Dawkins, 1976). Natural selection, the basis of Darwinian evolution, is a process of reproductive competition among members of a given species, and the attributes of an organism (including behaviour) which make a positive contribution to success in this competition are ultimately selected for. This leads on to the thought that organisms must have evolved strategies which maximize their reproductive success, and it may be useful to look at the differential sexual behaviours in this light. This way of considering the problem has been common among biologists at least since the classical studies of the British geneticist A.J. Bateman on fruit flies in the early 1940s.

It is clear that mothers typically contribute more nurture to each offspring, both prenatal and postnatal, both in point of time and in point of substance, than do fathers. Males also have an infinite number (almost) of sperms, while women have a very restricted supply of ova. Thus a female's reproductive potential is limited in two ways - capacity to provide nurture, and availability of ova. A male, on the other hand, can beget many more children than any one female can bear. Thus males gain from having many mates (polygyny), while females have nothing to gain from having multiple mates (polyandry). Males, investing little in each offspring, have everything to gain from sowing their seeds as widely as possible; hence they compete for the opportunity to fertilize women. Females invest considerably more in each offspring, and hence are predisposed to exhibit greater selectivity in their choice of mates. Men, of course, do invest parentally to some extent, and hence it is in their interest to protect themselves against cuckoldry, which would involve them in investing in the genes of other men! Males thus are much more involved in securing the fidelity of their mates than are females - if the male has intercourse outside marriage, this does not affect the security of his mate's genes embodied in her offspring. Note how neatly this explanation accounts for the greater promiscuity and impersonal sex attitude of males (Eysenck, 1976b). Several large-scale surveys, in different countries, have shown that some 50 per cent of men, but only some 5 per cent of women, said they would like to indulge in extramarital sex. We may recall in this connection the Coolidge effect, that is, the tendency in rats and other mammals for the exhausted male to renew its sexual interests when new partners are provided. Females do not show this effect; for them, the duration of sexual receptivity is shortened by copulation.

In human society, this concern with cuckoldry has usually shown itself in legal provisions which consider female sexual unfaithfulness much more serious than male. Furthermore, men are much more likely to seek divorce on grounds of adultery than women, although in actual fact men are much the more adulterous sex! Infidelity was twice as prevalent among the men in Kinsey's study as among the women (cf. Kinsey et al., 1948, 1953), yet it was a major factor in divorce twice as frequently for men than women - a fourfold disproportion, along the lines expected from the evolutionary argument. Female adultery faces the male with the presence of 'bastards' in his house, and the duty and responsibility to care for them and bring them up; male adultery at most leads to a withdrawal of the male's time, society and sexual energy from the wife. There is here thus a biological asymmetry, corresponding to the social asymmetries noted.

We can account along similar lines for the greater discrimination in sexual matters of females, as compared with males. In animals, the task of species recognition, and the avoidance of hybrid matings, is usually undertaken by females - it is they who lose more time and energy in a mismatch than does the male. In many species (e.g. crabs and ducks), females recognize appropriate males at first sight, but males have to learn to recognize females of their own kind. Thus male butterflies have been known to court falling leaves, and male frogs to mount galoshes. In a similar way, most sexual perversions in humans are the (almost) sole prerogative of males - fetishists, transvestites, exhibitionists, voyeurs, sadomasochists, necrophiliacs, frotteurs and the like are almost always men, and with most of the other categories (e.g. homosexuality, transsexualism, bestiality and pedophilia) men outnumber women to a marked degree. Men simply can afford to waste their seed, without reducing the number of offspring available to women impregnated by other, more willing males. If women wasted their reproductive potential in a similar manner, the danger to the species would be much greater.

If women are more choosey about their mates than are men, who tend to adopt the doctrine that 'all cats are grey at night' then this too is an evolutionary feature already found in animals. Mate quality is more important for the female than for the male, precisely because she invests so much more in the nurture of the offspring. This is so not only in mammals, but also in birds and insects; males are made to make gifts and other types of commitment, and the female only responds gradually to male courtship, thus protecting herself from philanderers whose parental duties elsewhere might lead them to abscond and neglect their implied support for her brood. It is for the same reason, one must presume, that financial provision is so important to females in selecting a mate among humans.

Society, in order to survive, has adopted the principle that these 'natural' tendencies should not be left to the accidents of genetic transmission and segregation alone, but that these biological determinants should be aided by precept and modelling; thus social norms in the vast majority of all societies we know have emphasized social and sexual roles very much in line with those which instinct dictated in any case. We thus have society and nature working in harmony rather than fighting against each other; the fact that all successful and surviving societies have taken this course suggests that if there had ever been any that took a different, contrary course, they would have perished in the struggle for survival. History certainly recorded no memory of them.

If this brief and inevitably speculative account of the development of sex roles is anything like accurate, what does it portend for the future? We must not make the mistake of imagining that because something has been biologically useful in the past, therefore we must without criticism or opposition accept it as a guiding principle for the future. Nature, 'red in tooth and claw' has certainly been a hard task-master in the past, and has shaped human behaviour in ways that none of us can tolerate without a loss of common humanity. Wars, pillage, rape, racism, ethnocentricism and xenophobia have been the laws of nature and scourge of our so-called civilized behaviour. It does not take a major prophet to foretell that unless we manage to overcome these trends we are not likely, as a species, to survive the next 100 years - if indeed we do not succeed in taking all creation with us into oblivion! There have certainly been hopeful signs that biological evolution is not the only guide for our behaviour, and that social evolution, that is the development of new and more promising types of conduct, can successfully take its place.

Saying therefore that our present masculine and feminine roles are deeply embedded in our biological nature is not to say categorically that no change can ever be brought about in this state of affairs. What is suggested is rather that such a change would be extremely difficult to produce, and that at the moment we certainly do not know how to effect it. Whether it is desirable to change the state of affairs that is acceptable and often deeply fulfilling for both men and women is of course another question; it is not a factual one, and therefore is not one within the remit of this chapter. Certainly the majority of women seem to delight in the feminine role, just as the majority of men delight in the male role; whether it is desirable to deprive them of this delight in the uncertain hope that both might find satisfaction in some form of unisex culture and role-playing activity seems very doubtful, but of course a decision on questions of this kind must be left to the individual.

The example of sex roles and gender identity has been discussed in some detail because it is typical of many other incidences in which there is a close interaction of biological and social factors, and where the majority of psychologists only pay attention to the social factors. An important counterweight to this one-sidedness has recently arisen in the new discipline of sociobiology (Wilson, 1975). This, being perhaps equally one-sided in the opposite direction, must be seen as a counterweight to the present stress on sociological and social factors; we are not likely to get a valid model of man from either extreme. To do that we must combine what is good and valid in both approaches, and refrain from neglecting, for ideological reasons, either the biological or the social determinants which fashion our behaviour. Most students of psychology will probably agree in principle that this is the right attitude, but will in practice deviate in either direction, depending on their interests, their prejudices, and their general beliefs. There certainly is no empirical support for any view which fails to regard man as a bio-social organism, or which attempts a piecemeal dissection of his behaviour, rather than trying to integrate it in some interpretation that emphasizes goal-seeking, with the goals again being partly dictated by his biological inheritance, and partly by social pressures. The almost universal failure to compromise between extremes, and emphasize the unity of man, and the unitary nature of psychology, seems to us by itself good evidence for rejecting the notion of man as homo sapiens; one-sided attitudes are more likely to be the product of limbic system involvement than of pure cortical activity!

The range of individual differences, genetically caused, and of personality factors is much wider than is normally recognized. As an example, consider social attitudes and values, or even ideologies like the Fascist and Communist ones. It is usually assumed that these social beliefs are caused exclusively by parental and societal precepts and teaching, and that personality and genetic factors have little to do with this. The evidence is very much against this point of view.

Eysenck & Wilson (1978) have assembled a good deal of evidence to show that genetic factors play an important part in the causation of differences in social attitudes; heritability contributes well over 50 per cent to the causation of both radical-conservative and toughminded versus tenderminded attitudes in this country, probably largely through the intervention of personality variables. Ideologies are closely related to these social variables, and to personality, and there is much evidence that people who embrace either of the two major ideologies of our time share common personality features, and are thus predisposed by heredity to adopt extreme points of view and an aggressive and emphatic manner. Here again it is not suggested, of course, that genetic factors account for all the phenotypic behaviour of such people; it is merely suggested that the almost uniform reliance on social factors is misplaced, and that we must take into account both biological and social factors in order to arrive at a reasonable model of political man.

We may take this argument a step further, at the risk of appearing to speculate in the absence of reliable information on which to build. It is not unreasonable to ask what the consequences of a state of affairs might be which allocates 80 per cent of the variance in intellectual excellence to hereditary factors, and 20 per cent to environmental ones. Two consequences would seem to follow, from the point of view of social organization. In the first place, we would expect that social classes would arise, dividing society into powerful and powerless, haves and have-nots. The universal presence of such classes in all societies of which we have a record suggests some underlying feature in human nature which is responsible for the existence of these class societies; inherited differences in intelligence would seem a reasonable candidate for this position. In the second place, we would expect a regression to the mean, a hereditary feature found in relation to IQ no less than to other heritable qualities, to produce social mobility within any class society, and thus prevent the creation of a caste system (unless such a caste system was artificially maintained by social forces, repression, etc., as in India). Thus it is possible to argue that major features of social organization and structure may be deduced from the sort of model of man we have been building up; the degree of credence one may give to such deductions will of course depend on such evidence as may be brought to bear on such a model.

Even more speculative are attempts, such as that of Darlington (1971), to interpret human history in terms of genetic characteristics of different peoples and races. We have been so conditioned to believe in the all-powerful effects of the environment as to disregard even the possibility that different ethnic subgroups, developing in different environments over thousands or even millions of years, without interbreeding, might develop along different genetic lines, and show innate differences in intelligence, temperament, personality, disease resistance, and many other characteristics. Such a denial, in the absence of empirical evidence, is as unacceptable as would be the unsupported avowal of the genetic determination of observed differences of a phenotypic kind. What is needed is unbiased research aiming to extend the boundaries of the model of man here developed; in the absence of such research little more can be said other than to beware of assuming as proven what in fact is merely fashionable to believe.

EDITED DISCUSSION

G. DELAFIELD: People who are incarcerated are not the only criminals. They are the ones who are caught. Self-report studies have not been so clear-cut in favouring genetic or environmental contributions to criminality.

H. J. EYSENCK: Several studies, particularly with children, have used self-reports, and they give the same kinds of results as those obtained from outsiders' ratings (such as teachers'), and they also give the same kinds of results as come to light when the children are called before the Magistrate for various misdemeanours. It does not make any difference which type of data you collect, you get exactly the same type of correlations with personality.

J. A. GRAY: I become particularly concerned when you begin to attribute Pavlovian conditioning to the middle portion of the triune brain. The best bet at the moment, I would have thought, is that classical conditioning is very diffusely represented in the brain. I would want to be cautious about specifying the number of layers in the brain and their various functions.

H. J. EYSENCK: I quite agree that the precise details of how conditioning works are still to be determined. Future progress, I believe, should be made through a recognition that the brain is not a unitary organ. While the different parts are interconnected, there are important ways in which they are not. In the neurotic, the cortex does not influence his conditioned responses: he knows perfectly well that his phobia is quite irrational, but he can do nothing about it.

J. A. GRAY: But you are assuming that knowledge is neatly parcelled up in the cortex, and we really cannot be certain of that. Exactly what the cortex does is the most mysterious aspect of brain physiology at the moment.

H. J. EYSENCK: If you abolish the cortex, you would not have much 'conscious knowledge', would you?

J. A. GRAY: Well, for example, we now know that the totally neo-decorticated rabbit is still capable of instrumental learning, and I am prepared to take such learning as evidence of intentionality. (Maybe John Shotter is not!) What is available after you remove the neocortex is still very much an open question.

M. JAHODA: I have always been puzzled by one thing in your very convincing account. You say that intelligence, personality, emotional disturbances and so on are largely determined genetically; and sometimes you put a figure of 80 per cent to it. You also say that you think behaviour therapy can produce changes; and there is some good documentation for that. Now, in behaviour therapy, you are obviously not manipulating the genetic equipment, but still you are producing a significant change in a relatively short time. Why couldn't a generally favourable environment, without your intervention, produce exactly the same effects? As Hebb suggested, one can proceed on the assumption that all behaviour is simultaneously 100 per cent genetically and 100 per cent environmentally determined. With the drosophila it works perfectly. If you breed them for a giant gene and then put them in a particular culture, they are not bigger than the ordinary drosophila. Considering the various phenomena you have studied, it has always struck me as slightly inconsistent that you should place such strong emphasis on genetic factors.

H. J. EYSENCK: The first point is that what you say is perfectly true. Genetic determination and quantitative estimates of heritability are population statistics: they apply to a particular group at a particular time. What I am saying is true of the United Kingdom here and now: it will differ across cultures and time. Given that these estimates relate to population statistics then, in theory at least, you could change the environment in hitherto unpredicted ways: heritability could then be zero or even 100 per cent. But of course such possibilities are purely theoretical; we have no idea of how we could change the heritability now observed. Your second point was about behaviour therapy. A person develops neurotic disorders primarily if he is high genetically on neuroticism and introversion. He then conditions a particular type of anxiety response with a particular set of stimuli, and that is his neurosis. Having conditioned it, it can be extinguished. But he will still be genetically weak as far as the exposure to traumatic situations is concerned. He has a perpetual, inherited, genetic weakness. This leads him, through interaction with environmental factors, to a particular neurotic breakdown which we can reverse.

K. J. CONNOLLY: It seems to me that this debate might be helped if one were to realize that neuroticism 'develops'. Certainly it is going to be influenced by the genes that the individual has, but it is also going to be influenced by the environment in which the organism grows. That also is true of a variety of morphological and behavioural characteristics in drosophila. You can vary it developmentally, but I think perhaps that one ought not to use the word 'determined': that can often be misleading.

H. J. EYSENCK: What you find in experiments on drosophila and other animals is an extreme of environmental manipulation that never happens with humans. My comments would not apply to a baby brought up in a black box. I am talking about the ordinary range of environments found in Europe, Scandinavia and North America.

K. J. CONNOLLY: If you take the condition phenylketonuria, we know that has to do with a recessive gene. We know too that if you raise children in an environment which does not contain phenylalanine, the likelihood of the extreme phenotypic disabilities will be reduced. So, I come back to my point about the development of the phenotype. You can have two individuals, both of whom are carrying the mutant gene. If you allow one to feed on phenylalanine then almost certainly extreme pathology will result. If you protect the other one by a special diet, you will almost certainly reduce that pathology.

H. J. EYSENCK: If I may say so, that is a good example of knowing what is inherited and bypassing it. I am suggesting something similar for neurosis. Like phenylketonuria, the genetic trap is always there, but you can get round it by not encountering the kind of stimuli which produce the neurosis.

Chapter 5

Naive parallelism: Simply synchronize several simultaneous models

A. Gale

No chapter in this volume can be as simple minded as this one. I set out in very straightforward terms, the case for a psychophysiological approach. Unfortunately this will be almost unrecognizable to many people who call themselves psychophysiologists (cf. Hassett, 1978). For the approach prescribes, quite specifically, the incorporation of subjective experience and notions of the social meaning of actions, into psychophysiological experimentation. First, let me present a brief discussion of models and their uses.

By 'model' I mean the borrowing of a conceptual framework from one domain of description, for use in another domain of description. This may be consciously done or unwittingly done, but the intention is not as important as the consequences. It can be done at the right time or at the wrong time, and can be seen to be right at the time it is done, or wrong at the time it is done. Thus the borrowing of a model has to be seen in its historical context. Perhaps the word 'judged' is better than 'seen'; for whenever this topic is discussed a good deal of emotion is discharged. Some of the proponents of models nowadays, particularly of new models, offer us a 'take-it-or-leave-it' approach which is not, I would submit, the best way of resolving complex issues. Exhortation and rhetoric outweigh coherent argument. I did not expect to leave the Models of Man conference any more confident about the answers to the questions to be put than I was when I arrived. For the topic under discussion is an impossible topic. One reason why we have a difficulty about the proper characterization of mankind is that no model, borrowed from any other domain of description, quite fits the bill. Nor in my view, will we ever achieve much more than an approximation to an adequate description. Mankind alters himself by altering his conception of himself. Mankind alters himself by ceaselessly tinkering with nature, by creating artifacts which in their turn recreate the nature of his experience. And there is no reason to believe that this process will stop. As mankind alters himself in unpredictable ways, so new models will be required, which will appear to fit in their time and which will even change the times into which they fit. The very use and exploration of models alters our experience, thus creating the need for new models. Since by virtue of this phenomenon we cannot sample such unpredictable futures, it would be wise to be cautious. But there is a paradox which I must mention, before leaving this inscrutable paragraph. The models which man uses to characterize man, are models which man himself has devised to characterize other classes or events within his experience. Thus he reflects upon himself his reflections of an external world. Yet surely, his reflections upon himself must presuppose an understanding of how he is able to reflect upon other things? For this he needs a model, independent in some sense, from that which he employs to characterize other aspects of his experience. Such a model would involve the sort of logical leap which requires tremendous endeavour.

Let me begin therefore with the statement that man is not a rat, a pigeon, an ape, a nervous system, a communication channel, a computer or, even, a scientist. Yet all these models, each of which contains more than a grain of truth but falls short of the whole truth, have been useful in their time. My criterion of usefulness is the increasing of our understanding and the generation of enthusiasm and even of vigorous contempt for these and other reflections of man upon his nature. Models have a crucial function in teasing, challenging, and stimulating - in creating ideas for us to play with. Models rouse us from our dogmatic slumbers. The scientific community needs models to chew upon and fight over. And society as a whole needs models for the creation of social policy and the allocation of resources. Models are not deities to be worshipped but tools which have a variety of functions. In science they help us to order our experience, in political life they determine the ways in which men respect each other. There is a danger that the psychologist, in using models for the former purpose, slips into the habits of the latter purpose, or unwittingly creates a justification for the latter purpose (Shotter, 1975).

The history of what we call 'the medical model' is instructive. In its time, it represented many good things: a humane approach to those who formerly had been considered to be wicked or possessed with devils and worthy of imprisonment, the introduction of systematic record-taking, the provision from the public purse of caring environments, the evolution of a profession dedicated to the creation of well-being for those in distress, and the development of the notion of asylum. Prisoners became patients. But now, in our time, patients are seen, by virtue of this very same model to have become quasi-prisoners. The psychiatrist is seen as an evil agent of social and political pressures, dominating his patient as the master creates and then dominates the slave, forcing compliance, denying individual responsibility, imposing rituals of institutionalization. Psychiatry has become a conspiracy. Psychiatry-bashing is an accepted norm for the psychology undergraduate - the model is seen to have outlived its usefulness. I am not convinced that psychology has a better model to offer, rather I believe it has a complementary model focusing on the consequences of illness rather than its causes; but certainly, our perception of the medical model has been altered by time and events. What was once seen as useful is now seen as misleading and even corrupt.

You may observe that I am standing too far back, am being patronizing towards the concept of a model, since from what I have already said, it will be clear that I do not believe we will ever find 'the right model' for I have suggested that there will never be one. There will only be models which arrive in a timely fashion, which guide, correct and reshape our reality, and then are seen to be irrelevant. What I am saying is that models can be and are useful and even that it is proper that, at the time in question, we should believe that we will find the right model. That is one of their crucial functions. Thus it is useful or it was useful, at some time in the development of psychology to think of man 'as if' he were a rat, an ape, a computer and so on. And in condemning any particular model we should be aware of the function it served in the development of new models. Since there is no fixed reality, each model must be looked at through an historical perspective.

My model of models is not new; it derives from one of my constructions upon what I take Kelly to mean by 'constructive alternativism' (Kelly, 1955).

Since for me, research, reading and writing are done for their own intrinsic fun, since thinking about the mind has become a functionally autonomous drive, I have to admit that I do much of what I do without thinking about it. Therefore, because I am known as a psychophysiologist, this chapter is a rather crude attempt to justify the psychophysiological approach to what I have called naive parallelism (Gale, 1973). Given the present state of our knowledge, there are certain ingredients of a psychological story which you just cannot do without. Psychophysiology, I believe, contains them all: man has a nervous system, he performs actions, he is sometimes a conscious agent, his actions and experiences take place in a social context, and finally, he is many 'hes', for each man differs from every other man. My argument is that psychophysiology recognizes all these aspects of man and is therefore a pretty good bet for advancing our understanding of man for the time being.

What is psychophysiology? Why was it necessary to invent a new name or a new label? Is psychophysiology really a new discipline? In what ways is psychophysiology different from biological psychology, neuroanatomy, neurophysiology and so on?

The first issue of the journal 'Psychophysiology' was published in 1964. There is a Society for Psychophysiological Research in the United States, and in this country, a Psychophysiology Society. Even since the early 1960s psychophysiologists have been keen to set themselves apart and distinguish their enterprise from that of their parent discipline, physiological psychology. They claim that in both conception and method, objectives and technique, there are fundamental differences in approach.

What does the physiological psychologist do? The physiological psychologist tampers with the nervous system, observes the ensuing behavioural disruption, and then draws inferences about its normal modes of operation. He cuts, burns, ablates, sucks out and even rewires parts of the brain. With the aid of chemicals he can induce reversible functional lesions and observe his experimental subject before, during and after his intervention. By observing how behaviour is changed he attempts to determine the normal role or function of the part which has been damaged.

This approach raises logical difficulties (Gregory, 1961). In a complex and interconnected system, damage in several places could cause the same outcome. Demonstration that damage to or removal of one particular part of the system, disrupts a particular function, merely demonstrates that the part in question is a necessary but not a sufficient condition for the satisfaction of that function. It cannot justify the assertion that the part in question is 'the' neural locus for the function. Clearly, it must be demonstrated that operations in other parts, do not lead to the same disruption, for damage in other brain areas might bring about identical effects. The best that can be said, is that the part in question is part of a larger system, which is dependent upon its integrity for the proper functioning of the whole. Damage to a complex or a simple part of one's television set can have either complex or simple effects.

When the physiological psychologist delves with his knife or electrode into the nervous system, he is not like the wireless engineer, probing within your transistor radio, or the car mechanic disconnecting this part or that. The engineer is able to do that just because he already knows how the system works. He has the functional block diagram in his head and he knows the modus operandi of every individual part and unit. The motor mechanic can tell you which parts have this or that effect on other parts. Regrettably, the neurosurgeon does not have in his head a block diagram of what you have in your head. Thrusting in a knife here and there can often be little more than putting a spanner in the works. The drawings seen in popular journals and Sunday colour supplements of 'how the brain works' are based upon an illusion. Such diagrams have been popular for more than 100 years, and have barely altered in conception since the days of the phrenologists, men who believed that psychological functions and their relative importance within the psychological make-up of the individual, could be determined by the magnitude and distribution of bumps on the cranium.

The fact that the frontal lobes of man have been associated with almost every psychological function in the book is a function of the logical insecurities of this approach. Each decade students learn that a new part of the brain is the repository of something or other which is the basis or the cause of some slice of behaviour or some behavioural disorder. The pineal gland, the frontal lobes, the reticular formation, the hippocampus, the amygdala and so on. At least, the presence of so many physiological psychologists of Jewish origin guarantees that we shall not be invited to believe that the seat of human intelligence is in the foreskin!

Needless to say, the experiments upon which much of physiological psychology is based, are experiments upon cats, rats and monkeys. A simple examination of the relative proportions of the cerebral cortex identified with sensory rather than integrative function at different levels of evolution warns us against extrapolating from animal experiments to human functions.

Of course, physiological psychological experiments conducted upon human subjects are subject to ethical constraints. I argue that even were the dreadful day to come when such constraints were removed, we would not be that much nearer to understanding the relationship between brain and mind. Certainly there are data from damaged human brains. Accidents, strokes and the surgeon's knife have all contributed to our understanding. But as we have shown, such data still provide problems of interpretation. Whatever function is affected by damage to a particular area, it is always logically possible that damage in another area will bring about the same effect. And of course, natural experiments bring their own difficulties. For rarely in the case of brain injury do we have sufficient knowledge of the individual before the damage occurred, to measure very precisely the effects of the damage. And where surgery is required because of a tumour or because of the need to remove an epileptic focus of long standing, the plasticity of the brain and its apparent capacity to reorganize itself, prevent us from knowing how much reorganization took place before surgery.

In all these studies the lack of sophistication in the measurement of behaviour change and the failure to be precise in the description of the psychological function disrupted, have left us in a state of confusion. Only recently have skilled psychologists turned to the detailed study of brain damage. The physiological psychologist, working within the confines of the animal brain, often talks for example of memory as the mere registration, storage and retrieval of information, and he searches for a simple key. He applies precision to physiology but reduces psychology almost to an 18th century notion of faculties. But for the contemporary psychologist, who devotes his professional life to the study of human memorial processes for their own sake, memory is much more complex than this. Correlations between sophisticated physiology and crude psychology are unlikely to yield sophisticated answers about the relations between mind and brain.

Physiological psychology therefore involves the use of physiological interference as the independent variable and behavioural change as the dependent variable. Experimental subjects are typically not human and the behavioural measures employed are, as a description of behaviour, barely removed from the vernacular. And, of course, observation is limited to the behavioural and physiological domains. Animal subjects cannot tell us how they think or feel. Finally, physiological psychology is concerned with general laws, it rarely concerns itself with differences between individuals in a population.

Physiological psychology, then, is more physiological than psychological. Clearly, there are grounds for a bridge between biology and psychology, but we must not be willing to cross that bridge too readily. In psychophysiology, a quite conscious decision has been made to place the psychology before the physiology - the 'psych' before the 'phys'. Psychophysiology presents a considerable contrast with physiological psychology.

In psychophysiology the approach is essentially correlational rather than causal. Rather than ask 'which part of the brain subsumes this or that function', psychophysiology attempts to integrate three universes of discourse, the physiological, the behavioural and the experiential: that is, what changes occur in our nervous system, what we are observed to do, and what we report we think, feel or imagine. An attempt is made to correlate observed events in these three domains, as parallel events on a common scale of time. This is what I mean by a 'naive parallelist' approach to the human mind. It has its problems and I attempt to tackle some of these in a moment.

The ideal psychophysiological experiment asks questions of the form: 'When S performs classes of action Xb, Yb and Zb, may we also differentiate parallel changes in classes of physiological state Xp, Yp and Zp and also in classes of experiential events Xe, Ye and Ze?' The subscripts (b,p,e) stand for behaviour, physiology and experience. X, Y and Z might be substituted for example by anger, fear and rage, which are of course related but differentiable.

I must emphasize that the psychophysiologist is not a reductionist. He is not committed to the reduction of all psychological realities to anatomical structures, or electrical, physiological or biochemical changes. While for historical and technical reasons, physiology has been granted more status, concern for the behavioural and the experiential domains has a sound conceptual basis.

In contrast with physiological psychology, experimental subjects in psychophysiological research are studied intact and rarely is any attempt made to tamper with the nervous system. The experimental subjects are human subjects and they can attempt to tell us what they experience, what they see and how they feel. They can perform for us those complex tasks which infra-human species are incapable of performing. The psychophysiologist does monitor bodily functions, but from outside the individual rather than from within the nervous system. With appropriate transducers and powerful amplifiers we may obtain a written record of brain activity, muscular changes, heart rate, blood pressure, skin conductance, respiration, and so on. These provide an immediate measure of the activity of an intact and fully functioning central and autonomic nervous system in a living and complete human being.

It is immediately apparent that the use of such techniques involves a considerable degree of technical expertise, in physiology, electronics, computerization of the analysis of complex analogue signals, and the mathematical and statistical skills required to characterize the activity observed and estimate changes and trends. In just a few minutes the zealous psychophysiologist can have enough data to generate a doctoral thesis. To help him cope and make sense of these data he must acquire mastery of these techniques. Thus, if you think my model is the right model for the moment, your acceptance will have implications for the undergraduate training of the psychologist. For if these are necessary skills for mastering part of my model, we will be obliged to change the ways we equip our students to handle the model. But I have not completed the picture yet.

Unfortunately, the history of psychophysiology so far has been a history of failure to realize its promise. I said earlier that psychophysiological research was largely human research. This means that there can be a rapprochement between psychophysiology and many areas of psychology, psychological studies of attention, information processing, skilled performance, aesthetic judgements, personality, psychopathology and social psychology. All these fields are already blessed with rich bodies of data and theoretical accounts of their own. This is where the major bridge can be built between the physiological and psychological traditions. Unfortunately, in spite of many brave attempts, this has not yet happened. Psychophysiologists, pre-occupied with technical concerns, have become technicians rather than theorists, have become a detached and postgraduate speciality, separated off not only from physiological psychology, but from the mainstream of psychology itself. Not only is there little psychophysiology in physiological psychology textbooks used by undergraduates, but there are few if any undergraduate degrees where psychophysiology is regarded as a basic subject of study in its own right. Psychophysiologists have been concerned with experimentation rather than with devising good experiments. They read their own scientific journals and have their own private controversies. The discipline is becoming strangled with the inertia of paradigms of its own devising. One of the key points I wish to make here is that psychophysiology has much to offer to psychology; indeed, that psychophysiology cannot advance without a firm basis in psychology and that psychophysiology might help to link the models used within the various subdisciplines of psychology.

The theoretical commitment to integration of psychophysiology (or at least, my version of it) might provide some integration within psychology. Most of the technical problems which obsessed the psychophysiologist of the 1960s and 1970s have now been overcome. Electronics and computing are now after all the mainstream of our culture. Psychophysiology could be ready to take off.

Let us return to some theoretical problems. I said earlier that psychophysiology is not reductionist. Is this a sensible view? Why is it not possible to reduce mind to body? Why does it not make sense to say for example that adolescent love and its painful pangs are merely a reflection of turmoil among the sex hormones, or that schizophrenia is merely a disease involving the malfunctioning of neuro-transmitters in the forebrain, or that complex functions of our social structure, such as the family or the legal system, are merely án elaboration upon the gene's selfish pre-occupation with its own reproduction?

I have two answers, which are not unrelated. If human experience is to be reduced to events in another domain of description, where do we stop? Surely, there is no logical limit to an infinite regression, from feelings, to behaviour, to anatomy, to physiology, to electrophysiology, to biochemistry, molecular biology and so on. What is the appropriate level of explanation?

The second argument focuses on what is lost by reducing one universe of discourse wholly to another. Imagine a rose. We may see it firstly in its full blush of colour. An object of aesthetic wonder and sensuous delight. What else would smell as sweet? Now see it robbed of colour and smell. It has form and complex structure. A reduced description of this sort has meaning to the artist and the art student, its surfaces have meaning to the topologist. But it has also a complex mechanical structure, with structural strengths and weaknesses, built to stand the extremes of climate, limits of stress tolerance - something to delight the engineer. At the same time, it also has a complex physiology which sustains its vegetative and reproductive functions. Do we need to make a further point about complex electrical fields generated within and about the rose, about its molecular structure, or indeed, its role within a living ecology, the rose's role among the flora and fauna of the garden? Yet look also at the brochure of a commercial horticulturalist. For him, roses are objects of love, but they are also a passport to a healthy bank balance. And then think of the cultural significance of the rose, its use in art and literature, the occasions upon which roses are given and received, when it is considered proper and not proper to present them. Finally, think of an individual rose, in the individual and unique past of one human being, who has plucked a rose in a certain mood, or received it from a particular person, on a unique and remembered occasion.

Thus a simple rose can have many meanings. A flower, something to draw, to smell, an efficient living system, an element in a food chain, with complex molecular structure, a source of income. It is given as an expression of love or a plea for forgiveness. It features in the emotional histories of numerous unique individuals. To tell the story of the rose, can we consider just one of these levels of description or must we take them all? Your immediate answer will be 'It depends upon what you wish to achieve, it depends who you are and what your ambitions: take those aspects which are relevant to these'.

The ambition of the psychologist is to understand the human mind. And I would submit that little advance will be made unless we attempt to come to grips at least with the integration of the physiological, the behavioural and the experiential domains. But this must also include a description of the mind in its social context, we must study events between individuals as well as within them. Finally, while devising general laws to describe and predict events in the domains of physiology, behaviour and experience, we must also determine those principles which explain how individual human beings differ. The variety of human experience is fascinating, if not more so, than predictable generality. Indeed only when we discover how general principles may be applied to the understanding of the individual will applied psychology be able to assist the individual qua individual.

The integration of these aspects of the person is the ambition of psychology. It is the failure to attempt this integration and the insistence that certain aspects may be studied to the exclusion of others which is in part responsible for the despondency among some contemporary psychologists. The brief so many psychologists have given themselves is so restricted that the answers to the questions they ask are limited. My moral is, they get into a muddle, because they stick to a model.

Take attempts to study the brain in isolation from its ecological context. Penfield showed long ago that one can stimulate the motor sensory strip of the exposed human brain and reliably produce motor twitches and movements in the man's limbs. Say we can reliably get a man to raise his arm by this means, is this an adequate account of why men raise their arms? The raising of an arm can mean many things, from a request to ask a question or to leave the room, as a mechanical means of raising a good brew to the lips, as a 'Harvey Smith' (V-sign) gesture of defiance and contempt, to a fascist salute. One gesture can mean many things. And of course the reverse is true; many apparently differing behaviours can have a common meaning. A common psychological criticism of psychiatric taxonomy is that different behaviours are seen as symptoms of different diseases. But a functional analysis of say the various symptoms of depression (sobbing, withdrawal, self-recrimination, hopelessness) may reveal that their variety disappears when one views the patient in the context of his immediate emotional environment (Ferster, 1974). The different symptoms are seen to have a common meaning. Taken out of context they seem so very different and various they have led the medical model of psychopathology down several garden paths.

A man may have many purposes in walking down the street - to take exercise, to post a letter, to get to work, or to meet a lover. Similarly, he may have many differing means of expressing bitter resentment towards his wife. The mere description of segments of isolated behaviours out of context is not enough.

Nor indeed will isolated segments of brain tell us much about the organization of our experience. Take a child's acquisition of the concept 'ball'. I choose this because it is a simple and common concept, and for most intents and purposes, the visual image cast by the ball is invariant and circular, unlike that say of another familiar construct in his immediate environment - a 'chair'. Take the visual mode. Balls have colour, are bright or dull, are small and large, maintain constancy in spite of varying distance and velocity. Balls are also heard; they bounce and create echos. Balls can hurt, and the pain may be caused by accident or intent. Balls are nice to touch and grip, they can be firm or squishy. They can taste rubbery or plasticky. Their surface can vary in humidity, temperature and texture. Balls are associated with muscular movements, manipulations both fine and gross, while stationary or moving. Balls obey the laws of gravity, they instruct us in lower-order concepts of ballistic expectation. Balls are given as presents. Balls are played with in conjunction with parents or peers. Balls are played with in private gardens and public parks. Balls are bitten by dogs and stolen. Balls are property. If all these elements go into the developing concept of 'the ball', can we expect to find an engram where that concept is stored, can we study the workings of the brain merely by working with the brain? Even the most simple concept dwells within an extended family of meanings.

Psychologists are beginning to get to grips with the observation of physiological and behavioural events in context, and recently the problem of describing the psychological meaning of situations and evaluating the importance of persons times situations interactions has received much attention (Magnussen & Endler, 1977).

But what of our experiences of ourselves and of the world; how can we come to grips with these? This is an area where psychology can benefit from the history of philosophical analysis of our experience of self and others. Indeed may I have the courage to suggest that we would benefit from such a bridge? Here we have an awful paradox. To persons like you and myself, experiential continuity, the awareness of a unique and private consciousness, the notion of being a self, is a matter-of-fact reality. Yet to many psychological traditions it has been an illusion. This is not just a fault of psychology. In our culture, training in the systematic observation and reporting upon the self, one's own inner states and the fine discrimination of thought and feeling, are not part of our educational practice. The educational experience is if anything second-hand and unsystematic, rather than direct, in the form of lessons in the appreciation of literature, poetry and theatre. Yet one might imagine a culture, and I know some of you will declare it to be logically absurd, where such instruction is part and parcel of even elementary education. But many psychologists have washed their hands of subjective experience as something which is unmeasurable, unreliable, and therefore conceptually unhelpful. There is some justice in this view, for in the absence of systematic training, human subjects have proved to be notoriously incompetent in reporting about their inner experience. The concept of the person as a conscious, striving and reflective individual has certainly not lost status in psychology, although it has recently undergone a muddled revival. As Gordon Allport put it: 'The individual has lost the right to be believed'.

Let us now return to our notion of naive parallelism. Is the term 'parallel' really justified? Are we really talking of three parallel worlds, with no causal link between them? Are the logical relations between these three domains really symmetrical? For example, is not the physiology-consciousness relationship asymmetrical with the consciousness-physiology relationship? We can say that there is no evidence of conscious experience in the absence of a nervous system, but does the reverse hold? What is the nature of the intersections in time between physiology, behaviour and experience? Theorists have varied between models of total correlation, partial correlation and even independence. Can we really devise units of description which are interchangeable between the three domains? Is it really straightforward to devise translation rules between the three universes of discourse, enabling mapping of one upon the other?

The analysis of these complex problems will be left for now! The resolution of the logical difficulties and the mastering of the technical challenges await the appearance of an Einstein of psychology. Regrettably I am not up to the challenge; therein lies the principal defect in this account.

But it is the tangibility and the apparent logical primacy of the biological domain which has proved so misleading. It has also provided a threat to human dignity.

More and more over recent years have we become aware of the biological side of our nature. Freud, so influenced by Darwin, believed that what we do and what we feel are determined by forces of which we are unaware. Unconscious drives, which owe their origin to the thrust and elaboration of animal instincts, dominate our lives and permeate our actions. Man according to Freud, is not rational, but a slave of his biological origins. In psychiatric medicine, we observe the extended use of chemical compounds to influence behaviour, mood and thought, by their action upon the nervous system. General practitioners, driven by the drug manufacturers and pressed for time, prescribe tranquillizers as a substitute for getting to grips with the patient's problems of living in a complex world. Medicine generally seems to favour the view of a machine whose defective parts are to be repaired rather than as a complex organism, living in a culture and whose behaviour might be more a determinant of health than his physiology. Totalitarian regimes attempt to change man's will by chemical invasion of the brain. Drugs have replaced religion as an instrument of the State (Lader, 1977). Biological scientists have popularized the notion of man as an animal. The simplistic, arrogant and logically fragile message conveyed by Desmond Morris is that man is an ape. Perhaps if he were to ask himself 'How was I able to write "The Naked Ape"?', he would not have written it. The works of Ardrey and Wilson appear to convey a vision of man as little more than a beast. And recently, the great biofeedback fraud, the popularized and inexact psychophysiological experiments of the transcendental meditation movement, and the abuse of so-called lie detector machines, have emphasized the primacy of physiological events. Poor psychophysiology has led to rapid and profitable commercial exploitation of people.

As psychology has evolved over the years it has adopted many images of man. But 'man as a nervous system' is a model for humanity taken out of context, just as Harvey's description of the circulation of the blood was borrowed out of context by Descartes for his psychological model of animal spirits.

It is because of the very uniqueness of the relationship between physiology, behaviour and experience that we have so much difficulty. The models and terminology borrowed from other contexts just do not ring true in the final analysis, although they have often proved to be devilishly enticing as the history of psychology has shown, still shows, and no doubt will continue to show.

It may be that we shall never be able to characterize the special relationship between physiology, behaviour and experience in a satisfactory manner. However, this does not mean that we may, in an arbitrary fashion, choose to ignore any one or even two of these universes of discourse.

Are the arguments which I have sketched out in this brief discussion logically intact or are they mere exhortations to practise psychology in a particular fashion? There are a number of classical problems in epistemology which have received scant reference here. The short and short-term answer must be that the proof of the pudding is in the eating. Unfortunately, it could be argued that there is not much pudding to taste at present. There is a considerable gap between the conceptual base of my version of what psychophysiology is, or should be, and the reality of hard data. But that is a story to tell on another occasion.

Let me summarize. (1) The psychophysiologist recognizes the biological part of man's nature, but he is not a reductionist. Physiology is seen as one way of viewing the person. (2) Physiological goings-on are seen to have meaning in the context of behaviour. (3) No description of human behaviour or human physiology is seen to be complete without reference to the world as experienced, felt and thought. (4) Physiology, behaviour and experience take place within a social context. Just as man is not a moral island, so also is he not a psychological island. (5) Psychophysiology is concerned with differences between people as well as similarities. It is concerned not only with general laws of the mind, but in asking the question 'Why and how do minds differ?' (6) It follows that psychophysiology can only advance by building bridges with all branches of psychology. The psychophysiologist must juggle with several models, must keep his feet in several camps at once, without tripping himself up. Over and above his skills in physiology, electronics and computing, he must be first and foremost a good psychologist. (7) The hallmark of psychophysiology is its commitment to integration between these various sources of knowledge and its openness to the philosophical analysis of the complexity of its subject matter. This, in my view, is its potential for the future.

The integration of these models of man is what I mean by the synchronization of several simultaneous models: physiology, behaviour, experience, social context and individual uniqueness.

It has to be recognized that the problems which the psychophysiologist has set himself may never yield understanding. In a sense there is no such thing as the brain or the nervous system. The brain has evolved over millions of years within a complex ecology, and each newly born brain develops within a new context. This reminds us that as well as past adaptations there will be new adaptations. The absorption into our culture of universal education and the revolution in mass communication must make human nature seem very different now from what it appeared to be even 100 years ago. The psychologist must recognize that the characterization of human nature will never be finite, will never be complete. As human nature appears to change so our views of brain function are likely to change. The one thing which we can be sure of is that man will find new ways to extend his mind.

CONCLUSION

Models should not be taken too seriously. They do not represent the truth; rather they urge us on, presenting alternative routes to the truth. The dyed-in-the-wool enthusiast, who moves heaven and earth for the love of his model is sure to fall - but his struggle serves to expand our understanding. Yet models can also be seen in retrospect to have deceived us, to have corrupted our thinking. No model will ever do, since man's conception of man will never be finite.

Psychophysiology moves between, and sometimes manages to integrate, at least five contemporaneous models: man as biological organism, as a conscious agent, as an observable actor, as a social creature, as a unique being. Perhaps this is too much for psychophysiology to cope with. But the psychophysiologist who tries to cope with less, deceives himself. How, for example, can the psychophysiologist present an intelligible view of schizophrenia without an awareness of all these domains of description? The alleged biological anomalies are accompanied by other causes and consequences. The patient behaves in a strange way, he reports unsupportable experiences of sensory invasion and distortion. He shows a lack of competence in social behaviour. He ascribes meanings which seem to us at the same time bizarre and yet governed by an unfathomable logic. And each patient has had his own life and his own interpretation of it. Much of what he does appears to be governed by tacit institutional rules, a reflection of the systematic patterns of reward which are part of the fabric of the ecology of the psychiatric hospital, or of his home.

In these circumstances, what sense does it make to identify schizophrenia with a malfunction in this or that bit of the brain? And indeed, what good will it do? I fear that some of my psychophysiological colleagues, in pursuit of the biological crock of gold, have forgotten that each schizophrenic patient is a person - just as the psychophysiologist is a person - and that the uniqueness of his experience and personal history will serve to modulate any normative generalization that the psychophysiologist will care to construct. I really do feel safe in predicting that my colleagues, if they persist in this confusion, will never reach the end of the rainbow.

What is the answer then? Does it really matter? The questions are probably wrong. Mindless men can get into hopeless muddles wondering about models of man. I am a naive parallelist and a happy pragmatist. I shall continue to juggle with my simultaneous models.

NOTES

Much of the content of this chapter is taken from an Inaugural Lecture entitled 'Psychophysiology: a bridge between disciplines' presented to the University of Southampton, 1979. In the original version, the initial statement (some of which appears here) was followed by a series of research examples designed to demonstrate the naive parallelist approach.

EDITED DISCUSSION

L. SMITH: I am not sure whether belief in parallelism can be sustained. You might sometimes search my conscious mind in vain for any mental experience which was an antecedent to an action on my part: for example, parrying a punch in a boxing match. Nonetheless, there would be physiological events going on. In other words, there may be something at one end of 'the bridge' but not at the other. How do you know that you can make good your claim about parallelism?

A. GALE: You seem to want things to be completed before one starts. My point is that, in psychophysiology at least, there is sometimes an unfortunate tendency to fail to acknowledge certain aspects of the situation: this can give a very misleading picture. I am not sure whether what you are suggesting is a technical or a logical difficulty.

L. SMITH: The point is not a new one: there may well be no correlation between behaviour, mental experience and physiology.

A. GALE: That is logically possible, but my scheme is more workable.

N. E. WETHERICK: I feel bound to say to Professor Gale that he cannot succeed in his enterprise. Quite apart from philosophical difficulties we have much empirical evidence to suggest: (1) the behaviour of his subject may not be what he thinks it is (i.e. the subject may be solving a different problem from that set by the experimenter, and there is sometimes no way of detecting this in the laboratory) and (2) what he tells us of his conscious processes may be a lie and, even if it is the truth as he understands it, may be wrong.

R. M. FARR: You pose a problem for some of us when you say in your chapter that you 'do not expect to leave (this Conference) any more confident about the answers to (various fundamental) questions' - because you have then gone on to tell us that you have to leave the Conference very shortly. So, those who want to convert you to a more philosophical pragmatism, for example, have to get in quickly! If there were time, I would want to suggest that George Herbert Mead merits very serious consideration in the context of the things you have described.

J. A. GRAY: I believe that the model of physiological psychology presented by Professor Gale is a straw man. Physiological psychologists do a great deal more than cut holes in brains (by whatever means) and observe the consequences. They also use methods such as stimulation of the brain (electrical and chemical); they do reversible lesions; they sometimes do not damage the brain at all, but they reverse the equation and look at the changes in the brain as a result of different types of behavioural experience; they sometimes look at electrical recordings of the brain, or biochemical changes in the brain; and so on.

A. GALE: But none of the examples you have given undermine the logic of Gregory's argument ...

J. A. GRAY: On the contrary, they do. The argument is that when you lesion the brain, you are studying a system which has been changed because of the part you have removed. But many experiments do not involve lesions at all. No one method on its own is satisfactory.

A. GALE: I would agree that they help to make the picture more coherent, but they do not overcome the distinction between necessary and sufficient conditions. Electrodes and chemicals are located at specific sites, largely determined by hunches.

J. A. GRAY: The aim is that eventually physiological psychologists, using different methods - different electrode sites, etc. - will examine all the possibilities.

F. FRANSELLA: Professor Gale seems to suggest that to be a 'psychologist' one has to have a technical expertise of physiology, electronics, computer analysis and so forth. Do you, Professor Gale, really see this as a central model upon which psychology might be based? If so, how do we inculcate these skills?

A. GALE: As a university teacher, I certainly think we are producing incomplete psychologists. We should indeed be teaching all of these skills to our students: they are basic.

Chapter 6

Neuropsychology and the relationship between brain and behaviour

E. Miller

Any comprehensive discussion of 'models of man' from a psychological point of view has to deal with the relationship between psychological functioning on the one hand and the nature of the biological organism on the other. This chapter is designed to explore certain aspects of this general issue from the point of view of a neuropsychologist. Because neuropsychology is a rather recent and complex subdiscipline it seems best to start by looking very briefly at the nature of neuropsychology and by describing the problems it raises that are of particular concern in this context.

THE NATURE OF NEUROPSYCHOLOGY

It is difficult to provide an adequate and concise definition of neuropsychology. This is partly because of the varied, and occasionally indiscriminate, usage of the term that can be found in the literature. Most investigators who would describe themselves as 'neuropsychologists' are concerned with the study of psychological functioning in subjects who have suffered some form of disease, damage or disruption of the brain. This does not provide a complete definition because some neuropsychological investigations do involve normal subjects. A common example is the tachistoscopic experiment in which brief visual stimuli are presented to the right or left visual fields so that the information is presumably processed initially by the right or left hemispheres of the brain. A common theme that runs through all neuropsychology is the relationship between brain structures and psychological processes. Some neuropsychology involves experiments on animals and has a considerable overlap with those areas of study generally described as 'physiological psychology'. In line with the overall theme of the book this chapter will of course be concerned with the neuropsychology of human subjects.

An obvious feature of neuropsychology is that it is a hybrid activity which covers the common meeting place of a small cluster of major disciplines. These include not only psychology but neurology and linguistics amongst many others (Hecaen & Albert, 1978). In fact a number of the leading figures in neuropsychology are not psychologists in terms of their initial training and major disciplinary affiliation. A consequence of this is that the psychologist who wishes to take a serious interest in neuropsychology must gain a reasonably competent knowledge of the relevant parts of the other disciplines which impinge upon this field. Particularly important is an understanding of some of the other neurosciences such as neuroanatomy and neurophysiology. An adequate appreciation of some of the work on aphasia is only possible with some knowledge of linguistics. On the positive side this mixing of disciplines can lead to stimulation and cross-fertilization. However this has to be counterbalanced by the fact that neuropsychology can run foul of some of the methodological problems of these other disciplines besides having to cope with the not inconsiderable conceptual and methodological problems inherent in psychology itself.

In very broad terms it is possible to detect two complementary approaches to neuropsychology (Miller, 1972). These can be referred to as the functional and the anatomical. The functional approach is primarily concerned with trying to elucidate the nature of the functional disturbances that can occur in memory, language, etc., as a result of brain damage. Little emphasis is placed upon the location or nature of the damage that produces the disturbance. Within this approach the common techniques and methodology are those of cognitive psychology. It can become what is in effect cognitive psychology carried out with an abnormal subject population. Because of the considerable overlap with cognitive psychology this approach is less likely to raise distinctive issues of underlying philosophy and it will not be considered further here.

The other main approach to neuropsychology is much more oriented to brain anatomy. It is concerned with describing the changes in psychological functioning that result from lesions in different parts of the brain. By extension from this the anatomical approach tries to draw conclusions about the functional significance of particular structures within the brain. Because it correlates changes in psychological functioning with damage to, or disruption of, particular brain structures the anatomical approach to neuropsychology is much more immediately involved in trying to relate brain and behaviour. In doing so it raises a number of underlying issues and assumptions. Some of these will form the major concern of this chapter.

As a starting point it is possible to consider one of the classical findings of neuropsychology. The Montreal case HM had the mesial portions of his temporal lobes removed bilaterally in order to relieve severe and intractable epilepsy. There was no depression of general intellectual functioning but the operation did produce what may well be the most marked amnesia ever recorded (for a general description see Milner, 1966). Other work has shown that left temporal lobe excisions are likely to result in verbal memory impairments and has confirmed that bilateral temporal lesions do produce very drastic memory impairments (Walsh, 1978). This evidence has in turn led to discussions of the role that mesial temporal lobe structures, especially the hippocampus, might play in the process of learning and memory (e.g. Horel, 1978).

For present purposes the point of this example is that some neuropsychologists have used this kind of evidence to argue that the hippocampus must be the anatomical location for certain parts of the overall memory process. Such a conclusion raises two fundamental problems. The first is whether psychological processes can be adequately identified with neural structures and be subsequently explained by activities that go on within these structures. This is usually referred to as the problem of reductionism. Even if a reductionist view of psychology is allowed there is also the rather more empirical question of the extent to which it is reasonable to expect the different parts of the brain to be specialized for different psychological functions.

This chapter now concentrates on the two issues of reductionism and the localization of functions. Reductionism is intimately related to the extent to which it is possible to view man as a form of biological machine. Assuming that this model of man does have some validity it is then incumbent upon advocates of the model to look beyond this and try to describe the kind of machine that is involved. The discussion about the localization of functions represents one possible means of approaching this latter problem.

Within neuropsychology reductionism is a problem that has received very little attention. This might be considered strange because neuropsychology has strong reductionist elements in its underlying philosophy. Possibly this is because neuropsychologists are not attracted to the idea of philosophizing about their work, but the neglect of reductionism as an issue probably has more to do with the fact that neuropsychologists working within or near to a reductionist framework see little point in arguing about it. On the other hand, reductionism has been much discussed by other psychologists and philosophers of science. It features as one of Westland's (1978) 'current crises of psychology' and is undoubtedly a problem of major concern to psychology as a whole. In contrast the extent to which psychological functions can be localized within the brain has been a significant and active issue for neuropsychology throughout its history. Unlike reductionism it is a debate whose underlying arguments have been well rehearsed within the subdiscipline, but the questions involved have been somewhat neglected by other psychologists.

REDUCTIONISM

Reductionism is a general philosophical problem which runs throughout the whole range of scientific endeavour (Turner, 1968; Weiss, 1969; Popper, 1977). The following discussion is naturally concerned with the possibility of the reduction or translation of psychological concepts, processes and theories to neural structures and activities. The general principles involved are undoubtedly similar to those arising wherever reductionist explanations are attempted in either the physical or biological sciences.

Within psychology it is possible to discern two diametrically opposed viewpoints. On the one hand there are those like Krech (1950) who argue that any real explanation in psychology must be reductionist in nature. Non-reductionist approaches may be allowed to have some place in psychology but according to this extreme view their value is limited and only temporary in nature. They are merely preliminary excursions on the way to a reductionist goal. On the other hand, there are vociferous proponents of the view that reductionist explanations are impossible in principle (e.g. Jessor, 1958; Bannister, 1968).

Underlying the more extreme views expressed on either side of this dispute, but rarely made explicit, seems to be an even more basic assumption. This is that there must be a single, 'correct' form of explanation in psychology. If this is the case it then follows that this form of explanation must be either reductionist or non-reductionist in nature (allowing of course for the fact that there are different possible types of reductionist and non-reductionist explanations). If this assumption is correct it logically follows that an argument for a non-reductionist form of explanation is also an argument against reductionist explanations and vice versa. It is part of the present thesis that there is no one 'proper' form of explanation for psychology. The appropriateness or otherwise of any form of explanation will depend upon the question that is posed and the context in which it is asked. It is further argued that both reductionist and non-reductionist explanations have a place in psychology and that their relative suitability depends upon the particular nature of the problem under consideration. In other words both reductionists and non-reductionists are right to argue the legitimacy and usefulness of their preferred forms of explanation but wrong in trying to go beyond this in an attempt to invalidate totally the other point of view.

As many writers on the topic have indicated reductionism is itself founded upon certain presuppositions. Jessor (1958) sets out four of these in a paper in which he strenuously argues against reductionism. Firstly, it is assumed that the various sciences can be hierarchically ordered from, say, physics at the bottom upwards through chemistry, biochemistry, physiology, psychology, and with sociology at the top. The second presupposition is that the concepts and laws of one science can be translated into those of another and adjacent science in the hierarchy.

Thirdly, this derivability of one science from another proceeds in one direction such that the concepts and laws of the 'higher' science are reduced to those of the 'lower'. Finally, Jessor argues that there is the assumption that the lower the level of the terms used in any explanation then the more basic and fundamental the explanation becomes.

The last of Jessor's (1958) presuppositions swings on the particular meaning that is attached to the phrase 'more basic and fundamental'. The position advocated in this chapter, that both reductionist and non-reductionist explanations are of value under the appropriate circumstances, does not involve any assumption that one form of explanation must always be valued more highly than the other. The notion that the various sciences can be ordered in a hierarchical way according to the level of the phenomena with which they deal has never been seriously disputed although Popper (1977) has cautioned that the hierarchical organization may not always be quite as simple and clear cut as it is commonly set out. In the present discussion the idea of the hierarchical organization of the sciences will simply be taken for granted.

The crucial issue for reductionism is the assumption that the concepts and laws of one science can be translated without residue into those of a science that is lower in the hierarchy. Those who argue against reductionism hold that there are situations in which the language we use to describe behaviour is not translatable without loss of meaning into the language of a discipline like neurophysiology. The type of simple example that is often used runs along the lines of the following. Consider the situation in which I am walking with my wife down one side of the street in a local shopping centre. For no reason that I can discern at the time my wife makes a gesture with her arm just as we pass somebody on the other side of the street. If I then ask 'Why did you do that?', not having recognized a person who lives in the same small village as we do, I would normally get a response of the kind 'Oh that is Mrs So-and-so who lives in the house next to the school'. Alternatively my wife could have given a response describing the neural pathways and muscle groups involved in moving her arm in a way that could be interpreted as a wave.

We then have two explanations of my wife's behaviour. One is in terms of waving to acknowledge a neighbour and the other is an account of the neurophysiological activities involved when this happened. It is readily conceded that under the particular circumstances in which the question was asked the neurophysiological account is inappropriate. The opponents of reductionism would want to go further and claim that the neurophysiological description is not only inappropriate but incomplete and in no way a proper explanation of the phenomenon.

The argument advanced for this stronger position is that once my wife's arm movement is described as a wave we imply a response to some external stimulus (seeing the neighbour in this case) and the language of neurophysiology, so it is claimed, cannot cope with situations occurring outside the organism itself. In fact some have taken the consequences of this viewpoint a little further by emphatically defining psychology as being concerned with the interaction of the organism as a whole and its environment. They then have a definition of psychology which on the basis of this line of reasoning specifically excludes the possibility of reductionist explanations. As Turner (1968) has shown the situation is not quite as simple as this. Neurophysiology is not powerless to cope with features in the external environment. In the example under consideration some visual image of the neighbour must have impinged upon my wife's retina otherwise the neighbour's presence would have been undetected. Physiological processes of some sort must have been involved in deciding that this stimulus had a certain familiarity and that a response of the type employed was called for.

One particular subset of behavioural descriptions that might appear to present a particular source of difficulty for reductionist explanations are those that rely upon what Ryle (1949) has described as dispositional concepts. Because nouns are often used to refer to particular objects it is easy to assume that concepts such as 'intelligence', 'memory', and 'extraversion' must refer to states or entities within the organism or within the mind. Ryle has argued that this is not the case. The use of a dispositional concept of this nature implies that the individual so described will behave in a certain way given appropriate circumstances. Thus to say that someone 'knows' or 'remembers' the names of all the teams in the Football League infers nothing about any mental or physical state within that person that may make recall possible. It merely means that when an appropriate question is asked, or relevant behaviour is called for, then the suitable response will appear. It is difficult, if not impossible, to apply such concepts to the neural structures that underlie behaviour and it might be argued that this places them beyond the reach of reductionist explanations.

In fact this is not the case. Although neurons, for example, cannot be said to 'remember', at least not in quite the same way as the intact human organism, this does not mean that the memory processes of the intact organism cannot be explained in terms of the structures that make such processes possible. This point may be made clearer by the use of a simple example. The ordinary domestic alarm clock (and what I have in mind is the old fashioned wind-up model rather than the more modern electric or quartz clock) can be described as 'telling the time' and 'waking up' its owner. Both of these are dispositional concepts which cannot readily be applied to the case, spring, cogs, balance wheel, and other constituents from which the alarm clock is constructed. Yet a simple knowledge of mechanical principles allows us to explain how these various components can be fitted together to make a device that will both tell the time and, it is hoped, rouse the sleepy owner on a cold morning. A similar situation that holds for the behaviour of the alarm clock must surely hold for human behaviour and the human machine.

It might be argued that the example of the alarm clock will cover simple dispositional concepts but will not do for the more complex concepts that are used to describe human actions. It would be quite usual to describe the owner of the alarm clock as 'intending' to get up at 7 o'clock but it would not be acceptable to describe the clock as 'intending' to ring its alarm at that time. Intentional concepts with their implications of goal-seeking are commonly used to describe human behaviour and are generally held to pose particular problems for reductionist explanations. Yet even simple devices, such as the thermostat, can show some elements of goal-seeking behaviour. The devotees of artificial intelligence (AI) are producing ever more sophisticated computer programs whose behaviour needs to be described in intentional terms (Boden, 1977) and which display more features associated with human intentionality. Nothing in the AI field has yet matched all the features of human intentionality and this leaves a quandary. Either it has to be accepted that the increasing sophistication of computers and their programs will allow this to happen or that AI can get so far in mimicking human characteristics but will then meet an impenetrable barrier. To me the first option seems more parsimonious and avoids the necessity of stipulating the point of no further advancement: a point that will no doubt be pushed farther and farther back as AI advances.

So far this discussion has emphasized the legitimacy of reductionism in psychology. As was explained earlier this is by no means meant to imply that non-reductionist explanations have no place nor that they are necessarily less useful in given situations. It is also not intended to deny that an approach solely based on reductionist explanations will have serious limitations. These points require brief amplification.

One advantage of non-reductionist explanations is that they can deal with phenomena for which the underlying neural mechanisms are ill understood. Given the present state of the neurosciences this is a predicament that is all too common. Even if the underlying neural processes are understood well enough a non-reductionist explanation may have advantages because it can describe and predict the phenomena of interest in a more economical way. In the field of verbal memory explanations in terms of the rather dated multi-stage model (short-term and long-term memory, etc.) or the now more fashionable levels of processing model may allow the prediction and control of the relevant phenomena much more economically than an alternative in terms of neural processes. The latter is of course not yet possible but, even if it were, the likelihood is that a description of verbal memory processes in terms of neural events would be very long-winded and tremendously complex. In applied psychology the relatively simple concepts and techniques of operant conditioning offer a much more immediate and sensible approach to teaching a severely mentally handicapped child to feed himself than working out the appropriate strategy by means of the neural mechanisms involved.

There is an extreme view of reductionism that goes beyond what is advocated here. My position is that the phenomena and laws of psychology can in principle be translated into a reductionist form involving a lower level of explanation but that this by no means ensures that such a reduction is either desirable or useful within a given context. The extreme position is that non-reductionist explanations are either not real explanations or are, at best, rather trivial in nature and that all explanations ought to seek a reductionist form. When pushed to its limits this line of argument, which seems to be advocated by writers like Krech (1950), runs into an infinite regression. If psychological phenomena can and should be reduced to those of neurophysiology the same argument can be applied again. The neurophysiological phenomena should in turn be reduced to those of biochemistry, and so on. Every explanation will then end up being expressed in terms of subatomic particles; an absurd position for psychology. The only way that the extreme reductionist can get round this problem is to make some arbitrary claim that explanatory virtue lies at one stage lower than the phenomena to be explained. This still leaves the seemingly ludicrous position in which explanatory models at a psychological level are perfectly acceptable to sociologists but must be firmly eschewed by psychologists.

In summary the main thrust of this section has been to establish the legitimacy of reductionism for psychology. In addition it has been claimed that all behaviour can in principle be explained in terms of neural structures and activities although in a given context it will not always be desirable or useful to do so. This argument is important because reductionism is often strongly attacked from within psychology and there are some who would regard any form of physiological psychology as a myth and an abomination (cf. Bannister, 1968). It is of interest to note that in recent discussions of reductionism by even those philosophers of science and scientists of other disciplines who particularly wish to stress the limitations of reductionism the value of the reductionist approach is still allowed (Thorpe, 1969; Weiss, 1969; Popper, 1977).

LOCALIZATION OF FUNCTIONS

Accepting the legitimacy of reductionism gives credence to a model of man as some form of biological machine. This just raises further questions. It is necessary to go beyond this and decide what sort of machine is involved and along what principles it operates. Any comprehensive discussion of this very broad problem would be way beyond the scope of a presentation of this nature. The second of the fundamental issues of neuropsychology with which this chapter is concerned covers just one small aspect of this major problem. This is the extent to which different parts of the key structure in the machine (the brain) are specialized for different psychological functions. If there is a high level of specialization or localization of functions within the brain then we are dealing with a machine which can to an appreciable degree be considered as the coordinated arrangement of a number of discrete units. These can then be explored independently. If the degree of localization is small or non-existent then some other kind of machine model is called for.

The topic of localization has been debated for a considerable length of time and can best be approached by setting out two diametrically opposed and extreme points of view. These contrary positions date from the earlier parts of the 19th century and arise from such pre-scientific activities as phrenology. A fuller account of the background is provided by Clarke & Dewhurst (1972).

One extreme position is that of equipotentiality which holds that all functions depend equally upon the working of the brain as a whole. There is no localization of functions within the brain at all. The alternative point of view is that the different functions can be quite specifically located in particular parts of the brain. Since this controversy began it has become well established that the basic sensory and motor functions are quite well localized within the brain. The basis of the argument has then shifted to the extent to which the so-called 'higher cortical functions' are localized.

As might be expected the equipotentiality theory was particularly espoused by the Gestalt psychologists and those who came under their influence. It received an appreciable boost from the work of Lashley (see Lashley, 1929). In a series of experiments Lashley studied the effects of brain lesions on brightness discrimination and maze learning in rats. He found that the effect on the dependent variable was related to the amount of brain tissue removed and not to which part of the brain the tissue was taken from. These results were formalized by Lashley as the principle of 'mass action'. This principle is of course the major prediction that would be derived from the idea of equipotentiality. Although initially very influential these results provoked considerable criticism and further investigations have shown the principle of 'mass action' to be untenable (Miller, 1972). Because subsequent critics have sometimes not been too correct in their accounts of Lashley's work it is worth recording that he was a careful experimenter who was always very cautious in drawing conclusions. In fact he later modified his position with regard to the principle of mass action to allow for some localization.

Modern neuropsychological research with human subjects also runs definitely against the notion of equipotentiality. The effects of right-sided lesions in the brain are quite distinct from those on the left side, and it is the left hemisphere which seems to be the one most specialized for speech (assuming the more commonly encountered right-handed subjects). This is evident both from the fact that left-sided lesions are associated with aphasic disturbances whereas right-sided lesions are not and from disturbances in hemisphere functioning demonstrated in 'split brain' subjects who have had the corpus callosum sectioned. This work is almost too well established to require any citations in its support but anyone with residual doubts is referred to Walsh's (1978) recent account of neuropsychology.

If equipotentiality is rejected, as it must now be, even if only applied to the 'higher functions', then how does a strict localization viewpoint fare? The answer appears to be that despite the overwhelming evidence for some degree of localization this is not good enough for the extreme localization position. There certainly appears to be no simple one-to-one relationship between the different psychological functions and identifiable parts of the brain (Miller, 1972). Language again provides a good example. Aphasic disorders are associated with lesions over quite a large extent of the left hemisphere. Despite many attempts it has always proved difficult to relate particular types of language impairments to lesions in definite parts of the speech areas of the brain in the rigid way that the strict localizationist would expect. It is probably fair to say that the fundamental question of interest is now not whether there is localization but in what way and to what degree.

There are at least three kinds of difficulty involved in trying to sort this out further. These can be loosely classified as methodological, conceptual and theoretical. The methodology involved in trying to establish that a psychological function can be related to a specific part of the brain is more complex than it might seem at first sight. It is well established that lesions of the left temporal lobe disrupt verbal memory (see Walsh, 1978). It is tempting to assume on the basis of this evidence alone that the left temporal lobe, or some structure within it such as the hippocampus, must be responsible for at least some aspect of verbal memory. As Gregory (1961) has argued it is not legitimate to draw a firm conclusion of this nature from evidence of this type alone. This can readily be seen from an analogy. If the workings of the motor car were being investigated it might be noted that removing the fuel tank left the car incapable of propelling itself forward. It would then be very misleading to conclude that the function of the fuel tank is to make the wheels go round. To return to the left temporal lobe it could be that this has no direct connection with memory processes. It could be that removing the left temporal lobe disrupts memory because it cuts an essential connection between two centres in other parts of the brain that do subserve memory.

Fortunately there are ways round this problem. The removal of a particular part of the brain resulting in a particular psychological impairment may not prove that the affected function is subserved or controlled by that part of the brain. Nevertheless this may remain an extremely plausible hypothesis when other information is taken into account. It is interesting that Weiskrantz (1968) argues that some of Sherrington's most important discoveries on the integrative action of the nervous system were made despite falling into just this logical trap. The most important technique for avoiding this problem is the use of Teuber's (1955) principle of 'double dissociation'. If it can be shown that lesions in other parts of the brain that might conceivably be involved in the particular function under consideration do not have any effect on that function then this strengthens the case for arguing a direct association between the function and the damaged part of the brain.

Another difficulty that has arisen is conceptual. Luria (1966) has pointed out that the term 'function' has been used in two quite distinct ways. It is possible to use this term in relation to the activity of small units; for example, the function of the rods and cones in the retina is to be sensitive to electromagnetic radiation of certain wavelengths. It can also be used to refer to complex activities like attention, memory and intelligence. As used in the former sense 'functions' are by the nature of things localized. In the second sense Luria prefers the term 'complex functional systems' and this emphasizes the fact that complex activities of this type demand a whole series of functions of the other type. For example, memory requires a whole series of subservient functions which start with the to-be-remembered information being registered by one of the sense organs, moving through phases of registration and storage and ending with the particular response indicating the recall of the information. It follows that functions, in the sense of Luria's complex functional systems, are unlikely to be strictly localized at one specific point in the nervous system. The situation is likely to be much more dynamic than an updated phrenology which merely identifies chunks of the brain and sticks functional labels upon them.

Following on from this another hindrance to understanding brain-behaviour relationships is the lack of good theoretical models of how the brain controls particular functions (i.e. of the 'complex functional system' variety). Although it has some inadequacies Geschwind's (1969, 1970) model of speech processes has considerable attractions. Instead of lumping speech into one or more parts of the left hemisphere this model implicates a number of different loci and the connections between them. It results in particular predictions about the kind of speech disturbances that will be produced by different lesions. For example, Geschwind's model leads to the prediction that deeper lesions within the left hemisphere which involve the arcuate fasciculus will lead to 'conduction aphasia' in which the repetition of speech is selectively impaired. Whilst the independent existence of conduction aphasia is a matter of some dispute (e.g. Luria, 1972) there is no doubt that this type of model could have considerable heuristic value in exploring brain-behaviour relationships. It is unfortunate that Geschwind has been one of the very few people to suggest theories of this type.

It is evident that the problems that have arisen from a consideration of the localization of the functions have still to be resolved. One of the most important advances that has been made is in the way in which the problem is conceptualized. The original 'either-or' controversy between the views of strict localization and equipotentiality now seems sterile. Neither of these two extremes is satisfactory. The emphasis is now on a more intricate and dynamic relationship between brain functioning and behaviour, but considerable conceptual, methodological and theoretical issues remain to be resolved. Finally, the understanding of the machinery of the brain is obviously something that will ultimately depend upon the integration of information from the whole range of the neurosciences - not just upon neuropsychology.

FINAL COMMENTS

With regard to 'models of man' this chapter has attempted to deal briefly with two highly complex issues. The first of these is a problem that commonly arises in discussions of the nature of man. It is often claimed that man is much more than a machine. If by 'more than a machine' is meant that man can usefully be described, and his behaviour often explained, in terms that are not directly applicable to the components of the machine then I would concur. If by 'more than a machine' is meant that behaviour can only be fully explained in terms that are in principle not capable of translation into those of the machine then this view is rejected. Whilst complete reduction of psychology is possible the present position does not deny the explanatory power and usefulness of other approaches. The position advocated here appears to me to be very similar to that set out by Medawar (1974) in discussing the problem of reductionism as it relates to biology.

Accepting the validity of a reductionist approach and a model of man that sees man as a form of biological machine makes it necessary to go on and specify just what sort of machine it is that we are dealing with. There is a need to describe the principles that govern its operation. This is a very difficult problem which will depend ultimately upon evidence that comes from the whole range of the neurosciences. This chapter has only been able to deal with one aspect of this that is central to neuropsychology and this is the question of localization of function. The pursuit of this question has developed from the position of trying to discriminate between alternative views of the brain as an undifferentiated mass as opposed to discretely organized functional units. The present view is of the brain as a much more intricate and dynamically organized system.

There is still a vast way to go in our efforts to understand the human machine and especially its control centre, the brain. It is the final claim of this chapter that the journey is more than worth while because in understanding the machine we understand ourselves.

EDITED DISCUSSION

I. ROTH: Several participants here advocate the principle of 'live and let live': models should not be seen as mutually exclusive, they say, but rather they apply in different domains. This may be right, but the problem that it poses is how do you know under which circumstances any model is appropriate? Other than on intuitive or ad hoc grounds, how do you, for example, choose between those domains in which a reductionist approach is appropriate and those in which it is not?

E. MILLER: There is no simple answer to that question. In fact I approach it as an applied psychologist, and then I adopt whatever method is likely to satisfy my particular goals.

J. SHOTTER: Your account of reductionism passed over completely the role of judgement and evaluation in human action. The example of waving, for instance, did not make mention of the fact that on any occasion waving is conducted in a particularly evaluative way - perhaps to obtain recognition. One may even decide not to return a wave so as to reject a friendly overture.

E. MILLER: This is obviously the sort of question that worries you more than me! To pursue the example of waving at a neighbour, I want to know what is going on inside the head, and presumably that is different according to the nature of the circumstances.

J. SHOTTER: And presumably the person who waves is making some sort of judgement on that basis.

J. A. GRAY: But she is her brain.

J. SHOTTER: That is where we really do disagree. I might be prepared to say she uses her brain.

E. MILLER: I do not see how she can use her brain and be separate from it.

J. A. GRAY: Exactly.

N. E. WETHERICK: John Shotter should be pressed on this point. He seems to want to avoid reductionism altogether (at the level in which he is interested), yet he maintains that it is possible to conduct a scientific investigation (at that level), and hence say things about the phenomena that occur (at that level). Presumably, then, this set of phenomena occurs in some law-governed entity which is not the same as the brain. That opens up a whole bag of questions which most of us believe are unresolvable. We appear in this context to be faced with no alternative to reductionism. Some light can be thrown on the subject by distinguishing between ontological reductionism and epistemological reductionism. Most of us are thrown back on ontological reductionism which postulates one existent ('matter', for want of a better term), all events being somehow functions of this one existent, since most of us find it impossible to account for the relationships between more than one existent. At an epistemological level, none of us is capable of conceiving a total science ranging from, say, subatomic physics to sociology. We are limited (probably as a result of our brain structure) such that we have to divide up the field of human knowledge. Thus there is an obvious epistemological sense in which reductionism is impossible: epistemologically we do not reduce the kind of phenomena about which John Shotter has spoken, because there would be no conceivable point in doing so.

N. FRUDE: Dr Miller, I wondered whether you were saying that if something is not reducible to brain processes then it is not psychology?

E. MILLER: No, I was saying that everything in principle is reducible. But that does not mean that the reductionist approach is necessarily the best one, or the most appropriate, for any given situation.

M. JAHODA: Would you therefore agree that your statement 'everything is reducible' is in the end a metaphysical statement? I do not have anything against metaphysical statements - indeed I believe that they are at the root of all our various approaches to psychology - but they cannot be 'argued'. A statement is made on the basis of your conviction, but there can be no argument about it: it is the necessary assumption from which your psychology proceeds.

E. MILLER: I have to agree with you about that...

L. SMITH: No doubt reductionism has considerable methodological value, but it is doubtful whether it has any metaphysical value. Let us take a specific example. In Piaget's class inclusion task, with seven marigolds and three roses, young children cannot say whether there are more flowers than marigolds: eventually they can. How would your reductionist program explain what goes on there without committing the homunculus fallacy - that is, attributing human properties to inanimate objects?

D. E. BROADBENT: May I intervene here? Because there are of course computer simulations of Piagetian processes based upon deduction systems. These do simulate class inclusion and the process of development from one stage to another. Presumably that counts as a reductionist explanation.

L. SMITH: I am not familiar with those, but I would like to be assured that they proceed without the use of any concept which we would normally employ in explaining how a human understands a logical problem. I refer to concepts such as 'understanding', 'knowledge', 'belief', 'argument', and so on.

D. E. BROADBENT: Those terms take on different definitions as people use them in different ways. You could say that a computer program in some sense uses them all, but naturally you have to apply particular definitions in order to say that.

Chapter 7

Energy, information and man

J. M. Brener

The genesis of modern psychology was marked by the development of models that attempted to provide fairly exhaustive descriptions of the whole man (e.g. Wundt, Freud, Watson, Lewin, James, Sechenov, Pavlov). To a greater or lesser extent these models represented an attempt to graft the framework of a burgeoning 19th century biology on to the roots of psychology that were buried deep in Western mentalistic philosophy. As psychology adopted specialized experimental methods, its emphasis switched from such comprehensive views of man to a concentration on microtheories that could account for particular aspects of human performance. The past two decades have witnessed the beginnings of an attempt to weave together into a scientific fabric the many threads that constitute psychology's history.

A comprehensive model of man would seem to require the consolidation of many different microtheories. The obstacles to this assimilation are profound. Not only must a common language be found to enable the sharing of knowledge between the various specialisms that constitute psychology but also a comprehensive understanding of man would seem to require an interface between psychological knowledge on the one hand and the vast bodies of knowledge associated with the more mature disciplines of physics and biology on the other.

It may be argued that the scientific endeavour and perhaps the entire intellectual enterprise is directed towards the development of ever-more efficient means of processing and transmitting information. This is reflected by the advances in knowledge that characterize the development of individuals and of cultures. The pursuit of knowledge, like other human activities, may be assumed to serve an adaptive purpose: it functions to support man's survival. The attempt by psychology to generate a language for describing the behaviour of organisms may be viewed as an integral part of this process. One idea about how the acquisition of knowledge promotes human survival is presented in this chapter. This idea incorporates a model of man that is cast in the terms science has generated to describe the universe man inhabits.

Although psychology, in conjunction with other biological sciences, has enjoyed much success in formulating generally accepted and comprehensible descriptions of subhuman behaviour, it has yet to settle on a standard language for the description of human behaviour. A fundamental problem here that is unique to psychology as a science is that all psychologists, before they become psychologists, have acquired a view of their subject matter: a view of man that is entrenched in their language, reinforced by the culture in which they live and which possesses many elements that cannot be assimilated by science.

The language of science and particularly 'the physical thing language' provides a very efficient means of communication. This is because the lexicon of science is comprised of symbols or terms that are unambiguous. Although this point seems indisputable, it is argued by some that the language of science is able to describe only a very narrow and 'trivial' range of human experiences. Very few people find satisfying metaphors for their thoughts and feelings in the language of the natural sciences. It either neglects or distorts those experiences that are central to man's image of himself as an individual member of a unique species. This view is expressed by Bergson (1911):

> ... not one of the categories of our thought ... applies exactly to the things of life ... In vain we force the living into this or that one of our moulds. All the moulds crack. They are too narrow, above all too rigid, for what we try to put into them. Our reasoning, so sure of itself among things inert, feels ill at ease on this new ground. (p. x)

The dissatisfaction with scientific descriptions of man is so frequently expressed that students of behaviour, even if they are unsympathetic with its underlying assumptions, are forced to acknowledge its expression as a ubiquitous component of human performance. As such, a comprehensive model of man should, inter alia, represent the processes that lead man to reject the framework of the natural sciences for his own description. This rejection appears to be based on the pervasive belief that mental phenomena are the fundamental sources of human behaviour. Such mentalism prevents meaningful discourse between psychology and other sciences primarily because it buries the sources of human behaviour within the individual and so obscures them from public view. Its concepts are so deeply embedded in the lexicons of Western language that attempts to expunge mentalistic explanations of human performance from the technical language of psychology have not been very successful. It would appear that the phenomenal experience of mentation is too vivid to be denied.

At the root of this problem is the apparent impossibility of adequately representing the phenomena of mental life within the constraints of science. In psychology, as in other sciences, the application of the scientific method functions to establish the meaning of its conceptual repertoire. Mental phenomena are not readily amenable to experimental dissection. The most direct public evidence of human mental activity is derived from the introspections of individuals. It is argued that because the validity of such reports of private experiences cannot be verified, they cannot be admitted as evidence in science. Although this argument is plausible and is widely accepted, it is not beyond dispute.

MENTALISM AND PSYCHOLOGY

The first and only really thoroughgoing attempt to use introspection in the experimental analysis of mental phenomena was described by Wundt and his students. The subsequent rejection of introspection as an adequate method of scientific inquiry may be justified more easily on pragmatic than upon epistemological grounds. It was not that introspection could not work but rather that it did not work.

The verbal reporting of both internal and external perceptions involves the labelling of (sensory) experiences. In other words the processes that provide, for example, an astronomer with the capacity to report the observation of a comet do not appear to be fundamentally different from the processes that enable him to report that he is feeling elated or depressed. Both sorts of reports require the individual to have learned to apply particular verbal labels to particular constellations of sensations.

From the standpoint of science, a critical difference is that the empirical sources of external perception lie more obviously in the public domain than do the sources of introspections. However, recent work on interoception (Adam, 1967) and visceral perception (Brener, 1977a), which has been aided by advances in knowledge about the internal sensory systems, establishes that the labelling of internal bodily states may be studied experimentally. Although the subject matter of this area of research may be accommodated under the general heading of 'introspection', because current technology provides the potential for identifying the physiological sources of internal perceptions, it also fits within the framework of experimental psychobiology.

The attempts of the early behaviourists (Watson, Pavlov, Sechenov, Holt, Perry, James, Hull, etc.) to define mentalistic concepts in terms that were assimilable by a scientific and natural view of man have received far less attention than they would seem to merit. These theorists generated descriptions of such processes as wishing, willing, purpose and knowledge that are compatible with biological principles. They therefore provided a means of identifying within the general framework of science those processes that are central to our image of man. It is not clear why these contributions are overlooked today. Perhaps it is because they conflict with man's apparent need to view himself as a supernatural phenomenon. Evidence of man's ability to control nature is all about us and it nurtures the concept of volition by which the exercise of free will apparently enables him to resist natural laws. The concept of volition lies at the root of our difficulty in generating a scientifically acceptable view of man. The belief that man can choose whether or not to obey natural laws is in direct conflict with the assumptions that underly a science of behaviour. As Blanshard (1958) has suggested: 'You are too much preoccupied with the ends to which the choice would be a means to give any attention to the causes of which your choice may be an effect' (p. 21). The concept of 'free will' closets the causes of human behaviour within the individual and thereby protects man's behaviour from scientific scrutiny. Much has been written on this subject (e.g. Hook, 1958) and some attempt has been made to study experimentally the mechanisms of voluntary behaviour (e.g. Brener, 1974a, 1977b).

Although 'cognitive processes' and 'symbolic activities' may be inferred on the basis of non-verbal performance, the use of this device has tended to foster anthropomorphic and mentalistic interpretations of the behaviour of subhuman animals rather than serving to demystify mental concepts. In the final analysis, the contents of consciousness may only be known through the introspective verbal reports of individuals. In fact, it is difficult to understand how the study of mental processes per se may be distinguished operationally from the study of language.

Whilst a complex language is the objective feature that most easily differentiates man from other animals, the case for language being a uniquely human capacity is not made as strongly today as it was a few years ago. It is clear that subhuman animals may be taught human language (Gardner & Gardner, 1969; Premack, 1977). Furthermore the traditional arguments against so-called S-R views of language seem rather implausible. For example, the capacity of organisms to generate an almost infinite set of functional movements does not seem very different from their capacities to generate an almost infinite set of meaningful utterances.

From a biofunctional point of view language is a very efficient and versatile means of organismic interaction. It may be employed to engage in commerce with the environment or to communicate information with minimal energy expenditure. Consciousness may be viewed as a by-product of human language which, like other facets of informational processing, serves an adaptive function. In other words, consciousness may be accepted not as the source of behaviour but as one of the many modes of activity that serves to sustain the individual and to perpetuate the species.

The maintenance of individual and species vitality depends upon processes that may be comprehensively described in biophysical terms. In particular, the survival of organisms depends upon their maintaining an adequate energy exchange with their environments.   By virtue of the intimate relationship between information and energy, human information-processing which is prominently expressed through language but which is also manifested phenomenally as mentation may be admitted to this biophysical scheme.

The concepts of 'energy' and 'information' have colloquial meanings and they also have closely circumscribed meanings within the framework of science. Let me endeavour to describe behaviour in the context provided by these concepts. Bioenergetics is studied by all branches of biology and information is a concept that is closely associated with human communication. However at a fundamental physicalistic level, energy and information are intimately related.   Shannon & Weaver's (1949) formula for entropy in communication systems is identical to Clausius's (1864) formula for entropy in thermodynamics (Tribus & McIrvine, 1971).

In a physical system, entropy is a measure of the degree of organization of system: the more disorganized and uniformly dispersed its elements are, the higher is its entropy value and the lower is the energy availability of the system.   Thus high entropy is associated with low energy availability.   In informational terms, entropy is identified with uncertainty.   We might say that the less our knowledge about a question, the greater is the uncertainty or entropy.   Information decreases uncertainty or entropy.   Thus Brillouin (1964) has used the term 'negentropy' (negative of entropy) as a synonym for information.   It may be argued that information is disentropic not only in the context of communication theory but also in the realm of thermodynamics (e.g. Brillouin, 1964; Singh, 1966; Tribus & McIrvine, 1971).   This may loosely be interpreted to mean that the greater the knowledge about a system, the higher will be the energy available from that system.   It is proposed to explore the implications of this notion for the analysis of behavioural processes.   The purpose of this endeavour is not to generate a specific model of man but rather to examine the application of a biophysical framework to the description of behaviour.

THE EVOLUTIONARY FRAMEWORK AND PSYCHOLOGY

Darwin's theory of evolution provided psychology with the fundamental assumption that behaviour is an expression of the process of adaptation.   The mechanics of the evolutionary process serve as a unifying model for the biological sciences.   Monod (1972, p. 33) proposes that 'the selective theory of evolution assures the epistemological coherence of biology and gives it its place among the sciences of "objective nature".'   Implicit in the mechanics of the evolutionary process is the important concept of 'teleonomy'.   This concept permits the use of purposive explanations in science without, as psychologists are prone to do, invoking future events in causal explanations of the present.   As Sherrington (1906) pointed out, Darwin's theory endowed all vital processes (not only the destiny of man) with purpose.   The structure of life forms enables the performance of functions which are concerned exclusively with maintaining that form of life (e.g. Dawkins, 1976). The purpose of all vital processes is the preservation of life and not the realization of particular end-points or goal objects.

Although current psychology owes its genesis to Darwin's theory of evolution, it has, since the turn of the century, drifted further and further beyond the constraints of the evolutionary framework.   Razran remarks, 'Unlike other life sciences and some social sciences (e.g. Anthropology), modern psychology has lost almost all commerce with evolution as integrator and arbiter of its research and thought' (1971, p. 2).   One might argue that Cartesian dualism which science has failed to excise from the conceptual framework of psychology lies at the root of this deviation.   The exclusive attribution of 'mind' to man served to distinguish him from other animals thereby isolating him from the world of nature and psychology from the biological sciences.

J. R. Kantor (1969) who has been writing books on psychology for almost 60 years points out that evolutionary theory did not weaken the mentalistic assumptions of psychology; rather evolutionary doctrine was assimilated by them. He observes that Darwin, Galton and Huxley all maintained classical Hellenistic views of a material mind. The functionalist school was also profoundly mentalistic. Lloyd Morgan whose attitudes were more characteristic of ethology than they were of psychology, made a far more radical interpretation of Darwin's theory than did psychologists like William James, Thorndike and Yerkes. It has been said that in the 100 years following 'The Origin of the Species' (1859) psychologists devoted themselves to discovering the man in animals. The emphasis is now shifting towards finding the animal in man. Since its inception, science has functioned to move man further and further from the centre of the universe and the current emphasis on sociobiology (e.g. Wilson, 1975; Barash, 1977) seems entirely consistent with this progression. Work in primate ethology (e.g. Van Lawick-Goodall, 1974) suggests that by relinquishing its intuitive, anthropocentric categories and by adopting observationally based biofunctional categories of behavioural analysis, psychology may generate a scientifically compatible description of human performance.

The renewed interest in evolutionary theory may also be evidenced in the changing emphasis of animal learning theory. Since the 1950s the conceptual and methodological contributions of the ethologists have gradually been accommodated by the theoretical analysis of animal learning. A recent and promising manifestation of this movement is Staddon's (Staddon & Simmelhag, 1971; Staddon, 1975) evolutionary analogue of the learning process. By using the principles of variation and selection this author provides a compelling analysis of superstitious behaviour in the pigeon. In the course of his analysis he shows that the previously accepted explanation of this phenomenon in terms of the 'Law of Effect' not only engenders a teleological understanding of the process but also that the predictions based on the empirical 'law of effect' are not substantiated. Another expression of the return to an evolutionary framework is contained in the recent interest in so-called 'Biological Constraints in Learning' (e.g. Rachlin, 1976). However one of the more ambiguous implications of work subsumed under this title is that only some learning is subject to biological constraints. This seems to be a manifestation of the view implicit in much psychological writing that biology deals only with genetically determined behavioural processes. The unwarrantable assumption that learning is somehow abiological fosters the view that man, who clearly has the most highly developed capacity to learn, is able to transcend nature. Traditional conceptions of learning such as Skinner's operant conditioning seem to involve little more than changes in the surface structure of the language describing volitional activity (Brener, 1974a). Like voluntary activities, operant responses are of unknown origin (emitted rather than elicited) and are influenced by their consequences. In terms of the perspective adopted here, learning is a process in which the communication of information serves to reprogram or restructure the nervous system so as to promote the organism's adaptation. It is a disentropic process serving the same function in the history of the individual as the processes of evolution serves in the history of the species (Verplanck, 1955).

BEHAVIOURAL BIOENERGETICS

The maintenance of vital functioning demands the intake, storage, conversion and expression of energy. The study of bioenergetics is common to all branches of biology and in biochemistry the study of metabolic processes crosses the boundary between biology and physics. Interest in these processes extends from mapping the molecular interactions that comprise the various pathways through which the body stores and releases energy as in biochemistry to the study of energy flow in entire societies and in the universe. It would seem that psychology, as a science devoted to understanding the behaviour of organisms, could profit substantially by studying the energy economy of organisms as they adapt to environmental demands.

However, despite the prevalence of energy concepts in the writings of psychological theorists from Freud to Tinbergen and the profound impact of the concept of homeostasis on the development of modern psychobiology, the direct investigation of energy processes in this science has been limited to the study of the regulation of food intake (e.g. Le Magnen, 1976). As Wahlsten (1972) has pointed out, such basic problems as differentiating motivational from learning processes cannot be solved in the absence of independent measurements of the energizing and selective functions of environmental contingencies. Theorists such as Freeman (1948), Duffy (1962) and more recently Notterman & Mintz (1965) and Collier et al. (1975) have expressed the need to study the regulation of energy expression in organisms.

The skeletal musculature is, of course, the effector system through which the organism engages in energy exchange with its environment. In describing his 'energy rule of skeletal muscle' Arshavsky (1972) discusses the anabolic negentropic functions of skeletal muscle activity. He presents data in support of the proposition that all other things (e.g. size) being equal, the life expectancy of particular species is directly related to the flexibility of their skeletal muscular systems. The learning capacity of each species is the major determinant of such flexibility and this capacity is, in turn, dependent upon the structures of its nervous system. In this context it is noteworthy that muscle systems which are involved in the most intricate environmental manipulations have associated with them the most prolific afferent systems and the most conspicuous central sensory projections. In the case of buccal animals like cows, the mouth is dominant, in monkeys it is the hands and in humans it is the speech apparatus (Paillard, 1960). The activities of these dominant effectors are also most easily modifiable by experience (Brener, 1974b, 1977b). Thus the structure of the nervous system reflects the intimate relationship between information and energy.

One characteristic of the process of behavioural adaptation is that with repeated exposure to a set of environmental demands, the activity of the organism becomes more energy efficient. The rate of external work performed by the individual may remain constant or increase whilst the individual's rate of energy expenditure actually decreases. This process, which is commonly observed during the course of learning, reflects the habituation or extinction of functionally redundant components of the individual's initial adjustment to the demands of the situation.

The adaptive importance of a more programmable and flexible nervous system may be viewed therefore as its capacity to enhance the profitability of the organism's energy exchange with the environment. In these terms, the functions of learning are realized as energy gains. This notion which has a long history in psychology (e.g. The Principle of Least Effort) is compatible with the relationship between information and energy expressed by Brillouin (1956) and Prigogine's (1965) theorem of minimum entropy production.

ENTROPY AND BIOLOGY

The drift of natural processes from the past through the present to the future, what Eddington referred to as 'Time's Arrow', is marked in the biological realm by the process of evolution and in the physical realm by the law of entropy increase. Carnot's second Principle of Thermodynamics states that in a closed system, energy is inevitably degraded until the system reaches a state of total equilibrium (heat death) in which no further work can be done. And this natural function of time is paralleled in biology by the evolutionary organization of more and more complex forms of life.

Superficially the principle of entropy increase seems to conflict with the principle of evolution. In trying to reconcile these apparently opposing tendencies Bergson (1911) remarked:

It has not the power to reverse the direction of physical changes, such as the principle of Carnot determines it. It does, however, behave absolutely as a force would behave which, left to itself, would work in the inverse direction. Incapable of stopping the course of material changes downwards, it succeeds in retarding it. (p. 259)

Although Bergson's notion that the processes of life might actually control the rate of entropy increase in a closed system cannot be accommodated by the principles of thermodynamics, local variations in the rate of entropy increase are quite feasible. Monod (1972) in commenting on the statistical improbability of species differentiation (and therefore its irreversibility) is led to the conclusion that 'it is legitimate to view the irreversibility of evolution as an expression of the second law (of thermodynamics) in the biosphere'. This is an appealing notion because it transgresses the boundaries between the physical and biological realms. Certainly the nature of the relationship between the natural entropic processes of the physical universe and the evolutionary processes of biology has stimulated much thought (e.g. von Bertalanffy, 1968; Nicolis & Prigogine, 1977).

Whether or not one wishes to find meaning in the apparently inverse relationship between the second principle of thermodynamics and the process of evolution, one is forced to recognize that vital processes are disentropic. In Schrödinger's words, '... what an organism feeds upon is negative entropy'.

Unlike closed systems which always move towards increasing entropy, organisms which are open systems may not only maintain a steady state but may increase their levels of organization as in ontogenetic and phylogenetic development. According to Prigogine (1965) entropy change in an open system is a function of a positive entropy factor associated with irreversible physical processes and an entropy transport factor which may be negative by import of matter carrying free energy. The primary energy source of all terrestrial life is solar in origin and it is stored in a biologically usable form as adenosine triphosphate (ATP). The processes of bioenergetics are fully reducible to physical descriptions. Singh (1966) puts this well. In comparing organisms with internal combustion engines he says, 'The only difference is the exceedingly low temperature at which it (biological combustion or respiration) is carried out so that life is quite literally an infinitely attentuated flame. The mechanisms of these subdued and smouldering fires of cellular combustion that sustain the processes of life have been studied in detail and found to conform in every respect to the fundamental laws of physics and chemistry including both laws of thermodynamics' (p. 81).

It has been suggested that information-processing is an integral part of the thermodynamic processes of biology. Brillouin (1964), for example, provides a comprehensive discussion of the relationship between information and energy. He points out that every experiment, every observation, involves the trading of negentropy for information and that information in turn increases negentropy. Although he cautions us against equating information in this sense with knowledge he does reach the conclusion that scientific laws are sources of negentropy in that they may be used to introduce structure to the system. Tribus & McIrvine (1971) express this idea in colloquial terms, '... it takes energy to obtain knowledge and it takes information to harness energy' (p. 121).

The argument so far is that the processes of life may be understood in terms of energy conversion. This assertion may be supported by reference to microscopic cellular processes or by reference to the energy economies of entire societies (e.g. Cook, 1971; Kemp, 1971; Rappaport, 1971). Furthermore it may be argued that biological systems maintain their vitality by reliance on negentropic information processes. This again appears to be true at all levels from the microscopic processes of genetic transmission to the macroscopic processes of cultural interaction. The final part of this chapter considers the extent to which this framework may be useful in describing some of the processes of human existence.

ENERGY AND INFORMATION AND SOCIETY

The fundamental thesis is then that the search for knowledge is a manifestation of the evolutionary tendency of life forms to manage energy resources in such a manner as to promote their survival. Implicit in the evolution of life forms is the development of information-processing capacities that permit optimal utilization of available energy resources.

Both inter- and intra-specifically, biological survival depends upon the efficient management of energy resources. Natural selection has clearly tended to favour the survival of species that can compete successfully for the available energy resources of the biosphere. Man's dominance on earth points to the adaptive advantages of a highly developed CNS that is capable of being reprogrammed by prevailing environment conditions. Leaving aside the question of species dominance we may concentrate on the relevance of the information-energy hypothesis to understanding the processes of dominance between and within human cultures.

At maximum efficiency approximately 25 per cent of the food energy consumed by an individual is expressed as work although the average gross efficiency is less than 10 per cent. For people in sedentary occupations, the efficiency is lowest - mental work consumes very little energy indeed. Although the neurochemical processes that underly information-processing consume very little energy, the knowledge they produce has obvious importance for the human conditon. Technology, which may be viewed as a material expression of knowledge, has greatly augmented man's control of the energy resources of his environment. Before man had harnessed fire his rate of energy consumption was equal to the energy equivalent of his food intake. Fire probably doubled it. The domestication of animals raised the per capita energy consumption to about 12,000 kilocalories per day. And each successive technological advancement has led to growth in the per capita energy consumption. The point to be made here is that knowledge, materially realized in technology, has served throughout history to amplify man's power output as measured in thermodynamic units. From 1700 when Thomas Savery introduced a steam-driven water pump with an output of 750 watts to the present, the power output of energy conversion devices has increased 1,000,000 times. By so harnessing natural energy the average 20th century man is able to produce a volume of work that is four orders of magnitude greater than an average 18th century man. The adaptive value of this process may be witnessed in the growth of the human population. From the birth of Christ until 1500 AD, the human population of the earth doubled. It is estimated that in the 75 years between 1925 and 2000 the population of the earth will treble.

The total muscle power output of the human race is estimated currently to be 1/25th of the total power usage under human control. Furthermore man's importance as a source of mechanical work is rapidly receding. It is estimated that at the turn of the century human mechanical work still accounted for 50 per cent of the total energy used in production whereas today it accounts for less than 1 per cent. These statistics have profound social significance. For example, although the average energy amplification ratio (energy under human control: muscle energy output) is approximately 25:1 for the human race, societal differences are great. In the USA an average energy amplification factor of 250:1 is estimated whereas in the subsistence economies of Central Africa it is two orders of magnitude lower. Furthermore, there is a direct linear relationship between per capita energy controlled and per capita work output as measured by the Gross National Product. This statistical relationship indicates that a twofold increase in per capita energy control gives rise to a threefold increase in per capita GNP (Starr, 1971).

This creates a situation in which technological advancement determines the social dominance hierarchy of nations.

Domination of one culture by another has always been made possible by differentials in technological development. The availability of superior weapons of destruction has since the beginnings of recorded history permitted the members of one culture to control the human and environmental energy resources of another. Science and technology have served to amplify man's constructive as well as his destructive powers. As was noted, in the modern world the virtue of man as an energy resource does not lie in his work capacity. This is maximally 5 kilowatt hours per day. However, by providing a man with a 20 horsepower drill for 8 hours a day or a combine harvester, it can be greatly augmented. The virtue of the human being as a source of energy lies in the negentropic, energy-managing properties of his brain power.

Fortunately it would seem that technological social domination contains the seeds of its own destruction. There are two reasons for this that are interrelated. First, technical artifacts such as combine harvesters and heat-seeking ground-to-air missiles model the systems of knowledge of which they are the products. As such they are very effective media for communicating information, perhaps more effective than are words. Therefore the act of social domination carries with it the process of cultural cross-fertilization: the dissemination of knowledge. Another factor has to do with the prediction that soon man's efficiency as a machine operator will be superseded by information machines. In a recent copy of a popular computing magazine, an interesting phenomenon in itself, it is recorded that at present in the USA there are 20,000 robots at work in factories and that the USA is behind Japan and several European countries in introducing manufacturing robots (BYTE, April 1979, p. 194). This suggests that soon humans will not be worth exploiting as a source of power.

The Industrial Revolution separated man as a worker from the medium on which he was working by a machine driven by harnessed natural energy. This machine had the effect of greatly amplifying the precision and power of man's manual output. Man's function was simply to direct the machine and as technology became more advanced, the nervous system acting through the motor organs of a single man came to control a greater and greater energy reserve. This advancement has been accelerated particularly over the past 30 years although during this period the energy efficiency of motive sources (electric motors, internal combustion engines, etc.) has not been very marked. It has come not by amplifying the mechanical force produced by human movements but rather by amplifying the precision and speed of man's machine-controlling responses. Man's information-handling capacity and therefore his capacity to manage energy has been greatly augmented by the development of computer technology. We are rapidly approaching a condition in which it will be possible to pack more information into a cubic centimetre of electronic circuitry than there are synapses in a cubic centimetre of brain tissue (see Scientific American, September 1977).

The development of information-processing technology and man's increasing reliance on it would seem to hold special challenges for psychology. For example, it may be anticipated that the social consequences of automation will require a considerable human adaptation that is likely to make new demands on applied psychology. It is also to be expected that psychology will be directly involved in generating the means of automation. Implicit in the development of robots is the modelling of human performance. This requires the participation of psychologists who in meeting the demands of the task will be provided with a means of simulating their models of man.

Turing (1950) suggested that one could test the adequacy of a computer simulation of human intelligence by the process of discrimination. An adequate model would be one that could not be distinguished from a human on the basis of verbal communication. Microelectronic technology would seem to be providing the means for the practical implementation of Turing's test. A prerequisite for carrying out such a test is that the processes to be simulated are described in explicit and therefore 'computable' terms. The discipline afforded by this venture may aid psychologists in applying the language of science to the description of man.

EDITED DISCUSSION

N. E. WETHERICK: Many of us here would argue that none of the early behaviourist accounts in fact works. I think behaviourism needs to be abandoned!

J. M. BRENER: The trouble with your position is that you imply that one has failed at one's theoretical task if one's description of mental processes does not conform to your preconceived notions of what the mental processes are. There is always a problem about assessing the validity of explanations.

H. PRICE: I would welcome a clarification of the relationship between psychology and bioenergetics. Writers for several hundreds of years have argued that man's dependence upon biological factors is becoming less acute. Has there not been a movement from the bioenergetic side of the scale to the social side?

J. M. BRENER: Well, I would dispute that man is now in control of nature. One of my 'articles of faith' is that man is a natural phenomenon and his interaction with the universe is proceeding in a way that is governed by natural laws. The task of the scientist is to make explicit these natural laws - to cast them in symbolic terms so that they can be communicated. I would argue that any aspect of human performance has a bioenergetic component to it.

K. D. DUNCAN: I am rather bothered by the linking of adaptability to the ability to capture energy. If we were adaptable in the way you imply then we would not be in the position that we are now where we are moving towards energy-hungry systems having scant regard to energy supply. I cannot see the survival value of that. But in animals, one can observe that before they over-crop their prey a control loop mechanism operates. To convince me of even a loose analogy for man you would have to show me a corresponding control mechanism.

J. M. BRENER: If you examine the significant jumps in technology which have led to amplifications of the human power output, these are always associated with very substantial leaps in the human population; and that is a standard method for measuring successful adaptation...

K. D. DUNCAN: But that disregards the size of territory and the resource upon which you are feeding.

J. M. BRENER: Well, I want to say that increasing information and knowledge leads to increasing energy.

J. H. CLARK: If the notion of the individual as a power source is to be pushed aside, what about accepting 'man as a programmer'? And will robots push aside unsophisticated programs produced by man? What happens when robots start writing programs that man cannot understand? And why should they bother to explain? What is the role of man in the evolution of the computer?

J. M. BRENER: Man is the father of the computer, and the computer shall inherit the earth!

G. DELAFIELD: You have made the point that information is rewarding and uncertainty is aversive. Does your analysis allow for uncertainty sometimes being rewarding?

J. M. BRENER: Well, yes, such situations obviously exist, and thereby one has support for The Principle of Least Effort: organisms usually work towards a more efficient accommodation to their environments.

G. DELAFIELD: Kelly's view of man as scientist seems to be diametrically opposed to man striving after the course of least opposition and effort ...

J. M. BRENER: ... and the course of maximum returns. The idea is that there is a continuous movement towards increasing negentropy and increasing profitability of the energy exchange with the environment - this supports the evolutionary process. So, they are not incompatible.

R. L. REID: There is also a bit of inconsistency between man-the-scientist and man-the-punter at the race-course.   He does not bet on favourites as often as one would expect.

A. P. BAILLIE: Dr Gray has criticized Dr Shotter's approach because it cannot explain intentions.   Does the bioenergetic approach similarly take for granted, and cannot explain, the purposiveness of living forms?

J. M. BRENER: I thought that was covered in the evolutionary assumptions.

A. P. BAILLIE: But assumptions are not explanations.

J. M. BRENER: No, but my 'articles of faith' are based on evolutionary assumptions, and the intentionality or purposiveness of behaviour is implicit in the evolutionary assumption that behaviour serves adaptive functions.

A. P. BAILLIE: Going back to the humanistic/mechanistic controversies that we have heard here, I think that you have not adequately demonstrated that the bioenergetic approach can totally explain the purposiveness of nature.

J. M. BRENER: That was not my intention.   I came here to present a plausible framework for examining human performance in a non-mentalistic, biophysical way.   Working out the fine-grain attributes of performance in terms of the parameters of the system is far beyond the brief that I set myself.   My chapter does not, for example, relate to why people bet at race-courses.   The casting of performance descriptions in bioenergetic terms, I maintain, can facilitate communication between scientists.

D. B. BROMLEY: Mine is a question that Popper might ask: what kinds of evidence would have to exist for your approach to be shown as false? For example, if a human society opted for de-industrialization would that run counter to your theory?

J. M. BRENER: That is a difficult question, and it does depend upon the prevailing knowledge about energy resources; but if a society did opt to return to nature then I would abandon the theory.

N. FRUDE: I am not sure how much your model of man can offer specific explanations of particular behaviours for particular people.   Does it help to consider people at extremes; say those with immense power and those with negligible power?

J. M. BRENER: People acquire access to power through knowledge about how to gain power, and in so doing they realize the negentropic consequences of their knowledge.

Chapter 8

Images of man in contemporary behaviourism

D. E. Blackman

To present oneself, as I do, as a behaviourist in a gathering such as this is surely to invite comparison with King Canute. What is more, the cold waters which I would wish to stem are by now lapping not just at my knees but at my ears. You will therefore understand if my presentation, in which I hope to defend behaviourism to some extent, has the qualities of a frantic gurgle and thereby fails to match the controlled eloquence which we may expect of other contributors.

It is not difficult to find in the psychological literature comments which are hostile to the broad approach of behaviourism. We all have our favourites. Amongst mine is Rowan's (1973) cautious assertion that behaviourism is 'wrong theoretically, wrong technically, wrong morally and wrong politically' (p. 648). Such opinions are, of course, to be expected from Rowan. But even that sober and respected commentator on the scientific status of psychology, Koch, has expressed the hope that 'when the ludicrousness of the position is made sufficiently plain, perhaps it (behaviourism) will be laughed out of existence' (1964, p. 20).

One difficulty in addressing oneself to such criticism centres on what exactly is in mind when 'behaviourism' is invoked. In the last 50 years there have after all been many psychologists who have described themselves as behaviourists of a sort. If we consider just a short list of such people, say, Watson, Tolman, Hull and Skinner, it is clear that these writers differ very considerably in their theoretical positions. Each found himself in different contexts in which to express his views, and each had different goals which he was seeking to achieve. It is surely important, for example, to appreciate the historical context of Watson (1924) more than half a century ago now when he asked 'Why don't we make what we can observe the real field of psychology?' (p. 6). He was at that time urging psychologists to adopt methods which had already proved effective in the established natural sciences. In so far as conscious experiences and mental life are essentially private and not open to public observation, the empirical methods of science seemed less appropriate for their study. Thus Watson, in asking psychologists to limit themselves to 'things that can be observed' in order to 'formulate laws concerning only those things', was seeking to transform the very subject matter of psychology as it was then evolving from the work of such pioneers as William James. This 'methodological behaviourism' therefore directed psychologists' attention to behaviour, and the reorientation proved modestly successful in providing a scientific domain for psychology. It was even possible to claim, as did Professor Mace, that we are all behaviourists now, and for this to be thought a constructive comment. I have noted with some interest that in departments of zoology which include the study of animal and human behaviour in their curriculum there is a tendency for the epithet 'behaviourist' still to be used in this innocent way, without frisson or embarrassment: for them, behaviourism is no more than the science of behaviour.

Skinner has distinguished between this methodological behaviourism as the science of behaviour and 'radical behaviourism', which he describes as a philosophical interpretation of that science. His book 'About Behaviorism' (1974) reflects on the relevance of this philosophical stance for psychology as a whole. It is this interpretative position which I intend to discuss in my paper, for I have found this general approach to psychology an exciting one to adopt for myself, particularly because it seems to me to have broadened my own horizons in psychology beyond those provided by the study of animal learning. Such a view is clearly not shared by Sutherland, who has contributed much to the science of behaviour, including of course to the study of animal learning. In reviewing Skinner's book, Sutherland (1975) had this to say: 'One can only suppose that the success, or perhaps one should say notoriety, of Skinner's works arises from the solace they afford to those who, for whatever reason, are opposed to the scientific approach to the understanding of ourselves. If the best that psychologists can do is to put forward a vacuous theory with no supporting evidence, to make unsubstantiated claims for the efficacy of their methods, and to produce works full of elementary philosophical howlers, then Koestler and his ilk can rest easily in their beds. This book will be a source of great comfort to Skinner's enemies, and I commend it to them, with the reservation that his approach is not characteristic of modern psychology' (p. 57).

In discussing the broad approach to understanding ourselves characterized by radical behaviourism, I am aware of a number of dangers, of which I may mention two.   First, I might be in danger of trying to give an exposition of radical behaviourism by expressing less adequately arguments which Skinner has himself developed at greater length. This would be fruitless, since I imagine that all the participants in this Conference have read the original in any case. Second, I feel in danger of branding myself as an unthinking disciple of another man. This has happened to me before, and I have always resented it: I have no desire to stand in defence of all Skinner's arguments and opinions, even though it is indeed true that I find myself in general sympathy with the approach advocated by him. For these reasons, I shall address myself here simply to some of the points in radical behaviourism which in my experience prove to be contentious or which seem to give rise to misunderstandings.

Perhaps the greatest barrier to a fair appraisal of radical behaviourism is to be found in its choice of terminology. Of particular concern here are the terms 'stimulus' and 'response'. The word 'stimulus' derives from a Latin word for which my dictionary offers a number of interesting translations, including 'a goad used for driving cattle or slaves' and 'a pointed stake to repel the advance of troops'.   Figuratively the word means 'a sting' or 'a torment'.   The word 'response' derives of course from 'respondere', meaning 'to answer'. These words seem to me to relate well to the 'innate reflexes' which form the basis on which Pavlovian conditioning may be built. Descartes (4th Discourse) suggested that the behaviour of animals was no more than 'nature working in them according to the disposition of their organs', and a clear example of such a stimulus-response relationship is provided by the unconditional or automatic salivation which answers the sting of dilute acid placed on a dog's (or indeed a person's) tongue. Such unconditional responses are no doubt the outcome of evolutionary pressures on species, and their predictability is such that it seems appropriate to term the environmental event a stimulus and the behavioural event a response. By extension, it seems not inappropriate to use these words in the context of an _acquired_ reflex. As a result of the conditions to which an animal or person is exposed in which there is a specifiable relationship between one event and an unconditional stimulus, and in as far as the first event may come to produce a similar pattern of behaviour to the original unconditional response, it is reasonable to term the first event also a (conditional) stimulus and the behaviour it elicits a (conditional) response.

A stimulus-response psychology such as this was, of course, of great interest to Watson, for obvious reasons. We can now recognize, however, that acquired reflexes must be built on innate reflexes which may be adaptively important but which certainly form no great part of the varied behavioural repertoire of humans. It is a tragedy that the terms stimulus and response have been too readily extended beyond the limited contexts such as those studied by Pavlov. Radical behaviourism, of course, puts greater emphasis on operant than on respondent behaviour. Operant behaviour is conventionally said to be emitted rather than elicited. Thus, if I may be allowed to restrict myself still to the behaviour of animals, a rat is in some sense free to press a lever when it is placed in a Skinner box. On first being placed in that environment, the rat's behaviour is unpredictable, though the behaviour of Pavlov's dogs was entirely predictable when an unconditional stimulus was presented for the first time. Although operant conditioners may refer to lever-pressing as an operant response, this terminology may serve to carry forward to a different context connotations of automaticity and inevitability which are appropriate only in conventional classical conditioning situations. A similar point might be made in connection with the term discriminative stimulus which is used in operant conditioning. If, for example, a continuous noise or light is presented in a Skinner box and sets the occasion for a lever-press to be followed by food, perhaps only intermittently, then the lever-pressing behaviour of a hungry rat will become predictable and may occur at high frequencies. Such a noise would be termed a discriminative stimulus, but it does not have the goad-like qualities of stimuli used in classical conditioning. Much unnecessary misunderstanding might have been avoided if operant behaviour had by convention been termed 'acts' or 'bits', and if discriminative stimuli had been termed 'cues', 'signals' or even 'antecedents' or 'circumstances'. The statement that in some circumstances specified bits of behaviour occur frequently is to my mind a more satisfactory generalization from operant studies than that some responses are produced at high frequencies by the presentation of discriminative stimuli. One particularly important feature of this admittedly ponderous alternative phrasing is that it begs fewer questions about causal relationships. This is not the moment to elaborate on the concept of causality, except perhaps to say that radical behaviourists would I think favour Humean analyses of cause. Cavalier use of the words stimulus and response inevitably invokes the suggestion that the former causes the latter, as inevitably as a moving billiard ball will cause to move another ball which it hits. The statement that behaviour is probable or even certain in some circumstances does not lead one so directly to the view that the circumstances cause the behaviour per se.

In addition, of course, operant conditioners often interpret the relationships between circumstances and the probability of behaviour in terms of the reinforcement which is forthcoming in those circumstances. The concept of reinforcement used in radical behaviourism seems still not to be fully appreciated by its critics, however. The point has been repeatedly made that reinforcers are defined functionally rather than in terms of any assumed characteristics that these events may have. An event is not said to be a reinforcer if it is nice or if it reduces a drive or need. Rather, it is defined as a reinforcer simply in terms of its sustaining effects on behaviour, which should ideally of course be demonstrated empirically. So, if in some circumstances a bit of behaviour is sustained when it is followed (perhaps only occasionally) by an event, then that event is defined as a reinforcer. It may be nice too - but in principle it could be labelled by the agent as nasty or it might not even be noticed. It might be added here that punishers may also be defined functionally, as events which lead to a reduction in the bits of behaviour which they follow (Azrin & Holz, 1966). Again, such a functional definition imputes no necessary hedonic qualities to a punisher. In this respect at least Skinner has been less consistent than other radical behaviourists, for he often seems to suppose that aversive stimuli act necessarily as punishers (1971).

We are now in a position to attempt to summarize the basic and fundamental stance of radical behaviourism, which may be applied with as much enthusiasm in attempts to understand human behaviour as in interpreting the behaviour of animals in laboratories. It is that behaviour may be understood by relating it (a) to the setting conditions in which it occurs and (b) to the consequences of the behaviour in those conditions. This statement has been represented in a more succinct and conventional form by Keehn (1969), who claims that radical behaviourism provides a distinctive paradigm in psychology, thus:

$$S^D \rightarrow R \rightarrow S^{R+}$$

where S^D = discriminative stimulus

R = operant response

S^{R+} = reinforcement

At the risk of appearing pedantic, I would favour different letters and indeed different symbols in an attempt to capture the important concepts in radical behaviourism and their relationships, thus:

A : B : C

where A = antecedent or setting conditions

B = behaviour (bits)

C = consequence

The colon relating A to B is intended to decrease any suggestion of automaticity, and represents simply the observable correlation between setting conditions and behaviour. The colon between B and C is again intended to reflect the nature of the relationship between behaviour and consequence, which may be only occasional, may not be immediate, may be relative, and indeed could be spurious rather than 'real'. The term 'consequence' is preferred to 'reinforcement' because it allows also for the situation in which consequences may reduce the frequency of behaviour: it may also be less liable to the misinterpretations which continue to be associated with the term reinforcement.

We have here a way of looking at behaviour, including that of humans, which is I think distinctively different from that favoured by most contemporary psychologists. It would perhaps be too easy to claim with Keehn that for this reason it represents a different paradigm in the Kuhnian sense. The approach does, however, put the major interpretative emphasis on the relationships between what we do and the environmental circumstances in which we do it, the antecedents and the consequences. The approach as summarized here is clearly not limited to rats in cages or indeed to humans in essentially restricted environments, though the experimental emphasis on restricted repertoires of behaviour is a reflection of the problems to be confronted in more ambitious settings. In general, radical behaviourism requires as a first step a sensitive and essentially descriptive analysis of human behaviour in whatever context it occurs: in back-wards of mental hospitals indeed, but also in schools, in social interactions between individuals, in group interactions, and in society at large. Such descriptive analyses of behaviour have not formed a prominent part of psychology over the years, and to this extent the continuing growth of interest in direct observation of human behaviour resulting from ethology and from ecological psychology is to be welcomed. Moreover, the emphasis in radical behaviourism on environmental influences on behaviour which are in principle publicly observable exposes the approach to the challenge of empirical test and thereby reveals the advantages and limitations of the approach pragmatically.

A particular source of tension between radical behaviourists and many other psychologists is of course to be found in the level of explanation which is sought for observed behaviour.   For radical behaviourists, the understanding of a behavioural phenomenon is to be found in the relationship between it and observed environmental events.   The behaviour is thought to be understood by identifying its environmental context.   Thus a person may be said to act because the circumstances provided for that action to be followed by a functional consequence in the past and such reinforcement increases or sustains the probability of such behaviour in those circumstances.   For many, this is clearly unsatisfactory.   They may (sometimes) concede that such an interpretation may have practical implications, but they will often not concede that any form of understanding has been achieved.   It is more usual to consider behaviour as an appendage to, or exemplar of, processes which are taking place at some other level within the behaver.   For example, Deese (1972) asserted that 'behaviour is only the outward manifestation of what counts' (p. 99).

'What counts' might of course be a reductionist's biological cause of behaviour, to be found in physiological or biochemical processes, for example.   It still seems to be the case that radical behaviourism is thought to be in some way opposed to physiological analyses of behaviour, even to believe that the organism is 'empty'.   In fact Skinner (e.g. 1974, p. 215) makes it quite clear that physiological studies may provide a bridge between environmental influences on behaviour and the current behaviour itself.   If the setting conditions or consequences of a particular act are changed, then the behaviour itself may change, and this is true whether or not any accompanying changes in physiological processes can be identified.   In biology, nobody would claim that evolutionary theory, which of course emphasizes environmental influences on the survival of species, provides the only way of understanding living creatures.   Inquiries and explanations at other levels are important too, but they do not displace any basic relationships which may be established between environmental characteristics and survival.   In psychology, nobody claims that analysis of the interactions between environmental events and behaviour provides the only way of understanding why people do what they do.   Radical behaviourists accept the reality of physiological processes - how could they not?   They assign no special causal or explanatory status to physiological processes, however, and they insist that the task of identifying such processes is the task of the physiologist.

Radical behaviourism, as expressed by Skinner, adopts a similar point of view in dealing with mental events.   A casual glance at Skinner's writings should be sufficient to dispel any belief that his analysis has no place for mental life.   However, the role assigned to such events in attempting to understand behaviour is unusual.   The main problem with mental events for any objective science is of course that they are by their very nature private, available to be seen or appreciated only by the one experiencer and not directly available to external investigators.   Skinner's system '... does not insist upon truth by agreement and can therefore consider events taking place in the private world within the skin' (1974, p. 16).   So, although such events are by nature private and to that extent subjective, it is important to realize that Skinner does not deny the reality of their existence for the individual - how could he?   But, as with physiological events, radical behaviourists do take the somewhat unusual position of not assigning any special causal or explanatory status to mental events in determining behaviour.   To do so would be to direct the attention of psychologists away from relationships between behaviour and environment which are open to public inspection and are therefore not merely of privileged access.

Skinner often discusses mental events as a form of behaviour, implying that they are subject to environmental influences like overt behaviour.   Thus consciousness is not seen as having some form of logical priority over behaviour. Just as our behaviour may be seen to be constructed by the contingencies of reinforcement (the A : B : C) to which we are exposed, so our very consciousness is constructed by the contingencies of reinforcement in our social communities. This idea is captured by Skinner in an epithet which would not be out of place in systems of psychology which are thought by some commentators to be the antithesis of any form of behaviourism: consciousness is a social phenomenon.

Skinner's paper 'Behaviorism at Fifty' with its subsequent addenda (see Skinner, 1969) remains in some ways the clearest and most succinct exposition of this view.   He distinguishes between 'seeing', for example, and 'seeing that we see'.   External observers may judge that I see a green light by noting any differential control over my behaviour when a green light is presented rather than red.   A correlation is sought between lights of certain physically specified wavelengths and particular patterns of behaviour.   Of course, the extent to which I 'see' a green light in this sense (or attend to it) is a function of the whole environmental context in which it occurs, the contingencies of reinforcement.   In some circumstances, there is a pay-off for my seeing green (at traffic lights for example); in others there may be little pay-off.   In the absence of differential control over behaviour, an external observer is not able to establish whether I 'see' the colour or not.

'Seeing that we see' goes beyond this simple objective analysis.   It involves additionally an awareness of private events or consciousness, and is said to be a function of the way in which our verbal or social community interacts with us. Other people will relate our verbal statements to the environmental situations in which they occur and are appropriate, and thereby shape us or construct us to 'see that we see' green in appropriate circumstances, that is, when lights of certain wavelengths impinge on our eyes.   In other words, we 'see that we see' green when certain environmental events impinge on us, producing in us sensations which are by their very nature private (though real) and when the community at the same time tells us that we see ourselves seeing green by its behaviour towards us.   Thus the verbal community may be said to be making its best efforts to establish the private event, to which it of course can have no access, as the appropriate setting conditions in which the reflexive verbal statement about awareness may be regarded as appropriate.   Lacking direct access to the private event, the community can use the physical world as its check on the 'authenticity' of the statement, and of course can do so quite reliably in this simple case.

Of course, people may claim to be aware of the colour green in unusual physical circumstances - perhaps with their eyes shut, or perhaps as in the McCullough effect when no light of the appropriate wavelength is measurable.   The verbal community may then take the report of their experience on trust as it were, and, depending on their history and on the circumstances, it may then treat them in the same way as if there were indeed the physical events which are normally open to public scrutiny when they report that they can see a green light.

In the simple example laboured above, the verbal community has the advantage of easy access to an external referent.   This is of course not the case in many situations, as sometimes for example when a person reports that a pain is felt, or when a person feels sad or in love.   It is in such situations that the verbal community is inevitably least efficient in shaping precise and consistent expressions of these private events.   Thus the private events, the experiences, are themselves diffuse, though real.   Radical behaviourism is rarely extended to applied problems in such areas of experience, but an interesting exception is to be found in an extended account by Fordyce (1976) of the behavioural treatment of chronic pain and illness.   His book may be said to be based in part on the view that awareness of pain is in some senses a social phenomenon, that pain in the patient is 'real' but nevertheless may be partly, and of course inadvertently, constructed by those around the patient.   It is important to emphasize that this book is not a facile recipe for ignoring a patient in distress or condemning a patient to suffering. The analysis of these problems expressed by Fordyce provides an unusual example of an applied radical behaviourist perspective on a facet of human experience which is often thought by its critics to have no place in behaviourism.

This discussion leads us to consider the view that in attempting to identify relationships betwen manipulable and scientifically respectable independent variables and behaviour, psychologists have overlooked the fact that the layman understands his own behaviour well enough. This view has been expressed by Joynson (1974), for example. It is perhaps allied to the suggestion that psychologists should seek reasons for actions rather than causes for behaviour (Shotter, 1975). Radical behaviourism is one implicit butt of such criticisms, for it places little emphasis on the inherent purposiveness of human behaviour as interpreted by the layman or by our new moral science of action. Indeed, Skinner has himself made much of the way both evolutionary and reinforcement theory interpret natural phenomena retrospectively rather than prospectively: 'Both in natural selection and in operant conditioning, consequences take over a role previously assigned to an antecedent creative mind. Before Darwin, the word was spelled with a capital M, and it was supposed to have produced the millions of diverse creatures found on the surface of the earth. In operant conditioning, the selective action of consequences generates behavior traditionally attributed to other minds' (Skinner, 1973, p. 264). Nevertheless, Joynson has a point, I think, in drawing our attention to predominant modes of thought. Radical behaviourists might suggest that the verbal community of which we are members generates self-descriptive and purposive accounts of behaviour in the way that it generates other forms of consciousness and feelings: we are asked what we are doing and why we are doing it, and the verbal community reinforces our answers in the ways which seem appropriate. If I say that my behaviour is purposive, perhaps others will look for the events to which it is addressed, by seeking events which follow the behaviour in question and which therefore support the assertions of purposiveness. In this way they may strengthen the future probability of my talking about these observable contingencies between my behaviour and the environment in terms of my purpose. The verbal community may therefore be said to teach us that we are conscious and to teach us that we are purposeful. The consciousness and the purposefulness are real but essentially private events. Radical behaviourists would see neither as independent or prime explanations for what we do, but would view both as the outcome of the environmental circumstances to which we have been exposed.

In this discussion so far, an attempt has been made to focus attention on some aspects of the radical behaviourists' approach to understanding human behaviour. It was perhaps inevitable, however, that a systematic approach to psychology which places so much emphasis on the relationships between behaviour and observable environmental events should have led to applications in clinical and other fields. The environmental events which serve as discriminative stimuli and reinforcers (or as setting conditions and consequences) may sometimes be quite easily manipulated, and as a result different patterns of behaviour may emerge. Applied behaviour analysis therefore gave rise to behaviour modification, and this in turn has prompted a feeling in some observers that radical behaviourism has proved to be manipulative and demeaning, a feeling that Skinner's repeated use of phrases such as 'behaviour control' does little to assuage.

The term behaviour modification is today used in a casual manner which has led to unnecessary confusion. This approach in clinical psychology may be traced to early attempts by radical behaviourists to extend their way of looking to specific clinical problems. Workers such as Bijou, Baer, Ullmann and Krasner were all well versed in the interpretation of human behaviour in terms of environmental influences and functional analyses (see, for example, Bijou & Baer, 1961). They were also aware of the empirical science of behaviour developing in studies of operant conditioning and learning in the laboratory. These studies gave rise to a number of specific techniques for producing changes in behaviour, such as conditioning 'appropriate' behaviour by means of positive reinforcement, extinguishing 'inappropriate' behaviour by withholding reinforcement, using techniques of successive approximation or shaping to generate new patterns of behaviour, using fading techniques to change the influence of setting conditions on behaviour, occasionally contemplating punishment procedures, and so on. Initially, attempts were made to restrict the term behaviour modification to the use of principles of learning derived from psychological studies within a broadly radical behaviourist perspective, the applied analysis of behaviour. For example, Krasner & Ullmann (1965) attempted to distinguish behaviour modification from other forms of 'behavior influence' such as psychotherapy, chemotherapy, psychosurgery, etc. Their efforts to prevent erosion in the term behaviour modification were not successful however.

Perhaps because of the initial impact of behaviour modification, which emphasized a potentially effective and an unusually direct role for clinical psychologists in the treatment of patients, psychologists of varying persuasions have increasingly been prepared to call themselves behaviour modifiers, and thus the techniques and theoretical bases of 'behaviour modification' have become increasingly eclectic. In a paraphrase of Mace, clinical psychologists might all claim to be behaviour modifiers now. At the same time there has been an increasing tendency for behaviour modification to become a pejorative term used, for example, by those opposed to any form of behaviour influence to identify any ethically dubious methods, whether these be based on learning principles, on irreversible psychosurgery or even on diffuse pressures brought to bear on individuals by institutions to produce greater conformity in residents' behaviour. The recent flurry of litigation about behaviour modification programmes in the United States has been marked by great confusions of this type, and in this country it is not without significance that an official inquiry into practices in a hospital which caused distress should have concluded with a call for ethical guidelines to regulate behaviour modification, although the practices investigated were based on a form of social psychiatry very far removed from applied behaviour analysis or radical behaviourism (see Bomford et al., 1973). In making this point one is not able to claim, unfortunately, that intervention programmes based fairly on principles of learning never give rise to ethical concern, for perhaps any treatment which proves in its own terms to be effective in changing or influencing behaviour can be insensitively used.

As an academic, I sometimes view the current enthusiasm in this country for 'behaviour modification' with some suspicion. To judge from published work at least, there has been no great concern in British psychology either for a behavioural science of learning and operant conditioning or for the interpretative stance within psychology of radical behaviourism. I remember with affection still the student on a clinical psychology course with (naturally) a good degree from a very reputable university who told me that she had 'done' Skinner already: he had discovered how to make rats press levers. My view is that the enthusiastic advocacy of the techniques of behaviour modification by some who have an unduly crude and ill-formulated view of contemporary behaviourism is likely to result in insensitive programmes. It is probably inevitable that other professions such as nursing and teaching will turn to behaviour modification merely as a set of effective techniques. If psychologists however brought more to the fore the interpretative framework in which these techniques could be best appreciated, perhaps some potential ethical excesses would be avoided. One thinks particularly here of the occasional use of painful events to 'punish' undesirable or dangerous patterns of behaviour which have not previously been analysed carefully in order to detect any environmental influences which may have generated or which may sustain the behaviour.

Behaviourism is frequently represented as being unidirectional, emphasizing as it does the influence of environmental events on behaviour. However, it is also clear that behaviour may in turn influence or affect events in the behaver's environment, a point relevant of course to the original choice of the word 'operant' to characterize such behaviour. This was amusingly captured in the well-known Jester cartoon in which the rat claims he has conditioned the behaviour of the experimenter. An obvious feature of human behaviour is that so many of its more interesting forms occur in the presence of other people. Such people provide events in our environment which may serve as setting conditions or consequences for our behaviour, and in turn our behaviour may serve similar functions for theirs. The behaviour of one person in a social setting is at one and the same time influenced by the behaviour of another person and exerting an influence on the behaviour of that other person.

I have already tried to suggest that radical behaviourism addresses itself to interpreting actions rather than responses, but in a more general view it would now be more appropriate to describe its focus as human <u>interaction</u>. Pretty examples of reciprocal interactions between people's behaviours or actions have attracted a good deal of attention in psychology in recent years - one thinks for example of the delicate interweaving of the behaviour of young infants and those who nurture them described by Bower (1974) as a 'dynamic interactive process that is called development in infancy' (p. viii). Such interactions, or those in non-verbal communication studied by Argyle (e.g. Argyle & Cook, 1976) or in verbal communication too, are as much grist to the radical behaviourists' mill as is the study of lever-pressing in rats. It is true of course that the interpretation of these interactions may put less emphasis than some might put on the potential causal influences at other levels than the environment. Many would favour interpretations of these behaviours in terms of the grammatical structure of the interactions between adult and infant, in terms of the goals of the socially skilled or by reference to the intentions of the speakers. It is becoming increasingly common in contemporary psychology to talk of the 'meanings' of interactions such as these. For the radical behaviourist, the meanings of all these actions, as with simpler behaviours, are to be found <u>in</u> the relationships between the actions and the events to which they are functionally related. Since such events are in these cases provided by the actions of other people, the meanings of the actions are in some sense in the interactions between people. I am trying here to extend a statement made by Skinner (1974, p. 90) in discussing language as an example of what he termed 'verbal behavior'. (Since his 'verbal behavior' was of course defined as behaviour reinforced through the mediation of other people, such an extension is legitimate: mother-infant interactions, social skills and language are all examples of such 'verbal behavior'). He suggested that language is usually considered different from other behaviours because it is an expression of something else: the words <u>mean</u> something. 'But meaning is not a property of a response or a situation but rather of the contingencies responsible for both the topography of the behavior and the control exerted by the stimulus.' Whether the actors in the interactions discussed above are aware or unaware of what is happening is also of course according to radical behaviourists constructed by, resides in, or results from the social interactions themselves, the contingencies of reinforcement.

The idea of reciprocity in radical behaviourist analyses of human conduct cannot be emphasized too strongly. Indeed, I take it that Skinner's much castigated book 'Beyond Freedom and Dignity' (1971) is an essay on this very topic. Of particular relevance here is his discussion of control and counter-control, terms for which you will expect by now that I would prefer to substitute influence and counter-influence. However, functional analyses and interpretations of dynamic interactions have not been handled well in the literature of radical behaviourism in my opinion (and I am sure I will fare no better!). We seem to need a static point of reference in discussing functional analyses of behaviour. In 'Walden Two' (Skinner, 1948) it has occurred to many that Frazier provides such a fixed point. Who influences his behaviour and his decisions for the community which he leads? I am aware that in my own halting discussion of consciousness earlier in this chapter I was in danger of suggesting that the behaviour of the members of the verbal community which constructed the consciousness of an individual may have appeared purposive and itself beyond functional analysis. Such a view is an over-simplification, of course. In a consistent radical behaviourist analysis, the behaviour of our conscious individual is indeed affected by the contingencies of reinforcement provided by the verbal community, but the behaviour of those in the verbal community is in turn influenced by the setting conditions and consequences provided by the individual on whom our discussion focused. Reciprocal, but not necessarily equal, influences result in a balance or equilibrium for interaction.

Skinner's discussion of what I have called influence and counter-influence (control and counter-control) can I think be appreciated better within this dynamic context than in the more static situation suggested by Chomsky's comment that Skinner had created a blueprint of hell. Skinner himself has put forward the view that moral questions emerge from interactions in which there is an inherent lack of balance, when one person is for some reason better placed to influence the behaviour of another than that second person can reciprocate. Interestingly, Skinner has also suggested that 'Control and counter-control tend to become dislocated when control is taken over by organized agencies' (1971, p. 171). An imbalance of interaction may of course sometimes be perceived by an external observer. But feelings of imbalance may arise within an interaction if aversive (or indeed obvious) procedures are used in an attempt to influence another. Such procedures may be perceived as coercive or as an affront to dignity, and may prompt additional mechanisms for adjusting the balance of interaction. However, Skinner goes on to argue that the balance of an interaction may be more insidiously distorted by procedures which use positive reinforcement to influence the behaviour of others. Our concepts of freedom and autonomy of action deflect us from recognizing the influence of positive reinforcers on behaviour. We are prevented by our literature of freedom to believe that individuals have a choice to conform or not in such circumstances, but the choice may be illusory in that our behaviour may in fact be quite predictable in those reinforcing circumstances. This is not to imply, of course, that the feeling of freedom or of choice is not real: it may be a private event shaped in us, as are other feelings and percepts, by the ways in which we interact with others in our verbal or social community. We may feel free and say that we do only what we want to do but, according to Skinner, the experimental analysis of behaviour has clarified the process of positive reinforcement which influences us to do what we feel like doing. It is particularly dangerous to dismiss this evidence, for the control exercised through positive reinforcement has no built-in source of counter-control to balance it. To me at least, and pace Rowan, such a view seems morally alert.

Behaviour modification as a movement in applied psychology seems to me to have been in danger of losing a valuable link with the general philosophy of radical behaviourism from which it originally developed. Thus there has been an emphasis on cook-book techniques of behaviour change, sometimes even without adequate analysis of the no doubt unstructured relationships between behaviour and the environment which may have conspired to produce the 'problem'. The initial challenge of dealing with the previously intractable problems in back-wards of mental hospitals led to interactions between psychologists and clients which were clearly lacking in inherent balance of influences. The behaviour of clients became viewed in too static a context which emphasized the influence of environment (and 'expert') on patient, and which placed too little emphasis on reciprocal interactions. The poor verbal repertoires of the early patients also protected behaviour modifiers from being reflexive. Fortunately, however, the increasing use of behavioural techniques in more challenging or more 'normal' situations, in schools, with verbal clients in social work contexts, in community planning, etc. (see, for example, Nietzel et al., 1977) and in programmes of self-control (Watson & Tharp, 1972), promises to correct the balance somewhat. The advent of contingency bargaining between psychologist and client emphasizes that it is not cheating to talk to a client or to take into account the client's hopes, aspirations or fears, and such developments place in a more sensitive context the ethical decisions that are confronted by anybody who would seek to influence the behaviour of others. Behaviour modification has certainly become more reflexive, and I hope that this in turn will feed back into a more sensitive appreciation of the philosophy of radical behaviourism in general. I may be disappointed, however. Current developments in my own field of animal learning suggest that as the lawful relationships which can be identified between behaviour and environment become more complex, there is an increasing tendency for theorists to dive 'inside' the organism to 'explain' these relationships by recourse to cognitive mechanisms (see, for example, Mackintosh, 1978).

In a short chapter such as this, I cannot hope to present the whole range of contemporary radical behaviourism. Also, of course, I have been able to address only a small part of the plethora of criticisms which have been directed towards current behaviourists. I have therefore chosen here to focus on just a few of the most obvious ways in which I believe radical behaviourism has been misunderstood (often perhaps through its own fault, particularly when aggressive or trenchant styles of writing have been adopted). I think that I have done no more than express in my own clumsy words ideas which have slowly developed in a progressive way in the literature of radical behaviourism in the last two decades. So strong are the prejudices against 'behaviourism' that if my arguments have had any force at all I suggest that I may be accused of not being a real behaviourist. I have never known quite how to cope with such a comment. For many reasons it would be politically and socially expedient for me to throw off the label with relief. Yet the ideas I have tried to express do seem to me to be distinctive in contemporary psychology (though probably not as far removed from many currently burgeoning systems in psychology as is popularly imagined), and so perhaps a name is indeed still called for. In calling myself a behaviourist, I do not accede willingly to the tired assertions that my image of man is based on the stimulus-response dynamics of the snooker table, that I believe man to be a mindless machine, a purposeless puppet pushed and pulled by forces beyond his control, or that my model of man implies that he is an empty organism unable to enjoy the richness of individual experience which plays such a prominent part in some other contemporary systems in psychology. Nor do I believe that my model of man applies only to other people, whose behaviour should be manipulated by confident but furtive technicians (though I do admit that some fields of application have come close to this). In fact, I suppose like everybody in this gathering, I believe that the approach which I favour is imaginative, far-reaching and indeed essentially humane (even humanistic?). It also enjoys some substantial empirical support in its own terms. I would not claim that it offers the 'right' way to see humans, but I believe it may be modestly useful in helping us to understand human beings a little better. Its emphasis on environmental influences on behaviour and experience should continue to play a role not only in academic terms but also in attempts to help people and in the field of social policy.

EDITED DISCUSSION

N. E. WETHERICK: Let me refer to your model 'A : B : C'. I take it that you do not intend this to be interpreted as meaning that the organism has learned in situations like A that when it performs behaviour B it gets a reward C. As you say, it is only the feeling of purposiveness in the organism which is real and not the purposiveness itself. So, granted that you do not intend an internal representation which is actually effective in mediating behaviour, the only argument that you give for this rather unusual way of looking at things is that it is consistent with a Humean analysis of cause. But this analysis has nothing whatsoever to do with science. What justification have you for adopting a theory of causation which is generally agreed to be irrelevant?

D. E. BLACKMAN: I must be reading the wrong books because I was not aware that Humean analysis is passé. What I meant was that, to some extent, causes precede effects and are in some sense contiguous with effects. The claim that radical behaviourism would make, I think, is that it is as reasonable to attribute influences on behaviour to environmental events as it is to attribute them to other events - at a physiological or a cognitive level. As far as animals are concerned, I adopt the stance of an external, objective observer. I cannot get inside the animal's brain or mind or whatever; and I do not have the advantage of being able to talk to him to see how he construes reality. If he were human, and had speech and so on, then it would be highly relevant to ask him about how he construes reality.

N. E. WETHERICK: He might tell you that he did something in order to achieve a particular goal, and you might say that his account was false.

D. E. BLACKMAN: No, I would not say that it was false at all.

N. E. WETHERICK: But why do you not refer to purposiveness, rather than feeling of purposiveness, as being real?

D. E. BLACKMAN: You are making more of a distinction than I would want to, and you have overlooked the pragmatic questions that can be addressed through radical behaviourism: questions to do with influencing the behaviour of the animal.

M. J. MORGAN: Could I ask you a direct question? Do you think that the relatively humane and subtle account of behaviourism that you have offered us is actually what characterizes the policy of the 'official organ' of radical behaviourism - the 'Journal of the Experimental Analysis of Behavior'? It is very hard to relate what appears in that journal to what you have said here.

D. E. BLACKMAN: That journal confines itself almost exclusively to experimental studies of animal behaviour. I suspect that the views that I have expressed are not typical of views expressed by most people who call themselves 'radical behaviourists'. Many may not be in sympathy with the kind of account outlined here.

R. L. REID: Yes, that is right. However, I would say that Skinner himself would be sympathetic.

G. THINES: I think the day has passed when one was either a behaviourist or not. It is only very recently that the important points of behaviourism are being recognized. There have until now been misunderstandings concerning conflicts between, say, ethological and behaviouristic approaches: in fact, there is no true radicalism on either side.

R. L. REID: Some of Watson's barely quoted work was very much in what we now regard as the ethological tradition.

D. E. BLACKMAN: I do so much agree with Professor Thinès that there is absolutely no reason for antagonism between an ethological and a behavioural orientation. There is no embarrassment for the systematic approach that I have adopted in the undoubted fact that different species behave in different sorts of ways. Nor is there any embarrassment over there being individual differences within a species.

J. A. GRAY: Going back to the argument between Dr Wetherick and yourself, it seems to me that what we next need is a mechanistic model which will explain the way in which, given A and given C, B will happen. You did not say anything about that. I am pleased that you allowed for the exploration of brain - I am not sure Skinner has been quite so keen to do that - but like Skinner you did not permit theory. We do need reference to the internal events which give rise to B. I would couch those events in terms of mechanistic theory, and then we need to relate that to brain events.

D. E. BLACKMAN: This raises the vexed question of theorizing within Skinnerian types of psychology, and this I think is consistently misunderstood. I wonder where you and I differ? Skinner argued, not that theories are undesirable, but that there is no strict necessity for moving towards understanding behaviour in terms of processes that were assumed to be going on at some other level ...

J. A. GRAY: The point that I would make is that you must move towards constructing a mechanism to account for your observations. Otherwise, Dr Wetherick is perfectly correct: his description in terms of reasons and actions, and your description in terms of causes of behaviour, are equivalent. Neither makes any advance over the other: both assume rationality.

D. E. BLACKMAN: But your mechanistic model might be couched in terms of systems which you believe to exist inside the organism, or in terms which serve as a mnemonic for your guessing as to what might happen in the future ...

J. A. GRAY: I meant the former - systems which one believes to exist and which are open to experimentation.

D. E. BLACKMAN: Well, that is a wholly praiseworthy endeavour which I would support to the hilt, since I do regard myself as being on the biological end of the continuum within psychology. But it still would not lead to a better understanding of relationships between biological events and behaviour. In the present-day study of animal learning there is a move towards interpreting the complexities of the interactions between environment and behaviour in terms of assumed cognitive processes in the animal. Now, that is a view with which I have no sympathy whatsoever. It redirects attention away from quantifying those aspects of the environment which may relate to behaviour, whatever is going on at a physiological or cognitive level.

N. M. CHESHIRE: Can you tell us, in a non-circular way, what your colons mean in the 'A : B : C' statement?

D. E. BLACKMAN: What I do not mean necessarily is what is captured in the conventional S→R arrow. Arrows seem to imply that in goes one thing and out comes another, and that it is automatic or inevitable. I conceptualize the relationships between A, B and C as essentially correlational.

K. D. DUNCAN: I would be quite happy to accept correlation for the status of colons. But I am still as puzzled as I was when Skinner originally eliminated intrinsic features of environmental events, so that a reinforcer was no longer defined in terms of any intrinsic feature. Are we not now in a situation where we are simply saying that behaviour is influenced by antecedent environmental events and consequent environmental events? And environmental events are not distinguished in any other way? In which case, why not just say behaviour is influenced by environmental events?

D. E. BLACKMAN: I think that is what I am saying. I am trying to unravel the different kinds of influences that those different kinds of environmental events might have. And they are different in terms of whether they are setting or consequential. For example, 'A' might be a sustained environmental event whereas 'C' is likely to be a discrete event: that is just one possibility.

M. JAHODA: I want the radical behaviourists to admit that there are certain phenomena which are excluded from their concern. They concentrate on the here-and-now condition in getting their information about man or animals. What happens to the 'A : B : C' arrangement if the contingencies of my past life are stronger than anything that I can be presented with now? Some phenomena are historical and not universal.

I. VINE: The weakest point in behaviourism, as I see it, is that it fails to throw any interesting illumination on the most interesting human phenomena. It deals, to some extent successfully, with some aspects of infant behaviour, with the behaviour of disturbed people and the mentally handicapped; and it deals quite well with animals in laboratory environments. But it simply cannot handle the complexities of normal human behaviour in any but the most forced and impoverished way.

R. L. REID: You mean that there are other theories that try to tell you more.

R. HARRE: Whenever I engage in discussion with someone who follows the Skinnerian position, in however muted the form, I feel that I do understand in the end; but that is only after it has been translated into another language. I wonder what advance is made, for example, by using the term 'emitted behaviour' instead of 'voluntary action'.   I think every term can be systematically translated into my language.

R. L. REID: One term at least cannot be translated, and that is 'reinforcement'. Apart from that, perhaps you are free to choose.

R. HARRE: Well, the issue between us then is a moral and political issue about whether we are going to have psychologies which, as it were, point towards larger possibilities for human beings, or whether they incorporate a picture of man which is rather narrower - narrower because of the reflexive way in which psychology tends to be borrowed by the folk and used by them to reconstruct themselves.

Chapter 9

The minimization of models

D. E. Broadbent

DOWN WITH MODELS

Every grand occasion needs a built in critic, like the slave who accompanied the hero of a Roman triumph, to whisper reminders of his death; or the Devil's Advocate in proceedings for the conferment of sainthood. My role in this gathering seems to be of this type, because I am doubtful both about models in general, and about holding a conference on them. Of course this is quite consistent with gratitude for the work and ideas of the organizers, since I am sure that much of value will be discussed, as it were incidentally; and equally that it will be certainly most enjoyable. In the same way, one might elect to go on a journey in a coach party of old friends; stopping to look at interesting views, and at pubs to refresh oneself, with a reasonable probability that at least part of the journey will have been covered by nightfall. The role of the critic, however, is to suggest that one would get there faster by the direct route, and there is even a danger that the scenic way will mean that one misses the goal altogether.

There are three main reasons for scepticism about discussions of this kind: (1) models are best discussed in a concrete context, rather than by abstract presentation; (2) emphasis on the development of a model causes actual distortion of data, which may put one on the wrong track; (3) even if one avoids this danger, an excessive use of models is a highly inefficient strategy for advance in a science and may delay achievements which could have been reached sooner by other means. For these reasons, models should as far as possible come at the end of research and not at the beginning. At the beginning, one should always be testing between alternative models, not operating within a single one. The next section expands on these arguments.

However, any reasonably sophisticated defence of this position must recognize why people do nevertheless want to have models. Briefly, the use of a model becomes important when one is considering a choice between actions. This is most obvious in the applied context; the use of one teaching method rather than another implies a theory of the way in which the student is going to be affected. It is true also in research, however, that the choice of problems and methods implies a pre-existing model. To reconcile this point with the dangers of models, we need to think about the minimum assumptions necessary, and make sure that we do not go beyond them. The third section therefore tries to lay down the minimum assumptions necessary for psychological research.

As already noted, however, abstract discussions can be very misleading. In the fourth and fifth sections of the chapter, therefore, I try to indicate one of the models which summarizes the results of contemporary psychological research.

THE DANGERS OF MODELS

Failures of communication

Many of the models of man which are used in everyday life and in some approaches to technical psychology, use words which are heavily ambiguous. The meaning is often clear to the person who generates the model, but the listener may understand him differently. It is even possible that the same person may shift the meaning of a term, perhaps without realizing it, between one occasion and another. Examples of such terms include the words consciousness, intention, desire, will and self. The ambiguity of these words is not merely an academic matter; a great deal of human suffering has been caused by the fact that the word 'love' means different things to different people.

Let us take 'self' as an example. Some people appear to use this term of the whole of another human being; others however clearly want to restrict it to part of the individual, as in the phrase 'my cold is still making my eyes run and my nose blocked, but I feel better in my self'. Some of the latter people appear to think of their 'self' as some kind of commander or pilot which sits in the middle of the head and moves levers causing the rest of the person to do things. This is illustrated by the phrase 'I myself have renounced alcohol, but my hand will not obey me'. If one holds that view, then this controlling or directing system would appear to be the one with which speech communicates; but in that case, why is the classic injunction 'know thyself!' regarded so highly? Presumably it implies that there are other parts of the control system, which are not necessarily known to the part which conducts conversations. If however the definition of 'self' extends to any controlling entity, without reference to communication by speech, then what about the autonomous hands of the drunkard mentioned previously? Furthermore, if we ask somebody to tick lists of adjectives or to complete rating scales about their self, they can distinguish very sharply between their actual self, and another self which can be described as 'as I would like to be'. Are each of these entities parts of a single whole, or is one of them truly to be described as the self and the other not, and in either case are they identical to the controlling agent or something different?

The point need not be laboured; there are obviously a very large number of alternative models, very different in their implications for everyday life and for psychological practice, hidden within the innocent phrases of English. It is unfortunately a mark of the philosophically unsophisticated that they do not see the need for an explanation of such words by concrete examples, but rather insist that the person who fails to understand them is either obtuse or being deliberately obstructive: 'After all, we all have selves so you must know perfectly well what I mean'.

The great merit of models which can be implemented on a computer, as discussed by Boden (chapter 10), is that they avoid many such ambiguities. I would firmly believe that in the long run any adequate account of human beings will have to be capable of computer implementation. The problem at the moment is rather that such models are not adequate empirically; none of them behaves quite like a person behaves, and this tends to be obscured when one discusses this without looking at concrete data.

It is for these reasons that discussion of models in the abstract is likely to be unprofitable. The meaning of the model becomes clearer when one sees the use to which it is put. The view I myself support has been expressed better than I could do it by Farrell (1975), in a review of a book concerned about the correctness of the psychological approach to human nature: 'my own recommendation to soft-liners, to all those in the romantic tradition from Leonardo to William Blake and beyond, is to avoid talking about science, and instead to continue practising their own brand, or brands, of inquiry. By their work shall we then be able to know and judge them' (p. 255).

Incorrect selection of information

This is the point at which to start thinking about why people do nevertheless adopt a model before they begin their research. The reason is straightforward; it is because any one man has limited resources. When he decides to start finding out about psychology, he cannot possibly observe all the facts about even one other person. Indeed, to look at only one person is itself a decision; ideally, one ought to look at every fact about every person who had ever been. Since that is impossible, we have to select. There are two kinds of selection in research, which interestingly enough show up also in our perception of the outside world (Broadbent, 1971). One kind of selection is to look only in certain places for information (filtering, cf. Broadbent, 1971). For example, one might decide to study only rats, to observe about each rat only the number of times that it pressed a bar, and to see whether it does so more often when the bar produces a food pellet than when it does not. The reason for doing so is, at the weakest, a belief that the facts so recorded will be especially interesting and important. The difficulty arises of course when the initial hunch is mistaken, and the data which are not recorded turn out to be crucial. Experiments done under the influence of a single theory which turns out to be false are not much good for supporting or rejecting any other theory.

The second way in which people cut down the amount of work they have to do is known in perception as pigeon-holing (Broadbent, 1971). What this means is that, if you have one pre-existing model which seems to you more likely than others, you do not demand very much evidence before you decide that the world does indeed agree with your model. On the other hand, you demand a very large amount of evidence before you decide that it disagrees. In the extreme case this can be a bit discreditable, and result in jeers at the rigidity of the scientific establishment in the face of new evidence. However, there is a sense in which it is very rational behaviour, and inevitable, given that one human being cannot do everything. For example, consider a choice-reaction experiment where the subject has to press one of 10 keys as soon as one of 10 lights comes on. If it were claimed that, after taking a certain drug, people could press the right key in less than 50 milliseconds, any competent psychologist would immediately start asking pointed questions about the number of measurements taken, details of the equipment, and if he could not immediately see something wrong with the experiment, would probably say 'Well, I'd like to see that repeated in a few other places by different people'. It is in fact more likely that an experiment with such a result is in error, than that all the studies by other authors and techniques are wrong. Bias of this kind is sensible therefore. When it happens to be wrong, however, it can be disastrous. There are all kinds of ways in which the bias of the author's thinking can affect the reported results of experiments; with the general result that the wrong model may actually lead to incorrect statements being accepted as fact and repeated on and on throughout the literature.

We are therefore landed in the paradox that all research is selective, and that there must therefore be some implicit model or models behind any investigation; but that if we use one model and it is wrong we shall be looking in the wrong place, and may even conclude that something is true when it is not.

Inefficiency of research strategy

Under these circumstances some people would argue that research is bound to be guided by a model, that one ought therefore to formulate it early and unambiguously, to draw predictions from it, and then to test those predictions by experiments. If a prediction is falsified, one would then drop or at least modify the theory; otherwise one would continue to find fresh predictions. Those who support this view can to some extent appeal to the authority of Popper (1935);

sometimes they may also appeal to Kuhn (1962). They may perhaps be especially likely to do the latter if they want to put forward a completely new model, since a good deal of Kuhn's thinking emphasizes the sharpness of the transition from one paradigm (perhaps, model), to another when somebody thinks of a new idea.

Unfortunately, looking at the actual conduct of scientific research does not encourage one in this kind of strategy. In the first place, it is of the essence of Popper's view that one ought to do experiments on the least likely predictions from one's model, so as to disprove it. But it appears to be a general rule of human nature that people do not do this.

For example, Dale (1958a) showed that radio repair men, looking for a fault in a set, would form the hypothesis that the fault lay in a particular component and immediately start the repair on that assumption, rather than testing that region of the set to see if it was working normally. The effect was not due to some quirk of the particular situation, because when he devised an abstract search task in the laboratory, the same thing happened (Dale, 1958b).

Again, Wason (1968) asked people to look at a row of cards, each of which had either a letter or a number on the side which was visible. They were told that the invisible sides also had letters and numbers on them; and were asked to test a hypothesis. That is, they might be asked to test the truth of the theory that if A was on one side of the card, then the figure 2 was on the other. By picking up certain cards, they could of course try to disprove this; for instance, they could pick up the cards which were showing a digit other than 2. In fact however they had a regrettable tendency to pick up cards which would confirm the hypothesis. That is, they looked at the cards which had a 2 on. Nothing that might be on the other side could disprove the hypothesis, and it could only confirm it.

When one looks at the psychological literature, one can see exactly the same process happening. Most of us will agree this about the past, and see that the theory of Hull (e.g. 1943, 1952) stimulated large numbers of experiments which gave results consistent with that theory. They were, however, also consistent with many other theories. The choice of experiments was such that it did not discriminate between theories, and therefore advance was slow.

The same thing is still going on, however. In the case of detection of signals, there are at least three completely different mathematical theories which will handle the majority of the experimental results, because they all make very similar predictions (Broadbent, 1956). The work of developing them has not been a waste of time by any means, since the results they all predict are completely inconsistent with a fourth theory, which is the one most of us have by the light of nature. The one model which is certainly false is that perception is all-or-none, with no degrees of confidence, so that errors of perception arise from random guessing. Whenever you see the words 'guessing correction' in the report of an experiment, you can be pretty certain that this false model is being used. It survives because the other models are so complex, and make such obviously different assumptions from each other, that some investigators give up the attempt to choose rationally between models and just assume the traditional one.

Anderson (1976), in discussing this problem, takes as examples the questions of search through memory, and of categorization of visual patterns. In each case many of the experiments have been guided by models which assume some theoretical mechanism; such as examination of each item successively, or of all items in parallel at a speed varying with the number being examined. In each case again different rules may be adopted for stopping the search. The experiments however do not discriminate between these alternatives, since each theory is perfectly capable of handling any of the patterns of results which have been obtained. This is even more true when one looks at the more complex models which have burgeoned in the last decade to represent the structure of knowledge in the head. The assumptions they make are extremely different; they may involve search rules of the type already mentioned, but also assumptions about the data structure. One might assume for example that memory for a complex sentence is structured about the main verb, with the agent, the object, the place, the time, etc., all linked to that symbol

(Norman & Rumelhart, 1975). Or one might assume that storage is propositional, with the verb being merely a part of one component of the proposition, and with all components linked to an abstract centre representing the proposition as a whole (Anderson & Bower, 1973). By a suitable combination of assumptions almost any data can be explained. Anderson (1976) ends by a positive affirmation that any one cognitive theory does not have a unique status with respect to the data, but could always be replaced by another equivalent theory. Models used in this way seem to fit neither the views of Popper (because nobody is trying to disprove them) nor those of Kuhn (because they are not in the least commonly accepted in the field). They seem to be an aid used by the individual for his thinking, with no outside validity at all.

It is important not to get depressed by this situation. I am not, because through the smoke I think I can see that steady progress is being made; though rather in the manner of a sleep-walker. On the one hand, the development of computer models is teaching us a good deal about the kind of processes and structures which are internally consistent, whether or not they have anything to do with the simulation of human behaviour. This is rather like progress in pure mathematics; it is worth while developing the theory of differential equations even if one has no idea whether, for instance, the tax rate in an economy controls the level of prices, the rate of change of prices, the acceleration of prices, or the rate of change of acceleration. To date, most progress in artificial intelligence has been of this type.

Secondly, a number of very simple facts about behaviour have been established. We now know a great deal about the dependence of search times in memory and perception on the number of items being searched. We know that the efficiency of somebody at recalling a sentence when he is given a word from it depends on the grammatical function of the word; he is not particularly good if he is given the verb, he is sometimes especially good if he is given the subject of the sentence but that depends on the previous sentences, the imageability of the word used as subject, and so on. These empirical facts are often quite irrelevant to the models of the people who discovered them, and sometimes flatly contradictory; but they are also often large effects, and if they were assembled without preconceptions I think they would get us quite a way towards a more adequate model of man. So there is progress; but I think it is slower than it need be.

The difficulty is, to summarize, that complex and detailed theories do not get tested at the really crucial points; and if data are found that contradict them it is too easy to add yet a further complexity and to go on believing in the theory. In many ways the complex theories of the past decade are worse than those of Hull in this respect because the complications of the theories are greater. There is correspondingly more difficulty in finding crucial experimental tests, and greater ease in finding some suitable escape if the experiment turns out wrong. Some advance in knowledge has taken place despite these theories, but I believe that it would have occurred more rapidly without them. The doctrines of Popper and Kuhn look much more plausible in old established sciences, for reasons which I have gone into elsewhere (Broadbent, 1956, 1958). They work extremely badly when applied simplistically to psychology. It is quite wrong and thoroughly dangerous to approach psychological problems with one existing model in mind.

THE ALTERNATIVE APPROACH

What follows is the credo of an applied experimental psychologist. Briefly, I do not believe that one should start with a model of man and then investigate those areas in which the model predicts particular results. I believe one should start from practical problems, which at any one time will point us towards some part of human life. In the places which we thus suggested, one ought to consider what actions could be taken; quite often this will eliminate the area from being worth investigation, because one can think of nothing which might be done. If there is only one thing to do, or one thing which is obviously better on the basis of existing knowledge, one ought to do it rather than waste time psychologizing. If there are a number of things to do, each of them will imply a different model of man. What one needs then is the experiment which distinguishes between these models, which makes one of them more probable than the others. Having got it, the resulting model can be used as a guide for action; it may also make other practical problems more tractable, so that the process continues. When one has been doing this kind of thing for a very long time, the number of models under consideration becomes quite small. It is at this point that an outsider might think the investigating scientist is 'testing a theory', when in fact he is discriminating between one or two surviving models which are very specifically defined. Sciences with a long history have reached this stage, and this is what makes a description of the procedures used in them misleading when one comes to psychology. People who set up a detailed model of man at the present day, and then act on it or try to test it by experiment, are rather like a Babylonian trying to guess in his armchair the full details of Einstein's relativity theory, in advance of the millennia of observations which eliminated all kinds of other types of theory.

This bald statement is of course simplistic. Let us fill in a few details.

The source of problems

The reason why one should work on practical problems is not to please the powerful, or get a lot of money for research; both of those can be very dangerous. Power and money go with a lot of pressure to come out with a conclusion favouring one model rather than another, which will distort the research (see above). Also, they may create pressure to work on problems when there is in fact nothing to be done at present and no likelihood of finding something no matter how heavily supported you may be. I am not (on this occasion) talking about social responsibility; I am talking about intellectual excellence. The point of practical problems is that they throw up the bits of human life which involve the major variables. Generations of academic psychologists have managed to fail to notice that one of the most important factors in human performance is the time of day at which it is observed (e.g. Folkard et al., 1977). This factor does not appear in any theory coming from pure psychology. It has finally fought its way uneasily into the edge of academic thinking because of the concern of the Royal Navy, British Rail, and almost every industry which has a continuous flow process. Again, academic psychologists managed for about 40 years to avoid all discussion of attention because that function did not appear in their models. It was only when applied psychologists were summoned to look at modern communication centres, and realized that there was nothing in the academic theory of the time to handle these problems, that attention had to be brought back into respectability (see, e.g. Broadbent, 1958). As another example, the whole contribution of dynamic and textural cues to depth perception was missed altogether by academic theorizing, until a distinguished psychologist spent the war years studying how pilots land aeroplanes (Gibson, 1950). The point of the real-life situation is that it stops you overlooking things.

The need for models at all

At first sight, you might feel that this approach leads to rejecting models altogether; surely the easiest way to decide between different courses of action is to try them all out, and look at the results. But that is very inefficient, for two reasons. First of all, it means that you will have no idea whether the solution which worked in one situation will then work again in another. In the case of the problems of attention in communication systems, the basic solution is to space loudspeakers horizontally; but whether or not this is a good thing depends upon the exact task the controller is doing, and the frequency with which he will have to get some kind of information from more than one loudspeaker. A conclusion drawn from one situation might be quite wrong for another. To make recommendations about the layout of loudspeakers in general, one needs a model of attention, and not just the result of an experiment in one place. I shall give another example shortly of the point that practical action demands a correct theory or it will be completely wrong.

In any case, next time there may be no chance to do an experiment. For example, at the time of writing (March 1979), there is an urgent problem of devolved government for Scotland and Wales. Research would be highly desirable; but cannot possibly take place within the time available. If we had a model of the interaction between larger and smaller scale organizations then we could act on it; but there is no time to construct one now. The point of a model is to avoid the need for experiment, even though the model itself arose from experiment. Ideally, applied psychologists ought either to know straightaway what to do, or they should do an experiment which will avoid the need to do one next time.

Metaphysical assumptions

If we have to have models in the end, then those who think we must have them in the beginning may suggest that our methods of gathering data presuppose at least broad classes of model; for instance, they might presuppose that we are going to have a model in terms of physiological events, or of connections between stimulus and response, or in terms of concepts derived from experience, or something of that sort. I can see no reason for being forced into one or other of these paths; there is really only one assumption which is necessary when using experiments to decide between models, and that is the assumption of causality. Let me make this abstract statement more concrete. I am at this moment interested in the degree of stress associated with various industrial jobs (Broadbent, 1979a; Broadbent & Gath, 1979). The people in any one job may give me experiential statements about their purposes in working, or their satisfaction with their job. They may also show certain kinds of behaviour, such as forgetfulness or waking up at night, which are known to be associated with mild psychiatric illness. It is also possible to look at their physiology, perhaps at the concentration of catecholamines in their blood. All three types of information are now known to differ between jobs; it would be ludicrous to deny oneself the opportunity of one source of data.

However, one does need to know which is cause and which is effect. We have found that in seven different work-groups, and for three different groups of psychiatric symptoms, there is in every case a correlation between the frequency of symptoms and the degree of dissatisfaction with the job (Broadbent & Gath, 1979). Does this mean that unhappiness at work produces neurosis? Or does it mean that people who have problems for other reasons complain about their work? If the first, we should change the job; if the second, some other line of attack would be better. We find that certain jobs show the same amount of satisfaction but different numbers of symptoms; this certainly means that the ill-health is produced by something other than simply dissatisfaction, and that is supported by the fact that we can find jobs where the satisfaction differs and yet the health is the same. So we ought to be thinking what to do about the job.

Perhaps we should select specially stable people for the jobs which seem to be associated with high anxiety? But that assumes that the job causes a rise in anxiety; it is just as possible that the job tends to be chosen by anxious people, or that they are the only ones who can stick it. It might well be a sign of mental health to opt for a quiet life, and conversely it might be that the tense and edgy individual keeps his balance by feeling that his job stretches him fully. If the causal relations run that way, and personality determines the job rather than the other way round, then we might be doing positive harm by picking stable people for stressful jobs. Before crashing into the situation full of our assumed model, we must check it against alternatives and find out which is true; the real world is less tolerant than universities are, where clever but false models are concerned. In the example, that means longitudinal studies to see whether the same person gets more or less healthy as the years go by.

The same kind of debate about cause and effect has to be carried deep inside the person, and may involve inference from events of different kinds. For instance, in certain cases of brain injury persons may be unable to report the identity of a word shown to them. They may nevertheless show that the word has been partially analysed because they are able to say other words related in meaning to the one presented. Similar effects can be found in normal people by showing the word obscured by particular kinds of pattern mask. Certain features of a word, such as the extent to which it is easy to form an image of its content, have effects on the ease of seeing the word with some techniques and not with others. These findings can be used to infer the causal chains which link the visual input, the report of conscious experience, the unconscious biases appearing in other actions or statements, the speed with which buttons can be pressed in certain tasks, and the location of certain physiological events within the brain (see, e.g. Allport, 1977; Marcel & Patterson, 1978). Thus experiential statements, actions, or physiological data may be used. Yet when we discuss the causal sequences we do not need to make any metaphysical assumptions about the events within those sequences. For instance, when we present the word 'doctor' to a normal person, and he consistently says 'doctor' and also is subsequently faster at reading the word 'nurse', we are entitled to claim that there is some event A which occurs within him. Event A is produced by a causal chain starting with the stimulus and in turn it starts a causal chain ending in his saying 'doctor'. If we had presented a blank flash of light, he would have said 'nothing'. Then event B rather than A must have occurred within him.

If now we present 'doctor' masked so that he cannot see it, and he reports 'nothing' then B must have occurred. But he is still fast at reading 'nurse'; so we know that A is not necessary for the effect on speed, but that some other event C, which also results from the stimulus, must lead to the benefit in reading 'nurse'.

We do not, however, need to know at this stage whether A, B, or C are concentrations of some chemical, or particular patterns of nerve impulses; or in the extreme case events occurring outside the framework of the known universe altogether. I think the latter unlikely, but it is worth emphasizing because it shows rather clearly the logical nature of what we are doing. The only important thing about A, B, or C is their causal relationship to earlier and subsequent events. The same abstract quality applies of course to formal computer models of behaviour; they do not require some particular machine, but could be implemented on many. The key element is only the causal structure.

Causality however is an assumption which is necessary for life in general, and not simply for psychology. The use of any statement, such as 'I have a headache today' implies that a correspondence exists between the internal state of the speaker, and the words uttered. If the speaker had said something different he would have felt something different (if only that he wished to conceal his headache, or that he felt there were more urgent matters to discuss!). The making of such a statement also implies a belief that it will select one state of mind in the listener, and not alternative states. The person who has just said he has a headache will be terribly surprised if the listener immediately turns up the radio or shouts at the top of his voice; indeed, he is likely to draw other inferences about the state of mind of the person addressed, such as hostility or at least inattention. All legal discussions of responsibility depend implicitly on the reliability of the causal connection between the internal states of the person and the overt actions; if that causal chain can be proven to be broken, then the law takes a different course, and does not regard the person as responsible for their actions.

More generally, the assumption of causal relations is at the basis of all human communication, by whatever means, and of all ethics or responsibility. It is therefore an extremely serious matter to discard it. It is surprising that some people wish to do so; perhaps without being facetious one could suggest that even if they think they are right, there is no point in their saying so, since they have no assurance that their intention will result in words, or that the words will produce any effect on the people they are addressing.

Given the assumption of causality, however, one can by combinations of experiment distinguish between alternative models of what happens within a person.

The simplicity of models

As already noted, some of those who construct complex cognitive models say explicitly that such models cannot be distinguished by experiment. This immediately suggests, from the point of view I am urging, that these theories have become elaborated beyond the point of what is useful. I must however meet the argument that a complete computer program to simulate, say, the entire processing of natural English will be enormously complicated. Some day we may get a true explanation of that process, or more likely find that different people process the same language in different ways; but the explanation for any one person will still be elaborate beyond our present imagining. It is not at all clear however what is the advantage of trying a complete conjecture for the entire system, at this stage. Different detailed models fall into classes; for example, there is a class of models of memory which are of a 'fragmentation' type (Jones, 1976). In such models if event B is recalled on presentation of A, then event A will be recalled on presentation of B. There are a number of different models within this class, but they differ from models in which the probability of recalling B given A is greater than the probability of recalling A given B. If one devises a complete model for the memory system, this involves an assumption about which of these classes is to be used. A similar choice has to be made at a number of other points, so that there are very many different complex models which might be devised. To return to my earlier views on the subject (Broadbent, 1956), it is extremely unlikely that one will make the right choice on all these assumptions straight off, in advance of experiment; if one is going to set up every possible complex theory and try and choose between them, this will take a very long time. Before setting up a highly complex theory incorporating a large number of assumptions, it is better first of all to test simpler antitheses and see which class of model is more probable. People do not like doing this; remember the work of Dale (1958a,b). In scientific activity it looks highly respectable to produce a psychological theory as complex as anything in physics or biochemistry; but I am afraid the feeling of superiority is an illusion. The reason why theories in physics and biochemistry have to be complex, is that broad and simple theories, such as all those which require the planets to have circular orbits, have already been eliminated. To repeat again what I have been saying all my life (e.g. Broadbent, 1956, 1958), the state of knowledge at any one time is consistent with a certain number of models and inconsistent with others. It can be shown that the rate of reduction of the unknown set is fastest if every experiment decides between equally probable sets of models; if the experiment can have only two outcomes, which is often true in psychology, this means that one can only test between two broad classes of theory, and this means that the theories are going to be very simple indeed. Such a procedure may look less sophisticated than the writing of a highly speculative model; it is however a quicker way to get to the truth in the end.

WHERE ARE WE NOW?

To be consistent with what I have been saying, I ought to give a concrete example of the kind of simple model which results from, rather than starts, research. It is also worth thinking about the way in which such simple models have developed with advancing knowledge; and reminding ourselves of the gaps and inadequacies in our present state.

Behind many modern researches in human experimental psychology, there is a general framework which looks something like a pipe-line or tube. Information goes in one end and travels along, undergoing various operations, until it emerges at the other end in an action. Not to be unpleasant to anybody else, let me take an early example of my own (Broadbent, 1957). In that model, the tube was shaped like a capital Y, with one branch at the bottom and two at the top. There was supposed to be a flap at the point where the upper branches joined, which could be moved across to close either arm; or it could hang free. Ball-bearings could be dropped down the arms and if only one was inserted it would simply knock over the flap and fall out of the bottom. If two were inserted simultaneously, they could both enter the branches, but could not simultaneously go out through the bottom of the tube. The flap could in that case be used by some higher control centre, to shut off one branch and select the other as the clear path through the system.

In this model, the balls represented information arriving at the senses and passing through analysis to response. The model would then represent the way in which two speech messages could not elicit responses simultaneously; and also the fact that two short messages could both be handled as long as one was stored temporarily and only produced a response after the other had been handled. There are some rather charming minor features, such as the suggestion that balls might be dropped into the tube with different amounts of force, so that the most violent would push the flap over and shut out the other; this would correspond to the attention-getting properties of loud sounds. There was also the point that the flap would naturally swing like a pendulum after the passage of a ball, so that the other branch would then have priority; this corresponded to the fact that a previously quiet loudspeaker, in a simulated control tower, was more likely to be heard than a previously busy loudspeaker. There were indeed a large number of experimental facts which implied properties of the person similar to those of the Y-tube.

At the time, this kind of model had a number of merits. The previous implicit model of many psychologists was more of the nature of an old manual telephone exchange, with stimuli and responses being connected to each other by links which went directly from S to R, without mutual interference or selection. To people who held such a model, the Y-tube communicated what was meant by an internal selective function, or by capacitative limits on a system; and that there was nothing particularly mystical or strange about such ideas. At the same time, the physical absurdity of the model acted as the strongest possible warning against taking it for hypothetical physiology, or for a complete account of all aspects of human beings. I still feel very attached to it.

However, as the years go by psychologists have got more and more involved in problems which make the old tubular model creak a bit. It is not so much that the analogy of a tube, pipe-line, or series of stages is false; within its limiting conditions, it is still true. It had to be, because it was inferred from observation, not used to generate observation. But it is awkward to handle certain phenomena with it, and the tube analogy biases one's habits of thought. There are perhaps three main difficulties with the model, although there are other minor ones.

First, the flow of information through people is not always in the same direction, from senses to muscles. Quite often it goes in the reverse direction. (Perhaps as if the flap was being moved automatically by a signal on the ball which had just gone past?) There is also evidence that higher-level processes modify and interfere with lower ones. (As if an outside controller was moving the flap?)

There is in fact clear evidence both for internal feedback loops (Broadbent, 1977a, 1979b) and for upper and lower levels of control (Broadbent, 1977b).

Second, it is a fallacy to seek for 'the' way in which people perform some operation. There is clear evidence that the same person may do the same task in different ways on two occasions, and that different people may do the same task in different ways on the same occasion. (A number of examples and a discussion of the implications are given in Broadbent, 1973.) This variable choice of strategies of processing is hard to accommodate within a tube analogy, and yet essential. After all, one would scarcely ask for 'the' way in which computers keep accounts; it depends on the program.

Third, and linked with the other two points, a tube analogy makes one tend to assume illegitimately that the system is inactive until some outside stimulus arrives. But this is clearly untrue in the case of people; important and crucial operations may be going on inside them while they are sitting apparently undisturbed.

As a typical example of the minor difficulties, one can consider the very specific effects of trying to combine two tasks. Suppose you ask somebody to learn a list of words while simultaneously saying some repeated nonsense phrase, so that he cannot mutter the words to himself. The amount of deterioration in the memory task depends on the length of each word in the list, and is greater at some parts of the list than others (Baddeley et al., 1975; Millar, 1979). The image of two ball-bearings squeezing past each other is scarcely adequate for that.

Let me therefore put forward a different simple model. Instead of a tube, think of a Maltese cross. Each arm of the cross has at its end a memory store, and information can flow in from the end of the arm towards the centre of the cross; but also out, from the centre to the end of the arm. At the centre of the cross is a 'processor', which does nothing except take information from one store and pass it to another; and it may pick any store as the start or finish of the operation. The choice is determined in a way which is explained in a moment.

The four arms of the cross each have their own special characteristics. One is an 'input buffer', which is fed from the outside world. It has different regions within it, corresponding to visual or auditory information; within each, there are regions corresponding to different spatial locations; and so on. When something new happens in a region, it wipes out the things which had happened there previously. So the last thing you heard tends to be retained until some other remark (in the same voice from the same place) comes in.

Another arm of the cross is an 'output buffer' which holds instructions for action, and can feed out to the outside world. Again this store is divided into regions; one important region is the part which holds instructions to the speech system. Others may be instructions for movements of the hands or feet. Again each region can be disrupted by putting a fresh set of instructions of the same kind into it. If no such wiping out occurs, the motor instructions need not go out into the outside world but are available for the processor to use in other ways.

These two arms of the cross can be studied by asking a person to remember something and then giving some irrelevant stimulation, or asking him to mutter some irrelevant words to himself while trying to remember. Because these conditions alter the efficiency of memory, in rather specific ways, we can tell that some of the items are in one kind of store and some in the other (see for instance Crowder, 1978, for a recent summary of the evidence which requires both). On the whole, for example, the early part of a list of words tends to be held in the output buffer and the later part in the input buffer; the length of each word tends to affect the output and not the input; and so on. These two arms, with the link between them, act rather like the pipe-line or tube of the older model; always remembering that material can travel back as well as forwards in this version.

There are however two more arms. One represents long-term associative memory; this is the memory which survives all kinds of intervening activity. Such activity must have required the person to take in stimuli and to emit actions, so that the other stores would be cleared. This is the store which, when fed with 'William the

Conqueror' comes back with '1066'. We know that such memory survives all kinds of irrelevant activities, and therefore by our causal principle we have to suppose that there is something inside the person which preserves memory and which is different from these representations which are abolished by chanting some nonsense words or hearing irrelevant words. Notice that this long-term memory is a third arm off the central processor; information does not have to go through the whole of the rest of the system to get there. That may surprise you, as it has often been assumed that we have to attend to things, or rehearse them to ourselves, if they are to be recalled long afterwards. But any item coming straight in from the input buffer and past the processor direct to long-term memory will do so with no context of previous or subsequent events. 'William' might be 'Rufus' or 'and Mary'; it might be 'Sweet William' or 'Just William'; it might be William Morris, or Professor Sir William Paton, FRS, or any of a hundred other identities. None of these others would be appropriate for '1066', and for the long-term memory to record an association between two events they must both be represented to the processor simultaneously; that is, they must both be present in one of the other stores at the same time. In fact we know that long-term learning can take place in a brain-injured patient who is severely impaired in short-term recall (Shallice & Warrington, 1970), so again by our causal principle we have to infer access to long-term memory without passage through short-term. More specifically, Flint (1979) has asked people to judge whether certain events occurred in a stream of attended stimuli. People are unduly slow at rejecting events which did occur but did so in a stream which was to be ignored. When however the task was to judge whether a particular association had occurred, people were just as fast at rejecting combinations which had taken place in the ignored stream as they were at rejecting completely new combinations. Although the event itself may be in long-term memory, its associations are not; unless it was held in short-term memory with them at the time it arrived. Since the long-term memory is by definition not erased by other events, there is a very large amount in it, and retrieval from it cannot be exhaustive as it is with the input and output buffers. Retrieval must therefore proceed by association and events which have not been rehearsed or otherwise associated in short-term memory are very hard to retrieve. A major role of the short-term buffers is to create, selectively, associations for entry into long-term memory; this principle has been well argued in a number of contexts by Flint (1979).

I have not mentioned the fourth arm of the cross; this is a work-space which can hold only a certain number of items and which is independent of input or output buffers. Thus a few events can be held in it even while the person proceeds with some other task involving intake and output of information, which would clear the buffers; yet these events are held only temporarily, because as soon as the experimenter says 'Now let's do this other task' they are cleared. I can illustrate the effect very easily; to what did the word 'it' refer in the last sentence? You must have known when you read it, but probably not now. This arm of the cross is the only one which is a little controversial; one might try to argue on grounds of parsimony that its functions can be performed by the input and output buffers, or just possibly by a subsection of the long-term memory. Some mechanism is needed however to explain why people can correctly assign pronouns in running speech; and to explain why the studies of Baddeley and his associates always find a residuum of working memory even after suppression of the output buffer; and why people can remember a list of words just as well while holding a couple of digits in mind throughout the problem. Yet whatever is postulated must be limited in capacity; because one cannot remember words just as well and hold six digits in mind (Baddeley, 1976).

A last, and fairly crucial point, which requires a working memory is the dependence of action upon the particular task which is being performed. As I come out of my garden gate, the stimuli striking my eyes are in essentials always the same. But if I am going to my laboratory, or to the local mental hospital, or to the factory where we did the study mentioned earlier, I turn left. But if I am posting a letter, or going to Birmingham, or to the agents for my motorcycle, I turn right. There must therefore be some representation within me of the task in hand, and this will change from day to day. It is only a temporary memory and yet it cannot be sensory or articulatory in character. The fourth arm of the Maltese cross models this type of temporary memory.

If you have found the abstract description of the Maltese cross hard to follow, you can (at some risk) think of it this way. Imagine a man sitting in an office. On one side of him are his 'in-baskets', into which people keep putting pieces of paper. This means that he can only read what is written on the last paper to arrive in a given basket, though papers may still drop into one of the other baskets without covering up the one in which he is interested. On the other side of the man are his 'out-baskets', into which he puts papers which are going to leave the office. Once again, he can still read what is written on the last paper he has put in a particular basket, until either somebody takes it away or he puts another paper on top of it. Papers might therefore arrive and be passed straight across to the appropriate out-basket, one after another. Or they might be held briefly in one or other of the baskets until that particular basket is used again. If the man wants to keep information more permanently, and without blocking the use of his baskets, then he uses a filing-cabinet which is placed behind him. Anything put into file is there until called for; but can only be found if one knows the correct file, if in other words it is associated with some other piece of information which is present when one is trying to make the retrieval.

The office therefore has in-baskets, out-baskets, and a filing-cabinet. But in addition the man has in front of him a desk on which he can put papers which he is using at the moment. Only a few papers can rest there, and they will be lost by putting any other papers on the 'desk-top', not merely by similar papers as in the case of the in- and out-baskets. But the chance to hold on to a few items without disturbing the flow of paper from 'in' to 'out' will let the man deal with interruptions and then go back to an earlier activity; all he needs is a note of which file to pull out or which basket to look in, once he has finished with the interrupting flurry of activity. Because he needs only a cryptic note, I have on occasion called the 'desk-top' by the more formal name of the 'address register' (Broadbent, 1971).

Now I come to the key point, and the reason why I have troubled you with this particular model. I said it was risky to think of the Maltese cross as being like a man sitting in an office. The reason it is risky, is that we are trying to model man, and yet there is a man in the model; if we are trying to analyse human function, we must not appeal to the thing we are trying to analyse. The really interesting thing about the Maltese cross is that the processor in the middle need not be a complete man with all his properties of foresight, memory, reasoning or purpose. It can be a totally passive robot which merely obeys instructions found in its four stores, at the moment when it reads them. Yet the whole office, the four places for keeping paper and the robot in the middle, could still behave in a highly active, purposive and deliberate fashion which the outsider could not predict.

This could arise because the filing-cabinet, the long-term store, holds instructions to the processor which tell it what to do in particular combinations of circumstances. For instance, the file could contain an instruction saying 'If a paper arrives saying that the garden gate is in sight and if there is a note on the desk saying that you are going to the lab, then put a note on the desk saying that you must turn "left".' There could also be a different but corresponding rule telling what to do if Birmingham was the destination. Notice that the instruction would not say 'put a piece of paper in the out-basket saying that a left turn must be made'. If it did, the system would run off mechanical and invariant sequences of actions, which would scarcely be good imitations of human performance. I do not turn right for Birmingham if the traffic is very heavy, because it is then quicker to turn left, go to the nearest roundabout, and come back along the road in the opposite direction. In the Maltese cross, there is an instruction in the filing-cabinet saying 'If there is an instruction to turn right on the desk, and if the in-baskets say that traffic is continuous, then put a paper in the out-basket saying turn left'.   I am not going to elaborate on the subtleties which allow a system of this kind to solve problems, respond to and emit natural language, or perform such tasks as seriation or class inclusion which Piaget has taught us to realize that humans achieve only with difficulty.   Others have done so in this volume, and there are a number of references for anybody who wants to follow them up (e.g. Broadbent, 1973, 1975; Boden, 1977).   The models advanced in artificial intelligence all involve the interaction of permanent and of temporary memories with a processor that is unintelligent and merely acts on instructions.   As I have said earlier, those models are not satisfactory in detail; but they have made the important contribution of showing that in principle a system like the Maltese cross could show the interesting, creative, and purposive features of human behaviour without resorting to a little man at the centre of the model.   Yet we know by causal inference from observation, not by hypothesis, that the formal properties of the Maltese cross are present in human beings.

In other words, at some point during the last decade or so we reached a major threshold in the development of psychology.   The pipe-line or Y-tube models had a tendency to make us think of people as driven passively by the stimulus, or else as having a little man inside the model to extract us from difficulties.   But we have now demonstrated enough mechanisms of the right kind to make possible a genuine analysis of human function.   A Maltese cross can handle the same problem in different ways; it can behave actively rather than passively; it can be humming with activity when nothing is going in or out, as information travels round from one store to another.   For the first time in the history of the subject, we now have a rough and ready framework for the working of the human system as a whole, rather than just the attention system, or visual perception, or motor control.   It is indeed rough and ready, but the areas now covered are far more important than those of earlier models.

LIMITATIONS AND QUESTIONS

It would be inconsistent with the scepticism I am advocating if I did not immediately point out some of the inadequacies even of the Maltese cross.   There are two main types of inadequacy; places where further detail is needed, and topics in psychology where we already know things that are not well handled within this model.

The needs for further detail are obvious, and I need not spend much time on them.   Is memory for instructions of the same kind as memory for other types of long-lasting information?   Are there constraints on the kinds of instruction which can exist?   What determines which instruction wins; are they searched successively in an order or by some other procedure (Broadbent, 1975)?   Of what kind are the limits on the 'desk-top', and could one justify the parsimonious view that its functions (though certainly performed) could be met by a combination of the other three stores?   What is the physiological basis of the various structures?   What are the cultural variations which can be created within them?   There are many other places where the reader can think of missing details.

More worth emphasis are the problems for which this model provides an awkward framework.   First, there is the question of randomness and statistical accumulation of evidence.   As noted earlier, we are already sure that perception and decision are not all-or-none processes, but rather that a succession of partially random events is cumulated to give rise to a final outcome.   In so far as the Maltese cross makes one think of a processor which works like a switch, either open or shut, that impression is bad and false to the data.   Most models in artificial intelligence have this deficiency, incidentally.

Second, the selective functions of the old Y-tube still need to be handled; they lie concealed in the way the processor of the Maltese cross selects which input buffer to examine, and also in the more complex statistical processes which bias it towards one decision rather than another (Broadbent, 1971, 1973).

Third, there is the question of practice or familiarity; we know that familiar sequences of actions are different from the same sequence performed when novel; the unskilled typist looks at one word at a time, while the skilled one takes in a whole phrase or sentence and starts to execute it while looking at or thinking of something else.   In the old Y-tube, this was met by identifying the balls with 'information, not stimulation', and regarding the limited part of the system as purely the decision-making part of the system, but it is doubtful whether most readers noticed that qualification.   In the same way, the Maltese cross might lead one away from thinking of the changes which take place with practice.   It is more natural, for that purpose, to think of handing over routine operations to peripheral lower-level processors rather than to think of everything going through a single processor at the centre of the cross.   An alternative model of this type can readily be constructed (Broadbent, 1977b) and again it can be shown that something possessing its formal properties must exist.   Neither model is really inconsistent with the other, but each is appropriate for different kinds of problem.   It is an essential part of the cautious or sceptical approach to models that one should expect to use different frameworks for different purposes, as long as they are not contradictory.

This leads me to a last major point.   One of the pressures to have a comprehensive model comes from those who want, not to do research, or to learn the best way of meeting a particular problem, but to find a general philosophy of life, that is, a religion.   I would be the first to agree that we all need such a philosophy, and that each of our lives probably implies a belief in one, whether we can consciously formulate it or not.   But the data which must be fitted by a philosophy of life are at present quite separate from those involved in the mental health of factory workers; or the layout of communication centres; and different too are the criteria of success.   Any claim to base a philosophy of life on current psychological knowledge is fraudulent, because our knowledge is still consistent with many models.   We should look outside psychology for a viable philosophy; and be clear that we are doing so.   It is of course important that the tentative models of man we use in the one field should be consistent with those we use in the other; in my own case, I believe they are (Welford, 1971; Broadbent, 1979c).   But the attempt to base one's life on one's knowledge of psychology distorts both the psychology and the life.

These cautions and qualifications are all of a piece with the general approach I have been advocating.   If I am right, then the sceptic's progress will be faster than that of the enthusiast for models.   On the record of the past 30 years, I am sure that is so.   I am content to abide by the verdict of the future.

EDITED DISCUSSION

R. L. REID: A point to which you have not referred is that one may well expect profound individual differences.

D. E. BROADBENT: But, of course, there are similarities between people too!

J. SHOTTER: I feel that there is a danger in taking problems from the situation as you find them.   Man is then seen as a mindless bureaucrat; and this applies, for example, in your Maltese cross model.   The whole tendency of our times is to demand a bureaucratic form of activity, and the danger is that applied psychologists are merely satisfying the demands placed upon them by their clients or society at large.   Hence they simply produce models which satisfy those demands and leave it at that.

D. E. BROADBENT: That can be said of any theory. Trades Unions, like myself, have a preference for cause-effect relationships. They are disinclined to favour theories of work organization which claim to give freedom to the individual but which require the breaking up of workers' organizations. Some disagree with their political views, but they are entitled to them.

H. J. EYSENCK: Physics has prospered with models that were wrong and even known to be wrong at the time, but physicists appear to be successful. So I am not sure how you could defend our not using models even if they turn out to be wrong. Second, you have given us very complex problems for which no realistic model could be expected at such an early development of our science. Even in physics models apply to relatively simple and clear-cut problems.

D. E. BROADBENT: Models being wrong but useful applies in psychology also. Signal detection theory is a case in point: this theory has been extraordinarily useful despite the fact that the axioms were known to be wrong from the outset. The theory's success arose because its predictions were inconsistent with an alternative theory: the same often applies in physics models. As for my use of complex examples, a good many psychological problems are complex when you start out. One generally arrives at simple situations after years of systematic analysis: you have to start from extremely simple models.

N. E. WETHERICK: Is it true to say that the Maltese cross model is consistent with every other model presented here?

D. E. BROADBENT: Well there are parts of the model that some would dispute.

N. FRUDE: Is there a confusion between implicit models and the deliberate construction of models? To talk about people having implicit models of man is quite different from constructing flow diagrams and so forth.

D. E. BROADBENT: The trouble is that if you take implicit models and make them explicit, they then become explicit models. So you cannot actually talk about models which are truly implicit.

J. A. GRAY: What we need to do is test a prediction which has got a very low a priori probability if the model were wrong. You suggest that we need to divide up the class of models and successively play 20 questions with nature. This means that, in advance, you have to identify all classes of possible theory, and perhaps that is one of the things AI is doing; but it could take a generation. The alternative approach, adopted to great effect by physicists, is to have a detailed model which is able to make predictions which are very specific and, in the best cases, to a highly quantifiable degree.

D. E. BROADBENT: But the probability in psychology is that the approach will not work. It is only really worth trying if you have already eliminated most possibilities: otherwise, on average, you are going to predict falsely.

Chapter 10

Artificial intelligence and intellectual imperialism

M. A. Boden

Intellectual imperialism, like the political variety, comes in aggressive and in paternalist modes. The aggressive mode is based in the belief that no approach to a particular area of debate is worth pursuing unless it is governed by a specific principle, or guiding idea, which alone has any intellectual authority. The paternalist mode tolerates, even appreciates, differently principled approaches. But it sees its own authority as relevant to all points within the given area, no distinctions being drawn between those things that are God's and those that are Caesar's. The arrogance and insensitivity of the aggressive imperialist are missing. But the paternalist shares the common imperialist belief that, within the area concerned, all inquiries could benefit from some allegiance to the preferred intellectual regime. Both types of imperialism may be manifest in crusades, and both foster resistance movements - but crusade and resistance alike are fiercer in the aggressive than in the paternalist case.

Crusades, and their respective oppositions, are hardly uncommon in psychology. If one thinks of Kuhn's (1962) account of scientific paradigms as a description of the rise and fall of intellectual empires, then psychology is all imperialism but no empire. For there is no normal science, in Kuhn's sense, no universally accepted way of conceptualizing theory and experiment in psychology. It is as though opposing armies were fighting battles in order to win the right to define the nature of the war. Humanists, phenomenologists, behaviourists, sociobiologists ... the armies are legion indeed. And the prize will be a power to influence basic presuppositions about human beings and society that are held by civilians no less than the militia. It is largely because the non-combatant population will be so intimately affected by the 'model of man' heralded by the victor that it is important enough to be a cause for battle.

Recently, a new intellectual force has entered the field. Its members see artificial intelligence (AI) as relevant to psychology, in so far as they take a computational approach to psychological phenomena. The essence of the computational viewpoint is that at least some, and perhaps all, aspects of the mind can be fruitfully described for theoretical purposes by using computational concepts. These concern rule-governed symbol-manipulations within information-processing systems in general, whether living or not. Computational processes, that is, are processes of symbolic transformation whereby information is stored, classified, and indexed; plans are formed, executed, and monitored; concepts are formed, extended, and linked; inferences are made and hypotheses tested; decisions are taken and later evaluated; memory is searched; problems are formulated and solved; interpretations are constructed; symbol-structures are compared ... and so on. Their clearest embodiment is in computer science and AI, wherein rigorously defined computational concepts can be used to specify qualitatively distinct types of data representation and transformation. This is why, although the computational approach in psychology is primarily concerned with these abstractly defined information-processes, writing and running computer programs is an important methodological weapon in the computationalist's armoury.

This new force has been called 'the artificial intelligentsia', a contemptuous term used by its opponents not merely to mark the influence of AI research on its members' thinking, but also to suggest something unnatural or inhuman (not to say anti-human) about their position. Specifically, the suggestion is that the model of man that is implicit in psychologies influenced by AI is inadequate to allow for - still less to explain - phenomena such as subjectivity, purpose, emotion, creativity and consciousness. Even intelligence itself, or so the suggestion goes, cannot really be illuminated by such an approach, which must necessarily ignore what is most distinctive and valuable in natural intelligence. The AI approach, it is said, involves an intellectual imperialism that rejects all other approaches to psychology as a waste of time, being based on sentimental and irrelevant models of man. On the contrary, say its critics, the computational viewpoint accepts a deeply misleading model of humanity that reduces us to the level of unthinking, unfeeling tin cans.

Do psychologists who are convinced of the relevance of AI necessarily believe that it is germane to all areas of psychology, and that no other approach is useful? And is their psychology implicitly dehumanizing in its implications? I shall address these questions by way of asking whether and in what sense AI leads to imperialism in psychology.

AI AND AGGRESSIVE IMPERIALISM

Let us admit it: there are people within AI, as in other psychological camps, who are imperialists of the most aggressive sort. Such people think, and sometimes tactlessly say, that traditional approaches to scientific problem-solving in psychology are essentially a waste of time. Behaviourists, Piagetians, Freudians, phenomenologists ... all are misguided in their different ways. The only way forward is a computational one. This imperialism is focused on the 'core' questions of consciousness, subjectivity, creativity, and emotion no less than on the more bread-and-butter issues of memory storage and motor skills. Far from being irrelevant to consciousness, AI is thought by proponents of this extreme imperialism to be the only approach that can throw light on the riddle of consciousness.

In so far as such attitudes are expressions of eccentric personalities or the arrogance (and ignorance) of enthusiastic youth, they bear no relation to the intellectual essence of the. computational approach. They may harm the computational cause in practice, because of the irritation and hostility they arouse in psychologists generally, but do not show it to be absurd in principle.

However, there is a more reasoned, and reasonable, version of aggressive imperialism which it is important to understand. This version typically gives credit to other psychological methods for the wide range of phenomena they have uncovered. But they see most psychologists as doing 'natural history' or fact-gathering rather than respectable theorizing:

> Computer science has brought a flood of ideas, well defined and experimentally implemented, for thinking about thinking; only a fraction of them have distinguishable representations in traditional psychology ... But just as astronomy succeeded astrology, following Kepler's discovery of planetary regularities, the discovery of these many principles in empirical explorations of intellectual processes in machines should lead to a science eventually. (Minsky & Papert, 1974, p. 25)

The reference to astrology should not lead one to think that these imperialists regard the traditional psychology of the past as a waste of time. For much of interest has been found out. With respect to the problem of consciousness, for example, many psychologists have contributed useful descriptions of conscious phenomena that will have to be borne in mind by anyone theorizing about it.

To mention just a few examples, work as diverse as Freud's and the experimental studies of subliminal perception sketch the range of influence on consciousness of unconscious processes of a kind significantly similar to those that we can introspect. Penfield's (1958) studies of the temporal cortex provide phenomenological support for the notion that a conscious memory of one and the same event may differ in nature according to whether it does or does not arise from (computationalists would say 'is or is not generated by') a complex system of associations in the mind, as opposed to an arbitrarily introduced physiological stimulus. And the many studies of perceptual masking and meta-contrast provide persuasive evidence that percepts are constructed within the mind, that the construction takes an appreciable time, and that certain processes within the overall constructive activity can be interfered with by others in various ways. Finally, the reports of clinicians dealing with cases of so-called 'multiple personality' have highlighted the strange fact that two or more apparently distinct minds can coexist within the same body; even stranger, these may be non-reciprocally co-conscious, in the sense that personality A may have direct access to the thoughts and experiences of personality B, being able to remember and report them later and sometimes to influence B's actions accordingly, whereas personality B has no knowledge of the existence of personality A except by hearsay.

Many other examples could be given, but the general point here is that AI-theorists may feel that we no longer have need of further facts such as these. Rather, we need to concentrate on seeking explanations that really are adequate to account for such phenomena, as the current 'theories' are not. Experiments in psychology thus tend to be regarded unfavourably by such people, who say either that they merely add more (unexplained) data or that they are theoretically uninteresting because of the conceptual vagueness and structural and procedural poverty of the theories they are supposed to be testing. In general, empirical studies based on the positivist dependent-independent-variable model are not well suited to capture the underlying generative structures and computational processes by which alone psychological phenomena can be theoretically understood. Even those studies that are aimed at underlying psychological processes typically fail to realize the existence of huge theoretical lacunae in their 'explanations' - lacunae which a computational viewpoint would at least have recognized, if not filled.

For instance, in commenting on the recent and admittedly 'fascinating' studies of symbol-using in chimps, a computational theorist has complained:

> In the long run we shall all learn more if we spend a little less time collecting new curiosities and a little more time pondering the deeper questions. The best method I know of is to explore attempts to design working systems that display the abilities we are trying to understand. Later, when we have a better idea of what the important theoretical problems are, we'll need to supplement this kind of research with more empirical studies. (Sloman, 1978, p. 4)

As an example of the 'new curiosities' referred to here, we may take the symbolically mediated cooperative problem-solving shown by chimps in experiments by Savage-Rumbaugh et al. (1978). Using arbitrary symbols that it punched on a teletype, and which were automatically displayed in the adjoining room of a second animal, one chimp was able to ask another for a specific tool required to reach some food hidden by the experimenter in the first chimp's room. Only this chimp knew where the food was, and whether a long pole, or a key, or a spanner ... was required to reach it, because while it was being hidden the window between the two rooms was covered. But only the other chimp had access to a toolbox. Both chimps shared the food once it was found.   Both animals had initially been individually trained to associate a given symbol with a given tool, as well as learning which tools were effective for which hiding-places.   If the teletype was put out of action, so that the first chimp was reduced to mere gesturing within view of the second chimp, the communicative success dropped drastically.   Moreover, the nature of the first chimp's reaction to a 'typing error' (noticed by it when the second chimp picked up the unwanted tool which had been asked for in error) made it quite clear that something of the symbolic function of the teletype was somehow understood by the animal.

Examples of the 'deeper questions' involved here include these: How is it possible for a creature (of whatever species) to form means-end plans for reaching a desired object, plans within which other objects are represented as instruments to the overall end?   How is it possible for an external symbol, as well as one in the internal representational medium of the creature's mind, to be employed by one animal and recognized by another as a request for a specific tool?   How is it possible for an animal (or a human being) to realize that the tool being selected is not the one that was intended, and that the way to overcome this obstacle is immediately to change the symbol displayed while gesturing to draw one's colleague's attention to the new symbol, rather than to the desired tool?   How is it possible for someone to represent to themselves that a long pole can be used in such-and-such a way to push a banana out of a tube, whereas a key used thus-and-so is required to get it out of a padlocked box?   And so on, and on ...

These questions were not treated as questions by the experimenters concerned, so much as as answers.   That is, these capacities were cited by them as explaining the observed cooperation between the chimps, as though these capacities were themselves psychologically unproblematic.   But the attempts to design working systems with comparable abilities show, to the contrary, how little is yet understood about their underlying psychological structure.   Psychological theories of a non-computational type characteristically take such human and animal competences for granted, whereas the basic psychological problem is to explain them.

For instance, Rumbaugh's experiments may surprise us by showing an unexpected degree of cooperation between chimps able to use external symbols.   But they afford no hint of how such cooperation can possibly occur, in whatever species, because they do not illuminate the nature of the organism's internal 'language' or representational medium, within which computational processes of inference and symbolic transformation take place to mediate complex experience and behaviour.

The aggressive imperialist insists that the only way of approaching such questions is to attempt to express our psychological theories as computer programs.   A program (or subroutine) which could offer appropriate instrumental advice to another program (or subroutine) encountering a specific type of difficulty in achieving its current goal would suggest how it is possible for such cooperation to occur.   Some relevant programs have already been written, which indicate the dimensions of the questions that need to be asked though they provide only the sketchiest of initial answers.   One of these embodies problem-solving procedures for classifying the nature of the problem, selecting a potentially fruitful method of approach, monitoring and evaluating execution of that method, changing tack to a preferable method, and even changing back again (with appropriate suggestions as to how to fix the hitch that initially led to abandonment of this method) in certain circumstances (Fahlmann, 1974; Boden, 1977).   Another incorporates a simple theory of how one goal-seeking system can cooperate with another only if each has some representation of the other's goal and current beliefs as well as its own (Power, 1976).   The AI-theorist would expect many of the representational and procedural constraints on problem-solving within cooperative programs such as these to be relevant also to the problem-solving that is going on in Rumbaugh's chimps.   That it goes on in the chimps is surprising, but how it goes on is mysterious.   The aggressive imperialist regards the production of surprises as no substitute for the illumination of mysteries.

Aggressive imperialism shades into the paternalistic variety, and might even be dubbed a 'paternalism of the past' in so far as it pays tribute to past discoveries in the 'natural history' of psychology.   But what is important and worth while now, according to this view, is to define the problems and outline possible answers in computational terms.   For only these are sufficiently rigorous to promise real theoretical advance.   The notion that new evidence might alert us to computational possibilities that otherwise we might have missed is assumed to be very improbable.   In sum, the best methodology is first to express psychological theories as computer programs, before seeking evidence of an experimental kind. The truly aggressive imperialist believes that the second methodological stage will not be reached for many years: meanwhile we will, and should, have our hands full trying to cope with the first.

AI AND PATERNALIST IMPERIALISM

Paternalist intellectual imperialism appreciates the contribution of different approaches, but like the more aggressive variety holds that there is no topic within the intellectual area concerned that cannot be illuminated to some degree by its own methods.   Applying this to what is commonly seen as the most intransigent topic for the AI-theorist, namely consciousness, paternalists will of course admit that various psychological approaches (some of which were mentioned in the preceding section) have contributed to our knowledge of consciousness.   And they will typically encourage further study along these various lines.   But they will insist that a scientific understanding of consciousness can be advanced by taking a computational perspective.   How could this possibly be, given the apparent gulf between conscious living creatures and mere tin cans?

Let us take as an example the phenomenon mentioned in the previous section, of non-reciprocal co-consciousness between the different 'personalities' within a case of 'multiple personality'.   This phenomenon is strange not only in the sense that it is very unusual (as would be a purple-spotted cow).   More interestingly, it is strange because our usual ways of thinking about consciousness give us no clue as to how it might be possible.   Still stranger, we are used to thinking about the mind and consciousness in a way that suggests such phenomena must be downright impossible.   The many claims within philosophical writings about the unity and indivisibility of consciousness, not to mention those which regard the higher mental processes as always open to introspection, bear witness to this.   If we saw a purple-spotted cow, we would hypothesize some genetic mutation, environmental pollutant, or practical joker with a paintbrush.   We would not regard the surprising creature as an existent impossibility, as a contradiction of the most basic principles of our thoughts about cows.   But this is precisely how the phenomena of multiple personality may strike us.

However, thinking of the mind on the analogy of a complex computer program may help to make these phenomena intelligible. The various subroutines within a complex program may have differential access to each other's operations, both in terms of information about the actions and effects of other's operations (mere monitoring) and in terms of possible interference with the actions of other subroutines, whether to help or to hinder.   Similarly, the data-base or information-store accessed by one subroutine may or may not be the same as that accessed by another, and changes in one may or may not be automatically copied into the other. Moreover, such structural features of the program can readily be varied at different times (and for different reasons) within the running of the program.   So two subroutines that 'normally' have access to the same memory-store and/or to each other's activities may 'abnormally' be dissociated from each other to some degree. Moreover, the AI-theorist would expect that at least some of the functional reasons that a programmer might have for building or for avoiding such a system might throw some light on the functional significance of dissociated personality in the human case. (Whether or not such clinical cases are the effect of experimenter bias, as has been claimed, is irrelevant: we are here concerned with the possibility of the phenomenon, not with its specific aetiology in actual cases.)

Similarly, the apparently paradoxical cases of aphasia, apraxia, and agnosia that are reported in the clinical literature, and that undermine our usual assumptions about the nature of consciousness, are more readily intelligible with the help of the computational metaphor. For example, programs that solve problems have to be provided with distinct procedures for distinguishing means-end hierarchies, for planning an overall sketch of the solution whose details must be filled in later, for translating such a plan into detailed execution, for monitoring the results of the action taken so far, for anticipating the effects of actions yet to be done ... and so on. Workers concerned with clinical agnosia are currently looking to these specific computational concepts to aid in the detailed structural description (and perhaps eventually the explanation and cure) of their patients' anomalous behaviour in situations of practical problem-solving (T. Shallice, personal communication). And theories of conscious and unconscious processes within the mind are commonly stated today with computational concepts to the fore (Shallice, 1978).

Someone might object that none of this even touches on, still less solves, the philosophical problem of consciousness. For computational theories, just like other psychological theories, 'bracket out' such philosophical questions, being content to take the existence of consciously experienced qualities as given. But the important point is that, even if one merely accepts experience as a given fact, the essential nature of such experience can to some extent be illuminated by a computational approach - as the example of dissociated personalities shows. And any adequate philosophical account of consciousness would have to be able to embrace and account for these clinical and everyday phenomena, which the Cartesian tradition (whether the Continental phenomenologist or the British Empiricist branch) strictly cannot.

Another example of a phenomenon that has seemed troublingly paradoxical to many psychologists and clinicians is the case of hysterical paralysis. As Charcot (watched by the young Freud) showed a century ago at the Salpêtrière Hospital, there is no neurological injury causing such paralyses. Even stranger, the limits of the paralysis correspond quite clearly to the patient's everyday concept of body parts, such as an arm, leg or hand. The neuromuscular distributions discovered by anatomists do not support the idea, for example, that an arm is an anatomical unit bounded by the line of the armhole of a sleeveless shirt. But this is how we usually think of an arm, and this idea evidently constructs the limits of the malfunction observed in the hysterical patient.

There could be no clearer example of the influence of mind on body, but such influence is inexplicable if not impossible for most psychological theories. Empiricists (whether introspectionist or behaviourist) cannot explain it, and though phenomenologists - who make much of the close mutual relations between mind and body - are happy to cite such cases, they cannot give any well-understood non-psychological analogy in terms of which to make them more clearly intelligible.

The computational approach, however, can. Suppose a robot were to be anatomically constructed with joints, wires, and levers paralleling the human pattern of nerve-muscle connections, and suppose that it were given the programmed capability of monitoring its own actions (for example, by visually inspecting the position of its body parts). It could be told to inhibit any incipient movement of its right arm, provided that the concept of its 'right arm' were defined for it (represented internally by it) in some way. Supposing that its inner representation, accessed by the inhibitory program, defined its arm as 'that part of my body distal to the sleevehole line', then it would exhibit behaviour comparable to that generated by the patient with a hysterical paralysis. Yet all its wires and levers would be physically intact. In short, the robot's internal representation of its arm, rather than any genuine anatomical feature of the arm itself, would be guiding its behaviour and inducing the functional paralysis.

It follows that some descriptions and explanations of the robot's beha (namely, those that are not purely mechanical and electronic, or 'physiologic would have to involve an irreducible reference to this inner representation. A have shown in detail elsewhere, such descriptions and explanations would share t various logical features characteristic of 'intentionality', which is so stresse by those theoretical psychologists who favour a subjective or hermeneutic accoun of the mind (cf. Boden, 1970). What the robot believes to be (or represents to itself as being) the case may be more important in explaining its behaviour than what actually is the case. The robot's arm is not an anatomical unit bounded by the sleevehole line, any more than is a person's, for as in the human case the wires and levers which move the robot's arm also move other parts of its body which are not affected by the functional paralysis. But the robot's representation of its arm as such a unit is crucial in mediating the paralysis.

In this, paralytic programs resemble Polish peasants: Thomas and Znaniecki's (1918-1920) seminal concept of the 'definition of the situation' similarly stressed the theoretical importance for social psychology of what is believed to be the case rather than what actually is the case. Hermeneutic psychologies in general take as theoretically basic the inner models of one's world and wants that make possible the subjectivity of experience and behaviour. The concept of 'representation' (and its close cognates, 'meaning', 'interpretation', 'construction' ...) being central to AI also, the AI-paternalist has a specific philosophical justification for accepting the relevance of hermeneutic approaches to psychological problems, and cannot be accused of a woolly-minded eclecticism that tolerates all views while basically respecting none. Hermeneutic, as opposed to behaviourist, views in psychology have in common with the computational approach that they emphasize the mental representations and transformational processes that guide intelligent, purposive action, and give to experience and behaviour their irreducibly intentional character.

For instance, surprising as it may be to people of a 'humanist' or 'anti-mechanistic' cast of mind, psychoanalytic and Gestalt writings are both closer to the computational viewpoint than are behaviourist theories, because they try to articulate some of the psychological processes and representational structures that underlie behaviour and consciousness. They encourage one to ask such questions as how is it possible for one and the same area of ink to be interpreted now as a young woman's chin, now as an old hag's nose; or how is it possible for a person to say 'Botticelli' when what they wanted to say was 'Signorelli'. The Freudian and Gestalt answers to these questions employ concepts of a broadly computational character, though they lack the rigour and specificity of symbol-manipulation concepts that are definable in programmed terms. Similarly, ethogenic and ethnomethodological approaches are basically compatible with AI in so far as they stress the underlying rules and representational metaphors (such as dramatic metaphors) that inform human behaviour. Social psychological concepts such as 'role', 'attribution', and 'dissonance' similarly focus on the use and construction of representations of social behaviour that are stored in the minds of members of a given society, some of which are of course more culture-bound than others. Even Laingian psychology stresses the guiding role of internal representations of Self and Other, and their reciprocal perceptions, in a way that one might express in computational terms, so that Laing's view of schizophrenia as an intentional construction rather than a physiological symptom is compatible with an AI-approach.

This is not to say that anyone interested in schizophrenia should rush to the computer terminal, eschewing all personal interaction with schizophrenics, and spending no time on statistically informed studies of possible hereditary and biochemical factors. The difference between proponents of the aggressive and paternalist modes of AI-imperialism is precisely that the latter expect some useful insights (theoretical as well as practical) still to be found by such methods whereas the former do not.

1
heral, AI-paternalists (unlike their aggressive fellows) are concerned to
methodological principles of validation whereby psychological findings of a
aditional or experimental kind may be matched against the performance of
x programs. In a recent discussion of the computational approach to
live psychology, Pylyshyn (1978) has detailed a number of methods whereby
tly psychological data can be used in the validation of programmed models.
even he, paternalist (and professional psychologist) as he is, expresses
npathy for the more aggressive view that 'these experimentally based methods are
latively weak and may be most useful after some top-down progress is made in the
inderstanding of methods sufficient for relevant tasks - such as may be forthcoming
from artificial intelligence research' (1978, p. 93).

(It is relevant to our example of consciousness to note that in an earlier
paper Pylyshyn, 1973, showed that the AI-approach is helpful even in the study of
mental imagery - hardly a topic beloved of the behaviourist. The recent upsurge of
interest in imagery arose from 'traditional' areas of psychology, but is
increasingly being pursued with computational concepts in mind. Some AI-
paternalist groups, such as Marr's at MIT, are specifically trying to integrate AI-
insights with psychological and neurophysiological evidence about vision, and are
writing their programs and formulating their theories accordingly: Marr, 1976.)

Pylyshyn reminds us that it is even difficult to know where attempts at
validation should start, quite apart from the difficulties inherent in interpreting
the result of a 'validatory' test. The reason for this is that a complex computer
program, even one written with the specific aim of simulating psychological
reality, will have many features that have no theoretical significance for the
psychologist -and it may be a 'formidable' task to decide which these are. Some
will be so obviously tied to the constraints of a particular programming language
or machine architecture that no one would be misled into assuming that they were
psychologically relevant (though even here, 'obvious' is a relative term: vide the
common confusions over whether the serial nature of current computers does or does
not make them essentially inappropriate for psychological simulations, Dreyfus,
1972). But others may be more questionable.

For instance, work on problem-solving and programming languages (including that
involved in Winograd's well-known language-using program) has shown the
computational value of carrying a continually updated 'context' through the task
and of storing it if and when backtracking is needed so that it can be used to
guide future choices in a task-appropriate way (Sussman & McDermott, 1972;
Winograd, 1972). This suggests that equivalent types of question might be fruitful
in the psychological study of the role of memory in problem-solving, but does not
settle the question of just how close to the original computational example (e.g.
the specific programming languages) the empirical psychologist should stay.
Similarly, computational considerations can show the advantages of first creating a
copy of a mixed-item list before trying to count the items of a given type on the
list. This clearly expressible computational notion can support and illuminate
psychological insights such as Piaget's (1966) when, in explaining the young
child's inability fully to understand class inclusion, he remarked 'if he thinks of
the part A, the whole B ceases to be conserved as a unit, and the part A is
henceforth comparable only to its complementary A'. (See Klahr & Wallace, 1972, and
Boden, 1979.) But whether one should expect the way in which this copy is made,
stored and accessed to be precisely the same in the human and any given
computerized case is another matter.

While we are still unsure about how to decide such issues of validatory
relevance, the practice of writing complex programs will carry the risk of leading
one into psychological irrelevancies which cannot even be clearly recognized as
such. Also, of course, much time will be spent on programming details which the
empirical psychologist may feel would be better spent (at least by all except
programming geniuses) in activities of a more familiar kind.

Largely because of these difficulties, some AI-paternalists require merely that
computational factors be kept in mind while theorizing and planning or interpreting

experiments, the writing of programmed simulations being unnecessary or counterproductive. But even these people insist that the psychologist shou some point undergo the intellectual discipline of learning to program, for awareness this will bring of the clarity required to express matters as progr. and the correlative unclarity of other forms of psychological theory. There more difference between an inexpert programmer and someone who has never attempt this exercise than between the expert programmer and the tyro, and this differenc is enormously helpful to any psychologist who wants to develop a feeling fc. clarity in psychological theorizing. Assuming that one does decide to sit down to write a program, the AI-paternalist is more likely than the aggressive imperialist to insist that psychological knowledge should be taken into account at every point, so far as is possible. Admittedly, ad hoc assumptions will have to be made, but the more the assumptions and constraints written into the program can be based on empirical psychological data, the better.

In sum, the AI-paternalist, who typically wishes to match programs against psychological data of more familiar kinds, admits that this validatory matching is not a straightforward affair. To some degree this difficulty is shared by any psychological, or even scientific, theory since the methodology of confirmation is a controversial area within the philosophy of science. But it is highlighted in the AI-context because the program itself, entire, is not a psychological theory and it may not be simple to distil out of it those features which do contribute to the theoretical position concerned. To insist that every aspect of a language-using program, for example, must be paralleled in the human case would be as blindly imperialist as to insist, not only that a postal system would be a Good Thing for a newly colonized society, but also that all its pillar-boxes must necessarily be red. But this cuts both ways: an opponent of AI cannot justifiably object that their system is a Bad Thing because its pillar-boxes are green, whereas ours are not.

CONCLUSION

It is important to realize that one may be convinced of the usefulness of the AI-approach in psychology without being an intellectual imperialist of either type I have described. In other words, one might be content to admit that there are some psychological phenomena that (certainly, probably, possibly) cannot be understood computationally. As Haugeland (1978) has pointed out in a recent critique of 'Cognitivism', such a position would be very tame unless at least some prima facie unsuitable phenomena were said to be intelligible in computational terms.

Psychological phenomena very commonly said to be unsuited to computational concepts, so lying outside any area open to AI-colonization, include consciousness, creativity, emotion, moods and motor skills. Suggestions were made in the previous section as to how consciousness might be illuminated to some degree, if not completely demystified, by thinking about the relevant data as being generated by computational processes. And elsewhere (Boden, 1972, 1977) I have defended the relevance of the computational viewpoint in each of the other cases also.

But even were such a defence to fail, it would remain an open question whether AI-resistant phenomena were intelligible in any other terms of theoretical psychology. By this I mean two things, first that the appropriate theory or explanation might be non-psychological (non-intentional). For instance, Fodor (1976) has argued that certain aspects of creativity and emotions might not be open to a computational explanation, being explained rather in physiological terms. But (admittedly because he defines 'psychological' in terms of 'computational' processes, and both in terms of intentional concepts), the upshot would be - surprisingly perhaps - that these matters were not within the purview of theoretical psychology at all. Second, there might be no appropriate theory, whether psychological or not. If it were the case that some aspects of the human

intelligible in general theoretical terms at all, but can only be
ne sort of insight (a position seemingly held by some proponents of
ction' and idiographic explanation in psychology, see Meehl, 1954),
y whatever could be adequate to characterize them. The most we could
that our individual human 'intuition' could be prompted and deepened by
dramatic insights, while scientific approaches of any sort would be
out of place. This view is popular in some circles, and it is difficult
some sympathy with it, but we should recognize its consequences. If
an mind is untheorizable, then AI is out - but so too are all other
al psychologies.
ally, and in connection with the charges of dehumanization that are often
d at the artificial intelligentsia, we must recognize that to see AI as
nt to psychology is not to assume that people are really computers. It is
misleading to say that it is to regard people as very like computers, because
basic metaphysical 'model of man' that is suggested in many people's minds by
is comparison is a thoroughly inhuman one. Computers are metallic machines, not
living creatures; and they owe their existence entirely to their being fashioned by
human beings for our own, human, purposes. As such, it is said, they can be
attributed none of the purposes or properties that concern psychologists. Even a
rat, a pigeon, or a lowly flatworm can prompt some degree of fellow-feeling, some
hope that their antics might be interestingly like our own and so worthy of the
psychologist's consideration. But utterly different attitudes and attributions, it
seems, are appropriate to computers on the one hand and living beings on the
other.

Tweedledum and Tweedledee made a similar point in relation to models made of
wax, not metal:

'If you think we're wax-works', said the one marked "DUM", 'you ought to pay
you know. Wax-works weren't made to be looked at for nothing. Nohow!'
    'Contrariwise', added the one marked "DEE", 'if you think we're alive,
you ought to speak.'

But speaking to one another, if we are indeed essentially no different from
computers, must surely be a radically illusory enterprise. Instead of effecting
sympathetic communication between living minds, it can only mediate basically
mechanistic and essentially meaningless responses, such as those elicited when the
teletypes of two 'language' programs are interconnected. There could hardly be a
more dehumanizing implication than this.

However, this depressing conclusion does not in fact follow from the AI-
approach to psychology, not even from the most aggressively imperialist form. And
this for two reasons, one 'positive' and one 'negative'.

The positive reason is that AI concentrates on the internal representations and
symbolic transformations that underlie various and changing interpretations of the
world (including the system itself). Intentionality is thus a core concept for AI,
as for humanist, hermeneutic, and cognitive psychologies in general. What is more,
far from forcing us to undervalue the mind, AI leads us to acknowledge its
staggering power and representational potential (Hofstadter, 1979). It points to
the awe-inspiring subtlety and richness of the human mind, a psychological
complexity that has been intuitively appreciated by many (though by no means all)
psychological theories, but which no other approach has illuminated in such
explicit detail as the AI-approach promises to do.

The negative reason is that the attempt to produce a theory to explain some
phenomenon is not the same as the attempt to build some simulacrum of that
phenomenon: a theory of the mind models but does not mimic it. Admittedly, if one
were interested in building a simulacrum of something, then one would expect the
theoretical representation of it to be highly relevant (so science is needed for
science-fiction). And some aggressive imperialists do believe that some imaginable
computer program could in principle merit the literal ascription of the entire

range of our vocabulary of consciousness (cf. Sloman, 1978). But then, though indeed like Alice we 'ought to speak', we would in fact be speaking to beings no less conscious than Tweedledum and Tweedledee (cf. Dennett, 1979). The AI-imperialist need claim no more, however, than that computational theories, like the solar-system theory of the atom, are analogies, which break down at a certain point.

I have argued elsewhere (Boden, 1972, 1977) that one important point where the computer analogy breaks down (and will always break down) is the artificiality of computers. Because computers can have no purposes of their own in the same sense in which human beings (and animals) have purposes of their own, psychological terms - such as purpose, knowledge, intelligence, speak, communicate ... - cannot be literally applied to any conceivable computer. This is of course not to deny that a computer could generate a 'purpose' that had not been foreseen by its programmer, or that went against the programmer's purposes. Nor is it to deny that many generations of self-modifying programs might separate the program in question from the original human programmers - who might even be dead, along with all their conspecifics. But, in the last analysis, computers are man-made as babies are not, and have no intrinsic purposes at all.

So there is a very basic human sense in which it would be as inappropriate to speak to a computer program, no matter how sophisticated, as to speak to a waxwork. But even if we cannot really speak to programs, but only 'speak' to them, as psychologists we can nevertheless learn from them.

EDITED DISCUSSION

I. ROTH: I should like to ask you about the criteria for validating or refuting theories in AI. You have, I think quite rightly, pointed out that there are few, if any, theories in psychology. But is there not a danger that with the enormous power of the computational approach there are actually too many theories and too few, or too unclear, criteria to choose between them?

M. A. BODEN: The aggressive imperialist would say that we cannot yet write even one program ...

I. ROTH: But in principle it is possible to produce a great range of solutions to a single cognitive problem. When you, at some time in the future, have that range of solutions, how do you choose between them?

M. A. BODEN: Well, first, this problem is no worse for the AI-approach than for any other. Second, every aspect of this theory is explicit. So that, for instance, if you had two programs which performed the same task, and where a particular feature was present in the one but not in the other, then clearly that particular feature would not be a universal computational necessity. Writing more and more programs should help clarify which features of the programs have theoretical relevance. Then it is a question of using your ingenuity and trying to plan experiments which will capture those features just as in any other case.

S. G. STRADLING: What exactly are the AI-imperialists better at? You gave us some nice examples about how these people claim that all questions in psychology can be 'illuminated', for example, by this approach; casting questions in computational terms makes problems more 'intelligible'; and the best way of 'thinking about' problems is in computational terms. Is it not the case that traditional psychology is equipped to do all the things you have mentioned - illuminating, making intelligible, thinking about, articulating, explaining?

M. A. BODEN: I do not think it is good on articulating. I think that it can do the other things, but then I am not an aggressive imperialist. If I were, you would get a different and slightly dustier answer. But certainly traditional psychology is not good on articulation. It is not even good on realizing when articulation is called for. That is the real strength of the AI-approach. It is an approach which gives a clearly specifiable way of imagining different ways in which psychological processes might go on. It gives a basis from which you can try to generate empirical hypotheses to test theories.

M . J. MORGAN: The computational approach, as well as making obsolete some of the traditional philosophical arguments in psychology, is doing it on a much wider front in biology. I am thinking here particularly of what it is doing for the study of embryology, which greatly resembles psychology in its state of development and even in the level of concepts used. The traditional argument in biology has been between mechanists and vitalists. That is similar to the one we have had to face. The vitalists pointed to the inability of simple mechanisms to account for what is going on in the developing embryo and, furthermore, they very reasonably asked what it could possibly mean to talk about genes containing characters. Well, the computational approach would now see the genetic influence upon development as corresponding to the nature of the program. The genes give the developing organism a program for development, and 'mechanism', in the old sense, would seem to be dead in embryology; and the controversy has gone with it.

J . A. GRAY: Dr Boden, I find your paper enormously illuminating for the problems we have been facing at this Conference. I think you pose in an acute form the question, 'What do the humanist psychologists want to get out of humanist psychology?' It is obvious from your paper that the concepts of 'intentionality' and 'subjectivity' are concepts which are manageable intellectually (and the humanists have already been telling us that) and which can be made to work on a machine. The example of the experiment by Rumbaugh and colleagues shows that the concept of 'intentionality' must be applied to animal behaviour as well. Some of the programs for human and animal behaviour will presumably have a great deal in common. The question for the humanist psychologist is, 'If it turns out that your humanist psychology is applicable to computing machines and to animals, will you give it up and try to produce some other kind of psychology which will only be applicable to human beings?' Let us take language as an analogy. Since Chomsky's original work, and as monkeys have been observed to do more and more of the things that were considered to be exclusively human, language has been successively redefined so as to eliminate from the definition anything a monkey can do. I have a second point. You disclaimed the notion that there is a single, central problem of consciousness. As I see it such a problem does exist: how does sensation arise out of a conglomeration of physical units? I do not see how AI can illuminate that one. On the other hand, I agree with you that nothing at the moment can.

M. A. BODEN: Taking the second point first: yes, you are basically right. But many aspects, even of phenomenological experience, which are commonly assumed to be totally mysterious philosophically, and certainly not compatible with an AI-approach, can be illuminated. Cases of 'multiple personality', mentioned in the chapter, apply here. Now your first point. Well we do have language in ways which chimps do not ...

J . A. GRAY: But, wait! You must tell me in which ways. Each way that Chomsky enumerated has subsequently proved to be wrong by what Washoe and other chimpanzees have been shown to do.

M . A. BODEN: Well, not each way yet: it is still an open question whether chimps (even Premack's Sarah) can use word-order as a generative syntactic device as we can; there is no evidence that Washoe can. In any event we can think of two programs, one of which is much richer in terms of structure, content and potential for inferential processes. In the same way human language is richer than that of chimps. We have a much richer understanding than chimps do. Questions arise then as to whether there are aspects of behaviour which are unique to human beings. Obviously there are: chimps do not form political parties, design and fly planes, or write books. The question then is, 'Are they inherently mysterious?' Now, there are psychologists who hold the view that they have a certain intuitive understanding of the human psyche which cannot possibly be expressed formally or theoretically.   If that is true then obviously AI is out, but so then is any other science of psychology.

J. A. GRAY: It seems to me that one has to distinguish between methodological and theoretical imperialism.   All scientific theories are imperialistic to the extent that they are good theories: the point of any scientific theory is to strive towards the greatest generality.   Methodological imperialism on the other hand imposes severe constraints on advancement.   It is inexcusable to try to impose just one method to the exclusion of others.   No one method on its own is likely to get us very far.   A second point is perhaps more fundamental to the Conference.   Concerning the discussion of intentionality and purposiveness in Dr Boden's chapter, there are strong parallels with my own presentation here (paper 2).   She has demonstrated how in AI the concepts which have been claimed to be special to conscious, intentional, purposive human behaviour can be instantiated in computer programs and run on machines.   She has also demonstrated how those same kinds of concepts have to be applied to animal behaviour.   Now, if it is agreed that both machines and animals are capable of displaying behaviour with all the features of intentionality which have been taken as specially human by humanist psychologists, then do humanist psychologists wish to erect some new fence to circumscribe that which is exclusively human?   That is essentially the problem that has been with us for the past 200 years: successively one has gone from spinal cord to brain, and so on (see pp. 318-321).

Chapter 11

The structure of effective psychology: Man as a problem-solver

C. I. Howarth

SYNOPSIS OF THE ARGUMENT

In this chapter I present a model of man as a problem-solver, based on the assumption that successful problem-solving involves the following three elements in a proper relationship:

(a) an agreed purpose to be achieved;

(b) well-understood resources to be brought to bear in solving the problem; and

(c) an effective strategy for making the best use of the resources available.

This simple model has several implications.

I argue that these three elements also describe the structure of effective psychology and that the psychologist's proper function is to act as a facilitator of human problem-solving. This view of psychology reconciles the apparently conflicting views of humanists and mechanists, since humanists tend to study human values and purposes while mechanists tend to study the limitations of human resources. Both are needed if we are to formulate strategic solutions to human problems. This structure is observable in the work of all effective psychologists.

The three elements of the model can be elaborated and extended into a theoretical structure of great power and complexity. Some existing theories of artificial intelligence (AI) already have this structure. The time seems to be ripe for a return to 'big' theories in psychology, but the complexity required can only be achieved by computer simulation.

This model of man is also a theory of knowledge related to the pragmatism of William James, John Dewey and George Herbert Mead. It suggests that ideas must be evaluated in terms of their effectiveness, and are only truly known when they have been evaluated.

Evaluation is ultimately a social process and the social structures within which it occurs have the same form as our model of man. This extends the pragmatic theory of knowledge and allows the effectiveness of the social structures themselves to be evaluated.

Finally, the model of man as a problem-solver enables us to formulate rules for the conduct of applied psychology. This creates a common theoretical framework for academic and applied psychology.

ARE WE REALLY UNCERTAIN ABOUT THE NATURE OF PSYCHOLOGY?

We are often told that psychology is in a state of crisis: that the old ways are bankrupt, or that a radical 'new look' will transform them. I am now old enough to have observed that the bankrupt procedures remain in business, and to know that 'new looks' become old fashioned as rapidly in psychology as they do elsewhere. Our subject seems to have a greater stability than is comprehensible from a study of alternative descriptions of it.   It may be the theoretical and philosophical accounts of the nature of psychology which are faulty.

Current practice seems to be richer, more interesting, and more coherent than any existing theoretical accounts of it.   I attempt here to describe this stability, which can be observed across quite long spans of time and also in the practice of many different kinds of psychology.   Psychologists already behave 'as if' they are working within a clearly structured theoretical framework and psychology appears to be 'preparadigmatic' in the Kuhnian sense, only because the paradigm has not been explicitly formulated.   By studying the structure of effective practice, we can see how the implicit paradigm could be made explicit. Fortunately we have many examples of effective practice in psychology and these examples have a pleasing coherence.   Their theoretical implications are both dramatic and simple.

Ideological conflicts in psychology

The implicit coherence is most strikingly demonstrated by the similarity in the practice of people who give the most divergent accounts of their own activity.   I follow Margaret Boden (1977), and almost every other contributor to this volume, in classifying psychologists into two opposing camps, the humanists and the mechanists. (Let us, please, avoid the ugly, germanic back-formations, 'humanistic' and 'mechanistic'.)   The differences between these two are very great at a theoretical, even ideological, level.   Humanists tend towards 'idealism': that is, they believe that the essence of knowledge lies within the ideas which we have about the nature of the world.   Mechanists tend towards 'realism': that is, they believe that the essence of knowledge is in the nature of the real world and that we possess knowledge only when our ideas match that reality.   Humanists prefer 'mentalist' and 'holist' explanations.   Mechanists prefer 'materialist' and 'reductionist' explanations.   Humanists believe in 'free will', mechanists deny its existence.   Humanists place great reliance on 'introspective evidence', while mechanists often adopt a dogmatic 'behaviourist' line.   Humanists are pre-occupied with human values and purposes.   Mechanists spend their time investigating human limitations and resources.

I would not expect any single psychologist to meet all these defining characteristics of either mechanist or humanist psychology.   Nevertheless these caricatured positions do correspond to the main ideological and theoretical divisions among psychologists today, and these divisions are often very unsympathetic to each other.   Humanists claim, with some justification, that mechanists provide only an impoverished account of human nature.   This may be because they deliberately cut themselves off from the rich descriptions of human nature which are to be found in the wider humanist tradition in our culture, which is of course not all psychological.   Mechanists claim, again with some justification, that humanists are careless in their attitudes to evidence.   This may be a consequence of taking an idealist view of the nature of knowledge.

In what follows, let me try to demonstrate that humanists and mechanists differ much less in practice than they do in theory.   They may attempt, for theoretical reasons, to establish clear differences in practice, but there is a strong tendency for their practices to drift towards each other (as has been described in the opening chapter by Joynson).   But before giving more examples of this I shall now present a simple resolution of the apparent conflict between humanism and mechanism. This argument is post hoc, in that it grew out of my observations of practice, but it is so simple that it now seems blindingly obvious, and it does provide a framework into which it is equally easy to fit either mechanist or humanist psychology.

An 'effective' resolution of the conflict between humanism and mechanism

It is possible to reconcile the humanist and mechanist approaches, if one assumes that psychology should be effective: that is, that it should meet the needs, theoretical or practical, of those who use it. This seems a relatively desirable and harmless requirement. There are of course alternative goals one could set. For example, one might wish psychology to be aesthetically satisfying or morally uplifting. My argument cannot be derived from these, but follows very simply from the requirement that psychology be effective. Hence the title of this contribution. To be effective implies making the best use of resources to meet a purpose.

It has already been pointed out that humanists tend to concentrate on human values and purposes, while mechanists study our limitations and resources. To be effective, a psychologist must clarify human purposes, making use of techniques derived from or related to the humanist tradition. He must also have a clear idea of human limitations and resources, derived from studies within the behaviourist and mechanist traditions. So, to be effective, a psychologist cannot be exclusively humanist or mechanist, but must be both. The two approaches are not in conflict, but are complementary.

In a military context, ways of achieving a purpose by making the best use of resources are called 'strategies'. The same word is used by many psychologists with exactly the same significance (e.g. Bruner et al., 1956). Moreover, the same concept is used, even more frequently, under different names such as 'plans' (Miller et al., 1960), 'hypotheses' (Krechevski, 1932), 'habit family hierarchies' (Hull, 1951), 'schemata' (Bartlett, 1932) or powers (Harré & Secord, 1972). The variety of words disguises the similarity of the ideas and may have prevented us from recognizing the coherence of present practice and its far-reaching theoretical implications. To be effective, psychologists must be both humanists and mechanists, and must conspire with their clients and subjects to devise effective strategies to meet negotiated purposes.

This view of psychology sees man as essentially a problem-solver and the role of the psychologist as a facilitator of solutions to problems.

A SOCIAL ANTHROPOLOGICAL AND 'HERMENEUTIC' STUDY OF CURRENT PRACTICE

In this section, I give some examples of the similarity in practice of different types of psychology. In it I adopt the approach of the social anthropologist, making use of my experience as a participant observer in some activities, and as a non-participant observer of others. Since most of the evidence quoted comes from the published accounts which psychologists give of their own work, this section could also be regarded as an exercise in 'hermeneutic' psychology.

Purposive concepts in mechanist psychology

Let me now try to demonstrate that purposive concepts can be found within the mechanist traditions, even when the word itself is avoided and the strongest possible protests made about the meaninglessness of such ideas as purpose and intention. In this endeavour, a prime difficulty is that different words may be used for the same ideas, while the concept of purpose can itself be subdivided into at least three different but related ideas. In order of increasingly humanist ambience, these are 'purpose-as-goal', 'biological purpose' and 'intentional purpose'.

The first of these refers to the end-point of an action, as when one says that the purpose of a thermostat is to keep the temperature of a room constant, or that the purpose of a batsman in cricket is to score runs. The word may be used in this way in relation to simple or complex systems, mechanical or human. This meaning of the word is now equally consistent with either a mechanist or a humanist position, although mechanists used to dislike it before the development of control theory during the 1940s.

The second meaning refers to the need to keep a system in existence, as when one says that the purpose of the mating instinct is to ensure the survival of the species. Because this concept is frequently met in a biological context, I have used the familiar term 'biological purpose', but we use the word in the same sense when we say that the purpose of a safety valve is to stop a boiler from blowing itself up, and destroying the valve in the process. For this reason, it might be useful to coin a less familiar but more general phrase, 'survival purpose'. This meaning of the word now seems to be equally compatible with either a mechanist or a humanist position, although it has created some difficulties for both in the past.

The third meaning, 'purpose-as-intention', is perhaps the one which is most commonly used in everyday life. In this sense it implies deliberate action taken in conscious knowledge of its consequences. This kind of purpose could only be exhibited by a very complex system with a degree of self-awareness, and humanists tend to believe it is an exclusively human characteristic. Some mechanists try to deny its existence, while others try to imagine how a machine might exhibit this kind of purpose. It is this meaning of the word which most divides mechanists and humanists.

I would now like to do two things, firstly, to demonstrate that there is no reason why mechanists should avoid using the concept of intentional purpose and, secondly, to give examples of their doing so, sometimes explicitly, sometimes in a covert manner.

The logical argument has been presented extensively by Boden in a number of publications. I shall therefore summarize it as briefly as I can (see also chapter 10, by Boden). Purpose-as-goal and intentional purpose are related, in that the latter always implies the former but not vice versa. Nevertheless, intentional purpose cannot be reduced to purpose-as-goal because intention implies a greater degree of complexity and some new relationships between the elements of the system. Boden (1970) has suggested that these will 'include reference to its perceptual classifications (which may be faulty), to its hypotheses and beliefs (which may be false), to the tricks and heuristics it relies on in situations of difficulty (which may mislead it)'. To put it more simply, the whole is greater than the sum of its parts because new principles of organization are required to deal with systems of greater complexity. These principles of organization, as in Boden's examples, can create entities which have no real existence except within the structure of the system itself. When the system is functioning efficiently, these entities (perceptual classifications, etc.) can be related to the structure of the environment in which the system operates. But when it is not functioning efficiently, these entities may have no relationship to the environment. The more complex the system, the more ways there are for it to go wrong. The greater the need, therefore, for monitoring the effectiveness of different forms of organization, and for making sensible choices between them. The concept of intention is related to this activity and the greater the complexity of intelligent machines, the greater the resemblance between the ways in which machines make these choices and the ways in which people make intentional decisions. In either case, it is impossible to describe what is happening without reference to those entities without real existence, which are the relationships between the elements in the system.

So much for the logical arguments. Now for some examples of the use of the concept of intention by mechanists. Overt uses of the concept are most frequently found when they are talking or writing metapsychology, that is, discussing the framework in which their work is done. A good example of this is Skinner's 'Beyond Freedom and Dignity' (1971). In that undervalued book, he argues that the 'literature of freedom and dignity' (which is largely humanist in the wider sense) helps us to protect ourselves from those who would control us by punishment and coercion, but leaves us at the mercy of those who seek to control us with rewards and inducements, such as advertisers, politicians and the entertainment industry. I am not here concerned with the rights and wrongs of that argument (although its interest and importance seem self-evident) but merely wish to point out that Skinner is making use of the concept of intentional purpose when he claims that, if we 'wish' to protect ourselves from all forms of exploitation, then we can do so by 'making use of' the technology of behaviourism. Skinner has never hesitated to write in this way. He would no doubt claim that he is using the words as a shorthand for complex but more intellectually respectable concepts.

I would argue that, even when paraphrased into clumsy behaviourist or mechanist language, the essential characteristics of the concept remain. This one might call a covert use of the concept of intention. These covert uses of the concept can be observed when mechanists and behaviourists are attempting to deal with complex forms of behaviour, which nevertheless may be considerably simpler than writing books on metapsychology. The more adequate the mechanists' attempts to deal with complex behaviour, the more difficult it is to distinguish mechanist and humanist language in operational terms. One example of this can be found in behaviourist accounts of depression. Seligman (1974) has compared depression with the 'learned helplessness' which is a consequence of repeated failure in both animals and men. It can be regarded as the negative aspect of 'learning sets' which were studied by Harlow (1949) and others. The humanist would regard both as expressions of the subject's willingness to attempt solutions to problems, to formulate hypotheses and try new strategies. This view is supported by the observation that recovery from depression, during treatment with either drugs or the type of behaviour therapy which Seligman recommends, usually takes some time. When asked about this, the patient may explain it by saying he was thinking about his problems and eventually sorted them out. He may even say, explicitly, that he 'decided' to behave differently or to interpret things differently. This kind of evidence for the reality and quality of mental life is both compelling and widespread. The behaviourist may deny the importance of the phenomena or the validity of the subjective evidence. He may then seek to explain the delayed effects of treatment in terms of the delayed effects of reinforcement, or the interaction of complex learned patterns of behaviour. The more successful these explanations, the more the language of the behaviourist comes to resemble the frankly mentalist language which other people use.

Seligman himself is not an extreme behaviourist, but what he describes as a 'subjective behaviourist'. The flavour of his particular combination of behaviourism and humanism is conveyed by the following quotation. Even, he writes, when 'the probability of the outcome is the same whether or not the response of interest occurs, learning will take place. Behaviorally this will tend to diminish the initiation of responding to control the outcome; cognitively, it will produce a belief in the inefficiency of responding, and difficulty at learning that responding succeeds; and emotionally, when the outcome is traumatic, it will produce heightened anxiety, followed by depression' (1974).

But even the most unrepentant behaviourist implicitly postulates entities without real existence when dealing with such problems as 'conditioned reinforcement' (also called secondary reinforcement) whereby an animal may be induced to work for an unrewarding stimulus because the latter has, in the past, been associated with a reward. It is difficult to escape the conclusion that the animal 'expects' that a reward may be associated with the conditioned reinforcer and that this 'expectation' is itself worth working for. Even when the behaviourist avoids using the word 'expectation' the concept is implicit in the (necessarily more complex) way in which he describes the problem.

The concept of 'anxiety' is one which (unlike the concept of expectation) the behaviourists have never succeeded in eliminating. It was first studied using conditioning techniques by Estes & Skinner (1941) in a paper entitled 'Some quantitative properties of anxiety'. They found that lever-pressing activity could be suppressed by the sound of a pure tone which had previously been associated with an electric shock to the rat's feet. Most important, however, was that the shock had never been given while the tone continued, only when the tone ceased. Nevertheless, lever pressing was suppressed during the whole of the time the tone was on, even if the shock never followed the tone when it was being used to suppress lever pressing. The last three sentences are deliberately written in aseptic behaviourist prose. They imply that something is going on when the tone is heard and that this something is interfering with the lever pressing. The concept of anxiety is unavoidable, and indeed Estes & Skinner did not, in this instance, try to avoid it. And if the concept of anxiety is unavoidable, so are the concepts of expectation and purpose, even if the words themselves are not used.

Behaviourists and mechanists are more willing to make use of the concept of biological purpose although it resembles in uncomfortable ways the vitalists' concept of the 'life force'. Like intentional purpose, it is based on entities with no real existence. For example, the purpose of mating cannot be explained in terms of the goal-directed mechanisms involved in sexual reproduction. Since evolution involves competition, biological purpose only has meaning in relation to alternative but less efficient ways of doing things. These may have real existence, in competing but less successful species, but in most cases the alternatives are entirely imaginary. No reductionist explanation of biological purpose can be given. Nevertheless, mechanists make frequent and effective use of the concept to guide and inform their research.

A nice example of this is to be found in Cowey's recent Grindley Memorial Lecture (1979). In it he describes his work on the architecture of the visual areas of the brain. He generously acknowledges his debt to Grindley who, when Cowey was a young research worker, posed him three questions about the topography of the visual areas of the brain. These were 'Why is there a map of the retina in the brain?' 'Why is there more than one map?' and 'Why are the maps mirror images of each other?'

After approximately 20 years' work, Cowey can justify some rather neat answers to the first two, but is still having trouble with the third. He suggests that a map is necessary in order to take full advantage of local mechanisms such as lateral inhibition. More than one map may be necessary beause several kinds of analysis need to be done on the visual signal, and cortical connections could not be kept short if all of them were done within the confines of the same map.

Cowey seems to dislike the word 'purpose' since he does not use it in his paper. This may be because he dislikes the unreal entities it implies. Nevertheless, his persuasive answers to two of Grindley's questions depend upon a comparison between the topographic organization which he observes in the brain, and other possible structures which do not exist.

Purpose-as-goal is now even more readily acceptable to most mechanists although this is a comparatively recent development. Many psychologists, such as Hull (1943), using words such as 'teleology' and 'entelechy' as synonyms for what I have called purpose-as-goal, derided the concept as totally unscientific, and even claimed that it would be impossible to build machines with such a property. Miller et al. (1960) who themselves played a big part in making the concept acceptable, acknowledged their debt to Rosenblueth et al. (1943) and to Ashby (1940), who showed that negative error feedback is essential to the design of all stable machines. Negative error feedback is yet another synonym for purpose-as-goal.

Error is itself an entity with no real existence outside the structure of the system within which it occurs. But this difficulty no longer worries even the most extreme mechanist. The behaviourist technique of 'shaping' an animal's behaviour by rewarding closer and closer approximations to the desired actions, is an explicit application of this concept. It is also central to all modern work on skilled movements.

Although all three types of purpose imply entities with no real existence, mechanists do not reject all of them. Historically one can see a steady erosion of their dislike of purposive concepts, as they have been translated into more acceptable language. The concept of intention is still not totally accepted although it may be used explicitly when discussing metapsychology or in a heavily disguised form when giving theoretical accounts of complex behaviour. If one accepts Boden's arguments, the mechanists' objections to the concept of intention are as unnecessary as earlier objections to the concepts of purpose-as-goal or biological purpose.

When discussing the different meanings of the word purpose, it is tempting to concentrate on the differences between them. But for our present discussion their similarities are more important. All life is a struggle against the 'final solution' implied by the second law of thermodynamics. Our rearguard action against the encroachment of disorder and decay depends upon the integrity of many interrelated feedback systems. As life forms have become more complex, the structure of these systems has become more complex. As their complexity increases, they develop characteristics which are not present in the simpler systems. Nevertheless, their stability depends, logically, on the presence of error feedback in their structure. In most life forms this stability is overdetermined, or to use Ashby's term, they are 'ultrastable'. This simply means that they have many different ways of preserving their stability. Compare, for example, the stability of a statue with that of a man. When the statue is pushed beyond its point of equilibrium it will fall over and remain that way. When a man is pushed, he will push back, or evade the blow. Even if he is pushed over, he will get up again. Each of these methods of remaining on his feet can be seen as an expression of purpose-as-goal, even when the action is unconscious. But to make the best use of all our resources requires some superordinate activity by which a choice can be made between the alternatives. It is in solving these problems that the phenomena of consciousness and of intention play their part.

Mechanist concepts in humanist psychology

It is a simple matter to demonstrate the use of mechanist concepts in humanist psychology, provided one accepts that a mechanism is something which can be used as a resource to achieve a purpose. Mechanisms are usually defined in terms of their relationship to the causal laws of physics or to finite state systems. In a later section, I try to show that these definitions are unsatisfactory and that a definition in terms of use is to be preferred. For the present, all I wish to do is to show that purposes can themselves be used as resources and in doing so take on the role of mechanisms.

For example, although Freud now gets more credit from humanists than from mechanists, he thought of himself as a natural scientist and his thinking was frequently of a mechanist kind. The conflict of repressed and conscious motives could be regarded as a misuse of resources. The resolution of conflicting motives during therapy serves the higher purposes of alleviating the patient's misery or allowing him to lead a more productive life.

Another example is the definition of values by law or by social convention. This is often done, not as an end in itself but as a means of achieving a higher purpose. To take some examples from work on road safety - the 30 mph speed limit, the definition of rights of way, and the law about responsibility for accidents on zebra crossings, all have the higher purpose of saving lives, although they act as guides to action when they themselves are regarded as purposes to be aimed at or observed. In my own work on road accidents involving child pedestrians, I have for many years looked for mechanist solutions in terms of better safety training and highway engineering. My colleagues and I have now come to the conclusion that, although worth pursuing, these remedies will never by themselves have a dramatic effect. We are now suggesting (e.g. Howarth & Repetto-Wright, 1978) that the best single way to save children's lives is to re-think the conventions of responsibility and blame. Drivers are now routinely excused responsibility because 'the child ran heedlessly into the road and there was nothing the driver could do to avoid the accident.' This excuse does not stand up to logical examination since, at the moment the driver was unable to avoid the accident, the child was equally unable to do anything about it. Observation of drivers shows that they do not modify their behaviour because of the possible presence of children. Common sense suggests that in these situations, which are dangerous to children but not to drivers, only a change in the law is likely to force the latter to behave with proper adult responsibility.

This way of thinking about the attribution of responsibility is related to Shotter's description (chapter 2) of persons as accountable elements in a social system. He may not welcome my description of his ideas and mine as essentially mechanist. But I think it is justified because we are both suggesting that the purposes and values of the individual must be related to social values in a hierarchical manner.

The growth of the concept of strategy

Since mechanist thinking can be found in humanist psychology and vice versa, we would expect to find some attempts at synthesis, and indeed there have been many. So many, in fact, that to try to catalogue them serves chiefly to reveal the limitations of one's scholarship. Dewey's paper on 'The reflex arc concept in psychology' (1896) is a notable example, but I suspect there are many earlier ones. Bartlett in 'Remembering' (1932), Miller et al. in 'Plans and the Structure of Behaviour' (1960), Deutsch in 'The Structural Basis of Behavior' (1960), Newell & Simon in 'Human Problem Solving' (1972), and Boden in 'Artificial Intelligence and Natural Man' (1977) are some of the authors who have had most influence on me personally. No doubt many more examples could be produced.

An interesting recent development has been the use of the concept of strategy to overcome difficulties in the study of human information processing. Following Broadbent (1958) and others, people who study human information processing have attempted to discover and describe mechanisms through which information is processed, such as iconic memory, primary acoustic store, working memory, attentional filters, pattern recognition devices and so on. Inferences are made about these mechanisms by studying the responses people make when presented with information varying in complexity and speed and when the responses make varying demands on memory or skill. In other words, the human is treated as an input-output device of unknown internal structure. The difficulty about this approach is that there is always an excess of theories to explain any data. An example of this is our difficulty in deciding whether information is being processed in series or in parallel. Serial systems can, under certain circumstances mimic parallel systems and vice versa. I have myself attempted to come to grips with this problem. Bloomfield and I suggested that 'In everyday life, we make economical contact with our environment by approaching it in an orderly fashion. The strategies we use in doing so have been largely ignored' and that 'theories of selective attention and information processing should be related ... to subjects' strategies for acquiring information, by making full use of studies of eye movements and other overt actions' (Howarth & Bloomfield, 1971).

This neglect of naturally occurring strategies is now a thing of the past. A good illustration of this is the book edited by Underwood (1978) on 'Strategies of Information Processing'. The power of this approach is illustrated in my own chapter in that book. In it (Howarth, 1978) is summarized the work of Beggs and myself on the relationship between speed and accuracy of skilled movement. Others, such as Fitts (1954) and Welford (1968), have taken a black box approach to this problem. In contrast we asked ourselves what overt strategies people use when trying to move quickly and accurately. The most striking finding was that people try to get as close to the target as quickly as possible so as to leave time to make small corrections just before hitting it. This led us to study the trajectory of the hand as it approaches a target and to our surprise we found that the form of the mathematical function relating speed and accuracy is entirely determined by the mathematical form of this trajectory. The essence of the process is not hidden within a black box. It is clearly revealed in overt and easily observed features of behaviour.

This approach can be generalized and enables us to see that many other features of skilled movement and spatial perception can be treated as strategic adaptations to problems we have in controlling our complexly articulated bodies. This led me to relate such diverse phenomena as autokinesis, ventriloquism and adaptation to spatial distortions, within a single theoretical framework. The study of strategies not only leads to easier experiments, it is also a powerful source of theoretical ideas.

Strategic concepts in applied psychology

Some of the clearest demonstrations of the complementary nature of humanist and mechanist approaches, and of their tendency to converge, are to be found in applied psychology. Purely mechanist or purely humanist applied psychologies have been relatively ineffective for reasons which seem obvious in terms of the argument presented in the section beginning on page 145. Recent developments in clinical, educational and occupational psychology can all be seen as moves towards a problem-solving approach.

Psychoanalysis could be regarded as a form of humanist applied psychology, although as I have pointed out, Freud himself was something of a mechanist. The basic tenet of psychoanalysis is that neuroses are caused by the conflict between repressed, unconscious desires and conscious, socially acceptable motives. The neurotic behaviour, such as hysterical paralysis, or loss of memory or anxiety, or depression, is believed to represent the repressed wish in a symbolic and therefore cryptic form. Analysis, by uncovering the nature of the repressed wishes or memories, cracks the symbolic code, so that the patient has the opportunity to resolve his conflicting, but now fully conscious desires.

This very attractive account of the relationship between conscious and unconscious purposes, fits the wider humanist tradition and, in 'The Interpretation of Dreams' (1900), Freud acknowledged his debt to it. Unfortunately, the results of psychoanalysis are not quite what the theory would lead us to expect. The bizarre symptoms of neurosis often persist even when their 'meaning' becomes apparent to the patient. Indeed, it has proved rather difficult to demonstrate that analysis has any beneficial effect on symptoms. A 'cure' may be claimed when the symptoms persist but the patient no longer finds them so disturbing.

There are several pieces of evidence suggesting that the insight produced by psychoanalysis is not the only source of the changes it produces. For example, Cartwright (1956) has shown that psychotherapy makes, on average, little difference in the rate at which people recover from neurotic symptoms, but that there is greater variability among those who receive treatment than among those who do not. In other words, psychotherapy helps some people, but makes others worse. Whether the outcome is good or bad does not seem to depend on the characteristics of the treatment, but does depend on the characteristics of the patient, the therapist, and on the quality of their relationship (Luborsky et al., 1971). The most successful therapists are warm, rewarding people. Moreover, Truax & Carkhuff (1964) have shown that the psychotherapist may unconsciously provide social reinforcement in a directed manner, which is not very different from the way therapists in a more mechanist tradition seek to modify their patients' behaviour.

The behaviour therapies can be regarded as a mechanist approach to treating neuroses. Their aim is to remove the uncomfortable symptoms without reference to the motives which underlie them and without seeking to increase the patient's understanding of himself. They use positive or negative reinforcement or simple habituation until the symptoms are abolished. Thus phobias are treated by desensitization (a form of habituation), alcoholism by associating nausea with drinking, and bizarre behaviours by rewarding normal and ignoring abnormal behaviour. The main problem with all behaviour modification is that the desired changes may be obtained in the place and in the circumstances in which the therapy is provided but that the symptoms may recur when the patient moves elsewhere. As in the case of psychotherapy, there is more variability in the results than can be accounted for by the procedures used. Again, the quality of the relationship between the patient and the therapist seems to be important (Meyer & Gelder, 1963). In order to reduce the context-specific nature of the relief of symptoms, some forms of behaviour modification are purely conceptual. Phobias may be treated by asking the patient to relax while thinking about the frightening object. Very recently, this has been taken further by the development of 'cognitive behaviour modification' (Kendall & Hollon, in press), in which the patient is asked to think about his problems, and is encouraged or rewarded when he begins to react more sensibly to them. The differences between this form of behaviour therapy and psychotherapy are very slight.

Both psychotherapy and behaviour modification suffer from the same assumption, that the patient can be treated in isolation from the social context in which he experiences his difficulties. A problem for both is the patient's relative inability to cope outside the therapeutic situation. More explicit, problem-solving approaches are now being developed (e.g. Smail, 1977) which solve this problem strategically by persuading relatives, friends, teachers, nurses or anyone else who spends a large part of the day with the patient, to cooperate in the therapeutic process. As a result, the therapy can be applied at least partially in the environment in which the problem arose and for a much greater proportion of the patient's waking life.

Community psychology (e.g. Rappoport et al., 1975) shows similar characteristics. It is based on the belief that psychological difficulties should not be attributed to weaknesses in the individual, or to deficiencies in the environment which shapes him, but to an inappropriate matching of one to the other. The solutions sought by community psychologists are therefore essentially strategic.

Clinical psychologists of all kinds are now beginning to regard themselves as social diagnosticians and problem-solvers. More and more they observe the patient in his normal environment, as well as discussing his difficulties with him. They consult relatives, friends and other professionals, such as doctors and social workers. Then having developed a picture of the whole problem they suggest strategic solutions to the patient's difficulties, which may involve discussing his feelings in group therapy (which has its main effect on the patient's self-image, motives and value systems, but may have a secondary effect on behaviour); or a predetermined regime of rewards and punishments (which has its primary effect on behaviour, but may have secondary effects on motives and values;) or training in specific social skills (which provide him with more effective strategies for solving his problems).

Very similar changes have taken place in educational psychology. The Child Guidance Clinics, which were created after the First World War, adopted a very psychoanalytic approach. The Schools Psychological Service which came into being after the Second World War, took a more mechanist line, using tests to measure children's abilities and personalities (a resource) and giving remedial teaching if these were not adequate. Neither approach was particularly successful.

Like the clinical psychologists, educational psychologists now operate more and more as social diagnosticians and problem-solvers (e.g. Gillham, 1978). They insist that when a child is in difficulties, the 'fault' may lie in the home or the school, rather than in the child, so that the best strategy may not be to provide therapy for the child but to intervene in his social environment. There is an increasing willingness to use other people as sources of information, or as media through which the child can be helped. Again, the intervention may be of a humanist or mechanist variety, or a strategic combination of both, depending on which is considered most appropriate. Wood has found that very different theories of child development lead to very similar practice in the classroom (see Wood, chapter 16). He goes into much greater detail about the nature of these similarities than I have been able to do. I suspect that if the practice of clinical psychology could be subject to the same detailed scrutiny, equally striking similarities would be found.

These changes in clinical and educational psychology were anticipated many years ago in occupational psychology. Although it has not aroused so much theoretical interest (and indeed has met with some ideological antagonism), the practice of occupational psychology has for many years been more clearly formulated than either clinical or educational psychology. It has developed a set of procedures which draw equally on the humanist and mechanist traditions and which facilitate the development of strategic solutions to the problems which people meet at work. These procedures include: (i) Task analysis - which defines the nature of the problem including the purposes to be achieved; (ii) Selection testing - which is a way of assessing the human resources available; (iii) Job design and training - which are strategic manipulations of the available resources; and (iv) Evaluation of the effectiveness of these solutions: the results are fed back into further modifications of the strategies used.

From this brief survey of the practice of different branches of applied psychology, it is apparent that there are great similarities between them. Indeed, the similarities are so great as to raise doubts about the justification for keeping clinical, educational and occupational psychology separate from each other in training or in practice. A recurring theme in all three is the abandoning of narrowly humanist, or narrowly mechanist approaches in favour of a more problem-solving approach.

THEORETICAL IMPLICATIONS OF THE CONCEPT OF STRATEGY

If the unity and coherence, which I have tried to outline, is a reality, then it demands theoretical explanation. After the disappointing results of earlier attempts to develop big theories, psychologists have been content to work with 'mini' theories (see Broadbent, chapter 9). If I am right, then psychologists ought to take up, once again, the challenge of constructing a big theory. If I am right, the new generation of big theories must be even more ambitious than those of the past. They must make proper contact with work on artificial intelligence, they must be consistent with an adequate theory of knowledge and they must describe the structure of individual experience and behaviour. This ambitious enterprise cannot be tackled here so I limit myself to sketching the kind of thing which might be attempted.

Implications for theoretical psychology and artificial intelligence

Some of the most important theoretical problems are at the junction of theoretical psychology and artificial intelligence (AI). Fortunately, a great deal of the necessary groundwork has already been done. Let me now simply list some of the issues which must be tackled.

(i) The theory must have the same basic characteristics at all levels, in its microstructure and its macrostructure. It must also be hierarchically organized so that the purpose or goal at one level of analysis becomes a resource or mechanism at a higher level. Miller et al. (1960) described a system of this kind more than 20 years ago. It could be called a system of 'nested hierarchies'. The example they gave, of knocking nails into a box, shows very clearly how such a system works. If one is analysing, at a lower level, the activity of hammering individual nails, then the purpose is to drive the nail into the wood and the mechanism is the activity of hammering. If one is analysing, at a slightly higher level, the activity of putting lids onto boxes, then driving the nail into the wood becomes the mechanism involved in achieving the purpose of putting the lid firmly on. At each level the mechanism is deployed strategically until the purpose has been satisfied. Progressively higher levels of analysis might include increasing the rate at which things are packed into the boxes, increasing exports, making greater profits or improving the well-being of the workers involved. Some of these may involve conflicting purposes leading to what has sometimes been called a 'heterarchy' rather than a hierarchy. Progressively lower levels of analysis might include hitting a nail on the head, controlling the muscles which move the limb, or nervous activity within the spinal cord.

Effective action, theoretical or practical, depends upon finding the appropriate level of analysis at which strategic changes can be made.

(ii) The system must be capable of learning. The weakness of Miller et al.'s system was that they did not say how it would be modified by learning. Systems which are capable of learning, such as Deutsch's (1960), Newell & Simon's (1972) and various perceptual learning devices (see, e.g. Hunt, 1975), tend to operate at a single level of analysis. We do not yet know the consequences of building a capacity for learning into a large system of nested hierarchies.

(iii) At higher levels of complexity, the system should be capable of resolving its own internal conflicts; that is, it should be able to operate on its own internal structure and 'learn' without overt experience. Problem-solving and theorem-proving programs already have this capacity (see Hunt, 1975).

(iv) Finally it must be capable of some degree of self-awareness and planning. Systems of this type are now being studied by both psychologists and artificial intelligencers (see, e.g. Eisenstadt & Kareev, 1977).

These last two points are the focus of a great deal of research in AI. They are not usually related to the first two. Instead they tend to be solved in rather ad hoc ways appropriate to one type of problem and a particular type of computing power (G.P.S. was not really a general problem-solver). My own hunch, which may not be worth a great deal, since I am not an expert in these fields, is that more general solutions to the third and fourth points will be achieved from advances in the first two. These ideas can only be tested by computer simulation. Theoretical psychologists must improve their understanding of the properties of complex systems.

Implications for theories of knowledge

The concept of strategy also has philosophical implications. For example, theories of knowledge range from idealism to realism but most of them take up some intermediate position. Since a strategy is a way of bringing together the idealist concept of purpose, and the realist concept of a mechanism, the kind of theory I am proposing is another of these intermediate theories of knowledge. Because of its dependence on the concept of effectiveness it is closest to the pragmatism of John Dewey, William James and George Herbert Mead (see Farr, chapter 13).

Its most interesting and original characteristic is its hierarchical (or heterarchical) structure. Strategic solutions can be attempted at any level. When one moves to a lower level of analysis one is attempting a reductionist explanation. When one moves to a higher level of analysis, one is attempting a holist explanation. If the present argument is correct, neither is more fundamental than the other. Instead of seeking fundamental explanations, we should be seeking effective ones, and these can be found at any level. The choice between holism and reductionism becomes a pragmatic one and different choices must be made in different circumstances.

I have also adopted an unusual use of the concept of a mechanism, regarding any resource which can be used strategically to achieve a purpose, as a mechanism. A more common definition of a mechanism is as something which 'can be explained by reference to matter and motion and their laws' (Encyclopedia Brittannica, 1954 edition). In other words, a mechanism is seen as a system whose operations can be accounted for within the laws of physics.

This concept of a mechanism is unsatisfactory because the laws of physics are not well enough known to give a complete explanation of anything, while even those things for which the laws of physics cannot at present provide any explanation, may in the course of time and with the increasing power of physical science, become amenable to physical theory. The laws of physics are themselves too uncertain and change too rapidly to sustain any 'absolute' concept of mechanism. This difficulty is avoided if we assume that the status of a system, whether it be regarded as a mechanism or not, depends upon the use to which it is being put.

An alternative definition of mechanism is to regard it as a device which can be treated as a finite state system (which is a mathematical concept). As in the case of the laws of physics, we do not fully understand the properties of 'finite state systems'. For example, Minsky (1967) has argued that the concept of a mechanism is as difficult to define as is the concept of life. Minsky and others have demonstrated that there are quite severe constraints on what can be achieved by finite state systems. Gauld & Shotter (1977) have suggested that since people seem to be able to transcend these limitations, people cannot be treated as finite state systems. The difficulty about this is that we cannot discover from these various arguments which aspects of human functioning can or cannot be regarded as mechanisms. If, however, we assume that a mechanism is something which can be used strategically to achieve a purpose, then all of these difficulties disappear.

Any pragmatic theory of the nature of knowledge must be able to cope with the problem of deciding between different criteria of effectiveness, and the equally difficult one of deciding who shall apply the criteria. These issues are most appropriately considered in relation to the sociology of knowledge.

Implications for the sociology of knowledge

Nested hierarchies can also be used to describe the social structures within which knowledge grows. The effective working of these structures determines, in part, the effectiveness of the ideas which circulate within them. Returning again to the standpoint of the social anthropologist, one can observe that the evaluation of scientific ideas is a social process which occurs initially within the social structure of science, then within a wider scholarly culture and ultimately within society as a whole. One can debate at which stage the most significant evaluations take place, but successful ideas do spread widely and may be evaluated in many different ways by many different kinds of people.

There seem to be three quite distinct types of evaluation. The first is 'empirical evaluation', the process by which ideas about the nature of the world are tested in terms of their effectiveness as guides to action. The second is 'theoretical evaluation', the process by which ideas are checked according to the effectiveness and consistency of their interaction with other ideas. The third is less familiar. It could be called 'communicative evaluation' and is the process in which ideas are judged by the extent to which they spread through a culture. Ideas which are effective in terms of communicative evaluation, but not in terms of the other two, are mere fashion.   Ideas which satisfy both empirical and theoretical evaluations, but are not effective in communication, are narrow and perhaps trivial.

Communicative evaluation is related to theoretical evaluation in that both depend on the effective interaction of ideas.   They differ, in that theoretical evaluation occurs within a well-defined unit of the social structure, and demands a high degree of logical rigour, while communicative evaluation occurs between units in the social structure and is usually less rigorous.   The most effective ideas satisfy all three criteria and spread widely throughout a culture.   The pragmatic view of knowledge avoids the need to make absolute judgements about the truth or falsity of any idea.   We need not worry if we find that an idea is useful for some purposes while an apparently contradictory idea is useful for different ones (as, for example, it is useful to treat electrons as particles when thinking about what they do when fired from the electron gun in a television set, but to treat them as waves when we are thinking about the diffraction patterns they produce when fired through thin sheets of metal.)   On the other hand, we are justified in feeling pleased when a single idea can be made to do the work which previously required two.

There are divisions in any culture.   Ideas sometimes get stuck within one division and are to that extent less effective.   An important classification distinguishes the levels of practical affairs, applied science and pure science.   Creative communication between these levels is an essential feature of the communicative evaluation of ideas.   Communication is equally important if ideas are to be used to achieve socially defined purposes.   The importance of applied science, as a mediator between the two, is often underestimated, particularly in Britain.   This reduces the likelihood that the solution of social problems will be facilitated by science or by our scholarly culture.

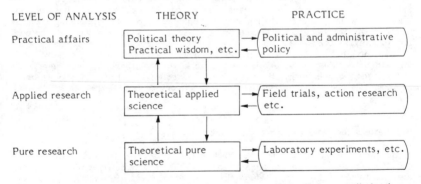

Figure 1.   The structural relationships between practical affairs, applied science and pure science.   Theoretical evaluations occur within the body of theory at each level; empirical evaluations in the relationship between theory and practice.   Communicative evaluations occur between the different levels, and at the same level between different sciences.

When describing the social structures within which knowledge develops and is used, we quickly discover that simple hierarchies are not enough.   As well as describing the structure of individual action, nested hierarchies seem to be needed to account for the complexities of social structures.   Figure 1 shows the schematic relationship between the levels of practical affairs, applied science and pure science.   They are presented as a simple hierarchy.   But parallel structures can be drawn for the many different branches of science, such as engineering and physics, medicine and biology, education and psychology, management, AI, sociology and economics. All of these interact with each other at any level. Moreover, the broad divisions of practical affairs, applied science and pure science can themselves be subdivided almost indefinitely. It is this degree of complexity which I have called a nested hierarchy. If more than one goal is being pursued at the same time then it will become a nested heterarchy. The consequences of this complexity are hard to foresee. The sociology of knowledge, like theoretical psychology, needs a better understanding of the properties of complex structures.

The implications for applied psychology

If we see psychology as a search for better ways to achieve our human purposes despite our limited human resources, then it becomes possible to make positive recommendations about the conduct of applied psychology. Previous codes of conduct have been entirely negative, enjoining us to refrain from harming the client or doing anything without his informed approval. In a forthcoming book (Howarth & Gillham, 1979), I have proposed eight positive rules for the conduct of applied psychology. These are based on the present analysis, plus the principle of generalization. The latter is the well-established finding that the greater the similarity between two situations, the greater the similarity in the behaviour they produce and in the subjective experience of them. The eight rules are:

(i) Help the client to clarify his purposes. Try to understand how he sees the problem and what he would regard as a solution. In this activity the methods of humanist psychology are appropriate.

(ii) Discover the nature of the psychological and other resources available to the client. In this activity the methods of mechanist psychology may prove to be the most useful.

(iii) Seek to understand the client's habitual strategies and life-style.

(iv) In investigating these things, do not work in conceptual or social isolation. Draw on as many sources of information as possible, using a wide range of mechanist and humanist techniques in a pragmatic fashion.

(v) Bear in mind the principle of generalization and study the problem in 'real life' rather than in a special clinic or laboratory.

(vi) Formulate with the client possible modifications of his strategic behaviour. This depends on agreeing with him the appropriate level of analysis at which strategic modification can be achieved.

(vii) Help the client to practise these modifications in the situation in which the problem exists, and as extensively (in time) as possible. Almost always, this will involve working with and through non-professional help.

(viii) Finally, the effects of the intervention should be evaluated with as much statistical scepticism as possible. But the ultimate criterion used in the statistics must be that the client and his associates are satisfied with the solution, provided it does not harm other people. In other words, the solution must meet culturally acceptable standards.

These eight rules, stated baldly, seem so obvious as to be totally banal. But a great deal of traditional applied psychology has violated some or all of them, either because it has adopted a restricted mechanist or humanist approach, or because it operates according to a different model of professional conduct, that of exclusive expertise. This latter assumes that the scientist, making use of truths discovered within his paradigm, develops professional tools which he alone can use and understand. To make effective use of these tools it is assumed that he needs a special environment, a clinic, consulting room or laboratory, and that the people who require his services should visit him there. This model of professional conduct may have some validity in other professions. In psychology it has almost none, because it ignores the client's own abilities as a problem-solver, and fails to take proper account of the social context in which his problems occur.

These rules also demonstrate how a model of man can guide the conduct of applied psychology.   As a result, the latter can now be seen as a genuine application of psychological theory and knowledge, rather than as an ad hoc collection of techniques, held together by nothing more than common sense and professional ambition.

MAN AS A PROBLEM-SOLVER: EVALUATION

This chapter has presented a model of man as a problem-solver. From it I have derived an outline sketch of a theory of psychology, its relationship to the philosophy and the sociology of knowledge, and some rules for the conduct of applied psychology.   None of these ideas is original, although I may be putting them together in a novel way and claiming more for them than their true originators would have wished.

How can these ideas be evaluated? Some of the people to whom they have been presented consider them too vague to be testable, in the sense that they could be modified to encompass almost any conceivable psychology. In other words, it is claimed that these ideas are not refutable. I do not accept this criticism. It seems to me that there are many ways in which these ideas could be shown to be wrong.

My description of the structure of effective psychology could be shown to be wrong by presenting only one exception, one example of successful practice which does not fit. Since I have claimed that all effective action must logically be based upon the strategic use of resources to achieve a purpose, then a logical disproof is possible as well as an empirical refutation.

The structure of the theory, based on nested hierarchies (or heterarchies), could be impossible, unwieldy, or may not have the properties required of it. Computer simulation could demonstrate this and provide powerful evidence against this model of man.

The pragmatic theory of knowledge may be found untenable on philosophical grounds. This would be strong evidence against the model. Equally damaging would be a demonstration that the social world within which knowledge develops and is used, does not have the structure or properties I have ascribed to it.

Finally, if it could be shown that the rules for the conduct of applied psychology are seriously misleading or ineffective, then I would be prepared to abandon the model.

It is quite easy to find people with attitudes which cannot be fitted into my framework. For example, in 1964, Koch wrote 'the continuing existence of psychology as a unified body of knowledge is a confidence trick based only on terminological rhetoric'. This is the most extreme example I know of a failure to recognize the coherence and stability of psychological practice over at least a hundred years. He was misled, as others have been, by the conflicting accounts which psychologists have given of their activities.

There is also a widespread feeling that psychology is still a 'promise of a science', that it is still in its infancy and that it has achieved very little. Such pessimism is based on a failure to observe the effectiveness of a great deal of psychology and on the setting of inappropriate theoretical or philosophical criteria of success.   As a discipline, we are currently passing through an extremely creative phase, which elsewhere I have dared to call a 'Golden Age' (Howarth, 1979). Our most serious weakness at the present time seems to be an inability to notice how well things are going.

In his Presidential Address to the American Psychological Association, Miller (1969) urged us to 'give psychology away', without formulating very clearly what it is we have to give. I am now suggesting that our gift to mankind should be a better understanding of man's dominant · characteristic, the ability to solve problems.

EDITED DISCUSSION

N. E. WETHERICK: It seems to me that you have advanced a theory of everything except psychology. As a human being my wish is that resources are put to the best use, by me and by the rest of humanity. But this is not what I am concerned with as a psychologist: I want to participate in the construction of a science. In wanting to teach people how to use resources you run the risk of being criticized for trying to tell them how to do better what they already know how to do. For that we require a general theory of problem-solving, and that we do not have.

C. I. HOWARTH: You and I seem to have different aims as psychologists: neither of us is alone. But in any case your brand of aims - your search for truth - can be incorporated in my model. Your aims and purposes can be clarified and understood - in terms of cultural and personal history and in the terms of my model. You need to make contact with the rest of society and that is where my analysis enters in.

A. STILL: You seem to take for granted what human purposes should be, but one could certainly imagine a society with purposes far different from our own. The basic postulates of your model might simply be inapplicable in such a society.

C. I. HOWARTH: I have talked more about evaluation than creativity because the latter is rather mysterious to me. But, if I do have to comment on it, I would say that it is partly a social process and partly it results from consequences of activity within complex systems - fortuitous but directed consequences. The complex system of society is one which we see generating new ideas: the generation of what I call 'negotiated purposes'. There is also creativity within each individual, because each individual is complex. The evaluation of ideas is also important in relation to creativity. It leads to a reordering of ideas, and some of those reorderings must be related to purposes. Remember that for me 'purposes' may become mechanisms; it depends upon which way you are pointing. I am quite happy to regress or ascend, indefinitely seeking for higher purposes, if the culture in which I exist demands that I do that.

P. B. WARR: In relation to 'negotiated purposes': first, I agree that it is possible to reconcile the humanist and mechanist approaches if one assumes that psychology should be effective (in your terms). But, second, I want to be clear on an issue more directly related to models of man: it concerns your notion that to be effective you need to meet the needs, theoretical and practical, of those with whom you deal. From this, it seems to me that some of the models of man which psychologists develop will be shaped quite significantly by non-psychologists. Do you agree with that implication; and, if so, do you see it as desirable (as I do) or not?

C. I. HOWARTH: I am entirely in sympathy with that. Psychological ideas should be evaluated by the extent to which they are attractive and useful to other scientists and to society at large.

G. THINES: You implicitly assume that psychology has consequences for the theory of knowledge - because psychology as you describe it, should be the basic science ...

C. I. HOWARTH: Oh, no, I am not a reductionist of any kind. The trouble with reductionism is that you work your way down to physics and then presumably to mathematics; but what then is your reductionist explanation of mathematics? Well it has to be psychology! So reductionism is a circle rather than a straight line. My pragmatic solution to reductionism is to be prepared to go either way depending on the circumstances.

M. M. GRUNEBERG: My comment is about the validity of your argument that we are now in the 'Golden Age' of psychology. While in occupational psychology we have experienced some limited success, we have also experienced some monumental failures. Surely we need more success before your position is tenable.

C. I. HOWARTH: There is a large number of negative instances which one can cite, but I believe that I can marshal sufficient evidence to justify my optimism.

M. JAHODA: Your formulation is very attractive, but I cannot really accept the imperialism. The model of man as problem-solver very quickly shades into the tension-reduction model. But there are ways of living which are to do with problem creating (which can be a lot of fun) or with just existing or playing. In that sense, I am doubtful that your model begins to get close to covering every aspect of man's activity. Naturally that is not to deny that your model is appropriate to clinical, educational, and industrial practice, etc., where there are overwhelming problems.

C. I. HOWARTH: My only answer to that is not one that I regard as satisfactory. It is the one used by sociobiologists and others - to say that altruism, play and all these apparently non-effective ways of behaving, are ultimately effective in terms, say, of the gene or perpetuation of the species. But that is almost metaphysics and it is not satisfactory.

J. TURNER: Returning to the point raised by Peter Warr, I am worried on three counts. First, there is a direct implication that the picture of man created by psychology will always be stamped with the particular views, theories, myths, prejudices, cultural biases and ideologies of a given society. That worries me from the point of view of applied science. It gives a very restricted picture of what psychology can achieve, and it implies that we can never transcend our own society. It implies that we cannot create any radical changes in it, in the ways that the technological advances in the other sciences have done. Second, the relations between science and society have not always been harmonious: it has been known for science to stand for enlightenment against prejudice. It would seem to me politically and socially wrong for scientists to 'negotiate' their version of the 'truth' in the way implied (based on evidence and rational argument). At some point it is possible that the picture of man that emerges from psychology is likely to threaten the ideological prejudices of wider society: do we then negotiate or not? The third point is a related one. The notion of political theory and society as a unified, consensual harmonious body is patently absurd. And it would be ludicrous to have as many psychologies as there are groups in society.

C. I. HOWARTH: I am not giving greater importance to communicating with non-psychologists than to psychologists, but I am interested in maximizing effectiveness over a wide range. However, problems to do with politics are not yet ones that I am trying to solve in my role as psychologist.

Chapter 12

The springs of action

P. B. Warr

This chapter is about what people do in their everyday lives. It examines the notion of an action and the kinds of reasons which people may have or appear to have for what they do, and it then moves on to consider some of the models which psychologists have developed to account for actions. It argues that each of these models is alone too restrictive, and that a more comprehensive framework of action psychology is desirable. I present the outline of such a conceptual framework and some models which may be contained within it, together with methodological and other implications of the perspective.

CONCEPTUAL FRAMEWORKS AND OTHER MODELS

In chapter 20 I suggest that the term 'conceptual framework' might be used for broad-ranging theoretical accounts, and I raise there the question of how a broad conceptual framework is logically and practically related to more limited theories or models. I observe that a set of limited theories can together form part of a conceptual framework, but that the framework itself goes beyond individual theories to guide thought and action in a very general way; it serves also to exclude certain types of thought and action. Conceptual frameworks do not usually have determinate empirical consequences, although their component models (limited theories) typically contain statements about reality which may be open to empirical test (Note 1*). I argue in that chapter that the 'bottom-up' development of limited theories should be supplemented by 'top-down' elaborations of broad conceptual frameworks, in order to provide more general yet systematic accounts of complex psychological processes.

The broad conceptual frameworks developed by psychologists in the first decades of this century naturally drew from earlier emphases upon the study of conscious experience to utilize a categorization of subject matter in terms of various mental elements and processes. Discussion was thus framed around instincts, sentiments, emotions and similar potentialities and responses. More recent developments have tended to elaborate types and features of observed behaviour and to examine the importance of social and other environments. These trends sometimes come together in the assertion that behaviour is a function of both the person and the environment, a proposition which is acceptable but bland. Empirical research aimed at its

*Notes are identified by numbers in the text and brought together at the end of the chapter.

elaboration has largely become set in an over-restricted analysis-of-variance mould (e.g. Ekehammar, 1974; Endler & Magnusson, 1976), and there is a need to expand the assertion into a comprehensive framework which may be developed in a 'top-down' manner to allow application in the scientific study of everyday life.

I attempt this below through the outline of an 'action psychology' framework. The primary components of the model are actions and reasons, the latter serving as the bases for explanation of the former.   The term 'reason' is used here in a general sense.   It is not intended to be juxtaposed with 'cause' or 'explanation', and my presentation assumes that reasons of several kinds are sought and provided in order to explain, or to answer why-questions about, actions. The model aims to cover an explanatory system of potential use to psychologists, rather than to describe merely the grounds for action which agents or lay observers may introduce, so that the appropriate types of evidence go beyond personal accounts and self-reports to include research information of observational, experimental or clinical kinds (Note 2).

THE CONCEPT OF ACTION

The formal definition of an action is not easy and has generated much philosophical discussion (e.g. Kenny, 1963; C. Taylor, 1964; R. Taylor, 1966; Care & Landesman, 1968; von Wright, 1971; Bolton, 1979).   The concept extends beyond observable bodily movements alone to include associated mental processes.   Furthermore, an individual movement (lifting a hand, for instance) is not the same as an action, since a variety of different physical movements may all represent the same action (waving goodbye, perhaps).   Some present or prior psychological process is therefore usually deemed to be central to the definition of an action (Note 3).

This psychological process is often described in terms of purpose, so that an action may be viewed as purposive behaviour.   Explanations of action may in consequence take a teleological form, defined by Boden (1972) to contain three principal features: reference to the future, to fundamental goals and to subjective psychological categories.   In the first place, teleological explanation requires prospective reference to possible future events, changes of state or goals.   This may be rephrased in terms of the need to avoid atomistic analysis in terms of separate small movements; an action gains its meaning from the purposive configuration of which it is a part.

The second criterion of teleological explanation identified by Boden is that such explanations in principle have a 'stopping point' in terms of some fundamental or ultimate goal.   Certain actions may be means to an end, but purposive sequences cannot extend indefinitely and there must be an action which qualifies as an end in itself.   Thirdly, teleological explanations require the introduction of subjective categories such as foresight, belief, striving and so on; actions are directed on a psychological object.

Among those subjective categories which are important to the explanation of actions are 'intentions' and 'wants'.   These two terms have much in common, although the former seems to imply a greater degree of deliberation or planning and the latter tends to give greater emphasis to immediate motivational pressures (e.g. Brandt & Kim, 1963; Boden, 1973; Alston, 1977; Davidson, 1978).   Both terms include the requirement that a person has some knowledge or beliefs about the world and about possible actions and their consequences.   Intentions and wants in this sense may constitute reasons for action, using 'reason' in the broad sense introduced earlier.   Note that wants and intentions may exist without being translated into action, and that adequate explanations of actions may sometimes be presented without direct reference to those specific terms.

Refinements to this outline interpretation may of course be suggested.   For example, Anscombe (1957) has emphasized that 'intentional action' presupposes that the agent knows that he or she is acting, and Gauld & Shotter (1977) have pointed out that an agent must somehow have knowledge of the criterion which an action may fulfil.   Boden (1973) has argued that intentions are linked with higher-order personal goal systems (Note 4), and has illustrated the connections between a given intention and associated goals and actions in the future and the past. Furthermore, 'it is essential to the concept of intentional action as it is ordinarily used that it be procedurally flexible in some degree, so tending to achieve the desired end by appropriate variation of means should obstacles to the goal arise' (Boden, 1973, p. 41).   Hollis's (1977) account of the elements of action goes beyond purposes and intentions to include the rules which a person follows; these rules belong to an external fabric of roles and interpretations which partly determine the significance of actions.

The conceptual framework to be presented here is consistent with these features of action and purposive explanation.   The 'reasons for action' which I review therefore tend to have a teleological flavour, but it would be unwise to exclude more mechanistic explanation.   For example, the importance of habits in shaping actions is introduced later, and it might be argued that habits serve as reasons for action in a classically mechanistic, non-teleological way.   This is not the place to argue whether in that case a purposive or mechanistic explanation is preferable, but it is important to emphasize that I myself have no objection to the latter within the broad framework under development.

A CONCEPTUAL FRAMEWORK : 10 TYPES OF REASON

Actions have been studied by psychologists in a variety of social and physical environments, and a number of limited models have been proposed. Let me introduce and illustrate some of these, with a view to including their principal features within a general framework.   This may be presented in terms of 10 classes of reason which an investigator might introduce to explain an action or set of actions:

(1)   The intrinsic desirability of an immediate outcome
(2)   The intrinsic desirability of consequential outcomes
(3)   Beliefs about outcomes
(4)   Trends in aspiration level
(5)   Social comparisons
(6)   Social pressures
(7)   Enduring motive structures
(8)   Role context
(9)   Spatio-temporal context
(10)   Motivational context

Note that as representations of different aspects of the commerce between people and environments these reasons may interact with each other in many ways. All the reasons may in principle be relevant to any action, but their relative importance is in practice likely to be systematically associated with the nature of the action itself; this point is taken up again later.   I should also emphasize that evidence about the involvement of a reason in an action may be acquired by an investigator in many ways; reasons are not restricted to those suggested by an agent personally (Note 2).

(1) The intrinsic desirability of an immediate outcome

The family of concepts such as want, intention, goal, purpose, motive and action contains within it the notion that some occurrences are inherently desirable, pleasant, attractive, rewarding or evaluatively positive.   Many actions are undertaken for the intrinsic desirability of their immediate outcome; for example, the intake of food, the viewing of a picture, the contact with friends, the reduction of pain, the response to moderate challenge, the use of well-practised skills.   The immediate attractiveness of these actions may be acquired through socialization or learning, or be a reflection of more ultimate goals or 'stopping points' of the kind mentioned earlier.

Intrinsic desirability has for centuries been viewed in terms of 'hedonic tone', and more recently the notion has been examined through studies and theories of 'cathectic orientation' (Parsons & Shils, 1951), 'sentiment' (Heider, 1958), 'arousal level' (Berlyne, 1973), 'psychological complexity' (Walker, 1973) or 'level of stimulation' (Eysenck, 1973).   Higher-order theories of motivation necessarily examine differential patterns of desirability: McDougall (1932) argued for the existence of 18 different instinctual 'propensities', Murray (1938) thought in terms of 20 'psychogenic needs', and Maslow (1973) suggested 14 'being-values'. A similar orientation is seen in theories of personality and attitudes, where people and groups are described in terms of values and behaviours which are relatively stable across time.   One final illustration: occupational psychologists have recently been strongly interested in intrinsically satisfying features of work (challenge, variety, feedback, etc.) in addition to extrinsic features such as style of supervision, working conditions and hours of work (e.g. Herzberg, 1966; Hackman & Lawler, 1971; Warr, 1978).

Using 'reason' in the sense introduced earlier, as a potential answer to a why-question about an action, we may therefore assert that some actions have as their reason the intrinsic desirability of an immediate outcome.   Such actions may exist relatively independently (swatting an irritating fly, for example) or be consummatory elements in a serial programme, but not all actions can be explained in these simple terms.   Furthermore this first element will often be part of a broader network of reasons.

(2) The intrinsic desirability of consequential outcomes

In addition to their own intrinsic desirability, immediate action outcomes give rise to subsequent occurrences which themselves vary in affective tone.   The personal value of a particular action is in part measured by the desirability of relatively distant events which flow from it.   For example, one may aspire to an initial outcome which is evaluatively negative or neutral in cases where consequential outcomes are likely to be intrinsically desirable.

The number and variety of possible consequential outcomes are often considerable, they are influenced by intervening perhaps unpredictable events, and their desirability might be contingent upon other occurrences.   Nevertheless, some theoretical progress has been made in the examination of consequential desirability and this is reviewed next.

(3) Beliefs about outcomes

Models of action necessarily assert the existence of desired goals (the previous two reasons) and also the presence of some beliefs associated with these goals (Note 5).   These three reasons in the present framework have been addressed by a number of investigators who have in common a focus upon people's predictions about outcomes and their expectations about the value to them of the predicted outcomes. Such research draws from an overlapping tradition of Lewin's resultant valence theory (e.g. Lewin et al., 1944) and subjective expected utility models of decision-making. Three current models of action of this kind are cited.

Occupational and organizational psychologists have made substantial recent progress in conceptual and empirical development of 'expectancy theory' (e.g.

Vroom, 1964; Porter & Lawler, 1968; Mitchell & Biglan, 1971; Lawler & Suttle, 1973; Mitchell, 1974; Warr, 1976).   The theory has several variations, but is built around three main components: (a) the expectancy that a particular act will be followed by a particular outcome; (b) the instrumentality of that outcome for future outcomes; and (c) the valence of all relevant outcomes.   'Valence' is viewed as anticipated value, or perceived desirability, and both expectancy and instrumentality are typically assessed in terms of subjective probability measures (Note 6).

Expectancy theory has been used to study occupational choice, work effort, production levels, job satisfaction and related variables.   The typical study uses a between-subjects design, in which each person is required to make a large number of responses in terms of expectancy, instrumentality and valence of a range of possible outcomes.   These responses are then combined according to some variation of the rule (expectancy times the sum of all instrumentalities-times-valences) to yield a predicted action tendency.

Research with expectancy theory gives rise to a range of problems, such as the need to obtain an excessive number of responses from each person, possible contamination between these responses, the difficulty of studying within-subject processes or between-subject idiosyncracies in valued outcomes, and a probable under-emphasis on current or non-deliberative reasons for action.   Results are of varying adequacy (e.g. Schwab et al., 1979), but the general notion that people often act in ways which are likely to yield desirable outcomes appears to be empirically supported (e.g. Warr, 1978) as well as psychologically sound.

A second type of model in this tradition has focused upon achievement tendencies in situations where some private and/or public standard of excellence is invoked.   McClelland (e.g. 1971) has particularly emphasized the higher-order features of dispositional achievement motives, and these have been incorporated into more precise models of microscopic action tendencies in specific situations by Atkinson (1957), Weiner (1972), Atkinson & Raynor (1974), Heckhausen (1977) and others.   These models have much in common with the expectancy theory approaches outlined above, but they are more likely to be examined through laboratory experimental manipulation, they give greater emphasis to inter-individual dispositional differences, and they tend to draw from educational rather than occupational settings.

Achievement motivation models were initially concerned with predictions of the tendency to attain limited goals, for example in ring-toss experiments where task difficulty and other local variables could be systematically manipulated.   The key features are measures of two tendencies: to achieve success and to avoid failure. The tendency to achieve success in a particular setting is treated as a multiplicative function of the dispositional motive to achieve success (measured through a projective test), the perceived probability of success in that setting (assessed through a person's own estimate) and the incentive value of success (perceived probability subtracted from unity, on the ground that success in more difficult tasks is more desirable) (Note 7).   A similar combination rule is applied to yield an estimate of the tendency to avoid failure, and this is subtracted from the tendency to achieve success in order to yield a measure of resultant achievement-oriented tendency.

Such a model appears to have reasonable empirical validity in limited laboratory situations.   It has given rise to a number of interesting questions, such as the relationship between resultant achievement-oriented tendency and belief about probability of success. There is general agreement that achievement tendency is lower in situations of very low and very high perceived probability of success, although the precise nature of this curvilinear relationship is open to some debate.   For example, Heckhausen (1977) has reviewed differences between groups of people who are identified as primarily success-motivated or primarily failure-motivated.   The former appear to prefer tasks slightly above their current performance levels (with probabilities of success between 0.30 and 0.40), whereas failure-motivated individuals have preferences which are contingent upon a range of external factors, for example concerned with an individual's mode of self-evaluation or concern for evaluation by others.

More generally, the need to incorporate factors external to the initial framework has led to an increasingly complex theory which is in that respect more satisfactory but correspondingly less determinate in its predictions. For example, achievement motivation theorists have come to emphasize that reasons for action may include the desire for social approval and for many other extrinsic outcomes, the motive to avoid success (supposedly particularly relevant for women), and future expectations of consequences and their value beyond the limited task under examination (see, for example, the historical account provided in Atkinson & Raynor, 1974). These extensions to the model are all individually plausible, but they illustrate the problems which arise with the 'bottom-up' development of a miniature model; I discuss these in chapter 20, for example in terms of the Christmas tree analogy and the cuckoo in the nest analogy.

It should be noted that both expectancy theory and achievement motivation theory include the influence of individual differences in ability level. A person's estimate of his or her ability is a major determinant of subjective probability judgements. Beliefs about outcomes (the focus of this third section) include beliefs about whether one has the potential ability to attain a particular goal, and such beliefs about one's own abilities in relation to a particular situation are important influences upon wants and intentions. However, ability in any situation is not only a function of personal skill level but is also determined by the severity of environmental constraints upon freedom of action. In cases of low constraint, where the agent is free to translate his or her wishes into action, it is likely that the correspondence between intention and action will be closer (e.g. Warr, 1978).

The third belief model to be described has its background in social psychology. Attitude theorists have increasingly emphasized how affective and cognitive processes work together to generate intentions to act. Attitudes may be viewed as relatively stable systems of wants, beliefs and values, and as such some general association with action is logically necessary (e.g. Audi, 1972). Simple attempts to correlate one attitudinal variable with one behavioural variable have given rise to more complex views about the structure of attitudes and the ways in which they lead into intentions (e.g. Schuman & Johnson, 1976). One such approach has been presented by Fishbein (1967), Fishbein & Ajzen (1975), and Ajzen & Fishbein (1977).

This model defines an attitude in purely affective terms (an evaluative orientation for or against something), treating attitudes as conceptually separate from beliefs (Note 8). The latter are studied in terms of subjective probability estimates about an attitude object and some related attribute. Attitude objects may be of all kinds (the people next door, honesty, Sheffield University, radishes), but are explicitly viewed as extending to possible actions. Attitudes towards an action are estimated by multiplying a person's evaluation of each attribute thought to be associated with the action by the subjective probability belief that the action will lead to that attribute. The products (belief-times-evaluation) are then summed to yield a measure of attitude.

Fishbein & Ajzen incorporate measures of 'attitudes towards an act' as one component of an equation which may be used to predict 'behavioural intention'. The latter is an intention to perform a specific act, and is predicted from the sum of 'attitude towards the act' (summed beliefs-times-evaluations, described above) and a 'subjective norm' (a measure of generalized social influence, see below). The two components (attitude towards the act, and subjective norm) are given empirically determined weights in their prediction of behavioural intention.

This model has been applied in a range of social psychological laboratory and field studies, and it has much in common with the two previous theories. However, it tends to focus mainly upon immediate outcomes (compared to the consequential outcomes separately assessed by expectancy theory) and has no place for dispositional personality measures (central to achievement motivation theory). All three approaches are formally restricted to the prediction of force to behave, action tendency or behavioural intention, although empirical research has often instead measured observable behaviour as the model's predicted variable.

(4) Trends in aspiration level

I have so far considered three possible reasons for action (the intrinsic desirability of an immediate outcome and of consequential outcomes, and beliefs about outcomes), and have illustrated how they have been incorporated into a number of psychologists' models. The fourth reason suggested earlier specifically introduces a temporal dimension

Trends in aspiration level were closely examined in the studies by Lewin et al. (1944) which gave rise to achievement motivation models of the kind described above. These and later studies have investigated success and expected success in moderately difficult situations of practical problem-solving or sensori-motor skill (e.g. Kuhl & Blankenship, 1979). A recurrent theme is that success at a task leads to raised aspiration levels, where these are defined in terms of how high to set the goal on the next attempt. This fact is usually interpreted in terms of a tendency to set progressively higher goals until success becomes uncertain or to set lower goals in cases of earlier failure.

However, the same point applies to wants and their satisfaction in many other areas. As rewards become familiar, and perhaps more easily attained, people adapt to them and seek out further rewards. Several models have been developed around this theme: Helson (1964, 1973) thought in terms of 'adaptation level' and Thibaut & Kelley (1959) wrote in terms of 'comparison level'. More macroscopic conceptualizations include Yankelovich's (1974) consideration of 'the psychology of entitlement'. For example, people at work used to wish that they might find a job which offered a pension on retirement, but they now consider this as an entitlement and their aspirations have been ratcheted up to a higher level. Conversely, there is evidence that repeated discouragements and failures can reduce motivation; for example, unemployed people who consistently fail in their attempts to find work may come to desire it less (e.g. Schweitzer & Smith, 1974), and educated workers whose aspirations for responsibility and involvement are continually frustrated may stop wanting these (e.g. Sheppard & Herrick, 1972). Lowered aspiration levels are also apparent in cases of depression and alienation (e.g. Stokols, 1975), and may be associated with more limited horizons in some cases of ageing.

Such processes are somewhat analogous to the operation of positive or negative reinforcement in animal learning studies, but the present account assumes the existence of some mental aspect to complex actions of the kind illustrated. Another concept from animal behaviour and physiological psychology which can be viewed under the current heading is that of habituation. Theories of habituation often assume two processes in opposition to each other, so that repetition of a satisfying action leads not only to a strengthening of the action tendency but also to its weakening (e.g. Walker, 1973). Solomon & Corbit (1974) have described an 'opponent process' model of motivation in which a primary and an opponent process are assumed to follow the onset of stimulation. They suggest that the opponent process (but not the primary process) is strengthened with use and weakened with disuse, and employ this and related postulates to account for a range of observations about emotional reactions. Landy (1978) has extended this model to encompass work attitudes, and it may be useful in other domains. However, its application to everyday actions does point up a principal methodological problem facing the investigator who moves away from microscopic behaviour in the laboratory; it is rarely possible to specify either the points of stimulus onset and termination or the level of stimulation which is present at any one time. Empirical examination of the opponent process model in everyday settings is therefore difficult, but the general theme of this section remains an important one: people's wants, intentions and actions are partly a function of the base-line to which they have become accustomed.

(5) Social comparisons

Interpersonal processes influence actions in a variety of ways. Many outcomes relevant to the reasons examined in earlier sections have an interpersonal content, and the importance of social roles is specifically considered below. The present section examines social comparisons, which are primarily a question of a person's perceptions of equality or discrepancy in relation to others. The following section ('social pressures') deals with more direct persuasive influences from other people.

Wants and intentions are strongly influenced through comparisons of oneself with others, and two main forms of social comparison may be suggested. The first is in terms of what goals might and should be pursued. There is a sense in which people want to want; they are frequently looking around for potential objects of interest, so that their wants can be both aroused and satisfied. Such learning is often achieved through comparisons with other people, who are sometimes seen to have aspirations and satisfactions which appear to open up new and attractive possibilities of action.

Freud's perspective was that a person develops through the attachment of 'cathexes' to different types of object, in part as a result of social learning. A more recent theme has developed around the notion of 'self-attribution' (e.g. Schachter & Singer, 1962; Bem, 1967; Laird, 1974; Gergen, 1977), where people may interpret their feelings and wants in terms of cues provided by the environment. Internal cues are sometimes ambiguous, and in those circumstances self-understanding may require inferences from the environment. We sometimes give meaning to our own wants by watching other people.

Another form of social comparison which may generate reasons for action is in terms of the desirability values which are accorded to certain outcomes. It is not always clear how one should evaluate the outcomes and potential outcomes of one's behaviour, and clarification may be sought through the activities and comments of others. This notion was classically formulated in Festinger's (1954) theory of social comparison processes, which covered the way people evaluate their own abilities and opinions through seeking out and responding to suitable comparison situations. In some circumstances there are relatively objective benchmarks against which to compare oneself (weight, performance in some specific tasks, wage level), but in many situations an assessment of that kind is not possible, and Festinger postulated that people tend to seek out encounters and interpersonal communications which can help them to anchor their own self-perceptions.

Many writers have noted that the motivation for social comparison may be of two different kinds, although in practice the two are likely to be interdependent (e.g. see reviews in Suls & Miller, 1977). One may seek information about oneself in relation to other people (the degree to which one's fear of flying or one's political beliefs are shared by similar others, for example), or one may wish for normative, self-enhancing evidence, that one is acceptable within a reference group or that one is relatively competent or attractive.

Research into social comparison processes of these kinds has been extensive, examining issues such as specific goals in particular settings, the person or group established as comparison target, the mechanisms of information seeking and integration, and the results of positive and negative assessments (e.g. Goodman, 1977; Suls & Miller, 1977). However, the research emphasis has remained upon the social interpretation of one's abilities and opinions, and there is scope for more comprehensive examination of wants and intentions in relation to those of other people.

In so far as social comparisons are in some sense unsatisfactory to the agent, he or she will tend to take steps to alter the situation. This basic feature of Festinger's original model has been of practical interest in studies of the perceived fairness of wage levels. Several forms of 'equity theory' have been developed, having in common the tenet that people compare their own inputs to a situation with those of other people and that they make similar comparisons of their rewards (e.g. Adams, 1963, 1965; Goodman & Friedman, 1971; Adams & Freedman, 1976). Inputs are typically seen in terms of effort, experience, skill, training, hours of work and so on, and rewards are in terms of the perceived desirability of differing levels of pay, status, esteem, material comforts and other outcomes subsumed under the first two headings in the present framework.

Many studies based on equity theory have been laboratory investigations which varied inputs in terms of task difficulty or participants' supposed under- or over-qualification, and simultaneously manipulated rewards in terms of pay received. The effects of perceived under- and over-payment on satisfaction and performance have been investigated for both hourly paid and piece-work experimental employees, revealing for example that underpaid hourly workers decrease their work inputs in order to restore perceived equity. Lawler (1971) has extended this laboratory approach to review field research into pay based upon equity theory, and a more wide-ranging view of social behaviour based upon assumed notions of 'distributive justice' has been presented by Homans (1961). The basic theme is that people tend to believe and act as if their net rewards in all areas of life should be proportional to their inputs; furthermore this ratio estimation process draws heavily upon social comparisons. A similar notion is central to Thibaut & Kelley's (1959) account of comparison levels and social judgement.

The widespread presence of social comparison processes in theory, research and everyday life argues for their inclusion as one category of reasons for action. In practice the distinction between this category and the next one is often a matter of degree rather than of kind.

(6) Social pressures

Any comprehensive theory of action must include among potential reasons the fact that people are subject to influence from other individuals and groups. It is a central feature of any cultural network that people surrender some potential freedom for the constraints and benefits of interdependence, and this feature has been embodied in a range of anthropological, sociological and psychological models.

This section concentrates upon relatively specific pressures for particular types of action. Social psychological studies of conformity and attitude change are of this kind, and an enormous literature has developed around empirical findings and possible explanations of these. It is clear that persons subject to pressure from respected others to alter their opinions or behaviour can experience unease, which they may reduce in a variety of ways, from direct conformity to rejection of the persons initiating the pressure.

Social pressures have been incorporated in several of the models already cited. For example, some variants of expectancy theory have included a term representing the agent's beliefs about the wishes of relevant other people. Such a feature does not fit easily within the elaborated interdependencies between miniature variables in the original expectancy formulation, usually appearing as an undifferentiated add-on factor which might impinge directly upon the expectancy-instrumentality-valence products. The analogy of a cuckoo in the nest seems again to be appropriate; all the fledgling variables have potential, but the late arrival may prove to be the most powerful.

The same point may be made about achievement motivation models, except that in these cases the cuckoo's egg does not always hatch. Extended achievement motivation models recognize that extrinsic goals may also be sought, for example in terms of social approval or affiliation. These goals tend to be noted as constraints upon the predictive accuracy of the detailed model but are not usually included as separate terms (Note 9).

Fishbein's model of attitude and belief differs from the expectancy and achievement motivation approaches in that it has a central component identified as a 'subjective norm'. This is the person's perception that most people who are personally important think that he or she should or should not perform the action in question. A subjective norm relevant to an action is measured in terms of the summed products of 'normative beliefs' and 'motivation to comply'. A normative belief is defined as the person's belief that a particular reference group or individual thinks that an action should or should not be performed, and motivation to comply is the agent's general willingness to accept influence from that group or individual. It is noteworthy that Fishbein sets this subjective norm feature separate from the more wide-ranging component, attitude towards the act. An alternative procedure would have been to include among the possible attributes (outcomes) of an act the approval or disapproval of respected others. However, this alternative is explicitly rejected, with a view to providing a bridge between individual and social processes (e.g. Fishbein & Ajzen, 1975, p. 305).

In more general terms we may include under the heading of social pressures those influences associated with requests, formal or legal instructions, advice sought or unsought, coercion, moral responsibilities and perceived duties (e.g. Vickers, 1973). Such pressures regularly constitute reasons for action, on their own or in conjunction with other features.

(7) Enduring motive structures

It is also necessary to include dispositional characteristics of the agent among possible influences upon action. There has in recent years been a reluctance to attempt broad explanations of behaviour in terms of personality traits, general motives, drives or needs, and yet the existence of trans-situational motive structures is undeniable.

In practice, few psychologists with an interest in dispositional personal characteristics would nowadays expect that trans-situational consistencies occur irrespective of context. For example, Witkin & Goodenough (1977) have reviewed studies of field dependence, a very general cognitive and interpersonal orientation, and have shown how it is only in certain types of contexts that behavioural differences between field-dependent and field-independent persons are observed. The achievement motivation models illustrated above go beyond a universal expectation that high and low scorers are always different from each other to introduce complex combinations of current conditions and dispositional motives.

Similarly, attitudes (a form of enduring motive structure) are now often thought to be related to actions only in circumscribed conditions or in interaction with other features (e.g. Schuman & Johnson, 1976; Warr, 1978). Fishbein's model has already been described, and the extension of attitude theory to specify degrees of correspondence between attitudes and behaviour is also noteworthy. Ajzen & Fishbein (1977) suggest that both an attitude and a potential behaviour may be viewed in terms of four elements: the action itself, the target (an object, person or institution) at which the action is directed, the context in which the action is performed, and the time at which it is performed. They argue that the strength of relationship between an attitude and a behaviour depends in large part on their degree of correspondence defined through the four elements. Ajzen & Fishbein's analysis has so far been restricted to the elements of action and target and they have examined 142 published relationships. Those studies with high correspondence and appropriate measures all yielded attitude-behaviour correlations of at least 0.40, whereas all except one of the studies with low correspondence produced non-significant results. An attitude towards a particular action and target is in this way shown to be predictive of that action in relation to that target, whereas attitudes and behaviours without such conceptual correspondence are unrelated.

Enduring motive structures do of course vary considerably in their scope, and it is essential to think in terms of hierarchies of systems. Such a wide-ranging possibility leads to a large number of relevant dispositional reasons for action, from lower-order to higher-order, with accompanying conceptual and methodological difficulties. Nevertheless, the complexity of everyday action is such that these difficulties must be faced in the development of appropriate models.

One type of lower-order structure which needs to be included within this framework of reasons is habitual. Habits have traditionally been studied by psychologists through learned behaviours of a relatively microscopic kind, but they are also evident in more complex motor skills and actions initiated in particular settings (e.g. Connolly, 1975) (Note 10). Many patterns of thought and action derive strength from the fact that they have become habitual, so that they are undertaken for their own sake rather than (or as well as) for their initial purpose. Allport's (1937) reference to 'the functional autonomy of motives' was a very appropriate one. People become accustomed to a particular routine or to the occurrence of particular events at particular times. A habitual sequence can become sufficiently important that deviations from it may cause anxiety and concern. By the same token, habits and other enduring motive structures can prevent the exploration of new and possibly more rewarding activities, thus constraining as well as initiating behaviour.

(8) Role context

The eighth item in my framework of possible reasons for action is concerned with the influences exerted through occupancy of a particular role. Such influences may sometimes overlap with the processes illustrated under 'social pressures' above, but the importance of action guidelines associated with role incumbency is such as to warrant their separate treatment.

The concept of role presents substantial problems of definition, partly because a role (like an action) can be of varying degrees of generality, each interdependent with but slightly different from the others. For example, the role of parent is much more wide-ranging than is the role of parent of a baby or parent of a teenager, mother or father, parent in a situation of conflict with one's child, or member of the school parent-teacher association. In outline terms a statement about a role indicates something about the actions and opinions which are expected of a person in a position. Roles may be formally designated (priest or prime minister for example), or informally developed (perhaps without explicit labelling) within particular social networks. Furthermore, a given individual is likely to move between roles, formal and informal, in the course of his daily life, some roles suggesting actions and opinions which conflict with the suggestions from others.

Roles often carry with them both rights and duties, and they are associated with formal or informal status differences and rewards of various kinds. For example, Hollander (1958) has illustrated how high status members of informal groups may acquire that status through valued competence and conformity, and how their high status carries with it 'idiosyncracy credit', the right to be deviant, innovative or moderately assertive.

Roles may also be viewed as clusters of rules associated with a position and a situation: rules govern the stock of available actions (Hollis, 1977, p. 119). A social rule is a limited statement of expectation: 'if in position P in situation

X, tend to do (think, say, etc.) A'.   Much recent research has focused upon the ways in which agents are influenced by their perception (explicit or implicit) of the role or rule requirements in a particular setting (Note 11).   One developed perspective of this kind is the 'dramaturgical standpoint', which builds upon naive role theory's examination of roles, performances, scripts, audiences and so on (e.g.   Biddle & Thomas, 1966) to classify roles and performances in a variety of ways (Harré & Secord, 1972; Harré, 1977).   In general terms, it is clear that a person's definition of relevant roles and rules often shapes the pattern of his or her actions.

(9) Spatio-temporal context

Other environmental influences upon action come from one's location in a physical setting or in a temporal sequence.   The former influences may be illustrated through Murray's (1938) examination of environmental 'press', where situations are seen to have the potential for harm or benefit and actions are shaped accordingly. A related theme colours the research of Barker and his colleagues (e.g. Barker, 1968) who showed how 'behaviour settings' such as a church service or a village community closely determine aspects of what people do (Note 12).   Other situational reasons may be associated with chance occurrences, in that a person may 'find himself' (or herself) in a situation which carries with it the potential for outcomes and actions which were not otherwise planned or pre-programmed. Furthermore,   the   potential   for   action   is   regularly   constrained   by   spatial obstacles, barriers or distances which prevent access to a goal object.   More generally environmental psychology is in part directed at the systematic explication of environmental influences on actions (e.g. Moos, 1976), and radical behaviourism emphasizes the importance of observable 'setting conditions' upon the determination of behaviour: the latter is thought to be understood by identifying its environmental context (Blackman, chapter 8).

The temporal structure of action is particularly interesting.   Some actions may exist relatively independently in the short term, James's 'ideomotor activities' for example (McMahon, 1973), but most are quite different from these.   The meaning of what one does often derives from the action's embeddedness within larger actions directed at long-term goals.   One way of looking at this is through the concept of a 'task' (e.g. Ryan, 1958, 1970), which once taken on (not merely for desirable outcomes, but also for other reasons of the kinds illustrated above) carries with it the requirement that actions will be developed, partly on a trial-and-error basis, until the task is complete.   Gauld & Shotter (1977) describe this in terms of the 'gerundive quality' of actions to which one has become committed.   A related notion is that of 'traction' (Baldamus, 1951): tasks have within themselves some power which draws us along once we commit ourselves to their execution.

The hierarchical nature of continuing tasks is conceptually very hard to work with.   Miller et al. (1960) introduced a number of valuable ideas around the concept of a 'plan', defined as 'any hierarchical process in the organism that can control the order in which a sequence of operations is to be performed' (p. 16). Plans are ever-changing across time and they can incorporate sub-plans with goals that are in themselves undesirable (see also Abelson, 1975; Schank & Abelson, 1977).   Such consequential instrumentalities were considered above in the discussion of expectancy theory, but that theory takes one specific action as the unit of analysis whereas the present focus is upon more macroscopic sequences of action.   These have been treated through 'ethogenic' analyses of social episodes by Harré & Secord (1972), Harré (1974) and others, but we should note that the same spatio-temporal features are relevant also in non-social activities.   Many of these have been examined by workers in the field of artificial intelligence (e.g. Boden, 1977; Schank & Abelson, 1977).

(10) Motivational context

Actions are also shaped by their location within a structure of motives and values which can inhibit or enhance commitment to particular sequences. Conflicts between potential actions may be viewed in terms of both lateral and vertical conflicts within a hierarchical system.

Lateral conflicts are between divergent tendencies of approximately equal scope, for example, wanting to go to the pub or to the cinema this evening. Their existence is obvious, but their theoretical treatment in terms of routine combination rules has often been over-simple. For example, the summations of expectancy theory fail to do justice to the complex ramifications of each decision outcome or to the vexing question of assigning differential priorities or weightings.

Vertical conflicts are between higher-order and lower-order reasons for action. The former may be in terms of enduring motive structures of the kind illustrated above where, for example, a strong achievement orientation may gain precedence over the more localized wants to go to either the pub or the cinema. However, we should also recognize the possibility of a more fundamental hierarchy of priorities, such as is embodied in Maslow's (e.g. 1970) theory of motivation. This assumes that higher-order needs such as for self-esteem become important only when basic bodily and security needs have been met to some reasonable degree. Alderfer (1973) has further detailed this idea in his formulation of 'existence-relatedness-growth theory', which makes rather more precise predictions about the ways in which those three types of motivational system may influence each other over time. Both models assume that the strength of any one want is in part determined by the degree of satisfaction of other wants, and this generalization seems to be of widespread applicability. It is of course associated with the aspiration level theories introduced earlier, where a particular want is set against the base-line provided by previous wants and actions in the same domain.

However, potential reasons for action do not only interact in a negative, conflicting way. They can also augment or recruit each other in the service of a common goal. The goal may be 'common' in the sense that two desirable outcomes are similar enough to operate as a joint goal at any one moment, but this may also be a question of means-end associations of the kind introduced in earlier sections: higher-order and lower-order objectives may combine to generate and sustain a long programme of action in the face of substantial obstacles.

Interdependence between reasons

Perspectives of the kind outlined above face the problem that reality does not lend itself to tidy compartmentalization: the reasons for action described here overlap in many different ways. For example, social comparisons can affect both aspiration levels and beliefs about outcomes. Social pressures and beliefs about outcomes also tend to work together to shape what people do. The intrinsic desirability of consequential outcomes and the wider motivational context both contribute to the influence of what I have termed spatio-temporal context. And the intrinsic desirability of immediate outcomes is strongly influenced by enduring motive structures.

Such interdependence gives rise to the question: what is the most appropriate level of differentiation for a conceptual framework of this kind? Should one strive for, say, 50 types of reason which are defined in ways which minimize their interconnections, or would five more global categories be preferable? The answer to that depends upon personal assessment of what is conceptually and empirically fruitful. My own belief is that for understanding everyday action the very atomistic examination and standardized combination of many small units which is required, for example, by expectancy theory is too differentiated a form of analysis.   My preference is for a less molecular, more configural approach.

The suggested 10 types of reason may therefore be appropriate for a conceptual framework at this level of generality; the important point is that all 10 reasons need to be included as potential influences in any one setting, although their proportionate contributions will vary from case to case.   Such a preferred degree of differentiation does not run counter to the use of a large number of elements in lower-order models of action; indeed the discussion in previous sections has illustrated how those more differentiated models have been applied.

What is the relationship between the several dozen miniature theories illustrated in the previous sections and the overall conceptual framework towards which I am striving?   It is important to recognize that the miniature theories are in a sense part of the overall framework, or more precisely have the potential to be components of it.   The brief presentation above was naturally at a rather abstract level, and working interdependencies were not fully spelled out.   What is now required are steps to provide greater texture by assimilating aspects of the many miniature theories into the single overall perspective.   The theories and associated metatheoretical features being pressed into such service will naturally require amendment, and such amendment in the interests of comprehensive theorizing is the primary benefit of 'top-down' elaboration of the kind I am advocating (Note 13).

PROFILE OF THE CONCEPTUAL FRAMEWORK

In chapter 20 I suggest 13 features by which models of all kinds might be characterized.   The features are likely to be differentially important for specific theories and to vary between broad conceptual frameworks and more limited models. Let me now comment on the present framework in terms of these 13 characteristics, recognizing that they too overlap with each other.

(1) Intended reference

The model is intended to cover everyday actions in contexts of many kinds, so that person-environment features are examined under 10 different headings.   This wide scope determines many of the other features to be discussed here, and also provides the basis for the model's evaluation: it should be assessed in relation to its objectives as a broad conceptual framework, not in terms of the requirements of, for example, a miniature theory.   Note, however, that the framework is intended to provide a psychological perspective, in this respect being narrower than Parsons & Shils' (1951) 'general theory of action', which aims to encompass psychological, sociological as well as anthropological features.

(2) Parsimony

By the same token, the present conceptual framework does not aspire to simplicity and parsimony.   Such a criterion is sometimes appropriate for limited models, although it might be argued that in their strong emphasis on the scientific value of parsimony many psychologists have been led to inappropriately simplistic views of psychological phenomena and procedures for their investigation.   'Appropriate simplicity' is the goal.

(3) Internal consistency

It appears to be a requirement of all broad conceptual frameworks in psychology to embody elements and processes which run parallel if not counter to each other. For example, there are several procedures which people may use to reduce cognitive dissonance; unconscious defence mechanisms may operate in many different ways, perhaps simultaneously or in opposition to each other; 'paths in psychological space' (Lewin, 1935) or 'belief-value matrixes' (Tolman, 1951) may extend in all directions; subjects in laboratory studies of cognitive processes bring with them a range of different strategies which may be implemented interchangeably.

Psychological research of many kinds has reached a point where we can identify principal elements and processes but cannot predict which of these will become operative on a particular occasion: we have achieved 'contingency models' which assert that 'it all depends', but have yet to specify systematically the patterns of these contingencies. This point has methodological implications which are reviewed below, but it also implies that broad-ranging frameworks like the present one will not be limited to single sets of predictions in the way which might be expected of miniature models of specific behaviour. Furthermore, internal consistency is itself not entirely desirable for models under development: it is by working on points of inconsistency that progress may be made.

(4) Degree of elaboration

The present brief account is clearly of a rather informal kind, lacking explicit definitions of terms and details of complex relationships. Further elaboration is needed when time and resources permit. One might begin by focusing upon parts of the framework (a subset of the 10 reasons) or one could attempt to synthesize principal themes from all 10 areas.

(5) Heuristic value

Irrespective of the characteristics introduced so far, scientific models may be important for their influence upon subsequent thinking and investigation. The many limited models encapsulated within the present framework have demonstrable value of this kind, but the overall framework has no such history. My hope is that the emphasis upon all 10 reasons for action will encourage wider conceptualization than is at present usual.

However, the heuristic value of a theory often depends upon the development of an associated methodology. Examples include rep-tests for personal construct theory, forced compliance experiments for cognitive dissonance theory, analysis of variance designs with standardized equipment for models in cognitive psychology, choice-dilemma measures for risky shift investigations, and comparative assessment of perceived causal origin for attribution theory. Such methodologies do not bear directly upon the empirical adequacy of the overall model, but they serve to increase its professional attractiveness. The present broad framework is thus more likely to prove acceptable if it becomes associated with a fruitful research paradigm.

(6) Actual and potential empirical support

The very considerable empirical support which has been gathered and is potentially available for the many limited models introduced above naturally has some bearing upon the validity of the broader conceptual framework although, as noted previously, frameworks of this kind are sets of working assumptions sustained through social acceptance and not themselves directly dependent upon empirical data.

Nevertheless, one theme of the preceding sections was that many restricted models of action are reaching the limits of their empirical application. Laboratory studies tend to emphasize immediate but not longer-term outcomes and necessarily omit several important influences upon everyday action. Attempts at precisely quantified prediction of everyday behaviour (e.g. through expectancy models or more sophisticated attitude theories) are valuable up to a point, but are troubled by potential response contamination, cyclical cause-effect processes and other well-known limitations. The problems of 'bottom-up' extension of miniature models have been illustrated here and in chapter 20 through the Christmas tree and cuckoo in the nest analogies.

(7) Implied research methods and types of evidence

What alternative methods and evidence might be suggested? I believe that one essential requirement for better understanding of action is the more widespread use of retrospective studies. Research psychologists tend to design investigations to predict future outcomes from specified manipulations, and such research is of course of great importance. However, when extended into investigations of complex actions these designs give rise to several problems of the kind noted above: it is often impossible to predict in detail sequences of future actions organized through time and modified on a trial-and-error basis to meet new situations.

Suppose we also attempted rigorous retrospective investigations to identify the configuration of reasons which led to particular actions. Such retrospective studies would be of a more idiographic kind than is customary and would examine contextual as well as personal processes. Evidence could be partly derived through people's accounts of episodes or from decision-making protocols, but would often need to go beyond these expressed reasons to look for features of which an individual may have been unaware or may have suppressed. Thus it is important that the 10 types of reason be examined from the standpoint of both the agent and the investigator. Evidence in terms of self-report and the agent's definition of the situation (here characterized in 10 ways) should be combined wherever possible with observational or experimental data derived by the investigator. The explanation so created will be based upon a synthesis of both types of evidence.

Case investigations in medicine provide some parallels here: the patient's stated symptoms and history are important for understanding, but so too are the investigator's inquiries and trained interpretations, as well as the performance of the patient in specially created test environments. Such medical case investigations of individual people are of course quite able to coexist with large-scale, quantitative, nomothetic investigations, and I believe that academic psychology has placed too much emphasis on the latter at the expense of the former (Warr, 1973, 1977).

One possible approach is to examine recent everyday actions with a view to classification in terms of such features as routineness, social embeddedness, amount of deliberation, freedom from constraints, personal salience, existence of public standards of excellence, or extensiveness in space and time, and to attempt to relate actions of varying kinds to different profiles of reasons. The 10 types of reason outlined above are likely to be differentially associated with certain categories of action, but these empirical associations have yet to be systematically explored and placed together into action taxonomies. A similar approach is possible in laboratory settings, where different subject strategies might also be related to different reason profiles. In all cases I would envisage the need to include qualitative accounts of certain features but also the collection of numerical data of appropriate kinds. Similarly, greater attention to the 'calibration' of different observers and their judgemental measuring instruments is often appropriate. Note that the goal of such research remains the understanding of people in general, but that this goal may sometimes be pursued through within-subject designs in order to generalize across subjects. Furthermore, aided experiments (Warr, 1977), action research methodologies (e.g. Susman & Evered, 1978) or 'action science' approaches (Argyris, 1980) are likely to be required to gain understanding of causal dynamics across time.

An associated question concerns the magnitude of the elements studied in experiments or other investigations. The emphasis upon single variables, closely defined and measured, may need to be complemented by studies which look at constellations of features, taking these in place of more limited variables as the objects of manipulation and observation. Meehl's (1977) discussion of 'syndromes' is very pertinent here. He points out how syndrome entities should be viewed as 'open concepts', whose components are not fully identified and which are linked to the constellation in varying probabilistic ways. Constituents may have different meanings as part of different constellations, each of which has an 'inner nature' requiring exploration in its own right and likely to be expressed in an observational language at a level different from that used for the constituents. I believe that psychologists would benefit by deliberate attempts to work at the level of syndromes as well as of variables (Note 14). Beginning illustrations of possible syndrome concepts include style, strategy, atmosphere, tradition and morale, as well as some dispositional features of persons and settings.

(8) Degree of quantification

The action psychology framework presented here is neutral with respect to quantification and the use of mathematics. There is undoubtedly a need to develop more sophisticated qualitative approaches along the lines outlined above, but there is also ample scope for the continuing application of quantitative measures of actions and their reasons.

(9) Compatibility with other perspectives

The framework is naturally at least partly compatible with those limited models which have been described, although I have from time to time illustrated what I take to be conceptual or methodological deficiencies in some of the approaches. Other comprehensive treatments which share many of the present features include Heider's (1958) 'common-sense psychology' approach to interpersonal relations (Note 15) and several models which have been developed from a social and experiential standpoint.

Attempts to characterize a particular model (as through this 13-item profile) should illustrate also what is excluded by the approach in question. The present conceptual framework appears to be incompatible with a strict behaviourist or reductionist standpoint, although biological underpinnings may quite properly be introduced into discussion of some of the 10 categories of reason. Entirely sociological constructions are similarly incompatible with the action psychology framework, since the focus is upon individual actions and experiences. However the present model is intended as an elaboration of the general person-environment interaction perspective, so that it naturally gives weight to important features of the social (and the non-social) environment. In these respects it has points in common with the broader theory of action outlined by Parsons & Shils (1951), although that theory's account of drives, need dispositions and 'behaviour psychology' now has a somewhat old-fashioned ring.

(10) Causal assumptions

The framework is clearly one which emphasizes complex, multiple causation, and I see no need to argue that, for example, mechanistic and purposive explanations are incompatible within the same model. Some actions are more prompted by mechanistic influences, others more by forward-looking goal setting. Nagel (1965) has illustrated four types of causal explanation in science (deductive, probabilistic, teleological and genetic) and I believe that we have to strive for procedures ,to admit all of these within models of action.

Classical philosophical debates about cause in terms of single conditions which might be necessary or sufficient for the occurrence of an event are often inappropriate for psychological events, where we need to work with a total complex of conditions present at the same time (e.g. von Wright, 1971). Mackie's (1974, p. 62) formulation of that type of causal relationship may prove helpful here. He points out that a causal field may contain single factors which individually are neither necessary nor sufficient to yield an occurrence, but which may be combined into several possible conjunctions of factors, one conjunction of which is in that setting sufficient for the outcome. Conjunctions may be illustrated as ABC, PQR, ABP, such that within each conjunction no single factor (e.g. A) is redundant with respect to potential causal influence of the overall conjunction. A single factor which alone is neither necessary nor sufficient is however related to the outcome in an important way, as an insufficient but non-redundant part of an unnecessary but sufficient conjunction. This gives rise to the acronym INUS. In view of the many possible conjunctions of factors which may arise, a plausible causal strategy is to seek disjunctions of INUS conjunctions, either ABC, or PQR, or ABP, or others as appropriate.

(11) Interdependence with action

Many psychological theories have no intended extra-theoretical implications, whereas others (e.g. normative theories of leadership or of man-machine interaction) are explicitly designed to suggest patterns of behaviour or designs for social and technological systems. The present framework has wide potential application, and indeed the more limited models cited have been extensively used in educational, organizational and social settings. One interesting possibility is in the area of rule breaking, legal restrictions and crime prevention, where social comparisons, trends in aspiration level, and beliefs about outcomes have clear potential influences upon action decisions. This conceptual framework might thus be used to interpret the impact of different legal or normative sanctions.

I am also interested in the possibility of using the model to examine mental health and psychological well-being, to develop interventions at the individual and institutional level to enhance these qualities or processes. For example, the concept of mental health extends beyond the absence of pain, unhappiness and discomfort to embrace optimistic and realistic goal setting, forward planning, and perceptions of reality (e.g. Jahoda, 1958; Warr & Wall, 1975). Such goal setting is at the heart of the action psychology framework outlined here, and the model might perhaps provide novel interpretations and prescriptions.

Another set of implications concerns psychologists' evaluations of the reports given by subjects in their own investigations. Such reports are actions in their own right. Consider a study of self-reported occupational strain, where employees are asked to characterize the degree of strain which they experience at work. Such deliberations cannot be based upon objective benchmarks, and might helpfully be examined through the reasons for action (including this self-report action) which were outlined above. For example, an assessment and public assertion of personal strain levels may be influenced by beliefs about and the perceived desirability of consequential outcomes of sustaining the present level, by uncertain social comparisons of others' apparent strain, by conceptions of role requirements, and so on.

(12) Beauty

The aesthetic qualities of a psychologist's model should not be left out of discussion, although the features which give rise to positive and negative assessments are likely to vary between observers. The present framework undoubtedly lacks elegance of the kind possessed by formally articulated miniature models. I myself find it attractive for its attempts to do justice to the richness and complexity of everyday life, but others might find the untidiness too much for their taste.

(13) Extra-scientific assumptions

A psychological model carries with it assumptions about the nature of man or of society, and these are nearer the surface of the present framework than is sometimes the case. The following characteristics are shared by some alternative models but denied by others.

People are viewed as active, self-aware, self-controlling problem solvers, who plan ahead to achieve goals and to maintain a positive self-conception against a background of changing conditions. They also respond to internal and external forces in a relatively limited way, being programmed to act with only restricted choice and control. A multi-level, multi-causal perspective is thus assumed.

And this brings me back to my title: the springs of action. The word 'spring' has a generic meaning in terms of origin or reason, but it also covers three main features which are common to human action. A metal spring has inbuilt elasticity, perhaps in the form of a coil which reacts in limited fashion to appropriate stimulation. In a more purposive sense, a spring is a leap forward to attain some self-generated goal. And, third, a spring is a stream of continuously flowing water. So it is with action: reactive, purposive and continuous.

Notes

1. The issue of testability is also discussed in chapter 20 where I illustrate how it is much less clear-cut than is sometimes presented in psychology textbooks. For example, 'any theory that is not susceptible to disproof is, of course, scientifically worthless' (Arkes & Garske, 1977, p. 227). Smedslund (1978) has argued a very different case, that many (but not all) psychological theories are open only to tests of logical consistency but are mistakenly presented as having empirical reference.

2. Despite the qualifications in this paragraph, I am still concerned that my use of the term 'reason' may be misunderstood. The term is widely employed in reference to the agent's stated reason for doing something: his or her own account of why it was done. This is certainly a valid use of the term (see e.g. McGinn, 1979; and Hargreaves, chapter 15), and is subsumed within my broader use here. 'Reasons' in this chapter go beyond personal accounts and self-reports to include interpretations made by observers (including research psychologists) to answer why-questions about actions. I have so far failed in my attempts to find a more adequate term with fewer misleading connotations, so would be grateful if the reader could guard against misinterpretation.

3. An alternative argument is that the meaning of an action is a function of the social context rather than any mental experiences of the agent; see Rubinstein (1977) and Farr's account (chapter 13) of Mead's conceptual framework. Hollis's (1977) approach emphasizes both psychological and social elements (rather than one or the other), as does the present framework.

4. In a similar way, wants are likely to be linked to higher-order attitude systems (e.g Audi, 1972).

5. The comment by Gauld & Shotter (1977) is notable here: 'without certain beliefs, intentions would disintegrate; without intentions or action tendencies, wants would collapse into idle wishes' (p. 145). And McGinn (1979) observes that 'desire without belief is blind, and belief without desire is purposeless' (p. 25).

6. Other labels for this model include 'instrumentality theory', 'expectancy-valence theory', 'expectancy-instrumentality theory' and 'the VIE model'.

7. This linear estimate of incentive value as a function of difficulty level is incorporated in Atkinson's version of the model. Heckhausen (e.g. 1977) has argued for a quadratic function.

8. The limited definition does not capture the full complexity of the concept of attitude, but the authors find it methodologically convenient and conceptually acceptable since it covers the 'most essential part' of an attitude (e.g Fishbein & Ajzen, 1975, p. 11).

9. Exceptions to this generalization are studies which examine the joint influences of achievement and affiliation motives (e.g. Sorrentino & Sheppard, 1978).

10. It is interesting how Connolly's analysis of motor skills is also applicable to the wide range of everyday personal and interpersonal actions which are the focus of this chapter.

11. The setting need not always be a social one for the person to follow a role or a rule; we often act and think in rule-related ways when we are alone. This point has been discussed by Schank & Abelson (1977), in their application of artificial intelligence concepts and methods to the understanding of plans and related processes: they illustrate a range of 'scripts' which are built around highly stylized rules of behaviour. Gauld & Shotter (1977, p. 29) draw attention to the similarities between grammatical rules and those rules applied (not necessarily with systematized awareness) in social settings.

12. Such influences may also be viewed in terms of roles and rules (above) or tasks (below).

13. An alternative way of presenting the material in previous sections is through a diagram in terms of labelled boxes with some interconnecting arrows. This is a widely used device for exhibiting psychologists' models, but I am not convinced that it always advances thought beyond a verbal account of the kind presented here. In practice, the meaning of the arrows in such representations (influence and/or information, for example) is usually unclear; the appropriateness of additional unspecified arrows beyond those in the diagram is often acknowledged, as is the need to incorporate more feedback channels; and empirical testing is often no more possible than for an account of interconnected processes of the kind outlined above. However, the choice

between a verbal account and a diagram to describe a model is largely a matter of personal preference; note that the conceptual framework outlined here could also be described in diagrammatic form, albeit loosely at present.

14. An approach through entities of this higher-order kind has something in common with top-down procedures for theory development advocated earlier. The analogy of policy and decisions (set out in chapter 20) is once again appropriate: A syndrome, like a policy, is more than the sum of its constituents.

15. Heider's analysis gives major emphasis to how perceivers interpret actions undertaken by someone else, but many features he described are naturally similar to those outlined here.

EDITED DISCUSSION

I. VINE: You seem to have come close to saying that logical inconsistencies can be a good thing in a model. Perhaps what we want to be emphasizing, in relation to conceptual frameworks, is that we are not necessarily going to demand, nor get, unique predictions. That aspect one can allow to be more flexible in the higher level models.

P. B. WARR: In some instances, if you cannot get unique predictions, it is because your model inconsistently predicts either A or B. Is that not the same thing?

I. VINE: But you can have a branching arrangement where the branch is more than two-way.

J. TURNER: I was going to make exactly the same substantial point as that made by Ian Vine. If one takes cognitive dissonance, for example, it may or may not be logically inconsistent, but that is certainly not demonstrated by the fact that under differing theoretically relevant conditions one can derive different predictions. Nor is it demonstrated by the fact that it may be we are not yet fully aware of all theoretically relevant conditions - we certainly are not; but that does not in any way demonstrate the logical inconsistency of the theory. That's my first point. Related to that, and more importantly, I am afraid that I simply cannot see any 'framework' or any unity in your analysis. There is an absence of any unifying principles or themes. I fail to see how you analysis adds up to anything more than the sum of its parts. In so far as I can see any role for developing conceptual frameworks, I would argue for going from the bottom down (rather than from the top down), in the sense that I would want to make explicit my broad working assumptions. Sometimes one finds that one can thereby give some theoretical content to those working assumptions. That in turn is sometimes very useful for doing the kind of thing advocated by Dr Broadbent: that is, delineating and organizing classes of mini-theories. That is a much more heuristic approach. If, on the other hand, you go from the top downwards, do you achieve anything more than an ad hoc list of mini-theories?

P. B. WARR: The difference between a framework and a list has exercised me not inconsiderably over the last few months. Presumably a framework has got to have some sort of working interdependencies: is this one of the points you are making?

J. TURNER: Well, a framework has to hang together.

P. B. WARR: In that case, I think I do have a framework. For me the concept of 'action' is central and everything hangs around that. To some extent I share your concern, but with somewhat different emphases. It is the working interdependencies that trouble me.

D. E. BROADBENT: I would advocate a heterarchy instead of the hierarchy which you have proposed for dealing with motives; and this is more in line with current thinking in Artificial Intelligence.   Let me give an example.   In journeying from Cardiff to Oxford, I adopt various subgoals: perhaps to get from here to the main road, from there to Swindon, and then to Oxford.   For each of those subgoals, there will be a number of lower-order goals: for instance, to reach my car, to drive out of the car park, and so forth.   Each of these might be seen as involving quite separate activities from those in the later parts of my journey.   But there are also other possibilities so that, for example, one goal (operating throughout the journey) may be to conserve fuel.   Another independent goal might be to drive safely.   So what I am saying is that these and other goals may simultaneously be held in appropriate representation in a multidimensional matrix structure.   This all has implications for your positioning of the conceptual framework at the top of your hierarchy.   The conceptual framework may be on another dimension that cuts across the various situations you are using.   Therefore it may be possible to go back into the same situations with a different conceptual framework, or to change parts of the conceptual framework while leaving the rest whole.   At the same time you may be serving other purposes on third and fourth dimensions.   The main practical implication of all this is that it is perfectly possible to cooperate with other people who have different higher-order goals.

P. B. WARR: On the first point, I had in fact intended that heterarchy should be represented in my analysis. So, I agree with you completely. The second theme troubles me a bit.   Before putting a conceptual framework on these cross-cutting dimensions I would like to work out what those dimensions are.

Chapter 13

Homo socio-psychologicus

R. M. Farr

In his background chapter on models Warr (chapter 20) notes the dearth of wide-ranging frameworks for research which extend downwards to incorporate some of the miniature theories which proliferate in contemporary psychology. It is just such a grand theory which I wish to propose here. This theory, however, has been around for some time without its relevance to psychological science having been noted. How this state of affairs came about is itself a curious fact which is worth exploring for the light it sheds on the historical development of our discipline. In discussing models of man it is necessary, I believe, to consider them in historical perspective. Joynson's contribution to this volume (chapter 1) helps to provide such an historical perspective. The theory which I wish to propose is to be found in the thought of a major American pragmatist philosopher: George Herbert Mead. It is, therefore, a system of thought rather than a theory which has been tested and validated by laboratory research. Ever since psychologists escaped the hegemony of philosophy they have been reluctant to turn to that parent discipline for inspiration or guidance. This may be one possible cause of the conceptual poverty which still characterizes much contemporary psychology. As a pragmatist model of man, of impeccable pedigree, it should commend itself to Howarth (see chapter 11).

My title reflects the influence of Dahrendorf's slim volume 'Homo Sociologicus' which he first published in 1958. In this early volume Dahrendorf wrestled with what he termed the 'vexatious fact of society'. Society is no less 'real' despite the fact that one cannot easily point to it or indicate either its nature or its existence to others. Many phenomena of a social psychological nature are similarly not open to immediate visual inspection. It is, therefore, easy either to deny their existence or to proceed as if they were of little, or no, account. The existence of individuals is fairly basic and much of psychology is centred on the study of individuals. It is all too easy, however, to identify the individual with his human body. Whilst the reality of individuals can scarcely be doubted the existence of 'persons' is more problematic and open to doubt. When it comes to adducing evidence for the existence of 'minds' (other than one's own) psychologists, like many philosophers before them, have been highly sceptical concerning the nature of such evidence. It is indeed an explicit part of the behaviourist programme within psychology to rid the discipline of such 'mentalistic' concepts. How 'mind' emerges out of social interaction and is an inherently social phenomenon is central to the form of behaviourism considered in this chapter. Perhaps one needs a theory in order to be able to 'notice' and to take into account certain phenomena. The absence of such a credible theory may account for the neglect of such phenomena in the past.   Eysenck observed in discussion at the Conference, that one becomes 'conscious' of a model when it goes against the prevailing Zeitgeist (see p. 307).   He made this point specifically in regard to the development of his own model of individual differences based on genetic factors.   I think that this is a significant observation.   My own 'awareness' of the social psychological model of man developed in this chapter arises precisely because it does run counter to the prevailing Zeitgeist.   Where Eysenck and I would differ, however, is that he would affirm, whilst I would deny, that the prevailing Zeitgeist in psychology is (or ever has been) social.   In my eagerness to assert the 'reality' of purely social phenomena in psychology I turned, in my search for a title, to Dahrendorf for inspiration (Dahrendorf, 1958).

The model of man which I wish to propose is one which was still evolving in the mind of G.H. Mead at Chicago right up to the time of his death in 1931.   Mead's system of thought has been characterized as social behaviourism (Mead, 1934).   It is safe to assume that Mead knew quite a lot about behaviourism in psychology as J.B. Watson had been, at one time, a junior colleague of his in the Department of Philosophy at the University of Chicago.   The implications, for Mead, of adding the adjective 'social' to qualify 'behaviourism' to characterize his own system of thought were quite profound.   I hope, in the course of this account, to identify a few of the distinctive features of his thinking and to assess their significance for research in psychology.   Mead's choice of the qualifying adjective 'social' serves also to highlight, for me, the non-social nature of that brand of behaviourism which has been such a dominant influence in the development of psychology and which has contributed so much to the prevailing Zeitgeist within the discipline.

The social psychological model of man, to which my title refers, is essentially that which Mead outlined during his annual course of lectures at Chicago on social psychology.   Mead delivered these lectures without the aid of notes.   After his death a class transcript of his 1927 lecture course was edited by C.W. Morris (who also added a valuable introduction to Mead's thought) and published under the title: 'Mind, Self, and Society: From the Standpoint of a Social Behaviorist' (Mead, 1934).   Before turning to Mead and his possible relevance to psychology I wish to make a few preliminary observations about the general utility, or otherwise, of developing 'models of man'.

MODELS OF MAN AND MODELS OF SCIENCE

There is an important sense in which a model of man may be little more than a declaration of intent to isolate certain phenomena for further, more detailed, study.   This declaration of intent is usually made to other members of the academic community.   By some such device the pioneer may seek to delineate his own distinctive contribution to knowledge and to declare the nature of the expertise he claims.   This provisional claim needs to be substantiated by subsequent research and scholarship within the newly identified field.   Academicians in other disciplines are likely to accord the results of such research a critical and qualified welcome.   The outcome of such exchanges can determine the context within which, in any one academic or research institution, psychology develops as a field of study.   Psychology is only one of several disciplines concerned with the study of man.   The models of man developed in psychology are therefore of interest to those in other related disciplines and there are theorists (other than psychologists) who develop models of man which, in turn, may be of interest to the professional psychologist.   I hope to discuss one such model in the course of this chapter but there are others: for example, Homo Oeconomicus, Rational or Logical

Man, Homo Loquens (Fry, 1977), Homo Sociologicus (Dahrendorf, 1958), and The Compleat Strategist of the Theory of Games (von Neumann & Morgenstern, 1944; Williams, 1954; Luce & Raiffa, 1957).

In a conference on 'Models of Man' it is important to bear in mind the interdisciplinary context within which psychology exists in our institutions of higher learning. Of the various psychological models of man available to those in other disciplines the most influential are not necessarily those enjoying the highest status within the discipline: for example, psychoanalysis is probably the most widely influential theory outside academic psychology. This may be because it is a model of man which reflects something of man's complexity and which is peculiarly suited to the needs of scholars in the Arts and Humanities in regard, for example, to the interpretation of literature, art, etc. Freud's psychology of the unconscious powerfully justifies the critic in his assumption that the artist is not necessarily the best interpreter of the significance of his own work. Academic psychologists have been particularly negligent in cultivating the many important links between psychology and subjects within the Arts and Humanities. In France psychology is accepted as a human science and enjoys an honoured status amongst the Arts and Humanities. This is much less often the case in Britain. It is an idiosyncrasy of the British university system that where psychology is fully accepted as a human science this is usually in those universities which were, until recently, Colleges of Advanced Technology and, hence, which lack a long tradition of scholarship in the Arts and Humanities. In many of the older universities, with a long-established tradition of research and teaching in the Arts and Humanities, psychology is often to be found only within the Science Faculty. When the study of language becomes a central topic of concern for the experimental psychologist links with the Arts and Humanities may revive. If the model of man outlined in this paper were to be generally accepted in psychology then the study of language would indeed become much more central than it is within contemporary psychology.

What happens, however, when scholars within a particular field become dissatisfied with the initial, though provisional, demarcation of their field of inquiry? They may stage a revolution within their discipline and adopt a new object of study to replace the one whose limitations have become increasingly apparent. When psychology commenced as a laboratory science introspection was used to study the contents of consciousness. The limitations of this approach rapidly became apparent. Dissatisfaction with introspection as an investigative technique, together with doubts concerning the feasibility of establishing a science on the basis of such 'subjective' data as introspective reports helped to prepare the ground for the advent of behaviourism. Whilst psychology started out as a mental science, it rapidly became a behavioural one. These two alternative models were regarded as being antithetical, with the latter being preferred over the former as it more closely approximated the canons of experimental orthodoxy in the natural sciences. I would want to argue that this antithesis was a false one and that it reflected an inadequate model of man. This was precisely Mead's position. He developed a purely behavioural account of mind. Any antithesis between the two, from Mead's perspective, would have been inconceivable. As an experimental discipline psychology was born within the false Cartesian dualism of mind and body. As such it was flawed at the outset by inheriting, as part of its legacy from philosophy, an inadequate model of man. An inadequate conception of behaviour does not necessarily compensate, I would argue, for having first subscribed to an inadequate conception of consciousness. In both instances the inadequacy stems, I would claim, from the non-social way in which, first consciousness, and then, behaviour, were conceptualized.

Wundt's conception of consciousness was inadequate in several respects. He was himself clearly aware of one of the most important of these limitations. He believed that it was not possible to study man's higher cognitive abilities in the laboratory by means of introspection. Introspection could be used to study the 'contents' of consciousness, but not to study either the nature of thought or consciousness itself. The futility of even attempting this latter task had been likened by William James to the experience of turning up the gaslight in order to see better the surrounding darkness. 'It is true that the attempt has frequently been made to investigate the complex functions of thought on the basis of mere introspection. These attempts, however, have always been unsuccessful. Individual consciousness is wholly incapable of giving us a history of human thought, for it is conditioned by an earlier history concerning which it cannot of itself give us any knowledge' (Wundt, 1916, p. 3).

Wundt could see that the controlled study of the consciousness of individuals within the laboratory needed to be augmented by a wider social or 'folk' psychology. Folk psychology originated in Wundt's conviction that there were important mental phenomena which could not be understood on the basis of a psychology which was restricted to the study of the consciousness of individuals. The focus of interest in Wundt's 'folk psychology' was on language, customs, magic and cognate phenomena. Wundt had this to say concerning his folk psychology: 'Its problem relates to those mental products which are created by a community of human life and are, therefore, inexplicable in terms merely of individual consciousness since they presuppose the reciprocal action of many' (Wundt, 1916, p. 3). Thus, for Wundt, the study of those higher cognitive processes which uniquely characterize man formed part of his folk psychology. Whilst Wundt is widely acknowledged, within psychology, as having been the founding father of psychology as an experimental laboratory discipline there is currently little, or no, trace within psychology, of his significant contributions to social psychology. Yet his model of man was such that he considered both types of study were necessary.

Wundt was forced, on grounds both of method and content, to separate his laboratory science from his social psychology. This was due, I would argue, to a widely shared assumption at the time that consciousness was a characteristic of individuals and hence was an inherently non-social phenomenon. Mead developed the whole of his social psychology from Wundt's conception of the human gesture. Wundt's concept of gesture, which he developed on the basis of Darwin's study of the expression of the emotions in man and animals, was part of his folk psychology. A gesture was a part-action which others completed. This was the behavioural basis of Mead's social psychology. Mead argued that the meaning of an action was to be found in the response which it elicits from others. His psychology was thus, clearly, a social psychology. An individual's behaviour comes to acquire the significance for himself which it originally had for others with whom he interacts. In thought man can anticipate the reactions of others to his own imagined actions. Individuals often 'intend' their actions to have certain effects. This notion of intentionality was an important topic of discussion at the Conference. It is important to appreciate that whilst Mead's model of man is a behavioural one it nevertheless incorporates intentionality as a distinctly human mode of action.

Mead directly challenges Wundt's assumption that consciousness is a uniquely individual phenomenon. Mead shows how man's self-awareness (i.e. his awareness of himself as an object in the world of others) arose from interacting with others in the course of his ontogenetic and social development. Thus it was that he demonstrated the purely social antecedents of individual consciousness. There was no theory of the human self implicit in Wundt's conception of individual consciousness. Mead's conception of consciousness is explicitly a theory about self-consciousness, that is, man's awareness of himself. The 'self' for Mead was a purely relational term; that is, it can be understood only in relation to the not-self. For man 'self' can be understood only in terms of a relation to 'other', that is, persons other than one's self. This makes Mead's conception of consciousness an inherently social one.

There were several unfortunate consequences to this failure, on the part of the early experimental pioneers in psychology, adequately to grasp the inherently social nature of man's consciousness:

(a) Social psychology became separated from general experimental psychology

This was as a direct consequence of Wundt's decision that they were separate, though complementary, fields of study. General experimental psychology became unnecessarily restricted to the study of individuals. A further regrettable consequence of this split is that Wundt's significant contributions to social science still remain unchronicled within the official histories of psychology as an independent experimental discipline. Boring noted the distinguished Americans who visited Leipzig and who returned to found laboratories of experimental psychology in their native land. Wundt, however, also influenced a large number of very distinguished social scientists (e.g. Malinowski, Boaz, Thomas, Mead, Durkheim, Freud, etc. - for a fuller exposition of this point see Farr, 1978b). For the purposes of this chapter I wish to confine myself to a single instance of this influence.

Durkheim visited Wundt at Leipzig and continued to be influenced thereafter by his writings in folk psychology (Lukes, 1973; Giddens, 1978). When Durkheim established his own over-sharp distinction between sociology and psychology he was, in effect, doing little more than amplifying the distinction which Wundt had previously made between his folk psychology and his laboratory science. With Durkheim, however, this now became a distinction between two academic disciplines; that is, sociology and psychology. Durkheim's 'social facts' and 'collective representations' are similar to those collective mental phenomena (language, magic, religion, customs, etc.) which were the focus of study in Wundt's folk psychology. For Durkheim, as for Wundt, these collective phenomena could not be understood in terms of individual consciousness. Classically Durkheim is the most anti-psychological of all major sociological theorists. Yet the psychology to which he was so strongly opposed was the psychology of the individual. He developed his own form of social psychology which was part of sociology rather than being part of psychology. The contemporary French school of social psychologists who study 'social representations' look back to Durkheim as their source of inspiration (Moscovici, 1961/1976; Herzlich, 1972, 1973; Farr, 1977, 1978b, 1979). They regard their social psychology as falling within the sociological, rather than within the psychological, camp.

As a consequence, there are now several different traditions of social psychology in social sciences other than psychology. These traditions have little or no contact with each other and have assumed different forms as a direct consequence of the parent discipline within which they have developed. The technical problems involved in reconciling these differing traditions are of quite a high order (see Farr, 1978b). We shall shortly see how Mead's social psychology came to be preserved within American sociology. Wundt's quite considerable influence on the development of social science now needs to be traced in British and American anthropology; in French and American sociology, etc. His writings in folk psychology remain unread and unappraised by the official historians of psychology.

(b) Only a highly restricted range of phenomena could be studied experimentally in the laboratory

We have already noted how Wundt's inadequate conception of consciousness precluded the study of man's higher cognitive functions within the context of the laboratory. Laboratory psychology was so narrowly focused on the study of individual consciousness that Freud was forced to describe his theory of the unconscious as meta-psychology as he was principally concerned with the analysis of phenomena which lay outside man's conscious awareness. Yet it is quite clear that Freud was developing a general psychology, and not a meta-psychology. Given the much fuller conceptions of man's awareness of himself which derive from Mead's social behaviourism and from Freud's psychoanalysis it is now possible to explore a much wider range of mental phenomena within the context of the laboratory. I am myself interested in using Mead's model of man in order to understand, and to re-interpret, the data of experimental social psychology (see Farr, 1976, 1978a). If we accept Mead's theoretical perspective it becomes possible, once again, to use experimental techniques in order to explore the nature of human awareness within laboratory contexts. The difference this time round lies in the fact that the analysis is now an inherently social psychological one.

Social psychologists might reasonably be concerned to ensure that the model of man which gains general acceptance within psychology should be social in nature. Their colleagues in general psychology might assume, with some reason, that social psychologists could produce just such a model of man. It may, therefore, seem strange that the model which I propose derives, not from social psychology but, from American philosophy. Mead's social psychology, it is true, is also preserved in the symbolic interactionist tradition of social psychology within American sociology. Social psychology on either side of the divide between sociology and psychology has developed in the context of two quite contrasting parent disciplines. The dominant bias in psychology is an almost exclusive focus on the individual. Social psychologists (especially those who use experimental methods of research) tend to counteract this bias by stressing the situational determinants of behaviour. Milgram (1974), for example, believes that the single most important lesson to emerge this century from social psychological research is: 'Often it is not so much the kind of person a man is as the kind of situation in which he finds himself that determines how he will act' (p. 205). The dominant bias in sociology is to stress the societal determinants of individual behaviour. Social psychologists within that discipline tend to counteract this bias by emphasizing the autonomy of the individual and by highlighting how social order is established and maintained through social interaction. Their model of man is thus a much more active one than the term 'subject' implies when used to designate the human participant in laboratory experiments. Mead's model of man rather precisely meets their needs. Sociological social psychologists prefer the term 'actor' to the term 'subject' and the focus of their theoretical interest is in 'action' rather than in 'behaviour'. It is interesting that several of the contributors to this volume should propose what are essentially theories of action. None, however, appears to be aware of the relevance of Mead to the type of theory which they propose. There might be much to gain if Mead's active model of man were to be used to interpret the data of experimental social psychology (Farr, 1978a).

A better integration of sociological and psychological traditions of social psychology could produce a more genuinely social model of man which might be valid throughout the various areas of research in psychology (Farr, in press). It is a curious failing of purely psychological social psychologists that their models of man are not really social ones at all. Moscovici can ask, with much reason: What is social about social psychology? (Moscovici, 1972). There is a persistent myth among social psychologists to the effect that psychology can only become social by moving to another 'level'; that is, to the level of groups. This way of thinking, I would argue, is the cause of, rather than an antidote to, the currently acknowledged non-social nature of social psychology. It was this type of thinking which originally led Wundt to separate his social, from his general experimental, psychology. The answer is to be found, I would argue, in adopting a social model of the individual. The sociological dimension is then incorporated within one's model of the individual. Mead provides just such a model of man. Had Mead's model of man been available there would have been no reason for Wundt to separate his social from his general experimental psychology.

Not only does the individual exist 'within' society but society 'enters into' the individual and actually constitutes the nature of mind. Man, for Mead, is a minded organism and mind is a purely social product. If psychology is, once again, to become a science of mental life then an adequate understanding of social phenomena becomes a critical requirement. If a social model of man, such as that proposed by Mead, were generally accepted in psychology and if all research contexts (especially that of the laboratory experiment) were explicitly acknowledged to be social then there might no longer be any need for a special sub-discipline of social psychology.   All of psychology would then be social.   At present, some of us are social psychologists only by virtue of what it is that our colleagues in general and experimental psychology leave out of their accounts.

It would be self-evident to most people that all research contexts in psychology are inherently social ones.   An explicit recognition of this fact may, however, provoke controversy.   The controversy might centre around the implications of such an admission for the type of science which psychology can claim to be. Whilst psychology is often classified, for administrative purposes, as a 'social science' few of its experimental practitioners accept such a classification.   This raises the important issue of one's model of science and how this might relate to one's model of man.   My reason for stating that psychology cannot escape being a social science is that man is both the agent and the object of study.   Physicists, at least since Einstein, have subscribed to a conception of the physical universe which includes man as an observer occupying a particular place in space/time.   When experimenters in psychology develop a conception of the experiment which includes their own location in space/time, then this will constitute an explicit recognition of the inherently social nature of all research contexts in psychology.   Mead read Einstein carefully and worked out the implications for philosophy of taking Einstein seriously.   Mead believed in the objective reality of perspectives.   For Mead a perspective was a point in space/time.   In his later work Mead preferred to talk of 'adopting the perspective of the other' in place of his earlier preference for 'assuming the role of the other'.

In the late 1950s Sigmund Koch edited a six-volume review of the status of psychology as a science.   He had this to say in the epilogue to his review: 'from the earliest days of the experimental pioneers man's stipulation that psychology be adequate to science (has) outweighed his commitment that it be adequate to man' (Koch, 1959, p. 784).   Here Koch identifies what he sees as a potential conflict between one's model of science and one's model of man.   Whilst the present volume is explicitly concerned with 'models of man' there is, nevertheless, a hidden agenda which concerns one's model of science.   In order to interpret the controversies and discussions one needs to be aware of this hidden agenda.   Koch also noted that psychology had become institutionalized as a field of study before there had been any consensus as to its content (i.e. whether it was the study of consciousness or of behaviour) and that its methods of research preceded its problems.   Koch thus saw a fundamental conflict between the potential contributions of psychology to the humanities, on the one hand, and to science, on the other.

Let us provisionally accept Koch's evaluation that scientific psychology has proved inadequate to the task of enriching our conceptions of human nature.   This criticism could not be levied, for example, against psychoanalysis.   Here the opposite imbalance between one's model of man and one's model of science may hold true.   We could claim, to parody Koch, that from the earliest pioneering days Freud's commitment that the new science which he was developing be adequate to man outweighed his stipulation that it be adequate to science.   That psychoanalysis has powerfully affected developments in the humanities is beyond dispute and has already been noted above.   It has done so because its model of man enriches, rather than impoverishes, man's understanding of himself and of others.   Freud took 'man' as the object of his new science and then fashioned a method of investigation (the psychoanalytic method) which was uniquely suited to the task of exploring his object of study, that is the unconscious.   This reverses what Koch thinks happened in the development of psychology as a science.   The contrast between behaviourism and psychoanalysis is quite stark.   By the criteria of science, which behaviourists and other positivists would invoke, psychoanalysis is found wanting.   By the criteria of whether a psychology enriched or impoverished one's conception of man, which those in the humanities might wish to adduce, then it is behaviourism which would be found wanting. Should psychology as a discipline be true to man or true to science?

Koch in his review of the status of psychology as a science, was primarily concerned with the limitations of behaviourism within psychology. It is here, perhaps, where the thinking of Mead might be most directly relevant to the future development of psychology. Mead had been clearly aware of these limitations some time before behaviourism had become an important force in the historical development of psychology. Mead believed that behaviourism in psychology was an important advance on the false psychophysical dualism of mind and body which had underlain Wundtian experimental psychology. Mead was as much concerned as Watson to banish introspection as the privileged method of investigation in psychology. He believed, however, that Watson had not gone far enough. He thought that Watson and others should have been able to come up with a behavioural account of mind and of man's higher 'cognitive' functions. Instead, the behaviourists in psychology had ignored mental phenomena as not being worthy of scientific investigation. In marked contrast to all this, Mead set out to account for these highly distinctive human characteristics. His model of man is thus much more complex, and better reflects the realities of human existence, than any model that might derive from either Watson or Skinner.

G.H. MEAD: THE MAN AND HIS MODEL OF MAN

His standing as a philosopher

As a professional philosopher Mead addressed himself to most of the main intellectual problems which have taxed philosophers ever since Descartes inaugurated the modern era in that discipline. He was much exercised with the task of working out the implications, for philosophy, of taking Darwin seriously. In the tradition of American pragmatism he sought to refute the false antithesis between body and mind which Descartes had formulated as a basis for modern philosophy. In many important respects Mead foreshadowed Ryle's much later démarche in proposing the behavioural bases of mental phenomena (Ryle, 1949). As a social philosopher Mead was much better able than the latter to conjecture how mind might arise out of social interaction with others in the course of social and ontogenetic development. Mead's thinking lies behind, and often goes beyond, that of other philosophers who are cited elsewhere in this volume for their possible relevance to the current debate within psychology concerning models of man: for example, Wittgenstein, Ryle, Austin, etc. Others who explicitly recognize the potential significance of this line of approach are as diverse in their contributions as Harré, Shotter and Hargreaves.

David Miller, a philosopher and former graduate student of Mead, has this to say concerning the scope of Mead's thinking and its relation to later developments in philosophy at Oxford:

> Under the influence especially of Ludwig Wittgenstein, philosophers at Oxford have become engrossed in a discussion about the nature and function of language, the theory being that it is an essential key to the solution of many problems in philosophy, notably the problems of meaning, perception, universals, private language, and subjectivity. Many of the beliefs that men at Oxford accept regarding these topics are sound, from Mead's point of view, but they are by no means new, since Mead deals with all of these topics and often comes to the same conclusions as do such men as Wittgenstein (in his later philosophy), Ryle, and Austin ... (Miller, 1973, p. 66).

At other points Miller notes 'it is one thing to hold that there can be no private language and another to show why there cannot be' (p. 69). 'It occurs to me that had Anthony Quinton taken into consideration Mead's "Mind Self and Society", he would not have said: "Finally, there is a theory of mind, the part of the Investigations in which Wittgenstein breaks wholly new ground, which interprets our descriptions of mental acts and states not as referring to something private within our streams of interior consciousness but as governed by criteria that mention the circumstances, behaviour, and propensities to behave of the persons described" '(Miller, 1973, p. 74). Ayer acknowledges that the pragmatists often came to the same conclusions that Wittgenstein was later to develop 'One of the debts that we owe to Wittgenstein, and before him to the pragmatists, is a realisation of the active part that language plays in the constitution of facts' (Ayer, 1963, p. 35, emphasis added).

My purpose in highlighting these links with Oxford philosophy is to convey the impression that, amongst philosophers, Mead was a major thinker. During the 1920s Mead was much influenced by the philosophy of Whitehead and he offered an occasional course of lectures at Chicago based on the latter's work. Whilst Mead was much pre-occupied in his early and mid-career with Darwin he was, at the time of his death, working out the implications, for philosophy, of Einstein's theory of relativity. The Carus lectures which he gave in 1930, just before his death, were primarily concerned with the notion of time. His background notes for these lectures have been published under the title 'The Philosophy of the Present' (Mead, 1932). Regarding this volume and 'Mind, Self and Society', A. N. Whitehead said 'I regard the publication of the volumes containing the late Professor George Herbert Mead's researches as of the highest importance for philosophy. I entirely agree with John Dewey's estimate, a seminal mind of the very first order' (Whitehead, 1934).

Brief biographical details highlighting Mead's links with psychology and sociology

Mead was born at South Hadley, Massachusetts in 1863 and died in Chicago in 1931. (For a fuller biographical account see Miller, 1973, xi-xxxviii.) He obtained a general arts degree in 1883 from Oberlin College where his father had been a professor of homiletics. After a period of 3 years working as a member of a survey crew for the Wisconsin Central Rail Road Company Mead enrolled at Harvard where he read philosophy and psychology. Whilst he was at Harvard he tutored the children of William James and lived in the James' household. In matters of philosophy he was, at the time, more influenced by the Hegelianism of Royce than he was by James. Henry Castle, a fellow student from his days at Oberlin College, was also studying at Harvard. Like many young Americans his generation Castle went off to Europe to help round-off his education. Mead then joined Castle in Europe where he studied, first at Leipzig and then at Berlin. In Europe Mead continued to study philosophy by way of psychology. Mead married Henry Castle's sister, Helen, in Berlin in 1891. It is not clear in which courses Mead might have enrolled whilst he was at Leipzig. It is clear, however, that he had studied Wundt's written works very carefully and he referred to them at length in 'Mind, Self and Society'. He borrowed from Wundt's social psychology the important notion of 'the gesture'. At Leipzig Mead met G. Stanley Hall, who had studied with Wundt. Hall influenced Mead in his decision to move to Berlin where he embarked on the study of physiological psychology.

Mead left Berlin in 1891 to take up an instructorship in philosophy and psychology at the University of Michigan. It was there, at Ann Arbor, that Mead and Dewey first met and became lifelong friends. At the memorial service for Mead in 1931 Dewey had this to say about Mead's pre-occupations in philosophy: 'In my earliest days of contact with him, as he returned from his studies in Berlin forty years ago, his mind was full of the problem which had always occupied him, the problem of individual mind and consciousness in relation to the world and society'. It is worth noting that Wundt had based his experimental laboratory science of psychology on the first of these notions and his 'folk psychology' on the other. Mead spent some 40 years of his life considering the interrelationship between the two. What Wundt had cut asunder Mead joined together.

Whilst he was at Michigan Mead also met and was influenced by C. H. Cooley who, at the time, was writing a doctoral dissertation in economics. Mead noted, on the basis of Cooley's work, how economic exchanges in everyday life proceeded more smoothly when the seller was able to assume the perspective of the buyer and vice versa. This 'assuming the role of the other' with respect to oneself is central to Mead's social psychology.

When Dewey was invited, in 1894, to become head of the Department of Philosophy at the newly established University of Chicago he accepted the appointment on the condition that he could bring Mead with him from Michigan as an assistant professor. Thus it was that the Chicago school of pragmatist philosophy came into being. The Deweys and the Meads saw a great deal of each other as families, with Dewey and Mead endlessly engaged in discussing philosophy and psychology. It was probably on the basis of such discussions that Dewey wrote his famous 1896 article in 'Psychological Review' on the reflex arc concept in psychology (Dewey, 1896). In the article Dewey warned of the dangers of adopting the reflex arc as the basic unit of behaviour in psychology. This was some time before behaviourism acquired its normative status within psychology. The ideas in this early Dewey paper were subsequently developed by Mead in his theory of human action (see Mead, 1938).

J. B. Watson went up to Chicago to study for his doctorate under Dewey. In his autobiography he claims that he never really understood Dewey and that he still did not. Instead, he completed his doctorate on animal studies. In his autobiography Watson had this to say of Mead: 'I took courses and seminars with Mead. I didn't understand him in the classroom, but for years Mead took a great interest in my animal experimentation, and many a Sunday he and I spent in the laboratory watching my rats and monkeys. On these comradely exhibitions and at his home I understood him. A kinder, finer man I never met' (Watson, 1936, p. 274). Whilst Watson may not have understood Mead I think it is highly probable that Mead understood Watson. Mead established in philosophy a much subtler and more sophisticated form of behaviourism than Watson was later to establish within psychology.

Mead first began to give his annual course of lectures on social psychology around the year 1900. Albion Small, the first head of the Department of Sociology at Chicago, was quick to appreciate the potential significance for sociology of this course of lectures offered in the Department of Philosophy. It was not long before he made this course a requirement for all students enrolling in the doctoral programme in sociology at Chicago. Chicago was rapidly to become one of the foremost centres for sociological research in the world. It was certainly the pace-setter in America. This was how Mead's social psychology came to be preserved within American sociology. This course of lectures became so central to the whole development of sociology in America that when Mead died in 1931 it was necessary to find a successor. It was Herbert Blumer who took over Mead's course of lectures in social psychology. It is important to appreciate that Blumer was a sociologist and not a philosopher. His interests were in social psychology rather than in the general problems of philosophy which Mead treated. It was Blumer who first introduced the terms 'symbolic interactionism' to characterize this particular form of social psychology. There is still, to this day, a healthy symbolic interactionist tradition of social psychology within American sociology.

There was, of course, much more to Mead than his 'Mind, Self and Society' course of lectures. I agree with Miller (1973) that if one reads the rest of Mead's philosophy then 'Mind, Self and Society' can profitably be re-read with a much deeper understanding of the issues involved. Indeed Strauss had something like this in mind when he edited other writings of Mead's for their possible relevance to social psychology (Strauss, 1956, 1964). I think there are some systematic distortions in the sociologists' understanding of Mead. In 'Mind, Self and Society' Mead was explicitly critical of Watsonian behaviourism within psychology. It is, therefore, easy to misread his social psychology as being an anti-behaviourist one or, more appropriately in the context of sociology, as being anti-positivist. The 'ethos' of the symbolic interactionist tradition of social psychology is certainly an anti-positivist one.

Any bias of an anti-positivist nature only makes it more difficult to appreciate that what Mead was proposing was, in fact, a form of behaviourism. He believed that Watson had not gone far enough. More than anything else, he believed that Watson over-simplified things. It was Watson's failure to come up with a behavioural account of mind which Mead found to be inadequate. It would be equally unfortunate if psychologists were now to discover Mead because his critique of behaviourism chimes with their own expressed dissatisfactions. To accept Mead is to accept some form of social behaviourism. Misperceptions of Mead's stance on the part of sociologists may be facilitated by the current tendency, following Blumer, to refer to his social psychology as 'symbolic interactionism' rather than as 'social behaviourism'. It is also difficult, I believe, for sociologists to appreciate the extent to which Mead developed his philosophy on the basis of a very close reading of Darwin. He even argued, convincingly to my mind, that it was inaccurate of Darwin to talk of animals 'expressing' their emotions. This said, however, it is greatly to the credit of the sociologists at Chicago that they could appreciate, better than the psychologists there, the significance of Mead's social psychology for their own discipline. Mead's own reading of biology, physiology and psychology was much more extensive than his knowledge of social science. His lectures should have been even more appropriate to psychologists than they proved to be to sociologists. It seems a pity, in retrospect, that the psychologists at Chicago appear to have been in the wrong classrooms for their ancillary subjects!

Why has the calibre of Mead's thinking not been more widely recognized? None of the books which now outline his thinking was published during his life time. His early publications were book reviews or occasional papers (e.g. there were a couple on Wundt's 'folk psychology'). He was in the habit of continually updating and revising his thinking through the medium of his various lecture courses at Chicago. He invariably delivered these lectures without the aid of notes. Mead was already well advanced in his career before his colleagues and students devised the strategy of hiring a stenographer to make a verbatim record of what he said in the classrooms. It is these fairly full stenographic records of his various courses and/or students' notes which have been edited and published posthumously as books. Even where manuscripts came to light after his death they needed to be carefully edited and introduced, usually by former graduate students of Mead who had attended the relevant courses. There is no reason to believe that they now appear in a form of which Mead would have approved. He clearly influenced those who heard him or else we would not now have even the inadequate record of his thinking which we do.

Perhaps the psychologists at Chicago under Angell (a prominent functionalist of his day) were too pre-occupied with gaining their own independence from philosophy and with gestating their own brand of behaviourism for Mead's thinking and teaching to have struck any responsive chords. We have already noted above that Watson, on his own admission, did not understand what Mead was talking about in his classroom lectures.

Mead's model of man

Mead set out to account for those very characteristics which set man apart from other species, that is human culture, human society, language, self-awareness and the human capacity for thought, etc. He was generally interested in man's higher cognitive processes; that is, those processes which Wundt had made focal in his folk psychology. These were also the processes which Watson had left out of account in his development of behaviourism. Regarding Mead's concern with man's higher cognitive processes, it is interesting to note that Thurstone, in his conception of human intelligence, acknowledged the influence of Mead. (I am grateful to my colleague Richard Rawles for drawing this to my attention.)

Mead was more interested in identifying those purely human phenomena which emerge in the course of evolution than he was in stressing the commonalities between man and other species. In this respect Mead provides the intellectual underpinnings for the view of man put forward in this volume by Reynolds (chapter 3). The model is one of man as a species and the time scale is that of man's evolutionary past. This is also where Mead differs so sharply from Watson. Both Watson and Mead accepted the Darwinian perspective but the one stressed the continuity, whilst the other stressed the discontinuity, between man and other species. This difference in emphasis gives rise to two totally different psychologies. The limitations of Watsonian (and Skinnerian) behaviourism are daily becoming as clear to us now as they were to Mead when Watson was first formulating them. Hence I would argue that Mead is peculiarly relevant, at this particular juncture, to the way in which psychology might develop in the future.

Mead had this to say of Watson's cavalier attitude to the task of accounting for consciousness and related phenomena: 'There remained, however, the field of introspection, of experiences which are private and belong to the individual himself - experiences commonly called subjective. What was to be done with these? John B. Watson's attitude was that of the Queen in Alice in Wonderland "Off with their heads!" - there were no such things. There was no imagery and no consciousness ...' (Mead, 1934, pp. 2-3). Morris, who introduced and edited Mead's 'Mind, Self and Society', was himself interested in the broader behaviourism which Mead was advocating. Indeed he himself went on to establish semiotics on a purely behavioural basis (Morris, 1946). In his introduction to Mead he charitably suggested that 'The judgment of time will perhaps regard Watsonism as behaviourism methodologically simplified for purposes of initial laboratory investigation' (Morris, p. xvii in Mead, 1934). Here Morris sees the narrower form of behaviourism as suited to the requirements of a laboratory science. The 'narrow' conception of behaviour came to replace Wundt's 'narrow' conception of consciousness as the basis for a laboratory science of psychology. In the earlier instance, however, Wundt could at least see the necessity of supplementing the narrow laboratory conception of consciousness by the broader study of mind in society. In the latter instance Watson remained oblivious to any need to supplement his own over-simplified view of behaviour.

Mead believed that Darwin's 'Expression of the Emotions in Man and Animals' was one of the important documents in the history of psychology. He thought that it was particularly important for any psychology of language. On the basis of Darwin's work Wundt had developed his notion of the 'gesture'. Wundt, unlike Darwin, placed the gesture in its social context. It was this aspect of Wundt's work which Mead picked up and developed. Mead discussed the 'conversation of gestures' involved in the dog and cat fights which Darwin had described so graphically in his book. Animals engaging in such 'conversations' strike postures and adopt attitudes towards each other. The term 'attitude' for Darwin (and hence also for Wundt and for Mead) referred to the often full-bodied orientation of one organism with respect to another. It is a matter of regret, in my opinion, that this purely behavioural meaning of attitude has fallen into disuse (see Fleming, 1967). One benefit which might flow from adopting Mead's model of man is the possible rehabilitation of this behavioural conception of attitude. A gesture was a part action which others completed. It was thus, for Mead, a social action. Mead then went on to develop the whole of his social psychology from this conception of the gesture. 'Mead specifically thinks of the gesture in social terms and from such gestures traces the development of genuine language communication. In one sense, then, Mead may be said to follow a path partially indicated by Wundt; and certainly Wundt helped him to correct the inadequacies of an individualistic psychology by the employment of social categories' (Morris, p. xiii in Mead, 1934). Mead's highly distinctive approach is to define the 'meaning' of a gesture or action as being the response which it evokes in others. In the course of interacting with others an individual's conduct acquires the same significance for himself that it originally had for those others. Meaning is thus central to Mead's behaviourism. It is peripheral to the behaviourism of Watson and Skinner. Much of the meaning in human affairs is conveyed through speech.

Wundt believed that possibly the most significant gestures to appear in the course of human development were the vocal gestures which underlay the development of speech. Mead developed this point much further and made language central to the whole of his social psychology. 'Mead's endeavour is to show that mind and the self are without residue social emergents; and that language, in the form of the vocal gesture, provides the mechanism for their emergence' (Morris, p. xiv in Mead, 1934). The individual is an object in the social world of other people. By interacting with others he becomes an 'object' to himself. This, in a nutshell, is Mead's theory of the human self. 'The self does not exist except in relation to something else. The word "itself", you will recognise, belongs to the reflexive mode. It is that grammatical form which we use under conditions in which the individual is both subject and object. He addresses himself. He sees himself as others see him. The very usage of the word implies an individual who is occupying the position of both subject and object. In a mode which is not reflexive, the object is distinguished from the subject. The subject, the self, sees a tree. The latter is something that is different from himself. In the use of the term "itself", on the contrary, the subject and object are found in the same entity' (Mead, 1936, p. 74). It is now my firm opinion that man is more truly reflexive in the auditory than he is in the visual modality (Farr, in press). Man rarely appears as an object in his own visual field but he can and does hear himself talk. It is interesting that one of the very few other models of man to contain reflexive components - the psychoanalytic model - should be the outcome of a careful listening to others talking about themselves.

The extent to which Mead and Watson in their respective behaviourisms emphasize different sensory modalities is worth highlighting. As language plays such a key role in his social psychology Mead attached a lot of importance to the processes of speaking and listening. Sometimes speaker and listener are one and the same person as in Mead's theory of thinking. The internal dialogues involved in the process of thinking reflect the symbolic interactions which occur in the wider society of the thinker. 'Behaviorism accordingly meant for Mead not the denial of the private nor the neglect of consciousness, but the approach to all experience in terms of conduct' (Morris, p. xvii in Mead, 1934). Gestures become, for Mead, significant gestures when they acquire the same meaning for the person making them that they evoke in others who respond to them. Language is an excellent example of an important class of significant gesture. Through language shared meanings are conveyed in a highly symbolic form. It is worth recalling at this point that the significant unit in Wundt's social psychology was that of the 'folk community' -the community of those who share a common language.

Man as an organism is finely tuned to surviving in his environment - but for man, to an extent that is almost unique in the animal kingdom, this environment is a highly symbolic one. It is easy to overlook the significance of this invisible environment. 'Mind', 'self' and 'society' - not one of these is visible to the naked eye. Yet each term refers to an important reality. Mead thought deeply about these realities over a period of some 40 years. As mentioned earlier, Dahrendorf in his early work 'Homo Sociologicus' wrestled in a similar way with what he termed the 'vexatious fact of society' (Dahrendorf, 1958). He neatly articulated the difficulties which arise in a discipline from not being able to point to the object of one's study. The realities of mind, self and society are easily ignored because they are unseen. This was Watson's great error. It is his sins of omission which now weigh heavily on psychology as a discipline. The decision to base the science of psychology on what was publicly observable was a deliberate and fully conscious one. Observable here meant 'available to visual inspection'. It was the verbal reports of the old introspectionist which were being discredited. Mead's behaviourism was much more flexible than Watson's had been and he attached considerable importance to the activities of speaking, listening and thinking. Mead, as a social psychologist, was centrally concerned with 'communication'. He was as critical of Wundtian introspection as was Watson. Unlike Watson, however, he was fully familiar with, and improved on, Wundt's social psychology.

I have traced elsewhere how behaviourism resulted in a radical reduction in the status of 'subjects' within laboratory contexts (Farr, 1978a,b; see also Adair, 1973). Under the influence of Watson and of Skinner language ceased to be the principal vehicle for the social conveyance of meaning and became instead mere 'verbal behaviour'. The verbal emissions of subjects participating in research were noted and logged by experimenters rather than being listened to and understood. The extent to which experimental psychology is still biased in favour of the visual mode of exploration may not currently be fully appreciated. An example of an early attempt to swim against the tide can be found in Broadbent's 'Perception and Communication' (Broadbent, 1958). It is true that much is now changing in experimental psychology and that Joynson (1974) can accurately enough refer to 'the return of mind'. In many laboratories behaviour (in the narrow sense of Watson and Skinner) is on the way out and mind, under the guise of 'cognition', is on the way in. The time is now ripe to recognize the distinctive merits of Mead's model of man as a suitable underpinning for contemporary experimental psychology.

That the visual modality of exploration is still a powerfully entrenched one is perhaps best appreciated when taking stock of what are claimed, by their proponents, as 'new paradigms' for research which involve little more than a switch in the sensory modality of investigation: for example, the plea by Harré & Secord (1972) that we should elicit and listen to the 'accounts' that persons can give of their actions. A paradigm shift, if there has ever been such a thing in psychology, is not a matter of substituting one type of data for another. We have already noted above how the either/or nature of the decision concerning whether 'consciousness' or 'behaviour' should be the subject matter of psychology led to the uneven development of the discipline. What is needed is an appropriate model of man of the both/and variety which can account both for consciousness and behaviour; both for 'reasons' and 'causes'; both for 'accounts' and 'actions'. Too much of social psychology is concerned either with attitudes or behaviour but rarely with the interrelation between the two. Interviews and interactions are studied quite independently of one another. Mead proposed a suitable model of man quite some time ago. It deserves our attention.

I do not wish to convey, in the immediately preceding paragraphs, that Mead was not interested in, or had not something useful to contribute to, the study of visual perception. I was seeking merely to indicate the advantages, within psychology, of adopting his model of man: the prospect of according speech and language a more central role in experimental psychology than they have enjoyed to date. Psychologists have not yet faced up to the challenges and excitements of integrating what they know about behaviour through visual exploration (scientific observation) with other evidence of an auditory nature which they may have about those same behavioural events. Amongst the physical sciences astronomy has become an exciting discipline in recent decades due to the challenge of integrating the knowledge derived from radio astronomy with the wealth of knowledge acquired over the centuries from the purely visual exploration of the universe. The exciting prospect of integrating different kinds of information about the same events lies in the future for psychology rather than being found in its past. I am referring here, of course, to cross-modal integration in the mind of the research scientist rather than to the already well-established field of study of cross-modal integration of information in the research subject.

There are whole psychologies based only on listening to persons talking. Psychoanalysis is probably the best example of such a psychology. Freud's training as a research physiologist was in the visual exploration of the natural world (amongst other things, for example, he was searching for testicles in the eel!). The switch in sensory modality to listening to clients talking about their problems must have been dramatic. The conflict throughout his professional career between the psychological language he was developing for talking about the human body and the physiological language of his earlier training is beautifully brought out in a book by Marie Jahoda (1977). The languages were incompatible. We are still here in the stage of either/or. Over half a century ago Mead was beginning to make some progress towards a both/and approach.

In relation to visual perception Mead was very much a haptic philosopher. The relationship between vision and touch was critical for him. His philosophy is certainly relevant to anyone with a contemporary interest in the answer to Molyneux's question. It is, therefore, surprising that a recent stimulating book on this fascinating question (Morgan, 1977) contains no reference to Mead even though the author covers several centuries of thought amongst philosophers on the issue. Mead's reading of Darwin led him to identify two emergent properties which set man apart from other species. The first was the human hand and the relationship, in the course of human evolution, between the hand and the central nervous system. The second characteristic was the development of the vocal gesture in the direction of speech and human language. By singling out and focusing on these evolutionary emergents Mead highlights what is distinctly human. His model of man emerges from a close reading of Darwin. It therefore represents a genuinely bio-social approach to the study of man. '... the problem as to how the human mind and self arise in the process of conduct is answered by Mead in biosocial terms' (Morris, p. xv in Mead, 1934). It has the distinct merit, in contrast to other biosocial 'syntheses' (e.g. Eysenck's contribution to the present volume, chapter 4), of treating the biological and the social as being of equal importance. To my way of thinking this makes Mead's form of behaviourism preferable to the behaviourism of either Watson or Skinner. His model of man really is a model of man. Too much of experimental psychology is still rather narrowly focused on what it is that man shares in common with other species.

EDITED DISCUSSION

R. L. REID: This is in the nature of a comment rather than a question. What Skinner says about understanding one's self is that you observe your own behaviour and its determinants in the way that you observe the behaviour of others. You learn to understand your own behaviour by answering questions that people ask about that behaviour. You give the kind of answer that you would give if it were to be someone else, but it happens to be yourself. Skinner would also say, and Mead would say, that you have privileged access to some facts that are not normally available when you deal with the behaviour of other people. I certainly conclude that the accounts of Mead and Skinner are very similar. Certainly Skinner is very much aware of the philosophy of Mead.

L. SMITH: I wonder whether Mead did anticipate the philosophy of Ryle and Wittgenstein? Ryle denied that he was a behaviourist and, even if he were wrong in that, his behaviourism is logical behaviourism. Ryle, for example, tries to explain the meaning of the word 'intelligent', and its meaning is explained by reference to various dispositions. That is very different from 'radical behaviourism' which tries to take certain events in the world, like behaviour, and to relate them to various other parts of the world - for example, what is going on in my environment. So, I wonder whether Mead is a forerunner of Skinner? Secondly, if I gesture to you right now, in this open discussion, I wonder what meaning you would confer upon the gesture. Suppose that I now make a thumbs-up gesture. You may tell me that it means good luck. But is that its meaning for Mead? My meaning might be quite different: for example, corresponding to that given to a Roman gladiator.

R. M. FARR: Well, a gesture elicits a response from others. Mead identified the 'meaning' of a gesture with the response it elicits from others. Hence his philosophy was a form of social behaviourism. Your gesture comes to have the same meaning for yourself as it originally had for others when they responded to it. It is not automatic. But the main mechanism by which meaning is conveyed is language. Language is absolutely central to the whole of Mead's social psychology. Wundt, influenced by Darwin, suggested that the most significant gestures for human development were the vocal gestures that led on to speech. Mead picked that up and argued that words when they are spoken have the same meaning for the person who speaks them as for the person who hears them. This is where the folk community enters again, and my own argument is that man is more reflexive in the auditory than the visual modality. (We are not an object in our own visual field; but we do hear ourselves talk.) This is very important in relation to contemporary, cognitive psychology. Mead provides the rationale for assigning language a central role. What I find intriguing is that the things which make man distinctive as a species cannot be seen. You cannot see words, 'mind', 'self' or 'society'; yet these are realities. The problem is trying to indicate why they are realities.

A. J. LOCK: I find a striking parallel between a lot of Mead's notions and those put forward by Vygotsky, despite the fact that these two were geographically far removed from each other. Both, for example, suggest that the self has to appear within the social process before it can be identified by the individual and become part of his consciousness. This trend appears to be important in Artificial Intelligence, and in what Rom Harré has said, and elsewhere too. I am interested in the general problem of how one starts representing these implicit abilities, before they are formalized into language, program, proposition and so on. How do you then build up a model of man to deal with these non-objective, implicit, non-propositional phenomena? In a sense they cannot be mechanistic but you cannot represent them in terms of what they are not.

R. M. FARR: In contrast to Watson, Mead focused on what makes man different from other species. He asked: how do we account for mind, self-consciousness, language and so forth? He would argue that his own overall perspective is not incompatible with explanations in terms of mechanism. He argues too that when something new evolves, you need to create a past to account for it. There is no such thing as a single past in relation to what happens. New events require the identification of new antecedents in order to account for them. As for the link between the thinking of Vygotsky and Mead, I would agree that there are great similarities, but of course neither could have influenced the other.

V. REYNOLDS: How would Mead deal with one's thinking about a personal problem, say a pain? Is his analysis in the least bit concerned with that?

R. M. FARR: How the individual comes to have a knowledge of his own physiology is an interesting problem. Presumably we learn about that from the outside: from the socializing community. Mead would be interested in the states of awareness between which we alternate - whether man is aware of himself as an object and therefore self-conscious or whether he is so engaged in an activity that he is not self-conscious about things. This latter state of awareness may actually be incompatible with the experience of pain.

R. HARRE: May I add a little footnote? The way in which one acquires a vocabulary for speaking of one's inner states is not by developing a private language. There is a difference between this as an observation about developmental psychology, to which I think the Vygotsky reference is germane, and as an observation about the way competent adults proceed. The latter proceed as if they have a private language, but from a developmental point of view we know that they could not possibly have a private language. The beauty of Vygotsky's ideas about 'becoming privatized' and Lichenstein's notions about the way language spreads across these barriers is that they enable us to solve the apparent paradox.

H. PRICE: Mead seemed to take a common-sense view of the relationship between mind and behaviour, much more so than Skinner did.   He looked at how mind developed from behaviour.

R. M. FARR: Mead was much more explicitly cognitive than Skinner.   With behaviourism there is a separation between the world as observed (behaviour) and the world of the observer.   Mead believed it was a mistake to focus so exclusively on what was publicly observable.   He says, for example, that the beginnings of an action are not visible.

N. E. WETHERICK: I find it difficult to follow your idea of the social origins of consciousness in view of the remarks that have been made about language.   I accept that we cannot possibly have a private language.   We learn language in a social context and we subsequently use language for private or social purposes. To me this implies that there is some consciousness that enables us to use this language, socially or privately as we determine.   How could this consciousness be determined socially?

R. M. FARR: Mead is not denying that animals have consciousness ...

N. E. WETHERICK: Animals may well have consciousness in his sense.   But if one is capable of thematizing one's consciousness so as to talk about it to oneself and to others, I do not see how that consciousness is determined.

R. M. FARR: Mead would claim that consciousness is different because of man's reflexiveness.   The fact that we each have a name which other people use is crucial.   We are an object in the social worlds of others and, through social interaction, we become an object to ourselves.   That is distinctively human. The nub of the matter is that 'meaning' is central in Mead's thinking; and it is socially constructed and socially mediated.

Chapter 14

Man as rhetorician

R. Harré

The word 'model' is sometimes used to point to an ideal or exemplar. In this sense the natural sciences have recently been taken as a model for psychology. But to use such a complex combination of intellectual techniques and empirical practices as exemplar some analysis must be presumed, revealing the salient features. But the natural sciences are far from transparent, and there are many rival views as to what are their salient features. Some of these views seem now definitely to be wrong. Unfortunately much of recent psychology has been based upon exemplars supposedly taken from natural science, but in fact reflecting some of these mistaken views. An obvious case is the setting up an ideal of simplicity. Despite the prestige of Einstein's semi-mystical neo-Platonism the history of science uniformly illustrates the contrary principle - later and more adequate treatments of a field of phenomena are more complex both in structure and in conceptual foundations than are earlier ones. So much for a general defence of the simplifications of radical behaviourism.

The natural sciences are neither inductive nor hypothetico-deductive. They do not develop by simple accumulation of accepted and verified fact. By the end of the 15th century discussions in the philosophy of astronomy had reached that conclusion. In 'De Stella Martis' Kepler demonstrated the non-inductive character of astronomy by revealing that he had not reached his hypothesis that planetary orbits were elliptical from a study of the known positions of Mars. He had tried that route and failed. Success had come from testing the consequences of an assumption that the orbits were elliptical. The temptation to use this case to support a hypothetico-deductive methodology was scotched by Clavius in his 'In Sphaeram de Sacrobosco' of 1600. He pointed out that there are infinitely many alternative theories from which correct descriptions of the known facts can be deduced. All but one of these are false. The chances of hitting on the true one, by the use of the hypothetico-deductive method alone are therefore as near as you like to zero.

So let us not burden a discussion about 'models of man' with naive pictures of science that are logical nonsense. Theories, it seems, are representations of hidden realities, the mechanisms which generate phenomena. At the same time our capacity to discern the phenomena are not independent of the theories we hold. The natural sciences are, in an important way, circular. Empirical work is not usually, perhaps not ever, the source of knowledge. It provides us with anecdotes to illustrate the explanatory and interpretative power of our conceptions. I too wish to model the human on the natural sciences, but on the latter as they really are!

BASES FOR A 'MODEL' OF MAN

We must choose the right sense of model. There is no more equivocal word in the vocabulary of metascientists, amateur and professional, than the word 'model'. In order to locate my remarks on adopting a model of man as rhetorician, I need to make, or perhaps remind you of, the basic distinctions in the use of that term.

The most universally applicable distinction is that between model as homoeomorph, that is a simplified representation of a complex reality; and model as paramorph, that is a simulacrum of an unknown entity standing in for the real thing by its capacity to behave in similar ways. A biological diagram is a homoeomorph; that is a simplified representation of a complex organic structure. The kinetic theory of gases describes a paramorph since a swarm of molecules can be seen to simulate the behaviour of real gases. A homoeomorph is modelled on its subject, while a paramorph is a model of its subject.

In sampling the other offerings for the 'Models of Man' Conference I was struck by how many proffer models which are not more than homoeomorphs, that is abstractions and idealizations of already 'visible' attributes of human beings. For instance the 'bio-social' model proposed by Eysenck is just such a homoeomorph. Homoeomorphic models depend on an identity between subject and source. A model boat is both a model of a boat and modelled on a boat. In the process of scaling potential information is necessarily lost. Of course homoeomorphs do have some pragmatically desirable features. They reveal structures that can be 'seen at a glance'. But in comparison with paramorphic models they are scientifically weak since they involve loss of content. Paramorphs promise its amplification. Since a paramorphic model draws on a source other than its subject, it necessarily and adventurously serves to amplify potential information about that subject.

Human beings and their modes of life are sufficiently complex to show 'cross-modelling'. One aspect of life, say, the use of language and other symbols for expressive purposes (rhetoric) can be used as a paramorph for some aspect of life apparently in the practical order, such as trades-union/management negotiations, so amplifying our capacity to grasp features of the model's subject by reference to features borrowed from its source. Thus we may come to see, under the guidance of the paramorph, man as rhetorician, that in many negotiations the ostensible matter of concern, say economic advantage, is not the central focus of motivation. The latter may be some expressive good, such as dignity or respect, definable only in terms of the model's appropriate vocabulary. In using one aspect of men's complex lives for explaining another, simplified representations of both are required. Each of these will be a homoeomorphic model of indefinitely elaborate reality.

In developing a theory in science a cognitive order is created among the materials germane to the problem. Let me show how to reveal that order with an analysis in terms of the paramorphic notion of modelling. In the cognitive structures behind the ostensible discourse of theorizing are three points of application for the notion of 'model'.

The phenomena of a field are complex and enigmatic, partially revealed through application of common-sense concepts embedded in ordinary language. An analytical model is required to carry further the disembedment of non-random patterns in our experience of a field of interest. For example, by systematically seeking for family relationships among plants and animals Darwin disembedded the properties of lines of descent of ancestral sequences of organisms. Since Boyle and Hooke thought of enclosed air as a spring they were able to pick out the relation between pressure and volume as the embedded pattern of interest from all the other properties that their samples of gas displayed.

Positivists stop there. Real scientists, imbued with the desperate need to understand, want to know how the patterns revealed by observation and experiment, informed by an analytical model, are generated. But at this stage in the life trajectory of a science the concepts and techniques that have guided the work are not usually able to reveal the generators. They must be imagined. An explanatory model must be created as a simulacrum of the real causal mechanism. In the terms of the general distinction above, it must be a paramorph (Harré, 1979).

The kinetic theory of gases is an old standby to illustrate the way a model of an unknown structure, namely the internal features of gases, is constructed.

Molecule ⇄⟶ Newtonian particle ⇄⟶ Material thing

The likenesses and differences of each item in this sequence control the acceptability of the molecule as a possible real entity. Newtonian particles are refined versions of material things, since certain properties of material things - for example their medicinal properties and their colour - are not treated when they are analysed as Newtonian particles. But molecules are themselves abstractions from the full prescription of a Newtonian particle since at least in their earliest forms they lacked volume and spin and a number of other plausible properties. Of course, as the kinetic theory developed molecules became more and more like Newtonian particles and their claim to reality consequently improved.

But this kind of construction is not confined to the physical sciences. One of the most beautiful applications of the method is to be found in Darwin's (1859) 'The Origin of Species by Natural Selection'. Darwin seems to have been in full control of this theory of theorizing and uses it quite explicitly.

Natural selection ⇄⟶ Domestic selection ⇄⟶ Breeding

Darwin considers the concept of natural selection as indeed derived through a sequence of likeness and difference relations from the breeding he observed being carried out by farmers and gardeners. Domestic selection is a schematized and abstracted version of breeding since the particular demands of the breeder are generalized to an abstract concept of adaptation to whatever requirements might be put upon the species. (There is a further refinement, one of Darwin's more beautiful philosophical analyses, in which he carefully distinguishes the concept of variety from that of species.) The move to natural selection, again via consideration of likenesses and differences with domestic selection, is the process by which Darwin's paramorphic model of the mechanisms of species change is actually developed, and he devotes considerable attention to contemplating the kinds of likenesses and differences that must obtain.

These cases are representative of thousands of examples scattered throughout the natural sciences. They illustrate the power of the source model in controlling the formulation of the paramorphic model whose description constitutes theory. In scientists of genius such as Newton, Faraday and Darwin, the source model is constantly before their minds; they devote considerable attention to its analysis and justification. It is in the source model that the metaphysical and moral and political aspects of sciences are most obviously realized.

However, source models are rarely explicitly formulated in day-to-day science and their idiosyncratic features are not usually publicly addressable. It is part of the virtues of introducing the model analysis for the content of theories that source models must be paid attention to, controlling as they do selection of likenesses and differences that go into the formulation of the central concepts of a theory. However, when source models do come to the attention of scientists, sometimes through the efforts of philosophers, the moral and political aspects are often striking. For example, in psychology, the most important distinction, I suppose, is that between the two source models 'Man as automaton' and 'Man as agent'. The political consequences of adopting one rather than the other of these sources have been made very obvious in some recent controversies. In developing the 'Man as rhetorician' model in the latter part of this chapter, I pay attention to the source model from which it is drawn.

Of course, source models are not the only controlling constraints on the formulation of explanatory models. 'A swarm of molecules' is an explanatory model for a gas because the imagined behaviour of the swarm is very like the real behaviour of a gas, though the model comes to be formulated just because physicists had at that time no idea of the constitution of gases. The adequacy of the theory, then, turns in the end on the balance between the behavioural analogy of its explanatory model to the behaviour of real-world objects and its material analogy to its source model. But all of this assumes that we know how to analyse the behaviour of gases. And that presupposes the existence of a coordinate analytical model. It is useless to pick out patterns among phenomena which could not be simulated by the explanatory models at hand. It is pointless to elaborate explanatory models that are appropriate to a simulation of patterns quite other than those the most powerful analytical models enable an investigator to discern.

Each model of man, and I would advocate allowing a hundred models to grow where one prejudice stood before, serves to pick out an aspect of a very complex reality, a reality which is essentially enigmatic; and this because it is very characteristic of human beings to reduce what they are doing as quickly and conveniently as possible to routine and even habit to free their butterfly minds for contemplating higher things such as sex, religion, fashion and motor cars. The mistake, I believe, of much previous psychology has been to become so fascinated with one model as to fail to realize that a special case has to be made for transforming it from the analytical to the explanatory mode, and then generalizing to a universal theory. As Secord and I argued some years ago, the only sensible procedure at this stage of the art, is to assemble an ensemble of models, to consider their power relative to both the analytic and the explanatory task, and then to engage in the theoretical exercise of looking at the possibilities of their being jointly applied (Harré & Secord, 1972). I believe that those possibilities can best be examined by relating each model to the cybernetic network which would be required to represent its system properties. Now what does the model of man as rhetorician pick out of the complex of our psycho-social activities?

In order to understand the force of this model we need to introduce the distinction between the practical order of society, which is concerned with the social organization of the production of the means of life, and the expressive order, the social organization of the production of such goods as dignity, pride, status, respect and their opposites, humiliation and contempt. Now I am not suggesting that these orders are ontologically distinct and that we stop studying the genesis of patterns of practical work and concentrate only on the study of face work. Every activity in which we engage ought to be considered with respect to its effectiveness as a practical act and as an expressive act. The distinction between these orders is analytic, not ontological. By choosing to operate under the model of man as rhetorician as opposed, say, to the model of man as transformer of raw material, or man as machine-minder, man as capitalist, or whatever, we direct our attention to action in the expressive order. At the worst we provide ourselves with an analytical scheme. With any luck we may find a coordinate explanatory system. We might look for the same kind of processes in the production of a strike, let us say, that we would look for in the production of a play. Just sometimes we might find them. The popular and powerful dramaturgical model for social/psychological investigations is primarily an analytical model; that is, it provides us with a set of concepts by means of which we can analyse an otherwise mysterious and enigmatic reality. One looks at a doctor's surgery, armed with Goffman's dramaturgical metaphors, and identifies front-stage, back-stage, props, costumes and so on. But, it would be a misunderstanding of the role of an analytical model to suppose that it could be immediately transformed into a coordinate explanatory model. For example, great light is cast on the organization of a clinic, by looking at it as the staging for dramas of character. It does not follow, however, that doctors are producing their activity like actors are producing theirs. The dramaturgical model is powerful analytically and rather weak explanatorily. In terms of another well-worn distinction analytical models are closely related to competence theories, while explanatory models are closely related to performance theories. With this distinction in mind we can now turn to the model I wish to advocate.

What is it, then, to say that we should treat man as a rhetorician? Certainly such a model must begin as an analytical model, that is, we should look upon speech and action in a human being as persuasive, as expressive, as being used for the purposes of getting others to see the events in the light that the orator, rhetorician, propagandist, etc., wishes them to be seen. I believe myself that this model provides us not only with analytical concepts, but can also become explanatory. To make that claim is to suggest that what are at least apparently other categories of action than the obviously rhetorical are produced by an individual actor in a manner similar to that and for similar purposes for which he produces explicit rhetoric. So that the mildly Machiavellian stance which a person deliberately engaging in rhetorical speech adopts to his listeners is, I would argue, part of the psychological conditions for a great deal of expressive activity that is not obviously rhetorical; as, for example, one might instance the choice of clothes, hair length, dishes to serve to guests, etc.

To say 'Man is a rhetorician' is to put before you an analytical model coordinate with an image of a human being engaged in talk - speaking of others so as to construct at least some part of his psychology, that is, of the many-faceted mechanisms controlling action, as he goes along. These constructions, it will turn out, are for certain quite readily identified social and expressive purposes. Of course, I am not proposing that man is no more than a rhetorician. Only that in order to understand our sort of men we must remember that a good deal of their time is spent, as I argue, in activities which can best be analysed within the science of rhetoric. However, to provide a convincing argument, this model should be amongst several that must be employed. I want to show what it is about the nature of human action and the societies in which it is deployed that leads one to adopt this model for certain purposes.

I suppose no one now would be so bold as to attempt any theoretical psychology without keeping a weather-eye on the philosophical criticisms which surround our subject. So I make no apologies for engaging in some discussion of recent philosophy of mind.

If we are to take seriously the view that people are partly creations of their own talk and other social practices, then since ordinary language and its embedded theories must have a rather central role in that activity, its analysis must be part of the science of psychology. In developing both analytical and explanatory models the conceptual systems of ordinary language must have priority over neologistic constructions and inventions. But this does not entail that common-sense psychology has any absolute hegemony. The folk may be deceived even about themselves, and in particular how far they have indeed succeeded in constructing themselves and their world of interactions in their terms. However, to discern any disparities one must know, so to speak, the ground point from which the folk have presumed themselves to have started.

We have become accustomed to trying to think of the science of psychology in terms of two elderly distinctions, that between inner and outer aspects or properties and states of a being, and that between the subjective and the objective standpoints from which these properties and states are viewed. Sometimes these dichotomies are treated as co-extensive. Traditionally, the methodological discussions which rend psychology from time to time have depended upon assuming the viability of the distinction, treating subjective/inner experience as incommunicable and then struggling with the apparent necessity of referring to and discussing the experience in explaining the pattern of outer behaviour objectively known. Recent philosophical authors such as Wittgenstein, Ryle, Coulter, Blüm and many others, have cast doubt on the very distinctions in terms of which the antique controversies about subjective states as elements in a psychological explanation are conducted. I shall not rehearse these very well-known arguments here. However, if we abandon the traditional Cartesian dichotomies as a way of locating mental concepts, nevertheless there are some important distinctions to be kept in mind to control the genesis of our models through correctly locating the concepts and principles of common-sense, implicit psychology.

By reducing the inner/outer, subjective/objective to a single dichotomy, and projecting the mental exclusively onto the inner/subjective component we get the basis of the traditional, post-Renaissance treatment of psychological processes and properties. At the same time we get all the traditional problems. How can the inner-subjective states produce outer-objective behaviour? How can inner-subjective states be reliably known if an observer can study only outer-objective properties of people? If the reduced dichotomy forms the basic structure of our conceptual system such expressions as 'the public aspects of mind', 'the social construction of consciousness' are meaningless self-contradictions.

Another beginning can be made by taking 'the one and the many' as a fundamental structuring principle, and considering the three phenomena of display, of the exercise of power, and of the existence of order. A separate argument would be needed to demonstrate the fundamental position of these three. Together they yield the three dimensions:

	One	Many	Leading associated concepts	
Display	private.........	public	knowledge	(persona)
Power source	personal........	social	causation	(responsibility)
Order	individual......	collective	structure	(relation)

Unlike the dichotomy of the traditional theory the three dimensions are continuous. The continuity of all three dimensions is mediated by language though each dimension has other mediators as well.

(a) It is important to defend the possibility of personal/individual conditions for action which are not within, in any sense, the individual actor, that is the acts are not private. For example, I might record my intentions in my diary, forget them and then depend on my secretary's use of my diary entry to guide my actions. Similarly, and most importantly, it may very well be that the knowledge that is required for the proper completion of some social activity is not represented completely in any one of the individuals who take part. Important conditions for social action may be collectively represented, though each component part may be in the possession of a single individual. There may be no public representation of everything the folk require to know. Cases could be multiplied readily enough to illustrate the whole range of possible combinations of dimensions.

(b) A second basic distinction of the greatest significance to psychology comes from linguistics. It has been argued that psychological investigation of speech and writing requires two distinctive kinds of theory - competence theories, which have to do with the organization of the knowledge needed by someone able to carry out the performance required by him, and performance theories, theories concerned with the causal generative mechanisms by which performances are produced on particular occasions. It has become clear that the true route to a non-behaviourist, that is genuinely scientific psychology, must be via the competence/performance distinction. But that distinction must be understood in the light of the three dimensions introduced above. For instance, the recent studies of football hooliganism (Marsh et al., 1978) are quite specifically aimed at the discovery of the system of knowledge which must somehow be distributed through a group of fans as a collective. Only individual fractions are represented in the cognitive structures of particular members. We have no idea how that knowledge is actually realized on particular occasions, on actual occasions of ritual and ceremonial action. In recent developments in the technique for studying individual production of action, pioneered by Hacker (1980) in East Germany, and von Cranach (1980) in Switzerland, we are beginning, I think, to get a whiff of a possible performance theory. Be that as it may, this distinction between competence and performance must be distributed over the combinatorial possibilities generated by our previous distinctions in that there are both private and public representations of knowledge, personal and social uses of it, and individual and collective locations of it. For instance, Derek Freeman has told me that in Brunei the Sultan has decreed that a large wall in the centre of Brunei City should contain a public representation of the social order of that state. Anyone can stroll down and locate his position in the complex status hierarchy. Etiquette books perform much the same function for us.

(c) Recent work on such important psychological concepts as intentions, wants and so on, has been much illuminated by studying the language in which they appear with the insights Austin (1963) pioneered in understanding and identifying the social power of speech. It emerges that most common-sense psychological predicates, those which are in use among the folk for constructing psychological claims as they go along are, as I would say, duals. They have a private personal aspect and a public social aspect. A simple example would be the way the performative formula 'I intend to ...' is used. This speech-form serves both to make a public social commitment and to indicate a private individual condition or state. Austin's most important contribution to the psychology of social action, apart from his discovery of the performative functions of speech, was to point out that the use of such formulae would be socially effective quite independently of whether they indeed did correctly describe a private individual state. For instance, an act of commitment may be remembered and its fulfilment insisted upon by the public before whom it has been made, even if the actor himself has quite forgotten the episode. A legal action for breach of promise was, I suppose, the most dramatic form this could take.

An important consequence of all the philosophizing which has gone on around the notion of human action and the possibilities of its explanation is that the inter-actor, be he professional psychologist or plain man, must taxonomize the actions of others, put them into categories, by reference to culturally shared assumptions about the intentions of the other and the conventions which he would be presumed to be using to produce his action. There is no universal one-to-one correspondence between the physical form of an action and its performative force or social effectiveness. Now this is, of course, a basic assumption to any ethogenic psychology. In consequence, there is the possibility of the actor altering the nature of his actions simply by interfering in the course of events with interpretative speech. For example, by declaring his intentions an actor influences the reading of the flow of his activities since he provides for inter-actor a ready-made classificatory scheme for interpreting what he is doing. Much, I would argue, of what is properly to be considered psychological, occurs in public space in the flow of public speech and public debate, in determinant social conditions, by means of which the activities of human beings are transformed from mere movement into meaningful action.

The example of an analytical model I am discussing, 'man as rhetorician', is intended to have its most direct application to social psychology.

It was a vice of the old social psychology to proceed either in ignorance of microsociological analyses of action or, worse still, in the light of naive, unexamined common-sense assumptions about the interpretation of the flow of action, assumptions which, as it turned out, were highly culturally specific. It seems never to have dawned on the vast army of social psychologists working the PhD machines of American universities that they were not discovering universal laws of human nature but reflections of local culture: for example, the use of cost-benefit schema to analyse the psychological basis of love. It is no longer permissible to carry out a psychological investigation without paying the closest attention to the anthropological aspects of the events considered. What are these events, socially speaking: that is, what do they accomplish? How are they related to the culture in which they are embedded?

(a) For the practical purposes of doing social psychology these reminders reduce to the observation that amongst the purposes of actors in engaging in social life and in particular in engaging in talk within it, is the continuous construction and reconstruction of social realities to suit their projects of social advancement, identity definitions and so on. Socially speaking, everything can be made and remade by persuasive talk. The structure and conditions of effectiveness of that talk is at last beginning to be understood.

(b) As the ethnomethodologists have pointed out, the real flow of speech between acting persons involves two different levels of address. There is performative speech, descriptive speech and so on, which is involved in what might be called the level of action. But, being human, actors are acting within and continuously creating a moral world. All that they do, in principle at least, comes up for the possibility of judgement. This introduces the notion of the accountability of actions. Actions divergent from habitual or normal sequences are inherently accountable. But they are actually challenged only occasionally. Sometimes the actor acts in advance of a challenge to pre-empt it by providing an acceptable interpretation of his doings. Empirical research shows that in those flurries there is the clearest revelation of social knowledge. In the twin acts of creating the warrantability and intelligibility of what is being done, are the very rules, conventions, interpretations and so on, that underlie the possibility of the action being understood, classified and so dealt with, by the inter-actor.

I want to illustrate the power of 'Man as rhetorician' as an analytical model, by looking at the phenomenon of rationality. Rationality, or assumptions as to its presence, pop up throughout the psychological sciences. They appear in consistency assumptions of various sorts. For example, consistency is assumed as a natural, personal property by cognitive dissonance theorists, information-processing modellists and so on. Now the criticisms of Festinger's (1957) cognitive dissonance theory have turned on two major matters. Is the notion of cognitive dissonance based upon a logical conception of consistency so that the dissonance arises from the perception of inconsistency between propositions in some representation or other? Or does the theory reflect some kind of processing problem where the dissonance is a feeling produced by forced malfunction, perhaps at the physiological level? Festinger's own version of the theory is systematically ambiguous with respect to these distinctions. In either case, rationality and its cognate property consistency are uncritically taken to be personal, individual attributes, probably universal in mankind.

This raises a further and deeper matter; namely, the endlessly tantalizing distinction between the assumption that man is a natural product and that regularities in social life reflect the workings of natural laws, and the conception of man as an artifact where the regularities in social life are products of culturally distinct, historically generated, rules, customs and practices. It is no secret that I would wish to defend a psychology which almost exclusively plumps for the latter since I can find no evidence whatever to support the former view. Could there be dyslexia, unless the culture required that we read, for instance? It seems to me obvious that a 'psychology' is a reflection of culturally distinctive systems of rules, conventions and meanings. If this is so we should be ready to contemplate the hypothesis that the ideal of rationality is a requirement of our culture, a demand of the expressive conventions by which we display ourselves as persons of public worth. We must show ourselves as rational beings. And that, of course, is a constraint upon, amongst many other things, our rhetoric. Our speech is rich in devices designed to create an impression of rationality, and by 'our speech' I mean the speech current in predominantly male, upper middle-class, intellectual circles, of the last two or three millennia in the Graeco-Latin West.

In order to see a little further into this we should distinguish between the problem of accounting for subjective rationality, that is, of finding social explanations for the appearance of rationality assumptions in theories of human functioning and social explanations of 'objective' rationality; that is, the appearance in public and later private talk of a rationality rhetoric. In my view, the former is strictly - and I mean strictly - dependent on the latter. What, then, is the extension of the concept of rationality?

(i) Social action always comes framed in some way, in an Umwelt imbued with distinctive social meanings, and usually occurs in well-defined settings.   This framing largely controls the range of interpretations which are available to the people present for the understanding of the activity.   It sets, as it were, an outer limit to consistency since, relative to local framings, actions must show the kind of consistency which enables them to be unproblematically taken as intelligible.   So, for example, sequences of events in doctors' surgeries, heavily dramaturgically framed, follow quite different rules from sequences of events in boudoirs.   Consider the very distinctive rationality constructions that would be erected around taking off one's clothes in each setting.   All this pertains to action.

(ii) But human life is not just a life of action. It is shot through, overlain and embedded in talk. And it seems quite clear that both the form and content of that talk is strongly constrained for many people by rationality requirements. It is not so much that talk should persistently show the highest levels of logical consistency, but that it should be couched in a rhetoric of reason.   This, as I understand it, is an expressive demand: that is, it has to do with devices by which we represent to others the kinds of persons we want them to take us to be. The young ladies of Kilvert's rural England were required to show a charming incoherence, an inconsistency of discourse.   Inconsistency and irrationality were taken to be a desirable presentational feature of talk and consequently heavily in demand as an expressive device for showing charm.   The adoption of similar rhetorical devices at the Conference would no doubt lead to social exorcism.

So, it seems, a case can be made for a dramaturgical analysis of the appearance of orderliness in action relative to local framing, and a rhetoric of rationality in speech. It should be quite clear that nowhere in this set of considerations is there the assumption that rationality is a natural feature of the intellect. Several consequences follow: even if some internal connections in systems of belief can be demonstrated this does not necessitate a hypothesis of innate subjective rationality.   The demonstration would have to involve a public display of coherence between action and speech.   If the general principle that the expressive order dominates social life is accepted, no inferences whatever can be made about the private, personal and individual properties of a human being from their publicly displayed, socially demanded and collectively located performances.   Citation of reasons is a public performance.   So there can be no inference without further consideration, from objective to subjective rationality.   Secondly, the assumption that there is a psychology independent of the history of the culture in which we find human beings of a particular sort functioning, must surely be called in question.   If there are historically and culturally generated features of public presentations, and if rationality is one of them, then this calls for historical analysis and comparisons, in particular with respect to the rhetorics of public self-presentation.   I have already mentioned the interesting case of 'female psychology'.   Inconsequentiality was valued in traditional middle-class models of social behaviour for women.   It is a nice question, for which I cannot see a means of formulating an answer just now, as to whether those girls who were clever enough to sustain a perfect representation of inconsequentiality and irrationality, were controlling that performance by a hard look at the consequences for themselves of so performing; were they using private, personal and independent rationality behind the scenes, demonstrated in the beauty of their performances as irrational, inconsequential beings on the public stage?   My guess is that if there were some way in which we could penetrate to the inwardness of a Victorian miss she would be as confused within as she was demonstrably charmingly disordered without.   Again, I can hardly recommend too highly the psychological analyses offered by the Reverend Kilvert.   Furthermore, in the works of our greatest native social psychologist, and in particular in his fine study of female psychology, 'Love's Labours Lost', the varieties of modes of female self-presentation are elegantly exemplified by Shakespeare.   But Rosalind's commentary invokes the possibility of Machiavellian arts open to at least the most designing and discerning of our sisters.   Perhaps the very idea of a 'female psychology' is itself a product of self-fulfilling, historically conditioned conventions.

METHODOLOGICAL REFLECTIONS

Where are we now in the geography of models? My last remarks suggest that we are not able to develop an explanatory model directly from the picture of 'Man (and Woman) as rhetorician'. In that model we have encapsulated an analytical scheme for dealing with the expressive order. When a science is in good form its explanatory models and its analytical models are highly coordinate. What then could serve as coordinate explanatory model for the analytical model I have just been developing? For example, what sort of explanatory model would one offer for the performances of football fans in their skilled use of a rhetoric of fights and bloodshed, which transforms metanymic and metaphorical violence for the purposes of public presentation? For the next stage we could return to the consideration of the practical order - the world of skilled performance and the manipulation of material things, initiated perhaps - though not wholly - for sustaining life. The superb work of Hacker (1980) and von Cranach (1980) has demonstrated the indispensability of both conscious self-monitoring and skilled automatisms in industrial and practical processes. It seems that the rule-following model and the automatic information-processing model are both required to understand, for example, wrapping a parcel, or putting together a piece of electronic equipment in a factory. This line of work seems to demand a general source model under which the conscious self-monitoring of the productive processes of action reveals rule-following and model-realizing in a highly specific form.

The comparison between the ways people make things and the way they generate formal and customary rituals suggests the use of the same cluster of source-models in social psychology for generating a coordinate explanatory model to the analytical scheme I have been arguing for in this chapter. Clearly, formal rituals are produced by conscious rule-following and the rules are publicly represented. But most customary rituals are not generated by conscious rule-following, nor are the rules publicly represented. By the time they are written down in etiquette books they are already out of fashion. But, von Cranach and Hacker have been able to demonstrate that when things go awry and the generative processes are represented in consciousness for repair, the same formal structure of rule-awareness and rule-following seems to be required to represent what is going on. So we find that in customary rituals in the social world where breakdown occurs and repair has to be initiated, the same sort of phenomenon appears. The drastic interferences encouraged by ethnomethodologists in the social world throw up explicit reference to rules, amongst other things, as the resources called upon in undertaking repair. Brenner (1978) has demonstrated the same thing for small-scale interactions where officials ask the folk questions.

The full working out of the consequences of the adoption of this interlocking set of models is far from complete. However, I think one can even at this stage answer affirmatively two searching and central questions.

(i) Is the rule-following agent idea as a source of explanatory models coordinate with the 'Man as rhetorician' idea as an analytical model? The answer I think is clearly 'yes' since the very idea of distinguishing a public performance from the inner world of contemplation, rehearsal and regret, allows for a general Machiavellianism. There may be social rules for the presentation of oneself as incompetent at rule-making. Hollis has recently explored this issue in his admirable book 'Models of Man: Philosophical Thoughts on Social Action' (Hollis, 1977): in comparing the prince as lion and prince as fox as complementary but contradictory presentations Machiavelli enjoins upon a ruler.

(ii) Can we form an explanatory model of the unknown generative process by which these public performances are created? Again the answer seems to be in the affirmative, borrowing the techniques developed in Eastern Europe, together with the work of Brenner (1978) and others in Oxford. This work suggests that conscious sampling of representations of various stages in the process does occur and that when this happens we seem to be in touch with a process which at least is functionally identical with the explicit and conscious activity of following rules. Of course, the next stage will be the empirical evaluation of the rule-following metaphor. We can be fairly sure that a functional identity between whatever is capable of generating speech which conforms to a rationality rhetoric and the iconic model of a conscious agent following a rule has been demonstrated.

The studies of representations sociales reported by Moscovici (1976) remind us of the reflexivity of psychology. If, as psychological beings, men are made not born, then their beliefs as to how they function are likely to become incorporated in their products - themselves and other men. The new discipline of historical psychology has already provided some intriguing hints of the degree to which psychological functioning, both private and public, is an artifact produced by the people-makers of a culture. Two striking examples are the growth of the practice of experiencing personal, private emotions, and of being or striving to be consistent.

From the point of view of the source-model of man as rhetorician the most interesting contemporary culture in which to observe socio-psychological reflexivity is the United States. I have no views on the resolution of the chicken-egg dilemma as to which started the cycle of a psychology based on automatisms and a culture of standardized routines. But it is clear that these are now locked into a progression it may be difficult to break into or halt, while the naive experimental conception of psychology continues to influence practitioners to seek to verify their theories in the very populations which have constructed themselves to realize them.

One can illustrate the point in the expressive order and with respect to the rhetoric model. Man as rhetorician engages in social interactions with his fellows as a spontaneous creator of meaning. Man as an automaton recites pre-programmed formulae. May I remind everyone of the ubiquitous repetition, over that whole vast continent, of the utterance of 'Have a good day, now'. What can one make of this? I suggest it is the product of the absorption into the community at large of a mode of psychological functioning, that of a programmed automaton that derives (dialectically perhaps) from a dominant psychological theory and its characteristic source-model. Perhaps we can help to free our cousins from their self-imposed thraldom by setting them another source-model. Perhaps man as rhetorician would do.

EDITED DISCUSSION

B. FLETCHER: As I see it what you are saying is that man observes the real world in terms of the 'texturing' device. But that in turn was generated from the source model or whatever. That seems to be circular.

R. HARRE: Well, analogies can and do break down under continuous pressure from experimentation. The whole thing is dynamically balanced between the constraints of theorizers working on the source model and the constraints produced by the experimenters working on the analytical model.

J. TURNER: It seems to me that you have been doctrinaire. What you have said is that the way experimental social psychologists are working is proving bankrupt and we should abandon our present styles in order to adopt something totally new. I personally am not aware of having a doctrine but, in any case, I would never allow one to dictate the course of my work. I would rather follow what seems, in the course of my work, to be effective in making sense of problems in which I am interested. (Of course, you implicitly use the same criterion yourself.) In fact, 'man as rhetorician' seems to me a very attractive notion which has worked for over 40 years in experimental social psychology. You must establish that in scientific terms your doctrine is fertile and productive before you may dismiss experimental social psychology.

R. HARRE: Well, I need you to answer fundamental questions. Tell me whether you think, for example, that processes like social comparison are automatic. Are you accessing habits, moment-by-moment processing ...? What is it that you are accessing? Experimental social psychologists do not answer such questions. People are not automatons: they are not motivated by the pressing of buttons. There is a lot behind all this, but the short answer comes in the form of two questions. What is the implicit model underlying what you are doing, and is it acceptable? Do the results of using that model give us any understanding of the social world?

V. REYNOLDS: I should like to bring in some physiology and contrast 'real-life' and 'laboratory' social psychology.   In our research, we find much more physiological responsivenesses in situations which correspond to real-life (e.g. giving a talk) than in laboratory simulations.

J. H. CLARK: Mine is a technical, educational point, relating to Mr Harré's talk - to its style rather than content. He put up a block diagram where arrows were essentially channels between static structures. In the oral delivery, his hand moved along the arrows, converting them from structural channels to rules. These were the functional rules of the system, showing events, including decisions, spread out in time. If he had shown us a flow diagram of these events, alongside his block diagram, then he could have discussed both structure and function, with us, at once.   A useful convention is to use 'hollow' arrows, formed from two parallel lines in block diagrams.   These suggest the channels which carry things between objects, in space. Then the single line arrows in flow diagrams merely denote the sequence of events in time.

J. SHOTTER: In giving your account of the scientific process you suggested that the dramaturgical analysis produces all sorts of patterns which you see as requiring explanation.   I see something quite different when I look at the social world. I am interested in human interchanges which have a developmental quality - rather than habitual things, or rituals and ceremonies. I want to be able to start with a different analytical model. This filters my perceptions in such a way that inevitably I see different things from you. The problem, then, is how can we justify taking such different points of view; and can we argue that they are equally legitimate?

R. HARRE: Well, as John Clark has just implied, what I have presented is highly static.   One way or another I have to put some dynamics into it so that the processes are recognized as dynamic. But to describe in books, etc., one has to freeze the whole thing. To answer your question I need to refer to a third dimension which was left out of my diagram.   There is a distinction between expressive and practical orders, and the extra dimension acknowledges that people engaged in the various operations have personal projects: some are practical (e.g. growing corn), some are expressive (e.g. making a move in the status game), and some are mysteriously interwoven. The moral order which you talk about can, I think, be incorporated quite well by talking about projects in the expressive order.

J. SHOTTER: What I want to say is that straight away you and I see different 'patterns' and, furthermore, you are precluded from seeing the same as I because of your original analytical model. So how can I put pressure on your analyses if your model filters out what I want to highlight?

R. HARRE: This problem is causing so much agony right now in philosophy of science - the problem of the paradigms, or something equivalent. I am afraid that I cannot answer the dilemma. But I do understand you perfectly well and I hope you understand me.

J. SHOTTER: But, therefore, is there not something fundamental to add to your analysis?

R. HARRE: Maybe, but let me add that the more complex the reality, the more likely you are to get workable paradigms which reveal different structures.

F. FRANSELLA: On a different matter, why should psychologists have to go down to physiology in the end, whereas physiologists apparently do not feel the need to come up to psychology?

R. HARRE: Well, physiologists jolly well should. The reason why I think that psychologists should go down to the physiology is that I have a metaphysical prejudice in favour of materialism. But I would warn that psychologists should delay going to that level until the cyberneticians tell them what questions to ask.

P. KLINE: I do not see how the findings of trait psychology could be fitted into the kind of model you have produced.

R. HARRE: Well, as you already know, I do not believe in a general psychology of traits. I think traits are products of the research process itself. What I do believe is that there are massive series of dispositions which are called upon from time to time and in different moments of life.

R. M. FARR: I should like to comment that there are attributional biases built into our methodologies.   There are two major attributional assumptions associated with two kinds of research. Experimentalists are biased towards making a situational ascription: changes in the dependent variable are brought about by changes in the independent variable.   Psychometricians do the opposite: through standardizing conditions of observation, they attribute variance in observed phenomena to individual differences.

P. KLINE: Well, first, science should not be a question of belief. Second, if traits were purely situational, you would not observe the correlations which do exist between test scores and a whole variety of criterion behaviours (see pp. 322-328).

J. SHOTTER: In the physical world it seems possible for us to agree about observations because they can have a formal identity.   In psychology, agreements have to be socially constructed. That is why it is easy for Rom Harré to disagree with Paul Kline.

R. M. FARR: Of course another important point is that behaviour can alter as a function of being observed, and in this way the subject matter of psychology is again different from the physical sciences. Persons and objects are different in that respect, and this has implications for the kind of science which psychology can claim to be.

R. HARRE: Psychologists themselves are part of the devices by which the world is constructed: everything they do filters out into the world and creates its own facts.

Chapter 15

Common-sense models of action

D. H. Hargreaves

> There are lots of different kinds of explanations of human actions ...
> In fact, however, we do discover the motives of other people. (Gilbert
> Ryle, 1949, p. 87)

> Requests for explanation are usually reflections of our ignorance
> about the particular rule or goal which is relevant to the behaviour in
> question (Richard S. Peters, 1958, p. 7, emphasis added).

'Science', said Alfred North Whitehead (1932), 'is rooted in ... the whole
apparatus of commonsense thought'. Yet it is commonplace for psychologists to
contrast scientific psychological theories and models of man with common-sense,
everyday or 'lay' theories or models. From this scientific point of view,
common-sense or 'folk' psychology is defective or unreliable; it is the task
of a scientific psychology to provide a true and superior account that will
correct common sense. Although psychologists often agree in this
dismissive attitude to common sense, they display startling disagreement
about the kinds of theory or model that are the proper or most useful ones
to advance psychological science - as many contributions to this volume
show. It is not merely that scientific theories and models compete with
common sense; they are in fierce competition with one another.
　　The spirit of this chapter is phenomenological. By this exceedingly woolly
term I refer to that perspective (or more strictly the version of that perspective)
in the social sciences which, in the famous words of Schutz (1932), 'sets as its
primary goal the greatest possible clarification of what is thought about the
social world by those living in it' (p. 222). Quite simply, such a scientific
phenomenology treats common-sense knowledge as the principal topic for study by
scientific methods and concepts; phenomenology is the scientific study of common
sense. Phenomenology thus refuses to set common sense on one side and is unwilling
to treat it as epiphenomenal. If men are guided in their actions by common sense
(amongst other things), then the study of human actions should include the
scientific investigation of common sense.
　　Science is concerned with explanation. In the case of the social and
behavioural sciences, however, there is the interesting feature that the object of
study, man, is also concerned with explanation, both of himself and of his fellow
men. It is these common-sense explanations that are the topic of this account.
Common-sense theories and explanations are organized; they rest upon particular
models of man. In this respect a phenomenological model of man is a meta-model; it

is a model of man's common-sense models. Special note must be taken of two features of common-sense theories and models. The first is that man is remarkably competent (by everyday rather than by scientific criteria) in explaining himself and others. Much of his life is spent in predicting, explaining and understanding the actions of himself and others in a relatively unproblematic way. When action proves to be momentarily puzzling, he reflects, hypothesizes and inquires in a manner akin to (but not identical with) scientific investigation. (See Fransella's chapter in this volume, chapter 17, for an exposition of George Kelly's elaboration of this theme). In rare circumstances man finds himself or others incomprehensible; he may then look to professional social scientists for their expert elucidations, or he may resign himself to the great mysteries of human conduct. But for the most part everyday life is negotiated and understood with few troubles. Man has at his disposal a vast range of concepts and recipes for action which, for all practical purposes, work. Because they work, they can be taken for granted and denied reflection and analysis. It is this 'obviousness' of common sense which the phenomenologist regards as a skilled accomplishment which requires elucidation.

The second feature of common-sense knowledge is that even though for mundane, routine events it works, and thus can be treated as trustworthy and unquestioned, it is nevertheless, from a wider point of view, 'incoherent, only partially clear and not at all free from contradiction' (Schutz, 1964, p. 93). In other words, a phenomenologist concedes the existence of those aspects of common sense which generate suspicion in the scientific psychologist. To put the matter another way, common sense does not consist of a single, unitary and coherent model of man. Rather, like scientific psychology itself, common sense contains multiple models of man, which from time to time may conflict and compete with one another. I suspect that all scientific models of man exist in some form in common sense; and so does the competition between models. When psychologists debate scientific models amongst one another they draw upon this competition between common-sense models. In science, as in common sense, models are partial and can be used effectively only in delimited fields.

My argument, then, is that the phenomenological approach to models of man is but one approach to the themes in this book. I shall try to show that it is an unduly neglected one, despite being one from which other perspectives could profit. Our starting point is man's explanation of man. There is an infinite variety of human actions to be explained and a vast number of possible explanations of these actions; common sense is astonishingly comprehensive in its scope. If these common-sense explanations of action are organized, does it not seem reasonable to hypothesize that there must be some basic conceptual machinery around which any specific common-sense explanation can be organized? If the infinite number of common-sense explanations can be regarded as 'the surface structure', what is the conceptual apparatus which forms the underlying 'deep structure'?

I believe that the most important signposts in this quest are to be found in the work of Fritz Heider (1958), whose work in social psychology, though relatively little of his extensive influence, is informed by a phenomenological perspective. It is worth recalling Heider's starting point:

... if we removed all knowledge of scientific psychology from our world, problems in interpersonal relations might easily be coped with and solved much as before. Man would still 'know' how to avoid doing something asked of him, and how to get someone to agree with him; he would still 'know' when someone was angry and when someone was pleased. He could even offer sensible explanations for the 'whys' of much of his behavior and feelings. In other words, the ordinary person has a great and profound understanding of himself and of other people which, though unformulated and only vaguely conceived, enables him to interact with others in more or less adaptive ways ... The task of conceptual clarification will be approached from two bases or starting-points: we shall make use of the unformulated or half-formulated knowledge of interpersonal relations as it is expressed in our everyday language and experience - this source will be referred to as common-sense or naive psychology; we shall also draw upon the knowledge and insights of scientific investigation and theory in order to make possible a conceptual systematization of the phenomena under study ...   Scientific psychology has a good deal to learn from common-sense psychology ... The fact that we are able to describe ourselves and other people in everyday language means that it embodies much of what we have called naive psychology. This language serves us well, for it has an infinite flexibility and contains a great number of general concepts that symbolize experience with the physical and social environment. After all, it is ordinary, non-scientific language that has served as the tool for writers in their representations of human behavior. However, this instrument lacks one important feature - a systematic representation - which is ultimately required by science (p. 27).

Heider's subsequent and brilliant analysis is organized around the central concepts of everyday language - can, try, want, cause, suffer, belong, ought, may and so on. This work has been immensely influential, yet it is astonishing how few British psychologists, despite occasional eloquent reminders (e.g. Joynson, 1974; Bromley, 1977), have made common-sense psychology and its systematization the focus of their studies.

There have, of course, been other approaches to this search for the general, or even universal, categories or concepts by which man makes sense of the world; one thinks readily of other psychologists (such as Osgood) or of the cognitive and structuralist anthropologists.   The line I wish to pursue has its origins in contemporary social psychology, especially where it has a sociological flavour. It is becoming common for social psychologists to use two basic models of man: as rule-follower and motive-avower.   My suggestion is that the social psychologists' use of rule or motive as a basic concept draws upon, elaborates and distorts the existence of these two concepts as part of the basic conceptual apparatus by which man organizes his common-sense explanations. Before this argument is amplified we must look briefly at the relevant literature.

The literature on man as a rule-following creature is extensive. In modern times this literature goes back at least to Kant, with his distinction between constitutive and regulative rules, but recent work shows the profound influence of Wittgenstein, especially on Winch (1958), whose book has been so influential on sociologists.   The most successful empirical application of this rule-following model has been in sociological social psychology, notably in the inventive and prolific writing of Goffman. In Britain, the most original proponent of this model among psychologists is Harré. As will become clear, my interest is not, as is true with some of these writers, in asserting an anti-determinist model of man as a rule-follower; my concern is that common-sense man operates a model of himself and others as rule-followers.   That is to say, man constantly invokes the concept of rule as a means of rendering action sensible.   The concept of rule may, then, be a clue to the 'deep structure' of common-sense explanatory models.

In their early work, the ethnomethodologists took a similar approach to the Goffman-Harré perspective.   But Garfinkel and Cicourel soon lost faith in this rule-following model, since it appeared to be dealing merely with the 'surface structure' of action.   There are, perhaps, two great achievements due to ethnomethodology. The first was to undermine the naive contrast that is sometimes asserted between common sense and scientific activities. It has been persuasively demonstrated that social and behavioural scientists constantly draw upon common sense in their scientific work.   They have no choice but to do so, yet it is accomplished implicitly and without acknowledgement or recognition. For social scientists common sense is an essential but usually entirely unexplicated resource in their work. This is related to the second achievement, the ethnomethodologists' recognition that social scientists often merely re-present common sense in a scientific form.   On this view Goffman's extensive studies of rules amount to a catalogue of surface rules operating in a wide variety of contexts. In consequence the ethnomethodologists lost interest in rules, potentially infinite in number, and began to search instead for the 'deep structure' of the small number of sense-making methods by which the world is made sensible. Common-sense man understands action as rule-following, certainly; but rule-following can be imputed only by means of the more basic 'interpretative procedures' (Cicourel, 1970) or sense-making practices. Ethnomethodology becomes a kind of cognitive sociology. Although I share the ethnomethodologists' scepticism concerning rule-following models of action, I believe they abandoned prematurely the search for a limited number of concepts by which action is common-sensically explained. I assume, however, that in documenting the model of man to be outlined shortly, common-sense man uses the 'interpretive procedures' to make the conceptual apparatus applicable in any specific case. This conceptual apparatus and the interpretive procedures I take to be the 'deep structure'; it is merely in the interests of brevity that I ignore the second aspect from this point on.

Carefully insulated from the literature on action as rule-following, there exists a literature which takes an unusual perspective on the concept of motive. On this view motivation is seen not in terms of physiological forces or drives (or 'higher-order' forms of them) which impel or energize action, which has been and remains the dominant perspective on motivation in psychology. Rather, motives are seen as linguistic forms, or social vocabularies, by which man makes sense of and explains (as well as controls) the actions of himself and others. Analytically speaking, the common assumption of both professional psychologists and common-sense man that motives are the 'springs of action' is suspended; 'motive talk', not motives themselves, becomes the topic for analysis and investigation. The pioneering statement of this perspective on motives is to be found in John Dewey's (1922) early social psychology; the most influential exposition and development of the idea is undoubtedly C. Wright Mills' (1940) 'vocabularies of motive' paper, so badly neglected by psychologists. In recent years both symbolic interactionists (e.g. Scott & Lyman, 1968) and ethnomethodologists (e.g. Blum & McHugh, 1971) have contributed to the perspective.

We have, then, two distinctive and surprisingly separate literatures; in one, man is a rule-following (and rule-breaking) creature; in the other, man avows motives and imputes them to others. Each model, I believe, represents an aspect of man's common-sense model of action. To grasp that common-sense model of action and its explanation we must restore both models to their original source. Let us consider each aspect in turn.

In recent times there have been several attempts to classify different kinds of rules, especially by Toulmin (1974) and the contributors to Collett (1977). In my scheme common-sense models of action distinguish at least four kinds of rule:

(1) Normative rules. This type represents the classical sociological and social psychological conception of rules as prescriptive. Such rules have a moral force or 'ought' quality and are designed to regulate conduct with sanctions. This type of rule covers general social norms, institutional and organizational rules, and situational rules. The major reference is to roles.

(2) Implemental rules. These rules are technical or procedural rules which must be followed if a person is to succeed in accomplishing a particular task. They are closely related to the concept of skill, for when a skill is exercised implemental rules are followed correctly. In accomplishing a task both normative and implemental rules must normally be followed. To drive a car well, both the skill of driving technique must be known (implemental rules) as well as the highway code (normative rules).

(3) Probabilistic rules. This is the kind of rule which, when followed, gives rise to regularity of conduct. When we say 'As a rule he catches the 9.15 train' we mean not that he ought to catch that train (a normative rule) but that he usually does so. The breaking of a normative rule leads to moral disapproval and to the invocation of a sanction; the breaking of a probabilistic rule leads merely to surprise at the unexpected. Probabilistic rules are linked to the concept of habit, not skill.

(4)   Interpretive rules.   Essentially these are the classificatory rules which dictate what will count as an instance of a given category or concept.   Little is said about them in this chapter.

I make no attempt to defend this typology as exhaustive or as containing mutually exclusive categories, for the distinctions are no more than analytical. The purpose is to reflect common usage of the concept of rule; and here, as Schutz noted, common sense is not all clear or free from contradiction.   Thus it is that the following of probabilistic roles (as in a habit) can soon acquire a normative quality where one feels that a man ought to be predictable in his habits.   In practice roles and habits are sometimes difficult to distinguish for analyst and layman alike.

The question I want to ask is this: why, on any particular occasion, does a common-sense man cite one type of rule, rather than another, to make sense of and explain human action?   The social sciences often separate the different kinds of rule into different models of, or perspectives on, man's conduct.   It is different branches of the human sciences which pay particular attention to one type of rule-following: roles, skills and habits have their own distinctive theories and research literature which stand in splendid insulation from one another.   Common sense appears not to make such neat divisions; all three types of rule-following commonly conjoin in relation to the same piece of human action.

Above I used the man catching the 9.15 train as an example of probabilistic rule-following (habit).   But an equally sensible answer to the question 'Why is he catching the 9.15 train?' would be 'He's got to get to work by 9.45 or he loses some pay' in which a normative rule (the worker role) is invoked as the explanation.   A further answer would be 'To avoid being late for work' in which implemental rule-following constitutes the explanation. The same action, then, can be explained in terms of three different kinds of rule-following behaviour; from slightly different points of view the same conduct can be seen as a role, skill and habit.   A little thought about the example I have used will show that the three different explanations interpenetrate in so far as the explicit explanation in terms of one type of rule-following tends to presuppose the other two types of rule-following at an implicit level.   The explanations which are artificially separated in psychological accounts are intricately interwoven at a common-sense level, even though the three types of rule-following are rarely mentioned explicitly.   This ellipsis is possible only because the type of rule and action not explicitly mentioned is tacitly understood by both questioner and respondent to be so obvious that it needs no mention.   As Nowell-Smith (1954) has pointed out, It would be excessively tedious if we had to give full explanations on all occasions'.

How, then, do respondents know which bit of the explanation (i.e. which kind of rule-following or breaking) to leave out in order to avoid a full and tedious account?   The answer appears to be that, as competent persons, both questioner and respondent know what aspects of the action are known by both parties and what aspect is under discussion.   Shared contextual knowledge provides clues to the precise meaning of the question.   The meaning of the question - and answer - will vary if we insert into 'Why is he catching the 9.15 train?' unstated contextual knowledge such as 'when we both know he normally catches the 9.30' or 'when that train leaves too late to get him to work on time' or 'when he's on holiday today' and so on.   Such contextual knowledge directs the respondent to explain the action by one type of rule-following rather than another.   Common-sense man, then, sees the same action as exemplifying multiple rule-following; the common-sense model of action integrates the rule-following which psychological theories disintegrate for analysis but then fail to reintegrate.

Typologies of motives are much less common than typologies of rule.   Schutz (1932) made a nice distinction between what he called the 'in-order-to motive' and the 'because-motive'.   The in-order-to motive refers to the intention or goal and is in the future tense at the time of the action.   'Why did he rob the bank?' - 'In order to get some money to buy a big car.' The because-motive refers to the causes or sources of the conduct and is in the past tense at the time of the act.   'Why did he rob the bank?' - 'Because he was brought up in a criminal environment.' Common sense permits both teleological and causal motive explanations.

Now I want to elaborate Schutz's distinction into a four-fold typology of motives as used in common-sense explanations. The motives are in a hierarchical chain; they pass backwards in time and each motive is in part generated by the motive lower in the chain.

(1) Intention. This type of motive is Schutz's in-order-to motive, a goal, purpose, or project. Beyond the immediate intention or goal stretches a chain of further goals, since immediate goals are often the means to the realization of larger ends.

(2) Reason. This type of motive refers to the state of mind of the actor at the time of the act. Its temporal reference is thus to the present (ignored by Schutz). Reasons are frequently affective in character - feelings, moods and other emotional states. To assert that he robbed the bank 'because he wanted some money' would be an example of a motive explanation by a reason. The reason arouses or stimulates the intention.

(3) Trigger. This refers to the highly situational events which 'trigger' or arouse the reason in the person. Thus our robber could claim that he robbed the bank because his friend asked him to help, or because his wife had demanded a new fur coat which he could not afford. The trigger need not be external to the agent: one can claim that one is hungry because one's stomach muscles are contracting or that one feels sexually aroused because one's 'hormones are racing'. Thieves may claim they experience an 'urge' to steal.

(4) Predisposer. Like the trigger, this is a form of 'because-motive' in the past tense. Unlike the trigger, it refers not to a relatively temporary or situational state of affairs but to a relatively stable, enduring or distant underlying state. A predisposer may be psychological (e.g. personality) or sociological (economic or cultural constraints) or a combination ('family background'). It is a predisposer which directly arouses the reason, or, when a trigger is present, permits the trigger to be effective.

From my preliminary studies - I am, in this chapter, using a fictional example for reasons of simplicity - such a typology of motives appears to be a rough guide to the common-sense model of motives. Motives are of different types, but they are closely linked to one another in a 'motive-chain' which is tied to time. This motive-chain, for most but by no means all cases, seems to find few problems with regard to the stumbling-block of the scientific psychologist - intention versus cause. In common-sense thinking these are generally not alternative ways of viewing action, the either/or view so common in discussions and debates among psychologists. Rather, both are involved in the same piece of action: all action has an intentional and a causal component. Thus it is that common-sense man can face up to the problems created by (and can often solve the tension between) freedom and determinism. Here common-sense man appears to adopt a model of man and action which is very close to the analysis offered by George Herbert Mead and Alfred Schutz. Mead (see Farr's original exposition of Mead for psychologists, chapter 13) developed a highly reflexive model of man, in which man could treat himself as an object. As a consequence of learning to 'take the role of the other', man can anticipate his actions before they are entered into behaviourally. Prospective lines of action can be mapped out, considered, criticized, amended, rejected. Because action can be rehearsed in advance, choices can be made. Schutz elaborates upon this by pointing out that an intention or project consists of an anticipatory fantasying of future conduct; the as yet uninitiated act is rehearsed in the future perfect tense. Yet precisely what is in fact rehearsed, and the choice among anticipated possibilities that is in fact made, are both conditioned by past events. Man experiences freedom to choose but the choices are severely constrained. Common-sense man's model of action and its explanation is much closer to the work of Mead and Schutz than to most psychological models which so often turn a mere part of this model into the whole model.

As in the case of rules, all four types of motive are presumed by common-sense man to be in operation in any given action; but again all four types are rarely mentioned explicitly in everyday interaction. Motives are traditionally linked to 'why' questions; and if one asks the question 'Why did he rob the bank?' any of the four types of motive could constitute a reasonable answer.

Intentions: (in order) to get some money.
                   (in order) to get rich quick.
                   (in order) to buy his wife a fur coat.

Reasons: because he wanted some money.
                   because he was short of cash.
                   because he got a kick out of stealing.

Triggers: because some criminal friends asked him to join them.
                   because his wife demanded a fur coat.
                   because he was being blackmailed.

Predisposers: because he was dishonest.
                   because he was brought up in a criminal home.
                   because he had learned that crime pays.

The different types of motive are not alternative explanations, for all four are interlocked aspects of the same explanation. Within each motive type, of course, alternative motives are readily available for any particular act, but the act is adequately explicated only when congruent motives from each of the four levels can be provided. The four types of motive, then, can be combined into varied constellations of motive explanation; but no action is ever adequately explained at the level of intention (or reason, or predisposer) alone.

In everyday life the motivational explanations provided explicitly seem very simple; this is again because, as in the case of rules, some of the motive types have to be taken by questioner and respondent as part of their presumed contextual knowledge. 'To get some money' is not an informative answer to the question 'Why did he rob the bank?' for this very reason. It is redundant information, which can be given only to children (who are still learning their common-sense competencies) or in the form of a joke. In adult interaction 'why' questions get their meaning from what is presumed to be shared knowledge among the participants. It is this feature which makes 'why' questions so dangerous when posed by psychologists to their 'subjects', for the psychologists may have no access to what is presupposed as shared knowledge (and therefore in no need of explicit mention) by the subjects. It appears that we get by in everyday life (and through research interviews) because sometimes the very way in which the 'why' question is framed gives the questioned person clues to the type of motive that is being investigated by the questioner. The question 'What did he have in mind when he robbed the bank?' directs one towards an intention or reason as a sensible answer, but steers one away from a predisposer; whereas 'What made him rob the bank?' draws one away from intentions, and perhaps reasons, to a more causal explanation at the level of trigger or predisposer. When the action to be explained consists of a series of repeated acts ('Why does he keep robbing banks?') the respondent is drawn away from the highly variable, situation-specific reasons and intentions and is pushed towards a predisposer which could arouse a variety of congruent reasons and intentions. Predisposers, both for common-sense man and for the professional psychologists so addicted to them, provide context-free motivational answers to multi-contextual questions.

Common-sense man, it appears, adheres to a more complex and elaborate model of motives, and the interrelations between different types of motive, than many psychological theories either themselves contain or concede to naive psychology.

Of course, my sketch of the common-sense model is rudimentary; I have said nothing about the attribution of responsibility for action, so important in everyday life. Clearly we need to investigate the different weights people assign to different types of motive in particular circumstances. It is not so much that one of the four types of motive is the 'real' motive - a game of motive-mongering laymen are happy to leave to professional psychologists - but the relative weight of predisposer, trigger and reason upon the intention and agent's readiness to turn intention into action. Common-sense man can never accept Eysenck's theories on crime and personality, since his account links predisposer directly to the action, and ignores the other three types of motive, especially the intention. It is not the correlations between personality and crime that the common-sense man would wish to dispute; it is that Eysenck's account is too elliptical, taking part of the story to be the whole story, and so damaging the well-tried common-sense model of man in the process. In this connection it is worth noting that whilst it is socially acceptable for us, as laymen or scientists, to attribute the conduct of others in part to the constraining power of predisposing motives ('What can one reasonably expect of someone brought up in such a criminal environment?'), it is seen as illegitimate for the person himself to make similar causal and deterministic avowals ('Well, your honour, I robbed the bank because I was brought up in a criminal environment, I have a criminal personality, and I have a monozygotic twin already doing time in Hungary') which deny or exclude intentional component in the motive chain.

The key issue remains; what is the link between the rule-based and motive-based analyses and explanations of action? Why, in psychological studies, do we so often get the one without the other, as in Harré's 'ethogenics' we get lots of rule-following but little in the way of motives? A wary reader may have already noticed that in the examples given earlier one type of explanation, rule-based or motive-based, could readily be translated into the terms of the other. Thus to the question 'Why did he catch the 9.15 train?' an answer making use of a reason ('Because he <u>wanted</u> to get to work on time') or predisposer ('Because he's an obsessively punctual person') is a perfectly sensible reformulation. (The reader can readily provide rule-based answers to the 'Why did he rob the bank?' question.)

This suggests a much closer link between motives and rules than their separate psychological literatures seem to allow. One may speculate that motive-based and rule-based explanations interlock within the common-sense model of action, man being taken as both motivated and rule-following. Sometimes one type of explanation can be translated into the terms of the other; sometimes each is complementary to the other. Thus, the suggested reason for robbery ('Because he wanted the money') makes sense (in the absence of more elaborate motives) if we know that the person has acquired the habit of stealing (probabilistic rule-following) and has the skills to effect a theft (implemental rule-following). To invoke a trigger motive ('His friends asked him to join them on a job') implies not only that we can fill in the unstated congruent reasons and predisposers, but that we also understand the obligations of friendship (normative rule-following). Both rules and motives seem essential to the common-sense model of action, and any scientific model which rests on rule or motive alone is likely to be an easy target for common-sense criticism. Yet we must inquire into the conditions under which one type of common-sense explanation, rule-based or motive-based, is sometimes the preferred form of explanation for action.

One possible answer, to pursue a line taken earlier, may lie in the precise form of the question which may direct the answer along a motive-based or rule-based channel, and in the contextual cues between questioner and respondent. It is in the light of these adult competencies that children's 'why' questions become so interesting, and to adults sometimes so irritating: one is simply unsure what kind of answer - motive or rule based, level of motive or type of rule - is being sought. As every parent knows, every answer can be followed by yet another 'why?' - in principle ad infinitum but in practice only ad nauseam.

It is probably also true that both rules and motives are seen to have a common source and linkage in what I have called predisposers. In common-sense theories, perhaps, both motives and our basic categories, roles, skills and habits have their roots in the deepest nature of man, both biological and sociological. For roles, skills and habits themselves become motivators, generating long-term goals and reasons (wants, likes). (From this complex whole behaviourists take physiological predisposer-reasons(likes)-habits as the central triad.) On this view rules and motives are sometimes merely different formulations of the same basic propositions. The same predisposer provides a dispositional motive, dishonesty, with its recurrent situational reasons and intentions and the desire to steal, and the rule-following tendencies of the criminal role and habit.

At the same time there appear to be some interesting situations where motive-based and rule-based accounts are not functionally equivalent but are used contrastively. For example, an action can be explained - and excused - on the grounds that it was done from 'force of habit'; that is, probabilistic rules were followed but without the conscious intent that normally accompanies such rule-following. Or an action can be explained - and again excused - by an appeal to accident, where the intention is held to be appropriate but the skill or implemental rule-following is defective and incongruent.

In this chapter I have sought to show, briefly and tentatively, that in the common-sense model of action both motives and rules are tied together in complex ways as part of the conceptual apparatus by which man explains himself and other men. The separation of these concepts (and the range of concepts with which they are associated) in the psychological literature is dangerous. Separation can easily be justified on the grounds that without it we could not simplify, study and experiment with the distinctive elements. But the failure to reintegrate these elements both between the branches of a single discipline as well as between disciplines cannot be so readily justified, for we then end up with partial and artificial scientific models of man of which naive psychology can be such a potent critic. We should face that critic more frequently and with more humility.

Whilst I believe that psychology as a whole has much to gain from further work of a broadly phenomenological kind into common-sense models of action and explanation, this should not be a missionary attempt to force the whole of psychology into a new way (the fallacy of a unified psychology) or the complacent development of a new and insulated branch of a diverse whole (the fallacy that progress is made when the subdivisions simultaneously move in different directions). A phenomenological analysis of common sense might help in the following four ways:

(1) If adults can display the competencies in the use of the complex common-sense models of action, how do children come to acquire these competencies? What problems are thereby posed for developmental psychology?

(2) Common-sense models of action may or may not rest on a relatively unchanging and underlying model or 'deep structure'; but certainly some aspects of common sense change from age to age. Following C. Wright Mills' work on 'vocabularies of motives', how are these changes in common-sense models to be explained and what are their consequences? How influential has the work of psychologists been in changing common-sense models?

(3) Cross-cultural analysis is essential. Are the common-sense models of action and explanations to be found in Western Europe and North America applicable to people in other cultures? What have psychologists to learn from anthropologists here?

(4) The practical application of psychological theory and research often requires man to modify his common-sense model. How can this change be effected unless we fully understand the nature of the model to be displaced? We know that man soon generates 'antibodies' to resist help and change derived from psychological work. Can phenomenology provide the needed immunology?

Heider (1958) expressed the general implications in his deceptively simple style over 20 years ago:

The study of common-sense psychology is of value for the scientific understanding of interpersonal relations in two ways. First, since common-sense psychology guides our behavior toward other people, it is an essential part of the phenomena in which we are interested. In everyday life we form ideas about other people and about social situations. We interpret other people's actions and we predict what they will do under certain circumstances. Though these ideas are not usually formulated, they often function adequately. They achieve in some measure what science is supposed to achieve: an adequate description of the subject matter which makes prediction possible. An explanation of behavior, therefore, must deal with common-sense psychology regardless of whether its assumptions and principles prove valid under scientific scrutiny. If a person believes that the lines in his palm foretell his future, this belief must be taken into account in explaining certain of his actions.

Second, the study of common-sense psychology may be of value because of the truths it contains, notwithstanding the fact that many psychologists have mistrusted and even looked down on such unschooled understanding of human behavior. For these psychologists, what one knows intuitively, what one understands through untrained reflection, offers little - at best a superficial and chaotic view of things, at worst a distortion of psychological events. They point, for example, to the many contradictions that are to be found in this body of material, such as antithetical proverbs or contradictions in a person's interpretation of even simple events. But can a scientist accept such contradictions as proof of the worthlessness of common-sense psychology? If we were to do so, then we would also have to reject the scientific approach, for its history is fraught with contradictions among theories and even among experimental findings (p. 5).

Psychologists tend to be insecure in their professional identity as scientists and this in part explains their persistent neglect of what is their principal source of inspiration ('hunches' which become theories and hypotheses) and a main topic for a systematic analysis, namely man's common-sense model of action and its naive explanation. When a phenomenological psychology takes its rightful complementary position with other psychological models and perspectives, we shall, perhaps, be in a stronger position to create a psychology which goes far beyond common sense.

EDITED DISCUSSION

D. E. BROADBENT: The main point that I would want to make is that, although common-sense man, as you say, can apply all four explanations, he does not actually do so on the one occasion. In fact the man-in-the-street exhibits much the same tendencies as the professional: some use one kind of answer and some use another. It might quite well be, therefore, that there is no common-sense man who thinks that all these explanations are simultaneously valid.

D. H. HARGREAVES: I would actually dispute that. People have a much more complicated system for explaining events than one would assume; certainly more elaborate than I had thought before my studies. What I did was to allow people to talk about a problem at some length, rather than pose sharply focused questions and expect neat answers.

G. THINES: I have two questions. Firstly, do you not fear that what you call 'data' are not in fact observations but are already interpretations? Secondly, why do you want to call your work 'phenomenological'?

D. H. HARGREAVES: On the first point, I regard any kind of observation as requiring interpretation. It is built in, and you cannot in my view have non-interpretative observations ...

G. THINES: What you are doing is a language analysis of possible instances, and that is quite legitimate research. However, without concrete instances it is not phenomenology in my opinion.

D. H. HARGREAVES: Well 'phenomenology' has many shades of meaning. I would regard my research, along with that of Heider for example, as being phenomenological ... But, then again, I do not like the term 'phenomenology' and would be happy to discard it.

N. FRUDE: It seems to me that the biggest differece between formal psychological theories and common-sense theories is that people using common sense do not accept what one might call a 'homogeneity' premise: that is, they are not happy to explain all cases in the same way. Formal psychologists put the question to nature, 'which of these possibilities is <u>the</u> explanation?' The lay person wants to discuss the individual case in detail.

D. H. HARGREAVES: You have triggered two thoughts in my mind. One is that common sense is interesting in that sometimes people certainly avow highly generalized explanations for action - so, for example, one comes across very general statements about the causes of crime - but then, when they consider a particular case, they switch to an answer which was not adduced in their general explanation. The other thought is that people will commonly reach the point where they are prepared to be quite agnostic about the explanation for an event: they might just say, 'I don't know and I don't really care'. Of course, the scientist will go on pursuing the answer for its own sake. What intrigues me is why and when people stop their accounts.

D. B. BROMLEY: The layman's explanatory concepts - trait, habit, role, expectation and so forth - are latent in common sense and can be produced whenever an appropriate occasion arises. The point that is being made is that scientists extract these notions, and they develop and use them.

D. H. HARGREAVES: If you could unearth the structure of common-sense thinking you might find interesting guides from which social scientists can learn. Inevitably we dredge into our own common sense, and we call that 'hunch'. We need to systematize the basis of our hunches.

Chapter 16

Models of childhood

D. J. Wood

The field of developmental psychology has seen an extremely active, controversial past decade as those possessed of different models of childhood have each sought to demonstrate empirically the value of their own hypotheses at the expense of those derived from competing theories. One aim of the present chapter is to try to evaluate the current status of our knowledge about children and their development in the light of this recent activity.

Which model rules? More specifically, we ask how far attempts to test different models of children's abilities in the laboratory have demonstrated the superiority of any one theory over another, only to conclude that such empirical work has not and arguably cannot be the basis for any such demonstration. Whilst laboratory and field studies have sharpened many of the specific issues which form points of conflict between different theories and have, in general, raised the quality of debate, their primary function has not been to invalidate one or other point of view. Rather, they have served to etch out the underlying assumptions upon which the different models are based, assumptions which are essentially untestable.

Investigations of models in practice and attempts to 'live out' theory in the classroom might also be expected eventually to support one theory over others. But, generally speaking, this has not proved to be the case. Effective practice has been derived from a number of models, so that success in application cannot itself provide an unequivocal basis for choice between them. More speculatively, I argue that these successes in practice are not due to the creation of different 'sorts' of children cast in the form of the different models. Rather, the effective practice derived from different models has converged on a common set of educational techniques and methods. Whilst theorists might construe the nature of what they do in different languages, the underlying actions and practices which they prescribe are similar. This leads us on to consider the wider relationships between models, practice and common sense. In the final section of the chapter I argue that the role of theory in the development of effective behaviour in adults is directly analogous to the role played by adults in the earlier development of the child. Both adult commentaries on the child's actions and theoretical descriptions of adult behaviour serve to raise consciousness. Both invite the actor to scrutinize and review his spontaneous behaviour and, ultimately, provide opportunities for him to act more deliberately and effectively in the future.

In the first section, I begin by examining some of the major issues which have arisen out of the debates between different theoretical perspectives on childhood and measure the contribution of contemporary empirical studies to those debates.

MODELS IN THE LABORATORY

The history of thought and argument about the nature of individual human development and its relationship to the society within which it takes place is at least as ancient as the written word itself. The Greeks, notably Plato, consciously derived their recommendations about the care and education of children from an image of the ideal society and the citizens best suited to inhabit it. Quintillion, less a philosopher, more a schoolmaster, urged his fellow Roman educators to pay more attention to the needs and the natural abilities of their charges - to beat them less often, praise them more, and, in the early years of their lives, to let them learn through play. Thus, by the first century AD and perhaps long before, many of the key educational issues had been raised - the role of political dogma in shaping our images of man and the child; the proper place for discipline and reinforcement in teaching; the balance between learning through instruction and discovery through play; and so on. Since the emergence of our own discipline, the continuing philosophical and political debates about the nature of man and his growth have been informed by an ever-increasing volume of empirical research - by experiment, systematic observation and, most recently, by planned interventions in the educational process itself.

Guiding much of this research has been the general question as to how far the child's thinking is radically different in kind from that of the adult. If the child thinks differently from his elders - as he did for Freud and does for Piaget - then the form of his mental activity and his understanding of the world cannot be founded in, nor directed by, social experience. Rather, it is governed by biologically constrained processes which are a natural and universal part of human immaturity. If the child conceives of the world in different terms to the adult, then the capacity of the mature to teach and inform the young child must be limited - since, by definition, they cannot think about the world in the way he does. So, in turn, adult language and actions can only have a secondary developmental significance since the meanings which underlie the one and the intentions which guide the other will only be understood by the child in his own terms. Only when the child is 'ready' will he come to understand what adults do and say in their terms. Development, thus conceived, is basically a maturational process demanding the selection and direction of experience by the immature themselves. The ideal process of education will, then, be paced and directed by relatively 'free' children.

Given the many fundamental educational implications which follow on this theoretical question, it is understandable that it has formed the basis of a great deal of our empirical work, and it is proper that it should also form the starting place for our consideration of models of childhood. Much of the recent research into the young child's mental abilities has been inspired, of course, by Piaget's integrated theory of knowledge and development. His wide-ranging observations of children's behaviour and his many studies of their problem-solving abilities form the basis for his central thesis, which is that all children develop through a series of stages before reaching adult intelligence and a capacity for logical thinking. In a novel integration of nativism and empiricism, he argues that the child must 'construct' a rational, integrated model of the world through his own actions on it whilst, at the same time, arguing that the natural working of the child's mind structures his experiences along biologically determined pathways.

In recent years, this position has come under increasing experimental scrutiny and, latterly, undergone serious criticism. Bryant (1974) has shown, for example, that it is possible to manipulate the conditions underlying Piaget's studies of children's reasoning to produce logically sound judgements from them. Where attention is paid to the child's information-processing limitations and care taken to ensure that he remembers all the information presented to him in a problem, a capacity to reason logically may be displayed. The child's logical abilities, Bryant and others argue, are essentially no different in kind from the adult's. What does differentiate adult and child is not a difference in basic competence but their differential response to factors like knowledge of what is likely to be relevant to a task, skill in selecting, coding and rehearsing this information long enough to work with it, and so forth. More recently, Donaldson (1978) has shown that changes in the language used to characterize a problem, the actual choice of task material, the manner in which the problem is presented and the way in which changes in the appearance of task materials are brought about, all interact to affect the child's performance and thus his apparent rationality. Her conclusion is that there exists no fundamental difference in logical abilities across age but rather the child lacks certain specific skills and attitudes towards abstract, unfamiliar problems. It is this relative lack of skills which leaves him less able to see, manipulate and solve problems. Other work, for example, by Walkerdine & Sinha (in press) also shows that a choice of task material is successful only if the expectations and mental operations which the child brings from his everyday experiences coincide with the logical structure of the problem. In other words, any failure is due to a lack of local knowledge not to basic differences in competence between adults and children.

Cross-cultural studies of reasoning processes in non-schooled illiterate people have led to similar conclusions (e.g. Cole et al., 1971; Cole & Scribner, 1974). Whilst people from such cultures often fail to solve formal, logical problems, the reasons for their poor performance are, it is argued, not to be found in terms of a different fundamental logical competence but, rather, in the absence of experiences and functional demands which engender the relatively specific skills and attitudes necessary for the solution of these problems. By looking elsewhere, to naturally occurring and ecologically valid contexts, evidence can be found of logical inferences being made by the same populations.

These and other contemporary studies of children's thinking are turning our attention away from a consideration of the logical structure of a task and the supposedly general rules of thought necessary to handle it, towards an emphasis on the actual content and appearance of the problem and the social context within which it is set. The same move away from general rules or processes towards an emphasis on the context of behaviour is also present in studies addressed to other general models of children's abilities - for instance, in examinations of Chomsky's theory of language.

Early tests of the 'psychological reality' of Chomsky's (1957, 1965) transformational grammar soon showed that semantic and pragmatic factors played a major role in the comprehension and production of speech. In other words, they showed that the ease and accuracy of communications between speaker and listener could not be accounted for simply in terms of a theory of syntax. Situational factors and expectations based in general knowledge of the culture helped to determine how readily mutual comprehension was achieved (e.g. Herriot, 1969). Whilst the earliest work following on Chomsky's formulations supported the notion of a language acquisition device and a universal linguistic competence, it soon became apparent that the fit between the transformationalist's descriptions of supposedly universal deep structure relations and the patterns found in early child language was far from perfect (Brown, 1973). The interpretations of children's early language, for example, rest not simply, nor even primarily, on the syntactic structure of the child's utterance, but on the exploitation of the context within which the speech takes place. Studies of interactions between adults and infants prior to the emergence of the child's first words now suggest that speech arises not from an innate, predisposition to process speech sounds in particular ways, but out of social interactions, in which the infant first develops or displays a capacity to signal his needs and intentions to another person (e.g. Bruner, 1975; Edwards, 1978). It is because that other person has the capacity to interpret those needs on the basis of the context of behaviour and a knowledge of the individual infant that the child manages first to achieve control of others through his actions and, ultimately, through his vocalizations.

Once again, then, the contemporary move is away from general models of behaviour expressed in terms of a relatively small number of universally applicable rules, to a greater emphasis on the role of the social and physical context in psychological growth. This same movement can be detected in research addressed to Bernstein's (1961) concepts of language codes and their relationship to social class. Bernstein's early writings were interpreted as putting forward the thesis that different sections of modern industrialized societies use language in qualitatively different ways. Early research following on Bernstein's thesis suggested not only that this distinction has some psychological and sociological reality but also, as he had supposed, that it was related to differences in methods of child rearing and, through these, to differential intellectual abilities in children (e.g. Hess & Shipman, 1965, 1968; Bee et al., 1969). This work suggested to some causal relationships between styles of socialization, language and cognitive development. However, further research has shown that language across social class is not so sharply delineated - varying as a function of the situation in which it is captured (Wells, 1975; Tizard, in press), the identity of the individual in conversation with the subject (Labov, 1970) and the actual objects or events being discussed (Robinson & Arnold, 1974). In these several different areas of research, then, a common theme emerges. Both in the empirical determination of an individual's abilities and in the identification of factors which influence the course of psychological growth emphasis has moved away from explanations in terms of large-scale rules or processes towards a recognition of the importance of local context. In fact, I would suggest that they indicate four sets of factors which, in addition to the formal or logical structure of the situation, interact to influence behaviour and its development. The way in which an individual will speak, act, think or learn is dependent upon: (1) the concrete (as opposed to the formal) structure and appearance of the task; (2) the institutional setting within which behaviour takes place; (3) the identity of the interlocutor(s) who directly or indirectly observe or elicit performance; and (4) the distribution of power and control between the actor and those interlocutors.

Although the various lines of evidence which I have been considering have grown out of attempts to test general models of childhood, it is not the case that their apparently contradictory findings serve to falsify those models. For in each case there are present in early formulations of the theory distinctions which can and have been elaborated upon to provide explanations for such 'unexpected' results. In Piagetian theory we find two distinctions which essentially preserve the theory from disproof. Piagetians distinguish between development and mere learning (e.g. Schwebel & Raph, 1974). It is possible to teach a child such that he comes to imitate the surface appearance of behaviour at a more advanced stage, but this should not be confused with development. For development, large-scale accommodations to experience beyond present levels of functioning can only occur when the child has developed through his own actions on the world to a state of disequilibrium, when contradictions between his old, dying view of reality and his newly emerging style of understanding come into conflict. Similarly, the concepts of vertical- and horizontal-décalage enable us to explain why a child, located at a given level or stage of competence, can display performances on other tasks at more or less advanced stages.

These distinctions, present in the early formulations of the theory, can be increasingly elaborated to provide an explanation for results which, on first sight, seem to contradict fundamental predictions from the theory.

Just as Piaget's stance about the relationship between performance and competence is essentially unfalsifiable, so too is the alternative position taken by Labov, Donaldson, Cole and others. They approach the analysis of competence armed with an abstract characterization of the nature of logical inference. On tasks in which they and members of their culture or subculture tend to bring this competence to bear, they find that others of a different age, socio-economic group or society do not. However, through sustained experiment or protracted observation they discover tasks on which what they take to be logically equivalent behaviour occurs, and then credit their subjects with a common basic competence. Thus any similar performance is proof of the possession of the same rule; any dissimilar performance has no implication for those general rules, being attributed to the absence of specific performance skills.

In relation to Chomsky's theory and the apparent refutation both of its ability to characterize mature speaker-hearer behaviour and to describe adequately the course of early language development, it can be pointed out that Chomsky himself (e.g. in 1968) stressed the distinction between competence and performance, warning that 'performance limitations' would render explicit predictions of behaviour hazardous. He also challenged assumptions underlying empirical work which held that the transformational rules he had identified were necessarily applied in a fixed temporal sequence, thus rendering any attempts to simulate the rule system to predict performance inadmissable as a crucial test of the theory.

Bernstein, in his more recent writings, has challenged many of the inferences which were drawn from his earlier work, particularly where it was used as a basis for the concept of 'linguistic deprivation' (e.g. Bernstein, 1970). He has come to lay more stress on the concept of 'frames' which, crudely defined, refers to the conceptualization which a given individual creates for a particular context. The relationship between codes and frames is not a simple one-to-one affair, so that in different situations or 'frames' the same speaker's language varies in code.

General models are not, it seems, falsified by contradictory evidence. Rather than contradictory evidence accumulating on the periphery of the theory, waiting to be swept up and re-interpreted in another paradigm, what seems to happen is that the model is progressively enlarged to accommodate it. In other words, large-scale models enable the user to explain findings that he could not predict - indeed, to explain findings which arise out of attempts to test and disprove the theory itself.

It can be argued, of course, that we should not seek to evaluate our models through attempts at falsification - that the test of a good model is its ability to be 'lived out' with predicted and desired consequences. This line of thought is considered in the next section. Before proceeding, however, two caveats need to be entered in order to guard against implications which may be drawn from what I have just said but with which I do not agree.

In the first place, in arguing that we have 'failed' to falsify any of the large-scale models in childhood, I am not also claiming that we have made no progress. Anyone reading Russell's (1926) essays 'On Education', for example, and measuring what he says there about the nature of infancy and childhood against what we now know about the abilities of the young, cannot help but be struck by the tremendous gap between his views, based in rational argument and casual observation, and the findings of psychological research over the intervening 50 years or so. Russell anticipated that the developing science of psychology would contribute greatly to our knowledge of childhood and one indication of his perspicacity is the extent to which we could now convincingly demonstrate the invalidity of some of his speculations. The constant debates between those possessed of different images of man may not deliver empirical evidence to disconfirm thoroughly any one point of view, but new findings surely raise the quality of those debates and force any theory to change. The language used to construe behaviour might continue unchanged, but the data to be construed continue to improve in quality and extent.

A second quite different implication which might be drawn, stems from the emphasis on the importance of contextual and social factors in human development. Whilst holding on to this emphasis, I do not want to imply that all the major determinants of human growth are environmental. We now have too much data about individual differences, some of which are observable at birth, to deny there is an important biological contribution to the development of the individual. However, I am primarily concerned here with our powers to manipulate and modify the 'contribution' of such endowments through deliberate changes in our institutions and our behaviour towards the developing generation. Eysenck, in chapter 4, speaks of the assessment of heritability of general intelligence as estimated '... at the present time and in our kind of society' (p. 52). There is no reason to suppose, of course, that we cannot vary the environment so as to manipulate heritability. Once one accepts that psychology may have a reflexible characteristic, acting back to modify the behaviour it observes, then the issue as to what we can achieve in the future remains an entirely open one. However, it is also clear that without much more knowledge about the potentially reflexive process of theory dissemination and its effects on ensuing behaviour, we can do little but argue in vacuo. In the next sections I examine some of the data - not all of them hard data - which relate to this question, to try to frame some preliminary hypotheses about the relationship between theory and practice outside the laboratory.

FROM THEORY TO PRACTICE

As psychologists have developed their general models of human development, it is predictable that, like the philosophers before them, they should begin to measure their images of the child against the practices of socialization and education in their own societies. And when theories about the relationships between experience, personality and intelligence meet with a political will to help change the achievements or abilities of segments of the populations in their society, as happened during the 1960s in the United States and the United Kingdom, the stage is set for practical tests of different models on a wide scale. Ideally, one might hope - on theoretical if not moral grounds - that one theory would prove effective where others failed. This has not been the case, however.

In the first, in all evaluations of ventures like Headstart in the United States and the Educational Priority Areas in the United Kingdom, the most reported finding was one of short-term gains in measures of IQ and language ability followed by rapid fading out as soon as active intervention ceased (e.g. Smith & James, 1975). More recent work, however, has looked more analytically at projects on an individual basis and produced more positive results (e.g. Rutter & Madge, 1976; Kellaghan, 1977; Lewin, 1977). Projects have been identified which have engendered enduring effects on children's achievements; effects which have lasted through the school years and into employment. But while it has been suggested that each of these successful interventions was characterized by possession of a strong theoretical framework (e.g. Bee, 1976), they did not possess the same theory. Consequently, even where success in practice has been achieved (in terms of the measures so far used) this success has not provided unequivocal support for the theory upon which it was based.

Although the effective programmes varied in their theoretical orientation, several studies have suggested that they nonetheless exhibit common characteristics - in addition to the possession of an explicit theoretical basis. In fact, the most common characteristic mentioned is fully in accord with the emphasis suggested in the last section - that on the role of interpersonal and contextual factors in determining the general path of development. It is reported that programmes which achieved success did so because they not only worked with the child but with his family and even his community. Where changes are made to the 'ecological setting' of the child's development, predetermined, lasting effects can be obtained. Where the structure of the relationship between the child, more knowledgeable others and a wide range of everyday contexts are manipulated, marked effects can be engineered in the child's measured achievements on various tests, his performance in school and, eventually, upon his employment prospects.

This emphasis upon the design of programmes which affected the social context of the child's life is also found in more detailed, analytic studies of the effects of different educational regimes on the child's development. In one study, for example, Karnes and his colleagues (Karnes et al., 1970) investigated the short-term effects of different pre-school environments on children's measured IQ, linguistic skills and perceptuo-motor abilities. Basically, what they found was that factors like encouragement of the child's play, his sensori-motor development and his social relationships with children of his own age, did not of themselves engender marked gains in linguistic and intellectual performance. On the other hand, programmes which encouraged sustained interactions between adults and children, ones in which adults were continually integrating their language with the child's activities, were associated with significant improvements in these measures. This same emphasis on the role of adult-child relationships in fostering intellectual development has emerged recently in a study of the effects of schooling on the academic and social behaviour of much older children (Rutter et al., 1979). It also emerges from more controlled laboratory and field studies of the development of learning skills, as can be seen in the next section.

EFFECTIVE PRACTICE

I have already drawn attention to the different emphases placed by various models of childhood on the role of adults in the development of children. Theoretically, the effects that teachers may have on children's knowledge, and the constraints they operate under in facilitating their development, vary substantially from one model to another. We might expect, therefore, that where educationalists have taken over a model and based their practice upon it, what they would do as teachers would vary substantially. Such, however, is not the case. When we examine the writings of researchers, teachers and educationalists working with Freudian, Piagetian, Vygotskian, neo-behaviourist, Brunerian or Bernsteinian models we find a marked convergence in their characterizations of the relationships between teacher and child and in their evaluations of the effects of different styles or regimes of adult control over the child. These points of convergence are identified and discussed below.

Child-centredness

As we have seen, models of childhood vary fundamentally in the scope or generality of the theoretical constructs they employ to characterize what goes on during thinking and learning. Piagetian theory and Freudian theory hypothesize large-scale structures or processes underlying functioning at any given stage of development. Theories like those of Bruner (1966, 1971) and Vygotsky (1962), on the other hand, lay greater emphasis on the tools, artifacts and objects of culture, arguing that the operations of mind are structured by and change with technological advances in society. At the extreme on this particular dimension are traditional forms of behaviourism which find no need for a system of complex constructs to model mental processes at all (e.g. Skinner, 1968).

We might well expect that models which argue for universals in growth might yield general principles to do with the teaching of children at a particular stage which are applicable to all learners at that stage. However, we have already noted in our consideration of laboratory tests of such models that whilst they may be able to explain a child's performance in a task after its occurrence, they often have no basis for predictions about how well or poorly that child will perform. And when we come to examine the writings of teachers who have based their classroom activities on large-scale theories we find a similar, common emphasis on the inability of models to predict behaviour. They stress the need to work carefully with an individual child - to try to fashion hypotheses about his hypotheses or ideas by working directly with him, preferably on a one-to-one basis. One of Piaget's ex-students, returning to teacher-training speaks thus about the relationships between his theory and her practice:

Even if I did believe that Piaget was right, how could he be helpful? ... we might ... keep in mind the limits on children's abilities ... when deciding to teach them at certain ages. However, I found this an inadequate criterion. There was so much else to keep in mind. The most obvious reason, of course, was that any class of children has a great diversity of levels. Tailoring to an average level ... is sure to miss a large proportion of children. (Duckworth, 1974, p. 261)

A general model may well present an integrated and coherent theory of knowledge, but it is clearly of limited value in deciding what to do in relation to a particular child in a given context with a specific task. Clearly, the practice which develops must move beyond the limits of the model, extending it to fit context, as Duckworth points out:

A theory of intellectual development might have been the basis of a theoretical framework of a curriculum. But in making things work in a classroom it was but a small part compared with finding ways to interest children, to take account of different children's interests and abilities ... and so forth. So, the burden of this curriculum effort was on classroom trials. The criterion was whether or not they worked, and their working depended only in part on their being at the right intellectual level for the children. (Duckworth, 1974, p. 261)

Effective practice, then, demands a substantial involvement with the individual child. The general or universal processes identified in theory are an inadequate guide to what a child may be thinking or doing and, hence, of limited value in shaping the teacher's hypothesis about the pupils' needs:

For me, through my experience with Piaget, working closely with one child at a time and trying to figure out what was really in his mind, I had gained a wonderful background for being sensitive to children in classrooms. (Duckworth, 1974, p. 262)

Another Piagetian makes a similar point about the essential individuality of the teaching process:

The task of the teacher is to figure out what the learner already knows and how he reasons in order to ask the right question at the right time so that the learner can build on his own knowledge. (Kamii, 1974, p. 203)

By basing the teaching episode on the social and physical context facing the individual learner, the general model is thus extended in practice to accommodate those four factors identified above as instrumental in the assessment and development of behaviour.

A similar position is taken by Isaacs (1930) in developing a method of schooling based on Freudian and Kleinian theory. Whilst taking issue with Piagetians over the supposed illogicality of the child and rejecting their 'dehumanized' vision of knowledge, she nonetheless places a similar emphasis on social and physical context in the determination of behaviour. Whilst her work is often remembered for its emphasis on play as the basis for fulfilment and ablation of fantasies, there is in her method an acknowledgement, even a stress, on the role of the adult in helping the child to bridge the gap between fantasy and reality. The adult is cast as vicar of the 'reality principle', but in actual behaviour his or her role is similarly defined to those above - taking a lead from the interests, questions, perceptions of the individual child and through interaction and conversation bringing him nearer to a logical appreciation of reality.

For me, the school has two main sorts of function:
  (a) to provide for the development of the child's own bodily and social skills
       and means of expressions, and
  (b) to open the facts of the external world ... to him in such a way that he
       can seize and understand them. (Isaacs, 1930, p. 20)

The school is ... simply a point of vantage for the child in his efforts to
understand the real world, and to adapt himself to it. It should be a place of
shelter for him; but not in the sense that it shuts out the larger world away
from him.   The school, the teacher and the teaching alike are simply a
clarifying medium through which the facts of human life and the physical world
are brought within the measure of the child's mind. (Isaacs, 1930, p. 22)

The way out from the world of fantasy is through the constant appeal to
objective reality to physical and social facts, and to interests and activities
directed upon these ... in our school our constant aim was therefore to throw
our own weight always on the side of an appeal to the world of objective fact
and to stimulate intelligent observation and judgement on the part of the
children. (Isaacs, 1930, p.33)

We shared all the children's interests actively, joining in their making and
doing, their digging and painting, their experiments and discoveries; as well
as in their games ... Together we and they explored the outer world and
together we devised ways of expressing the inner world of fantasy. We were
fellow workers and playmates. In general, however, we took our cue from the
children. (Isaacs, 1930, p. 35)

Thus, from models which warn of the potentially disruptive effects of adult
involvement in the child's intellectual or emotional experiences, practices are
derived which portray a similar active role for the adult and their knowledge in
the child's growth.   They lead the child to greater understanding but they try to
take their lead from him.   This notion of the child taking a lead through his
questions, interests and play is further developed in these and other accounts to
provide more specific descriptions as to how one actually proceeds in being
effective as a teacher.

Discrepancy

Although some theorists argue that development is paced by inner processes whilst
others reply that it is determined more by social or environmental influences,
there is a general consensus that development can be led or at least accelerated.
And a primary basis for this acceleration is the engineering of 'discrepancies',
'conflicts' or 'contradictions' for the child.   For the Piagetians these conflicts
arise out of competing mental activities based in two sources - one in a decaying,
passing view of reality and another in a newly emerging stage of understanding.
For Vygotsky (1962) they are not so directly paced by maturation and can
potentially be engineered by adults who, with skill, can bring the child to make
competing predictions from his repertoire of 'complexes' - his pre-scientific,
inconsistent concepts of reality.   For Bruner (1968) and his colleagues they are
'manageable problems' based in the 'recognition production' gap (Olson, 1966, 1971;
Wood et al., 1976).   For Isaacs too, the central metaphor is one of learning as
problem-solving with an acknowledged debt to Dewey (1933) for his initial
formulation of the principle of teaching by engineering problems.   The following
quotations illustrate the point:

... it is as easy to ask trivial questions as to lead the child to ask trivial questions. It is also easy to ask impossibly difficult questions. The trick is to find the medium questions that can be answered and that take you somewhere. This is the big job of teachers and textbooks. (Page, quoted in Bruner, 1966, p. 40)

Piaget believes that a child is more likely to accommodate his behaviour to solve a problem when the new behaviour that is required differs only slightly from those already in his repertoire. If parents, day-care workers, and other adults caring for infants understand what the infant is trying to do they may be able to facilitate learning by providing just the right environmental input or match between what the child is able to do, and what he cannot yet do. (Birns & Golden, 1974, p. 128)

Contingency

The learner, then, has to be in a specific mental state or, for neo-behaviourists, the right 'mood' (Meichenbaum & Asarnow, in press) for learning. He must appreciate some gap between his current state of knowledge and a particular phenomenon or event. The teacher's task is to look out for and help to engineer such problems. When we examine specific descriptions as to how a teacher effectively proceeds in fulfilling this task, another common theme emerges. It is argued that the child must not be swamped by demands which are too complex for him, nor plunged into apathy by not being challenged. And the accounts given as to how one operates in order to reach these states in the child, exhibit a shared emphasis on the contingency of teaching (Wood, in press). Where the child starts to fail or lose interest, the teacher should immediately simplify the situation to a level at which the child can succeed. Given success, the teacher should stand back and leave greater room for initiative. The following selection of quotations illustrate the argument:

Learning involves getting feedback and encouragement by instruction adjusted to performance. (Haavind & Hartmaan, 1977, p. 21 - working out of a Piagetian framework)

Later the same authors write:

In the beginning (of task activity) the child may easily become passive. It is therefore important quickly to introduce concrete and easy tasks. The sequence of (teaching) is not fixed but determined by events. All through the training one has to balance the quantity of new information against the child's receptivity. Some will get bored if they have to listen to too many examples and explanations. Others are less sure and need examples and concrete tasks before acting themselves. If the child is unsure or acts against the rules, it is best to interfere quickly and try to alter the child's behaviour. (Haavind & Hartmaan, 1977, p. 48)

Thus error demands a speedy increase in teacher control, success is a signal to stay silent and step back in order to offer the child greater scope for error.

(The) training sequence was individually tailored to the performance level and instructional needs of each child. Consequently, the difficulty level ... on each trial was determined by the S's performance on the previous trial. (Cognitive Behaviour Modifiers, Meichenbaum & Asarnow, in press)

LANGUAGE AND THOUGHT

There has, of course, been a great deal of argument about the role of language in development. For Piaget, it only comes to have fundamental significance as the child achieves formal operations. For Vygotsky, Bruner and Bernstein, on the other hand, language helps to shape thought, creating 'inner speech,' 'internal dialogues' and 'codes' for thinking. However, when we examine descriptions of the relationships between teacher language and child learning we find again a marked measure of agreement in practice. First, it is generally agreed that concrete precedes abstract, and that, ideally, teacher talk should be integrated with the child's ongoing behaviour - it should be 'contextualized' by, and contingent upon, his activities and interests, as in the description given above of successful practice by Karnes and his colleagues.

Verbal reasoning is no more than wave-crests upon the flow of young children's thought, taking its direction from concrete understanding. (Isaacs, 1930, p. 84)

We thus use speech chiefly to provoke active exploration of the world and make its results clear and precise. We did this because, after all, words are only tokens of experience, and are either empty or confusing to the children until they have had enough immediate experience to give the words content. With young children, words are valueless unless they are backed by the true coin of things and doings. They have their own place as aids to experience, and to clear thought about experience. (Isaacs, 1930, p. 40)

Trainers and teacher trainers have made some progress in recognising the importance of concrete experiences prior to words. (Kamii, 1974)

Neither the child's own organising activity nor the extrinsic influence of speech forms ... independently produce progress ... whereas speech and action incorporated together by discussion with the teacher is effective. It seems that such guided dialogue helps the child to formulate and thus synthesise ... relations. This reciprocal formulation has to be made in terms of the listener's point of view. (Heber, 1971, supporting Vygotsky's emphasis on dialogue in the development of scientific concepts)

Piaget points out that logical thinking is primarily non-linguistic, derived from first imitating and then performing actions ... (but) does not deny that social interaction and the resulting language acquisition are important. Verbalisation may sharpen contradictions in the child's thinking and help ... propel him into a higher level of thinking. Language, according to Piaget, permits the child to evoke absent situations and liberate himself from the restrictions of the immediate, so as to extend and deepen his understanding. (Schwebel & Raph, 1974, pp. 23-24)

The emphasis on the 'distancing' or 'de-contextualizing' function of language when a teacher comments on a child's actions is now being emphasized by educationalists working within a Piagetian framework. This is also, of course, a primary theoretical concept in the writing of Bruner (1971) who sees schools and school-language as the vehicle for 'distancing' the child from concrete experience. It is also central to the ideas of Vygotsky (1961) and Luria (Luria & Yudovich, 1971) who see language as the primary basis for de-contextualizing experience. It also figures in socio-linguistic accounts of the relationships between language codes and styles of thinking and problem solving. Recent developments in behaviour modification have also embodied a stress on the role of language as the basis for generalization of experience. This emphasis is related back to Skinnerian principles by the concept of 'self-management operants'.

Cognitive behaviour modification is thus cast as:

> approximate(ing) a kind of Socratic dialogue with the child helping by analysing his or her own cognitions, contributing to the model package, reacting to the model and the like ... the trainer and then the child 'tried on' suggested rules. This interplay has enmeshed in a cognitive-modelling and overt and covert rehearsal format. (Meichenbaum & Asarnow, in press)

> ... the child would say to himself, 'I must stop and think before I begin. How would it work out if I did that? What shall I try next? Have I got it right so far? ...' (Douglas et al., 1976, p. 408)

In recent work arising out of Piagetian theory, the role of skilled linguistic instructions is integrated back into the general body of Piagetian theory by use of the concept of 'de-centration'. The commentaries of a more knowledgeable other, at the right moment, help a child to de-centre himself from his experiences, to examine the relationship of what he is doing to what he might do, what he has already done, and so forth. The characterization of effective and ineffective styles of instruction which emerge from this empirical work is strikingly similar to the earlier work by Hess & Shipman (1965, 1968) and others working from Bernstein's concept of codes - as the authors of this new work (Haavind & Hartmann, 1977) acknowledge themselves.

In practice, then, language is given the dual role of sharpening thought and providing for generalization of learning. The theoretical interpretations of what language is achieving may differ, but the actual use of language in practical contexts would seem to be similar.

What does practice converge on?

The model of effective adult support for the developing child which emerges from attempts to apply various theories of development to the practice of teaching thus exhibit a number of common characteristics. There is a common emphasis on the role of language in directing and structuring the child's learning, and in helping him to 'distance' or 'de-centre' him from his immediate experience. There is also a shared emphasis on the importance of working out from the child's immediate actions and interests - letting these form the immediate basis for teacher suggestions, instructions, feedback and so forth. The recognition that a careful choice of task material and an effective social relationship is an important basis for engineering discrepancies between what the child already thinks and what he may comprehend in a new experience is also widespread. In short, whatever is said of the processes going on in the child - whether these are seen as paced by maturation or structured through social interaction - it is acknowledged that only through individual, contingent interactions with a particular child in a given context can the teacher derive effective hypotheses about how and when to help that child.

Thus, from recent laboratory studies, from descriptions of individual studies of teaching and learning and from attempts to apply psychological principles in the creation of educational changes, we find a recurring emphasis on the importance of contextual and social factors, not simply as a determinant of immediate behaviour but also as a primary basis for learning and development in general. This emphasis may not have been present in the earliest presentation of some of the models considered, but in the face of practical demands and a need to evaluate success, this emphasis is incorporated or accommodated in developments of those models. It is not the case that any educational practice is effective, but what evidence we have to date suggests that where practice is successful it exhibits the common characteristics just outlined.

Had only one theory of human development produced success in interventions we could have concluded that this alone presented a 'true' or useful model of the child. Had none of them produced any success we might have been tempted to conclude that none had any validity or value and question our traditional methods for constructing models. However, neither of these alternatives has come about. Rather, what we have is a common measure of success where practice exhibits certain characteristics. So what is the nature of these characteristics and what relationship do they have to the models upon which they were initially based? Put another way, what is the relationship between theory and practice if, as I have argued, theory is modified in practice and practice modified by theory?

One possibility, of course, is that those who have attempted to apply models have simply come round to common sense. The models have been expanded to cover or account for factors which were underplayed or not represented in the original theory - do theories, then, simply deny common sense only to return to it in practice? The answer, I believe, is negative. In the first place, common sense itself is not a single, coherent line of thought. As Hargreaves argues (chapter 15), there is not one contemporary common sense about the nature of man (or the child) but several. At a more fundamental theoretical level, common sense is limited and even defective in ways which can be overcome by effective theory and observation. Even where individuals are acting effectively in the world it is unlikely without conscious, systematic observation and analysis that they would be able to articulate and communicate their common-sense knowledge. There is such a variety of evidence for this assertion, from the inability of people to describe their systematic strategies in problem-solving (e.g. Bruner et al., 1956) through to attempts to get people to articulate their everyday goals and practices (Wood & Harris, 1977), that I need not dwell on it here.

In saying all this, however, I am not trying to belittle the importance of common sense, nor, in Hargreaves' words, to argue that it is all 'defective and unreliable' (p. 215). The failure of common sense, if I may use that expression, is selective. It is most likely to occur when we ask an individual to step out of his context or out of his own perspective. So, for example, general statistical statements about the frequencies of certain occurrences in his behaviour, may well come as a surprise to him (Wood & Harris, 1977). Similarly, he may be unable to scale his performance relative to that of others. The fact that his eyes point forward, that he hears that which fits in with his immediate interests, means that, like all of us, he misses much. Another set of sensory receptors or a recording device enables him to adopt another stance relative to what was going on and again can be a source of surprise.

All these, quite familiar characteristics of human behaviour underline certain weaknesses in common sense. To be sure, they may be offset by collective evaluation of experience, but they profit more clearly from systematic observation. There are also other, less obvious barriers to self-knowledge. So much of our behaviour, to use Hargreaves' term, is 'triggered' rather than intended. And the triggers often go unnoticed. Once we step out of one context into another, then the triggers may be irretrievably lost. Here again common sense can be amplified and changed by external scrutiny. The first stage in the explication and potential development of common sense is a raising of consciousness about our existing experience. A theory or systematic description serves to raise self-awareness in the mature in much the same way that the commentaries of adults serve the developing child. A theory distances people from their own habits and practices; it invites them to consider or reconsider the relationships between their goals, their actions and their effects. Where this reveals intuitively acceptable or empirically sound insights the actor may proceed more confidently and deliberately in the future. Just as another's commentary on a child's actions helps transform his spontaneous, largely unconscious activities into conscious plans for the future, so too a theory helps to transform and change habits and practices to strengthen those that are adaptive and uncover those that do not meet with intended or desired consequences.

A model, thus construed, helps to mobilize and constrain change. It will be useful to the extent that it enables people to formulate and recognize goals and discover those procedures and practices which enable them, in their current institutional and social milieu, to operate more effectively in the achievement of those goals. It is, perhaps, in this relationship between theory and practice that convergence can be understood. In all the descriptions, interventions and even experiments explored above, there is a common, usually tacit, set of aims. The goal of teaching is to engender greater control by the child over his own affairs - to increase the temporal scope of his thinking, make him appreciate that the past may be relevant to the present, that he should look ahead to anticipate difficulties and consider alternative lines of action. It is taken as self-evident that the child should not be apathetic, demoralized or powerless but that he should be free and able to manipulate his environment and other people in it to achieve his ends. At a deeper level, then, all models-in-application respond to basic social sentiments and reflect the character of our culture and our times.

It is not my concern here to explore the question as to how far these goals are culture-bound. It can be argued, with force, that the ability to plan, remember, to dictate the course of the future and bring the past readily into the service of the present are basic attributes of human intelligence, selected and honed through generations of social and biological change. It can also be argued that these adaptations in mental abilities are culture-bound, arbitrary and according to at least one theorist politically unacceptable (Dittmar, 1976). Our society, however, seems to value and wish to improve the intellectual, linguistic and social abilities of children. Another question is raised by Eysenck's bio-social model of human abilities. In chapter 4 Eysenck talks of the 'sociological fallacy' (p. 51), the assumption that correlation means cause. Because adult socializing behaviour is correlated with child performance we cannot infer a causal path from one to the other. Clearly, this is right. However, several studies, some mentioned above, looking both at local learning in the laboratory (Sonstroem, 1966; Heber, 1977; Wood et al., 1978) and in the classroom (Wright & Nuthall, 1970) together with intervention studies of effects on more general variables like IQ and tests of linguistic ability (e.g. Karnes et al., 1970) have each used predefined patterns of teaching/interventions to achieve their effects. In other words, they have shown that we can 'wrest causation from nature' in the sense that we can have some predictable effects on the progress of a group of children. However, this does not mean, of course, that they have solved the question as to how the initial correlations came about, spontaneously, in the 'natural' population. Such correlations may well be the consequence of the biologically based streaming about which Eysenck speculates in his chapter. However, they do illustrate the reflexive nature of psychological knowledge and the powers of the mature to exert some influence over the future achievements of children. What this implies for heritability estimates we cannot say, since interventions have only worked with relatively low-ability groups - it may well be that such concentrated efforts on 'higher-ability' bands would lead to even more dramatic effects, we simply cannot say at the present time.

The exciting and challenging prospect to which this conclusion leads - that psychology can act back to modify that which it studies - is, of course, the central concern underlying the chapters by Shotter (chapter 2) and Harré (chapter 14). As they have argued, psychology is, in part, in the position of transforming everyday behaviour - rendering the 'enigmatic' explicit, an object of knowledge and a focus for potential change. However, if attempts to apply models of childhood are any guide, it is an activity which is severely, and rightly, constrained by existing physical and social realities.

SUMMARY

I have argued that where individuals possessed of quite different general models of the child have translated their ideas into demonstrably effective practice -

whether by revealing that practice in laboratory studies, through correlations between social and educational factors or by direct intervention in the educational process at both micro- and macro-levels - there are some interesting and non-trivial convergences in their practice. Although the different perspectives I have considered diverge in relation to such fundamental theoretical issues as the role of the mature in the development of children and the part played by language, when they come to work with an individual child in a particular situation, what they do is similar.

I have also argued that what emerges as effective practice cannot simply be accounted for as a return to common sense. What, then, is the nature of the convergent activity? For the Piagetians, the influence of one individual's comments and actions on another's experiences serves potentially to 'de-centre' the second individual from that experience. It leads him into a process of reflective abstraction, encouraging him to treat his own behaviour as an object of scrutiny to be inspected and evaluated from the perspective of the onlooker. Thus, fundamental processes of development - disequilibrium, de-centration and reflective abstraction - may be rooted in interpersonal processes. For workers in a Bernsteinian perspective, the influence of different styles of speaking to the developing or learning child serve to construct different inner cognitive frameworks - elaborated language, for example, leads to a de-contextualization of experience. 'Distancing' is the equivalent metaphor in Bruner's theory of instruction. The more linguistically differentiated the teaching or controlling commentary is, the more it is linguistically well formed, then the more easily it can be manipulated in time, related and contrasted with other experiences and so forth. Similarly, for Vygotsky and Luria, the 'inner-dialogue' shaped from the commentaries of others produces a more or less differentiated second signal system which underlies the individual's ability to operate mentally and relatively free of context. For cognitive behaviourists, the construction of 'plans for plans' or 'self-management operants' in the form of inner verbal responses enable learning to generalize more effectively and more widely.

In all these accounts, then, the tacit aims are to increase the individual thinker's awareness of self and, simultaneously, his effects on others; to increase his ability to plan and to bring past experience to bear on immediate problems. An increasing internalization both of mentally represented actions on the physical world, and perspectives and dialogues derived from the social world, thus increase the individual's powers to free himself from his immediate perspective and experience.

It may be that an emphasis on the nurturing of capacities for anticipating consequences and evaluating fruits of action is merely one aspect of one, culturally determined vision of man's future. I personally find it difficult to believe that such skills will not be vital to the perpetuation of the species and it is a vision which seems to be shared by many developmental theorists possessed of a variety of models of man.

EDITED DISCUSSION

D. WALLIS: I should like first of all to thank Professor Howarth for stepping in to read Dr Wood's paper, and I am sure we all wish Dr Wood a speedy recovery from his illness. Let me now invite you to make comments and observations in an open, general discussion.

R. B. JOYNSON: I am in a position, I think, to ask a question of Ian Howarth. In his remarks immediately before presenting the paper he indicated that the conclusions drawn by David Wood are far from consonant with those drawn by himself from the same data. Do you believe that David Wood is of the same view? I have the impression that all three of us are in substantial agreement.

C. I. HOWARTH: Well, evidence from convergence is used by me to justify constructing a rather grand theory (see chapter 11). That same evidence is used by David Wood in a more limited and specific way. His way may be more useful; but then again it may not. The commonalities extracted by him I find to be extremely illuminating. Probably they could be fitted into my framework but for the moment I am not sure of the value in that.

N. E. WETHERICK: I have a comment, or at least a worry, that I would like to air. It is one that always occurs to me when I hear accounts of convergence in theories of child development and so forth. The accounts seem to rule out the possibility of anyone obtaining a good education by rote learning enforced by beatings.   They also seem to rule out the possibility that, like the philologist Joseph Wright, one can work in a wool factory from the age of 6 to 15, decide that it would be a good idea to learn to read, and then perhaps go on to a chair at Oxford.   Such things would seem to be impossible on the account of development which is given by the theories just outlined.

C. I. HOWARTH: You cannot be sure about that until you discover how Joseph Wright structured his own learning world. Some people do structure their own learning environment.   Certainly it would be evidence against David Wood's view if you could not find anything of relevance in Wright's experience.   Similarly, if you could find evidence that beating plus rote learning was just as effective as a more enlightened technique or system, then that would work against David Wood's position.   But of course he does cite much evidence in support of that position, and I think that evidence is compelling.

Chapter 17

Man-as-scientist

F. Fransella

George Kelly suggested that not only are scientists human, but humans can also be construed as scientists. His personal construct psychology, published in 1955, is a theory about the personal theories of each one of us - and possibly of all organisms, but the theory's range of convenience has yet to be tested that far. In truly reflexive manner, the theory applies equally to the theoretician himself as to the rest of humankind. This theory was put forward by a man who had a degree in physics and mathematics and who worked for a time as an engineer. Small wonder that such a man should pick the psychological model of 'man-the-scientist'.

It is also not surprising that Kelly felt that scientific activity was proving itself to be one of the most exciting and rewarding enterprises that human beings have involved themselves in. He did, however, wonder why it should be that only those with university degrees should be privileged to feel such excitement and reap the rewards.

THE MODEL

Kelly took the unusual step of discussing, in detail, the essential features or 'model' of the individual organisms he was seeking to describe. The purpose of this chapter is thus to describe that model, to note how it relates to the theory and then to outline some of the sorts of activities these have led psychologists to undertake. The model is best described in Kelly's own terms:

> The long-range view of man leads us to turn our attention toward those factors appearing to account for his progress rather than those betraying his impulses. To a large degree - though not entirely - the blueprint of human progress has been given the label of 'science'. Let us then, instead of occupying ourselves with man-the-biological-organism or man-the-lucky-guy, have a look at man-the-scientist.
>
> At this point we depart again from the usual manner of looking at things. When we speak of man-the-scientist we are speaking of all mankind and not merely a particular class of men who have publicly attained the stature of 'scientists'. We are speaking of all mankind in its scientist-like aspects, rather than all mankind in its biological aspects or all mankind in its appetitive aspects. Moreover, we are speaking of aspects of mankind rather than collections of men. Thus the notion of man-the-scientist is a particular abstraction of all mankind and not a concrete classification of particular

men.   Now what would happen if we were to reopen the question of human
motivation and use our long-range view of man to infer just what it is that
sets the course of his endeavor?   Would we see his centuried progress in terms
of appetites, tissue needs, or sex impulses?   Or might he, in this perspective,
show a massive drift of quite a different sort?   Might not the individual man,
each in his own personal way, assume more of the stature of a scientist, ever
seeking to predict and control the course of events with which he is involved?
Would he not have his theories, test his hypotheses, and weigh his experimental
evidence?   And, if so, might not the differences between the personal
viewpoints of different men correspond to the differences between theoretical
points of view of different scientists?   (Kelly, 1955, pp. 4-5)

THE PHILOSOPHY

The model of the person as well as the theory's basic postulate and 11 elaborative
corollaries, are all derived from the philosophical standpoint of constructive
alternativism.   Reality is going on all around us, yet no one of us can grasp it.
We can only place our own interpretations upon it and these interpretations are
determined by the constructs we have developed on the basis of our individual
experiences up to this point in time.   Our personal system of constructs Kelly
likened to a pair of goggles through which we gaze upon the events milling around
us.   If the goggles start not to fit events too well, we need to alter them and
hope to get a better fit.
    By saying that we each construe, or place interpretations upon, reality, Kelly
was pointing out the creative nature of his psychology.   We create our own
constructs to represent our environment rather than merely being organisms that
respond to it.   In this way it accounts for the great variability found both within
and between groups of human beings.
    The philosophical statement is essentially optimistic in that it states 'We
assume that all of our present interpretations of the universe are subject to
revision or replacement'.   This does not mean that we are totally free and able to
change our interpretations at will.   Change is often fraught with dangers and
difficulties, sometimes so great that the change we desire is impossible.   The
statement simply implies that the potential for change is there in each one of us.
No one need be a victim of his or her biography.   Many others, of course, have
thought in similar vein (e.g. the 'Schema' of Bartlett, 1932).   But Kelly takes
this philosophical position as the starting point for his theoretical statements
concerning a total psychology.   For this is not a theory of personality, but is a
psychology of the whole individual.

THE THEORY

The construct

The central unit of Kelly's system, the construct, is likened to an hypothesis set
up to account for perceived events; it is a means whereby we can place an
interpretation on those events and from there, put the interpretation to the test.
This is formalized theoretically in the Fundamental Postulate and the first
corollary.   These state that 'A person's processes are psychologically channelized
by the ways in which he anticipates events' and 'a person anticipates events by
construing their replications'.
    By noting that people with glasses say erudite things whereas those who do not
wear glasses by no means always do so, we come to anticipate that a stranger
wearing glasses will say erudite things.   In effect, the construct 'says erudite

things - does not say erudite things' is 'lifted out' of our construct repertoire and 'placed over' a stranger.   The stranger is then slotted to one pole of the construct according to whether he or she is wearing glasses.   Of course, this is not the only construct that may be seen as relevant through which to peer at that stranger.   If the stranger is female, a man might pull out a construct about making passes at girls with glasses.

Erudition or the lack of it is not something that is a basic component human beings carry around with them, something there to be discovered.   Rather, it is a construction placed upon one person by another.   The notion of similarity and contrast is an inherent feature of each construct.   If all people were construed as erudite, there would be undifferentiated homogeneity.   If all people were construed as non-erudite or stupid, there would be undifferentiated heterogeneity.   This is formalized in the Dichotomy Corollary as 'a person's construction system is composed of a finite number of dichotomous constructs'.

It is often thought that this construing of similarities and differences is a verbal process.   But it is important to realize that this is not necessarily so. Construing is an act of discrimination.   There seems to be no good reason why one should deny to the child, the dog, the rat or the ape the ability to discriminate between aspects of their environments.   Constructs are discriminations each set up to give shape and meaning to the otherwise haphazard events in our environments. These discriminations may, but need not, have verbal labels attached to them.

Constructs by which we impose meaning on our world, are not discrete, separate units, but are arranged in a hierarchical manner, some being subordinate to the superordinacy of others.   The Organization Corollary states that 'Each person characteristically evolves, for his convenience in anticipating events, a construction system embracing ordinal relationships between constructs'.   We can thus attempt to trace networks of implications so as to arrive at a statement of the meaning a particular construct has for an individual person (Hinkle, 1965).

By using the word evolves, Kelly underlined the view that constructs are not static but are potentially in a constant state of motion.   Kelly (1962) argues from this that there is no need for a concept of motivation in psychology.   The need arose in the first place from the desire of psychologists to emulate the physical sciences.   These studied static matter and therefore some construct of energy was necessary to explain why it moved.   Freud extended this idea to his psychological model of man by employing the construct of 'psychic energy'.   Kelly suggested that we are ourselves forms of motion, since this is the essence of living matter, and so no separate construct of motivation is necessary.   The directions in which we may move are explained in the Fundamental Postulate and Choice Corollary.   We choose our action in order to define or extend or elaborate the system of construct channels, so that we become more and more able to anticipate events.

Kelly placed a great emphasis on each one of us having a unique perspective of the world of events (Individuality Corollary).   This is because no two people can play precisely the same part in the same event.   For instance, in a given event, each experiences a different person as 'the other' and each experiences a different person as the central figure - it is oneself.   But experiences can, of course, be shared as when we construe some of the similarities and differences in our street in the same way as does our neighbour (Commonality Corollary) and we may well also construe him as having experience similar to our own.   Social intercourse is underway when we attempt to construe how another is construing things (Sociality Corollary).

The prediction

In the discussion of his model of the scientist, Kelly asks: 'What is it that is supposed to characterize the motivation of the scientist?' He answers himself: 'It is customary to say that <u>the scientist's ultimate aim is to predict and control.</u> This is a summary statement that psychologists frequently like to quote in characterizing their own aspirations' (Kelly, 1955, p. 4). Thus, as scientists, we note the repetition of events, and hence construe them, and are then able to predict future events. (Kelly does not distinguish between the terms anticipate and predict, so I will use the latter as the more 'scientific' term.)

However, we rarely, if ever, predict that the future event will be repeated in its entirety. For instance, predictions can vary along a time scale. Some may be tested only once, others are constantly being tested. The statement, 'I, like every other living creature, must die' is a prediction few seek to validate. On the other hand, some predictions are tested many times a day. Every time I walk on a floor I predict that, amongst other things, it will be solid and not opaque water vapour or porridge. Other predictions are tested once a day, like Kelly's own example of the prediction derived from the construct 'day'. What is being predicted is not that today's day will be like yesterday's in what we eat, drink, wear or do. But it will be like yesterday's and tomorrow's in that the sun will rise in the morning and set in the evening. If such a prediction were ever to be invalidated we would indeed be in chaos. It is interesting that in some literary descriptions of attempts to extract information by force, it is the invalidation of such basic predictions that is particularly effective. By making light and dark occur at irregular intervals, by lengthening or shortening days, by disrupting sleep patterns and meal times, the physical world can be made an unpredictable and hence alarming place. Theoretically, our person-as-scientist is made anxious by the awareness of being confronted by events which he is unable to construe adequately.

Predictions can also vary as to the number of properties in the future event that will need to be present for us to accept it as evidence validating our prediction. The man who goes through life looking for a wife who is the replica of a mum, may well have a riotous social life going from girl to girl. But he may leave each sadly because there is always something that is not mum-like in her make-up. This man could well end up an embittered bachelor blaming womanhood and life for conspiring against him. Another young man may be less certain about his future mate, and may have fewer dimensions to define her, but for him, sure enough, along comes a girl who psychologically 'fits'.

If our predictions are constantly validated, does this mean that we have established a truth? The answer must be no. For we may come to apply other constructs to the situation at a later date. Although people wearing glasses all do seem to talk in erudite ways, we might come to consider what we actually mean by erudite. This in turn may lead us to see that some bespectacled people are pretentiously erudite and others creatively erudite. Any construct is only a best-fit for events that we have available at that moment. With any luck further constructions will be devised in the future that will do the job better.

If our predictions are invalidated, then we have to do something about it. We may acknowledge the inadequacy of that aspect of our system and reconstrue. However, we do not always respond to invalidation by changing our construing so as to increase our predictive efficiency. Sometimes we cannot contemplate the magnitude of the revision confronting us. In this case we may show hostility and make sure that our predictions are validated. We fix the experimental outcomes. If I go up to a colleague whom I construe as a fool, and ask him a question in an area in which I know he is ignorant, he will give me an ill-informed answer. I have thus validated my prediction that he behaves in fool-like ways. But fixing of outcomes or reconstruing are not the only ways of dealing with a validational problem. Sometimes we are reluctant to test our predictions at all. How many people delay going to the doctor to inquire about the nature of a 'lump'? They keep the event to themselves. For, if the prediction is correct, they are threatened (aware of imminent comprehensive change in one's core structures) or flooded with anxiety.

It is this awareness that our constructs are not a good fit of the events with which we are confronted that is the basis of most of what we call emotional experience. The place of emotion within Kelly's framework has recently been elaborated by McCoy (1977) and discussed by Bannister (1977). Personal construct psychology is not only a cognitive theory. Its model person can just as easily feel passion and despair as he or she can think, for the model knows of no dualism - we are not a body and a mind, but an indivisible whole.

So much for our own attempts to predict events on the basis of past construed experiences. But what of the psychologist's dream of being able to predict the behaviour of others? We can only hope to predict (and hence make understandable) the behaviour of others in so far as we are aware of the constructions that those others place upon events. A piece of behaviour may appear extraordinary to the observer, but be totally comprehensible in the context of the person's own world view. To understand the behaviour of others, we have to know what construct predictions are being put to the test.

Behaviour

So far we have our scientist with his ideas, his predictions and his ways of assessing outcomes. But something is missing. Where is the experiment, so essential to all scientific ventures? For Kelly, behaviour is the experiment. Whether it is observing the rising of the sun, the walking on floors or approaching the bespectacled stranger, we are behaving to test a prediction. From Kelly's standpoint, all behaviour is an experiment.

> In the restless and wonderful world of humanistic endeavor, behavior, however it may once have been intended as the embodiment of a conclusive answer, inevitably transforms itself into a further question - a question so compellingly posed by its enactment that, willy nilly, the actor finds that he has launched another experiment. Behavior is indeed a question posed in such a way as to commit man to the role and obligations of an experimenter. (Kelly, 1970, p. 260)

For each of us, as individuals, behaviour is the independent variable, whereas for many psychologists it is more often the dependent. This aspect of the 'man-the-scientist' model has particularly important implications for psychology. But to understand fully the behaviour of others we must remember that constructs are bipolar. A prediction not only says what will happen, but also what will not happen. It always involves a negative forecast as well as a positive expectation. Kelly argued that behaviour only has meaning in the context of relevance. A particular act is brought into relevant perspective by our awareness of what it might have been. The bipolar nature of our constructs means we have rejected one way of acting in favour of another. Because of this, we can never claim to have an absolute understanding of a person's behaviour since we rarely know what the other possibilities were. Kelly saw this criterion of relevance as also important for the discipline of psychology:

> I am not greatly disturbed by the fact that I have proposed a criterion for understanding human behavior that makes stable conclusions about it virtually impossible. As a matter of fact, I hope the criterion of relevant contrast will serve to keep us from deciding once and for all that our confirmed predictions of any man's acts encapsulate all that may ever be expected of him. A science that respects relevance simply cannot rest upon conclusions, save as tentative grounds for further questions. And I think there is no place where this is more true or more pertinent than in the science of human behavior. So I hope my criterion will keep all conclusions quivering on their empirical foundations and will confront us with such disturbing questions about the potentialities of man that all sorts of imaginative inquiries will be provoked. (Kelly, 1969a, p. 13)

Behaviour thus becomes the problem we seek to solve in coming to understand another person, and it is also our own key to solving it.

Control

Besides aiming to predict and perform experiments to test predictions, scientists are said to aim at 'control'. In Kelly's language, construing events enables us to make predictions which our behaviour puts to the test. The more often our predictions are validated as opposed to invalidated, the more often we can be said to have control over those events and over ourselves. Yet, even being able to control events or another's behaviour does not necessarily mean we understand those events or behaviours. Smearing dirt on the hand of a person with obsessional ideas about contamination, will very predictably lead to washing rituals - predictable both to the observer and the distressed person. But this in no way means that the person concerned or the psychologist understands why this behaviour happens.

In the truly reflexive context of the theory, we may ask not only what control do we have over events (and we certainly do have some control over them - with or without understanding), but to what extent are we ourselves controlled by our construct system? Kelly argues that we are both determined and free 'it depends which way you are looking'. We are determined in the sense that the constructs that make up our total system for interpreting events in our world, are all we have at that point in time - it is a finite system. Maybe we will develop others tomorrow, but that will be no good for predicting events today. No matter how hard we try, we cannot step outside our existing system for construing events.

However, within that system, we have some freedom of choice. Each construct is dichotomous. Each provides us with a channel along which we may move. We can always change the pole of the construct we normally use to construe particular events for the other, so as to extend or better define the construct system. This allows us to see what sort of difference it makes to view things another way; what sort of experiments it leads us to create and what sort of outcomes it yields.

Kelly also invoked the notion of control in his description of the decison-making process which involves the self. This C-P-C Cycle 'is a sequence of construction involving, in succession, circumspection, pre-emption, and control, and leading to a choice which precipitates the person into a particular situation'. One first circumspects the field in a general way, then pre-empts since she cannot 'mount her horse and ride off in all directions'. She next selects what she considers to be the essential or important issue and disregards the rest. This is her control - she has come to a decision.

THE NATURE OF SCIENCE

Although Kelly was quite explicit in his description of the model of person-as-scientist, he said very little in his 1955 work about what he thought science to be. However, in 'The language of hypothesis: man's psychological instrument' (1964), he had more to say concerning the scientist's approach to life. He argues that scientists cannot avoid making subjective judgements and that they should therefore regard subjective thinking as an essential step along the road of increasing understanding of the universe.

He suggests that the language of hypothesis would lead to greater inventiveness. By this he means the use of the 'invitational mood' or 'as if' philosophy of Vaihinger (1924). At some point in the scientific sequence of events, the scientist has to look beyond the obvious. By saying 'let us look at these data as if ...', the scientist may entertain seemingly preposterous hypotheses, but if they make sense to the scientist, he may go ahead and quietly experiment within the laboratory until there is some 'hard' evidence to present to colleagues.   These new so-called 'facts' may show that a previous set of 'facts' is invalid and hence a new theory is born.

Perhaps it would be interesting to look at the other models of the person being discussed in this volume in the invitational mood.   What do we see if we regard people 'as if' they were rats, pigeons, apes, a nervous system, a communication channel, a computer, a scientist, a moral being, or a rule-follower? Perhaps we could go to a higher level of abstraction and regard models 'as if' they were the psychologists' game of 20 questions but without there necessarily being a correct answer since, if we are indeed self-creating organisms, we may have changed before we get there.   The discussion of our models can be looked on 'as if' it demonstrated the personal constructs each of us is using to define the nature of psychology - and these constructs will have different implications for each of us.

RESEARCH STRATEGIES

Strategies for psychologists

In his discussion of the strategy of research, Kelly (1969b) dwells on the fact that it is necessary to adopt a particular approach if all behaviour is to be viewed 'as if' it is a question.   In the past, science has been seen as progressing step by step with each fragment of 'truth' being likened to a piece in a jig-saw puzzle that will one day be completed.   Each piece of the puzzle being regarded as part of the final answer.   Kelly called this strategy 'accumulative fragmentalism'.

In an interview Harvard's Professor of Philosophy, Hilary Putman, explained that the traditional idea of scientific knowledge focused on the use of the scientific method and accumulation (Magee, 1978).   But, when Einstein found there to be a human component to 'truth', the idea of science changed.   Putman argued that science is now a term for the successful pursuit of knowledge.   Magee summed up this part of the interview by saying that for two or three centuries man thought of the universe as consisting of matter in motion and that science:

> consisted in finding out more and more about this matter, and its structure, and the laws of its motion, by a special method known as 'scientific method'. If it went on doing this for long enough it would eventually find out everything there is to find out.   This view of science has now been abandoned by scientists - but that fact seems not yet to have got through to the majority of non-scientists. (Magee, 1978, p. 227)

Kelly points out that if one takes the view that in an experiment a person is testing predictions, then the answer one gets simply confirms or disconfirms that the hypothesis is working well at the moment.   The constructive alternativist knows that he or she may one day come up with a much better hypothesis, one that will account for the data in some way that will be an improvement on the present.   He will thus always be looking for new questions to ask of his world, seeking to follow up implications of ideas that occurred to him during his last experiment.

One implication of this for such a person, contrary to that for the accumulative fragmentalist, is that new ideas and new hypotheses can be tested out experimentally without the old hypotheses first having to be discarded.   Kelly explains the difference thus:

> To the accumulative fragmentalist the next step is to find another nugget of truth ... To the constructive alternativist the next step is to see if he can improve his hypothesis, perhaps by formulating his questions in new ways or by pursuing the implications of some fresh assumption that occurred to him when he was writing up the conclusions to his last experiment.   But for the

accumulative fragmentalist the only grounds for entertaining further questions about the matter is evidence that he was wrong. Since this kind of nuisance may pop up at any time he is careful to replicate his experiments and make sure the answer to his question is absolutely, positively, and irrevocably right!... But to the constructive alternativist it is a matter of no more than momentary interest whether his colleague's findings are disconfirmed or not. To propose a new question does not require the denial of an old answer. Indeed every neat answer makes him wonder what would have happened if the question had been posed differently. (Kelly, 1969b, p. 126)

Strategies for persons

Because of the reflexive nature of personal construct theory, this description of the strategies of scientists at work is also a description of the person-as-scientist at the work of living.   The philosophical stance of constructive alternativism means that there are always alternative ways of looking at events; we also do not have to give up a working hypothesis before we test out a new one.

On the other hand, there are people who achieve control over their lives by collecting nuggets of truths.   They accumulate fragments; firm opinions; habits; they punctuate their conversations with phrases such as 'everybody knows that ...', or 'I always say that ...' or 'it's common sense ...'. If something in life makes them doubt the validity of all these 'facts' they have acquired so painstakingly, then life becomes very difficult. If the whole pyramid of facts starts to crumble, they are faced with potential chaos.

Kelly, was, of course, not saying that all those who do not follow his own line of thinking about people generally are the 'seekers after nuggets of truths' and all those who agree with him in looking at people 'as if' they were scientists are the 'questers'.   Nor was he describing personality traits.   He was describing strategies we may operate, professionally or privately, at certain times in our lives and for dealing with certain aspects of our personal worlds.

Tyler (1978) summed up her view of Kelly's contribution to our understanding of research as follows:

If the subject matter of psychology is not a finite collection of behaving objects but rather the limitless domain of human possibilities from which generation after generation of individuals draws without depleting the resources, then our science cannot be content with models borrowed from physics and chemistry. We must create new models, new rules for playing the game of scientific inquiry, new guidelines for our research.   George Kelly realized this. (Tyler, 1978, p. 130)

THE PSYCHOLOGICAL EXPERIMENT

Looking at each of us 'as if' we were scientists, has implications also for the psychological experiment. Traditionally, subjects are expected to behave at the behest of the experimenter - The Scientist. As psychologists we have some theory about how subjects should respond to certain experimental stimuli. We then check up on their responses to see whether they have or have not validated our predictions. Or rather, not whether 'they' have or have not, but whether their behaviour has.

Kelly's model of man in no way argues that we should not be concerned with behaviour. Behaviour is, after all, our way of conducting experiments and the behaviour of others is all we have to go on in our unceasing attempt to gain greater predictive control over our environment. But instead of viewing behaviour as some fact of life to be objectively viewed in our psychologist-as-scientist terms, we might try to find out from our subject-as-scientist what it is he intends by his behaviour - what is it that he is testing out? If all behaviour is to be regarded as an experiment, then the subject is experimenting along with the experimenter.

Following this line of thought, we might see the subject as one who is desperately trying to construe the construction processes of the psychologist. Most of us will have been subjects in experiments as students and found ourselves saying in silent desperation 'what the hell is she trying to get me to do?'. We try our various hypotheses until we think we have the right one. In experiments on the advantages of binocular as opposed to monocular vision, we might learn more about the human process by going beyond the success rates of subjects under each condition. We could ask what is it in the way subjects perceive (construe) the objects with two eyes that enables them to do 'better' than with one? What does 'better' mean to each person? Why do subjects occasionally do 'worse' with two eyes? They are doing more than being 'errors'. They may be saying that such psychological experiments are useless and a waste of time; they may have something wrong with their eyes; or they may be concentrating on the man they are going out with that evening. Whatever the reason, each is behaving in a meaningful way - meaningful to him or her that is, but it is error to the experimenter.

Taking each person as a scientist in their own right leads one to look at subjects as persons and not as organisms in a situation, so controlled, that ideally only one piece of behaviour will vary.

But what of the experimenter? As Mair (1970) says, psychologists are human too. In a sense we could say that Kelly's model will not lead to the psychologist being seen very differently, since he started out as the scientist - unlike the subject. But is that necessarily so? We know, for instance, that female subjects are smiled at considerably more often than male subjects and that it takes more time to collect data from females (Rosenthal, 1967). We do not need research data to tell us that we take a more jaundiced view of our subjects when we have a hangover than when we are feeling that life is good. Subjects also seem to behave more stupidly than usual when we (as experimenters) have personal worries or have an important appointment to go to ourselves. But if we wished to pursue this further, might we not investigate the construing of our experimenters (psychologists) and look, perhaps, to see whether those who think women are inherently more stupid than men obtain lower scores on some relevant task than those who have no such stereotype? For, let us not forget, our model person uses behaviour as an experiment and thereby tests out his hypotheses.

Commitment

If we, as persons or as psychologists, have a vested interest in some areas of construing - such as 'women are not as good as men' then, if we are in danger of having to revise that construct in view of the incoming evidence, we may cook the books. We may show hostility in Kelly's sense and extort validational evidence for a form of social prediction that has already proved itself a failure. We have to cook the books because, if we were to hold that women are inferior to men (which conversely makes men superior), then to hold that women were equal would rob men of their superiority at the same time. Not all men can contemplate that fall from on high. Not all have such views about the place of women in the human hierarchy, but some of us do feel strongly about our role as experimenters - and good ones at that. It is well documented that researchers often get results supporting their hypotheses, and I suppose this could be expected since we have, after all, chosen that particular experiment because it stands a good chance of succeeding. But now we have suggestive evidence from Rosenthal (1978) that more errors occur in data analyses supporting hypotheses than one would expect by chance. Ruling out dirty deeds and chance, it would make sense that this were so. We are, indeed, often personally involved with the successful outcome of our research and so may give our point of view an 'unconscious' helping hand.   To get too many negative results might lead to the unwelcome idea that we are not good researchers.

As we go along conducting our professional experiments, we have committed ourselves to these particular courses of action.   But many psychological experiments are conducted without personal commitment, without an understanding of what it would be like to be the subject.   Just as Harry Lime looked down from a great height on the seething masses below and argued that he could have no feeling for those ants and so was content to make himself rich by selling them heroin, so are subjects in psychological experiments viewed by some psychologists.   There are those dedicated to manipulation in psychology, just as there are in daily life.

If there were personal commitment this could not be.   But commitment is a real handicap.   For if we are committed to our research, and if we are carried along with our enthusiasms, we may find that we have risked too much and have behaved in a way that is at odds with our essential view of what sort of person we are.   If this happens we experience the unpleasant feelings of guilt (aware of dislodgement of the self from one's core role structure).   So, if we decide to become committed to our professional work as we are committed to our private actions, we are involving ourselves in personal risk-taking.   The model of the person-as-scientist means we must accept such commitment, and we thereby take responsibility for the well-being of our subjects.   Salmon (1978) argues that the lack of personal commitment in our professional experiments may be due to the fact that a distinction is made between human experience and behaviour.   With a dichotomy between experience and behaviour, traditional psychology has research:

> clearly assigned to the behaviour pole.   This has meant that research has been viewed as being about the explicit and observable behaviour of subjects, with the method of enquiry being the explicit and observable behaviour of the investigator.   By the same token, what has been defined as experience has been excluded.   So what subjects think and feel about the investigatory situation - as opposed to what they observably do - has been viewed as irrelevant to the 'real data'; concomitantly, the investigator, as an experiencing person, with concerns and investments in the research, has been totally absent in any account given. (Salmon, 1978, p. 40)

Experience and behaviour are not two poles of a construct with a man-the-scientist model.   One investigates the total person, and shows concern for the personal meaning of the behaviour for an individual.   Salmon advocates a form of psychological research that is truly about subjects.   It is about the process whereby we come to make sense of our world and the constraints we impose upon it.   Being about process, it is thereby about change.   It also becomes a truly social psychological research since subject and experimenter are expected to interact.

THE NATURE OF CHANGE

When we focus on change from the point of view of the person, things look very different from how they appear when we look at behaviour alone.   It was around the awareness of the need to change that Kelly built his theory of emotion.

Our scientific endeavours, whether professional or personal, are rooted in change when they are viewed as questions put to nature, and when behaviour becomes a means and not an end.   With this emphasis on behaviour as one of the most important concerns of psychology, it is not surprising that Kelly has been regarded by some as a behaviourist.   But the part behaviour plays in daily living for man-the-scientist is very different from its role in behavioural or psychoanalytic approaches to understanding the person.

When our personal experiment fails - that is, when the outcome is other than that predicted - there are several ways in which we can deal with this invalidation.   We can say our experiment was poorly designed - this leads us to improve the design and put our question to the test again. Or we can accept the unpredicted outcome and say that it was just one of those chance events and put the same question to the test once more. Or when, for instance, we come up against an audience which is unexpectedly hostile to our views, we can accept this but manage to convince ourselves that the listeners are all fools or all bigots and that there is no need for us to take them seriously. Or else we can accept the invalidating evidence and reconstrue. That is, turn it round on ourselves and say that we must now agree that our views are not acceptable to all and that they do not have the limitless appeal which we had at first supposed.

Or we can resist change and refuse to accept the invalidation for what it is. We thereby show hostility.   As personal or psychological scientists, as psychotherapist or teacher, as worker or boss, as parent or child, we often 'make' the events support our predictions.   One reason for this refusal to accept the invalidatory evidence could be that to acknowledge the stark reality staring us in the face would require personal change of such enormity that we could not contemplate it.   It is too threatening.   To spend a professional lifetime in the belief that what one is doing is of profound importance, not only to psychologists but to mankind, and then to read of, or listen to, ideas that invalidate our cherished beliefs, would mean we would have to acknowledge that our past life has been unwisely spent.   There is only one course of action that will protect our personal integrity - we must show to ourselves and others that these new ideas are no good, poorly constructed, unscientific, fit only for lower people and yobbos, or whatever strategy seems most appropriate to us. It is in this manner that threat can lead to hostility. Few of us are willing to accept the need for radical change. Occasionally some do. For instance, it was a heartening experience to hear A. J. Ayer discuss his role in the rise and fall of Logical Positivism:

> INTERVIEWER: But it must have had real defects.   What do you now, in
> retrospect, think the main ones were?
> AYER: Well, I suppose the most important of the defects was that nearly all of
> it was false.
> (Magee, 1978, p. 131)

Change can be disturbing in other ways as well. It can make us very anxious (aware that the events with which we are confronted lie outside the range of convenience of our construct system).   We can be plunged into anxiety if the outcome of our experimentation was such as to place us in a relatively meaningless situation.   Supposing our experiment produces results in the opposite direction from the one we predicted. What are we to make of it? It might have been all right if our prediction had simply been invalidated, but to be significantly wrong in the opposite direction! Where are we to go from here? What possible meaning are we to place upon it? We may be faced with an event we find impossible to construe. We can now make no predictions and so are rudderless. We have to be able to place some interpretation on the events confronting us before we can behave in relation to them.

Kelly argued that the dichotomy erected between cognitions and emotions was detrimental to the understanding of the whole person. He explained his position in the following way:

> ... in talking about experience I have been careful not to use either of the
> terms, 'emotional' or 'affective'. I have been equally careful not to invoke
> the notion of 'cognition'.   The classic distinction that separates these two
> constructs has, in the manner of most classic distinctions that once were
> useful, become a barrier to sensitive psychological inquiry.   When one so
> divides the experience of man it becomes difficult to make the most of the
> holistic aspirations that may infuse the science of psychology with new life,
> and may replace the classicism now implicit even in the most 'behavioristic'
> research. (Kelly, 1969c, p. 140)

SOME APPLICATIONS OF THE MODEL

If we truly looked upon ourselves 'as if' we were scientists, not only would our research and experimental enterprises look somewhat different, but so would our attempts to understand ourselves and others in the name of psychology.   To demonstrate the point, I could cite studies of the student (e.g. Radley, 1975); of the traumas encountered by us all in confronting the notions of death and dying, or by the few in the contemplation of suicide (e.g. Landfield, 1976); of the world of management and managers (e.g. Boxer, 1978); or the commune dweller (e.g. Karst & Groutt, 1977); or of the religious (e.g. Todd, 1977).   It is a model that is appealing to many groups other than psychologists.   It is a model that generates questions in abundance.

In order to clarify the point further we can look at the broader areas of child development, social and clinical psychology.

Child development

From the standpoint of personal construct psychology, the study of the developing child is a bit odd.   It normally seeks to identify 'stages' through which she goes before reaching the period of time when she stops developing - around adolescence; or 'milestones' which clock up her progress through the development years; or 'critical periods' which dictate that if she fails to find in the environment the vital stimuli necessary to enable her to develop a particular skill, then she will find it increasingly difficult to take advantage of those stimuli as the years progress.   Psychologists have thus tended to look for psychological stages, physical milestones or environmental stimuli to map out the progress of this strange developing organism - the child.

I want to emphasize once again that the construct is a discrimination.   It is a way in which a person has found it useful to categorize events in the environment which are similar in some respects and thereby different in others.   This discrimination may have a verbal label attached to it or it may not.   Thus the model of the scientist is not a model that can only be used for people who have language at their disposal.   It is equally applicable to the dog, the cat, the rat, and the ape, not to mention the foetus and the deaf-mute.   All can be viewed as organisms that construe.   As long ago as 1932, Tolman talked about the rat having an hypothesis, an expectation in relation to a particular situation.   These hypotheses he thought were weakened if not confirmed (invalidated) or strengthened if confirmed (validated).   Likewise the foetus can be construed as discriminating between events within its cosy environment.

Taking the model of 'person-as-experimenter' leads one to approach the study of development in very different ways from those of Piaget, Skinner or Freud.   I think most would agree with Piaget's use of the clinical method of inquiry and his focus on trying to understand what the child itself thinks it is doing, but we would part company with him, as with Freud, in trying to classify children in terms of set stages through which they should progress.   Maybe I will be proved wrong about this.   Perhaps the similarities and differences the personal construct model leads us to perceive in the development of children's construing will impinge itself on us so forcibly that we will come to talk of different stages in the development of construct system integration, differentiation, and any other '-ations' that we can think of.

Some of the research findings suggest that this may already be happening (see Bannister & Fransella, 1979, for a more detailed discussion).   But Kelly's scientist is an individual who is similar to and different from all other individuals in certain respects, and it is this individuality that many people who like the person-as-scientist model would seek to follow.   Salmon (1970) suggests that we might seek to understand child development in role terms.   For our model person this means construing the others' construction processes. The child starts out by construing its mother's construing of him and then elaborates this as he comes into contact with other people who are like his mother or with other children who are like himself.

Shotter (1974) describes a period he calls psychological symbiosis during which the mother sees her baby's behaviour as being the result of the ways in which he is interpreting that part of his world. She attempts to construe what it is that he is intending by his actions. Likewise, the mother has intentions about what her baby should do and he attempts to construe her intentions. They thus have a full role relationship in operation from a very early age. By acting together, the child becomes able to discriminate between 'them' and 'the rest of the world'. In time, the child becomes able to distinguish between himself and his mother and so develops his own self-construct system.

In his chapter in this volume, Shotter (chapter 2) talks of a child 'inheriting' social behaviour at birth, but is unable to state the mechanism. Since constructs are discriminations organisms invent to give meaning to (or enable them to relate to) events, the child scientist could be seen as discriminating between the mother's different tones of voice, smiles, gestures and so forth - with no verbal labels attached to these discriminations. Construct theory can thus provide one explanation of the mechanism whereby children 'inherit' the social language of their culture.

Social psychology

Although Kelly describes psychotherapy as the focus of convenience of his theory, it is almost equally at home in the field of interpersonal relations. The mother-child, subject-experimenter, client-therapist - are all also social interactions. Any event in which, as the Sociality Corollary states, one person attempts to construe the construction process of another, is of interest to the social psychologist.

In the field of attitude studies, prejudice comes to be looked on as a constellation of constructs providing a strategy for the individual, designed to preserve his present personal identity; stereotypes are subsystems of constructs used in a constellatory and pre-emptive manner - 'if a man is a Negro it necessarily follows that he must be lazy, musical, highly sexed, low on washing and high on laughter' (Bannister & Fransella, 1979); studies on cognitive complexity-simplicity arose directly out of construct theory (see Adams-Webber, 1979). What can be done with viewing the person 'as if' each were a scientist is also well illustrated by the work of Duck (1979) on friendship patterns.

As well as bringing an altered perspective on old issues, the theory has been of value in extending other theoretical frameworks. For example, Durkheim's notion of the 'representation' is, in a sense, the linch-pin of French social psychology. By viewing the representation 'as if' it were a construct, it is possible to relate thought with action or behaviour (Fransella, 1979).

Yet, in spite of its evident fruitfulness in social psychology, there is a need for more reflexivity. That is, there is a sense in which personal construct psychology says too little about the impact of society upon the development, extension and maintenance of individuals' construct systems. It is here that a link with, perhaps, the social psychology of Mead (as outlined by Farr, chapter 13) could be of great value.

Clinical psychology

It is in this field that most of the early work based on the theory was carried out. For, if one views the person 'as if' they are scientists, then diagnostic categories, disease notions of process and treatment all take on a very different look. For instance, Bannister's work (e.g. 1962, 1965) with those diagnosed as schizophrenic was concerned, not with what they said or how they behaved, but with their process of construing. He demonstrated that the construct subsystems they have to do with construing people, are unusually 'loosely' tied together. This work leads not only to the usual end result of aiding diagnosis, but suggests a form of psychological treatment.

Within a construct theory framework, the stutterer comes to be seen as a person who has never developed a construct subsystem to do with communicating with people in a fluent manner. Help then takes the form of guiding him in his elaboration of his view of himself as a fluent speaker (Fransella, 1972). But the model of the experimenting person takes one beyond the changing of behaviour. It is only when, for instance, the stutterer can speak with some fluency, or the agoraphobic is able to do some going out, or the obese or anorexic is approaching normal weight, and so on, that each can start to look at life from this new vantage point. Far too often, the person does not like the look of what they see and prefers to return to the old, though undesirable, position. Each has to be persuaded to be a constructive alternativist, to view their personal theories as being only one way of looking at their world so that they can start experimenting by behaving differently.

The bipolar nature of the construct also enables one to ask what it is that a person is not doing while they are behaving as they are. New light can be thrown on many personal problems in this way.

Rowe (1971), for example, showed how a depressed woman was being not 'bad'- she saw people who are depressed as 'good'. It was reasonable to predict from this that such a person would not change very readily.

There are now many examples of the different views one takes of psychological disturbances by asking different questions. Instead of asking 'what symptoms does this person have?' so as to place them in some diagnostic category, one asks 'what is it in this person's way of viewing the world that leads them to behave in this particular way?'. It is sometimes surprising the answers one gets.

Physiology and psychology

Bannister (1968) argued that physiological psychology was a myth since it was a form of reductionism that tried to equate two very different language systems. It is certainly not appropriate to talk of focusing on the person, the scientist, and then to look at how certain parts of the brain influence behaviour. But Harré (chapter 14) provides a possible solution for those who feel that dualism is not a useful concept to apply to us as persons, yet find it difficult to incorporate our experienced physiological activity into our man-as-scientist model.

Harré suggests that a cybernetic model may provide the means for translating from psychological to physiological language. Those in the field of artificial intelligence are already taking an interest in Kelly's theory. For instance, Aleksander & Morton (1979) have worked their way through the Fundamental Postulate and intend to proceed to all Corollaries. Kelly has made their task as simple as possible by defining each of the words he uses. To date, the only problem these workers have encountered is with 'events' (a person's processes are psychologically channelized by the ways in which he anticipates 'events'). The problem is to determine where the first constructs come from to allow such anticipations to take place.

Harré's suggestion and the work of Aleksander & Morton are promises for the future. But there seems no theoretical reason why a person's physiology should not be studied along with construing. For instance, the person's ability to control his or her own physiological functioning can be approached by looking at feedback as a device enabling the person to discriminate between aspects of the inner workings. By construing, say, blood pressure, the person is sometimes able to bring the level under control. The research that Peter Fonagy and I are at present carrying out along these lines seems similar to the 'naive parallelism' model suggested by Gale (chapter 5). But with us it is subjective experience and behaviour which are seen as likely to be paramount.

DOES MAN-THE-SCIENTIST EQUAL ADAM-AND-EVE?

A strong reaction has developed against Kelly's use of the term 'man' in his man-the-scientist model. There has also been some discussion of the implications of the title of this conference. We are constantly being told that 'man' embraces 'woman'. If that were the case, then surely 'he' and 'she' should be equally applicable after the term 'man'. We can reasonably say that 'man-the-scientist describes her in her scientist-like aspects'. But we do not often do this. Or, likewise, we could say 'all men are mortal, Miranda is a man...'

The source of the problem has been well documented by Miller & Swift (1976). English originally had the word 'Mann' to describe both the human being and the male sex.

In view of Kelly's choice of term, it is reasonable to ask whether it truly encompasses women in the generic sense. A glance at some of his writing leads one to suspect that he fell into this chauvinistic man-trap along with the rest of male-kind. For instance, he gives a long account of the relationship of Adam and Eve to help portray his ideas concerning the nature of 'man'. He says:

A long time ago, so the story goes, Man made a fateful decision. He chose to live his life by understanding, rather than obedience ...
It should be said, I suppose, that Man probably would not have had the initiative to take this fateful step if he hadn't had some encouragement from his girlfriend. (Kelly, 1969d, p. 207)

In this example, Kelly clearly meant Man to mean man and not woman, since why else is it necessary to specify the girlfriend separately? He continues:

Without her he would probably have been content to do what he was told, as men are inclined to be when they are part of an all-male society ... But when women are around, or you can't get your mind off them, material security and inner contentment don't always add up to the same thing. (Kelly, 1969d, pp. 207-208)

Poor, discontented man, having to rush around to make money to buy the things that will make his woman secure. Yet more follows:

Now, about this woman! She was not altogether a disobedient young thing herself, but she had had her feelings stirred up by something or other she had interpreted as rather suggestive - something symbolic, no doubt. And while, as frequently seems to be true of the opposite sex, she was disinclined to take any improper action herself - a fact that must be held to her credit - she was, nonetheless, disposed to drop the intriguing issue into the midst of Adam's idyllic contentment, just to see if he might not want to do something about it. This bit of domestic strategy is known as 'sharing your problems'. The upshot was that Adam did do something about it, and, as a dutiful mate, she went along with the deal. And, I am sure, something like this is what still makes man's world go round and round instead of standing still in obedient contentment, and what, more and more, turns it into the fascinating and fearsome puzzle it has come to be. (Kelly, 1969d, p. 208)

Try and sort the man-the-human from man-the-male from that lot. After a few pages in which 'man' is clearly meant to encompass both sexes, he points out that the Garden of Eden story is much the same as the psychology of the laboratory. 'So, just as in the Eden project, our experiments, also, fail to confirm predictions, our women get neurotic, our nations go berserk.' No neurotic men here, only women.

In spite of the obvious sex bias in the examples Kelly gives, there seems only to be a bias in the theory in terms of emphasis. Kelly argues philosophically, that all events are subject to revision and replacement and that no one need be a victim of his biography or paint himself into a corner. Our 'man' goes out into his sea of events, construes their similarities and differences, makes predictions about subsequent events and so gains control over that aspect of her life. If she finds her predictions invalidated or comes to dislike aspects of herself or her life, she can reconstrue - here lies the freedom. I would only suggest that our social climate may make this easier for more men than women.

What about the working-class woman with six children under five years of age? She finds herself tied to her home, acting as a very underpaid drudge to her children and her husband. She resents this bitterly and becomes depressed (Brown & Harris, 1977). Not only does she resent being a drudge but she resents not being able to study some subject that has always interested her. She gives up the unequal struggle. She appears to be a victim of her biography - to have painted herself into a corner.

How does she set about reconstruing? What does she reconstrue? She can change her construction of herself as a wife and mother with concomitant implications of duty and so forth. She can come to see that she owes a duty to herself, and others must take second place. So she ups and leaves knowing that the social system will not let her children starve and knowing that her husband earns the money with which he can keep himself. But where does she get her money from? She has no training, presumably she may find work in some factory - woman's work - low paid work. Out of this she has to pay for somewhere to live and for her food. Where now is the time to go in for the studying she wants to do. She has no 'wife' to look after her and see to her needs, so that she can study when she comes home from work. It is all too much. She again gets depressed.

Her medical practitioner puts her on some pills to reduce the depression. But her life is still unbearable. So she is sent to a psychiatrist who thinks psychotherapy will help - she needs help to reconstrue. Her present life is miserable so all agree that it is probably best if she were able to fulfil her role of mother and wife. So she reconstrues and returns home. The therapy was successful. So often psychotherapy for women is directed toward persuading them to reconstrue in order to better fulfil their female role rather than toward seeing how they can best fulfil their own personal needs.

I do not think that any of this radically affects the theory or the model of the scientist - a model which I, personally, find intensely exciting and continually challenging. But if the 'as if' model proposed is at a sufficiently high level of abstraction to make a separate model of woman-as-scientist unnecessary (as discussed by Beloff, chapter 18), and I think it is, then a way must be found to deal with what can be considered a language problem with far-reaching implications. I have thought long and hard about this and come up with nothing better than the rightly criticized 'person-as-scientist'. If more people accept that a problem exists, someone may soon come up with a better alternative.

CONCLUSIONS

I would like to end with a quote from a 1966 paper of Kelly's which sums up his view of the effects of looking at each of us 'as if' we were scientists, using behaviour as our experiment to ask questions about nature:

To ask a question is to invite the unexpected. If any man seriously asks the question of what his possibilities are - as indeed men are now doing at an accelerating pace - something shocking is likely to come of it, as indeed it has. The very process of posing questions about himself with deeds rather than words transforms the questioner, even before he is aware of any rewarding answers. As long as most men were so overawed by nature that they treated events as stimuli to which their behavior must be attuned, man appeared as an object so vestigial that psychologists could explain him as a tail wagged by the dog of antecedent events. But no modern man, no race, no people - its fears and its scholars notwithstanding - accepts this post-Darwinian premise indefinitely. Instead, behavior that probes his possibilities transforms a man beyond the scholar's recognition - as it is known to transform a child. The bolder the questions the more remarkable the transformation. And what is psychology to say about that! (Kelly, 1969a, p. 8)

EDITED DISCUSSION

H. COWIE: You called one of your books 'Inquiring Man'. 'Inquiring woman' has quite different connotations, of someone who is rather nosey, curious and inquisitive - rather than scientific. I wonder if you would want to retain the original title of your book?

F. FRANSELLA: No. I have personally evolved since then! But the snag is that there is no way of changing the title. I do not know what the alternative would be, but I do feel strongly that it should be changed.

P. KLINE: Kelly's model is supposed to contain the seeds of its own destruction. In some people's opinion if it really did have that property it would have been destroyed long ago. It is very difficult to see what value the theory has had except for practitioners of grids and similar techniques that are bound up with it. So, could you tell me what scientific facts, ideas or concepts, or anything of value, that has come out of it?

F. FRANSELLA: There are a number of answers, and it is important to note that interest in the approach has really only developed in the past 5 years. One explanation for that is that the theory is excessively complicated. Another explanation is that it represents for many psychologists a quite different orientation from the one in which they were trained: therefore, it often requires a considerable amount of rethinking on their part. These factors account for the slow development. As for facts, by their very nature they are interim things; and I am not sure that the theory is designed to find out facts. Do we not want to assess a theory by its usefulness in generating ideas, in leading people to explore things in fresh ways, and in finding interim facts? If so, the theory has been of immense value: for example, in clinical, child and social psychology.

H. WEINREICH-HASTE: Kelly offers something which Piaget also offers (and which is apparent in Professor Wright's paper - see pp. 313-317), and that is a very active model of the person. That is in contrast with traditional models which have implicitly or explicitly made the person passive in the face of either biological or environmental influence.

F. FRANSELLA: Yes, that is quite right. The other attraction is that it is a very explicit and elaborate theory. You can go to it with a 'problem' and you can find an explanation within the theory: you do not have to go outside it.

L. SMITH: One difference between Piaget and Kelly is that Piaget can explain the origin of structures but Kelly cannot explain the origin of constructs. How does the first construct come about? If you say that reality is understood only through a construct, and also that any construct arises because of some behaviour in the world, you have the problem of explaining how the first construct arose.   The idea of an innate one seems to me to be self-contradictory.

F. FRANSELLA: Maybe an integral feature of all living matter is that it construes its environment.   Plants can be said to construe in that they discriminate between good and bad soil, and light and dark.

J. SHOTTER: You must admit that Kelly's scheme is a metaphysical one, just providing the terms within which one can begin to seek facts of a certain kind to discriminate one kind of construct system from another ...

F. FRANSELLA: That to me is a very high level of abstraction, but I would agree with you.

J. SHOTTER: That is so in just the same way that mechanism is also a metaphysical system within psychology.   There are no facts which can prove either approach to be wrong.   They live or die by their usefulness - the way they fit in with different enterprises in life generally.   I think that many people here are misleading themselves if they think your position is weakened because you cannot provide the vital 'facts' to prove your system correct and theirs wrong.   Requests for facts ought to be phrased in a much more subtle way.

F. FRANSELLA: Fundamental postulates and their corollaries are statements of faith.   What you can prove and disprove, or validate and invalidate, are the hypotheses that are derived from those statements.   If they all turn out to be inadequate you would say that it is not a useful 'as if' model.

J. SHOTTER: Indeed, we have heard many statements of faith from the 'other side' here.

Are models of man models of women?

H. Beloff

Why should we have this chapter at all?

This is a genuine question. While men are male, man is our species. I am not suggesting that it should have been 'models of persons' - or even 'of people', which at least sounds less bureaucratic. But clearly somewhere in our discussions we must come to the point that our population of man does come from two subsamples.

We must consider how the pattern of biological differences is reflected in our social and psychological modes, and how these modes are important to our models.

In one sense there has arisen in the last few years, of course, a whole new psychology - of M/F differences. In that plethora of discussion and empirical study, do we need another analysis? Are we perhaps even coming to the reaction in the dialectic? After all, Fran Lebowitz (1979), that sensitive feeler of the social pulse, has recently written, 'Being a woman is of special interest to aspiring male transexuals. To actual women it is simply an excuse not to play football' (p. 144). And indeed the spirit of reaction is shown in another swing. Men are voicing their rejection of the male stereotype (Pleck & Sawyer, 1974; Tolson, 1977). First the women cried out in pain at their procrustean overcoats, now it is the men. A lot do not fit.

But it is not the minutiae of individual differences, however carefully surveyed and annotated, that are our concern here. Although even there it is not irrelevant for us to note that, following the earlier era when differences were searched for and found, lately there has been a drawing back and a realization of non-differences, if one can use that awkward term. The authority of Maccoby & Jacklin (1974), for example, points to the fewness of essential differences psychometrically confirmed, and except in one case (aggression), to their specificity and indeed triviality.

If, like Eysenck (chapter 4), we accept that difference in aggression, or more broadly assertion, there remains the question of the relative variance that might be attributed to it by historical and cultural convenience, in relation to its reflection of biology. As Eysenck himself has so often stressed, in another context, individual differences do not imply absolute divisions between groups. There is still the possibility of a 'delight' in a variety of adjustments among and between all kinds of classifications of people. And for once, Eysenck will agree with Freud (1932), that while our nature is part determined by our sexual function, 'an individual woman may be a human being apart from this'.

But seriously, if we consider our topic in terms of form and content - individual differences surely count as content - then we are here to think of

form.   In terms of form, of models, there are three questions we must ask
ourselves:

    Models of Women: Do we need one?
                     Do we want one?
                     Do we have one?

DO WE NEED ONE?

This is obviously the main question and the basis of my arguments comes from a
variety of sources and contexts: developmental psychology; the history of art; the
study of common parlance; a model of man from one of the gurus of our culture - all
as examples of our subject matter.

    Right at the outset some of us might be prepared to say that we need not make
heavy weather at all; gender differences are not fundamental in our personal
interactions.   This is an attractive view, but on fundamentals, studies of early
development are often very pertinent.   And on that question of fundamentals I might
not be the only psychologist who has recently been pulled up by some evidence in
the developmental literature.   I refer to the reports of Lewis & Brooks (1975) that
infants seem able to recognize the gender of other infants.   To put it most simply,
they look longer at their same-sex peers, finding, it is thought, some element of
'like me' there.

    Now we know that infants can already distinguish between their father and their
mother, and also between strange men and strange women.   This is, of course,
presumed to be a perceptual skill based on the visual cues of dress and hair, and
auditory cues of voice.   In so far as greater fear is usually expressed of strange
men, this might have a rather clear biological function.   But what are we to make
of that supposed biological function when it is displayed by infants at the ages of
6 and 12 months, towards other infants of those ages?   Consonant with the current
challenge to reduce the age of reason further and further - to show that infants
are already sentient, not to say sensible, people - they have been shown to
distinguish their like and unlike peers in this way.

    And the matter is more complicated than a simple connoisseurship of pink and
blue, or dolls and toy cars.   Stuart Aitken (1977), working with Tom Bower at
Edinburgh, has been able to demonstrate that babies 'prefer' other babies of their
own sex not only in the ordinary way of things, but when they are accoutred as the
inappropriate gender.   That is, babies will look longer at others of their own sex,
even when the boys seen are dressed as girls and playing with dolls, and the girls
dressed as boys and playing with a drum.   The babies are not responding to
stereotypical cues.   In fact, the study indicates that the cues involved are
movement ones, because the 'preference' cannot be elicited with still photographs.

    Whatever else we may conclude, this sort of evidence certainly suggests that
sex differentiation is a fundamental component of our psychology.   Some of the more
sophisticated among us may reiterate that they make no distinction by gender in
interactions - that is often right and good - but they once tended to.   Accepting
then that we have some intriguing evidence that sexual differentiation is not a
superficial or a purely culturally convenient matter - we must begin to see what
kinds of images of women and men we have and have had, in order to find our answer
for the 'do we need it' question.

    We could consider the big differential psychology literature to see what of
fundament lies there.   There are a number of excellent surveys.   I have already
mentioned the impressive documentation of Maccoby & Jacklin (1974).   There are
balanced and dynamic scrutinies of biological and cultural variances like that of
Lloyd & Archer (1976).   Surveys of real-life contexts and implications (Chetwynd &
Hartnett, 1978) and useful reflexive analyses of scientific stereotypes (Weinreich
& Chetwynd, 1976) complement the hermeneutic account of what we know about how
women actually see themselves from Fransella & Frost (1977).   However, I myself

consider that even in the face of this erudition and scientific respectability it might just be worth while to stand back from psychology and consider, perhaps, the broader sweep that other kinds of scholars have made. It might be good to see gender differences out there in another world.

The three themes, already mentioned, which I hope will stimulate us, are based on the work of scholars who have looked about, trying to uncover what has always been there, and what has, at the same time, never been noticed. Sometimes such uncoverings have ignored gender in the time-honoured way, sometimes they have focused on it in crucial ways. We shall see what they tell us about model needs. I suggest that we could approach our subject from a particular strand in the texture of everyday life - by examining models of man in the literal sense. Let us look at the history of life painting - of the nude.

There has recently been a particular interest in the analysis of the history of the nude, not only in terms of the pure aesthetic values involved, but because the artistic representation of the human figure provides a marvellous set of raw data - large samples over the millennia, frozen and unadulterated by time. Those provide then a survey of the natural history of images of men, and women, and also of the relations of men and women. From our point of view, too, it is a set of samples of profound studies of male/female differences, of the history of the stereotypes that men have had of their own and of women's character. And we refer not only to their characteristics as seen objects, of course, but as human ideals in a fundamental sense, as embodiments of religious ideology, as stimuli of sexual excitement, and of the relations between the craft of production and the demands of the consumer.

It is on Margaret Walters' recent 'The Nude Male' (1978) that I draw with most enthusiasm, but the groundwork for psychological interest was laid already by John Berger in his enormously influential book 'Ways of Seeing' (1972). There he sets forward what one must call a set of sonorous postulates that state, more vividly than any psychologist has ever done, the polarity between men and women:

A man's presence is dependent upon the promise of power which he embodies. A man's presence suggests what he is capable of doing to you or for you ... a power which he exercises on others. By contrast, a woman's presence expresses her own attitude to herself, and defines what can and cannot be done to her. (pp. 45-46)

To be born a woman has been to be born ... into the keeping of men. The social presence of women has developed as a result of their ingenuity in living under such tutelage within such a limited space. A woman must continually watch herself. She is almost continually accompanied by her own image of herself. (p. 46)

One might simplify this by saying: 'men act' and 'women appear'. Men look at women. Women watch themselves being looked at. This determines not only most relations between men and women but also the relation of women to themselves. Thus she turns herself into an object - and most particularly an object of vision: a sight. (p. 47)

It is worth noting that Berger goes out of his way to proclaim the particularity of this 'model' to the European culture. In Indian, Persian and African art, the theme of relations and attraction is shown typically as active sexual love between two equal people. The women as active as the man, they being absorbed in each other. So it is at this point sensible for us to make the general proviso - in our culture.

This is the broad sweep. Let us look at Walters' more detailed argument. And also note before we go further - let us make clear that although we are in the realms of art, for about two thousand years (until the 18th century) it was entwined with scientific curiosity. It was scientific curiosity that motivated artists in their work, curiosity not only about the structure of the body, but about the meaning of its divinity, about its central place in the universe, about the differential meaning of manhood and womanhood. They simulated human beings, lifelike but idealized, principally of men, but differentially of women also.

Let us apply a kind of social science approach to these 'data'. Let us consider the incidence (or prevalence) of male and female figures, consider the size of the subsamples. Surprisingly for us now, for whom the word nude conjures up for sure, a woman - from Renoir, or Russell Flint, or Pirelli - we must know that for all the time between prehistory and the last two hundred years - the nude human figure was pre-eminently a man. (Renaissance artists you will remember, even used male models for their female figures ...) We begin to see ourselves in a familiar territory ...

What about the characteristics of these models? The males are public; the male nudes are not only worshipped in church, but guard public buildings, they stride through city squares; whilst the female exists for an individual capitalist, in his study, for his private delectation. Again one must say that the message of the male is potency. He is the symbol of the phallus, he has its power. He is the embodiment of a culture. And since the Venus of Willendorf - the woman has been passive - beautiful (but not more so than the man), calm, playful but modest, receptive, mysterious. (As Walters says, when the male becomes the focus of Christian art and its masochism, it is a clearly feminized male body that appears, albeit nailed to a phallic tree.) As the heroic nude, man has been presented in three archetypes: Narcissus, Apollo, Hercules. But the separate virtues of youth, virility and massive strength remain essentially unchanged. It is only their salience that varies. The male artist sees that his body's integrity is maintained. It is the women that he makes that must shift and change - in order that their power to titillate may remain always fresh. They are indeed passive too, in the hands of their creators. And it is in their comparison over time that we can best appreciate the magnitude of their deformations - from the emaciated, pregnant women of Lucas Cranach, to the fat and pink and smiling Rubens 'Hausfrauen', and the adolescent fun girls of Watteau and Boucher, to the freaks of Picasso. (Note that for him it was always the women that suffered the greatest sea-change, the most monstrous assaults.) Indeed here is reinforcement for the point that it is women who have been subject to the strongest moulds by the demands of the European high culture. And there is reinforcement for the argument that the role of women is to function as a foil, a reciprocal of the masculine ideal.

How is the activity and potency of the male but enhanced by the passivity, by the dependence, by the appeal in every sense, of the woman? And this again is a function of the fact that men have been the principal producers of art. The non-history of women artists is, of course, being actively rewritten, with documentation of their contribution ranging from the illuminated manuscripts of the mediaeval abbesses through every school until we reach the better-known figures like Mary Cassett and Käthe Kollwitz. As the archivists Petersen & Wilson (1978) write, The only places we have not found women artists are where we have not yet looked (p. 6). This still does not place women on the highest reaches of creativity and innovation in the visual arts. Maybe they have lacked the intellectual power. However, even a little familiarity with the history of the taboos within the art guilds and academies suggests other factors.

It was naturally in the arena of life drawing that the hardest struggles ensued. Especially telling perhaps is the story of Angelica Kauffmann - who was denied attendance at the Royal Academy life studios, and when she produced her fine nudes was accused of extra-curricular study of an immoral kind. And let us appreciate the position of the young women students at the Pennsylvania Academy of Arts in 1883 who practised their life painting with a cow. It is hard not to believe that over-determination occurred here. The barriers were erected in order to maintain intact the purity of women artists - perhaps. Might we not also suppose that there was an implicit acknowledgement by the men that in painting the male models, women might in their turn evaluate, judge, assess, not only the male models, but men? There might be a clearer, colder, reciprocal appraisal not only of the reality, but its relation to those ideals, and of the ideals themselves.

Then the source of the appraisal of those male models would no longer be tinged with narcissism, but be made in terms of the needs of women, and more importantly in the long view, in terms of the coming together, of the cooperation, the interactive lives of men and women. (And I do not mean only the sexual coming together.)

No one is here assuming that women would want to turn the tables in the simplest sense. We will not necessarily want to see our nude male as another kind of landscape to be explored and possessed; or to make it play peek-a-boo with those bits of gauze; or ourselves to stride in that blatant, shameless way through the Piazza della Signoria. In the present, women artists are showing a humanistic kind of image of man and men that is startling and awakening. It is totally different from the tradition - vulnerable, individualistic, open and expressive - themes that I come back to. We would come to a broader appraisal than the traditional one which has described the male image in art as noble, austere, rational, objective, public-minded and revolutionary, while the female displays frivolous, shallow intimacy; family affection, the graces of life, melting colours and silky textures.

If that is one summary of past themes - we would conclude that tradition surely dictated and exemplified separate models. The present suggests that they are not the only ones, and that we might re-negotiate without great misalignments if only we accept that a female as well as a male perspective might be drawn.

Perhaps now it would be good to come to a domain closer to home - which I have called common parlance. Here seems to be one of those 'innocent' topics from text-books - gender differences in speech, which might take their place with class differences, age differences, national and other cultural comparisons. Examined more closely, as have indeed those other innocent chapters, their validity as well as their interpretation is fraught with difficulty.

One approach here is that of the attribution of differential value, interest, intellectual power and, of course, our old friend attraction, to the female voice. This is pregnant with interest and has been the object of most useful and ingenious study (Giles et al., 1977), but is not relevant to our discussion here. I refer rather to the attention that is now being given to the hidden languages, or more particularly to the 'grammar' of the hidden language of women, that is being written by some linguists (Hass, 1979, presents a neutral summary). It is now formally stated that there are in fact two tongues within English (and indeed in many other languages) - one known and spoken by women, the other by men (although the latter will sometimes use certain women's usages to, and in the presence of, women). Two postulates then follow:

(1) That each language reflects in its pattern of usage the roles of men and the roles of women - and the relation between them.

(2) That we are largely unaware of these patterns, and as a corollary of (1) - that we must (now) open them out.

(That opening out is a highly dynamic process.)

What are the languages? Much of the masculine form hardly needs me to specify it. It is the 'ordinary' English of colloquial usage, which we take for granted. It has certain limitations of vocabulary and idea. But it has the crucial plus of the Anglo-Saxon words and expletives, which I as a woman know nothing about, and therefore cannot exemplify or describe. (It is perhaps interesting to note here that I in fact learnt more about it recently - from my adolescent son, who is, of course, insufficiently socialized as yet to keep the tribal secrets in their proper place.)

It is women's language that is the bone of contention. Let us follow Lakoff's (1973) celebrated 'translation', and consider three prongs of her attack. Women's language:

(1) It is marvellously polite.

(2) It has a number of elements that are simply gender specific.

Sometimes these are parts of a vocabulary that belong to a social class/gender group, and hence have easily lent themselves to becoming the objects of satire.

('Divine' is a passé example, 'gorgeous' perhaps a more contemporary one.)   But here are included a much more interesting set of classifications, and possibilities of fine appreciation with respect to sensory, or aesthetic, and I would add, of psychological modalities.

One might reiterate Lakoff's example, which seems slightly amusing to us here perhaps – that an American man will not seriously consider using the word 'mauve'. To do so would be to admit to a preoccupation with matters that are outside the domain of permissible interest of a virile person.   More seriously I would put it to you, and more persuasively I think, that most men would be uncomfortable giving fine consideration to that beautiful definition of sexuality which George Klein gave us – as 'a distinctively poignant pleasure experience'.   I believe it is the term poignant that is the stumbling block. Men's language lacks many words – not for snow – but for the graces of life: women enjoy them.

(3) Women's language eschews not only 'bad' language, but strong language. That means for Lakoff, that a man will say, 'Shit, you've put the peanut butter in the fridge again.' And a woman, 'Oh dear, you've put the peanut butter ... etc.' But, also, this means that women will embroider (yes that is an appropriate term) their statements with many a little signal of modesty, deference, ingratiation – tag questions, conditionals – 'I wonders ...', and 'you knows', to demonstrate that she is unsure of her position, needs social support and is unwilling to assert her view.   I believe that without spelling out tedious details of the demographic evidence for these assertions, we can accept that the argument is broadly valid. Nay, I assert that!

I have presented this evidence and this position in some detail, not only because I find them provocative in their own right, but because there is clearly more than one position one may take with regard to their implication.   More than the one specified at the beginning of this section.   What are some of the possibilities?

(1) The status quo is not only de facto – but desirable. Vive la différence! This is psychologically not as boring a position as it might first appear.   From the male perspective it is indeed simple.   It is held by them as a rational strategy which removes women from the action. Let women continue queens in their domain of the finer civilization, the graces – social, aesthetic, spiritual and moral.

But it is held often equally strongly by women themselves. Held not rationally some of us would say, but as a comfort. We cannot obtain real power (we implicitly know), therefore let us satisfy ourselves with our traditional empires – of etiquette and social relations.   We accept the bribe of 'superiority' for our inferiority.   Surely this is a variation of Mies' provocative, 'Less is More' – Worse is Better. But we shall return to this form of dissonance reduction.

(2) In making this transition from an essentially, implicit, oral tradition to a formal 'grammar' we women will want to change our language, and in changing our language will be in the process of changing ourselves.   The process of 'opening' already involves us deeply in the process of change – inextricably of the language and of ourselves. Then women unlearn their present language, speak like a man, and become part of the power elite, because, of course, the argument that men's language is that of the power elite is compelling.

Men are assertive, they do not need to ingratiate themselves to get what they need and deserve.   They are not polite because they are clear, logical, rational and succinct.   The fact that they are also rude is not important. They do not need to concern themselves, either with the finer points of fashionable descriptive terms, nor with the evaluation of those matters of arts or human relationships that cannot be covered by the more popular bipolar adjectives of the Osgoodian semantic space.   Anything more acknowledges that it is only peripheral to real-life space, and outside the arena of serious concern.   Women are pre-occupied with the subtleties because the realities are not theirs.

And, finally, that use of 'fuck' and 'shit' shows that men are indeed as 'strong' as their language – that assertion and laying about oneself in an immediate and impulsive way is what a man can do.

This is indeed the tactic that Lakoff herself advocates, and she does so persuasively. Women are polite because they are insecure, not to say frightened, by the rough and tumble of social intercourse. They are indeed concerned with etiquette because business, government, technology, affairs and learning were traditionally closed to them. Purity, and avoidance of language contamination just reinforce the taboos. We need no special model. But there is a third alternative strategy.

(3) We understand the present position - we make some choices of a more subtle and specific kind, not in terms of an all-or-none tactic, but in a careful evaluation of the function and meaning of our position and our purpose. Who would deny her cri-de-coeur: '... Because I came into the world with two X chromosomes, I have no choice but to be an arbiter of morality ...'. But if we take language at all seriously, if words still have actual meanings for us, if we have a feel for language - do we constantly want to associate the image of shit with the peanut butter, or indeed other facets of our lives? That is surely done by people who lack visual imagery. Need we be ashamed of precision or richness of vocabulary - and therefore of our concepts? Are polite forms always symptoms of anxiety? They may be so. Empty adjectives (charming), tag questions (isn't it?), and those constant uses of hedges (you know ...) are. And they are a waste of time. But some of us draw back from the use of tooth and claw for positive reasons.

Goffman (1972) has described better than I can, the sacred ritual and ceremony of deference and demeanour played in our social circles. In that ritual game it is better that we play diplomatically, that we cope honourably. But the position is surely that situation and task is a better guide to right action than personality and demography. There are indeed contexts demanding courtesy, and others that demand not only assertion but ruthlessness.

We turn not only to situationism, but to the goal of flexibility and choice. There are limitations in the traditional adjustments of men and women. The fact that women's has not been ideal, does not mean that that of men is.

Does this begin to mean that one model, two models, is not what it is about? If we are prepared to go beyond psychology - there are various benefits. Let us consider next a model constructed by a polymath - and a polymath with the courage no academic would have to construct a model that is universal, indeed cosmic - based on an analysis of evolution, anatomy, history, culture and, come to that, psychology. I refer to the Janus of Arthur Koestler (1978). The model Janus is the final figure of Koestler's interpretation of the human condition, seen with the inevitable, logical pessimism of a veteran of the European intelligentsia towards the end of the 20th century. Let us summarize the dimensions of Janus, and then evaluate him and his problems from our point of view. Whose problems are they anyway? Might we be able to offer other solutions?

Koestler starts with the old argument that we have within our power the simple potential for destroying not only our enemies, not only our enemies and ourselves, not only civilization, but civilization and the whole human race. This potentiality is brought towards actuality in Koestler's view by the paranoid streak, as he calls it, that homo sapiens has revealed in his past record. He sees the imminent end of life on this planet, ended by the pathological and paradoxical combination of our unique talents for technological achievements and our equally unique clumsiness in the management of social relations. He tells that familiar story with great vividness. Who can forget his example, that man can leave the earth and land on the moon, but cannot cross from East to West Berlin? The power of his argument rests, then, on the development that he brings to his model of Janus in the middle of those paradoxes.

Basically the predicament that he addresses himself to is the evil in man. And that predicament, of all others, has had many explanations - from the Fall, through Freud's Thanatos, to our recent friend the Territorial Imperative. They all centre on the aggression of man to man. Perhaps the problem is more subtle than that. It is worth considering in some detail the particular paradigm symptoms that Koestler himself enumerates.

(1) The Abraham and Isaac complex - that is the Western European version, but it is a single example from a host of stories of human sacrifice, and sacrifice of some pure and guiltless, weak and defenceless member of the group; these sacrifices being carried out not in anger but in sorrow, acts of supreme love for some authority. Note that it is not a bizarre curiosity, but a widely known ritual.

(2) The symptom of our lack of biological safeguards against the killing of conspecifics, about which Lorenz has taught us so much. Koestler here refers not only to warfare, but more potently because more personally, to those embellishments of torture from the practice of crucifixion to electric shock and the 'chemotherapy' of dissidents.

It is phenomena like these, set within the context of our divide between reason and emotion, and the parallel divide of high achievement in technology and the slow, low development of ethical and moral rules and behaviour, that leads Koestler to present his Janus and his explanation and amelioration of our wretched and unstable condition. And it is here that he takes his fascinating lateral step. He suggests that it is not in fact an excess of aggression or sheer hostility that is at the root of our trouble. On the contrary, it is an excess of selfless devotion. We begin to see the two faces of Janus.

His argument is easy for a psychologist to follow. He starts with the old point that we, as animals, have an extraordinarily long period of helplessness and dependence. This enables us to have that highly sophisticated socialization experience, to learn much new culturally devised information, many skills, and crucially complicated values. All these we learn from a series of less and more formal authorities, without whose ministrations we would not be here at all. Those benign authorities encourage us to continue as willing recipients of ready-made beliefs. We come nearer and nearer the point that our trouble is not our hostility alone, but our loyalty, our adherence to our group. It is indeed our altruism and its service that is at the centre of our problems.

These two themes of aggression and selfless devotion are developed within the ground of another fundamental biological idea - that of hierarchy. The hierarchy which describes life, of a cell and its components down to subatomic particles; and also a cell and its superordinate tissues and organs; as well as a functioning individual person and their superordinate groups.

At all levels we find a holon, which is stable and independent in its own right but which faces, on the one side upwards towards a higher order of which it is a part, but also downwards towards its own parts for which it is a whole. All elements in nature are thus Janus faced. As people we are holons, autonomous, self-governing from some points of view, but also in some sense partial, members of a family, a class, a nation - to whom we stand in a particular relation of allegiance and loyalty, love and obligation.

There are two themes in our lives, our wholeness and our partness; our self-assertion and our self-transcendence; our autonomy and our integration. We maintain both, and jealously. Ideally these themes are finely balanced. Assertion enough practised to keep the individual intact; transcendence enough to maintain group membership. This is the aim that we have as persons, as families, as nations. But that fine balance is hard to maintain. The pathology of self-assertion, aggression, hostility; the pathology of the holon as individual has been salient in our thinking. As we have said, it has been the pre-occupation of many social planners, ethical teachers and moral rule-makers. The pathology of individual and group assertion leads to vivid social sanctions. Its excesses put us beyond the pale. And yet our problems remain.

What of the excesses of self-transcendence? These are the heart of Koestler's contribution. If we are too self-assertive we outlaw ourselves from the hierarchy of society. The true believer, on the other hand, comes more closely knit into it. Socialization is all about the sublimation of self-assertion. Not so for self-transcendence. Its forms of the civilized values of cooperation and altruism, on the contrary, are idealized. Its form of loyalty is the motive power of our social organizations and fundamental groups. It is in our group memberships that its vagaries show themselves most clearly. The group holon is more than a sum of its individual parts. There are new polarities, because the self-assertive behaviour of the group is based on the self-transcending behaviour of its members. The egotism of the group feeds on the altruism of the members.

We come to the paradox that the virtues we value so highly in the individual - loyalty, discipline, self-sacrifice - are the very properties that lead to the engine of war and which tie men to malevolent systems of authority. It is the pathology of self-transcendence that Koestler contributes as his idiosyncratic explanation for our 'evil'.

The pathology of integration. If that theme of our holon, its partness, its selflessness, cannot be fulfilled - we will submit wholly to a father/leader, we will identify with a group unqualifiedly, we will accept an ideology uncritically. A credo then will mediate for us - wars, repression, torture, punitive 'social hygiene', destruction, murder - all engaged in, not in anger but in sorrow. We prepare ourselves for submissive, painful, self-denying, self-transcending suffering altruism. It is a pathology often met in Man - or is it in men?

At last we come to see what the fit of the model is for Man, for men, for women. And surely then it is that dramatic lack of fit for women that is important both in its own right and for the validity of the Koestler position. Women are indeed not to be found within the deeper recesses of hot ideologies. They are to be characterized more often by a piecemeal, pragmatic, empirical position - exemplifying British empiricism at its most spirited. Characteristically, they neither partake of the pathological extreme of self-assertion and aggression, nor of the pathology of uncritical, unqualified identification with flag, dogma, credo. But then the model does not fit in its substance because, perhaps, women are not unsatisfied in their integrative themes. Their integration may be more mature. They do indeed balance their reason and their emotion because they are able to express their taking and giving of dependence, their cooperation, their balance of centrifugal and centripetal tendencies. We see here the positive function - personally, socially and biologically of their affiliation, their social interest, their expressiveness, their much-maligned 'warmth'.

Koestler's pessimism is historically justified. It is rational though only as long as we consider the status quo. We can see new possibilities if we consider Man to be both men and women. Koestler's model is of men. It does not admit the existence of women. Janus loses power from that. (Could there not be the face of a man and the face of a woman?) Here one might profitably enumerate Koestler's own set of polarities which describe the two themes:

integration	self-assertion
partness	wholeness
dependence	autonomy
centripetal	centrifugal
cooperation	competition
altruism	egotism

What does that list remind us of? The feminine versus masculine qualities. Exaggeration of either theme will lead to conflict and disaster. If many societies have found effective curbs, physical and moral for the extremes of self-assertion, we must look for balance of integration. In the pharmacological curbs that he posits? Or in the possibilities for the positive functioning of dependence and integration and altruism that women have traditionally found? And, of course, this is the argument for bisexuality. It is an old argument that has in fact never been taken seriously. This is obviously a point to which we must return in answering those questions we have set ourselves about models.

So do we need a special model of women? Tradition would say yes. Feminists would say no. On reflection we see that we will have to negotiate a delicate argument and counter-argument which centres on potentialities as well as actualities, and situations as well as personalities.

DO WE WANT A SPECIAL MODEL?

I want to posit that this is not simply a trivial form of the previous question. It is not just a personalization of the deeper logical question. And it is no easier to answer by yes or no!

Again there is the platform that says the trouble is that we do not have one - we want it. And there are other people who say our trouble is that we do have one - we despise the fact. But, of course, we have come through the background of that argument by now.

If there has been no specific notice of gender it is likely to be because the woman's position has been entirely ignored. Then we often find that the conclusion is not right, not in some way. However flattering it may seem not to be seen as different - it must be admitted that in our difference there may be a positive contribution. When there has been a model of women it has been given us. And that given model has been patronizing.

Beyond aesthetics, beyond language, the notorious image (some of us might say mug-shot) has been that presented by Freud (1932). Here he shows his own Janus head. Facing on the one side forward with eagle eye, shrewd, unafraid and able to see through mere appearances - but on the other, looking backwards at women through a veil of his own cultural conditioning, seeing their traditional socialization as essential destiny. His specification of femininity, formidable in its list of defects and deficiencies is surely well known enough to require no detailed rehearsal. Women are narcissistic (needing to be loved more than to love), vain, excessively modest, having little sense of justice, a weak social interest, and a staggering psychological rigidity. All these stem, of course, from our inexorable penis envy, our unresolvable Oedipus complex, our lower possibility of sublimation and its following weaker super-ego. Freud admits that it might not be an altogether flattering portrayal; we must logically agree that it may have been a de facto true list for his patients. However that proviso is hardly emphasized, and the final insult surely comes from his plain statement that while women have contributed but little to the technology of civilization, they did invent plaiting and weaving - thus imitating nature's veil for our genitals, and improving on that tangle by fixing the hairs permanently together!

At this point we surely come to a problem that other 'minorities' have experienced - other people stigmatized in the power imbalance - the physically handicapped, Blacks, Jews, Catholics - we join the conceptual group of the White Negro (Mailer, 1957).

First one seems to want assimilation, then defiant separatism, but, in the end, ad hocery might turn out to be most satisfactory and most satisfying. But we have to come too close to the politics of liberation - which I have tried not so much to eschew as to take for granted. I believe that we might best move forward now in the broad conceptual perspective of Tajfellian intergroup theory.

It will be remembered that Tajfel (1974) is making a particularly dynamic contribution to two topics, that of social identity and its relationship to group membership, and to the topic of social change. Let us apply his kind of analysis both for the understanding of the existing adjustments which women are enjoying (sic) and for the solution of our titular question. The theory starts with basic postulates which relate social identity with group membership. Accepting that we all wish to attain the most positive self-image possible, we make a series of social comparisons, judge the satisfactions to be achieved with our group affiliations, and point social comparisons with psychological distinctiveness. When the outcome of such identity work is basically negative, the individual tries to change some term in the nexus in order to improve their lot.

Womanhood forms a fundamental ascribed group status, and stereotypes of traditional femininity are, in a vital way, the rules of group membership. A person who follows those rules is an integral, paid-up member of the group; one who does not is marginal. We begin to see what the power of the analogy to racial groups might become. As White Negroes, models of women might be negotiated as have the models of Blacks.

In the substantive discussion here, we have seen that the status of women has been effectively ignored (Koestler), or their position has been described from a masculine perspective with their definition standing in a reciprocal relationship to men (Berger, Walters, Fransella & Frost provide examples); or their part in the game has been to rules designed for a special creation (Lakoff). Whether we perceive the present position most saliently as a form of power game with a crucial submission/dominance dimension or not, it is clear that some dissatisfaction is likely to be raised with respect to the holding of a strong, secure, highly valued social identity. One might also suggest here that interesting kinds of cognitive dissonances will also arise. It is in the deductions which can be drawn from the basic theory that Tajfel makes his specifically social contribution. Intergroup comparison and its dynamics with respect to social identity can help us to understand several adjustments which women have made, and will help us to answer our questions.

Do we want a special model? Consider the answer – 'No'. The firm answer that women are not a fundamental creation, nor have they a special social contribution to make, is seen in the intergroup context as a form of 'passing'. 'Passing' is, of course, a fine, traditionally hallowed example of bypassing the membership rules for groups, of achieving an illicit kind of upward social mobility. In this case a version of the male identity is assumed and one kind of self-satisfying adjustment is made. It is a process used by members of inferior groups to assert their rights as people, and to partake of the benefits of the superior club - which benefits the individual - but does not change the status quo, of course.

From our point of view, as well as for others, it is an answer that does not answer any problem - it does away with it. It says that whatever the frills (!) attached to womanhood - they are inessential. It asserts that existing differences between men and women are unimportant, psychologically irrelevant, the products of arbitrary social pressures, or all of these. It suggests that if women only choose to do so, they may join the great society. It states that the idiosyncratic adjustment of women does not, cannot and should not contribute anything of value to the community. Passing does have a long history, and one must tell here again the story of its most dramatic, and surely most tragic protagonist. Nearly 50 years before Elizabeth Garrett Anderson, the 'first' woman doctor in Britain, another woman had graduated from my own university's medical school, and served with distinction in the Army Medical Department, rising to the rank of Inspector General - her forced idiosyncracy being, of course, that she lived as Dr James Barry. In an active, not to say hectic life as a highly regarded professional and humanitarian reformer, she had been chosen to change the outward show by a group of liberated, dissident intellectuals under Lord Buchan and General Francisco de Miranda (see June Rose, 1978). (And moreover the fates satisfy our inevitable question. During a tour of duty in the Crimea, Dr Barry did meet Miss Florence Nightingale. They quarrelled. How could they tolerate each other's strategies - when Miss Nightingale saw Barry as 'the most hardened creature I ever met throughout the army', while she herself averred that 'A woman obtains that from military courtesy ... which a man ... partly from temper, partly from policy is effectually banned.')

Less extremely, one cites the role-play of those women who are doing work, being competent and assertive, while taking care not to embody those characteristics of affiliation, tact and expressiveness which might label them as women. The social and intellectual skill that is required for this act is sometimes formidable. One might gauge this from the sometimes rough social performances of our predecessors - the blue-stockings. Gender differences are denied. Their discussion is anathema. No problem.

Do we want a special model? Consider the answer – 'Yes'. Here the dissonance reductions are more subtle and involve sophisticated variation. Social identity adjustments take place within the specification of feminine group membership. Here differences in orientation are given due emphasis, are often seen as fundamental and often therefore they are related by social evolution to the critical biological functions of child bearing and child rearing. In accepting the fundamental difference, at least two translations or interpretations of them are possible, again common processes as seen through intergroup theory.

One such adjustment involves simply the due evaluation of the group's characteristics. We have met it already in the female speech discussion. Here the hallmarks of female speech are not seen as indices of absence from the arena of action, of insecurity, of inferiority. They are accepted and avowed as really meaning that women are indeed morally superior. From outside, it is usually seen by other women as a tactic which makes a virtue of necessity. It is despised by free women as symptoms of a washed brain. It is acceptance of the bribe that men have thrown to women, to maintain their own position intact. It is par excellence an example of false consciousness.

A second re-evaluation involves another kind of appraisal where a difference is translated into a newly positive, important contribution which advances the goals of the whole society. If men have been superior in innovation and material manipulation, women are superior in affiliation, nurturance, and cooperation. Who is to deny that the latter are as important, as functional as the former from either the social or the biological point of view. Indeed in the present era, following either Arthur Koestler or E.C. Schumacher, are they not more valuable? Separate models are then required - separate but equal.

And lastly one might mention the 'naked and unashamed' position. Here members of a 'minority' group define themselves saliently and loudly as different, emphasizing even stereotypically despised characteristics.

It is a stage of transition, which is a kind of falling over backwards. It is a tactic that may shame the dominant group into a better recognition of the minority, and is designed to enhance the social identity of minority members by denying the negative evaluation of their nature through their proud proclamations of it. You will recognize the 'Black is Beautiful' movement. That redefined the self-identity of Negroes without overt reference to the White group - but admitted differences and revalued them positively by own group standards. This works first for 'home', in-group consumption, but then, of course, combines changes in self-esteem with changes in intergroup interactions to produce changes in dominant group estimations. It is another kind of making a virtue of necessity, but reduces dissonance in a non-defensive way, and involves social changes. For American Blacks it has had positive outcomes. For women it is a current stage of transition - witness as Glynis Breakwell (1979) has noted, all those publications on menstruation, on the menopause, on mothers and daughters, which may again be useful, but which are also likely to provide some ammunition for the threatened group of men.

DO WE HAVE A MODEL?

My conclusion has become clear and plain through this discussion. I am suggesting that we will always be involved in a series of negotiations for conceptual descriptions that will sometimes involve a special perspective, adjustment, orientation; sometimes the feminine perspective being salient, sometimes the masculine; sometimes no differences of any kind are important.

There are a variety of arguments against the neat pair of tailor's dummies - one with a bosom and the other with broad shoulders. The demonstrated differences between men and women are hardly deep enough, broad enough, absolute enough to warrant such a neat distinction. Where differences exist we are not in a position now to speak authoritatively about the origin and therefore the meaning of these differences. Further, we have the problem of the best fitting test for fit of the models. Is it to be simply and solely the 'scientific', objective one, or a more humanistic, moral, meaningful one? Consider the vexed question in the following form: are the images we have considered stereotypes, or are they pictures of a well earned reputation?

Let us recapitulate the arguments we have raised. In the history of art, we, as outsiders, might most easily be willing to say that the images are expressions of fantasy, of ideals, and indeed are most importantly expressions of the aesthetic canon. However, I maintain their significant analogy to our psychological inquiry when we consider the works of artists in terms of power relationships in the production and consumption of art. Then the potence of the male image and vanity of the female one are differentiations which match the needs of the male artist producing them, and certainly the demands of the capitalist consumer. They may also be reproductions from a stereotype that happens to be faithful to reality, but one begins to doubt this seriously when we see how vividly and persuasively current women artists have presented the narcissism, the vulnerability, the gentle tenderness of the nude male - see the works of Sylvia Sleigh and Martha Edelheit in particular.

In speech and language, women's talk may be an illustration of that special lack of assertion on which Eysenck has so strongly insisted. However, it might at least as easily be seen as the result and the index of the enforced lower status that women have been assigned and have to a large extent accepted. Here, as we tried to argue, are obvious areas of choice, negotiation, specificity for both men and women. (And, of course, we remember that Lakoff herself avers that not only all academic men, but Englishmen too, do not sink to the lowest depths of her characterization of American non-intellectuals. Men readers have had acknowledged their subtleties of thought and word - even 'mauve'.)

In Koestler's account of all our ills, I tried to show that his argument was indeed powerful, having a power unacknowledged by Koestler himself. The paradox of the evil of our altruism, the pathology of our integration is a problem of men. It is their style of power that contains it. And therein surely lies our hope. If we do not subscribe to the ideology of absolute masculine political and social control, or rather not to the masculine style of power ideology, then we may begin to be free of that evil also. And might we not speculate that other styles of assertion and social exchange may lead to other kinds of interaction?

There can be no argument for a model of woman, nor for a model of man. We will surely end with holograms rather than anything more concrete. We have some material to work with, but have hardly started to consider the possibilities. I am looking for a discussion about conceptions that work. Conceptions that work in biological and intellectual and social modes, that are working hypotheses not only for social scientists, but for people. There are more roles in more scenarios than ever before. But still men and women will have biases in making a hologram that satisfies them - again both in their roles of social scientists and as people. While we talk in terms of some objective, empirical evidences, it is the peculiar nature of psychology to have other tests. A model has to 'fit' as well as to be logically useful and consistent. And as Shotter (chapter 2) has told us, people then become not just the objects of study and evaluation, but are in those very studies also the sources of information and evaluation.

Freud's model of women might indeed have been validated by some sharp psychometrist of a personological turn of mind who lived before his time. It certainly seemed to 'fit' Freud's own ego needs. The critique of the interpretation of those statements about immaturity, childishness, waywardness has come from women. While one cannot deny the possibility of the truth of his statements of individual differences, the speculation of their fundamental quality is certainly open to debate. Here his bias crosses with ours. This is not a reason for dismay or the deploring of a nihilistic end. It is part of the fascination of psychology.

As this discussion I have presented has tried to be logical, it is informed still with a particular evaluation and not divorced from my values. As Marie Jahoda (1977) has written, 'It is doubtful whether any systematic thought is ever produced without the stimulant of such personal involvement' (p. 174). And most importantly, she goes on to say, 'It is the examination of the logic of the argument and counter-argument which in the end decides where a personal bias is constructive and where destructive (p. 174).

Those arguments and counter-arguments have been monopolized by men so far. The values of women and the values of men, and their logical efforts must meet. And, as so often in psychology, that is a postulate that once grasped, is self-evident.

EDITED DISCUSSION

J. A. GRAY: I was not convinced by your survey of art. There are surely a large number of instances where male images are distorted too. I wonder if you have not given us a very selective look at artistry which does not really represent any fundamental differences in the pictorial representation of male and female bodies.

H. BELOFF: The argument about distortion of women's bodies being greater is persuasive to me. If we take artistic representations as our data, indicating differences between men and women, we come to the conclusion that the male is potent and the female is passive. But my argument is that we see this only if we take the stance of a man.

A. STILL: Distortions in sculpture and paintings are something of a projective test. In novels it is more clear cut. The distortions are very interesting psychologically.

H. BELOFF: Certainly the nudes that are now being painted by women have, for example, this very strong difference that figures of men are seen as individuals rather than as representations of ideals, and this is an important development. An actual person can never be as strong as a type.

P. KLINE: I should like to refer back to the question you raise about the quality of the data upon which are based your statements about language. Are they not stereotypic versions of men and women? What is the data base? Are these middle-class women talking between themselves in private, or when they know that they can be overheard; or are they mill women in private, or what?

H. BELOFF: Well, from a social class point of view, the data are of course extremely biased.

H. WEINREICH-HASTE: We have seen through psychological studies the very negative, implicit model of woman which is held in society, and which also has been held by psychologists. How can one change the psychologist's model of woman? Another question has to do with man and woman as scientists. Being a woman scientist brings conflicts of roles very sharply into focus, and this in turn brings into focus problems that men have over their images as scientists. The question of how a woman can become a scientist, given the essentially masculine image of a scientist, is a microcosm of the problem - 'How can a woman become an effective person in our society?' There is of course evidence that the really top scientists acknowledge characteristics which are non-masculine or stereotypically feminine.

H. BELOFF: Taking the last point first, the argument for some version of bisexuality being an ideal is not a very new one. Those working in creativity, for example, would suggest that it is very important. But it is the kind of thing to which lip-service is paid, and then everyone carries on regardless. As far as gender images are concerned, in psychology and elsewhere, ultimately changes will come through women occupying roles and doing things. It is not a question of propaganda: it is going to be a question of fact. Now, young girls may be deterred from becoming scientists because of the masculine image of the scientist, but simply bringing these stereotypes into the open is itself emancipating.

H. WEINREICH-HASTE: But then to what extent do you end up with the 'honorary man' syndrome?

H. BELOFF: Well, I suspect that the early suffragettes were to some extent honorary men. This may well be a necessary state of transition, and the question is whether 'transition' is a valid concept or whether you want to reach your goal straight away.

Chapter 19

One model of man or many?

M. Jahoda

The contemporary scene in psychology clearly reveals the existence of a fairly large variety of models of man; some - though not all of them - are presented as the only appropriate one around which psychology should be unified. The debate about this issue is not only about the current state of the discipline but also about its development in future. From that point of view the desirability, even the possibility, of a unitary model of man is an open question. The gist of what I have to say consists in arguing that a pluralism of approach is not only desirable but inevitable.

The argument proceeds in the following way: I first introduce a terminological clarification and spell out its consequences. This raises the question of how, if at all, it is possible to justify a choice between existing models, a question of importance for the education of psychologists. That a variety of models can be justified does, however, not imply that one has to take them as they stand; they are amenable to improvement. The need for improvement is demonstrated in discussing some models and a suggestion for what is required in this respect for a broadening of models in social psychology is made.

Let me begin, then, with an apparently trivial distinction. Models come in two basic forms: as faithful replications of reality, such as the prototype of an aeroplane, and as conceptual tools for thinking about aspects of reality. Psychology has no need for the former; there are enough exemplars of the real thing about - some think too many; of the latter there are several in psychology - and once again, some think this is too many - even though they are, as a rule, left implicit in the research literature. It seems to me useful to emphasize this rather obvious distinction because in the heat of the theoretical controversy in psychology the conceptual and the ontological are occasionally confused.

Such confusion is all too easy. For, like everyone who reflects on the human condition, psychologists carry in their minds an ontological model about the essence of being human; as scientists they add to this a conceptual model, which incorporates the point of view from which they look at man systematically. The ontological and the conceptual model can influence each other or be miles apart. But whatever the degree of their integration, they are analytically distinct: an ontological model rests on metaphysical assumptions; a conceptual model is a tool for thought.

Conceptual models contain the basic categories of thought applied to the study of man. They are the basic questions one wishes to tackle and therefore broadly prescribe the methods to be used in research as much as the categories of answers which will be found acceptable. If the conceptual model directs curiosity to the relation between behaviour and physiology, an S-R answer will not be forthcoming.

We do not know much about the process by which a psychologist arrives at his conceptual model; it certainly cannot derive from the state of his discipline which is so rich in contrasting conceptual approaches. Basic metaphysical assumptions, personal preferences and conformity pressures in postgraduate education are more likely candidates for explaining individual choices. Whatever the case may be, conceptual models lead to theories which are both more concrete and more precise in as much as they establish testable propositions linking categories in the conceptual model.

As a rule, psychologists remain silent about their ontological and often also about their conceptual models, while being explicit about their theories. It is this conspiracy of silence about the non-scientific reasons that lead to various directions of psychological research that encourages confusion of the two basic forms of model. For one can distinguish good concepts from pure fantasy only by reference to what there is, and once one has some evidence it is only a small step to asserting that what one's concepts lead one to see is all there is to be seen and thus to define what man is; Robert Borger (1970), for example, in his friendly exchange with Charles Taylor confidently asserts: 'I am a mechanism' (p. 80). He and we know better, even though he is fully entitled to think of himself as if he were nothing else. But the very fact of making this ontological statement gives the show away: no mechanism could make it. It takes a mind to do so.

Borger's statement implies, of course, a decided stand on the metaphysical problem par excellence that plagues all discussions about models of man: the body-mind problem. It has been with us as an unsolved problem for a long·time and shows no signs of disappearing. Nothing that I can say will help its demise. But it is surely not too much to ask that it be recognized for what it is: a metaphysical issue. And it is a metaphysical decision, an act of faith in monism or dualism or any other philosophical approach to the problem that has ever been suggested, that forms the rock bottom of every model of man.

Sutherland (1970) recognizes this explicitly when he says 'Just as there is no proof that behaviour cannot be explained in terms of physical events, there is equally no proof that it can be so explained' (p. 137). This leaves the ontological question open, even though conceptually he has, I believe, taken a stand similar to Borger's. There is a parallel here to Gödel's theorem: the ultimate assumption remains unprovable.

My own metaphysical commitment on the ontological issue consists of a belief in the essential indivisibility of body and mind. I cannot conceive of psychological phenomena independent from or outside an organism, even though I realize - sometimes uneasily - that in their religious beliefs probably nine-tenths of mankind can, including some scientists. Uneasily, because I know, we all know 'with Cartesian certainty' (Warren, 1978, p. 56), that to conceive at all of body and mind, divisible or indivisible, requires above all a mind. There is here a first indication that in psychology the relation between the ontological and the conceptual is not as simple as it looked at first glance.

The body-mind problem is not the only occasion in psychology that tempts one to confuse what there is with how to think about it, as I try to show below, but it presents the most often recognized split in basic assumptions. This is the reason why the suggestion is frequently made that all we need is two models, one committed to the language of the natural sciences and one speaking the language of 'mental life', to use George Miller's phrase. Even forgetting the gratuitous slur that some advocates of the natural science model bestow on everybody else, the situation is more complex. To the extent that psychologists deal with man - and not all of them do - the languages, as much as the procedures implied by these languages, tend to get confused. Little Albert showed 'fear' of furry objects, 'extraversion' and 'introversion' are basic personality concepts; none of these terms fit the language of the natural sciences. I do not regard such mixture of languages as high treason against a principled stand; it is the only reasonable stance when faced with an unsolved, perhaps insoluble, problem: we do what we can rather than yearn after the impossible. As Medawar (1966) said, science is the art of the soluble. A more important argument than the inevitable confusion of languages against adopting two dichotomized models stems from the fact that a multiplicity of models has de facto been produced on either side of the great divide presenting as many differences in basic assumptions within each camp as between them. They have not disappeared because the positivists in the past called for a unification of all sciences; they will not go away now, though the call has been repeated; they cannot go away because all science is inevitably a simplification of the phenomena in the real world.

Conceptual models are indeed limited points of view applied to the complexity of what there is, tools for the purpose of increasing knowledge. This implies that they must be shown - sooner or later and not necessarily by the originator of a model - to match with some aspect of the real world. At first glance this requirement appears to have the aspects of saving grace and the promise of reducing the multiplicity of possible conceptual models to the one with the best fit to reality. But only at first glance. For here we are faced with a difficulty peculiar to the study of man. While even in the natural sciences, as also in psychology, one sees only what one looks for - in other words, one is guided by conceptual models - in psychology alone there is the possibility that the model influences not only what one sees but also what there actually is to be seen. I well remember a woman factory worker who once told me that she had been interviewed by an industrial researcher who had asked her what she thought about while working. She found it difficult to answer him, and so he probed: 'Do you ever think of how nice it would be to travel all over the world?' To me she said: 'I had never thought of this before; but ever since he asked me I do'.

What the anecdote illustrates is that ideas, including conceptual models of man, have consequences in the real world just as what there is influences our concepts. By looking at the world in a certain way we change the phenomena themselves, which in turn influence our concepts. What we think and what there is therefore cannot be kept fully apart, though we should not take one for the other. This is in sharp contrast to the natural sciences. While we must assume that the behaviour of matter and particles did not alter because Einstein thought of curved space and of time as a fourth dimension, the parallel assumption for psychology simply cannot stand. Nonetheless on this issue opinions are sharply divided. Toward the end of 'Beyond Freedom and Dignity' (1971) Skinner emphatically asserts that 'no theory changes what it is a theory about' (p. 213). The opposite point of view I once heard Hannah Arendt formulate epigrammatically when she said: 'The trouble with behaviourism is not that it is wrong, but that it could become true.' If psychology could exist as a secret science, the odds might perhaps be with Skinner, but no psychologist in his senses, certainly not Skinner himself, entertains this as a possibility.

Indeed there is ample evidence that conceptual models of man have influenced the way people, not just psychologists, think and act. The changing fashions in bringing up children whether by those who believe that Watson or Freud had the last word or by those who took the early or the revised Dr Spock as the bible, must surely have had some impact, as has the unquestionably successful application of Skinner's conceptual model on making the management of some mental patients easier or helping some schoolchildren with learning, notwithstanding his claim that theories have no consequences on what they are a theory about.

This does not dispose of Skinner's model as a conceptual tool, one among others. Since we have to abstract and simplify whatever the object of study, it is perfectly legitimate to look at man as if he were a reinforced mechanism only. The trouble begins when it is claimed that this conceptual model has universal ontological validity, that man is nothing but what a particular conceptual model presents. This leads to statements which are flagrantly wrong, as when Skinner says 'a person does not act upon the world, the world acts upon him' (1971, p. 211). Even Churchill, no great psychological authority, knew better: 'First we shape our buildings, then our buildings shape us', he said in a speech after the bombing of the House of Commons. The point of quoting a layman in psychology is to emphasize that there exists an enormous amount of psychological knowledge in the collective experience of mankind about what it means to be human. This is no substitute for systematic psychology, of course, but in statements about what man is, common sense is less confused than some models tend to be; we ignore it at our peril.

The argument against Skinner's ontological statement has, however, also been made on the professional level, best known perhaps from the Skinner-Chomsky controversy about the acquisition of language. Other models of man have abandoned the idea of an empty and passive organism, shaped from the outside-in. Piaget's assimilation and accommodation are conceptual formulations paralleling Churchill's phrase; the systematic study of the behaviour repertoire of newborn infants reveals attributes of the organism which Skinner's conceptual scheme cannot handle and which contradict his slip into ontological assertion.

The relation between what there is and how we think about it is subtle and complex; to assume that the conceptual is identical with the ontological amounts to denying the major problem in theoretical psychology.

Three things follow from this effort at terminological clarification: first, metaphysical assumptions and personal preferences are not very far removed from psychological research. Second, conceptual models - I take them to be the subject matter of this volume - cannot be verified or falsified; only the theories stemming from them can be so tested; and third, because the conduct of research stemming from a conceptual model has the power to alter people's ontological models of themselves - even their very way of being - a unitary model cannot last; the object of study changes, and not only because of the activities of psychologists.

The untestability of the basic point of view from which a psychologist looks at man raises the question of whether one therefore has to accept every conceptual model on equal terms, whether one is as good as the other. To answer this question affirmatively would lead to an extreme relativism, which would invite chaos; to qualify the answer is, however, not easy. At this point one is tempted to envy the large army of researchers who manage to proceed without bothering about their model of man, who have apparently learned their lesson from the fatal consequences which ensue if you ask the centipede how it moves - until one realizes how inconclusive, fragmented and often trivial such studies can be, based either on blind empiricism or on mini-theories unrelated to the broader issues in psychology. Though not suggested by proverbial wisdom, the possibility remains that if the centipede did investigate its own behaviour he might double his speed. So the question must be faced: what is a good model?

Criteria for evaluating conceptual models or, at least, for comparing them are inevitably judgemental. The criteria suggested here furthermore overlap to some extent; they are nothing but a first guide for comparative purposes.

A first criterion is whether research based on a model remains true to that model. This is an internal criterion, as it were.

A second criterion is external and concerns the degree of inclusiveness of a model: are there psychological phenomena which a model cannot handle? If the answer is 'yes' such a model is not invalidated in itself, but additional models are clearly called for. I shall apply these criteria first to a broad category of models which come in many variations: the natural science model. One version of it is strongly recommended by Eysenck (chapter 4) as a unitary model for psychology. It is indeed an impressive one, grounded in biology and extending via personality differences to social issues. But its characteristic feature - looking at man as an object - is shared by many mainstream psychologists, and it is the general, not the specific model, which will be briefly examined.

Taking the natural sciences' approach to be emulated by psychology invites comparison with that approach. Not with their achievements, of course. For though it has become unfashionable to claim that psychology's lesser achievements are the result of its relative youth, the fact remains that our achievements are to date simply of a lower order of magnitude. Whatever the reasons - youth, greater complexity of subject matter or the power of psychological concepts to change human experience and behaviour - a comparison of the approaches of natural science type psychology and the natural sciences shows some significant differences. In the natural sciences research appears to be much more a search process than is the case in much natural science oriented psychology. Medawar in 'The Art of the Soluble' (1966) illustrates this search process by describing the shop-talk that occurs in his biological laboratory. Of course everybody has to begin with a hunch or hypothesis and choose methods to tease out its correspondence with reality. But if the methods do not work, others are tried; if the idea begins to look dubious, it is reformulated. Because natural scientists are more problem-centred, they seem to change and develop their methods continuously to adapt them to the problem in hand. Of course, there must be much mechanical application of well-established methods in the natural sciences too; but their achievements seem to come about because a reformulation of a problem has led to redesigning methods or inventing new ones. Research based on the natural science model in psychology, notwithstanding its power and clarity, does in that respect not emulate the natural sciences. With firmly established and useful techniques the most diverse problems are tackled resulting as a rule in the confirmation of the theory which originally gave rise to the technique. This is why the empirical data, essential in any type of psychology, so often produce a déjà-vu experience in the reader rather than providing a new illumination of the complexities with which we deal.

The method-centredness of the natural science model in psychology results in blind faith in the virtues of experiments and statistical manipulation of data obtained by standard techniques, in contrast to the procedures of the natural sciences proper. The virtue of experiments as a logical control of thought and discovery is, of course, unquestioned. But experiments are just that: a logical control, nothing more, nothing less. If there is no thought or discovery, the logical control becomes an empty shell. Much the same goes for statistical manipulation of data. More often than not they are cook-book fashion mechanically applied, every step being rigidly determined from the outset without considering the possibility that what becomes visible during the research process may be better captured by other techniques. That this need not be the case, that statistical manipulation can be conducted as a cognitive search process where data manipulation can lead to new ideas which, in turn, lead to new analysis, has been demonstrated by Bailyn (1977) in her paper entitled 'Research as a Cognitive Process: Implications for Data Analysis.' But this is an exception rather than the rule. More frequently research based on the natural science model of man has not - at least not yet - learned to emulate the natural sciences in this respect.

This in itself does not yet amount to an argument against this model as the one and only in psychology, only to an argument for its improvement and development. The case for more than one model is further strengthened by the application of the second criterion for the evaluation of the appropriateness of a model, its degree of inclusiveness.

The natural science model is, as a rule, a reductionist model; that is, it often assumes that the best and most complete explanation of human behaviour, actions and experiences lies in the discovery of their biological coordinates. While I do not believe that reductionism is a sin against the Holy Ghost, while on the contrary I believe that Penfield or Sperry, for example, have made significant and dramatic psychological discoveries - it all depends on what you want to know - there is a price to be paid for reductionism in psychology. On the practical level psychologists who put their ultimate faith in biological explanations are arguably working in the wrong field, creating their own frustrations unless they manage to switch the basis of their expertise. But this is secondary to the other price they have to pay. This model imposes severe limitations on the subject matter of psychology: it seems to compel its advocates to think of man as fundamentally passive, being pushed by a variety of drives into behaviour, never acting or engaging in choice and thereby eliminating the question of the role of consciousness; it has difficulties in dealing with concepts such as purpose, intention or expectation - Skinner apologizes for his mentalistic language while realizing that he cannot get his point across without it; it assumes linear causality; and it regards the interpretation of meaning, once mechanisms have been established, as 'mere' understanding and thus relegated to be outside the province of science.

In its reductionist version the natural science model is also compelled by its own assumptions to ignore the phenomena of psychological change and ontogenetic development. One reason for this, it seems to me, lies in the different time perspectives appropriate for the study of differing phenomena. The laws of nature have validity for astronomical time spans, though even the universe has a history (Toulmin, 1965) and will in the very end disappear in a black hole, or so we are told. Within millions of years, this change can be ignored. Biologists use evolutionary time spans; what they discover can be assumed to be valid for thousands of years, if not millions. Psychological phenomena occur within the lifespan of an individual. The phenomena of the social world within which the individual lives occur within historical time, the most erratic of all - now rushing ahead at incredible speed, now appearing to stand still. I have more to say later about the trouble historical changes create, particularly for social psychology, but in connection with the reductionist model the thing to note is that it is unable to accommodate the shorter time spans of individual lives or of history. As a result, once a high IQ, always a high IQ; once an extravert always an extravert.

In summary, then, the natural science model does not quite implement the first criterion, remaining true to itself; and, as a unitary model, it fails on the second criterion by its severely limited inclusiveness. Those of us who therefore reject it as a unitary model for psychology, as I do, would, however, be foolish indeed not to recognize it as one major and powerful approach which has probably led to more knowledge than research based on other models has so far produced. What is wrong with it is above all its claim to be 'the' way of thinking in psychology.

What about other models? There is a large variety to choose from. For example, Kelly's model of man as a scientist continuously engaged in confirming or refuting his own constructs about how the world works (see chapter 17); there is Piaget's cognitive developmental model assuming a continuous interaction between development from within and influence from without (see paper 1); there is Heider's common-sense model (see chapter 15) from which stem, directly or indirectly, several theoretical developments - balance theory, cognitive dissonance theory, attribution theory; in its original form it dealt with mental life only. And then there is, of course, a whole host of psychodynamic models, all going back to Freud, but so diversified at present that their common origin is easier historically than conceptually traced. In addition, other human sciences have introduced their own models of man assuming, as some economists do, a perfectly rational man maximizing his utilities (Note 2) or, as some sociologists do, inevitably driven by historical forces and external circumstances.

Some, though not all of these models, also claim to be the best way of thinking about man. Each of them can be critically examined in the light of the two criteria, but it would be tedious to do this here. The very existence of models which do not necessarily claim exclusive status gives one last chance to the notion of a unitary model for psychology: why not take the essential features of all compatible models and construct an umbrella model within which psychologists could place their own constructions, explicitly recognizing that for their own research purposes they are guided only by parts of the comprehensive model?

It sounds an attractive idea, but I know of only one effort in the history of psychology that aimed for unification on such a grand scale, including both sides of the body-mind problem: that effort - Freud's - failed. I have suggested elsewhere (Jahoda, 1977) that the examination of this failure offers crucial lessons for psychology that need to be learned and could be acquired at less costs than are incurred by ignoring Freud or repeating his inconsistencies or belittling his several powerful contributions to psychology as a science. Notwithstanding these contributions, his effort to construct an all-embracing conceptual model of man does not come off.

Freud called the elements of his model metapsychological points of view. He insisted that a full explanation of man required that all six inherent in his work be used. They are: the dynamic; the economic (dealing with the distribution of energy); the topographical; the genetic; the structural and the adaptive point of view. In terms more familiar in academic psychology: motivational conflicts, instinctual drives and their strengths, degrees of consciousness, development, personality, and interaction with the environ ment. The energy point of view regards man as a passive tension-reducing organism; in contrast the topographical view - the continuum from unconscious to conscious - and the structural view - personality conceptualized as id, super-ego and ego - combines active and passive aspects of man. There are other inconsistent assumptions if one compares these stances in more detail, but these will do to demonstrate the difficulty: the energy point of view requires that we conceive of man as passive and mechanically determined; it is a natural science model. The concept of the ego leaves room for reality testing in interaction with the environment and hence for choice, that is, for deliberate and rational direction of actions. Freud repeatedly declared himself to be an arch-determinist. But he also said that the aim of his treatment method was to break the determination by the past and replace it by rational choice: 'Where Id was, there Ego shall be.' Like Skinner, he used two languages: that of the natural sciences and that dealing with concepts for which the natural sciences have no need. But in contrast to Skinner he did not apologize for that second language, but tried to combine it with the first. When one reads his case studies, however, where he is predominantly concerned with the elucidation of meaning but also introduces his mechanistic concepts, it emerges that the two remain side by side without integration. The great riddle of how mechanisms translate into specific meanings and meanings into mechanisms is highlighted rather than resolved by the juxtaposition of two incompatible languages.

As indicated before, the natural science model resolves this puzzle by the arbiter dictum that biological explanations are better, more profound, more 'scientific' than others. Freud, on the contrary, insisted on the equivalence and combination of his various explanatory principles. From that point of view his model does not meet the first criterion I have suggested for evaluation: it does not live up to its own stipulation, the combination of a natural science language with a language of psychological meaning, even though his ceaseless search for this combination led him to design a language in which there was room for understanding the body as a psychological experience.

Freud's model fares better on the second criterion: I cannot think of any psychological phenomena that could not find room in one or the other of Freud's various points of view. Are we then back at the idea of two models only? Admitted that Freud did not succeed in combining a natural science model with psychological explanations of meanings, do his remaining elements of a model form an appropriate umbrella for psychology? Perhaps in a very formalistic fashion this could be said to be the case for there is room in it for asking questions about learning, thinking, perception, memory, motivation, emotion, development, degrees of consciousness, personality, social psychology, etc. But it would amount to underselling both Freud and other models to leave it at that. For there is more to the Freudian points of view than a mere collection of topics, as there is to most explicit models. These pre-theoretical conceptions prescribe the broad categories of possible answers to basic questions. If one seeks for environmental or for biological determination alone, for behaviour rather than action and choice, answers will come - if they come - in these categories. Now it is characteristic of each Freudian point-of-view (excepting the energy concept) that it excludes such over-simplifications. This makes research more difficult, but where it succeeds it says something about human beings; simpler models make research easier but often result only in statements about variables; they are based on a model about behaviour, not of man; or in statements about supermen, when based on a model about action and conscious choice alone.

What I have learned from Freud in this context consists largely of two points: his metapsychology, taken altogether, aimed at a universal conceptual model of the mind; it failed as such because it did not achieve internal consistency; it is nearer to a metaphysical view of man, accepting inconsistency as inherent in our existence.   Secondly, it leads me to considering a third criterion for the evaluation of models.   Taking each of his points of view as an independent conceptual tool and comparing it with other available models, I find them to differ in degree of simplicity.   Freud's various points-of-view appear to me nearer to an optimal complexity than competing models, particularly in their efforts to combine mechanism and meaning, multiple causes and reasons, passivity and active choice, cognition and emotion.

As I now turn to social psychology I sense a tendency to prefer over-simplified and static models.   Cognitive dissonance theory is a case in point, even though the underlying models are, as a rule, not made explicit but must be teased out. Festinger's (1957) original formulation was clearly based on a model of tension-reduction; he did leave room for more complexity, in stating that dissonance resolution was not all that motivated man but could be counteracted by other powerful drives.   This has occasionally been overlooked in the subsequent debate about the theory, but in any case it does not change the tension-reduction nature of the underlying model.   Virtually innumerable experiments have followed the original publication, many of them obviously only yielding to the seductively ingenious experimental set up - the method once again having precedence over the problem - and have often confirmed the original evidence.   As always with postulated drives no one has yet been able to identify it or measure its strength. It remains an assumption in the model.   Some, however, have gone beyond replication and modified the theory in line with their own more or less explicit, more or less complex, models of man.   One outstanding contribution to the development of the theory is Bem's radical behaviourism (1967), that eliminates the drive concept and proceeds explicitly on the basis of a Skinnerian model, excluding the organism and relying alone on the concept of reinforcement.   This amounts to substituting a simpler model.   There is a nice give-away of the over-simplification of this model in a casual remark in his interesting discussion: 'When the answer to the question "Do you like brown bread" is "I guess I do, I am always eating it" it seems unnecessary to invoke a fount of privileged self-knowledge to account for the reply' (p. 190).   Agreed.   But what about my answer which is 'I love it but I hardly eat it since it is here not as good as it was in my youth in Vienna'?   One way of distinguishing a model from a theory built on it is that the former should have room for the non-hypothesis-confirming recalcitrants.   They exist, of course, in every experiment, but the habit of discussing mean differences between experimental and control group only relegates them to the inexplicable.

Bem, who has since then changed his position, introduced a simplified model. Sometimes subsequent researchers have proceeded on the assumptions of more complex models of man.   The conceptual vocabulary of dissonance theory has been enlarged to encompass notions outside the vocabulary of tension reduction: expectancies, incentive and attribution theory concepts stem from a cognitive model of rational man; commitment, defensive projection, self-confidence and moral values seem to be based on models including rational and irrational components as well as introducing aspects of personality (conceived of as a result of an individual's past history), and contemporary factors which transcend the 'here-and-now' feature of the experimental situation.   As far as I can see there is at present available a large number of empirical studies but no comprehensive dissonance theory, because the basic assumptions which produced this rich yield are left in their incompatibility implicit; the attempts to increase the complexity of the model resulted only in a switch of models.   The various elaborated theories of cognitive dissonance, taken singly with their corresponding models of man, have an additional price to pay for their increased sophistication in theory and experimental manipulation: perhaps inevitably they have more and more neglected concern with external validity.   But in the long run the ultimate justification for what we do in a laboratory is, after all, to regard it as a means to the end of explaining what happens outside it. Psychology must aim at more than the establishment of sophisticated rules for a game that professionals play with each other in the laboratory. I think the newer versions of cognitive dissonance theory have moved further away from this goal.

There is no reason, however, to be pessimistic about the state of experimental social psychology. The very vigour of the controversies it produces periodically over various theoretical or experimental innovations promises to counteract any tendency to an ossification of models. But this should not lead to underestimating what seems to me a major intellectual problem in social psychology with regard to external validity. Granted that the bare bones of a social psychological model are inevitably more complex than, say, physiological or purely cognitive models, because they regard the human organism as inseparable from its physical and social environment, the necessary fleshing out of the bare bones requires conceptual tools both for people and for this environment. But we are not very good at doing both; it is either one or the other that is assumed as given without further conceptualization. As a result, soon after social psychology became of age it appeared reasonable to split the subject in two: a psychological social psychology and a sociological one, each producing interesting research but neither being true to the basic stipulation of the model.

One major reason for the difficulty of using a more appropriate model lies in the fact that individuals and social factors operate with differing time perspectives. There exist, for example, many studies on differences between social classes in attitudes or socialization procedures. For what historical time period can we assume the results to be valid? One way to answer this question is to say for a limited period only; that amounts to making social psychology a historical descriptive discipline, as Gergen (1973) has suggested when he raised doubts about the transhistorical validity of social psychological results. Another way is to reduce environmental concepts to purely formal notions such as social influence, cross-pressure or opinion leaders, and claiming longer-lasting construct validity at the expense of losing external validity and meaningful content in the here-and-now real world. Perhaps we cannot do better at the moment than opt on hunch for one or the other of these positions, though neither one is wholly satisfactory.

It seems to me that we should be able to do better if in our social models of man we were more concerned with asking questions about what we assume to change very slowly and what relatively quickly. It is not only a question of recognizing that attitudes are more easily changed in the laboratory than outside and that no available attitude change theory can claim external validity, let alone help those who continuously assert that attitude changes are required in the population by telling them how this can be achieved. There is some evidence for showing that even underlying processes, generally assumed to be longer lasting than the direction of an attitude are not stable over time. This, at least, I infer from both, success and failures to replicate experimental findings after a period of years. Waly & Cook (1966) replicated a study of the impact of attitudes on learning and forgetting; since Levine & Murphy had demonstrated in 1943 that people recall best matters congruent with their own attitudes this had been accepted as a relatively stable process and was confirmed by Jones & Kohler in 1958. The replication conducted 5 years later, however, failed to confirm the result. The subject matter was racial attitudes. The intervening 5 years saw dramatic developments in awareness of racial issues in the U.S.A. Were they responsible for the change in the underlying process? The authors rightly point out that the original results were in line with the assumption that there are unconscious elements in attitudes. Do the current results mean that dramatic events can make unconscious elements subject to conscious control or do they eliminate the notion of unconscious elements?

I have no answer to these questions; but they appear to me to be legitimate questions which require greater concern in our conceptual tools with the different clocks that regulate time in psychological and social matters. In a recent review of what we know about the psychological impact of unemployment in the 1930s and the

1970s (Jahoda, 1979) I was struck by the implicit assumption in some contemporary statements that there is no difference and I tried to show that some elements in the situation must be assumed to have changed while others persist - I do not know for how long.   All I can say is that in a social psychological model whose main component is the interaction between people and their environment the possibility of change in either component should be more systematically included than is now often the case.   Whether social psychology is a historical discipline cannot be answered with a simple 'yes' or 'no'; rather we shall have to ask ourselves what remains relatively constant and what changes.

This brings me to the last point I wish to make. I have come to only one firm conclusion: a rejection of the idea of one unitary model of man for psychology. I do not believe that we should or even could strive for it.   We should not for moral reasons: potentially the power of psychological thought to influence psychological reality, for the conceptual to have consequences for the ontological, is enormous and dangerous; there is some safety in pluralism.   We could not - and this is the better safeguard - because the ultimate questions about human existence cannot be decided by science.   New interpretations of the old riddles will give rise to new questions demanding modified conceptual tools.   This does not, however, amount to advocating that psychology be split into a variety of disciplines as several writers have suggested.   I believe that the recognition of the possibility of a variety of models within psychology is more fruitful in the long run, never mind if it gives rise to continuous controversy.   Rubbing shoulders with other models, and being confronted with what they can and cannot achieve, serves as an invaluable reminder that there are no final answers, that the ultimate questions require a metaphysical commitment and that what our concepts have led us to observe is inevitably the result of our tacit or explicit models.   The observable itself is infinitely changing.

NOTES

1. I want to thank Neil Warren who read an earlier draft of this chapter; I have profited much from his criticisms.

2. The concept 'utility' in economics resembles 'reinforcement' in psychology; both are hard to define in a non-circular fashion.

EDITED DISCUSSION

N. E. WETHERICK: I am worried that you display a poor opinion of humanity when you say another human being might accept my 'expert opinion' that he was wrong in believing that he was responsible for his own behaviour. I cannot concede that man is the creature of his environment to that extent.

M. JAHODA: Are you not overlooking the power relations in humanity? Let us not forget 'Walden Two' and '1984': 1984 is very close!

N. E. WETHERICK: Well, I still find it impossible to believe that you could bring about a genuine change such that people who once believed that they were responsible for their own behaviour no longer held that belief. They may be prepared to pretend for various purposes.

R. L. REID: I agree with almost everything you have said, Professor Jahoda, but the attitude expressed about behaviourism so many times at this Conference is reminiscent of the resistance towards Darwinian ideas: to believe in Darwin was somehow considered to make man out to be some kind of monkey. In fact to believe in behaviourism is in no way to dehumanize man or to reduce his status (see pp. 354-355).

R. HARRE: I should like to take up the question of historical change and psychological functioning.   This is an area which is ripe for empirical investigation.   There is already good evidence that social practices affect mental capacities in the late renaissance work on memory methods.

M. JAHODA: Yes. I quite agree.   I have recently had occasion to compare what is known from the literature about the impact of unemployment in the 1930s and 1970s (Jahoda, 1979).   People in the 1970s write about the psychological consequences as if the world had stood still.   So much is this so that they quote a contemporary study and then, to make the point more explicit, they quote from a study conducted 40 years ago.   That is extraordinary!   There is, in this respect such a blindness in social psychology; and I believe that is, to some extent, because most social psychologists have sold their souls to experiment and, therefore, to the here and now. We are ignorant about the time dimension in social life.

H. WEINREICH-HASTE: A question that has occured to me during this Conference is, if as psychologists we can bring about change, do our various models of man predetermine the types of social change that are possible?

M. JAHODA.   Well, first of all, we certainly can bring about social change. Take Freud, for example.   Whether you think for better or worse, he has made a profound difference to the way man experiences himself.   So too Watson and behaviourism have had an enormous influence ...

H. WEINREICH-HASTE: But some models are more worrying than others - socially and politically.

M. JAHODA: That is the social reason for the undesirability of a unitary model. From all sides, you need opportunities for everyone (not just psychologists) to be reflexive about themselves, and to change, and to use whatever little help science can give them in that process of change.

D. E. BROADBENT: It does seem to me important to air a contrary point of view. It is one that has not been mentioned much at this Conference, and it is that the psychological model may be the ideology which justifies the existing economic system.   I am afraid that some people do think that the doctrine of unrestricted autonomy is the official rationalization of the capitalist system. It is the justification that is put forward by British companies for paying very low wages to Black workers in South Africa.   There are obvious intellectual connections between certain political thinkers and academic researchers, in terms of their believing that you should leave everyone totally uncontrolled.   Maybe this sort of view really does represent the final kicks of a dying culture.   It gives rise to the idea that we should not intervene and discover the pre-existing causes, say for crime or mental illness, but should instead leave people to sort things out for themselves.   It is too simple to suggest that if you want to investigate causes as well as intentional relations that you are necessarily in favour of a reactionary and regimented society.

J. SHOTTER: I would like to offer an integrative note, because I think we have heard far too much 'either/or' discussion and I am sure that most of us can coexist.   Rom Harré has told us that, in order conceptually to grasp anything at all, we have to freeze it.   The freezing process can be illustrated in ambiguous figures where you switch between figure and ground.   We must freeze our entities, for thinking about them, but at the same time we must realize that they are in a context.   The type of causal approach just advocated is then perfectly acceptable.

M. JAHODA: I am all in favour of peaceful coexistence as long as it includes as much controversy as is conceivable.   There are so many models in psychology that some people have gone so far as to suggest that the discipline should split into several parts.   Now, as psychologists, it is essential that we examine our metaphysical assumptions and their relation to what we actually do; and we will never do that unless we are confronted, in peaceful coexistence, by somebody who can argue as sharply against us as possible.

Chapter 20

An introduction to models in psychological research

P. B. Warr

The term 'model' has many meanings and generates much confusion. In its most general sense the word refers to a representative device through which some features of an object, person, process or structure can be characterized. In this general sense 'models of man' may be of many different kinds, having in common the fact that they all contain some assertions about what people are like. The title of this book is thus equivalent in generality and alliteration to 'perspectives on people'.

Such a broad use of the term 'model' is quite proper. However, the word is also employed to refer to specific types of perspective, and it is important to examine the principal features of these more limited models. This is the aim of the present chapter. I introduce some central characteristics of scientists' models and I attempt to relate the concept to others such as theory, conceptual framework and paradigm. In doing this I draw in part from the philosophy of science literature, exploring some potential applications for psychology. The views of philosophers are of course often conflicting, and my intention is to find broad areas of agreement rather than to examine detailed issues of dispute. I do not wish to prescribe how terms should be used, but hope to summarize and clarify the ways in which they frequently are used.

The principal section of the chapter examines two major meanings of the word 'model'. This requires a previous examination of theory, and introductions to conceptual frameworks and paradigms. These four are collectively referred to as 'perspectives'. Finally, 13 differentiating characteristics are identified as a basis for possible comparisons within and between the perspectives, and the problems of jointly constructing broad conceptual frameworks and miniature theories are explored.

HISTORICAL BACKGROUND

It is helpful to be aware that we are in a period of transition. Much discussion of theories and models in recent decades has been from the powerful and well-developed perspective of logical positivism. This needed to find a special status for theoretical statements since they contained terms whose referents could not be directly observed; the statements were thus deemed metaphysical and of uncertain meaning. This special status was achieved in philosophical discussion by construing scientific theories as self-contained axiomatic calculi with no direct reference to the world of observation. Theoretical calculi were to be mapped on to observational statements through 'correspondence rules' which aimed to provide explicit definitions of theoretical terms and specifications of admissible empirical procedures. The calculus was otherwise viewed as independent, cohering through its own internal logic, and having no direct reference to reality. Explanation of a series of facts in terms of a scientific theory was thus thought to be a matter of linking (empirical) observation statements into the (non-empirical) deductive calculus through application of the separate correspondence rules. This was usually discussed in terms of the subsumption of events under increasingly general statements, sometimes referred to as 'covering laws'.

The doctrine that scientific theories must have a deductive structure was linked with the recommendation that the method of science should be a hypothetico-deductive one, in that investigators should establish hypotheses which were deductively interrelated. More limited hypotheses were to be logically derivable from more general ones, and the overall calculus should yield (through the correspondence rules) specific predictions which were open to empirical test.

Suppe is one writer who has examined the history of this 'received view' of the logical positivists, that scientific theories are no more than axiomatic calculi which are given a partial observational interpretation by means of correspondence rules. He points out that almost every major development in the philosophy of science between the 1920s and 1950 was in some way based upon the received view.

> In the 1950s, however, this analysis began to be the subject of critical attacks ... By the late 1960s a general consensus had been reached among philosophers of science that the Received View was inadequate as an analysis of scientific theories; derivatively, the analysis of other aspects of the scientific enterprise (for example, explanation) erected upon the Received View became suspect and today virtually have succumbed to skeptical criticism. (Suppe, 1977, p. 4)

Awareness of these developments is important in an examination of models, since so much analysis in the area has inevitably been within the perspective offered by the received view (Note 1*). More recent approaches have paid greater attention to the processes of model-making and theory-building and given less emphasis to a single formalized conception of science and scientific method. Note however that the features and processes described and analysed by the proponents of the received view are not wholly discredited by later thinking. Some models may take the form of axiomatic calculi, some scientists may proceed by a hypothetico-deductive route, and some theories may make no direct reference to the world of observation. Abandonment of the received view as a comprehensive doctrine is significant in that the class of scientific theories is no longer formally defined in an exclusive manner; other types of scientific reasoning and theoretical structure in addition to those of the received view are now generally also accepted as appropriate.

A related issue which has had a substantial impact upon psychology concerns the function of empirical evidence in tests of a theory. Despite the long recognized problem of justifying inductive inference, the traditional view (retained in the positivist doctrine summarized above) has been that science advances by confirming generalizations through the observation of supporting instances. An alternative position has been influentially argued by Popper (e.g. 1959, 1963): that evidence is valuable in science only if it has the potential to falsify general statements. The latter are not verifiable (capable of being shown true) by any accumulation of observational evidence, but are informative to the extent that they are falsifiable.

*Notes are identified by numbers in the text and brought together at the end of the chapter.

Since theories can only be falsified and not confirmed, scientific method is said to be pre-eminently a matter of developing theories and methods which can be placed together in attempts to eliminate some theories through empirical refutation.

There has sometimes been a tendency in psychology and elsewhere to infer from Popper's argument that theories which are not immediately open to refutation are somehow non-empirical, non-scientific or metaphysical, although such an exclusive approach to what is a theory is now less common than previously. This point is taken up again later; it is made here to introduce the central importance of confirmation and refutation, and to illustrate a historical trend away from tight definitions and prescriptions towards a more flexible approach to the nature of theory and scientific method.

CONCEPTUAL SIEVES AND MOULDS

In general terms we can see that models, theories, conceptual frameworks and paradigms all serve to organize thinking and action: they give differential priority as well as structure to ideas and practices. This point can be illustrated in terms of conceptual sieves and moulds.

Scientific models and the other perspectives act as sieves in the processes of thought in the sense that they allow some items to pass but disallow others; a sieve selects some things over others, rearranges things (e.g. Swanson, 1966) (Note 2). This is partly a question of models suggesting potentially valuable ways of thinking and acting in the domain in question, but an equally important feature is the way in which the perspectives close off certain areas of inquiry and exclude alternative styles and content of thinking. In a sense, then, a model or one of the other perspectives begs the question of what should be considered, what is to count as a fact and how facts are to be distinguished from one another. In doing this it has the converse benefit of advancing thought about the questions which may be accommodated within the perspective.

This is partly achieved by allowing the sieved material to settle and become firm within moulds, as in the preparation of custard or jelly. Our conceptual moulds give shape to our thinking, establish systems of meaning, and create familiar patterns which we can manipulate and work with. Conversely, the structures which they give rise to can become too solid or too difficult to change.

Such conceptual sieves and moulds are familiar to psychologists in perception, remembering and habitual social attitudes, but they are also central to their own use of models, theories, paradigms and conceptual frameworks. The economy, guidelines and objectives provided by these scientific perspectives are of clear benefit to an investigator, yet their negative aspects, limited focus and restricted notions of what is worth while, need always to be kept in mind.

CONCEPTUAL FRAMEWORKS

The several perspectives to be examined here have many points in common, and it is sometimes difficult to distinguish between them in a consistent manner. However, the broadest term of the four appears to be 'conceptual framework'. This is appropriately used to describe a perspective which is wide-ranging and which extends into and connects with more limited theories or models (Note 3).

A conceptual framework provides a technical language system, a set of interpretative principles, and important benchmarks for guiding thought. It carries with it epistemological assumptions and prescriptions, so that different frameworks may contain different notions of knowledge and how to increase understanding as well as divergent statements of fact and assertions of priority.

A researcher's conceptual framework is likely to have been developed within a particular professional culture and internalized in such a way that the members of that culture can easily communicate among themselves, can share a common evaluative structure and can routinely frame research questions and possible ways to find answers.

Most psychologists will share a broad conceptual framework with certain other members of their profession, but it may of course happen that an individual researcher has a framework which to a greater or lesser extent differs from those of his or her colleagues. A conceptual framework is thus appropriately thought of in individual terms, but is normally to a large extent socially determined. Many chapters in this book illustrate the features of such frameworks, and later in the present chapter I return to the question of their empirical reference. For the moment note that a broad conceptual framework may not be directly testable against specific facts.

PARADIGMS

A similar term applied to scientific thinking which also has many non-scientific applications is 'paradigm'.   Recent discussions of this notion have often been influenced by Kuhn's (1962) argument that science evolves in a discontinuous way through 'paradigm shifts' interspersed with long periods of 'normal science'. Unfortunately, Kuhn uses 'paradigm' in a wide variety of different ways (Note 4), so that it is difficult to draw from his work a single satisfactory characterization.   Shapere concludes that according to Kuhn's presentation 'anything that allows science to accomplish anything can be part of (or somehow involved in) a paradigm' (Shapere, 1964, p. 385).

Nevertheless, it would appear that one necessary feature is that a paradigm consists of a 'strong network of commitments - conceptual, theoretical, instrumental and metaphysical' (Kuhn, 1962, p. 42).   Within psychology such commitments are illustrated through types of research methodology (laboratory experimentation or action research, for example), through contrasting approaches to personality (idiographic versus nomothetic paradigms, for instance), and through different styles of clinical treatment (e.g. behaviour therapy versus verbal psychotherapy).   This book contains many more instances, both explicit and implicit.

Kuhn has recently (1977) revised his position to argue that the two principal notions which are separable within the concept of paradigm are 'exemplars' (concrete problem solutions accepted by the scientific community as good illustrations) and 'disciplinary matrixes', which are the shared elements which assist professional communication and encourage unanimity of professional judgement.   The components of disciplinary matrixes are symbolic generalizations, shared beliefs, values and exemplars.   Kuhn's emphasis has been upon the social nature and impact of paradigms, but it is of course possible to ask of an individual scientist what is the paradigm with which s/he is working.

We may also ask how a scientist's paradigm differs from his or her conceptual framework.   Recognizing that both terms imply the operation of sieves and moulds, the two types of perspective clearly have much in common.   The difference seems to be one of emphasis, in terms of conceptual or methodological guidance.   A scientist's concepts and methods are closely interdependent, but common usage seems to see a research paradigm somewhat more than a conceptual framework in terms of methods and activities; the paradigm suggests 'how to do research' in a particular area, and the conceptual framework suggests 'how to think about' that area.   This may be rephrased to say that a conceptual framework may on occasion stand without implied methodology, but a paradigm cannot exist without instrumental or methodological components (Note 5).

THEORIES

The literature on theory within the sciences is enormous, and opinions and arguments are very varied (e.g. Rapoport, 1958; Achinstein, 1968; Colodny, 1971; Harré, 1972; Suppe, 1977). In common usage the term seems to have evolved so that theory is contrasted with practice and activity, and a core meaning has been associated with reflection or speculation (Williams, 1976). This contrast was preserved in the received view of the logical positivists, described earlier. Here the statements of a scientific theory were denied any empirical meaning and the theory was thought to stand on its own merely as a formal logical calculus. Current philosophical thinking seems to be that it is inappropriate to seek an ideal view of how a theory should be formulated; instead attention should be directed to the characteristics of theories as they are actually used by scientists. The sharp distinction between theory and practice, formal and empirical meaning, may now be less readily sustained.

Scientific theories take many shapes and have many purposes but they all involve a systematic set of conjectures about part of reality. Some of these conjectures may be quite well established, others less so, and others again merely possibilities which are awaiting exploration. Theories may however also contain descriptive statements of fact. Most theories have a mixture of factual statements and conjectural assertions (sometimes referred to as 'hypotheses'), and if the theory proves acceptable over a long period of time a growing proportion of the latter become members or near-members of the former; additional conjectures may of course be added later so that the set of potential components of a theory is not usually fully determined in advance. Theories may be employed in order to attempt explanation, prediction or systematic description, but no one theory necessarily has all these tasks. By definition the truth of parts of a theory has not been ascertained, and theories naturally vary in the extent to which it is plausible to believe them true.

It is important to identify principal ways in which theories differ from each other. However, the major differentiating characteristics are likely also to be applicable to the other scientific perspectives under discussion (conceptual frameworks, paradigms and models), so let me defer their introduction until later. For the present, how in global terms may a theory be said to differ from a conceptual framework and from a paradigm? It shares with them the features of a sieve, both excluding from thought a large number of options and guiding thought about material which is allowed to pass. And the perspectives have in common the fact that they contain moulds into which thoughts are pressed and preserved.

However, there appear to be two main distinguishing features between a theory and either a conceptual framework or a paradigm; neither is unequivocal. These are the extent to which the perspective is open to empirical test and its degree of specificity. In general terms a theory is more likely to be considered liable to confirmation or refutation through observation than is a conceptual framework or a paradigm. Certain features of the latter two may receive detailed empirical examination, but their whole structure operates more as a set of working assumptions and guidelines sustained primarily through their place in a cultural network. On the other hand, psychologists tend to believe that one of the criteria for a good scientific theory is that there are empirical procedures which can be applied and which in certain circumstances have the potential for showing the theory to be false; this point was introduced in an earlier section.

Yet many theories within psychology are in practice not open to refutation in the allegedly orthodox way. Meehl (1978) has suggested 20 different reasons why this is so, and in addition has drawn attention to a general philosophical issue raised by Feyerabend (1971), Lakatos (1974) and others. This concerns the crucial role of 'auxiliary theories' in tests of substantive theories. It is often impossible to derive an observational test of a theory from that theory alone: we require a set of complex auxiliary conjectures and also the establishment of

particular conditions in which observations can be made.   Illustrations of
auxiliary theories include the assumptions that a certain test accurately
operationalizes a psychological variable, that an associated process peripheral to
the theory (e.g. short-term storage) operates in a certain way, that a given
variable is stable across time and across changing conditions.

This means that in attempting to falsify a theory, T, we are in effect
examining the complex conjunction of the theory (T), the auxiliary theory (A) and
the specific conditions (C).   A negative test of a prediction cannot therefore
directly falsify T, but only TAC, so that T itself is in the absence of further
information not directly refutable.   In some cases where we have accumulated
considerable knowledge about important characteristics of A and C, the observed
data may allow unequivocal conclusions about T, but in many cases acceptance or
rejection of a theory in the light of evidence is often a matter of personal
judgement rather than the outcome of applying a simple decision rule.

Lakatos has stressed how research often proceeds successfully despite apparent
disconfirmation in specific empirical tests.   This methodological attitude of
treating as <u>anomalies</u> what Popper would regard as <u>counter examples</u> is commonly
accepted by the best scientists.   Some of the research programmes now held in
highest esteem by the scientific community progressed in an ocean of anomalies'
(Lakatos, 1974, p. 317, emphases in original).   'The scientist lists anomalies but
as long as his research programme sustains its momentum, he ignores them' (Lakatos,
1974, p. 318).   In this sense many psychological theories are retained for their
overall heuristic value despite localized empirical failings, and the similarity
between theories, conceptual frameworks and paradigms is thereby enhanced.   Other
theories may be closely specified and limited to certain conditions where auxiliary
theories are less essential or already fully supported.   In these cases their
refutability may be less in doubt, and this distinction between a theory and the
other two perspectives may then be more clearly drawn.

The second distinguishing feature introduced earlier was in terms of
specificity: a theory is similar to a conceptual framework or a paradigm, but it
often has a more specific focus, a narrower range of questions to answer, and
greater precision of inquiry.   This difference in scope appears to be illustrated
in common usage of the terms, but as noted previously there are exceptions;
'stimulus-response theory' and 'psychoanalytic theory', for example, are extremely
wide-ranging.

Differences in scope suggest the possibility that theories may be subsumed
within or at least linked to the broader perspectives, and this is undoubtedly
often the case.   A particular theory of limited scope is likely to be consistent
with a larger set of metatheoretical positions.   This partly accounts for its
initial development, its momentum, and its continued acceptance in the light of
partial disconfirmation.   Theory and metatheoretical perspectives are to some
extent mutually supportive, but the latter (in this discussion, conceptual
frameworks and paradigms) tend to be wider in conceptual scope and practical
influence.   This point is taken up again in the final section, where it is argued
that psychologists have paid insufficient attention to the relationships between
limited theories and broader frameworks.

MODELS

How should the term 'model' be viewed within this discussion?   Let me introduce a
discussion of scientific models (using this term in its restricted meaning rather
than in the general sense of 'perspective' outlined in the first paragraph of the
chapter) by first drawing attention to some non-scientific uses of the word.   There
are two main types of model, distinguishable in terms of their emphasis upon direct
representation or upon importation from elsewhere.

The first type in everyday life is illustrated through scale models of trains or aeroplanes. These are direct representations (usually simplified) of the original object; the object existed first and was subsequently represented by the model. Let us refer to these as models-1. Other illustrations of models-1 (direct, simplified representations) include children's dolls, working models of equipment displayed in museums, or early mechanical calculators which modelled numbers and transformations through ratchets and the movement of cogwheels (Note 6).

The second set of models in everyday life is identifiable in terms of the importation of analogues from some other domain in order indirectly to give meaning and to assist thought in a puzzling or difficult area. The gods in classical literature were modelled upon men, and contemporary science fiction writers characterize social relations among non-humans through imported features from human life. In these model-2 cases the models are used to describe and explain an unknown domain in terms of analogues imported from a more familiar world. This is quite different from the first use of the term, in which a model is more a simplified representation of a familiar object, structure or process.

The distinction between the two types of model has been presented by Harré (1970) in terms of 'homoeomorphs' and 'paramorphs' (see also chapter 14). In the former case (model-1, above) the source and the subject of the model are the same: a child's doll (the subject) is a model of a baby (the source) but it is also a direct representation of that source. In the case of paramorphs the subject and the source are different: classical gods and men are quite separate groups, yet the former (the subject of the model) may be viewed in terms of men (the source).

We should also note that everyday models of each kind may be to varying degrees value-laden. Thus a statue, a painting or a fashion model may serve to represent currently desirable attributes, and a parable or a plan of action are value-laden representations of what is or what might be. Similarly a model student or a model answer provide clear evaluative indications, whereas a model aeroplane or a model yacht tend to be representations in terms of descriptive simplification.

In summary, the non-scientific uses of the term are capable of separation into:
Model-1: simplified representations of a part of known reality.
Model-2: imported analogues to assist thinking about the unknown or unfamiliar.
Both types of model may be more or less value-laden.

This characterization is similar to the distinctions which are emerging from philosophers' discussions of scientific models. Many detailed characterizations are possible (for example, uniform, difform; material, iconic, mathematical, sentential; micromorphic, macromorphic; see, for instance, Harré, 1970; Wallace, 1974; Collins, 1976; Suppe, 1977), but of fundamental significance is the distinction between model-1 and model-2 which has been developed by Hesse (1963, 1967; see also Leatherdale, 1974).

Model-1

One major category of scientific models contains what might equally well be termed theories. The models are systematic conjectures about a part of reality and they attempt to simplify that reality within a network of thought. Note that in this use of the term, the reality is examined first and the model is then generated to interpret what is known and perhaps to suggest what might also be the case. The model is likely to take a symbolic (verbal and/or numerical) form, but in some cases it might be represented through physical devices or working mechanisms.

In designating their framework a model rather than a theory, scientists seem to be affirming its limitation at the present time. The theory may be restricted in scope (purposefully, perhaps), or in number and richness of components, or it might have only a small amount of evidence in its favour, being in effect a provisional theory. This major sense of a model as a limited or provisional theory has a long history and widespread use in psychology and other sciences. For example, much fruitful research has been developed around the congruity model and other accounts of information integration, models of specific animal behaviours, models of association learning or information retrieval, models of reflex action, proactive inhibition theory or the similarity-attraction hypothesis.

In examining and assessing models-1 in psychology, we naturally should use the parameters of theories in general; some suggestions about these are offered later. Two points should however be noted here. The first is the fact that models-1 tend to have a place within a wider metatheoretical framework in the way suggested in the earlier discussion of theories. They operate as systems of sieves and moulds which tend to be consistent with established conceptual frameworks and paradigms (and therefore sometimes consistent with other associated theories and models-1), and they derive much of their strength from these relationships.

The second point is a differentiating qualification of the first. Psychologists' use of the term 'model' for limited or provisional theories seems often to include the notion that a model can have a relatively more isolated existence than a theory. Whereas theories are expected to cohere with other bodies of fact and conjecture, a limited model is more likely to be accepted for a while on its own terms whether or not it draws directly upon a metatheoretical framework: rejection of a theory is more likely to damage a metatheoretical structure than is rejection of a model.

The second type of scientific model has a number of features which make it rather different from models-1.

Model-2

Many scientific models exist separately from theories; they are analogues with an independent existence (in thought or in the world) which can be imported from some other area of experience to provide a new structural or interpretative framework. Hesse suggests that such a model-2

> exploits some other system (such as a mechanism or a familiar mathematical or empirical theory from another domain) that is already well known and understood in order to explain the less well-established system under investigation. This latter may be called the explanandum. What chiefly distinguishes /models-2/ from other (Note 7) kinds is a feature that follows from their associating another system with the explanandum. This is that the /model-2/ carries with it what has been called 'open texture' or 'surplus meaning' derived from the familiar system. The /model-2/ conveys associations and implications that ... may be transferred by analogy to the explanandum; further developments and modifications of the explanatory theory may therefore be suggested by the /model-2/. (Hesse, 1967, p. 356)

Leatherdale points out that 'models-2 range from simple concepts or complexes of concepts drawn from ordinary experience, with connotations which are not normally precisely, exhaustively or formally stated, to extensive formal systems of propositions. At its most formal and skeletal a model-2 may be a calculus, comprising relata defined only and related purely by logical or mathematical relations' (Leatherdale, 1974, p. 51). The latter form of model-2 was much discussed within the logical positivist framework, for example in terms of Braithwaite's assertion that 'a theory and a model for it ... have the same formal structure since the theory and model are both represented by the same calculus' (Braithwaite, 1953, p. 90); the two are isomorphic in that there is a one-to-one correspondence between elements and between relations between those elements. Note however that Braithwaite took a strict hypothetico-deductive view of scientific theories, and that many models-2 are in practice more informal attempts to increase understanding in terms of an object, process or idea which is more familiar and intelligible than is the domain under investigation.

The key feature of this endeavour derives from the use of analogy. A model-2 is necessarily different in some respects from the explanandum to which it is applied, but the resemblance must be strong enough to suggest its fruitful importation: we proceed 'as if' the model-2 were appropriate. The set of similarities between the imported model and the object of investigation may be described as the 'positive analogy' and the set of differences as the 'negative analogy'. Thus 'billiard ball' models of molecules have structural similarities with the objects they represent (these constitute the positive analogy), but they are also quite clearly different in terms of size, materials, colour, origin, location, etc.; these differences comprise the negative analogy.

The scientist's activities with a model-2 have in these terms been described by Hesse.

> The model is first proposed because there is some obvious positive analogy ... between it and the explanandum. But the /model-2/ that results from ignoring the negative analogy has more than simply a remaining positive analogy with the explanandum. If this were not so, the /model-2/ would be identical with the explanandum and not richer, as we have required. In addition to the known positive analogy, there is a set of properties of the model whose positive or negative analogy is not yet known. Let us call this set the neutral analogy. Exploitation of the model consists in investigating this neutral analogy and in allowing the neutral analogy to suggest modifications and developments of the theory that can be confirmed or refuted by subsequent empirical tests. (Hesse, 1967, p. 356)

In practice,it seems likely that the theory can also sometimes suggest modification of the imported model, so that there is a process of interbreeding between theory and model-2, often with reference to empirical observation.

This process may be illustrated through the structure of elements in Figure 1. Suppose that a theory (in row 2) is confirmed by observation in respect of

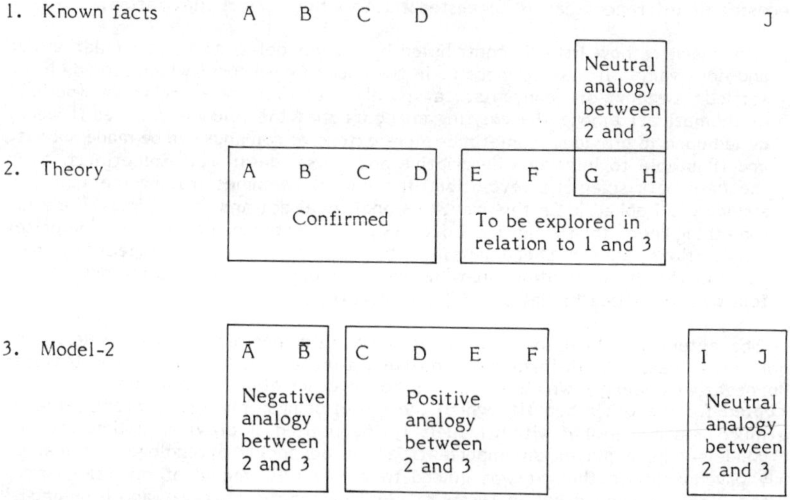

Figure 1. Illustration of possible relationships between known facts, theory and model-2.

components A, B, C and D, but that the status of theoretical components E, F, G and H is currently indeterminate. Then suppose that a model-2 is introduced which has the following relationships to the theory and the known facts:

(1) Components A and B of the theory and of the facts are distorted by the model to the extent that it is in these respects an incorrect representation; A and B thus comprise the negative analogy.

(2) Components C, D, E and F are present in both the theory and the model-2 (being the positive analogy), but of these components only C and D correspond to previous observations.

(3) Components G and H are present in the theory but not in the model-2, and components I and J are in the model-2 but not in the theory, although these correspondences have not so far been denied. Suppose also that J, but not G, H and I, falls within the set of known facts. These four elements comprise the neutral analogy.

Scientific progress may be possible in this situation by some or all of the following activities:

(A1) Components E to H of the theory may be explored through empirical tests. This may lead to the adequate confirmation of expectations (resulting in inclusion of the components in row 1), or to failure of expectations, in which case further tests may be attempted, or the theory may be modified or rejected.

(A2) Components E to H of the theory may be explored in relation to the model-2.   Of principal interest here is the exploitation of the neutral analogy: can G and H be found to fit within the model-2, thus extending the positive analogy and perhaps leading on to new insights and developments?

(A3) Conversely, components I and J of the model-2 may be examined for potential interbreeding with the theory, perhaps increasing the positive analogy by expanding the theory.

(A4) Component I from the model-2 may be treated as an expectation about reality (even though it is not currently part of the theory) and thus subjected to observational inquiry.

The value of the model-2 in this illustration is highlighted through activities A2, A3 and A4; A1 is the routine application of procedures to test theoretical expectations. Note however that in practice the interactive exploration of facts, theory and model-2 is often a much less mechanical comparison of features and processes of inference than is suggested through this formal illustration.

> How much or how little is contributed by the /model-2/ to the formulation can and does vary. It may be merely, in the case of a /theory/ which already has a settled system of concepts, a purely abstract new relation (perhaps mathematical) among the existing concepts that the /model-2/ is, as it were, called upon to provide. Sometimes more extensive demands can be made upon it, and it is able to introduce descriptive and causal detail ... Sometimes, as in the case of a scientific revolution, the /model-2/ comes trailing metaphysical strings ... Looked at in this way, the analogical act and the /model-2/ provide something more than a limited inference, more even than a new relation or set of relations among phenomena.   They provide a new perspective, new possibilities of description, new horizons to explore, novel inferences to be followed up. (Leatherdale, 1974, pp. 22-23)

The extent to which some or all of these outcomes arise will of course vary from case to case. In all instances, however, a model-2 will contain some features (the negative analogy) which are known to be descriptively wrong but which are accepted for the other benefits which the model brings; manifestly wrong features are much less acceptable within models-1, the limited or provisional theories.

Models-2 have played an important part in advancing psychologists' thinking. Early psychoanalytic thought was guided by a hydraulic model of mental energy, Tolman (1951) viewed needs in terms of electromagnetic charges, and ethologists' studies of drives were partly based upon the notion of an operating water cistern.

Broadbent describes in chapter 9 his ball-bearing and tube model, introduced in 1957 with subsequent impact on many studies in experimental psychology. More recent importations have often been in terms of concepts and systems from information theory and computer science; and models-2 in social psychology have come from sociology and anthropology as well as dramaturgical models from the theatre. Models-1 in one part of psychology are often transferred to become models -2 in another part: concepts from, say, speech perception may be imported into thinking about memory, or the perception of people may be treated as analogous with the better understood perception of objects.

The process of interbreeding which takes place during sustained application of a model-2 to a prior theory often begets a framework in which the origin of the components is no longer clear. In effect then, whether a structure is better identified as a model-1 or a model-2 is partly a function of its location and purpose at the time. The same structure may switch its class membership through importation, and models may exist within models in a network which makes it very difficult to apply an overall description: model-1 or model-2.

Scientific models of all kinds are often examined in terms of their use of metaphors (e.g. Black, 1962; Swanson, 1966; Leatherdale, 1974).

> The metaphor works by transferring the associated ideas and implications of the secondary to the primary system. These select, emphasize, or suppress features of the primary; new slants on the primary are illuminated; the primary is 'seen through' the frame of the secondary. (Hesse, 1966, pp. 162-163)

This is particularly obvious in the discussions of some social and clinical psychologists, where ideas or images have rich and varied meanings and uncertain boundaries, but metaphorical features are also central to the use of more formalized mathematical or logical models. In his examination of the language of physics, Hutten has observed that 'models thus resemble metaphors in ordinary language ... when words normally used in a given context fail, we seek help through words which, usually, belong to another context' (Hutten, 1965, p. 84).

A currently important growth area in psychology is artificial intelligence (AI), where computer programs and programming techniques are used to cast light on the principles of intelligence in general and human thought in particular (e.g. Boden, 1977; see also chapter 10); this approach extends into social and clinical areas which are not immediately suggested by the rather restrictive reference to 'intelligence'. AI models take the form of computer simulations of behaviour or experience, allowing precise examination of assumptions, interrelationships and possible predictions.

Such models illustrate the role of metaphor in psychological research, not merely through the use of single metaphorical assertions (as emphasized in the quotation from Hutten above, and apparent through statements that a computer program has 'perceived' or 'decided'), but also through the more global metaphor of a programming language as a whole. These languages provide their own conceptual framework, in the sense introduced earlier, in that they not only attempt to represent some verbal expressions of what is being modelled but also determine the shape and content of the account which is provided. Each programming language and system has its own principal concepts and forms of control, and the choice of language (or of the computer metaphor in general) naturally influences how the scientist proceeds in his thinking and empirical investigation.

Computer simulation models often illustrate a point made earlier, that researchers may see their model as relatively independent of observed data. It is often argued that to develop a computer program which undertakes a task effectively represents a major step forward in its own right. A model may in this way show itself to be internally consistent and sufficient as a system, and it is sometimes thought appropriate to evaluate the model merely in these terms. More generally, AI models bring out clearly the difficulties of assessment: which criteria (internal consistency, empirical support, simplicity, etc.) are most appropriate for assessing or choosing between models? This point is taken up again in the final section.

Computer simulations may be of the model-1 or the model-2 type depending on their developmental history. In the former case a psychological process is first examined and then modelled in program terms, whereas the model-2 approach to AI imports procedures and concepts from computer science to examine their potential value in psychology. An illustration of how models-2 may contribute to and shape research in a range of quite different areas is provided by Rapoport's comment on mathematical systems models:

> It sometimes turns out that the model fits some other situations better than the one for which it was formulated. If so, then the systems theorist is led to wherever the model leads him. In short, he is as frequently in the market for situations to fit the model he has investigated as on a quest for models to fit a given situation. (Rapoport, 1966, p. 520)

In both cases, the expanding structure and detailed interconnections of the computer program are likely increasingly to determine the later model-building stages, so that the system becomes particularly resistant to major change. It may also be difficult to disentangle the components with psychological theoretical interest from those features required by the nature of the computer system or programming language.

Although AI researchers are developing increasingly sophisticated forms of non-numerical symbol manipulation, computer models are frequently explicitly mathematical. Indeed, mathematical formulations are widespread in psychological theorizing of all the kinds examined in this chapter. There may be value in distinguishing such mathematical models from statistical models, in the sense that the latter are concerned to examine observed statistical distributions against expectations derived from features of probability theory.

The simpler type of statistical models may be illustrated through procedures to describe averages and variances and to assess the probability that observed sample distributions are drawn from different populations. In more complex examples a researcher may set up an analysis of variance model or a putative factor structure against which to test observed data: the goal is to learn how much of the data can be systematically accounted for by the model. Recently developed statistical models have been used to test causal assertions about non-experimental data through path analysis and other forms of structural equation model, involving the regression of particular variables on other 'causal' variables (e.g. Blalock, 1971; Goldberger & Duncan, 1973). Causal statistical models of this kind may include estimates of the influence of unmeasured, latent variables as well as measured observables. For example, Bentler & Huba (1979) have examined possible causal models of love, introducing latent constructs such as attraction towards and thought about a person in addition to directly measured manifestations of these processes.

Statistical models come close to the independently existing formal calculi analysed within the logical positivist framework for scientific theories. The models themselves have no direct reference to specific factual domains and their internal coherence within a broader probability theory is of primary importance. In cases where observed data cannot be accommodated within a statistical model, the model itself is not disconfirmed, but merely its applicability in a particular context. However, it is important to note how the use of a statistical model to assess one's data has the effect (common to all perspectives described here) of conditioning the facts which are admitted and the data which are gathered. Although statistical models differ from some other types employed by psychologists in that they are logically independent of observable reality, their use still shapes the psychologist's view of that reality and influences the way it is studied.

DIFFERENTIATING CHARACTERISTICS

In examining this family of four perspectives (conceptual framework, paradigm, theory and model) I have suggested that the former two are usually granted wider meaning in psychology than the latter two. Furthermore, a conceptual framework and a paradigm are themselves partly distinguishable in that the first tends more to suggest 'how to think about' a particular area and the second 'how to do research' in that area.

I have argued that a theory, as a systematic set of conjectures about part of reality, is usually more focused than a conceptual framework and a paradigm and is sometimes more open to empirical test. Models-1 are direct representations, limited or provisional theories, whereas models-2 have a rather different role as analogues which are imported into theories or models-1. Theories and models tend to be located within metatheoretical structures, but the interdependence may be relatively less strong in the case of some models. Scientists' thoughts and actions are associated with these several single perspectives, as well as moving in complex ways between them.

In examining, comparing and creating the perspectives, we need to be alert to their principal differentiating characteristics. In what terms should we compare two theories, for example; or in what further respects can we contrast broad conceptual frameworks with more limited theories? The following interrelated parameters appear to be central:

(1) INTENDED REFERENCE Which features of reality does the perspective aim to cover and how widely set are its boundaries? The models presented in this book vary considerably in content and scope, and their intended reference needs to be identified in any attempt at assessment or comparison.

(2) PARSIMONY Scientific theories are often assessed in terms of their parsimonious use of concepts and assumptions. However, what is an appropriate degree of parsimony may vary between different kinds of perspective.

(3) INTERNAL CONSISTENCY It is essential to a well-formed logical calculus that the elements be internally consistent. Such a characteristic appears in principle to be desirable in scientific models, although it may not be completely necessary at every stage of development, since progress often comes through tackling points of inconsistency.

(4) DEGREE OF ELABORATION Some models have explicitly stated assumptions and detailed elaboration of relationships between parts, whereas others are presented in a looser, less precise form.

(5) HEURISTIC VALUE Irrespective of the previous features, a model may be important for its influence upon empirical and conceptual developments.

(6) ACTUAL AND POTENTIAL EMPIRICAL SUPPORT The amount of supporting evidence is clearly important, as is a model's potential for generating expectations open to empirical test. Note however that not all perspectives of the kinds illustrated in this chapter require detailed empirical validation.

(7) IMPLIED RESEARCH METHODS AND TYPES OF EVIDENCE The epistemological assumptions embodied in scientific perspectives often lead to divergent styles of research and types of appropriate evidence. This is clearly illustrated throughout the book, and it is important to separate this parameter from the previous one, which is concerned with the amount of empirical support irrespective of its type.

(8) DEGREE OF QUANTIFICATION A further differentiating feature is the extent to which individual models are presented and applied in mathematical terms.

(9) COMPATIBILITY WITH OTHER PERSPECTIVES A model may also be viewed in terms of its consistency with others. This is partly a question of coherence with metatheoretical perspectives, such as the very broad 'mechanist' or 'humanist' approaches which are discussed in several parts of the book, but links with other models at the same level of generality as the one in question also require examination.

(10)   CAUSAL ASSUMPTIONS A related feature is the type of causal processes (if any) which are assumed. For example, some perspectives explicitly deny the possibility of teleological causation, whereas others contain that as a central feature.

(11)   INTERDEPENDENCE WITH ACTION Many psychological theories have no intended implications for personal or societal action, whereas others (for example, normative theories or statements of 'praxis') carry with them recommendations for action or change.

(12)   BEAUTY There is no doubt that scientists view models in terms of their attractiveness, elegance, and other evaluatively tinged notions. This may be captured in the general statement that theories vary in their beauty, but that beauty lies partly in the eye of the beholder.

(13)   EXTRA-SCIENTIFIC ASSUMPTIONS This final feature covers the moral, ideological or metaphysical aspects of a scientific model. These are difficult to introduce briefly and may pervade all the previous items. The essential feature is that a psychological perspective often contains assumptions and implications about the nature (actual and ideal) of man or society. Psychologists' questions and models can influence how they and other members of society think about themselves. One general feature of this kind is a model's optimism or pessimism about people's potential for initiative and self-development. Another aspect is the extent to which a psychologist's perspective appears consistent or inconsistent with the contemporary Zeitgeist.

In applying these 13 characteristics to individual conceptual frameworks, paradigms, theories or models, it is inappropriate to prescribe any generally desirable level or content of each attribute. For example, parsimony is differentially valuable as a function of many other features. Furthermore, comparative examination of psychologists' perspectives might attempt to describe not only the observed variations in the characteristics but also the preferences or importance attached to each characteristic by the holder of the perspective. For example, many psychologists value a high degree of quantification whereas others prefer to avoid this; uncovering and describing such values and preferences appears to be part of the task of comparative description.

For the present I would like to draw further attention to some issues which arise from variations in intended reference (item 1 in the list above). What are the principal interrelationships and tensions between a theory or model of limited scope and a more wide-ranging structure in the same domain? Most research published in psychological journals is explicitly intended as an examination of limited theory, and precise operationalization and specification of appropriate conditions are thus expected. Such miniature theories can yield exciting investigations within their restricted scope, and recent decades have seen a strong preference by psychologists for bounded thinking in contrast to some earlier attempts at 'grand theory'.

One motivation behind the concentration on limited theories may be the hope that they will gradually expand in scope and power, eventually giving rise to or coalescing into more comprehensive frameworks. Such a belief might be supported through the 'covering law' notions of science, described at the beginning of this chapter, where statements within a theory are thought to be deductively interdependent and therefore of increasing generality at higher levels. That formalized view of science is nowadays less widely accepted (Note 8), and I would like to question how far one can generate comprehensive theoretical accounts merely by attempting to expand miniature theories; perhaps a systematic 'top-down' endeavour should also be encouraged to complement the more common 'bottom-up' approach.

Two principal arguments support this view, one in terms of lateral relationships between models of approximately equal scope and one concerned with vertical relationships between limited and more comprehensive perspectives. First, how may miniature theories of approximately the same level of generality become combined? This is often extremely difficult because of differing metatheoretical settings. A major theme of this chapter has been that theories both guide and restrict thought and action; the restrictions are supported by socially acceptable metatheoretical assumptions which are not always made explicit. Two limited theories within different metatheoretical structures can be quite incapable of interbreeding. This may be illustrated through experimental social psychologists' models and those in the same domain developed by their more experiential counterparts; each type of theory is of value but they are predicated upon such different conceptions of valid knowledge that mutual assimilation appears to be ruled out.

That may be a somewhat extreme example. However, the difficulties of lateral integration are seen within experimental social psychology and also within cognitive psychology. Several commentators in the latter field have noted the fragmented nature of the subject and the surprisingly few interconnections between limited theories at the same level of generality. Whereas one might hope for cumulative progress through the placing together of separate theoretical 'modules' to form a larger structure, this does not seem to happen to any large extent. Thus Newell concludes that 'far from providing the rungs of a ladder by which psychology gradually climbs to clarity, this fragmented form of conceptual structure leads rather to an ever-increasing pile of issues, which we weary of or become diverted from, but never really settle' (Newell, 1973, p. 279). Allport also views cognitive psychology with dismay at 'the near-vacuum of theoretical structure within which to interrelate different sets of experimental results, or to direct the search for significant new phenomena' (Allport, 1975, p. 152).

I cite these authors not in order to be critical of the field they are reviewing, but to illustrate how separate miniature theories are very difficult to combine, because of their focus on different phenomena, their use of different concepts and measures, and a pervasive difference in metatheoretical perspectives. Each of these differences may itself be quite small, but the overall effect is sharply to reduce the probability of lateral convergence between limited models.

The second possibility introduced earlier was to strive to build an individual model vertically, to attempt to develop its generality from the starting point of the localized account. This is a sensible procedure which may be fruitful up to a point, but it has logical and practical limitations. The gradual expansion of a restricted model changes its nature in ways which point up the wider inadequacy of both the original and the expanded model, so that in due course it is necessary to abandon both in favour of a completely new structure. Researchers tend to be reluctant to take that step.

I have in mind here the fact that expansion often consists in adding new variables and processes which tend either to take precedence over the original concepts or to fit only uncomfortably with them. For example they may be drawn from a different domain, perhaps being concerned with contextual, structural or social constraints upon the original phenomenon or laboratory behaviour. Furthermore expanded versions of limited models often require different styles of empirical research, of a kind which the investigator no longer feels competent or inclined to undertake.

These themes are further illustrated in chapter 12 and elsewhere in the book. The problems of vertical elaboration of a miniature model may here be couched in terms of two analogies:

THE CHRISTMAS TREE ANALOGY The clear initial structure of a model becomes lost through the repeated addition of unconnected decorations and refinements, so that it eventually lacks the coherence of a purposeful configuration.

THE CUCKOO IN THE NEST ANALOGY The initial features of a model may be joined by a new variable which proves to be more powerful than the original ones and which makes redundant the considerable attention lavished upon them.

I suspect that a 'bottom-up' approach to the development of wide-ranging theories cannot succeed on its own. Miniature theories are in practice only loosely linked to the comprehensive models, conceptual frameworks, 'grand theories' and so on with which they might be consistent. The vertical link is certainly not of a straightforward deductive kind, where the premises state the conditions which are logically sufficient for the truth of the conclusions. Instead there are conceptual and practical screens between the different levels, and throughout a large and comprehensive theoretical structure it is necessary to introduce specific qualifying conditions, the provision that 'other things are equal', probability estimates, assumptions about correlated features, proposals for measurement, assertions about constancy or variation, and similar ad hoc characteristics.

The relationship between a wide-ranging conceptual framework and a more limited theory is like that between a general administrative or legal policy and specific decisions associated with that policy. Decisions in particular circumstances may be consistent with a policy but they are not usually directly derivable from it, since so many local contingencies and other, possibly contradictory, policies come into play; conversely a policy is more than the sum of associated decisions. A policy guides thought and action in a very general way, and serves also to exclude certain types of thought and action. Conceptual frameworks in science have the same role, and in similar fashion they do not usually have determinate empirical consequences, lacking detailed texture in terms of both content and structure. They are not themselves directly predictive; rather they provide guidelines to help generate predictions. This suggests that there is a gap between the miniature theory and the wide-ranging conceptualization which cannot be bridged by ever-broader inductive reasoning and empirical study.

Kendler (1968) has made a similar point in his examination of stimulus-response theory, arguing that, despite its title, the perspective is not one which yields empirical predictions. S-R theory is what I have here called a conceptual framework, itself non-committal about detailed empirical relationships.

How then can we bring together such broad perspectives and the more limited predictive models? Perhaps we should accept that concepts, measures, language, and criteria of adequacy must vary in nature at differing levels of abstraction: the extensiveness and detail of concepts and evidence needs to be proportional to the extensiveness and detail of the features to be covered. There is a sense in which, once a broad conceptual framework has been developed, the associated miniature theories are part of that framework and share some of its features, just as specific decisions are in a sense part of an overall policy. This means that the contents of a broad framework and its associated theories will be of several kinds, and we may need different notions of knowledge at different levels of abstraction.

To determine the form of these different kinds of knowledge and the research methods associated with them is one of the major challenges facing psychology. Whereas we are clearly influenced by conceptual frameworks and paradigms which serve as metatheoretical structures to support and assist more limited theorizing, these comprehensive structures are not usually articulated as potential explanatory systems in their own right. Such an articulation requires more detailed consideration of the nature of wide-ranging frameworks and how they might be extended in top-down fashion to embrace miniature theories and their empirical referents.

NOTES

1. Thus Swanson observes: 'Almost all contemporary writers on models ... assume, as point of departure for their analyses, the hypothetico-deductive position on the nature of scientific theories ... But of course science in general is not axiomatised, give or take a portion here or there'. (Swanson, 1966, p. 303)

2. I am using 'sieve' here rather than 'filter' (the term used by Swanson) to avoid confusion with psychologists' filter models outlined elsewhere in the book.

3. The task of characterization is made difficult by the fact that many wide-ranging perspectives of this kind have acquired the label 'theory'. Thus stimulus-response theory, association theory, Gestalt theory or cognitive consistency theory appear to possess the features of a 'conceptual framework' rather than of a 'theory' in the more limited sense in which that word is frequently used. This point is taken up in the final section of the chapter.

4. Masterman (1970) identifies 21 different meanings of 'paradigm' in Kuhn's writing.

5. Anticipating the later discussion a little, one might say that a paradigm is a model of science rather than a model in science.

6. Incidentally, psychological experiments might be viewed as models in this category, since they aim to be simplified versions of situations and processes in which people find themselves in their daily lives.

7. Although the distinction between model-1 and model-2 appears to be widely accepted in the philosophical literature, several different labels have been used. When quoting from other authors I have therefore introduced the basic terms between solidi in place of the original wording where this differs from 'model-1', 'model-2' and 'theory' as used here.

8. Nagel is worth quoting here: 'Despite frequent claims that all explanations must be of the deductive type if they are to be satisfactory, the explanations actually available in many areas of inquiry are rarely of this form. Indeed, most students in certain branches of science ... do not even aim at achieving strictly deductive explanations'. (Nagel, 1965, pp. 14-15)

EDITED DISCUSSION

P. B. WARR: An important question recurring through these proceedings is one first identified for us here by Bill Joynson. It is the distinction between mechanistic and humanistic psychology. Surely this cannot be described in terms of a single dimension, but requires a multidimensional space. I think that this space can be characterized by four major features: (1) focus of research - the mechanistic approach places a greater emphasis on quantified, observable behaviour, while the humanistic approach is rather more concerned with experience; (2) the size of unit of analysis - the humanistic psychologist works on a more macroscopic level; (3) the type of evidence allowable - on the whole, the mechanistic psychologist tends to emphasize experimental manipulations, whereas humanistic psychologists tend to use a wider range of sources of evidence; and (4) the nature of scientific explanation - mechanistic psychologists tend to assume that scientific explanatory structures are of the axiomatic-deductive kind, whereas humanistic psychologists adopt a looser notion of what an explanatory system looks like.

R. P. KELVIN: I am appalled by the damage which has been done by the very concept of 'models of man' (see pp. 345-347). I believe that the notion itself is responsible for the dichotomy between mechanism and humanism, and this is an inherently fallacious, misleading and destructive way of looking at human behaviour. It arises from, if not ignorance, then ignoring the history of ideas. As long as we conceive some other field as the basis of a model, or set of models, of man, it will be the case that psychology is in a state of logical primitivism. To think in terms of models is primitive. We should look for the phenomena for which we have to find an account. The real problem is to try to understand how a biological and physical system can lead to the messy kind of organism and social system which gives rise to historical and social patterns and forces. The argument between humanism and mechanism is a nonsense.

G. THINES: In my opinion it is wrong to think in terms of an opposition in <u>methods</u> between 'humanistic' and 'mechanistic' psychology. There are questions posed which deal with man's images of his own destiny: those are different from 'scientific' questions, but they are psychological questions. Some such questions may, of course, become 'scientific'.

L. SMITH: Yes: there need be no conflict between the humanists and mechanists. The humanists are bringing forward ever-better phenomena - redescribing and refining - using intentional concepts which one hopes will eventually be couched in terms of theory.

I. VINE: In the case of phenomena described by humanists, there is much more reliance on the coherence theory of truth. In more traditional, natural law phenomena, one can adhere more to the correspondence theory.

R. P. KELVIN: It is unfortunate that we do not have available systematic data collected over a period of time. Until we have such data, there will be whole dimensions of human behaviour to which we will not have systematic access. With those data, some answers, which at the moment are described as intentional, metaphysical or whatever, might actually be amenable to some kind of archival verification.

N. E. WETHERICK: How do you decide what kind of data to collect?

R. P. KELVIN: Well, sometimes, by simply having a look. Take unemployment. We have negligible systematic data. So we cannot answer even simple hypotheses, such as, 'do attitudes to unemployment change as unemployment increases?' We need content analyses of archival evidence.

K. D. DUNCAN: As an applied psychologist, it seems to me that anyone who does not work with contrived tasks is very vulnerable to having their reports questioned. But, of course, the design of tasks affects the eventual generality and applicability of the results. It is only latterly that ethological studies, which have attempted to examine non-contrived situations systematically, have made any advances in psychology. These strike me as being rich for hypothesis generation. Experiments, on the other hand, are powerful when it comes to hypothesis-testing.

J. A. GRAY: I should like to propose a short, provocative, empirical generalization: there exists a strong negative correlation between the amount of time spent talking about models and theories and the amount of construction of actual models and theories. That is observable across time and people within professions, and across institutions generally. It is not yet a well-verified generalization!

A. STILL: Maybe we would save a lot of time if we thought about how to determine ways of deciding between models (see paper 5).

J. A. GRAY: My impression is that there are fields of psychology in which rapid advances <u>are</u> being made, and they are the fields in which people are not asking themselves questions about what ought to be the criteria for models and theories. Instead those people are busy dismissing models that have not worked and then substituting better ones. They are not asking metatheoretical questions.

J. GREENE: I do not see any reason why one necessarily has to make a choice between models. You have to choose to work within a general theoretical framework (e.g. information processing) and you have to choose between mini-models within that framework, but in so doing you do not have to dismiss other approaches to psychology.

A. STILL: But a whole conceptual framework may be wrong.

J. A. GRAY: Yes. It can be logically inconsistent in terms of its own axioms; and it can generate untestable theories ...

N. E. WETHERICK: And it can fail to apply to its subject matter.

P. HERRIOT: One of the major criteria by means of which we choose at the macro-theoretical level has to do with the range of human activities about which we hope to talk. Actually we have barely begun to look at the diversity of human activity.

H. J. EYSENCK: I think we are running away with ourselves and using the term 'model' very loosely. For example, we have been calling Artificial Intelligence a 'model' when it is nothing of the kind: it is a 'tool'. You should be able to construct a model, and you cannot construct AI.

A. STILL: I agree that computing is used as a tool, but Margaret Boden in my view has presented a computational model. Man operates computationally: a theory was stated in computational terms.

J. GREENE: No. We may have theories of self, of memory, of perception, and so forth, using AI to make them more specific and possibly more testable; but the model is not about Artificial Intelligence. I totally agree with Hans Eysenck about that.

P. B. WARR: To me AI would be a paradigm.

B. FLETCHER: And to me a model is a tool!

K. D. DUNCAN: I am sympathetic to the notion of hierarchy introduced here by Peter Warr. It seems to me that if we adopt, from the top level, a single conceptual framework (perhaps related to natural selection, for example), then this could pay handsome dividends. But the danger is that it could rule out, at the lower levels, lots of things we ought to be looking at. Operating at a higher level has important consequences for specifying what the lower-order components amount to. Unless you operate in that way, however, you do not know whether you are being efficient or not. The progress from Hullian research, for example, has indeed been massive, but it might have taken place more quickly if the problems had been formulated at a higher level.

P. KLINE: May I point out that psychoanalytic theory seems to fit very precisely the kind of prescriptions we have heard from Peter Warr. At the top there is a metatheory - the psychoanalytic theory in general. From it, you can derive a whole subseries of theories, many of which are testable and have been tested.

R. L. REID: What I have to say supports Jeffrey Gray, but perhaps only up to a point - the point where things start to go wrong. When research is progressing well, the last thing you want to be doing is to be thinking of the whole general framework: you just plough ahead with experiments. When they go badly, you wonder about changing gear, and then you have to look up and try to get a better conception of what you are doing.

J. A. GRAY: I am entirely with you on that.

N. E. WETHERICK: What has not been recognized is that an experiment is not a path to knowledge unless it is combined with a phenomenological analysis.

G. THINES: A good epistemology must be heuristic and must be predictive, and what is needed for a good psychology is the minimum of philosophizing. You see, the origins of a question may not become apparent to the psychological researcher until late in the day, and that is all to the good.

H. J. EYSENCK: I believe it is useful to think about models. If you do not have an explicit philosophy then you have an implicit one; and the same goes for models of man. And an implicit model of man can be very damaging if you do not know what you are doing. For the last 30 years the Zeitgeist has produced a model of man which is entirely abiological, which leaves out genetic factors, and which is entirely socially oriented; but the people who work that model are entirely unconscious of so doing, and their research cannot answer the type of questions which I think should be answered.

H. WEINREICH-HASTE: Are we confusing models of science and models of person? We should try to tease out our implicit assumptions about the nature of the person and our implicit assumptions about what are legitimate and effective ways of doing research. As it is, there are examples of people doing essentially mechanistic-type research in humanistic fields and humanistic-type research in mechanistic fields.

D. H. HARGREAVES: I think that one descriptive point that Kuhn makes is that when science is proceeding normally the philosophers of science are ignored. When crisis occurs between paradigms it is then that their views are sought. It is perfectly clear that some people here are in crisis - others not! The others then are with us under sufferance to some degree, and they are saying, 'what is all the fuss about?' Those in crisis are saying, 'Come on, let's get some philosophizing done'.

J. GREENE: Even if all the theories from one approach - or model of man - appear to be true, that approach could still not illuminate every psychological aspect of man.

J. A. GRAY: If you are saying that the normal methods of scientific investigations do not apply in certain branches of psychology - and that is certainly what appears to have been claimed by some people here - then I await evidence of that. I also await evidence that there are any methods, other than the normal methods of science, for producing publicly agreeable theories.

C. I. HOWARTH: I should like to hear some more discussion about the nature of refutation. We ought to discuss what 'refutation' means, and perhaps we should begin by acknowledging that at the outset we need to delineate and clarify the data which a theory is expected to encompass. Jeffrey Gray claims, for example, that John Shotter's theory cannot be refuted because it is descriptive rather than explanatory or predictive. This may appear to be true if we use a very narrow focus. But large-scale theories are not refuted by detailed empirical evidence. They are judged by their success in relating a wide range of different phenomena and activities. In their own terms they may be as vulnerable to evidence as any scientific theory, and it is not without significance that John Shotter has changed his mind several times in the past 15 years. During that time Jeffrey Gray's ideas have remained relatively static. This is not a criticism of either of them. The kinds of small-scale theory favoured by Gray and others are refutable only in the small scale. The larger framework within which the theories are formulated are too vague to be easily testable. When someone like Shotter attempts to clarify ideas on a larger scale it is inevitably difficult to test them in relation to evidence at a microscopic level. In terms of refutability it is not at all clear who are the 'good guys' and who are the 'bad guys'.

R. HARRE: One has to acknowledge that the nature of falsification is quite different depending upon the nature of the theory which you are operating under. If a theory has a well-established deductive structure, then the refutatory process is roughly speaking logical: it is shown that an element in the deductive structure is false, but the particular element is not identified. That applies to what we have been calling 'mini-theories'. More interesting are theories which contain a double-analogy structure. These theories are not deductively related to their consequences; as I have explained (chapter 14) they do nevertheless provide a conceptual system in terms of which we can understand events.

M. JAHODA: One must always bear in mind that it is refutability in the theoretical formulation which is crucial. It cannot be expected that any individual should devote his efforts to refuting his own theory.

H. WEINREICH-HASTE: I cannot think of any theory in psychology which has been refuted by anyone at all, let alone its creator.

R. HARRE: Survival by a thousand qualifications is what goes on. Cognitive dissonance theory provides a beautiful example of that.

R. L. REID: Surely, at some point, we would say that we have a different theory; and, in any case, it is quite proper that we should move forward step by step.

R. HARRE: Indeed yes, but I am saying that has nothing to do with the logic of the process.

B. FLETCHER: At least some theories are probabilistic in nature, and you can say that these are verified as long as tests of those theories are positive more than 50 per cent of the time.

C. I. HOWARTH: Yes, Fisherian statistics are better at refuting theories than establishing their truth. I like Bayesian statistics because they are intended to compare the likelihood ratio of the probability of two different sorts of theories being correct.

B. FLETCHER: So, we should be more concerned with the nature of the distribution of probability that we are talking about.

C. I. HOWARTH: Exactly so.

K. J. GERGEN: I am not certain that is possible to think in terms of refutation or falsification of any theory if that theory is looked at as an abstract system for which there are no obvious exemplars; and I think that most behavioural theories are looked at in that way. We can negotiate the meaning of any particular observation in virtually any direction - so we have theories of aggression - but we can never be certain that we have identified a particular act of aggression. In effect any theory can be sustained so long as you have a capable negotiator of reality - in such a way that you can get people to agree that the analysis is plausible.

S. G. STRADLING: I think we are overlooking three vital points. Kenneth Gergen has just touched upon the problem of classification: the first stage in any science is the classification of phenomena under investigation - psychology has singularly failed to do that. That is my first point. Secondly, surely the basic, defining characteristic of the scientific method is not testability but replicability. Thirdly, if logic plays no part in the construction of modes - if we have not yet refuted anything, but theories are discarded - then what process have we employed?

I. VINE: Perhaps we are focusing on the wrong issues. The point is surely that our subject, psychology, must do justice to human beings first. We can worry about precise methodologies later.

D. B. BROMLEY: The word 'model' has been used in all kinds of different ways in our proceedings - at least eight, by my count. The word has been used: (1) to refer to some kind of conceptual framework, like Darwinism; (2) to refer to a methodological framework, like factor analysis or computer simulation; (3) to talk about ideologies where facts and values are mixed up; (4) to pick out single facets of interest in human behaviour, like socialization or decision-making; (5) to talk about middle-range theories, like Dr Broadbent's Maltese cross, which at least have the advantage of presenting some kind of rational analysis into which empirical findings are embedded; (6) to refer to simple analogies; (7) to refer even to the kinds of psychological processes that go on when people are making models, and that includes the models as they have come up in the history and philosophy of science; and (8) as a checklist for doing good research. That leads me to think that debates of the kind at this Conference may not be altogether desirable. They tend to lead to polarization. Of course the speakers' papers were precirculated in full, but I am inclined to think that to get anywhere in science one has to sit down with the actual arguments set out briefly and succinctly on paper. Then, step-by-step, you have to work through the fine detail of the arguments. When this is done you often find that half the argument is missing: one is being presented with an incomplete model. Also this process allows you to pursue the methodological ramifications and so forth.

R. L. REID: Yes, arguments about 'behaviourists', 'humanists', 'mechanists', 'existentialists' and so on are futile unless you specify what you mean by those terms.

N. M. CHESHIRE: I agree very much with Professor Reid: debates cast in terms of '-isms' can be fruitless. Also, I agree with Professor Bromley: we should look at particular instances of issues if we are to make genuine progress. I think that there would be fair agreement that a debate that has recurred here has concerned the reconciliation of the 'Nottingham School', on the one hand, and advocates of the 'scientific method', on the other. I agree with Dr Gray that maybe the 'Nottingham School' would be more fruitful if it did have some theoretical underpinning. Now, it does strike me that there are psychodynamic theories, of a developmental sort, which have relevant characteristics (see pp. 356-358).

G. JAHODA: Let me outline some prejudices which I have heroically refrained from voicing until now. I have two points, and the first is the more specific. It is that in constructing models which apply to a particular domain it is very often assumed that the kinds of behaviours that we are analysing are universal. But cross-cultural psychologists have been able to show that this is not invariably the case. I won't pursue that point here. My broader point is that in several of the models presented there have been either misconceptions/over-simplifications or concealed cultural assumptions; and these would be worth pointing to. I would begin by distinguishing between 'culture' and 'Culture' (see pp. 336-339).

P. KLINE: I want to put the case of a psychometric model of man (see pp. 322-328) ... Second, we have had an amazing fascination with Artificial Intelligence. We have been told by Margaret Boden and other proponents that one of the really important features of AI is that things have to be written down in computer language. But what is so special about computer language? Why should such a language be better than languages developed over thousands of years? Well, the answer is that huge areas of human experience are left out; but that, of course, is a complaint levelled against behaviouristic psychology!

D. WALLIS: I would want to endorse Paul Kline's appeal for a wider consideration of psychometric models. But my chief concern relates to the choice of criteria for judging between models (see pp. 340-342).

D. E. BROADBENT: What John Clark said earlier (e.g. see p. 212) about block diagrams is perfectly true: on the blackboard, they are static, and almost any process could be going on. There is a sense in which this issue (and similar issues) is the cause of this Conference: there is a communication problem. It is an even worse problem than he implied. For example, if you write out one flow chart that would merely be the way that the model would operate on a single set of circumstances. If, for instance, you used production systems (as do many AI workers) you would have many possible sequences of operation within that. How can you possibly summarize them all? The list of the productions that a computer has in long-term memory allows an almost infinite number of flow diagrams within a single block diagram. It is very difficult for a human being to grasp that. So in parallel with Rom Harré's excellent idea about looking at the possible consequences of the development of psychological notions in the culture, I believe we need some work on how we understand complex systems. That is necessary if we are to understand people; after all, they are complex systems. All too often one looks at a static expression of a system without understanding the dynamic sequence that will result from it. Of course this means that we have to struggle, to negotiate, and so on; and I am sure that this Conference has been a great help getting us a little further along that way.

A. P. BAILLIE: Professor Wright's comments about Piaget (see pp. 313-317) offer an interesting perspective on the proceedings of this Conference. Many problems raised here have been taken to be problems arising from adopting different models of man; but Piaget's position would argue that they arise from different theories of knowledge. Perhaps, therefore, the Conference should have been entitled 'Models of Knowing'. Communication might be facilitated if the various issues were examined from that perspective.

D. S. WRIGHT: I agree. A missing element in our discussion has been any attempt to explain the fact of what we are doing here. Man is a model-maker and we have not tried to deal with that. Piaget's epistemic model would be helpful if we did try to do so.

Section II

Discussants' and Chairmen's commentaries

Epistemic and moral man, Piagetian style

D. S. Wright

We have been well taught to be scathing of untestable theories. The favoured target has of course been Freud. I have heard it argued that not only is Freudian theory untestable but the evidence does not support it either. The fact that some of us can agree with that argument points up the fact that the testability of a theory is a variable, not some kind of absolute characteristic. I think I would want to say of Piagetian theory that though, like all 'grand designs', it is basically untestable, yet there is a good deal of evidence to support it. Now if Freud is these days of historical interest only, some of us are still in the process of digesting Piaget - and getting ulcers as a result. And it hardly seems fair in a conference on models of man that his point of view should not have at least a footnote. For at the very least he has drawn attention to certain phenomena which have been somewhat ignored and provided a language, of sorts, to talk about them.

Of course he has done much more than that. In his recent monographs he has given tentative expression to what might perhaps not unjustly be called a vision of man and his place in nature, a vision which appears to have been present throughout his adult life. Let me give a short account of what I understand to be the heart of that vision, and then turn, with it in mind, to moral development, an aspect of development he has left in a very undeveloped state.

The main thrust of Piaget's work has been to chart the development of epistemic man - a curiously bloodless creature, defined, minimally, as the centre of functional activity, where the activity concerned is cognitive construction, or knowing. Of course it is not as simple as that, for in Piaget's terms knowing is a kind of doing, and doing a kind of knowing. In these terms, the amoeba has some knowledge of what is good for it, though presumably it does not know that it knows. In the evolutionary as well as the developmental sense, know-how precedes knowing. Piaget's declaration of the continuity between the knowledge implicit in overt action and representational knowing involves an extension of the concept of knowledge which raises problems, but we will not linger on them now.

It is convenient to begin the story at its end, developmentally speaking, for this is the point where, historically, Piaget appears to have begun, namely the distinction between necessary truths and contingent or empirical truths. As Piaget rounds off his system it becomes clear that of the two it is the former which is the more significant for his theory. The points about necessary truths that are relevant to Piaget are as follows. (1) They are generated by self-contained systems of 'pure thought', the systems axiomatically based on mathematics and propositional logic. (2) Though these systems have been enormously productive of empirical knowledge when applied to empirical problems, they are not themselves derived from empirical knowledge - though of course their construction may be stimulated by empirical problems. That is to say they are not learned from the world about us but are the instruments of our understanding of that world. Matnematicians and logicians continue happily to develop their disciplines without reference to what the world is actually like. (3) According to Piaget these systems or structures are capable of indefinite development by virtue of the process of their creation, reflective abstraction, a process to which I return. (4) These structures are so to speak eternally true and stable, and when simpler structures are elaborated into more complex ones they do not lose their integrity but are reintegrated into more comprehensive systems. And lastly we might add that logicomathematical systems offer the inquiring mind an endless succession of moments of 'acquired self-evidence', those tremors of the mind at a fresh deduction, the excitements of perceived necessity - or as Freud might put it, the mini-orgasms of the intellect. Though quite properly and decently, Piaget stresses that such delights are empirically contingent upon the acquisition of operational structures in thinking.

So Piaget's problem is where do these logicomathematical systems come from. And even if that problem does not personally grab you, at least you may concede it is a problem. Indisputably they come from living organisms - even mathematicians and logicians are alive. But how come living organisms produce them, and how come, having produced them as it were independently of the real world, do they prove so useful in understanding that world?

May I first make a slight digression into one of the denser parts of the Piagetian jungle to draw attention to one of the many confusing circularities in Piagetian thought. If logicomathematical systems are highly effective tools of empirical investigation, then we might expect Piaget to use these tools in empirically investigating how they came to be created. But as far as I can see this is not what he does. To make clear what he does do it is useful to follow him in clearly separating two things. There is first M, by which he means the consciously and collectively created systems of mathematics and logic which are in the intellectual sense objectively self-subsistent. Then there is G, by which he means those structures inferred to be present in the actual thinking of people (or indeed in the instinctual know-how of animals). What Piaget then does is use M, or more accurately certain general features of M, as his formal model of G, his means of characterizing or representing G. But M is the product of G, and produced by the process of reflective abstraction. Now the point about reflective abstraction is that it is thought which learns not from studying the empirical world but from studying itself. In conscious thinking what we are aware of in some degree is the functioning of the underlying structures, not of those structures themselves, for these are in effect defined as the organized and systematic aspects of the cognitive unconscious. Reflective abstraction is the process whereby we consciously create, by thinking about thinking, new and conscious structures of thought which literally reflect or are isomorphic with, the unconscious operational structures. But this new conscious thought presupposes its own unconscious operational structures, which in turn can be consciously reflected or realized, and so on ad infinitum - hence the potential limitlessness of mathematics. In brief, M is used as a formal model of G on the one hand, and on the other M is said to be created by G consciously realizing itself. The circle seems complete. (Is there anything wrong with circles?)

But if this is crudely how Piaget accounts for how mathematicians make mathematics, we still have to look at his account of how people become mathematicians.

Piaget's account of the development of formal operations is now very familiar. My present concern is only with this process as it relates to logicomathematical knowledge. It embodies his central psychological, or perhaps better biological, doctrine.

This doctrine asserts that the operational structures, G, the reflective abstraction of which constitutes M, are not acquired from the environment in the sense of learned from it. However far back down the ontogenetic scale (indeed phylogenetic scale) we go, knowledge of the environment, whether perceptual and figurative, operational, or instinctual know-how, is always the assimilative functioning of a system or structure. And the development of these structures, though stimulated by non-balance induced by the need to accommodate to the environment, is itself a function of equilibration processes inherent in the systems or structures themselves. It is this equilibrating characteristic of structures which always brings to the knowledge of the environment, at whatever level, an element that is not present in it. They always, so to speak, go beyond the given in assimilating it. As he looks back down the development process Piaget finds at every turn evidence of the partial isomorphisms, in the most general and formal sense, between the structures that know and logicomathematical systems - for example in the perceptual constancies, in a two-year-old child's ability to move freely and in coordinated fashion about a room, in the sensorimotor beginnings of the conservation of the object, and beyond that in physiological organization.

At the same time he wants to reject the idea that the structural development which culminates in formal operations is genetically determined in the sense of being a function of information encoded on genes. At this point he takes up Waddington's claim that the genotype itself is a system, and that genetic transmission cannot be understood as the transmission of a sort of aggregate of informational units, but only as the functioning of a self-conserving system, the formal properties of which, of course, can be understood in logicomathematical terms. Thus in addition to the transmission of genetic information there is also, as it were in the nature of things, the absolute continuity of the organizing function - everything exists in systems. You trace mathematical knowledge back to its roots by tracing back the development of the form or structure or systems character of the subject who has it.

It is not my purpose here either to bury Piaget or to praise him - though the more you examine this account of his the more it exhibits in complex form the kind of circularity I mentioned earlier. But at the beginning I used the word 'vision', and it is appropriate to sum all this up in suitably romantic and visionary language (surely a man who spent nearly 70 years on the same problem is a romantic visionary at heart!). One could say that in logicomathematical knowledge, nature, through man, consciously realizes the formal properties of its own structures, and in the process makes possible both on the one hand an ever-widening empirical knowledge of itself, and on the other extends those structures in forms which may have no empirical embodiment but which, in the intellectual sense, are immune from the decay and death organic structures are subject to. And that is either a revelation or a resounding platitude - or perhaps both. Either way it is the detail that counts, and I have no choice but to ignore that here.

With that I want to turn to the question of moral development to point out a job which waits to be done. It is to supplement Piaget's account of epistemic man with an equally detailed account of moral man in his terms. Piaget has of course already given the briefest of sketches of what might be involved in such an undertaking. But there seem to be several reasons why it might be worth while to build upon his beginning. In the first place Piaget's speculations in this area have been largely neglected. Interest in his monograph on the moral judgement of the child has focused mainly upon his pilot empirical work. Then Piaget's own conceptual scheme seems to need such exploration for its completion. He has repeatedly emphasized the importance of social interaction for cognitive development, and at least implicitly he acknowledges that subjects form relationships with other subjects which themselves can be regarded as systems - one aspect of which is the moral rules which conserve, regulate and develop them. If Piaget's main work has been to show how the subject realizes his own structure in logicomathematical knowledge and utilizes this for understanding his world, then to complete the story it would seem necessary to examine in similar terms the systematic relatedness of subjects with each other. Thirdly, what has been called the cognitive developmental approach to moral development, which is mainly associated with Kohlberg, has tended to ignore mainstream Piagetian theory and perhaps as a consequence has run into problems which it could have avoided.

All I can do here is to resurrect three themes (I hope not hares) which Piaget started and never pursued. They are the issues of theoretical and practical morality, personal relationships, and conscious realization or prise de conscience.

Kohlberg's cognitive developmental approach has been criticized for its inadequate treatment of affect and action. With Piaget the issue is a good deal less clear cut. In the first place cognitive structures are said to be structures of action. Then his treatment of affect is somewhat ambiguous. In some places he talks of emotions as forming structures and in doing so becoming the will. At other times he asserts that affect and cognition are two sides of the same coin, that there is never one without the other. Affect creates value, cognition creates knowing, and knowing is always value laden. In his study of moral development he sets out explicitly to explain the roots of moral obligation. The young child delights in regularities. When these regularities are social, and especially when they are contained within relationships of respect, they begin to be experienced as obligatory. When these regularities are cognitively structured as rules, they are from the start charged with obligation. Extrapolating beyond Piaget we might say that, cognitive structures, when operational, generate logical, deductive compulsion, so when the subject enters the two-person relationship system he begins to experience moral compulsion or obligation, the strength of this moral obligation presumably depending upon the stability and involvement in the relationship system. That explanation is at least simpler than one that invokes Oedipal complexes, repression and mental organs like the super-ego.

As everyone knows, Piaget proposes a dimension along which relationship systems vary from unilateral respect at one end to mutual respect at the other. Though these terms remain obscure and undefined, there are several points to be made about them. First, we are here talking about personal relationships rather than role relatedness - or, given the ubiquitous and promiscuous use of the concept 'role', the personal dimension of role-relatedness. Then, second, despite the persisting tendency for people to equate unilateral with child-adult relationships, and mutual respect with peer relationships, Piaget explicitly rejects this equation. For him they are conceptually idealized ends of a continuum which is conceptually independent of, though it may be empirically correlated with, status difference. Third, relationships of unilateral respect are inherently unstable systems and tend always to move towards the equilibrium of mutual respect. Just as the developmental equilibration of cognitive structures is central to the development of necessary and contingent knowing, so the progressive equilibration of relationships is at the heart of moral development, though the equilibration process may be more fraught with problems.

Piaget draws a distinction between constitutive and constituted rules. Constitutive rules refer to the structural features of the relationship itself. Constituted rules refer to those manifest in the functioning of the relationship. The parallel in epistemic development for constitutive rules are the unconscious cognitive structures, for constituted rules the parallel is the functioning of those structures in conscious thinking and knowing. In the case of relationships of unilateral respect the constituted rules derive from one party to the relationship only and are accepted and submitted to by the other; in mutual respect relationships, the constituted rules are arrived at by negotiation and mutual consent.

However, the real thrust of development in the individual is through the processes of conscious realization and reflective abstraction which are intrinsic to constructive equilibration. Piaget proposes the formula that theoretical, or consciously held, morality is the conscious realization of practical morality. This can be restated in the following way. The equilibration process in moral development is a function of the progressive conscious realization of the constitutive rules that structure relationship. In the case of unilateral respect relationships, especially in their extreme form, the constitutive rules assert that one party is the source of and authority on morality and that the other is the submissive recipient, and therefore that the moral judgements and thinking of the recipient are of no value. The inherent instability of this relationship lies in the fact that as the recipient consciously realizes these constitutive rules they begin to conflict with his valuing of his own thinking, his self-respect if you like, an autonomy of thinking manifest in the conscious realization itself. Such instability is reinforced to the extent to which the individual also experiences relationships of mutual respect, the constitutive rules of which imply that both parties to the relationship are equally respect-worthy and equally valued as sources of moral judgement and thinking.

The concept of 'relationships of mutual respect' is an idealized one; actual relationships only approximate to it in varying degrees. But the experience of such relationships, and the conscious realization of their constitutive rules makes possible a more idealized concept of their nature and the formalization of their rules in terms of natural justice, truth telling and the like. Since rooted in real relationships, these principles carry with them their value charge, and become the morality of the good.

As I said, this paper is a kind of footnote. So much more needs to be said. But my purpose is very modest. To remind you that Piaget exists, and also, perhaps, remind you that he is worthy of attention.

Paper 2

Criteria for consciousness: The soul in the spinal cord revisited

J. A. Gray

Behind the innocuous title of this Conference, 'Models of man', there lurks, I suspect, the oldest and thorniest of psychological problems: that of the relation between mind and brain. I am not so foolhardy as to address that problem with any hope of contributing to its solution. The purpose of this paper is more modest: to draw attention to a controversy which occupied the attention of physiologists during the 18th and 19th centuries, and which still has some lessons for us today. This controversy was about the criteria one should use for the attribution of consciousness to an organism - or rather to a part of an organism. The debate concerned spinal reflex action.

Anyone who has wrung a chicken's neck has seen spinal reflex action. That is to say, they have seen that the spinal cord can control integrated patterns of movement in the absence of the brain. More formal observations, entering this fact into the records of science, were reported by Robert Whytt in Edinburgh in 1751, though he used frogs. In the next century Marshall Hall (1790-1857) demonstrated in the spinal cord centres of nervous control (besides the bundles of nerves travelling to and from the brain which, in the dominant view of the time, were all that the cord contained). But, having shown that the cord can integrate reflex action on its own, without the brain, what inferences shall we draw about the locus of consciousness or mind? Shall we allocate these mysterious entities to the brain and the spinal cord, to the brain but not the spinal cord, or to neither?

This debate, difficult enough in its own right, was made worse by the fact that much of the discussion was in French or German. In neither of these languages do the key terms (l'âme and die Seele) make the invaluable English distinction between 'soul' and 'mind'. Thus the protagonists in the debate described the central issue as that of the existence, or otherwise, of a 'soul in the spinal cord', no less. In English, it is easier to keep psychology and physiology separate from theology. We find it safer, therefore, if less dramatic, to think of this question with 'mind' or 'consciousness' substituted for 'soul'; though there is no doubt that the actual course of the discussion over the years was strongly influenced by theological considerations.

The out-and-out materialist answer to the question, 'where is the mind?', is 'nowhere'. But the first materialist move was to take mind away from the newly discovered centres of nervous control in the spinal cord. Whytt had drawn the opposite inference from his experiments on spinal reflexes: he had concluded that the mind might be everywhere in the body. At the same time, however, he emphasized the distinction between voluntary movements, said to be dependent on the brain and will, and involuntary movements, which were automatic and dependent on the spinal cord alone.

Hall, in the next century, agreed that spinal reflexes were involuntary and automatic, but added that they were independent of feeling and consciousness. Hall's view was in turn attacked by the German physiologist Pflüger (1829-1910), who argued that consciousness is a function of all nervous activity, in the cord as well as in the brain. If, he said, you divide the spinal cord of a cat into two parts, the cat acquires two 'souls'. Liddell, writing in 1960 about these beliefs of Pflüger's is scornful, as would have been the majority of 20th century scientists or philosophers. Yet, shortly after, exactly the same problem re-emerged in modern guise with reports of the 'split-brain' operation carried out in human beings for the treatment of epilepsy. In this operation, the commissures (bundles of nerve fibres) connecting the left and right halves of the brain are severed. It then turns out that the two halves of the brain can (under appropriate experimental conditions) each separately carry out very complex functions of which the other half apparently remains unaware. What do we do now? Do we say that there are 'two foci of consciousness' (the modern equivalent of 'two souls'); or treat one half of the brain (no doubt, the speechless one, normally on the right) as 'merely reflex', and the other as the only conscious one?

These issues are too important to be left to the ebb and flow of fashionable belief. Criteria are needed by which to distinguish the conscious from the unconscious. The controversy between Pflüger and Hall cast up some suggestions for such criteria. Pflüger defended his own position by pointing to the purposeful nature of spinal reflexes. After decapitation, a frog's leg will scratch the exact point where its skin is irritated by the application of acid. Only a few years later, in the monograph 'Reflexes of the Brain' (1863), that was to make such a profound impression on the young Pavlov, the Russian physiologist Sechenov turned Pflüger's argument on its head and treated purposiveness as the veritable hallmark of reflex action. He defined involuntary (i.e. reflex) movements as follows: 'Involuntary movements are always expedient. By means of these movements the animal tries to prolong a pleasant sensory stimulation or attempts to eliminate the stimulus by avoiding it.' There can be little doubt that, at least under some circumstances, Sechenov's move is descriptively correct: what is there more purposeful than the reflex movement by which the hand is withdrawn from the flame, an example already used in the 17th century by Descartes? And the development of cybernetics and the engineering of control systems has provided a lucid mechanistic account of how this can be so.

If reflexes are purposive, purpose cannot be used to distinguish reflex from non-reflex action. The next move tried during the 19th century was Lotze's proposal that, while reflexes are apparently purposeful in a normal environment, they do not adapt to changing circumstances. Only consciousness, according to Lotze, can enable action to go beyond reflexes by adapting to change. But it was then demonstrated by Auerbach that adaptation to change can occur in a decapitated frog. In this experiment, Auerbach amputated one of the frog's legs. If acid was not applied to the flank on the side of the missing leg, the remaining leg made only ineffectual efforts to remove the acid. Its reflex function was apparently confined to its own side of the body. Now, however, Auerbach made a slight change in the conditions of the experiment. He put a drop of acid on both sides of the frog's body. The result was that the one remaining leg swung up and removed first the acid on its own side, and then the acid on the opposite side of the body. Here was good evidence for the capacity of a reflex to adapt to changed circumstances - the loss of one leg - provided the conditions were right.

It was, however, Pavlov's discovery of the conditioned reflex which finally disposed of Lotze's proposal. The conditioned reflex is nothing if not adaptation to a changing environment. If conditioned reflexes do not require consciousness, then consciousness is not necessary for adaptive behaviour.

But perhaps conditioned reflexes do require consciousness. The conditioned reflex is, after all, very different in some respects from the simple spinal reflex with which we - and the history of our problem - began. And it gets even more different when Pavlov (like Sechenov before him) treats all behaviour that is not a spinal reflex as a conditioned reflex or 'reflex of the brain'. The term 'reflex', whether conditioned or not, calls forth the image of a slot machine, or of the mechanical toys which first inspired Descartes' mechanistic theories of the behaviour of animals: insert an appropriate stimulus and the corresponding response fatally occurs. But there is much in common experience that this image fits badly, if at all. We all know what it is to think about what to do, solve a problem, make a decision, and so on. This kind of behaviour not only does not feel like a reflex, it is precisely in opposition to it that we recognize as reflex a blink of the eye or a sneeze in sudden sunlight. Tell us that both kinds of behaviour are reflex, and we feel puzzled. And, if we believe that there is a non-material world to which mind gives access, a world perhaps charged with spiritual significance, the puzzle may become outrage or panic.

We must consider seriously, therefore, whether the conditioned reflex ought really to be regarded as a reflex at all. Is it, say, the same sort of thing as the jerk of the knee which follows a tap on the patellar tendon?

At one level we shall only be able to answer this question when we have fully understood the neural machinery which controls both kinds of reaction, conditioned and unconditioned reflexes. But a little thought shows that the conditioned reflex is indeed, for the purpose of the present argument, a reflex. When my mouth waters at the sight of my favourite dish, or even at the thought of it, I do not ponder whether or not to salivate, I just salivate. It is for this reason that conditioning techniques are so successful when applied to neurotic behaviour. For the hallmark of this kind of behaviour is that the patient cannot deliberately do anything about it. He knows that it is absurd to fear a cat, but the fear comes anyway. That is why he needs therapy.

Pavlov, then, was justified in aligning the conditioned reflex with the spinal reflexes described in the previous century. Certainly, there must be important differences in the detailed machinery by which the two kinds of reflex work; and Pavlov spent much of his scientific life attempting to discover those differences. But the conditioned reflex does not require consciousness or volition, any more than the unconditioned kind. So adaptation to change, the raison d'être of the conditioned reflex, is of no more value than purposiveness as a criterion of mind or soul.

By the time Pavlov had done his work, the soul in the spinal cord had been forgotten. Yet it should not have been. For, if none of the criteria that had been proposed as distinctive features of consciousness can in fact discriminate between spinal reflex action and the activity of the brain, one is left with two equally logical alternatives. One can decide, with Sechenov and Pavlov, that neither the spinal cord nor the brain possesses (what shall we say?) 'soul' - that will meet with the agreement of many; 'mind' - that will meet with the agreement of some; or 'consciousness' - that will meet with the agreement of hardly anyone, for we all know what consciousness feels like, when it is in the brain at least. But one can equally well decide, with Pflüger, that consciousness lies in the spinal cord, as well as in the brain.

This view has a less heretical sound about it now than it would have had two decades ago. For, in the interim, we have become familiar with the remarkable results of the split-brain operations performed in California and described by Gazzaniga in his book, 'The Bisected Brain'. Roughly speaking, when the commissures connecting the two cerebral cortices are divided, both half-brains can perform highly adaptive and purposeful behaviour, but only one of them has fully developed language capacities. And, furthermore, it is apparently possible for each half-brain to remain unaware of what its separated twin is doing. Faced with such extraordinary observations, the temptation is to call upon yet one more criterion for consciousness - that of language - in order to preserve the unity of consciousness. One could then say that the speaking, understanding half-brain is fully conscious, the other 'merely reflex'. But this move consigns all the animal kingdom (except perhaps Washoe and a few other fortunate, talking chimpanzees) to the outer, unconscious darkness. And this new division between the human species and all others must be regarded as unacceptable by any scientist who takes the theory of evolution seriously. There would seem little alternative, therefore, to the conclusion - difficult though it is to grasp - that the split-brain operation produces two foci of consciousness. But, if so, why not also a soul in the spinal cord?

Perhaps Pflüger was talking nonsense a century ago, and I am talking nonsense now. But the therapy that linguistic philosophy offers for this kind of nonsense has not yet convinced me that, behind the undoubted difficulties of grammar and vocabulary that abound in this field, there are not also real, empirical problems awaiting scientific theory and experiment for their solution (see Gray, 1971). Until we have some glimmer of understanding of how they might be solved, it is premature to construct anything so grandiose as a model of man.

NOTE

This paper is closely based on material contained in my book 'Pavlov' published in the United Kingdom by Fontana Books and in the USA by Viking Press (1979).

The psychometric model

P. Kline

In my view, the psychometric model presented in this paper is indubitably the most simple of all of the models discussed in this volume. Furthermore, unlike the majority of these models it can be (and has been) easily applied and, as we shall see, is able to predict behaviour with some degree of success.

THE BASIS OF THE MODEL

From the factoring of individual differences since the time of Spearman, it is generally agreed (a rarity in psychology) that three classes of factors have been revealed (e.g. Cattell, 1973) - abilities, temperamental traits, and dynamic traits. In addition more volatile mood and state factors have been found. Factors belonging to these different universes tend to be uncorrelated with each other.

The psychometric model claims that any given behaviour is a function of these ability, temperamental, dynamic and mood factors interacting with the particular stimulus situation. From this bare outline of the psychometric model it is clear that it is a variant of a trait model - that our behaviour is a function of our traits. The difference lies in the fact that the traits are specified and by definition quantified. They are specified in that the traits are those found most powerful in the sense of accounting for most variance through factor analysis, and they are quantified because, by virtue of their identification through factor analysis, they must have tests loading on them.

Definition of ability, temperament, dynamics and mood

Although there is little argument as to whether a factor belongs to one category or another, as Cattell & Warburton (1967) point out, rigorous definition is difficult. However, an operational approach which is effective defines an ability trait as a trait on which the population mean changes most (relative to the population variance) in accord with changes in the complexity of the environment. A dynamic trait changes most with changes in the incentive features of the environment, while a temperamental trait remains stable in the face of changes. States can be distinguished from temperamental traits which they resemble (e.g. anxiety) by their greater lability over time and by their emergence from P and Dr factor analysis the analysis of individuals over time and changes in scores between occasions). Traits, on the other hand appear only in R factor analysis (analysis of tests), as is fully discussed in Cattell & Kline (1977).

As can be seen, these operational definitions are rigorous, but at the same time they fit the tautologous, intuitive distinctions often used by psychologists, namely, that ability traits refer to what a person can do, temperamental traits to how he does it and dynamic traits to why. In addition such clear examples of each category as intelligence and numerical ability, anxiety and sexual drive fit the operational definitions. Such then are our reasons for categorizing traits into these spheres in the psychometric model: they are conceptually and statistically separate.

Choice of variables

An obvious objection to a general trait model is how is the decision to be made as to what traits to include. Do we include courage or bravery, or both, or are they synonymous? Do we include general intelligence and verbal ability; almost all would say 'yes'. But what about pea-pushing ability (beloved of Beachcomber) or the ability to gauge the ripeness of cheese?

The psychometric model (as defined here) based upon factor analysis overcomes these problems at a stroke because factor analysis is a statistical technique which selects out the most important variables. Since factor analysis, despite its long history in psychology, is still not well understood, at this point in my paper, let me summarize what is now generally agreed by experts in the field (e.g. Cattell, 1978; Nunnally, 1978) concerning the nature of factors, although, of course, only relevant points will be mentioned. A full discussion of these can be found in Kline (1979).

(1) Factors can be seen as fundamental dimensions underlying the variables which load on them. They can have causal status in some instances. These dimensions are constructs defined by their loadings.

(2) If, as in the psychometric model, factors are used as mapping devices, indicating the most important variables, it is essential that the universe of variables be properly sampled, as well as subjects.

(3) The problem that there is an infinity of solutions to a factor analysis, thus making it impossible to trust one rather than another, as opponents of the technique have claimed, can now be countered.

(4) The Thurstonian notion of simple structure deals with this difficulty, its rationale being that if each solution is regarded as a hypothesis to account for the observations, then the simplest is (Occam's Razor) the one to choose. Rotating to simple structure is, therefore, an application of one of the precepts of the scientific method.

(5) How rotation to simple structure is to be achieved is still to some extent a matter of debate. Nevertheless the main issue is clear.

(a) Either, as Thurstone (Thurstone, 1947) has advocated and Cattell has long supported, oblique factors can be obtained by maximizing the hyperplane count, that is the number of zero loadings in the hyperplanes of the factors. This produces factors with a few high loadings and the others negligible. Various objective computer programs can carry out this type of rotation; for example, direct oblimin (Jemrich & Sampson, 1966). Such simple structure solutions have been shown by Cattell (e.g. 1978) to be replicable and stable.

(b) The other approach is that of Guilford and his colleagues (e.g. Guilford, 1959). Guilford prefers orthogonal solutions, that is, with the factors uncorrelated. He argues that a set of uncorrelated albeit complex factors is more parsimonious than a set of correlated but simple factors. Ultimately this is a matter of scientific judgement. However, two points cause me to support Cattell's claims, one theoretical, the other empirical.

(6) First, it would seem unlikely that in the real world, fundamental, possibly causal dimensions, are uncorrelated. Thus an oblique solution is a priori more likely.

(7) Second, empirical criterion data in the real world have strongly supported some of the oblique factors in the Cattell systems, both in the ability and personality sphere (see Cattell & Kline, 1977, for a summary of this work). This is by no means the case with Guilford's orthogonal factors and the work of Horn & Knapp (1973) indicates that the ability factors of Guilford are indeed artifactual - of the Procrustes rotation program used in the research.

(8) From this we conclude that into the psychometric model should be inserted the main oblique factors in the various domains derived from investigations where simple structure was properly obtained.

(9) The choice of variables, therefore, can be made by sifting through factor analyses and extracting those factors which have been properly located in factor space. This means (a) that simple structure had been reached, (b) that variables and subjects had been fully sampled and (c) that marker variables were included in the study.

(10) This last is important. For example, a factor analysis can show clear simple structure, but the location of the emerging factors vis-à-vis E and N in the field of personality is essential if the factors are to be properly identified.

In summary, therefore, it can be said that the psychometric model will utilize the factors that have emerged as most important in the four spheres of ability, temperament, dynamics and mood. These factors will be those obtained in simple structure rotations.

A comment on simple structure

Whether simple structure is obtained or not depends not only on the proper rotational procedures. In addition as Cattell (1973) has stressed a number of other technical demands have to be met in the factor analysis. Highly important here are the numbers of factors rotated. Under-factoring can lead to the emergence at the first-order of what are really higher-order factors. Over-factoring, on the other hand, generally produces a solution that is not simple. Similarly the ratio of variable to subjects is important although there is little agreement what this should be. Guilford is the most liberal (Guilford, 1956) suggesting a ratio as low as 2:1. Nunnally (1978) the most severe - his claim is 10:1. Thus in examining research we must feel certain that the technical criteria for good factor analysis are met, if we are to utilize the results.

THE FACTORS IN THE MODEL

Precisely which are the most powerful factors in the different fields is still a matter of dispute, even though there is some agreement on some of the factors. In general the position can be thus summarized: the disagreements concern the stability and nature of the primary factors, that is the factors loaded on the psychometric tests. There is far less dispute concerning the higher-order factors, that is factors accounting for correlations between factors. Fluid ability and extraversion are typical higher-order factors.

Kline (1979) has attempted to clarify the position and has shown that in both the ability and temperament fields there are so many primaries that a workable useful model would involve so much testing time that it would not be viable. If a model were to be used for any practical purpose, higher-order factors would have to be used.

Thus in this paper, I insert into our psychometric model the best established higher-order factors in the various factorial domains. However, it must be understood that as psychometric research continues these factors are likely to be changed. Indeed this is one of the advantages of the model. Different combinations and sets of factors can be tried and those giving the best predictions can be retained until other new factors are shown to produce superior predictions. However, for the purposes of understanding the model, what particular factors are inserted is unimportant. In principle, we put in those that work best.

Ability factors

In a study which meets all the technical criteria for attaining sound, replicable simple structure and in which a wide variety of ability variables was sampled, Hakstian & Cattell (1974) obtained 19 factors and this by no means constitutes the total possible list. Second-order analysis of these factors (Horn & Cattell, 1966) reduces much of this ability variance to five factors and, these, we argue, constitute the ability variables that should go into the psychometric model. These are:

(1) gf: fluid intelligence, conceived of as basic reasoning ability.
(2) gc: crystallized intelligence, fluid intelligence as evinced in a culture.
(3) gv: visualization, the skill employed in tasks where this is helpful.
(4) gr: retrieval capacity or fluency, the ability stressed by Guilford in his well-known model.
(5) gs: cognitive speed, this is the speed in carrying out tasks, writing or collating data, for example.

It should be pointed out that these factors accord well with the experimental analysis of abilities carried out by Hunt (e.g. 1976) and his colleagues.

Temperamental factors

Kline (1979) found in his survey at least 100 factors with some degree of research support. However, careful study of investigations in which some of these variables were factored together and rotated to proper factor structure revealed the following second-orders and other factors to merit inclusion. The choice is somewhat arbitrary, although it has elsewhere been fully justified (Kline, 1979) and it is certainly the case that future research is likely to some extent to change our views. Indeed Barrett & Kline (in preparation) are engaged in exactly this - attempting to produce a reference set of temperament factors where the structure is replicable and which embrace almost all known factors. A pious research. Nevertheless the factors to be included in the model are:

(1) E: Exvia or extraversion. Too well known to merit comment, as is
(2) N: Neuroticism or anxiety.
(3) P: Psychoticism - toughness, lack of empathy, sensation-seeking.
(4) Cortertia: A Cattell second-order factor: the toughmindedness of William James.
(5) Obsessive traits: A factor which regularly appears and which no second orders seem to cover (see Pollak, 1979).
(6) Masculinity⎫ These are two factors which seem important and which as Kline &
(7) Femininity⎭   Storey (1978) showed were quite independent of the Eysenck and Cattell factors.

These variables would appear to cover the most important temperamental variance. However, as stated above, other than the first two factors, future research may well contraindicate all these variables.

Dynamic factors

The only serious factorial psychometric work here is by Cattell and colleagues at Illinois, summarized in Cattell & Child (1975). In this domain the second-order structure has not been explored with any precision and it would appear sensible to use in our model the most important ergs (basic drives) and sentiments (culturally moulded drives) as measured in the MAT test. The rationale for this, as we shall see, is that these variables do work in a specification equation. However, it must be stressed that with future research, many of the factors in this domain will be changed. The factors to be used are:

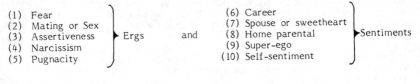

(1) Fear
(2) Mating or Sex
(3) Assertiveness   Ergs   and
(4) Narcissism
(5) Pugnacity

(6) Career
(7) Spouse or sweetheart
(8) Home parental   Sentiments
(9) Super-ego
(10) Self-sentiment

Moods and states

Factorial work in moods and states is far less advanced than in the previous domains so that a definitive list of factors in this area is not possible. However, Cattell & Kline (1977) were able to report that anxiety stage, stress, fatigue arousal and certain depressive moods seemed to be important.

It is to be noted that moods and states, transient and volatile compared with traits, are unlikely to be important in the prediction of long-term behaviours, for example, job success or academic performance. Of course, moods and states are important in the prediction of a discrete event, for example, behaviour at a party. However, from the viewpoint of our model, what is essential is that some measures of moods and states (at present far from ideal) go into the equation.

The situation

Mischel (1973) has tried to deny the importance of traits, a view which renders the psychometric model worthless, arguing that the situation determines our behaviour. However, more recently that extreme case has been withdrawn (Mischel, 1977), and he admits that there is an interaction between situation and individual, a statement with which the psychometric model is in full accord.

The situation in the psychometric model is dealt with in theory rather than in practice, for this is a new field of research. Thus it is assumed that for each mood or state there is a state liability trait and that there are individual differences in these state liability traits. This liability value is transformed by a modulator expressing the average stimulation of a given stimulus for a particular state. Thus, to take a somewhat pornographic example, it is assumed by most editors of magazines of this ilk, that the female pudenda with pubic hair have a high stimulus value for sex and that a 50 year old matron in twinset and pearls with a corgi and supermarket trolley has a low value, but chacun à son goût.

Thus the situation is dealt with in the model by developing situational indices to modulate state liability traits. At present little of the necessary situational measurement has been done so that the practical effects of such modulations on predictions has not yet been completed. We shall not include these, therefore, in our equations.

Two comments

(i) The psychometric model is a linear additive model. As Cattell (1973) has argued until the first simplistic model is shown not to fit the data, it would be unrealistic to try to develop one with more complex relationships.

(ii) Some of the values of the variables in the equation can be negative. Thus, if we were planning to do something about which we felt guilty, the super-ego and self-sentiment values would be negative. If these were sufficiently so, we would, of course, decide not to carry it out, as Macbeth said 'If 'twere done when 'tis done, then 'twere well it were done quickly'.

THE PSYCHOMETRIC MODEL

The psychometric model to be discussed is that proposed by Cattell, although it is so general that its provenance is not perhaps important. As I have argued, the terms to be inserted into it will be finally decided upon as research proceeds.

The basic equation

In the behavioural specification equation any act or behaviour is estimated for a given individual by taking his score on the major psychometric factors and weighting it according to its importance for the given criterion behaviour. Thus to estimate an individual's (i) behaviour (J), for example, being a successful physicist, the basic equation is:

$$a_{iJ} = b_{J1A}l_i + ... b_{JkA}k_i + b_{J1T}l_i + ... b_{JkA}k_i + b_{J1D}l_i + ... b_{JkD}k_i + b_{J1S}l_i ... + b_{Jk}s_{ki}$$

where A1-k are the K ability traits, in serial order, T1-k are the K temperamental traits in serial order, D1-k are the K dynamic traits in serial order, and the S1-k are the K states in serial order, (K, of course, can be a different value in each of these domains). The bs are the weights, obtained from factor analyses of the criterion behaviour and the variables. Thus, into this equation we should insert the results of factoring all the variables set out in our section, 'Choice of variables'.

This model we have referred to as the basic psychometric model, because as Cattell (1973) and Cattell & Child (1975) show it can be elaborated (a) to take into account the claimed integrative function of certain of the dynamic factors, such as the self-sentiment, and (b) as we have stated to compute the effects of the situation with state liability traits. However, these are Cattellian elaborations of the model, elaborations largely speculative and certainly with no empirical basis. Our purpose here is to present the psychometric model rather than a particular version of it, however brilliant.

It must not be thought that abandoning the state liability traits means that the psychometric model ignores the situation. In fact, the beta weights from the factor pattern do take this into account. Thus, if the behaviour is one where, for example, anxiety plays no part, its weight will be nil. This, of course, is not to say that the psychometric model will not be improved by proper measurement of situations and stimulus.

Test of the model

In this volume there is much debate about the problems of testing models, and generally, it would appear to be extremely difficult. Happily this is not the case with the psychometric model. If the model were perfect, we should obtain multiple correlations of 1 between the behaviour and the weighted variables in the equation. If we do not (and we do not!) then the fault must lie in the variables put into the model, the model itself or both. In fact, the only research done with this model is that carried out by Cattell and colleagues, work spread over nearly 40 years and fully summarized in Cattell & Kline (1977). Here we can find multiple correlations with varied criteria ranging from around 0.6 with educational achievement to around 0.2 or 0.3 with various different occupations. I shall not elaborate further on these results because (a) they were done with a set of variables in the model which reflect Cattell's natural predilection for his own tests and (b) because the full equation including all domains was not used.

CONCLUSIONS

However, the fact that any success was achieved at all enables us to draw the following conclusions. (1) The psychometric model of man does allow worth-while predictions of behaviours even when theoretically incomplete and when using a set of variables that may not be the best obtainable. (2) From this it follows that it is a model which cannot be dismissed as Harré did at this Conference by claiming that he does not believe in traits (p. 213). In fact, the success of the model supports traits and reduces the force of the situationalist argument. (3) Indeed it can be concluded that psychometrics is able to produce a model of man that enables practical and theoretical psychologists to advance knowledge systematically. A great research task lies ahead to identify the major variables in the domains, to quantify situations and stimuli and to improve our psychological and environmental measures, and always there is a criterion of how far we are succeeding - the rise and fall of our multiple correlations. In the light of this, to decry psychometrics is foolish and reports of its death are premature.

Homo temporalis

A. J. Lock

The 'hero' of Hermann Hesse's 'Steppenwolf' (1965) contends that were there an adequate psychology his story need never have been written. He goes on to characterize man as:

> an experiment and a transition. He is nothing else than the narrow and perilous bridge between nature and spirit. His innermost destiny drives him on to the spirit and to God. His innermost longing draws him back to nature, the mother. Between these two forces his life hangs tremulous and irresolute.

The chapters and discussions in this volume tend to vindicate the Steppenwolf's view. To take just two examples, the duality of nature and spirit is reflected in Reynold's realms of mechanism and 'moral autonomy' (chapter 3), and Shotter's two worlds of action (chapter 2). Here nature and spirit certainly receive their dues, yet one is left with the feeling that the motive for the telling of the Steppenwolf's tale still remains.

I will take two further words from the opening quotation to characterize briefly a developmental perspective on man: 'transition' and 'bridge'. It is not just man who must be characterized as a dual being, but every individual man. It is generally accepted that the roots of (our) reason are embedded in language: an ability we do not possess at birth. Without language we have no reason, we are children of nature, and are thus open to classical scientific investigation. When we have language, then maybe a different investigatory mould is required, for we are now children of the spirit.

But the individual himself makes the transition from the one form to the other; he is his own bridge, linking the two. He is Homo temporalis, developing from one mode to another, as if climbing the rungs of a ladder. Nothing emerges fully fledged, but each step grows from the last, progressively reaching 'higher and higher into the realms of abstraction' (cf. Romanes, 1887). Thus, neither mode of explanation will suffice, for the individual is not an either/or being, but a transitory one. And thus he requires a transitory, a temporal, a developmental psychology.

Sanborn (1971) has argued that language development should be thought of as a 'genetico-historical process with adult language as its end point'. This motto will well serve for a developmental account of any adult faculty. If, for example, adults can indulge in meaningful linguistic communication, or act intentionally, then three questions must be posed:

(1) What is the nature of these abilities?
(2) How might they have developed?
(3) What kind of account of this development can be put forward, given that individuals do not possess such abilities to begin with?

Space precludes dealing with any of these questions in detail, so for practical reasons let me concentrate largely upon question (3).

I will sketch what such an account might look like by taking a number of questions arising from the following example: 'I don't know what that means, I just made that up'. This was said by one of the participants of the Conference while drawing a diagram on the board to illustrate a point to his audience. In the course of doing one thing he produces another, something new. But it appears to have meaning: it is definitely not a mistake; hey, there might be something here. What might there be? And where? Well, it will need thinking about. The apparent (how are they apparent?) implications of this creation need working at to be made explicit. Something (what could it be?) has momentarily been indicated (how can that be?) and how can one work towards something when one does not know what it is, and then know when one has found it?

In a series of papers, Smedslund (1978, in press) has indicated that there will not be a causal link to be found between the something pointed at and the indicator pointing at it: but a logical one. It will follow necessarily, logically. The same point is posited by Popper (1972) in his theory of World 3; before that by Romanes (1887) in his account of man's mental evolution; and yet earlier in Euclid's geometry: that the logical implications of a particular set of concepts follow necessarily from the possession of that set of concepts. But this does not mean that the individual who possesses those concepts has any awareness of their implications. They exist somehow beyond him at this present moment.

Elsewhere, I have tried to show at length how this approach may be applied to language development (Lock, 1980). My argument there is that any activity generates implications that the individual actor is unaware of; that these implications are ordered hierarchically according to principles which are by no means fully understood; and that language development progresses in an orderly fashion, uncovering these implications in their fixed hierarchical order, and thereby making them explicit. I am suggesting here that the same will apply to our present speaker.

Let me take a question raised earlier to expand on this suggestion: something (what could it be?) has momentarily been indicated. Let us assume for the moment that conceptual structures have, for example, a spatial structure, and that these structures have some form of symmetry, or tend towards it, for their stability. An example of a stable structure is shown in Figure 1:

A   B

            C

D   E

Figure 1

Suppose now that concept E in this structure is not part of an individual's explicit knowledge, but that concepts A, B, C and D are. For the sake of simplicity only, assume further (for this assumption is unlikely to be anywhere near the truth, even in this simple model) that these concepts form the conceptual structure shown in Figure 2:

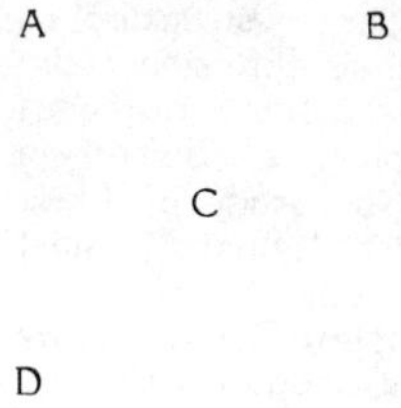

A   B

              C

D

Figure 2

Clearly, this figure is unstable in this orientation. For it to be stable E must, in this simple example, be created. I propose then, that it is this instability which leads to the momentary insight that something (E) exists - exists by implication of the ordering of A, B, C and D.

Staying with this spatial analogy (a little further) and adding a little more sophistication, let each concept (A, B, C and D) possess a directional implicational force - a sort of sophisticated valency as usually found in organic chemistry formulae. These are represented for the individual concepts in Figure 3.

Figure 3

A—
B

D—
C

Figure 4

Let us now go back to the individual who possesses these concepts, and assume he has attempted to put them into the stable conceptual structure shown in Figure 4. As can be seen, while spatially the structure has stability, it is going to be under a distortional stress imposed upon it by the imbalance of the directional implicational forces which are an integral part of each concept. The detection of these distorting stresses by the agent will lead, in this model, to a shift from the structure shown in Figure 4 to that of Figure 2, which will imply, as noted earlier, the existence of concept E (or the process might happen directly under the influence of these distorting forces which are then not detected by the agent: in this case only the resulting structural imbalance is detected). Furthermore, since the conceptual structure A B C D E will be located within the larger 'structure' of knowledge, any changes in this structure may have repercussions throughout the whole system. But there again, they may not: factors from the linguistic codes available to an individual to his 'personality' may all conspire to prevent an already organized system from undergoing reorganization. The study of these logical relations existing within conceptual systems is only just beginning, and I take Hargreaves' contribution (chapter 15) as representative of this line of work.

Thus, in this view, knowledge is essentially always incomplete, continuously open to further development. And its further development is quite strongly determined - though not by any causal laws - by the state of the system at any given time: through the logical implications it engenders. It is this incompleteness which leads to many of our problems in dealing with others in everyday life and in scientific research. In everyday life I may impute motives to you based on my interpreting your behaviour as implying the knowledge you are acting upon; yet even though your activity implies such knowledge you may nonetheless not possess it, and hence your motives will not be the ones I impute to you. In scientific research concerning infants and young children this raises problems concerning the ascription of knowledge and intentionality that are so obvious as not to need discussion.

Indeed, it is this incompleteness that puts intentionality at the centre of the stage in any understanding of human activity. It is the essential component of Brentano's (1874) discussion of intentionality, echoed by a number of contributors to this volume, that mental activity is inherently aimed at, points toward something beyond itself. Yet, while intentionality is central, it is most difficult to pin down: it has that ineffable quality of the Peace of God which is beyond human understanding: and quite literally beyond, as the implied temporal 'gap' in our conceptual systems which is continuously motivating their restructuring. We see in intentionality the 'driving force' noted by the Steppenwolf. By contrast, the forces of inertia - brought about by the dynamics of attitude consistency and the like - will put a brake on our development. And perhaps the resulting tension will then 'drive' us back to nature.

There is, then, in this sketch of a developmental psychology a peculiar blend of determinism and indeterminism. An individual does not know what will come next, the world may appear indeterminate and formless, requiring him actively to impose himself upon it if it is to become comprehensible to him: yet what will come next is already determined logically by implication from his present state. The psychologist, for example, may not know what stage of development the subject of his study has reached - that stage is essentially indeterminate: but he may well perceive what will come next - for that is culturally, historically and logically determined as well.

Man, then, as Homo temporalis is a being in transition. His psychology must therefore be based in time, putting the concept of intentionality at centre stage. There is, though, room in this plot for both the 'empirical scientist' espousing determinism and objectivity, and also the 'humanist' with his emphases on indeterminism and inter-subjectivity.

NOTE

Space precludes a full discussion of the cognitive structures and dynamics outlined. I accept, then, that words such as 'stable' and 'unstable' may appear ambiguous, and sometimes inappropriate in relation to the figures shown.

On the problem of deciding between models

A. Still

One question that was seldom raised at the Conference was how one might decide between models of man. Some of the models described (e.g. Broadbent, chapter 9) are testable, and hence may be falsified. But there are other kinds of model (truly 'models of man') which are not directly testable. Such broad models provide frameworks within which narrow testable models can be formulated, and they do this, in a way that became clearer during Harré's paper (chapter 14), by providing a source of concepts to be used in explanations. An example is the information-processing model, where Artificial Intelligence (AI) and related disciplines provide a source of concepts. The human information-processing model is implicit in many of the chapters, but was not seriously questioned, except when, as a representative mechanistic model, it was contrasted with non-mechanistic humanist models. But it is not the only kind of mechanistic (or, better, biological) model, and therefore it is important to examine the possibility of deciding between this and the other broad models that are directly testable but could be an alternative source of concepts to go into the construction of narrow testable models. Alternatives of this kind are those of radical behaviourism and J. J. Gibson (1966), and I shall consider the latter since it was not discussed at the Conference. Thus my motivation in writing this paper is twofold: first, to raise the unresolved problem of how to decide between alternative models of man; and, second, to give an airing to the views of Gibson since, in my view, a conference on models of man that failed to do this would be incomplete.

For present purposes, the important differences between the two models (information-processing and that of Gibson) are as follows. An information-processor interprets inputs by constructing appropriate representations. These representations are of the world which is the source of the inputs, and they enable the organism to act appropriately upon the world. The inputs are meaningless in themselves, and are described in terms of physics, light waves and sound waves, for instance, which are transduced by the sense organs from one form of energy to another. In Gibson's theory emphasis is not on 'inputs', but on the stimulus invariants which exist in the organism's environment, and which are picked up by means of perceptual systems, where a system includes a transducer (e.g. the retina) but also the capacity to bring that transducer into contact with the environment for the purposes of picking up information (e.g. the visual control system which includes the capacity for directed eye, head and body movements). This is a holistic view of the organism, which sees limited usefulness in studying the elements of the perceptual system in isolation. The information-processing view, on the other hand, is atomistic in that it studies interfaces with the environment, memory banks, central processors, etc., in relative isolation from each other, a way of proceeding that has generally found support from the practice of experimental psychologists. The information-processor constructs the world of meaningful objects from sparse information provided by the inputs, while on Gibson's holistic theory the world of objects is the world of invariants, and we can do no more than aim to pick up these invariants, either literally or metaphorically. By presenting stimuli which are themselves representations (such as pictures in a tachistoscope) experimenters can create an illusion of construction when subjects are made to guess what is represented. But stimulus invariants are not representations, so this laboratory procedure misses the essence of perception.

The following are three general ways of deciding between broad models such as those of human information-processing (IP) and the information-seeking (holistic) theory of Gibson.

(1) WHAT ARE THE RESPECTIVE SCIENTIFIC FRUITS? In terms of the simplicity of designing experiments, and the sheer number of experiments carried out, the IP model wins easily. This is important, but could be an inevitable result of being able to separate out, for experimental purposes, distinct psychological functions and faculties. It is easier to study the retina as a transducer (even one with information-processing properties of its own), than to study it as part of a perceptual system. The holist would have to argue that there is a dangerous temptation to sacrifice validity for the sake of neat theories and proliferating laboratory experiments. He would certainly admit that such theories and experiments may be important, only to the physiologist, rather than to the psychologist (or even to the biological psychologist). But the holist is on weak ground here, and eventually his model must bear fruit.

(2) HISTORICAL AND PHENOMENOLOGICAL EVALUATION. One might criticize the IP model with its idea of a cognitive elaboration of sparse and meaningless input, as a modern expression of a bad old habit of thought, with roots in the philosophical theories of both empiricism and Descartes. The mind, the processor, is separated from the world, with which it contingently makes contact through the senses by means of sense data, or sensations, or sensory input. Criticisms of such approaches in general will apply in particular to the IP model and some of the most cogent criticisms have been made by phenomenologists. Following this historical approach with a phenomenological analysis, Merleau-Ponty (1962) was led to conclude that mind and body are inseparable from having a body and hence from being in the world. If he is right, the bodiless abstractions dealt with by AI and IP may be of limited importance to psychology. AI can, as Boden points out (chapter 10), include the concept of intentionality (central to phenomenologists) as the relationship between a representation and what is represented. But such a relationship involves contingent links between mind and world, links that are imposed from outside on to the polarities of representation and what is represented in order to forge them together. This does not accord with the phenomenological analysis of intentionality, in which it is an essential attribute of most forms of consciousness. This view is paralleled by the holistic view that perception cannot be understood in isolation, as the accessing of a representation, but only as part of a perceptual system concretely directed towards the world.

(A parenthetical word about phenomenology seems in place here. It is not the same as introspection, but at its best is an attempt to show how the truth of mathematical, scientific and other systems can be recognized through experiences that are prior to the acceptance of the systems. The analyses are often rigorous and systematic, sometimes more so than the now common self-criticisms of experimental psychologists, which may indeed be thought of as a kind of phenomenology. Psychologists puzzled about the possible role of phenomenology might read Tragesser's, 1977, attempt to use phenomenology to decide between alternative logics.)

(3) COMPATIBILITY WITH OTHER THEORIES, ESPECIALLY THE THEORY OF EVOLUTION. A first impression is that AI turns evolution on its head. There are

programs that play chess like minor champions, and others that solve the most intricate problems in logic, but there is great difficulty in designing a program that could control a robot to find its way about its environment in the way an animal does. In the way an animal does 'without thinking', one is tempted to say, for it does not seem to be a matter of thought, certainly not an intractable computational problem (sometimes referred to by workers in AI as the 'frame problem'). For if it were, and most vertebrates can manifestly solve it with ease, why do they not have equal facility with chess and mathematical logic? It could be argued (cf. Rozin, 1976) that animals do have programs for finding their way about the environments, and that these programs use enormous computational capacity, but that they cannot be readily plugged-into to aid the solution of problems in other areas, such as mathematical logic. Such convenient plugging-in is a trick learned during the course of evolution.

The holist alternative is that evolution is of perceptual systems, and an account must be given of the rather complex business of the selection of systems rather than organs. It is through such systems that an animal is so thoroughly at home in its niche, and this is the starting point of the cognitive elaborations of human thinking. Being at home in the world cannot itself be explained by cognitive elaboration. Thus there is a crucial distinction here that is not acknowledged by IP theories, but is close to the distinction contained in the phenomenological concept of a pre-reflective mode of being. I think it is a distinction that could be studied empirically even if a nice 'knock-down' experiment is inconceivable.

It may seem that the grander implications of 'models of man' have been forgotten in this afterthought. In one sense a 'model of man' guides interactions with people and perhaps one should feel less complacent than is usual about the split between the everyday model and the model apt to be taken on as the scientist enters the laboratory. As an effort in this direction, I would suggest that on Gibson's theory, suitably spun out, a scientific psychologist's account of man (or any animal) must include an account of the environment, using the kind of ecological language being developed by Gibson; and that it is this necessity which makes the psychologist's task different from that of a scientist of physical systems. The environment is obviously relevant in the IP theorist's account, but it does not have the same necessity in that the workings and essential structure of his model can be described independently of an environment. The distinction is similar to that made above between necessity and contingent intentionality, and in its implications it distinguishes two models of man in the grandest possible sense.

Comments from a cross-cultural perspective

G. Jahoda

An academic discipline often tends to be a self-contained world with few windows to the outside. It seems to me that this was to some extent reflected in the present Conference. In spite of the fact that the general quality of the contributions was most impressive, few of them acknowledged explicitly the existence of cultural differences or that psychology is merely one of a group of disciplines concerned with man. I therefore thought it might be useful if I played the role of an outsider looking in and commented accordingly.

Let it be said at the outset that psychologists are not the only ones to suffer from disciplinary myopia, and as an example I cite an (admittedly atypical) anthropologist:

How is human behavior to be explained? ... Man's behavior is fully (sic) explained by culture. Man learns to think, feel, believe and strive for that which his culture considers proper. (Freilich, 1972, p. 1)

Surprisingly, something like this view was echoed at the Conference by Harré (chapter 14) when he said 'it seems to me obvious that a "psychology" is a reflection of culturally distinctive systems of rules, conventions and meanings' (p. 208). There is a sense in which this statement is a truism, and in that sense it is applicable to all sciences - presumably this is not what Harré meant; but if he is suggesting that psychology, in contrast to the physical and biological sciences is 'nothing but that', he has in my opinion not made out his case. On the other hand the implication that psychology as we know it is shot through with Western cultural assumptions is undoubtedly correct. I would hazard a dual generalization in relation to levels of behaviour: as one moves up from the predominantly biological to that involving the higher mental processes and complex social interactions, so cultural elements become increasingly important both in governing actual behaviour and influencing the nature of the explanations formulated to account for that behaviour.

Before going any further it will be necessary to say a few words about 'culture', an extremely elusive term. Without entering the jungle of innumerable definitions proposed (cf. Kroeber & Kluckhohn, 1952), I just wish to clear up a confusion all too common even in the literature. First of all there is Culture in general, with a capital C, as in the Lévi-Straussian opposition between Culture and Nature. This aspect is discussed by Reynolds (chapter 3) in an evolutionary context and refers to certain elements without which man would not be human. As an anthropologist has dramatically phrased it:

Men without culture would not be the clever savages of Golding's Lord of the Flies thrown back upon the cruel wisdom of their animal instincts; nor would they be nature's noblemen of Enlightenment primitivism or even, as classical anthropological theory would imply, intrinsically talented apes who had somehow failed to find themselves. They would be unworkable monstrosities with very few useful instincts, fewer recognizable sentiments, and no intellect: mental basket cases. (Geertz, 1975, p. 49)

In this brilliant essay Geertz argues against what he calls the 'stratigraphic' conception of human nature whereby one could peel away culture and be left with psychological and biological aspects of man. Culture influenced the evolution of the brain itself, and in this important respect as well as others is intrinsic to man. Other factors involved in Culture-in-general may be certain universal aspects of socialization, though what precisely these may be is still far from clear.

Culture-in-general has become differentiated into numerous particular cultures with a small 'c' which vary widely in beliefs, values, customs and so on. It is these specific variations I am primarily concerned with here, because their consideration suggests that some of the supposedly pan-human models may in fact be Euramerico-centric.

Several examples could be cited, but I shall have to confine myself to a few selected ones, the first being Eysenck's 'bio-social' model (chapter 4). While admiring the coherence and elegance of this model, it seems to me that this is achieved by some over-simplification of the facts based on a strong biological bias. This is particularly evident in his discussion of sex differences where, incidentally, I share his view that it has become fashionable to underplay their biological foundations; at the same time I am not ready to go as far in the other direction as the following passage implies:

Society, in order to survive, has adopted the principle that these 'natural' tendencies should not be left to the accidents of genetic transmission and segregation alone, but that these biological determinants should be aided by precept and modelling; thus social norms in the vast majority of all societies we know have emphasized social and sexual roles very much in line with those which instinct dictated in any case. (p. 58)

The suggestion that culture merely follows biological dictates at once raises the question, familiar from the incest debate, why it should be necessary to reinforce natural tendencies in that way - after all, there are no social norms telling us that we must eat and sleep! In fact Eysenck paints a seriously misleading picture which greatly exaggerates the uniformities across cultures. Sex roles vary considerably, such variations of course not being random: they can usually be shown, as Reynolds mentioned, to constitute adaptations to particular ecological settings and the corresponding modes of subsistence. With regard to sexual customs and behaviour this has recently been demonstrated by Goody (1976). In general any bio-social model should give appropriate weight to both aspects and avoid being thinly disguised biological determinism.

Another very different model that seems to some extent open to similar criticism is the Piagetian one presented by Wright (see pp. 313-317). In the course of the discussion of this paper a link was suggested between the logic of sets and the development of the ability to handle formal logicomathematical operations. This sounds plausible, until one remembers that Piaget's concentration on these types of intellectual skills is merely a consequence of the scientific and technological culture in which his biologically oriented theory originated. It has led to the view being put forward that people in traditional cultures are incapable of reaching the level of formal operations. Elsewhere (Jahoda, 1980) I have tried to show that this is an absurd conclusion, arising from a confounding of structure and content. If one defines formal operations in terms of logicomathematical skills it is true, but trivial. First-hand experience of the capabilities for abstract reasoning of individuals in traditional cultures, albeit in the social and juridical spheres, clearly contradicts such views.

There is an interesting parallel here with the history of cross-cultural intelligence testing, where it was anthropologists in close contact with indigenous peoples in their everyday lives who cast doubt on the validity of such comparisons at a time when psychologists were still persuaded of their scientific 'truth'. The reason for these and many other misconceptions is probably at least partly the persistence of sterotypes about 'primitives', which date back to the 19th century when the Victorians bathed in the comforting glow of their moral and intellectual superiority. Echoes of this are even to be found in the challenging presentation by Shotter (chapter 2) who, I hasten to add, clearly has no wish to denigrate peoples of other cultures. Nonetheless the quotation below he presented from Buber (1970), characterizing the 'magical world-image of primitive peoples', corresponds to an older outlook:

> ... to anything which stirs activity within them they are prepared to attribute existence and power: to the moon and the 'dead' who haunt them at night, to the sun that burns them, to the beast that howls, to the chief whose glance compels them, and to the Shaman whose song fills them with strength for the hunt.

In discussing this (see p. 15) Shotter wishes to suggest that even we 'civilized' Europeans have feelings and experiences of this kind, which is no doubt true. Yet this is presented in strictly individual terms, just as the beliefs of the 'primitive' are listed as though they were a collection of strange bits and pieces of individual feeling and thinking. In reality such beliefs are the result of cultural transmission; usually far from isolated, they form part of what Shotter himself called a 'world-image'; such cosmologies are often not merely coherent, subtle and complex (as for instance in the case of the Dogon), but can sometimes be shown to constitute an efficient form of adaptation to the environment (Reiche-Dolmatoff, 1976). On the other hand such systems in intact traditional cultures are invariably monolithic; and where no alternatives are available - perhaps, as some have suggested, they are literally unthinkable (Horton, 1967) - the kind of cross-checking by looking at alternative accounts mentioned by Shotter cannot occur; it is a luxury, or perhaps a burden, confined to the heterogeneous cultures of industrial countries.

The crux of my argument is that psychologists of varied persuasions tend to operate with an implicit model of 'homo Euramericanus' when formulating their theories, taking insufficient account of variations in behaviour across the globe. A second point is that the characteristic research strategy of psychology is not always the most appropriate one for the more complex forms of behaviour displayed in social life. This reinforces the critique made by Harré, though I cannot agree with his solution of studying people's own 'accounts' of their behaviour. This is something anthropologists do all the time, but far from regarding such 'accounts' as the final product, they treat them as the raw data from which they move to a higher level of generalization. The contrast in the approaches has been epitomized by Richards (1970):

> ... there is the salient difference between the psychologist who arrives in the field to test a hypothesis and the anthropologist who is initially, at any rate, trying to describe a system, whether of social relationships, activities, symbols, or world views. (p. 23)

She correctly indicates that psychologists are, by and large, concerned mainly with fairly restricted segments of behaviour, while anthropologists view the person as a whole in a broad systems context. This, incidentally, is the reason why anthropologists find few psychological theories helpful in their work, with psychoanalysis as the major exception; for it is what Kluckhohn called the only theory of 'human nature in the raw'. If we wish to wean them away from Freud, we shall have to be in a position to offer an alternative theory of the same kind.

These remarks have sketched out what I regard as some limitations of psychological models, viewed from a cross-cultural perspective, and taking into account the work of anthropologists. From such a standpoint it seems a little presumptuous of us to pretend that we can offer models of man; possibly anthropologists, who after all publish a journal called 'Man', have a better title to this! Perhaps we should call our next conference 'models of behaviour'.

Comments on criteria for judging models of man

D. Wallis

I want to make a fairly brief and perhaps belated comment first, and then append a suggestion. First of all the comment.

It seems to me that during most of the Conference we discussed criteria for evaluating models of man, rather than describing actual models. A marked feature of this discussion was that, despite the ritualistic refutation of Cartesian thinking about body and mind, we seemed unable to avoid dualisms of one kind or another; for example, mechanistic versus mentalistic models, scientific versus humanistic, cognitive versus social ones. And, excepting Howarth's thesis (chapter 11), there was an unfortunate tendency to reject utterly the conceptual basis of the one approach if one happened to be a proponent of another. We encountered variants of materialism and vitalism, but rather little dialectics.

I also found it remarkable that at least some of the formal criteria by which theories or models tend to have been judged in the past, are no longer judged applicable to psychology or perhaps to any science. I am thinking here of refutability, which seems now to be either impracticable or irrelevant; similarly so for explanatory power, the ability to account coherently for otherwise disparate facts and data; and even internal consistency which was also challenged during our proceedings.

Without wishing to comment on the foolhardiness or otherwise of rejecting these particular criteria, I find it difficult to discern from our contributors that there are any clear alternatives by which to judge our various models. However, there is at least one criterion which to me seems of quite fundamental importance in psychological as in any other scientific model-making. That is the criterion of intelligibility and communicability. I think a case can properly be made for saying that no model is of any significance, except perhaps to its originator, until and unless it can be communicated in an intelligible form for the purposes of criticism and further development. I have to admit that I have found some of the models presented here very hard to understand; and I have an uneasy suspicion that in their struggle to represent, or perhaps to create, reality in a new guise, some of our model-makers may be trying prematurely to express the ineffable.

However, let me turn now to my belated suggestion. It offers yet another way of looking at models of man. I hesitate to claim the status for it of an all-purpose criterion by which to choose among models: but here it is anyway. It arises from the standpoint of an applied psychologist, rather than from that of a theoretician or philosopher. Put at its simplest, mine would be like the criterion an engineer adopts in relation to the theories of physics. It is a pragmatic criterion. Does the model or theory 'work': that is, does it work for someone like me, as an applied psychologist?

I ought to say something of what I mean here by 'working'. An alternative expression might be to ask: is the model relevant? Is it useful? Now these emotive and possibly disreputable notions of relevance and usefulness are very rarely adopted in relation to theoretical models. I would want to say that at any rate for applied psychologists (and there are many of us nowadays) a model should be judged worth while if it helps to guide, justify, or explain, professional practice and problem-solving in the real world. Conversely, a model which neither contributes nor seeks to contribute anything to these objectives is not worth spending much time on. (Whilst denying the worthwhileness of a model of man on this criterion, I would not of course wish to exclude its having value in a purely intellectual and self-indulgent sense; constructing a model could well be more satisfying intellectually, and personally, than engaging in crossword puzzles or philosophical debate. Both of these are enjoyable and eminently worth while, but from quite different standpoints.)

Applying this pragmatic criterion of mine, I would wish to dispense with any model of man which does not permit, even in principle, 'naive interactionism' - as distinct from 'naive parallelism'; or one which does not give prominence to cognitive and affective experience; or which does not take sensible account of individual differences; and which neglects or tries to explain away what Warr called the 'springs of action': that is, motivation, intentions and purposive behaviour. Now I am afraid that physiological psychology goes out more or less completely on this account, being reduced to its proper status as physiology and not as psychology. I am happier with behaviourism, which has obvious implications for clinical and perhaps other applied psychologists; but the model has to be a very 'radical' one. Humanistic models like Shotter's may also have regretfully to be set aside, as examples more of literary and ethical philosophizing than of psychological modelling. On the other hand, the psychometric models of which we heard little (see Kline, pp. 322-328), the models based on 'trait and factor' concepts which are so unpopular now, still have a good deal to offer. At least they acknowledge explicitly the reality and relevance of individual differences. I fear also, in view of my claim that motivational factors are critically important to an applied psychologist, that personal construct theory (as distinct from the repertory grid techniques which have emerged as a valuable by-product of it) is largely irrelevant. I do, however, thoroughly approve of Howarth's notion of man as a problem-solver. Observation of man's behaviour in the real world lends clear support to this view; though I do not think it lends much support to Kelly's idea that man's ordinary problem-solving is analogous to the way a scientist behaves. I would also commend Warr's conceptual framework to encompass everyday actions; yet even this does not incorporate what to me is another central and crucial feature of man in real life - and that is a 'limited model' of skill and competence.

We have also been offered a number of most helpful historical analyses of how certain models of man have arisen in our subject. In this context, I should like to reiterate my view that models of man which do meet the criterion of usefulness, relevance, and indeed of intelligibility also, are and indeed always have been very variable as regards durability. Models of man which were valuable 30 or 40 years ago no longer seem so now. Yet it may be worth just recalling some of those models which seemingly exerted a powerful influence upon those like myself whose work has been concerned with psychological problem-solving in real life. I must confess to some surprise that not one of these models, so far as I can recall, was featured in our discussions until the final review session.

The formative years in Britain for professional application of psychology in the educational and occupational/industrial areas, and to a large extent in the clinical area too, were the 1940s. In this period, the most powerful model of man was that based on the psychometric, structural approach to human abilities and personal qualities which stemmed from the work of factor analysts like Spearman, Thomson, and Burt in this country, and of Hotelling and Thurstone in the United States. This model was the basis for practical work in assessment, selection and training in most of the fields of government and public service where applied psychologists first made a mark. It achieved its peak in the form presented in a series of texts by P. E. Vernon in the 1950s, though it is better known through the rather different versions produced by Cattell and Eysenck.

However, by the time the 1950s were upon us, and the problems faced by applied psychologists (at least in the occupational and industrial areas) were those of demands from a rapidly changing technology and accompanying manpower shortages, the models of man which took root and soon became as influential as the structural ones, were variants of the human engineering, servo-mechanistic, and information-processing, models. Attributable at least in this country to the wartime work of Craik, Hick and other researchers under the direction of Bartlett, these models were highly influential and indeed particularly useful to those psychologists engaged in what has since become identified as the field of ergonomics. Incidentally, just as there are persisting fragments of the psychometric model in our present-day applied psychological thinking and practice, so too are there residuals of the information-processing models I have just mentioned.

In the 1960s as a consequence partly of the upsurge of practical interest in education and training, indeed of human learning in general, we encountered models of man based upon operant conditioning on the one hand, and on cybernetic principles on the other, as very powerful influences within the applied psychology of training research and educational technology. In the same context, and perhaps of more lasting significance for models of man as a problem-solver, the notion of man as a 'planning' organism was incorporated from a seminal text by Miller et al. (1960). By the 1970s, however, the interest of many applied psychologists working in industrial and other occupational contexts, had been seized by what are sometimes called the problems of organizational behaviour: that is, of people working in organizations. So it is that the most influential models nowadays for these applied psychologists are ones based on motivational and social interactional factors. We heard some references to them at the end of the Conference.

This brief representation of an idiosyncratic point of view can have very little impact, I am sure, at this stage of our general proceedings. But perhaps I am not alone in thinking that psychologists, and psychology as a discipline, will be moving down a slippery slope towards intellectual isolation, if not self-destruction, if they spend too much time creating models of man which ignore the criterion of 'workability', or relevance to practical human affairs, for which I have offered this belated claim.

Reflections of an applied psychologist

K. D. Duncan

A lucid analysis of the origins of present-day disputes about the appropriate model of man was provided early in the Conference by Joynson. From the many possibilities he chose, as anchor points, the Locke view of man, and the Leibnitz view of man. The usefulness of his chapter is not only its historical illustration of two major competing models of man, but also its argument that the major schools from behaviourism, through Gestalt theory, psychoanalysis, to factor analysis may be regarded as lying on a dimension roughly corresponding to the complexity of the human functions with which they deal.

The notion of a continuum between Leibnitzian man and Lockeian man seems to me to be a useful one for students of applied psychology. If we take the contrast in Allport's terms, which Joynson cites, Leibnitzian man is the source of acts, whereas Lockeian man is passive till roused (or stimulated) from without. The student of human skill may recognize here the difference between the early stages and the later stages of a psychological process. Initially the novice is essentially respondent, his behaviour is plausibly explained in closed loop, mechanistic terms, indeed he may be so hypnotized by his environment as to appear and indeed sometimes to feel scarcely human (e.g. the well-known feeling of having things happen to you while struggling in the early stages of learning to drive). At a later stage, however, when a degree of mastery of the task has been achieved, the picture is very different. The subject actively initiates, makes predictions, anticipates future events, but above all is nothing like as pre-occupied with the task as he formerly was - he is in fact free to talk about other things, think about other things, and generally to behave, in a word, in a peculiarly human way.

The point of this digression is simply to reinforce Joynson's argument that the Lockeian and Leibnitzian models can be seen as extremes of a dimension. Indeed they are, in my view, wrongly identified, in the light of our current knowledge of how skills and capabilities are acquired, as models of man between which a choice should be made. They simply represent different stages of an ubiquitous psychological process.

Not all the contributors attempted to put forward a model of man. On the one hand, the papers by Shotter, Blackman, Beloff, Fransella, Eysenck and Farr took this daunting task very seriously. On the other hand, the various other contributions are perhaps best described as research perspectives, rather than models as such. Models of man, from those brave enough to attempt them, were forthcoming and, to say the least, provocative. However, had the title of the Conference, with the wisdom of hindsight, included the term 'research perspectives', or something of that kind, then perhaps other perspectives might have been represented besides those which were represented in the event.

One perspective which emerged in several contributions was that psychology should adopt the approach of other natural, especially biological, sciences even to the point of reconciling the increasing intricacies of human and other biological systems with the second law of thermodynamics. Although it was not a viewpoint shared by all or even most of those present, and although it was seriously and explicitly challenged, nevertheless, several misrepresentations went unscathed. For instance, scientific method was by implication identified with experimentation. The point was not brought out that psychology, even in its most slavish imitations, has not sought, and not surprisingly has failed to reach, the achievements of the well-established natural sciences in at least two important respects:

(i)   psychology has signally failed to develop and to interact with a vigorous technology as have other well-established natural sciences;

(ii) psychology has only recently turned its attention to observational methods; its achievements in this regard are primitive; when it comes to ordering and classifying human behaviour we still await a psychological Linnaeus; certainly psychology has not taken seriously the importance of non-experimental disciplines such as astronomy.

It was thus relatively easy for those participants of an experimental persuasion to attack 'the rest'. It was not acknowledged that experimental psychology has the immense advantage of contriving and specifying beforehand the task which subjects will perform, as indeed does psychometric testing, and that neither has to contend with the intellectually taxing problem of rigorously describing complex sequences of behaviour which occur in 'real life' or, more formally, in situations which are not of the psychologist's contriving. One might add that the danger of basing psychological theories on behaviour in situations wholly of the psychologist's contriving was not sufficiently acknowledged either.

The problem of choosing an appropriate level of description which bedevils most applied psychologists attempting to solve problems (which they did not invent in the first place!) was at one stage almost written off. We were told that we could with confidence take a Watsonian line and regard, as units of analysis, such disparate events as, on the one hand getting married or, on the other, drawing lines. Still more depressing to me was the argument that there is really no need for any conceptual structure of a higher order than let us say an experimental paradigm - although it was very clear that there was considerable disquiet among participants about the style of psychological research which proliferates experiments on variations of an arbitrary task without any explicit, and presumably therefore higher-order, rationale for so doing. Concept learning was the subject of this particular criticism, yet we were assured that just such an approach was to be commended. In another context it has led to that extremely useful body of work on schedules of reinforcement by Ferster.

It is one thing to arrange a meeting in which people with widely differing viewpoints can state their positions. It is quite another matter to expect or hope that entrenched positions will not be adopted, and that sterile, holier-than-thou debates or, as Howarth laconically put it, the 'I am more refutable than you' contest will not dominate the scene. By the end of the first day, beginning as it did with Shotter's paper and ending with Blackman's, the lines were drawn, the meeting had met, in a tired phrase, its moment of truth. But happily someone voiced a simple view which seemed to stop the several sides in their tracks. The protagonists, argued this commentator - and suddenly the argument seemed to seize everyone's attention - are disturbingly assured. They are apparently without worries or doubt. I do not know who made the comment, but no more apposite comment could have been made. One could almost hear the thoughts racing : 'doubt - yes, surely systematic doubt is the very stuff of science - careful!' From that moment, what was frequently referred to as goodwill prevailed between the opposed points of view. In this regard the Conference like the Battle of Waterloo, was a 'damned close-run thing'.

The search for models is a delusion

R. P. Kelvin

I want to convey, albeit briefly, my deep conviction that, except for one important but essentially trivial purpose, the use of models of man - the zealous search for them, the passionate defence of those adopted - has stunted the development of psychology, not promoted it. I therefore go further than Broadbent (chapter 9): for where he counsels merely restraint in the use of models, I would plead with you that if ever Occam's Razor were to be appropriate, if ever the 'law of parsimony' were to be invoked, it should be in relation to models of man - not simply in terms of the sheer number of models which appear to be used, but in terms of the very use of any model at all. The use of models reflects the immaturity and inadequacies of psychology as a science, not the creative imagination of psychologists as scientists. If we look at the history of other sciences, it becomes quite clear that we shall not gain the intellectual maturity of an intellectually independent body of knowledge and theory until we stop playing games with models - and stop using them as a means to spurious respectability-by-association with, physiology, ethology, engineering, the logic of science, or whatever other 'established' discipline is available as a host to our conceptual parasitism.

To digress in order to clarify: it is essential to distinguish between what I suggest we call 'pedagogic' and 'parasitic' uses of models. By 'pedagogic' I refer to the use of models as aids in the communication of ideas between those already conversant with them and those still trying to grasp them - as, for example, in the use of billiard balls to demonstrate molecular structures. This pedagogic function of models is clearly very valuable, but it is also fundamentally trivial, in that the role of the model here is to serve as an illustration not as a source of ideas. Which brings me to the second, much more serious, and dangerous, parasitic use of models - whereby one discipline, as it were the 'host', provides the conceptual and intellectual structure for the dependent other discipline. And so we have models of man as an information-processing system, or man to be understood through the common ancestral ecology he shared with wolves, or man-the-scientist, or man to be conceived as conditioned by processes manifested in dogs, rats, or pigeons, or as a product of his social environment or economic system - and so forth through the plethora of models which may be derived from the physical, biological, engineering and social sciences.

Given this widespread use of such a wide range of models of man, and given that most of these models have at some times made at least some contribution to our understanding of man, it may seem singularly perverse of me to cry 'Stop'. Yet if we consider the history of psychology in relation to the history of science in general, it becomes quite clear that to free ourselves of our models is precisely what we must do if the psychological study of man is genuinely to advance.

The fundamental problem of the history of psychology is actually a problem in the history of science: why did it take so long for psychology to emerge at all? It is not sufficient here to trot out the traditional answer that psychology was embedded in theology and philosophy. Although superficially plausible, this answer is inadequate: first, the kind of psychology encompassed by theology and most of philosophy (except aspects of epistemology) scarcely falls within what would today be regarded the domain of psychology; second, the most prominent of the physical sciences, and especially astronomy, perhaps the earliest, were also suffused with theological and philosophical assumptions. All sciences in fact have theology and philosophy as common ancestors; and the question therefore remains as to why it was that the physical and biological sciences developed so much earlier than psychology. It is at first sight all the more a puzzle because whereas advances in these natural sciences were inherently dependent on sophisticated developments in technology, for most of psychological research - 'most', not 'all' - technology is a convenience rather than a necessity. The ancient Greeks could have investigated most of the phenomena which concern us in visual perception; Aristotle in his 'de Memoria' came close to postulating Hull's intraserial learning curve; any moderately competent circus trainer could have anticipated Skinner; any politician could have set about the systematic study of attitudes, leadership, organizations - to mention only a few of many possibilities. In effect, when we consider what technology is inherently necessary for psychological research, and particularly when we consider the technological requirements of 19th century psychology which is, as it were, our immediate forerunner, one truth becomes most evident: most of the basic topics of psychological research could have been pursued well in advance of the actually much earlier rise of physics, chemistry or anatomy and physiology with their much greater inherent dependence on technology.

Why then was psychology among the last and not among the first of sciences to emerge? Since the answer cannot be through its being uniquely enmeshed in theology and philosophy, and since the answer also cannot be its technological requirements, I suggest that it lies at a conceptual level - in the way we, as human beings, look at nature and, ultimately, at ourselves within it.

Very simply, for most of the intellectual history of mankind, man himself was the model in terms of which he sought to gain a systematic understanding of nature. Man is the model which underlies the manipulations of the 'motives' of natural forces in primitive ritual; man as the model is the source of the science of classical Greece, from its cosmology based on notions of 'perfection' to the purposive implications of the Final Cause in Aristotle's theory of causation; anthropomorphism is at the root of the mystical elements of alchemy. The pattern is clear: the attempt to arrive at a systematic understanding of nature ultimately reduces to the attempt to gain a systematic understanding of causation; in the initial phases of such an attempt we look to what we believe we know, as a guide or model for exploring the unknown; 'pre-scientific' man manifestly took himself as that model, using as his axioms what he believed he could take for granted concerning human emotions and purposes; he thus produced theories about natural causes which were either directly or at only very few removes attributions of personal motives. And precisely because the model was man and his motives, these accounts of causation were inadequate. The sciences, as we know them, only developed when they abandoned man as their model and came to consider and work only in terms of the functional relationships which could be observed between phenomena within their respective domains or levels of analysis. And this was also the necessary condition for the emergence of psychology, and for two reasons: first, as long as man was himself the model he was to that extent the source of unquestioned axioms; second, I suspect that until there were at least some sciences which were essentially self-sufficient - which did not require man-as-model - so long as there were also no models-for-man to provide the starting-point for the study of man. In effect, just as mankind needed a 'psychology' of man as the initial model for other sciences, so some other sciences (mechanics, chemistry, physiology) had to become sufficiently independent to provide the models to launch psychology.

Please note that although I counsel the rejection of models in order to attain conceptual maturity, I do not deny their usefulness in the initial stages of the development of ideas by particular individuals.   It is however essential to distinguish the methods we adopt in trying to think from what we are thinking about. We have need for models only to the extent that we have not yet understood the complexity (or simplicity) of observed patterns of phenomena in their own right. Thus although a model may indeed be powerful in the range of phenomena which it can represent, however 'powerful' a model may be in that sense, the need to use it is itself a symptom of the immaturity and inadequacies of the initial stages of an idea or a science.

All this is not just an academic nicety, to be pushed aside on the ground that psychology is a 'young' science; after more than a century of growing activity the constant search for models makes it sometimes look sickeningly like an ageing adolescent in a pathological crisis of identity. Models of man based on other sciences are not merely a sign of conceptual inadequacy, they positively hamper development by inevitably leaving out the fundamental question for the psychology of man. On the one hand, models derived from the physical and biological sciences are ultimately (and quite properly) grounded on the assumption of 'universal' laws, that is, on the assumption that the regularities in the relations between the phenomena of the model under review are independent of place and time. Some social scientists may claim similar 'universality' for their 'laws', but in many other instances the stress would rather be on the social, cultural and, therefore, historical determinants of human behaviour. So, models based on the natural sciences essentially assume the universality of the processes in question, whereas those derived from the social sciences essentially assume historical contingency. Both types are inherently inadequate as models for the psychology of man: for the fundamental problem for this psychology is to understand how this physical or biological system, the human being, operates in terms of both 'universal' and 'historical' processes. (By 'historical' here I do not mean only 'the influence of the past', which is also manifest in the evolution of species and in any acquired behaviour of any individual lower organism: by 'historical' I mean not just the influence of the past, but awareness of a past, whether in the form of history or myth.) And a central task of psychology, as I see it, is to try to identify what aspects of human behaviour are 'universal', which are 'historical', and to what extent one kind of process sets limits to the operations of the other. Certainly no social psychology can simply withdraw into either a natural sciences or a social sciences model.

In the final analysis, we regard those disciplines as well established which do not have to rely on models from other sources to make sense of the phenomena of their domain; and which can resolve new problems by an extension or modification of their existing theoretical or conceptual framework, without having to invoke models from other fields.   This, however, requires looking at and conceptualizing the problems with which one is concerned in their own right, and not 'as if' they belonged to some other level of analysis. To use a metaphor, not a model: to see things in terms of a model is to see them as through a glass, darkly, as it were filtered; this may make it easier to look, but it does so by cutting out much of what is there to see; in the long run it therefore hampers our progress, rather than helps it.   To arrive at a psychology of man we need to look at the nature of man sui generis, and observe, chart and try to relate the patterns of his behaviour, and their functions, for what they are in the domain of man, and not as if they were something else in some other area of natural or social science. Only thus can we ever develop an adequate psychology of man - precisely because no model from other sources can represent man adequately.

Why not psychological psychology?

N. E. Wetherick

Discussion of the papers presented at this Conference often polarized round the distinction between natural science psychology (Blackman, chapter 8; Brener, chapter 7) and humanist psychology (Shotter, chapter 2). Throughout there was also an undertow of satisfaction with the present state of affairs in psychology coupled with the belief that we cannot have and should not want any kind of general theorizing except what is capable of being derived directly from psychological practice (Howarth, chapter 11). I find myself at odds with all parties since I believe that the distinctions on which they rely are based on a false analysis of science in general and of psychological science in particular. Broadly all parties subscribe to a form of empiricism which holds that science must be derived from observational evidence. Science must of course be consistent with observational evidence but cannot be derived from it. What is required (and practised in all the sciences except psychology) is the imaginative construction of putative real entities that lie on the other side of sensory experience and account for the fact that some experiences but not others are and will be available to us. Experimental science as it is actually practised would be impossible on empiricist assumptions (Bhaskar, 1975). One supporting quotation must suffice. Einstein wrote to the philosopher Schlick 'I tell you straight out: physics is the attempt at the conceptual construction of a model of the real world and of its lawful structure'.

The attempt to observe the canons of empiricism (which are, strictly, philosophers' fictions) has had dire consequences for psychology, the most important of which is that the knowing agent at the centre of psychological function has been left out of account. Books on the philosophy of science do not normally state in so many words that every science ought to try to account for the phenomena with which it purports to be concerned; the fact is considered too obvious to need stating; but in natural science psychology (behaviourism) the phenomena of the knowing agent (with which surely psychology purports to be concerned) are relegated to the sphere of extra-scientific activity, and the psychologist concerns himself with problems which are as much the concern of the physiologist or the zoologist, while in humanist psychology these phenomena are equally relegated to the sphere of extra-scientific activity and the psychologist concerns himself with problems which are as much the concern of the social anthropologist and the social and political theorist. The difference between the natural science psychologist and the humanist psychologist lies in the fact that the former believes that the relegation is temporary, in the end man will be brought in toto within the sphere of natural science, while the latter holds in effect that the relegation is permanent. If it were true that the phenomena of the knowing agent could in principle be reduced to law in the empiricist sense, the natural science psychologist would hardly be blamed for not as yet having established what the laws are, since they would cover what is certainly the most complex body of phenomena known to man. But it seems certain that the reduction is, in principle, impossible; an argument going back at least to F. H. Bradley shows that if we are capable of knowing laws that purport to govern our behaviour then it makes no sense to deny that we may also be capable of overriding them as they apply to us. We are not passive spectators of our own behaviour. This is not to deny that some of our behaviour may be governed by laws of which we are not aware, only to assert that if and when we become aware of any such law we can, if we choose to do so, override it. The usual natural science reply to this argument is that when a law appears to have been overridden, what has happened is that another law has supervened which predicts the behaviour which was actually observed. But this law too could have been overridden if it had been known to the knowing agent and so on ... The proposition that behaviour is law-governed becomes a proposition in metaphysics not a proposition in science, whatever happens there is a law predicting that that will happen and not something else.

We may distinguish here between the layman's interpretation of his own (and other people's) behaviour and the natural science (behaviourist) alternative. The layman holds that, knowing from past experience that in a given situation he can obtain a given result by behaving in a certain way, he behaves in that way in the given situation if and when he desires the given result. The behaviour in his account is purposive; it is initiated by the behaver in order to obtain the result. The behaviourist account of the same phenomenon asserts that in the given stimulus situation the behaver has previously been reinforced following behaviour of the specified type, the stimulus situation therefore elicits the behaviour as a consequence of the behaver's reinforcement history. The behaver's 'feeling of purposiveness' (Blackman, chapter 8) is real but illusory. Notice that, from the point of view of an external observer, no distinction can be made between the two accounts, the sequence of sensory events for an observer is the same whichever account is true. What the layman regards as features of the stimulus situation enabling the behaver to predict that a given type of behaviour will produce a given result become in the behaviourist account stimulus events that elicit the behaviour. The layman's account is intuitively so convincing that we are entitled to demand very good grounds for believing that it is really false, that it is only the 'feeling' of purposiveness that is real. The grounds we are offered are that the behaviourist view is consistent with science which the other is not, since it involves the postulation of 'private' events and, by admitting that behaviour may be 'initiated' by organisms, seems to take it out of the realm of law-governed natural science phenomena.

Like the behaviourist I favour material monism as a view of the nature of reality. I should be loth to admit the necessity of mental/material dualism but the first priority must be truth to experience. Science must direct its attention to the phenomena with which it purports to be concerned and not rule out classes of phenomena on a priori grounds. If it were true that no 'scientific' account of behaviour was possible that allowed equal reality to the activities of humanist and scientific psychologists then so much the worse for science, we should have to accept a version of dualism, but I believe that this is not true. A genuinely scientific psychology is possible based on material monism like the other sciences, but behaviourism is not that science. It fails because it resorts to denying the reality of phenomena which legitimately fall within its purview because they cannot be accommodated within a simplistic empiricist framework. The equation to which behaviourists often subscribe between Darwinism in biology and behaviourism in psychology is false. Darwinism was good science and prevailed against irrelevant extra-scientific objections, behaviourism is bad science and will not prevail against relevant scientific objections. I pointed out earlier that observations of behaviour are always capable of interpretation in either lay or behaviourist terms. In retrospect a behaviourist interpretation can be offered of any behavioural event but in prospect the interpretation is invalidated because of the behaver's capacity to override laws which purport to govern his behaviour if he is aware of them and chooses to do so. It is of course very easy to ensure that the behaver will not choose to do so (e.g. by using a hungry animal subject and a food reinforcer). The behaviourist account will then appear to have predictive validity but the need to eliminate everything to which the animal could possibly wish to attend except the stimulus nominated by the experimenter testifies to the fact that for the prediction to work any real possibility of choice on the part of the subject must be excluded. The experimental results obtained by behaviourists will not be lost; they can all be reinterpreted according to the layman's model, though it must be admitted that many of them then take on the appearance of 'blinding glimpses of the obvious'.

All the other sciences were developed by gentleman amateurs to the stage at which they could usefully be institutionalized; no one depended for his living on the practice of these sciences until a general structure had been established which could usefully be developed piecemeal. Psychology omitted the preliminaries since empiricism seemed to guarantee the utility of any data whatsoever provided certain methodological principles were observed. Unhappily, the behaviour of organisms (particularly human organisms) is infinitely richer as a source of data than the behaviour of any other class of entities with which science is concerned. Brief perusal of the journals of 20, 40 or 60 years ago will convince the reader that the phenomena discussed are different but in no sense logically prior to those under discussion today; as Newell (1973) points out there has been no genuine progression of ideas. I would add that there is equally no reason to believe that future data collection will succeed where past data collection has failed. A genuine science of psychology will have to confront the phenomena of consciousness and of human agency. If it is possible in principle for psychology to do this without losing contact with physiology then both humanist and natural science psychologists can continue in their present courses undisturbed. The central concern of psychology will not however lie either in humanism or in natural science but in the mind, the nexus between the one and the other. The question to be answered will be what sort of thing is it that can do what we know human beings can do and experience what they can experience and at the same time constitute itself in the kind of physiological structure we know organisms to consist of? The need for such a tertium quid was identifed by Harré (1971) though I believe he was wrong in thinking that access to it is immediately available through the medium of language. Unfortunately the cognitive psychologists who should be concerned have sold out for an unending but scientifically unproductive stream of fascinating behavioural observations. Only the AI-theorists address themselves to the central problem (Boden, chapter 10) and they avoid employing the principal mode of access available to us to the structures in which they are interested. However, advances in our understanding come only when appropriate concepts are available. We did not come to understand the operations of the musculature until we understood levers nor the operations of the heart until we understood pumps, perhaps we will only come to understand the mind when we have derived appropriate concepts from attempts to simulate its function, though it would in my opinion be a mistake to assume that the concepts at present in use are 'appropriate' in the required sense.

In the light of contemporary philosophical analysis a genuine science of psychology is wholly possible and would require no procedure not already employed in the established sciences. It could handle the problem of consciousness by taking consciousness to be a pattern of activity in neurons from the point of view of the organism of whose nervous system the neurons form part. (From the point of view of another organism, for example an experimental physiologist, this activity is merely 'activity in neurons under observation' but as a conscious state of that other organism it is a pattern of activity in neurons that form part of its nervous system.) It could handle the problem of agency by allowing that a pattern of neural activity which corresponds to the perception of a particular object in the organism's immediate perceptual environment (IPE) may be triggered by an internal state of the organism as well as by the particular object. An organism which lacked this capacity would not be precluded from learning, it could for example form conditioned responses from a series of reinforced trials, but non-reinforced trials would simply be wasted time from a learning point of view because what it learned would be that a state of its IPE (the conditioned stimulus) predicted the imminence of reinforcement (the unconditioned stimulus) (see Asratyan, 1973; Bindra, 1974). Such an organism could learn nothing, either positive or negative, from a non-reinforced trial because it could not recognize that the trial was non-reinforced. Recognizing a reinforced trial is no problem because the reinforcement is present in the IPE and can have whatever effect it has directly, but recognizing a non-reinforced trial in order to learn from the fact that it is non-reinforced requires an organism that can have the reinforcement in mind on entering the situation. Such an organism has a considerable advantage, since it can count non-reinforced trials against reinforced trials and thus sometimes avoid taking chance associations between stimuli as evidence of potentially valuable non-chance associations. It can also extinguish a relation between stimuli that was valuable but is no longer and thus avoid the handicap of learned responses that are no longer relevant. Bitterman's (1975) evidence suggests that fish may be incapable of having the reinforcement 'in mind'. They learn slowly, extinguish slowly and, when presented with a black/white discrimination in which black is reinforced 70 per cent of the time and white 30 per cent, distribute their responses at random but in the same proportion thus getting the reinforcement only 58 per cent of the time. The rat on the other hand learns quickly, extinguishes quickly and responds to black on every trial thus getting the reinforcement 70 per cent of the time. All of which is consistent with possession of the capacity to have the reinforcement 'in mind' and thus recognize that it is absent as well as that it is present. The phenomena are of course explicable in other terms, usually derived from Pavlov's concepts of conditioned and unconditioned internal inhibition. Anything whatever may be explained in these terms by setting the parameters of variation at appropriate values. Reactive inhibition was originally postulated to explain the fact that experimental extinction occurred without supposing that the organism could recognize the absence of reinforcement, since to suppose this implied that the organism had some kind of effective internal representation of the reinforcement and such a supposition was necessarily 'unscientific'. We have seen that there is nothing necessarily unscientific about this supposition, it is indeed required by our intuitions of our own behaviour for organisms like ourselves. The evidence above suggests that rats may represent the lowest level of phylogenetic complexity at which it is present and that fish may be below that level.

The ability to 'have in mind' the reinforcement involves the ability to be consciously aware of something that is not present in the IPE, something whose representation is drawn from the memory store. It is here beginning to be possible for the organism to detach itself from its IPE. This is the first step on the road to the evolution of the capacity to operate on the IPE and draw conclusions about it; thus when an organism has evolved to the point where it can have in mind a present state of the IPE and a state no longer present, comparisons become possible; that observation of similarities and differences between perceptual events which is the foundation of language. It is not necessary to postulate such a capacity to account for the behaviour of any organism below the level of the primates but there is evidence that primates have it in a rudimentary form. Human beings have it in a highly developed form, it is essentially what makes them human in the humanist sense. Thus it may be said that behaviourism can in principle account for the behaviour of organisms below the level of the rat that are unable to detach themselves from their IPEs and are thus in the same relationship to their environment as billiard balls are to theirs. Above that level, behaviourist accounts may seem to apply when the organism is prevented (or in the case of a human subject dissuaded) from using whatever capacity he may have to detach himself and this is often an unremarked side-effect of the imposition of rigorous experimental controls. Behaviourism is of value in demonstrating the essential continuity between species, but mammalian species appear to possess capacities which preclude the explanation of their behaviour in terms of S-R laws. These capacities (though largely as yet unexplained) do not appear likely to require resort to any extra-scientific principles for their understanding.

At the level of complexity attained by the human species the ability to detach oneself from one's IPE has resulted in the construction of numerous systems of thought, theories of the operation of the real world, works of art, etc., some of which are the province of humanism and some of the non-psychological scientific disciplines. It is important to avoid any suggestion that psychology will take over from theology as the Queen of Sciences. Such an implication is not far beneath the surface in some humanist psychologies, at least with regard to the problems of everyday living, and Howarth (chapter 11) seems to suggest that psychology may have contributions to make to every discipline, scientific or other. Such a suggestion is unlikely to be acceptable to specialists in other disciplines and is also in my opinion unlikely to prove well founded. Psychology has its own object of study, the mind, the nexus between the body (the sphere of the physical and biological sciences) and the mind's products (the sphere of the arts and the human sciences).

Psychology, like other sciences, faces difficulties unique to itself resulting from the specific characteristics of the entities with which it is concerned. These difficulties result from the fact that the mind is essentially a model-making structure; there is no more reason to doubt that the mind has a structure of its own than there is to doubt that a computer has a structure separate from that of the programs run on it but this structure's function is to model other structures so as to provide the organism with a predictive basis for interaction with the real world of persons and things. The only observational evidence available to the psychologist is the behaviour of the organism, which is determined by the model made by that organism for use in that particular situation. The structure of the mind, the model-making entity, has to be deduced from the models it makes in different situations. The nearest analogy is perhaps with X-ray crystallography, with the additional complication that the situation is defined in part by the entity under investigation not wholly by the investigator. It could be argued that the interposition of a model originated by the entity under investigation between that entity and the behaviour from which its structure has to be deduced makes the deduction strictly impossible and that therefore no science of psychology is possible. This argument neglects the opportunity offered by the fact that individual minds have special access to their own mode of operation, to the models they make. This is not to suggest that direct introspection is necessarily of value but the phenomena revealed by introspection are as capable of analysis as are empirical phenomena. It happens that British and American psychologists are so closely identified with the analysis of empirical phenomena as to have forgotten that there is an essential preliminary, the identification of a phenomenon as a phenomenon worthy of study: not all phenomena are. Phenomenology is specifically concerned with this problem and has a contribution to make to all sciences but its contribution to psychology is of special significance because of the unbounded scope of the mind as a model-maker. Which of these models are potentially informative as to the structure of the mind itself? The mind can make a model to enable the organism to play noughts-and-crosses: will the behaviour depending on this model necessarily permit the deduction of any important characteristic of the mind itself? If not there is no point in making noughts-and-crosses behaviour the subject of experimental investigation. Phenomenology can accomplish little alone, but as much is true of experiment; a genuine science (and in particular psychology) requires both.

To conclude, there appears to be no obstacle to the construction of a science of psychological psychology. Like other sciences this will be based on material monism and employ the scientific methods appropriate to the investigation of material phenomena. It can allow the entity which is the object of the investigation an efficacious consciousness and the freedom to operate as an initiator of behaviour. This will be insufficient to meet the theologian's criteria for 'free will' (these criteria cannot be met in a material monist framework) but sufficient to allow the reality of all the phenomena with which the humanist psychologist is concerned. At the same time it will postulate only structures which can instantiate themselves in a nervous system having the characteristics we know the nervous system to have. It will however be reducible to physiology only in the same sense that chemistry is reducible to physics and physiology to chemistry. That is, in the ontological sense that all these sciences are concerned with aspects of one material reality.

Is man an ape or an angel?

R. L. Reid

Disraeli asked the question, and answered it by declaring himself to be 'on the side of the angels'. The date was 1864 and the controversy over Darwin's assertion of the mutability of species was acute, acrimonious and not wholly rational.

Behaviourism shares some features with evolutionism. Phylogenetic shaping by contingencies of survival is echoed in the shaping of individual behaviour by contingencies of reinforcement. Both processes are demonstrable and both principles of selection can be used speculatively and in retrospect to explain how the present state of affairs happened to come about. But what brings to mind the infamous 'apes and angels' debate is a similarity in the reaction against evolutionism and behaviourism, rather than any direct correspondence between the theories themselves. Of particular interest are the Victorian fulminations against Darwin, suggesting that to accept the theory of the descent of man would be to precipitate an actual descent to ape-like behaviour. Only believe that your ancestors were apes and you would risk throwing off civilization and becoming an ape yourself. Darwin was seen to aim a blow at morality and human dignity. A similar danger has been and surprisingly still is discerned in behaviourism. Only believe and you may change men into machines. Even more alarming is the thought that although behaviourism may be wrong it could still have the power to make itself come true. Such ways of thinking give a peculiar piquancy to the title of Shotter's chapter 'Men the magicians'. Are there things that we had better not talk about, not investigate, not know? The principle of natural selection was once thought to have diminished man's stature. Is reinforcement the next apple on the tree? Nothing has been the same since the earth ceased to be the centre of the universe. I believe that knowledge is always enriching and that the great risk is to put barriers in the way of the method of free inquiry which characterized the older forms of humanism.

It is doubly irrational to fear behaviourism if it is taken to be a doctrinaire account of the muscle twitches of rats, formulated 60 years ago. This bogey would be exorcized if ordinary standards of scholarship were to be observed. Contemporary behaviouristic psychology is about operants, acts shaped and defined by their effects, more akin to voluntary actions than to those 'muscle twitches' conjured up by the critics of John B. Watson. No one 'denies consciousness' - but the meaning of the phrase is obscure except in referring to Watson's denial of the existence of a conscious mind such as Titchener had tried to describe. In the special case of human action it is obvious that an account of the acquisition of a language has to be attempted in terms of non-linguistic processes. Thereafter the influence of language on other behaviour can be studied within a behaviouristic psychology, making a distinction between 'rule-governed' and 'contingency-controlled' behaviour, as does Skinner. Among the most important tasks of psychology is the analysis of the interaction of words and deeds, whether in Skinner's terminology or not, and at least one area of interaction, self-control, has been studied intensively and effectively by operant psychologists.

A number of points about contemporary behaviouristic psychology are set out lucidly by Blackman (chapter 8) who mentions an embarrassment that tends to recur in the professional lives of those who are regarded as behaviourists. A critic of behaviourism, becoming convinced by discussion that one's point of view is sensible and intelligent, then decides that he cannot be talking to a real behaviourist after all. This may be a move in a welcome direction but it only goes part of the way towards the conclusion that behaviourists, in the stereotyped sense, do not exist. A label like 'behaviourist' is useful and acceptable only if it is allowed to change in meaning as knowledge increases, and it has to be defined by those who accept the label. (Being told what one must necessarily believe because one is known as a 'behaviourist' is like being told how to pronounce one's own name.) But it is doubtful whether by now the word 'behaviourist' is useful except perhaps as a term of abuse, meaning someone who believes what McDougall thought Watson believed.

With relief at changing my label, I join the ranks of the empirical or experimental psychologists, where I think I belong, and note that one outcome of the Conference was to show that most such psychologists see no pressing need for a reorientation or a radically new conception of man. Psychology is in crisis for some, who seem to want to redefine it, while others see steady, although perhaps undramatic progress being made and believe that, in spite of differences in techniques and attitudes to theory within different fields, no great difficulties stand in the way of fitting them together. Within the empirical camp (to invoke one of the many warlike metaphors of the humanistic/dramaturgical/magical psychologists) there is plenty to do by way of obtaining more information, using ideas that have not yet outlived their usefulness. It does not seem likely that the problems that interest empirical psychologists will cease to be problems through the sudden discovery of a new model of man. New systems of thought are expected to emerge from research rather than be superimposed from above, reflecting the growth of knowledge rather than changes in fashion.

A revival of interest in theoretical/philosophical issues adds a welcome variety to psychology although the grandiosity of the approach may not be to everybody's taste. When Darwin's theory first came out, discussion was confused because it was difficult to know whether to reply to it in theological or in scientific terms. A similar bafflement was felt during the Conference. What are the rules for judging the jumbo-sized models? Their exponents seem to concentrate on criticizing other points of view without demonstrating what is so good about their own or even saying how its worth is to be judged. Sheer criticism is an ineffective irritant and contributes only to our reputation for trying to stand on the faces rather than on the shoulders of our colleagues. The problem of judging a model is made peculiarly difficult when its author disavows any intention of predicting behaviour. In that case, are we to judge the model as literature or are we being asked not to judge at all? And finally, how could the Conference as a whole be assessed? By the proportion of participants who changed their minds?

Project for a humane psychology: Science and personal agency

N. M. Cheshire

Any informed attempt, however belated, to lead psychology out from the Dark Ages of doctrinaire experimentalism, and into the Renaissance of a realistic study of interpersonal action and experience, should no doubt be given aid and comfort. Throughout the Conference, we found ourselves making frequent reference to Shotter's efforts in this direction (see chapter 2); and, much as I sympathize with them, I wonder if he does not overstep the mark and provoke unnecessary disaffection. In his concern to demechanize psychology, he seems to err in the direction of hypomechanization in so far as he makes a mystery out of things which, relatively speaking, are scarcely mysterious at all.

For instance, his example of hand-shaking, which he takes to depend upon some sort of quasi-magical interpersonal 'accommodation' and 'equilibrium' (to impose Piaget's terms), is conspicuously romanticized. We do have the equipment, both conceptual and experimental, for distinguishing behaviour which is over-learned, and for that reason no longer consciously monitored, from actions that are in some important way intuitive; and we understand that the latter lack conscious monitoring for a different reason, namely that they never were consciously monitored in the first place. The further question whether, and how, such intuition is 'learned' is a separable and examinable issue (which Shotter and others do, of course, tackle elsewhere). This being so, is it not gratuitously obscurantist to give the impression that we do not know how to sort such matters out? For this kind of reason, I regret that some aspects of Shotter's 'alternativism' appear not so much 'constructive' as almost perverse.

If some such demystification had been undertaken, by reference to existing theories and techniques, it would have served also to draw the teeth of a second objection. Gray complained that Shotter's message seemed to lack a coherent theoretical substructure (see edited discussion pp. 32-34), and it is difficult not to share some of his irritation on this point. But my reasons for irritation are, I suspect, different from Gray's: for him this lack seems to be a sign that the whole enterprise is intrinsically misguided or at least impossible to assess, whereas for me it means that the message is less persuasive than it would otherwise have been. Naturally it might be premature and unrealistic to expect Shotter to have produced a novel and rigorous conceptual framework of his own; but there are a number of psychological theories which have some of the characteristics he seems to need, and it would give us some helpful conceptual bearings if he were to tell us how his own theoretical scheme, implicit though it may be, is like them and how it is unlike them (to borrow the immortal words of the Terman-Merrill test).

To be sure, we can see from his quotations that his attitudes are in sympathy at various points with such thinkers as McMurray, Merleau-Ponty, Buber and Lao Tsu. But this much is absurdly vague, because when he talks about the construction of 'self-images', he might equally well have quoted from Freud on the 'ego ideal', from Solveig's dialogue with Peer Gynt at the very end of the play, or from that Apostle who writes that 'it doth not yet appear what we shall be' (I John, iii, 2). In order to use these allusions constructively, we need to know as well where Shotter's 'model of man' differs from those of these other authorities, and this amounts to identifying what the conceptual model-builders call 'the area of negative analogy' (Hesse, 1966; Cheshire, 1975).

I ventured in discussion at the Conference to advocate a psychological theory which does seem to capture many of the aspects of interpersonal conduct and experience which fascinate Shotter: the Kleinian system of 'object-relations', with its central concern for the essential object-orientation of mental life, for fantasy and magical thinking, and for the infantile development of social learning and apperception (Segal, 1964, 1979). Indeed this volume contains remarkably little about psychodynamic 'models of man' of any kind, though Marie Jahoda (chapter 19, pp. 282-284) does discuss the supposed failure of the Freudian models. One fears that this may be to some extent because the recurrent counterfactual folklore about the untestability, and hence the scientific unrespectability, of such theories has become institutionalized; and Gray did in fact oblige at one point by explicitly verbalizing this legend. However, just as psychological news used to travel slowly in Cambridge, as Joynson illustrated, so evidently some news still travels slowly to Gray's department in Oxford. For there has accumulated over the last 40 years or so a considerable literature about the empirical testing of psychoanalytic notions, and a handful of Gray's audience have actually been contributors to that corpus or to its study, as Kline's newly revised critique shows (Kline, 1980). (A striking case of 'I see no ships'!) The fact that such misleading pronouncements continue to be made, and have indeed to a great extent become part of the subculture in which psychology students are trained, touches upon another pervasive pre-occupation of the Conference, namely our concern that the activities of psychologists be 'scientific'.

Following Reid and Bromley, who reminded us that controversies which are cast in terms of '-isms', '-ologies' and abstractions can often be rescued from sterility by substituting representative questions framed in particular and concrete terms (see edited discussion, chapter 20, p. 309), I used an example from the history of 'real science' to try to expose the confusion and artificiality inherent in some of our tendentious contrasts between what is 'scientific' and what is not (see Note). Let us apply this same lesson to another dispute which arose in the course of discussion, and try out one further therapeutic technique of the linguistic philosophers; for another source of defective reasoning which they have instructively exposed is the implied but misleading contrast on which an argument may tacitly trade (Warnock, 1962).

Brener was at one point pressing Fransella to say 'yes' when asked 'Is man a natural phenomenon?' (or rather he was in effect defying Fransella to answer 'no'), his purpose being to set up the inference that the appropriate methods of study in psychology would therefore be those of the 'natural' sciences. Now, since man is a member of the animal kingdom, a product of evolution and so on, it seems unreasonable to deny that he is part of nature and in that sense a 'natural phenomenon'. But as psychologists, we do not deal with 'man' in the abstract: we deal with particular aspects of the functioning of particular people. What happens then if we particularize the question and make it concrete? 'Is man a natural phenomenon?'; and more realistically still, since we are concerned with particular things that people do (don't do, think, feel, expect, worry about, remember, don't remember, perceive, etc.), the question becomes more like 'Is Mrs Smith's overprotectiveness, or John's fear of failure, or Mary's verbal facility a natural phenomenon?'

Already the reformulated question is beginning to sound awkward and unreal. So let us now expose the implied logical contrast: 'natural phenomenon' - as opposed to what? Interestingly, this move coincides with applying Kelly's 'personal construct' scheme, which Fransella herself would advocate (see chapter 17), by asking what is the implicit pole of the construct being employed whose emergent pole is 'natural phenomenon'? The term 'natural' may derive its semantic and psychological impact from being contrasted implicitly with a great variety of other terms, and a clear understanding of the direction of this contrast is crucial to a coherent and fruitful argument.

According to whether we are concerned with cream, flowers, sex, religion, chickens, inflexion or anxiety, some typical candidates for the 'polar term' would be: synthetic, artificial, perverted, supernatural, battery-reared, consciously contrived, pathological. In the case of interpersonal actions in a social context, however, a traditional contrast for 'natural phenomenon' (at least since Vico and the rise of the social sciences) has been 'culture-determined phenomenon'. Now, on the one hand, we will not answer 'no' to Brener's question if that commits us to saying that 'man' and his behaviour are essentially synthetic, supernatural, battery-reared or perverted, etc. On the other hand, against the background of the nature/culture antithesis, it may well make very good sense to give that answer in order to signal that a particular action, attitude or anxiety (such as Mrs Smith's overprotectiveness, or John's fear of failure, or Mary's verbal facility) is in important ways a product of their culture rather than of 'nature'.

This would be to open up again the time-honoured debate whether nature-based as opposed to culture-based paradigms, with their familiar long German names, are the more appropriate to our subject matter. Or rather, it would be to ask what purposes in psychology are served better by the one sort of paradigm than by the other. And this can be a proper and productive debate, provided that its own internal contrasts are themselves kept under scrutiny, and provided that we do not assume, pace Eysenck (chapter 4), that one alternative has the monopoly of pathways to valid discovery.

NOTE

The example concerned Kekulé's much-quoted daydream about cannibalistic snakes, and its 'scientific' status in the discovery of the structure of the benzene ring.

Conference overview: And is the question of models an unavoidable issue?

G. Thinès

The word 'model' is a fascinating one for psychologists because, quite apart from the functional role it may play in locating research and promoting creative thinking, it sounds technical and it immediately conveys the impression that one is engaged at the outset in some serious scientific endeavour. Nonetheless, the word is ambiguous and may serve to designate many different things. If our Conference has solely contributed to making the participants aware of this, I feel that a major objective has been achieved, if not the essential one. A striking example of the ambiguity in the meaning of 'model' may be found in the fact that the very title of the Conference is literally identical to that of three books: one was published by Simon in 1957 and deals with computer simulation of behaviour, the other was published by Dagenais in 1972 and is devoted to a phenomenological critique of some paradigms in the human sciences. More recently, Hollis (1977) produced the third book bearing that title. A thorough search in the vast literature on models may perhaps lead one to discover other books and articles bearing similar or identical titles.

Such similarities in wording may be claimed to be unimportant and to result simply from historical circumstances which tend to impose particular expressions in various fields of knowledge for reasons of facility and clarity, and most of all because such expressions subtend a wide range of concepts endowed with some common fundamental features. However, since the eventual rules of congruence underlying the supposedly homologous phenomena are not known at this initial stage and, moreover, since in each field considered these particular phenomena may still be themselves approached in a pre-scientific manner, these so-called common features result in fact from pragmatic decisions which materialize in some kind of overall working intentionality. The danger in such cases lies in the fact that no principle whatsoever is available as a sufficient criterion allowing us to appreciate with precision the momentary stage of systematization reached by the fields of knowledge tentatively brought together in the model in question. This is mainly due to the historical dimension of scientific domains, according to which the pragmatic decisions mentioned above are never expressed in a clear-cut fashion and appear mostly in the literature under the form of implicit statements, as if the underlying evidence were to be accepted as a matter of course. Worthy of notice in this respect is the following quotation from Wundt's 'Grundzuege der Physiologischen Psychologie' (1903): 'In the same fashion as physical and chemical phenomena, or law and state, or again society and history do not refer to entirely different factual substrates but only to different points of view, from which we consider natural phenomena, the latter covering in our case some complex forms of mental life, physical and psychic phenomena do not refer to different substances, though the requirements of scientific analysis oblige us to consider them apart' (p. 764, author's translation). There is here an indirect assumption that 'some complex forms of mental life' would belong by their very essence to the realm of natural phenomena.

I selected an early psychological text because it is directly linked with the foundations of psychology at an initial stage of its history, a time at which basic questions concerning psychology's epistemological autonomy were perhaps more crucial than in the present-day context. As to the objection that today's views on the 'natural' essence of psychic phenomena are expressed within a radically different framework, or even that the problem as such has become obsolete, I may be tempted to answer that reductionism is still very much alive and that many of our so-called models are often based on assumptions concerning subjective components of behaviour which have not developed much since Wundt's epoch, even if we do now refrain from speaking of 'mental life'. The above instance may at least help us to become aware of a dangerous illusion; viz. the assumption that a model is always at the outset a purposeful and logically well-structured set of propositions. If this is indeed the aim which is ideally to be reached in every possible case, we must examine to what extent such a conceptual construct is actually meant, intentionally or explicitly, whenever the word is used in psychology and other human sciences. For reasons of accuracy and clarity I use Bunge's (1973) terminology in the sections below.

THE MODEL AND THE A PRIORI

If we agree to include under 'model' every initial representation of a problem one sets oneself to solve, we have to turn to the question of the role of the a priori. Philosophical reflections on the nature of psychology as a science meet a growing interest among empirically inspired as well as phenomenologically inspired psychologists. This testifies, in my opinion, to an increasing awareness of the role which the represented tasks play in the tentative realization of a particular piece of research. If we consider with Bunge (1973) 'model objects and theoretical models as hypothetical sketches of supposedly real, though possibly fictitious, things or facts' (p. 91), there is a structural difference between the models defined in this fashion and any sort of a priori. There is also, in this case a structural difference between the a priori and the hypothesis. The a priori is the minimal starting-point of any thought process; that is, of any organized sequence of concepts obeying a minimum of syntactic rules and leading eventually to some logically or factually coherent new concept. Such a starting-point may be considered as basically unimportant, as evidenced by the widespread conviction that many major scientific findings emerged from haphazard incidental observations and also by the traditional philosophical conviction according to which every sort of thought process is initially rooted in intuition. Serendipitous discoveries leading to later well-structured models of a given aspect of reality are considered to have been 'haphazard' because they are unexpected in terms of subjective probabilities - but not because they belong, as provisionally unexpressed structures, to a purely random order of phenomena. The opposite view seems on the contrary more appropriate, since an event can only be said to be unexpected if some other event was actually expected; that is, if some well-defined hypothesis had already been formulated in another direction. In this case, the minimal a priori is only remotely present and some model object has been formed.

Intuition refers to all possible unexpressed subjective experience leading in an undefinable fashion to the first expression (or eventually proposition) in a particular domain. The trouble with intuition is that, in philosophy, there has been a consistent temptation to stress the uselessness of every attempt to pass from the unexpressed to the expressed, suggesting thereby that there exists within consciousness some radically inexpressible reality.   The well-known Bergsonian thesis opposes intuition as continuous experience to the objective fragmentation of conceptual language (Bergson, 1963). In such a perspective, the idea of model is seen as a rather negative construct, since it is supposed to prevent that peculiar kind of communication with reality whose essential feature is supposedly devoid of any language-character. This and related immanentist views need not be developed further for our purpose, since they do not even allow us to refer to the initial a priori stage.

Intuition has however another sense in philosophy, which brings us back to the question of models as related to the founding moment of every act of knowledge. I suggested above that a kind of primitive model is always elaborated in the genesis of hypotheses on the basis of the a priori moment. Turning to phenomenology, it should be recalled that in Husserl's view, the role of intuition is not to be limited to the realm of immanent inexpressible qualities, but on the contrary to serve as a synthetic founding act aiming at further object characterizations. In other words, whatever the ulterior theoretical construct may be (i.e. be it empirically inspired or not; say, a perceptual description or a mathematical structure), the initial step is intuitive in the sense that it has the character of a direct pre-scientific exploration, even if it implies at that very moment the existence of a definite kind of categorization transcending pure perceptual experience. A typical instance of the last-mentioned case may be found in Meinong's analysis of real or ideal complexes as related to perception on the one hand, and to description or logical statements on the other hand. The intuitive act and its first categorial consequences amount to a delineation of the 'state of affairs' (Sachverhalt) concerning any kind of object under study. As Spiegelberg (1960) puts it in connection with Reinach's theory of the phenomenological a priori:

> A priori states of affairs are universal for all possible examples, and they are necessary in the sense that the a priori property contained in the Sachverhalt belongs to its carrier by an essential necessity ... Universality and necessity are for Reinach only secondary characteristics of the a priori; they follow from the more basic fact that there are essential connections which are immediately intuitable and which can be given with complete adequacy. Thus 'a priori' means at bottom nothing but the fact that a certain property is necessarily entailed by the essential structure of an object and can hence be understood as such. (p. 199)

It is of interest for our purpose to refer to Husserl's own theory in order to investigate whether the concept of model (in the sense of Bunge's model object, if nothing else) may be framed in his conception of founding intuition. According to his descriptive characterization of the object-profiles, no phenomenon, from perceptual structures up to mathematical entities, is given in its totality, but only under one particular profile (Abschattung) at a time. Each profile, however, acts as an indicator of the essence of the phenomenon, the essence being ideally the final integrated totality of all possible profiles.   Intuition is founding because it actually grasps pre-scientifically a set of properties which cannot possibly be inferred at that stage; it therefore deals with the most primitive mode of subject-object relation and can thus be said to deal with the essence of phenomena. This calls for two comments. (1) The relation just described amounts to evidencing object-properties which are directly dependent on the constitutive capacities of subjectivity.   Consequently, any model object is defined at the outset in its structure as being at the same time the minimal and the maximal set of describable properties. (This corresponds in fact to necessity and universality as postulated by Reinach.) (2) The essences of phenomena, as resulting from what Husserl calls 'eidetic intuition', place them in a regional ontology.   In other words, every a priori has wider implications than the mere delimitation of a given field of knowledge within which further constructs are elaborated: it implies necessarily a minimal conception of reality. This means that the a priori, even when unformulated (which is mostly the case), exists as a particular profile of a more general image or model of the subject's world, in the absence of which the intentional core of the act of knowledge concerned would be devoid of sense, if possible at all.

In conclusion, we see that there exist some peculiar relationships between the a priori and the concept of model; the latter referring here to the structure of subjective acts and their necessary context at the initial stage of cognitive elaboration under the form of representation. From this point of view, we may answer positively the question put in the title of this paper: under its primitive intentional form, the idea of a model is an unavoidable issue. Needless to say, if I feel entitled to use the term at this stage of my analysis, it is only because I want to stress the fact that this widespread concept can be used to describe not only the structure of a hypothesis or of a theory, but also the primary structure of the noema-noesis relationship which allows them to emerge at a given moment. At this stage, the structure of this relationship has not yet given rise to any definite construct.

ACCURACY, CONGRUENCE AND HEURISTIC VALUE

At the a priori stage, the only fact which may suggest some link with the idea of model is thus the existence of a representation of some kind. Bunge (1973) stresses the fact that the modelling relation - that is, the adequacy of the principles of the system intended as a model (e.g. a mathematical function) to the actual set of facts under study - generally resists representation and is thus unavailable at that level as an organized structure. It can thus be said that at the level of initial intuitive acts, as tentatively grouped under the a priori, no specific rules of structuration and transformation are explicitly present. To be sure, even if intuition is liable to give rise to a well-structured hypothesis after a while, its postulated relation to real structures rests on what the same author calls a 'semantic assumption'. Since formal languages have no prescribable content at the outset, this assumption must be made as precise as possible, in order to ascertain that a manipulation of the model may be assumed to correspond to a manipulation of the real thing. Bunge (1973) writes further:

> An explicit exhibition of the modelling relation will not only indicate what one is talking about but may also constitute a reminder that the object model, though hoped to represent a certain thing, is not the same as it. It is never useless to insist that every model object is an idealization of a system or a fact taken to be real or realizable. There are as many idealizations as idealizers, data and goals. Even if two model builders have access to the same empirical information, they may construct different models, for model building is a creative activity engaging the background, abilities, and taste of the builder. (p. 96)

These remarks concerning the conditions in which a model object may be generated, apply also, and even more specifically, to the tentative idealization process characterizing the intuitive a priori. What follows - that is, when a hypothesis has been put in proposition form and when, further, a theoretical and eventually mathematical model is in view - is an accurate picture of reality, congruent with what observation yields and heuristic, that is capable of generating new hypothetical propositions. A rather difficult aspect of this overall process is the essence of the construct itself. Accuracy concerns the rules of the formal language as such, and is therefore readily obtained if the language is correctly used. Congruency will be obtained if the language used conveys information relevant to the object, as required by the limits of utterance defined by the semantic assumption. Heuristic value will in its turn be obtained if, after a given sequence of descriptive propositions, a non-descriptive proposition can be uttered.   In other words, a model becomes heuristic as soon as it generates propositions which do not deal with contents referring significantly to its own past or present state as a system.   Considering the way the system functions at a given moment, it may comply with the conditions of accuracy and of heuristic value, without being congruent.   But congruence raises a paradox as far as scientific reality coincides with the construct itself.   How is it then thinkable that we may require that the construct or model should correspond to reality?   Clearly, this indicates that the word reality, as applied to the referent of the model, does not designate any piece of scientific knowledge, but rather some perceptual and/or cognitive non-formalized elements prior to modelling.   Moreover, since heuristic value is lost as soon as the model in progress turns back to its previous or present state, these elements cannot be looked for in that particular part of the overall process either.   We must thus conclude that the reality of the referent can only be found in the intuited a priori or, at best, in that non-formal part of the hypothesis which defines the general intentionality of the process which has led to the modelling itself.

For these reasons, I think that a phenomenological approach to the problem of modelling is not gratuitous speculation about the accurate realizations of scientists, or at least of non-phenomenologically oriented workers.   The point is, I believe, that no reference to reality, and hence no model-congruence can be discovered if one discards the problem of the subjective constituents of representation.   There is, therefore, some naivety in assuming that accurate knowledge is at hand by the very fact that some kind of modelling is going on.   If models are an unavoidable issue, it is first and foremost because they are pressed upon us by the very acts through which we establish some intentional relationship with noemata, and because they include, as such, a certain amount of pre-scientific phenomena present in our experience in spite of our eventual pretence to be rigorous at the outset.

GENERATING AND TESTING THEORIES IN PSYCHOLOGY

These remarks about the rootings of modelling in representation and its subjective constituents need not be developed further, because they concern only the origin of modelling intentionalities and not their actual outcomes; viz. the theoretical models or specific theories as they are currently formulated in psychology.   It is outside our brief to ask here whether these founding intentionalities amount to an acceptance or rejection of psychologism in the Husserlian sense, though the accusation of psychologism made by Husserl against mentalistic realism, was ultimately aimed at destroying some coarse models of man, namely the associationist and the Fechnerian ones.   Considering the developments of psychology since the period when phenomenology began to question the fundamental character of scientific psychology, we cannot avoid asking whether our present-day models are truly less coarse than the early ones.

But what allows us to speak of a coarse model as opposed to a more refined one? At first sight, a coarse model is one which, after reduction to its basic constituent parts, proves to make sense only at the level of representation initially needed to permit its elaboration.   Thus, in psychology, the concept of trace, for instance, which is still widely used in memory studies, refers initially to physical phenomena such as magnetic remanence or to chemical ones, such as the persisting presence of contaminating molecules in a solution which has undergone various stages of purification.   Psychologists expect to give an accurate account of memory by assuming that, according to the universality principle, there is little, if any, chance that the still undefinable properties of organic substrates allowing information recall or retrieval, may behave otherwise than as physical entities.   This assumption has remained up to now a matter of faith, since no theory to date has succeeded in bridging the gap between the facts of genetic transfer of information and those related to ontogenetic information recall.   This faith or belief may conveniently be said to be synonymous with a wide set of unverified hypotheses. The difficulty does not lie at the level of theoretical reductionism as such (because there would be no sense in looking for an explanation of memory processes by discarding the idea of one or several molecular information carriers at the outset), but rather in what seems to be the impossibility of achieving an actual test of a hypothesis formulated in such terms. In other words, the unavoidable character of the memory model elaborated in this fashion sets an absolute limit to the development of a theory requiring that all phenomena (physical, physiological and cognitive) linked with the permanence of events in time, should be connected on a single continuum. A similar problem was encountered in the tentative assessment of the generalized isomorphic model proposed by Gestalt theorists. These and other well-known instances lead to the conviction that reductionism in psychology has the peculiar feature of generating models which resist testing by their very nature. Thus, physicalist models of perception and memory presuppose causal mechanisms which are coarsely figured at the level of representation and which only make sense if the same coarse representation is found back at the end of the process of scientific investigation. Hence we have the non-heuristic repetitiveness of many theoretical constructs currently elaborated in psychology and related fields of human sciences.

The widespread impossibility of establishing the continuity postulated by object-models between psychic phenomena and their supposedly corresponding causal mechanisms, has been a constant stumbling-block in the search for psychological models endowed with congruence. In such conditions, the modelling tendency in this field has evolved paradoxically in two main directions: (1) a search for quantitative accuracy as a sort of compensatory displacement of scientific interest making for the loss of congruence and heuristic value; (2) a qualitative displacement from organically bound analysis to more autonomous psychological systems. A steady trend in the first direction may be observed, in which assimilated mathematical procedures easily provide face validity for coarse model objects (mostly not recognized as such). Good instances are some over-simplifications of cybernetics in experimental psychology and the colonizing of psychology by linguistic analysis. The second tendency is at work in Gestalt models and in various clinical hermeneutics. An intermediate solution is now attempted in cognitive psychology, where the qualitative displacement hybridizes both with formalistic approaches and some epistemological concerns. These redirections may be considered paradoxical because the modelling falls back, perhaps unnoticed, to the level of intuitive representation (under the form of a persistent model object) in spite of its pretence either to be exact science, or to be subject-centred descriptive analyses.

The well-entertained illusion here is that one or several models of man's psychic organization will emerge, and perhaps one or more may prove adequate. However, there is up to now no compelling reason to suppose that adequacy may be unequivocally defined and that, if such a definition could be formulated, even in very general terms, it would allow us to define further the minimal criteria needed to accept or reject the emerging model(s). The implicit assumption made by many at the Conference was that many models may be found acceptable in the end. If proposed models are to be tested, they should take the form of theoretical models (or specific theories, as proposed by Bunge). As far as general theories are concerned, they should, according to the same author, only be taken into consideration if they can 'generate reasonably true theoretical models' (1973, p. 113). This being granted, let me now examine to what extent the various accounts presented at the Conference actually tackled the question of 'models of man'.

CONSTRUCTS AND COMPROMISES

Reading through the various contributions my first impression was certainly not that of a structured whole converging towards a central ideal liable to be used as a guideline in appreciating the adequacy of possible models of man. Perhaps this is due to the fact that I felt somewhat diffident at the outset about the legitimacy of trying to establish one or several models of 'man'. Tentative modelling in specific fields of research, such as perception, learning or brain mechanisms in behaviour, is a legitimate and necessary practice because in these and other specific frameworks, the a priori representation is liable (and bound) to form some model object by the very nature of its act. But it seems doubtful that any corresponding cognitive operation may actually be possible when 'man' is the issue.

This is not merely a question of words. For one thing, I do not see how the concept of man could be framed in a general theory - not to mention specific ones - without being framed in another one on the basis of different or even contradicting postulates. This is clear when one considers for instance the respective merits of biological versus psychological interpretations of man's place in 'the' or 'his' world, not to speak of all supposed answers given to the problem by various beliefs. More deceptive, however, are the not infrequent attempts at elaborating models of man in human sciences, which may eventually prove to be nothing else but cultural images. If human scientists are tempted to accept this state of affairs as corresponding to their ultimate objective, they should first try to investigate epistemologically whether they can rely on the kind of objectivity belonging to their own disciplines, in the line of Strasser (1963) and other phenomenologists. This is a crucial point, if only because phenomenologists refuse to reduce their endeavour to any sort of philosophy of culture (see on this point Husserl's 'Philosophy as Rigorous Science'). More importantly, the peculiar tendency of some psychologists to use unwittingly in their analyses cultural derivatives of scientific concepts borrowed from natural sciences must warn us against attempts at interpreting cultural images as models in the technical sense of the word. For the above reasons, it is neither sure nor excluded that some 'models of man' may belong to such a class of concepts.

Reviewing the various chapters presented in this volume, one can see how this general theme did indeed give rise to some ambiguities at the Conference. However, as they stand, the contributions fall into fairly distinct categories. A first category deals with the overall impact of models on psychological thinking (Warr, chapter 20; Broadbent, chapter 9; Wood, chapter 16; Jahoda, chapter 19). A second category deals with man as involved in the creative process of modelling (Harré, chapter 14; Fransella, chapter 17; Brener, chapter 7; Shotter, chapter 2; Reynolds, chapter 3; Hargreaves, chapter 15; Howarth, chapter 11). A third category includes studies on the social and ethical aspects of scientific psychology and some of their epistemological consequences (Eysenck, chapter 4; Wright, paper 1; Farr, chapter 13; Warr, chapter 12; Beloff, chapter 18; Boden, chapter 10). The fourth category stands a little apart since it deals with epistemological issues in the field where the modelling urge is perhaps most evident; viz. physiological correlates of behaviour and behaviouristic theory (Miller, chapter 6; Gale, chapter 5; Blackman, chapter 8). These subdivisions are only quasi-logical and therefore somewhat arbitrary. They are however necessary if one wants to get, as much as possible, a clear picture of the many different and sometimes discrepant views expressed. However, since it is impossible to give a detailed account of all papers and comments, let me limit myself to the discussion of some salient issues, apologizing at the outset for omissions or possible misinterpretations.

While stressing the usefulness of models in psychological research, some critical analyses express serious doubts concerning their value as heuristic tools when they are accepted in bulk as a basic requirement; that is, without making any distinction between the various degrees of structuralization they may attain. In this perspective, Warr (chapter 20) rightly insists on the necessity of conceiving models as sieves capable of enhancing the primary selection of working hypotheses. This, as I said before, is the first necessary and unavoidable function of the model: it helps to formulate the 'state of affairs' in a precise manner. Since this operation requires a definite reference to some kind of conceptual framework, one is tempted to say that, at its initial stage, model building refers to nothing other than intuitive representation focusing on one or more potential lines of analysis in a given field. The danger at this stage is to ignore the analytic potentialities of the conceptual framework itself. If we assume that the latter has the form of a general theory, the obvious requirement is then to submit it to a minimum of epistemological inquiry in order to ensure, not that the contents of the theory, as such, will eventually generate useful paradigms, but that, given its level of abstraction and its corresponding internal coherence, it is liable to generate paradigms at all, with all their necessary methodological consequences. Only then may the subsequent building up of a specific theory prove possible. This corresponds roughly to Warr's (chapter 20) warnings on the difficulties in passing from type-1 models (coarse object models) to type-2 models (importing analogues of the a priori kind) without losing sight of the paradigmatic potentialities of the conceptual framework (which may reduce, at the limit, to ideological items). In this respect, the analyses Warr devotes to the frequent inconsistencies which exist between general theories and miniature ones and the practical impossibility of bridging the gap by pure inductive thinking or empirical study open the way to a better understanding of the tasks of a sound scientific philosophy, including the epistemological bases of general theories of phenomena. Phenomenology is only one of them but it at least has the merit of recognizing itself as a general framework aware of its limited paradigmatic fruitfulness at the level of 'regional' ontologies. The fact that phenomenology as a general conceptual framework evolved historically through a fundamental criticism of causal explanation is beyond our considerations here, but it is not unconnected as a historical fact to Warr's remark that the jump from general theories to miniature ones cannot be justified by sheer (and endless) empirical work. Here again, the idea is that models are important in helping to arrive at a minimum of concise and clear-cut formulation of the intuitive a priori. They are not universal devices liable to furnish both the basic propositions necessary to the initial structuration of hypotheses and the technical means of analyses which are naively thought of as leading automatically to a specific theory. This childish view is nevertheless held quite widely. It has, among other things, led many psychologists to expect causal explanations from refined statistics and other mathematical tools; as if, for instance, causal relations could emerge from correlations; and, generally speaking, as if senseless questions could gain sense just by being translated into formal language.

It is for kindred reasons that Broadbent's account (chapter 9) appears to me as one of the major contributions to this volume. In spite of its negative title, his analysis shows the positive functions of models in a particularly convincing fashion. Let me select, from among the many fundamental issues tackled, some points which I consider to be particularly important. First, the injunction that 'models should as far as possible come at the end of research and not at the beginning' (p. 113). This is a principle which warns against the illusion that hypothesizing necessarily refers to the acceptable propositions of a previously well-tested specific theory, and which suggests correlatively that the starting-point of many research programmes belongs to classes of overall untestable statements of general theories. The consequent rule is thus: beware of unwittingly confounding a particular facet of your conceptual framework with some allegedly concrete hypothesis. This and the necessity stressed by Broadbent to proceed at the beginning by tentatively 'testing between alternative models' fits very well, in my opinion, with the idea expressed above that the unavoidable modelling occurs at the initial stage of specifying the intuitive a priori. Second, and much in the same line, a model must be selective (a 'sieve' according to Warr; a 'filter' according to Broadbent) and should not favour any single theory to the extent that one risks supporting it whatever the outcomes. This reminds us that there exists a direct relationship between selection and falsifiability and, moreover, that if selection is actually practised, '... there must ... be some implicit model or models behind any investigation; but that if we use one model and it is wrong we shall be looking in the wrong place, and may even conclude that something is true when it is not' (p. 115).

In discussing the inefficiency of research strategies, Broadbent rightly argues that if a model is formulated 'early and unambiguously', there is a greater probability that new ideas will appear during the development of the initial hunch. Indulging in my own philosophical axiology, I am tempted to see in this remark an opportunity to bring together the idea of the Husserlian a priori (as generating the rules of specific regional fields of research) and the Kantian a priori judgement (as being the source of newly discoverable attributes or properties). This, I hope, would not be discarded by Broadbent as unnecessary metaphysics. If, as he puts it, 'the point of a model is to avoid the need for experiment, even (if) the model itself arose from experiment' (p. 119) and if, considering metaphysical assumptions, 'there is really only one assumption which is necessary when using experiments to decide between models ... the assumption of causality' (p. 119), a somewhat overlooked aspect of model making emerges: its primary function is to enhance creative thinking. This being granted, the initial, or rather founding, models have little, if anything in common with models which are elaborated within the framework of simulation procedures, although any model object formed at the a priori stage simulates in some fashion a certain expected reality. If, as Broadbent remarks, a computer model is useful in itself in clarifying 'processes and structures which are internally consistent' (p. 117) and may be compared in its essence to a piece of research in pure mathematics considered apart from its eventual future application, the initial 'simulation' characterizing intuitive representation does not necessarily obey homologous rules of development, at least in time and in the successive partial 'decisions' taken within the system. This is why such human software processes are so easily challenged by scientists as being metaphysical, despite the fact that computing simulation rests ultimately on tentative 'models' of this sort.

Concerning 'models of man', we may stick to Broadbent's remarks about his own examples, namely that 'we are trying to model man, and yet there is a man in the model' (p. 125). Apart from its concrete functional meaning, this sentence applies to all situations in which the device required by the model - be it an actual behaviour pattern or a purely intellectual operation - is supposed to decide by itself what the observer or operator normally decides in ordinary life. Finally, we must beware of mixing up non-technical extensions of models and actual concrete modelling operations. This danger is inherent in the endeavour of arriving at some model (or models) of man satisfying a wide range of axiological attitudes; and it leads, in my opinion, to ideological and ethical distortions of scientific model building. This justifies the dual title of this last section of my comments: do we actually construct models according to some accepted rules dictated by the subject matter of our research topics, or do we compromise and put together in heterogeneous wholes (such as woolly psychological theories) bits of pre-scientific and scientific experience in order to meet the pragmatic urges of individual or social life? If this proved to be the case, there would be little sense in expecting that the theoretical evolution of psychological systems should lead by itself to some ultimate unified model. It may be that there is no place for such an expectation and that the minimal degree of convergence which may reasonably be expected, may only result from pragmatic similarities. This is apparently what Wood (chapter 16) suggests when he argues that the hypotheses that attempt to solve the same applied problems within similar social contexts tend, where successful, to converge on common practice. However, when the author defines a useful theory as heuristic devices for gaining access to patterns and regularities in social practice, one may fear that, in these conditions, heuristic value may be sought irrespective of the level of internal coherence and congruence attained since access to social structures and functions can be secured even if the 'heuristic' tool reduces to a schematic simulation of current behaviour events. In brief, such pragmatic work can be performed without requiring a specific theory and the 'useful' theory is then synonymous, either with a general untestable theory, or with an intuitive a priori. But efficient context-linked work of this sort provisionally proceeding that way is not excluded.

Wood insists on convergence, implying at the outset that taking the context into consideration imposes indirectly that plurality of points of view and of modes of analysis.   Much in the same line, Jahoda (chapter 19) argues that over-simplification in psychological models mostly results from splitting apart the individual subject and the social subject, and thus the model arises from an uncritical acceptance of a plurality of analytic points of view.   If further, 'psychological concepts (as opposed to biological ones) applied to people may have the power to change them' and if 'there is ample evidence that conceptual models of man have influenced the way people, not just psychologists, think and act' (p. 279), one has to agree with the author when she claims that a unitary model is impossible.   To me, the important consequence is that, multiplication of models being the rule, the need for selective epistemological work in this field seems once more to be the basic task.   This being the case, Jahoda's rejection of ontological models rests upon a conception of the metaphysical issues of the scientific act which I would be tempted to reject or at least to moderate.   To be sure, if the epistemological analysis concerns the possibility of delimiting a regional ontology (i.e. the necessary ontological implications of the scientific field in question), then conceptual models are always endowed with ontological properties.   The problem is therefore to build up models which do not contradict their necessary ontological prerequisites.   In this perspective, the above-mentioned dualistic treatment of the subject as individual or as social being can be eliminated by referring to the necessary links between subjectivity and inter-subjectivity as the unavoidable postulate of any form of psychology, even if axiological choices are at work to orient some psychologists towards the study of lived experience and some others towards the analysis of interpersonal interactions.   In stating this, I refer to a conceptual framework whose extension should be made precise, but whose epistemological impact could eventually lead one to ask to what extent conceptual frameworks really differ from regional ontologies in the Husserlian sense.

Keeping in mind Jahoda's idea of the dualistic over-simplification, there is no doubt that Harré (chapter 14) is right in stressing the necessity of avoiding both the old objective-subjective distinction and the more recent individual-social one.   His suggestion that man is a rhetorician actually engaged in manifold expressive or practical intentional endeavours, is a useful one because it refers every attempt at building up models of man to the founding function of his symbolic language.   Reading Harré's chapter confirmed my conviction that the theoretical work of psychologists proceeds all too often as if the human subject were reduced to silence as soon as he is confronted with the devices of the scientists who paradoxically assume that he is endowed with communication capacities in order to perform successful experiments.   This, I think, indicates that, in spite of the diversity of points of view, scientific psychology tacitly assumes in the vast majority of controlled situations that more is to be expected from the initial hypotheses than from the subject whom it helps to approach.   In other words, the scientist easily believes that the particular language he uses is the only founding one and that he is bound to discover heuristic propositions concerning man if he deliberately ignores the active intentionalities of the subject.   This is perhaps the most general intuitive model to be found in psychology since its positivistic origins.   Such criticism against reductionist pretences has been voiced repeatedly by phenomenologists.   Harré's reminder of the active properties of the subject falls into this line of analysis and raises, once more, the epistemological question whether scientific language must be considered solely as a subsystem within the overall founding activities of the human subject.   Such a conclusion may be considered as historically sound, since man was surviving long before the language of science became the main source of his power over nature and his fellow-men.

It appears from Fransella's contribution (chapter 17) that man the rhetorician is liable to generate that particular subspecies which she calls (after Kelly) 'man-as-scientist' without losing contact with the facts of life if 'behaviour is the experiment'.   However, the hope that spontaneous human relations may form the basis of a truly efficient construct is slight because, as Fransella herself rightly remarks, the model of the experimenting (or psychologizing in any particular field) takes one beyond the behaviour. In such conditions, the idea of model is, once more, an extended a priori leaving aside systematization rules as such.

I am much tempted to make similar comments regarding Shotter's (chapter 2) suggestive contribution concerning the structure of man's moral worlds. Here again, the idea of model is immersed in the complex whole of axiological decisions unceasingly taken by individuals within the social context, without specifying at the outset in terms of systems which kind of programme each individual is liable to generate or to admit. Shotter's chapter seems to me to offer a rather heterogenous compromise between issues (observational for some part) pertaining to human ethology and to the theory of values. Speaking of moral commitments, one should not forget that it is man's adaptive capacity to generate at the one time behavioural rules (biologically founded) and corresponding meta-rules (symbolically founded), the latter expressing the obligation to comply to the former. This is why I feel that in Shotter's analysis of the relations between joint action and intentionality, neither of them can be given priority. This being so, there is no need to refer to man as a 'magician', to use Shotter's own word, to describe the constraints he meets in his constitutionally unavoidable attempt at bridging the gap between his lived subjective world and the inter-subjective world as systematized in institutional realities. If this attempt is to be considered as defining a model of some sort, its meaning cannot be made precise by referring to intentionalities considered as values founding our moral worlds, because values have no predictable content. There is therefore some illusion in believing that the people's actions can be explained on the basis of this moral dimension. This does not mean that Shotter is wrong in thinking that the current framework of human actions should be considered as the ultimate source of psychological issues; he just expects too much of it in his attempt to build up sufficiently heuristic models; because any model, whatever its level of refinement, requires a minimum of invariance in the facts to be described or eventually explained and this is precisely what intentional values can hardly offer.

In this sense, I see some complementarity between the reflections of Shotter and those of Howarth. Howarth (chapter 11) argues that there are many reasons to be optimistic about psychology's future. In his opinion, man as a problem-solver offers a general model or strategy liable to be applied in nearly all sectors of psychology. However, it must be asked whether such generic qualification may effectively help us to formulate specific issues in an adequate fashion. Here again, the idea of one or several models of man coincides with the general intentional act of the psychologist when faced with the heterogenous aspects of human action, both from the individual and the social points of view. What is to be feared is that the intentional may be reduced to a wishful attitude rather than being recognized as the a priori with all its epistemological founding implications.

A solution to this problem is tentatively attempted by Hargreaves (chapter 15). It is worth noting that Hargreaves is the only contributor to this volume who states at the outset that his approach is phenomenological. Referring to the work of Schutz and Heider, the author asserts that 'phenomenology is the science of common sense' (p. 215) and outlines a semi-pragmatic programme liable to place scientific psychology within man's lived world as a discipline coping with man's actions according to a given set of subjectively accepted 'rules'. The idea that psychology should be centred on the subject's 'Lebenswelt' is indeed the general point of view of phenomenologically inspired psychologists, but here again this overall intentionality must act as the background of specific and testable questions. One must agree with Hargreaves' criticisms of the prerequisites of scientific psychology and corresponding current practices. This, in fact, is up to now the major <u>negative</u> theme of phenomenological psychology, but one is bound to look for constructive proposals. It should not be forgotten in this respect that neither classical scientific psychology, nor phenomenological psychology coincide with common sense in so far as any kind of heuristic model is tentatively elaborated. In my opinion, equating phenomenology with common sense amounts to confusing a conceptual framework with the objects it helps to bring to the analytical level. This is why I entirely agree with Hargreaves' seemingly self-destructive conclusion that 'when a phenomenological psychology takes its rightful, complementary position with other psychological models and perspectives, we shall, perhaps, be in a stronger position to create a psychology which goes beyond common sense' (p. 224) - granted, of course, that we do not mix up general theories with specific ones and coarse models with explanatory ones. In this respect, Wright's (paper 1) reminder of the Piagetian endeavour to build up an overall theoretical framework relating the genesis of operations to a fully fledged genetic epistemology, contains many comments which are well to the point.

INTEGRATION VERSUS COMPROMISE

Considering man's insertion in the social context on the one hand and the theoretical foundations of models of man on the other, it appears to me that the main difficulty encountered during the Conference was to reconcile the reality of everyday behavioural issues with a minimum of constructive rigour. This explains, in my opinion, why several contributors decided in favour of the various possible compromises that I have just outlined. In other cases, there has been a definite attempt at presenting an elaborated whole stressing the general conditions at which such compromises may be considered legitimate. In this sense, the well-documented and highly critical accounts by Eysenck (chapter 4), Warr (chapter 12), Farr, (chapter 13), Boden (chapter 10) and Beloff (chapter 18) must be considered as formulating the problem of modelling in sufficiently strict terms to allow a sound appraisal of what may be gained or lost in the understanding of the human subject by choosing to submit him to constructive analytic degrees of reductionism. Due to their length and to the fact that their contents cover an extended range of psychological issues, a detailed account of these chapters is beyond the scope of this final discussion. Boden's (chapter 10) analysis of the limits of artificial intelligence procedures deserves special mention however because it makes it clear that the 'dehumanizing' of the subject in such a perspective is not an unavoidable consequence of models endowed with a high degree of operational accuracy.

   This leads us to consider briefly the standpoint of experimentalists. As I suggested before, psychologists studying causal mechanisms of behaviour at the organic level are often believed to be the kind of human scientists who are more readily engaged in modelling than others. This opinion is certainly a remnant of the early conviction that there is little controlled work going on in psychology outside the laboratory. What most psychologists working in other fields quickly forget is that comparative and physiological causation is not justified by the crude fact that the experimenter has a supposedly direct access to the anatomo-physiological substrate. It should certainly be remembered that direct access to the organism is rather a metaphoric expression, because there is no physical privileged dimension in the organic reality which includes, as such, both the organized behaviour patterns and the organized underlying anatomo-physiological mechanisms. Thus, if we believe that modelling is a more obvious and more compelling practice in this field, it is just because we readily give more importance to the conditions of behaviour than to the emergent properties of behaviour themselves. Coming back to my previous analyses, I think that the real difference lies in a basically more favourable possibility for the biologically oriented psychologist to define his initial a priori within a limited field of potential scientific acts. This, however, is greatly dependent on methodological constraints, in the sense that it is practically impossible to dissociate methodological designs and corresponding (instrumental) techniques as soon as the subject is tackled through the register of organic potentialities. That it nevertheless makes sense to study subjectivity through the very structure of the organism and its corresponding founding actions on the surroundings, is evident when one considers the work of Sherrington on receptors in relation to the animal's field, or the work of Buytendijk on active and passive touch, to quote two famous instances. Unexpectedly enough, a model of subjectivity seems to be more easily attainable in these conditions than in some humanistic contexts, where language is the only possible object offered to the investigator.

Hence the analyses Blackman (chapter 8) devotes to the contemporary status of behaviourism are to be appreciated within a framework of this kind, because they show very well that, first, the current image of radical behaviourism is grossly over-simplified and, second, that rigorous psychological systems do not exclude adequate hypotheses concerning subjective components of behaviour, granted that 'man' is more than a cultural image. In fact, the real trouble is that cultural images distort both the object of human sciences (i.e. 'man') and these sciences themselves, in so far as one is ready to stick to epistemological criteria allowing for an acceptable distinction between 'science' and 'non-science'. Much in the same perspective, Gale (chapter 5) rightly argues that the ideal of the human scientist is not 'the' model at any cost, but a multiple set of convergent analyses in which 'the psychophysiologist must juggle with several models' (p. 71), so that 'the hallmark of psychophysiology is its commitment to integration between these various sources of knowledge and its openness to the philosophical analysis of the complexity of its subject matter' (p. 71). Referring to Miller's (chapter 6) remarks on the equivalent value in principle of reductionist and non-reductionist explanations, one may be justified in thinking that laboratory experimentalists are increasingly aware of the exact potentialities of their models, so that perhaps the ultimate question amounts to asking whether it makes sense to dissociate models of man from models of the organism. Here again, it is one of the tasks of epistemological inquiry to make a clear-cut distinction between biological and cultural models and to examine under what conditions they could eventually converge.

Psychobiologists, clinical psychologists and social psychologists are all concerned with emergent properties. This is why I fully subscribe to Gray's critical comments regarding pure linguistic analyses of behavioural facts versus experimental investigations, however limited they may seem when compared to the programmes of social sciences. To me, the question is not to know in which part of the nervous system consciousness is localized, because 'consciousness' is a symbol which I use to qualify an aspect of organic life without being certain at the outset that the word calls for a biological reality whose specificity would correspond precisely to a particular supposedly unequivocal word of my language. I therefore think that Gray (pp. 318-321) is right in considering that building up 'models of man' is premature and that a lot is to be learned from experiments before we are in a position to decide what belongs to man as a functioning structure and what belongs to man as a symbolic creator of language-linked superstructures. If the word 'man' used in the expression 'models of man' proves ultimately to have homologous meanings at the biological and at the cultural levels, then a great deal of psychology's ambiguities would be eliminated and the plurality of models would probably be seriously reduced. We may then agree with Reynolds (chapter 3) when he claims that the model of man which we need to operate is thus one that has to combine organic features, sociological features, features relating to understanding of our environment both social and physical. At the present moment, however, the semantic confusion which still pervades human sciences makes it difficult to imagine that the various categories just mentioned are truly distinguishable on the basis of epistemologically founded criteria.

CONCLUDING REMARKS

In adopting an epistemological standpoint, I do not pretend that one can fully appreciate scientific endeavours in psychology from a philosophical point of view detached from the actual work (theoretical and practical) of psychologists and other human scientists. However, as soon as one takes up the question of models, one raises a philosophical problem. The kind of epistemology I have in view is of the 'vigilant' type; that is, it concerns the necessary implications of the scientific work as it is actually performed. This is why I referred at the beginning of this paper to regional ontologies - in other words, to the unavoidable ideas about reality which govern our intellectual decisions when we tackle a particular question and consider, as much as possible, the consequences of these decisions within the general framework of our investigations. Now, as we have seen, models may equally concern general frameworks and specific subfields within them. This means that studying the conditions of elaboration of models could not but raise the fundamental problem of the philosophy of human sciences. Proof of this may be found in the fact that many authors have tackled philosophical issues as a seemingly necessary consequence of the specific treatment of their subject. As far as I am concerned, the frequent use of phenomenological terms does not imply any dogmatic attitude on my part: it just happens that this vocabulary belongs to a philosophical movement which devoted an exceptionally great amount of analysis to the problem of the foundations of psychology.

There is one final point which I want to stress. My frequent contacts with Anglo-Saxon psychologists during the last 10 years have convinced me of their growing interest in epistemological issues - issues which were considered for a very long time as belonging typically to some of their continental colleagues, namely to those trained in phenomenology or at least influenced by this movement. The growth of interest is important, both in the United Kingdom and in the United States. What the meaning of this evolution may be is hard to say, but I cannot refrain from thinking that it heralds a renewal of empiricism as a general conceptual framework and that it is bound to have far-reaching theoretical and practical consequences in psychology and in other human sciences.

Bibliography

Abelson, R.P. (1975). Concepts for representing mundane reality in plans.
In D.G. Borrow & A. Collins (eds), Representation and Understanding: Studies
in Cognitive Science. New York: Academic Press.

Abelson, R.P. (1977). Persons: A Study in Philosophical Psychology.
Basingstoke: Macmillan.

Achinstein, P. (1968). Concepts of Science. Baltimore: Johns Hopkins
University Press.

Adair, J.G. (1973). The Human Subject: The Social Psychology of the
Psychological Experiment. Boston: Little, Brown.

Adam, G. (1967). Interoception and Behavior. Budapest: Akademiai Kiado.

Adams, J.S. (1963). Towards an understanding of inequity. Journal of Abnormal
and Social Psychology, 67, 422-436.

Adams, J.S. (1965). Inequity in social exchange. In L. Berkowitz (ed.),
Advances in Experimental Social Psychology, vol. 2. New York: Academic
Press.

Adams, J.S. & Freedman, S. (1976). Equity theory revisited: Comments and
annotated bibliography. In L. Berkowitz (ed.), Advances in Experimental
Social Psychology, vol. 6. New York: Academic Press.

Adams-Webber, J. (1979). Personal Construct Theory: Concepts and
Applications. New York: Wiley.

Aitken, S. (1977). Gender differentiation and the emergence of a sex role
concept in infancy. Unpublished MA thesis, University of Edinburgh.

Ajzen, I. & Fishbein, M. (1977). Attitude-behavior relations: A theoretical
analysis and review of empirical research. Psychological Bulletin, 84,
888-918.

Alderfer, C.P. (1973). Existence, Relatedness and Growth. London: Collier-
Macmillan.

Aleksander, I. & Morton, H. (1979). Personal Construct Theory and Artificial
Intelligence. Third International Congress on Personal Construct
Psychology, Breukelen, Holland.

Allport, D.A. (1975). The state of cognitive psychology: A critical notice of
W.G. Chase (ed.), Visual Information Processing. Quarterly Journal of
Experimental Psychology, 27, 141-152.

Allport, D.A. (1977). On knowing the meaning of words we are unable to report:
The effects of visual masking. In S. Dornic (ed.), Attention and
Performance VI. Hillsdale, New Jersey: Lawrence Erlbaum.

Allport, G.W. (1937). Personality - A Psychological Interpretation. New York: Holt.

Allport, G.W. (1955). Becoming: Basic Considerations for a Psychology of Personality. New Haven: Yale University Press.

Alston, W.P. (1977). Self-intervention and the structure of motivation. In T. Mischel (ed.), The Self: Psychological and Philosophical Issues. Oxford: Blackwell.

Anderson, J.R. (1976). Language, Memory, and Thought. Hillsdale, New Jersey: Lawrence Erlbaum.

Anderson, J.R. & Bower, G.H. (1973). Human Associative Memory. Washington: Holt, Rinehart & Winston.

Anscombe, G.E.M. (1957). Intention. Oxford: Blackwell.

Arendt, H. (1959). The Human Condition. New York: Doubleday Anchor Books. (Originally published, 1958.)

Argyle, M. & Cook, M. (1976). Gaze and Mutual Gaze. Cambridge: Cambridge University Press.

Argyris, C. (1980). Inner Contradictions of Rigorous Research. New York: Academic Press.

Arkes, H.R. & Garske, J.P. (1977). Psychological Theories of Motivation. Monterey, California: Brooks/Cole.

Arshavsky, I.A. (1972). Musculoskeletal activity and rate of entropy in mammals. In G. Newton & A.H. Riesen (eds), Advances in Psychobiology. New York: Wiley Interscience.

Ashby, W.R. (1940). Adaptiveness and equilibrium. Journal of Mental Science, 86, 478-483.

Asratyan, E.A. (1973). The causal conditioned reflex. Soviet Psychology, 11, 112-129.

Atkinson, J.W. (1957). Motivational determinants of risk-taking behavior. Psychological Review, 64, 359-372.

Atkinson, J.W. & Raynor, J.O. (1974). Motivation and Achievement. New York: Wiley.

Audi, R. (1972). On the conception and measurement of attitudes in contemporary Anglo-American psychology. Journal for the Theory of Social Behaviour, 2, 179-203.

Austin, J.L. (1962). Sense and Sensibilia. G.J. Warnock (ed.). London: Oxford University Press.

Austin, J.L. (1963). How to Do Things with Words. Oxford: Clarendon Press.

Ayer, A.J. (1963). The Concept of the Person and Other Essays. London: Macmillan.

Azrin, N.H. & Holz, W.C. (1966). Punishment. In W.K. Honig (ed.), Operant Behavior: Areas of Research and Application. New York: Appleton-Century-Crofts.

Baddeley, A.D. (1976). The Psychology of Memory. New York: Harper & Row.

Baddeley, A.D., Thomson, N. & Buchanan, M. (1975). Word length and the structure of short-term memory. Journal of Verbal Learning and Verbal Behavior, 14, 575-589.

Bailyn, L. (1977). Research as a cognitive process: Implications for data analysis. Quality and Quantity, 2, 97-117.

Baldamus, W. (1951). Incentives and work analysis. University of Birmingham Studies in Economics and Society Monograph A1.

Bandura, A. (1977). Self-efficacy: Toward a unifying theory of behavioral change. Psychological Review, 84, 191-215.

Bannister, D. (1962). The nature and measurement of schizophrenic thought disorder. Journal of Mental Science, 108, 825-842.

Bannister, D. (1965). The genesis of schizophrenic thought disorder: Pre-test of the serial invalidation hypothesis. British Journal of Psychiatry, 21, 229-231.

Bannister, D. (1968). The myth of physiological psychology. Bulletin of The British Psychological Society, 21, 229-231.

Bannister, D. (1977). The logic of passion. In D. Bannister (ed.), New Perspectives in Personal Construct Theory. London: Academic Press.

Bannister, D. & Agnew, J. (1977). The child's construing of self. In A.W. Landfield (ed.), Nebraska Symposium on Motivation 1976. Lincoln, Nebraska: Nebraska University Press.

Bannister, D. & Fransella, F. (1971). Inquiring Man. Harmondsworth: Penguin.

Barash, D.P. (1977). Sociobiology and Behavior. London: Heinemann.

Barker, R.G. (1968). Ecological Psychology: Concepts and Methods for Studying the Environment of Human Behavior. Stanford: Stanford University Press.

Barrett, P. & Kline, P. (in preparation). Comparison of rotational methods in obtaining simple structure in the questionnaire realm.

Bartlett, F.C. (1932). Remembering: An Experimental and Social Study. London: Cambridge University Press.

Beach, F.A. (1977). Human Sexuality: Four Perspectives. Baltimore: Johns Hopkins University Press.

Bee, H.L. (1976). A Developmental Psychologist Looks at Educational Policy: or The Hurrier I Go the Behinder I Get. Aspen Institute for Humanistic Studies, New York.

Bee, H.L., Van Egeren, L.F., Streissgutt, A.P., Nyman, B.A. & Leckie, M.A. (1969). Social class differences in maternal teaching strategies and speech patterns. Developmental Psychology, 1, 726-734.

Beit-Hallahmi, B. & Rabin, A.I. (1977). The Kibbutz as a social experiment and as a child-rearing laboratory. American Psychologist, 32, 532-541.

Bem, D.J. (1967). Self-perception: An alternative interpretation of cognitive dissonance phemomena. Psychological Review, 74, 183-200.

Bentler, P.M. & Huba, G.J. (1979). Minitheories of love. Journal of Personality and Social Psychology, 37, 124-130.

Berger, J. (1972). Ways of Seeing. London: British Broadcasting Corporation; Harmondsworth: Penguin.

Berger, P. & Luckman, T. (1967). The Social Construction of Reality. London: Allen Lane.

Bergson, H. (1911). Creative Evolution. Edinburgh: R. & R. Clark.

Berlyne, D.E. (1973). The vicissitudes of aplopathematic and thelematoscopic pneumatology (or the hydrography of hedonism). In D.E. Berlyne & K.B. Madsen (eds), Pleasure, Reward, Preference. New York: Academic Press.

Bernstein, B. (1961). Social class and linguistic development: a theory of social learning. In A. Halsey, J. Floyd & C.A. Anderson (eds), Education, Economy and Society. London: Glencoe.

Bernstein, B. (1970). A sociolinguistic approach to socialisation with some references to educability. In D. Williams (ed.), Language and Poverty. Chicago: Markham.

Bhaskar, R. (1975). A Realist Theory of Science. Leeds: Leeds Books.

Biddle, B.J. & Thomas, E.J. (eds) (1966). Role Theory: Concepts and Research. New York: Wiley.

Bijou, S.W. & Baer, D.M. (1961). Child Development I: A Systematic and Empirical Theory. New York: Appleton-Century-Crofts.

Bindra, D. (1974). A motivational view of learning, performance and behavior modification. Psychological Review, 81, 199-213.

Birdwhistell, R.L. (1970). Kinesics and Context. Philadelphia, Pennsylvania: University of Pennsylvania Press.

Birns, B. & Golden, M. (1974). The implications of Piaget's theories for contemporary infancy research and education. In M. Schwebel & J. Raph (eds), Piaget in the Classroom. London: Routledge & Kegan Paul.

Bitterman, M.E. (1965). Phyletic differences in learning. American Psychologist, 20, 396-410.

Bitterman, M.E. (1975). The comparative analysis of learning. Science, New York, 188, 699-709.

Black, M. (1962). Models and Metaphors: Studies in Language and Philosophy. Ithaca: Cornell University Press.

Blalock, H.M. (ed) (1971). Causal Models in the Social Sciences. Chicago: Aldine-Atherton.

Blanshard, B. (1958). The case for determinism. In S. Hook (ed.), Determinism and Freedom in the Age of Modern Science. New York: New York University Press.

Blum, A.F. & McHugh, P. (1971). The social ascription of motives. American Sociological Review, 36, 98-109.

Boden, M.A. (1970). Intentionality and physical systems. Philosophy of Science, 37, 200-214.

Boden, M.A. (1972). Purposive Explanation in Psychology. Cambridge, Massachusetts: Harvard University Press.

Boden, M.A. (1973). The structure of intentions. Journal for the Theory of Social Behaviour, 3, 23-46.

Boden, M.A. (1977). Artificial Intelligence and Natural Man. Hassocks, Sussex: Harvester Press.

Boden, M.A. (1979). Piaget. Fontana Modern Masters. Glasgow: Collins.

Bolton, N. (ed.) (1979). Philosophical Problems in Psychology. London: Methuen.

Bomford, R.R., Roberts, J.M. & Greene, J. (1973). Report of the Professional Investigations into Medical and Nursing Practices on Certain Wards at Napsbury Hospital, near St. Albans. London: HMSO.

Borger, R. (1970). Comment on Charles Taylor. In R. Borger & F. Cioffi (eds), Explanations in the Behavioural Sciences. Cambridge: Cambridge University Press.

Bower, T.G.R. (1974). Development in Infancy. San Francisco: Freeman.

Boxer, P.J. (1978). Reflective analysis. Unpublished MS, London Business School.

Braithwaite, R.B. (1955). Scientific Explanation. Cambridge: Cambridge University Press.

Brandt, R. & Kim, J. (1963). Wants as explanations of actions. Journal of Philosophy, 60, 425-435.

Breakwell, G. (1979). Woman: group and identity? Women's Studies International Quarterly, 2, 9-17.

Brener, J.M. (1974a). A general model of voluntary control applied to the phenomena of learned cardiovascular change. In P.A. Obrist, A.H. Black, J.M. Brener & L.V. DiCara (eds), Cardiovascular Psychophysiology. Chicago: Aldine-Atherton.

Brener, J.M. (1974b). Factors influencing the specificity of voluntary cardiovascular control. In L.V. DiCara (ed.), The Limbic and Autonomic Nervous Systems: Advances in Research. New York: Plenum Press.

Brener, J.M. (1977a). Visceral perception. In J. Beatty & H. Legeuise (eds), Biofeedback and Behavior. New York: Plenum Press.

Brener, J.M. (1977b). Sensory and perceptual determinants of voluntary visceral control. In G.E. Schwartz & J. Beatty (eds), Biofeedback: Theory and Research. San Francisco: Academic Press.

Brenner, M. (1978). A critical approach to survey research. In M. Brenner, P. Marsh & M. Brenner (eds), The Social Contexts of Method. London: Croom Helm.

Brentano, F. (1973). Psychology from an Empirical Standpoint. London: Routledge & Kegan Paul. (Original publication, 1874; translation by L.L. McAlister.)

Brillouin, L. (1956). Science and Information Theory. New York: Academic Press.

Brillouin, L. (1964). Scientific Uncertainty and Information. New York: Academic Press.

Broadbent, D.E. (1956). The concept of capacity and the theory of behaviour. In E.C. Cherry (ed.), Information Theory. London: Butterworth.
Broadbent, D.E. (1957). A mechanical model for human attention and immediate memory. Psychological Review, 64, 205-215.
Broadbent, D.E. (1958). Perception and Communication. Oxford: Pergamon Press.
Broadbent, D.E. (1967). The relation between theory and experiment. In Les Modèles et le Formalisation de Comportement. Paris: CNRS.
Broadbent, D.E. (1971). Decision and Stress. London: Academic Press.
Broadbent, D.E. (1973). In Defence of Empirical Psychology. London: Methuen.
Broadbent, D.E. (1975). Cognitive psychology and education. British Journal of Educational Psychology, 45, 162-176.
Broadbent, D.E. (1977a). The hidden pre-attentive processes. American Psychologist, 32, 109-118.
Broadbent, D.E. (1977b). Levels, hierarchies, and the locus of control. Quarterly Journal of Experimental Psychology, 29, 181-201.
Broadbent, D.E. (1979a). Chronic effects from the physical nature of work. In B. Gardell & C. Johansson (eds), Man and Working Life. Chichester: Wiley.
Broadbent, D.E. (1979b). Priming and the passive/active theory of work recognition. In R.S. Nickerson (ed.), Attention and Performance, vol. 6. Hillsdale, New Jersey: Lawrence Erlbaum.
Broadbent, D.E. (1979c). Genesis 1, 27. University sermon preached, 11 March 1979, Oxford.
Broadbent, D.E. & Gath, D. (1979). Chronic effects of repetitive and non-repetitive work. In C.J. Mackay & T. Cox (eds), Psychological Response to Occupational Stress. London: International Publishing Corporation.
Broadhurst, P.L. (1975). The Maudsley reactive and nonreactive strains of rats: A survey. Behaviour Genetics, 5, 299-319.
Bromley, D.B. (1977). Personality Description in Ordinary Language. Chichester: Wiley.
Brown, G. & Harris, T. (1978). Social Origins of Depression: A Study of Psychiatric Disorder in Women. London: Tavistock.
Brown, R. (1973). A First Language: The Early Stages. London: Allen & Unwin.
Bruner, J.S. (1966). Toward a Theory of Instruction. New York: Norton.
Bruner, J.S. (1971). The Relevance of Education. New York: Norton.
Bruner, J.S. (1975). The ontogenesis of speech acts. Journal of Child Language, 2, 1-19.
Bruner, J.S., Goodnow, J.J. & Austin, G.A. (1956). A Study of Thinking. New York: Wiley.
Bryant, P. (1974). Perception and Understanding in Young Children. London: Methuen.
Buber, M. (1970). I and Thou. (Translation, W. Kaufman.) Edinburgh: R. & R. Clark.
Bunge, M. (1973). Method, Model and Matter. Dordrecht & Boston: Reidel.
Buytendijk, F.J.J. (1953). Toucher et être touché. Archives Neerlandaises de Zoologie, 10, Supplement 2, 34-44.
Care, N.S. & Landesman, C. (eds) (1968). Readings in the Theory of Action. Bloomington, Indiana: Indiana University Press.
Cartwright, D.S. (1956). Note on 'changes in psychoneurotic patients with and without psychotherapy'. Journal of Consulting Psychology, 78, 403-404.
Cassirer, E. (1944). An Essay on Man. New Haven: Yale University Press.
Cattell, R.B. (1973). Personality and Mood by Questionnaire. New York: Jossey-Bass.
Cattell, R.B. (1978). The Scientific Use of Factor Analysis in Behavioral Life Sciences. New York: Plenum Press.
Cattell, R.B. & Child, D. (1975). Motivation and Dynamic Structure. London: Holt, Rinehart & Winston.

Cattell, R.B. & Kline, P. (1977). The Scientific Analysis of Personality and Motivation. London: Academic Press.

Cattell, R.B. & Warburton, F.W. (1967). Objective Personality and Motivation Tests. Urbana, Illinois: University of Illinois Press.

Cavell, S. (1969). Must We Mean What We Say? Cambridge: Cambridge University Press.

Chamove, A.S., Eysenck, H.J. & Harlow, H.F. (1972). Personality in monkeys: Factor analysis of rhesus social behaviour. Quarterly Journal of Experimental Psychology, 24, 496-504.

Cheshire, N.M. (1975). The Nature of Psychodynamic Interpretation. Chichester: Wiley.

Chetwynd, J. & Hartnett, O.M. (eds) (1978). The Sex Role System: Psychological and Sociological Perspectives. London: Routledge & Kegan Paul.

Chomsky, N. (1957). Syntactic Structures. The Hague: Mouton.

Chomsky, N. (1965). Aspects of the Theory of Syntax. Cambridge, Massachusetts: MIT Press.

Chomsky, N. (1968). Language and Mind. New York: Harcourt Brace Jovanovich.

Cicourel, A.V. (1970). Cognitive Sociology. Harmondsworth: Penguin.

Clarke, E. & Dewhurst, K. (1972). An Illustrated History of Brain Functions. Oxford: Sandford Publications.

Cole, M., Gay, J., Click, J.A. & Sharp, D.W. (1971). The Cultural Context of Learning and Thinking. London: Tavistock/Methuen.

Cole, M. & Scribner, S. (1974). Culture and Thought: A Psychological Introduction. New York: Wiley.

Collett, P. (ed.) (1977). Social Rules and Social Behaviour. Oxford: Blackwell.

Collier, G., Hirsch, E., Levitsky, D. & Leshner, A.I. (1975). Effort as a dimension of spontaneous activity in rats. Journal of Comparative and Physiological Psychology, 88, 89-96.

Collins, L. (ed.) (1976). The Use of Models in the Social Sciences. London: Tavistock.

Colodny, R.G. (ed.) (1971). The Nature and Function of Scientific Theories. Pittsburgh: University of Pittsburgh Press.

Connolly, K.J. (1975). Movement, action and skill. In K. Holt (ed.), Movement and Child Development. London: Heinemann.

Cook, E. (1971). The flow of energy in an industrial society. Scientific American, 225, 134-144.

Cowey, A. (1979). Cortical maps and visual perception. The Grinley Memorial Lecture. Quarterly Journal of Experimental Psychology, 31, 1-18.

Crowder, R.G. (1978). Audition and speech coding in short-term memory: a tutorial review. In J. Requin (ed.), Attention and Performance, vol. 7. Hillsdale, New Jersey: Lawrence Erlbaum.

Dagenais, J.J. (1972). Models of Man: The Hague: Nijhoff.

Dahrendorf, R. (1973). Homo Sociologicus. London: Routledge & Kegan Paul. (Original German edition, 1958.)

Dale, H.C.A. (1958a). A field study of fault-finding in wireless equipment. Cambridge Applied Psychology Unit Report, no. 329.

Dale, H.C.A. (1958b). Fault-finding in electronic equipment. Ergonomics, 1, 356-385.

Darlington, C.D. (1971). The Evolution of Man and Society. London: Allen & Unwin.

Darwin, C. (1859). The Origin of the Species by Natural Selection. London: Murray.

Davidson, D. (1978). Intending. In Y. Yovel (ed.), Philosophy of History and Action. Dordrecht: Reidel.

Davidson, L. (1979). The Sociology of Gender. London: Rand McNally.

Dawkins, R. (1976). The Selfish Gene. Oxford: Oxford University Press.

Deese, J. (1972). Psychology as Science and Art. New York: Harcourt Brace Jovanovich.

Dennett, D.C. (1979). Why can't you make a computer that feels pain? In Brainstorms: Philosophical Essays on Mind in Psychology. Hassocks, Sussex: Harvester Press.

Deutsch, J.A. (1960). The Structural Basis of Behavior. Chicago: University of Chicago Press.

Dewey, J. (1896). The reflex arc concept in psychology. Psychological Review, 3, 357-370.

Dewey, J. (1922). Human Nature and Conduct. London: Allen & Unwin.

Dewey, J. (1933). How We Think. New York: Heath.

Dittmar, N. (1976). Sociolinguistics: A Critical Survey of Theory and Application. London: Arnold.

Donaldson, M. (1978). Children's Minds. London: Fontana.

Douglas, V., Parry, P., Marton, P. & Garson, C. (1976). Assessment of a cognitive training program for hyperactive children. Journal of Abnormal Child Psychology, 4, 389-410.

Dreyfus, H.L. (1972). What Computers Can't Do: A Critique of Artificial Reason. New York: Harper & Row.

Duck, S.W. (1979). The personal and the interpersonal in personal construct theory. In P. Stringer & D. Bannister (eds), Individuality and Sociability. London: Academic Press.

Duckworth, E. (1974). The having of wonderful ideas. In M. Schwebel & J. Raph (eds), Piaget in the Classroom. London: Routledge & Kegan Paul.

Duffy, E. (1962). Activation and Behavior. New York: Wiley.

Durham, W.H. (1978). The coevolution of human biology and culture. In N. Blurton Jones & V. Reynolds (eds), Human Behaviour and Adaptation. London: Taylor & Francis.

Eaves, L.J. & Eysenck, H.J. (1977). Genotype-environmental model for psychoticism. Advances in Behaviour Research and Therapy, 1, 5-26.

Edwards, D. (1978). Social relations and early language. In A. Locke (ed.), Action, Gesture and Symbol: The Emergence of Language. London: Academic Press.

Ehrenfels, C. von. (1890). Ueber gestaltqualitaeten. Vierteljahrschrift fuer wissenschaftliche Philosophie, 14, 249-292.

Eibl-Eibesfeldt, I. (1970). Ethology, the Biology of Behavior. New York: Holt, Rinehart & Winston.

Eisenstadt, M. & Kareev, Y. (1977). Perception in game playing: Internal representation and scanning of board position. In P.N. Johnson-Laird & P.C. Wason (eds), Thinking: Readings in Cognitive Science. Cambridge: Cambridge University Press.

Ekehammar, B. (1974). Interactionism in personality from a historical perspective. Psychological Bulletin, 81, 1026-1048.

Endler, N.S. & Magnusson, D. (1976). Toward an interactional psychology of personality. Psychological Bulletin, 83, 956-974.

Estes, W.K. & Skinner, B.F. (1941). Some quantitative properties of anxiety. Journal of Experimental Psychology, 29, 390-400.

Eysenck, H.J. (1965). Fact and Fiction in Psychology. Harmondsworth: Penguin.

Eysenck, H.J. (1967). The Biological Basis of Personality. Springfield, Illinois: Thomas.

Eysenck, H. J. (1969). The technology of consent. New Scientist, 26 June, 688-690.

Eysenck, H.J. (1973). Personality and the law of effect. In D.E. Berlyne & K.B. Madsen (eds), Pleasure, Reward, Preference. New York: Academic Press.

Eysenck, H.J. (1976a). Genetic factors in personality development. In A.R. Kaplan (ed.), Human Behavior Genetics. Springfield, Illinois: Thomas.

Eysenck, H.J. (1976b). Sex and Personality. London: Open Books.

Eysenck, H.J. (1976c). The Measurement of Personality. Lancaster: Medical and Technical Publishers.

Eysenck, H.J. (1977a). You and Neurosis. London: Maurice Temple Smith.

Eysenck, H.J. (1977b). Crime and Personality. London: Routledge & Kegan Paul.

Eysenck, H.J. (1979). The Nature and Measurement of Intelligence. London: Springer.

Eysenck, H.J. & Eysenck, S.B.G. (1976). Psychoticism as a Dimension of Personality. London: Hodder & Stoughton.

Eysenck, H.J. & Wilson, G.D. (1978). The Psychological Basis of Ideology. Lancaster: Medical and Technical Publishers.

Eysenck, H.J. & Wilson, G.D. (1979). The Psychology of Sex. London: Dent.

Eysenck, M.W. (1970). Human Memory. Oxford: Pergamon Press.

Fahlmann, S.E. (1974). A planning system for robot construction tasks. Artificial Intelligence, 5, 1-50.

Farber, L.H. (1976). Lying, Despair, Jealousy, Envy, Sex, Suicide, Drugs and the Good Life. New York: Basic Books.

Farr, R.M. (1976). Experimentation: A social psychological perspective. British Journal of Social and Clinical Psychology, 15, 225-238.

Farr, R.M. (1977). Heider, Harré, and Herzlich on health and illness: Some observations on the structure of 'représentations collectives'. European Journal of Social Psychology, 7, 491-504.

Farr, R.M. (1978a). On the social significance of artifacts in experimenting. British Journal of Social and Clinical Psychology, 17, 299-306.

Farr, R.M. (1978b). On the varieties of social psychology: An essay on the relationships between psychology and other social sciences. Social Science Information, 17, 503-525.

Farr, R.M. (1979). The nature of human nature and the science of behaviour. In P. Heelas & A.J. Lock (eds), Indigenous Psychologies: Implicit Views of Mind and Human Nature. London: Academic Press.

Farr, R.M. (forthcoming). A Social and Reflexive Model of Man: Theory and Evidence. London: Academic Press.

Farrell, B.A. (1975). Review of the cult of the fact. British Journal of Psychology, 66, 253-255.

Farrell, B.A. (1978). The progress of psychology. British Journal of Psychology, 69, 1-8.

Ferster, C.B. (1974). Behavioral approaches to depression. In R.J. Friedman & M.M. Katz (eds), The Psychology of Depression: Contemporary Theory and Research. New York: Wiley.

Festinger, L. (1954). A theory of social comparison processes. Human Relations, 7, 117-140.

Festinger, L. (1957). A Theory of Cognitive Dissonance. New York: Harper & Row.

Feyerabend, P.K. (1971). Problems of empiricism, part II. In R.G. Colodny (ed.), The Nature and Function of Scientific Theories. Pittsburgh: University of Pittsburgh Press.

Fingarette, H. (1967). On Responsibility. New York: Basic Books.

Fishbein, M. (1967). Attitude and the prediction of behavior. In M. Fishbein (ed.), Readings in Attitude Theory and Measurement. New York: Wiley.

Fishbein, M. & Ajzen, I. (1975). Belief, Attitude, Intention and Behavior. Reading, Massachusetts: Addison-Wesley.

Fitts, P.M. (1954). Information capacity of the human motor system in controlling amplitude of movement. Journal of Experimental Psychology, 47, 301-391.

Fleming, D. (1967). Attitude: The history of a concept. Perspectives in American History, 1, 287-365.

Flint, C. (1979). PhD dissertation in preparation, University of Oxford.

Fodor, J.A. (1976). The Language of Thought. Hassocks, Sussex: Harvester Press.

Folkard, S., Monk, T.H., Bradbury, R. & Rosenthall, J. (1977). Time of day effects in school children's immediate and delayed recall of meaningful material. British Journal of Psychology, 68, 45-50.

Fordyce, W.E. (1976). Behavioral Methods for Chronic Pain and Illness. St. Louis: Mosby.

Fransella, F. (1972). Personal Change and Reconstruction. London: Academic Press.

Fransella, F. & Frost, K. (eds) (1977). On Being a Woman. London: Tavistock.

Freedman, D.G. (1974). Human Infancy: An Evolutionary Perspective. Hillsdale, New Jersey: Lawrence Erlbaum.

Freeman, G.L. (1948). The Energetics of Human Behavior. Ithaca: Cornell University Press.

Freilich, M. (1972). The Meaning of Culture. Lexington, Massachusetts: Xerox College.

Freud, S. (1900). The Interpretation of Dreams. Standard Edition, vols 4 & 5. London: Hogarth Press, 1953.

Freud, S. (1932). The psychology of women. In New Introductory Lectures. London: Hogarth Press.

Friedman, M. (1967). To Deny our Nothingness: Contemporary Images of Man. Chicago & London: University of Chicago Press.

Fry, D. (1977). Homo Loquens: Man as a Talking Animal. Cambridge: Cambridge University Press.

Gale, A. (1973). The psychophysiology of individual differences: studies of extraversion and the E.E.G. In P. Kline (ed.), New Approaches in Psychological Measurement. Chichester: Wiley.

Gardner, R.A. & Gardner, B.T. (1969). Teaching sign language to a chimpanzee. Science, New York, 165, 664-672.

Garfinkel, H. (1967). Studies in Ethnomethodology. Englewood Cliffs, New Jersey: Prentice-Hall.

Gauld, A. & Shotter, J. (1977). Human Action and its Psychological Investigation. London: Routledge & Kegan Paul.

Geertz, C. (1975). The Interpretation of Cultures. London: Hutchinson.

Gergen, K.J. (1973). Social psychology as history. Journal of Personality and Social Psychology, 26, 309-320.

Gergen, K.J. (1977). The social construction of self-knowledge. In T. Mischel (ed.), The Self: Psychological and Philosophical Issues. Oxford: Blackwell.

Gergen, K.J. (1978). Toward generative theory. Journal of Personality and Social Psychology, 36, 1344-1360.

Geschwind, N. (1969). Problems in the anatomical understanding of the aphasias. In A.L. Benton (ed.), Contributions to Clinical Neuropsychology. New York: Aldine.

Geschwind, N. (1970). The organization of language and the brain. Science, New York, 170, 940-944.

Gibson, J.J. (1950). The Perception of the Visual World. Boston: Houghton Mifflin.

Gibson, J.J. (1966). The Senses Considered as Perceptual Systems. Boston: Houghton Mifflin.

Gibson, J.J. (1967). Autobiographical study. In E.G. Boring & G. Lindzey (eds), A History of Psychology in Autobiography, vol. 5. New York: Appleton-Century-Crofts.

Giddens, A. (1978). Durkheim. Fontana Modern Masters Series. Glasgow: Collins.

Giles, H., Smith, P., Browne, C., Whiteman, S. & Williams, J. (1979). Women speaking: The voice of feminism. In R. Borker, N. Furman & S. McConnell-Ginet (eds), Language and Women's Lives: A Feminist Perspective. Ithaca: Cornell University Press.

Gillham, W.E.C. (1978). Reconstructing Educational Psychology. London: Croom Helm.

Goffman, E. (1972). Interaction Ritual. London: Allen Lane.

Goldberger, A.S. & Duncan, O.D. (eds) (1973). Structural Equation Models in the Social Sciences. New York: Seminar Press.

Goodman, P.S. (1977). Social comparison process in organizations. In B.M. Staw & G.R. Salancik (eds), New Directions in Organizational Behavior. Chicago: St. Clair.

Goodman, P.S. & Friedman, A. (1971). An examination of Adams' theory of inequity. Administrative Science Quarterly, 16, 271-288.

Goody, J. (1976). Production and Reproduction. Cambridge: Cambridge University Press.

Gray, J.A. (1971). The mind-brain identity theory as a scientific hypothesis. Philosophical Quarterly, 21, 247-252.

Gregory, R.L. (1961). The brain as an engineering problem. In W.H. Thorpe & O.L. Zangwill (eds), Current Problems in Animal Behaviour. Cambridge: Cambridge University Press.

Guilford, J.P. (1956). Psychometric Methods, 2nd ed. New York: McGraw-Hill.

Guilford, J.P. (1959). Personality. New York: McGraw-Hill.

Haavind, H. & Hartman, E. (1977). Mothers as Teachers and Their Children as Learners. Reports from the Institute of Psychology, University of Bergen, Norway: No. 1.

Hacker, W. (1980). Subjective and objective organization of work activities. In M. von Cranach (ed.), Approaches to the Study of Goal Directed Action. Cambridge: Cambridge University Press.

Hackman, J.R. & Lawler, E.E. (1971). Employee reactions to job characteristics. Journal of Applied Psychology, 55, 259-286.

Hakstian, A.R. & Cattell, R.B. (1974). The checking of primary ability structure on a broader basis of performance. British Journal of Educational Psychology, 44, 140-154.

Hare, R.D. (1970). Psychopathy. Chichester: Wiley.

Harlow, H.F. (1949). The formation of learning sets. Psychological Review, 56, 51-65.

Harré, R. (1970). The Principles of Scientific Thinking. London: Macmillan; Chicago: University of Chicago Press.

Harré, R. (1971). Joynson's dilemma. Bulletin of The British Psychological Society, 24, 115-119.

Harré, R. (1972). The Philosophies of Science. London: Oxford University Press.

Harré, R. (1974). Some remarks on 'rule' as a scientific concept. In T. Mischel (ed.), Understanding Other Persons. Oxford: Blackwell.

Harré, R. (1977). The self in monodrama. In T. Mischel (ed.), The Self, Psychological and Philosophical Issues. Oxford: Blackwell.

Harré, R. (1979). Social Being. Oxford: Blackwell.

Harré, R. & Secord, P.F. (1972). The Explanation of Social Behaviour. Oxford: Blackwell.

Hass, A. (1979). Male and female spoken language difference: stereotypes and evidence. Psychological Bulletin, 86, 615-626.

Hassett, J. (1978). A Primer of Psychophysiology. San Francisco: Freeman.

Haugeland, J. (1978). The nature and plausibility of cognitism. Behavioral and Brain Sciences, 1, 215-226.

Hearnshaw, L.S. (1964). A Short History of British Psychology. London: Methuen.

Heber, M. (1977). The influence of language training on seriation of 5-6 year old children initially at different levels of descriptive competence. British Journal of Psychology, 68, 85-95.

Hecaen, H, & Albert, M.L. (1978). Human Neuropsychology. Chichester: Wiley.

Heckhausen, H. (1977). Achievement motivation and its constructs: A cognitive model. Motivation and Emotion, 1, 283-328.

Heider, F. (1958). The Psychology of Interpersonal Relations. New York: Wiley.

Helson, H. (1964). Adaptation Level Theory. New York: Harper & Row.

Helson, H. (1973). A common model for affectivity and perception: an adaptation-level approach. In D.E. Berlyne & K.B. Madsen (eds), Pleasure, Reward, Preference. New York: Academic Press.

Hendrickson, A.E. & Hendrickson, D.E. (1978). The biological basis and measurement of intelligence. Paper read at XIXth International Congress of Applied Psychology in Munich, August.

Herriot, P. (1969). The comprehension of active and passive sentences as a function of pragmatic expectation. Journal of Verbal Learning and Verbal Behavior, 8, 166-169.

Herzberg, F. (1966). Work and the Nature of Man. New York: World Publishing Company.

Herzlich, C. (1972). La représentation sociale. In S. Moscovici (ed.), Introduction à la Psychologie Sociale, vol 1. Paris: Larousse.

Herzlich, C. (1973). Health and Illness: A Social Psychological Analysis. London: Academic Press.

Hess, R.D. & Shipman, V.C. (1965). Early experience and the socialisation of cognitive modes in children. Child Development, 36, 869-886.

Hess, R.D. & Shipman, V.C. (1968). Maternal influences upon early learning: The cognitive environments of urban pre-school children. In R.D. Hess & R. Bear (eds), Early Education. Chicago: Aldine.

Hesse, H. (1965). Steppenwolf. Harmondsworth: Penguin.

Hesse, M.B. (1963). Models and Analogies in Science. London: Sheed & Ward.

Hesse, M.B. (1966). Models and Analogies in Science. Notre Dame University: Notre Dame Press.

Hesse, M.B. (1967). Models and analogy in science. In P. Edwards (ed.), Encyclopaedia of Philosophy, vol. 5. New York: Macmillan.

Hofstadter, D. (1979). Godel, Escher and Bach: An Eternal Golden Braid. Hassocks, Sussex: Harvester Press.

Hollander, E.P. (1958). Conformity, status, and idiosyncracy credit. Psychological Review, 65, 117-127.

Hollis, M. (1977). Models of Man: Philosophical Thoughts on Social Action. Cambridge: Cambridge University Press.

Homans, G.C. (1961). Social Behavior, its Elementary Forms. London: Routledge & Kegan Paul.

Hook, S. (ed.) (1958). Determinism and Freedom in the Age of Modern Science. New York: New York University Press.

Horel, J.A. (1978). The neuroanatomy of amnesia: a critique of the hippocampal memory hypothesis. Brain, 101, 403-445.

Horn, J.L. & Cattell, R.B. (1966). Refinement and test of the theory of fluid and crystallised intelligence. Journal of Educational Psychology, 57, 253-270.

Horn, J.L. & Knapp, J.R. (1973). On the subjective character of the empirical base of Guilford's Structure-of-Intellect Model. Psychological Bulletin, 80, 33-43.

Horton, R. (1967). African traditional thought and Western science. Africa, 37, 50-71; 155-187.

Howarth, C.I. (1978). Strategies in the control of movement. In G. Underwood (ed.), Strategies in Information Processing. London: Academic Press.

Howarth, C.I. (1979). The structure of effective psychology: Is this our Golden Age? Bulletin of The British Psychological Society, 32, 199. (abstract).

Howarth, C.I. & Bloomfield, J.R. (1971). Search and selective attention. British Medical Bulletin, 27, 253-258.

Howarth, C.I. & Gillham, W.E.C. (in press). The Structure of Psychology. London: Allen & Unwin.

Howarth, C.I. & Repetto-Wright, R. (1978). The measurement of risk and the attribution of responsibility for child pedestrian accidents.   Proceedings of the Royal Society for the Prevention of Accidents Conference, Harrogate, May.

Hudson, L. (1972). The Cult of the Fact. London: Cape.

Hull, C.L. (1943). The Principles of Behavior. New York: Appleton-Century-Crofts.

Hull, C.L. (1951). Essentials of Behavior. New Haven: Yale University Press.

Hull, C.L. (1952). A Behavior System. New Haven: Yale University Press.

Hunt, E. (1975). Artificial Intelligence. New York: Academic Press.

Hunt, E. (1976). Varieties of cognitive power. In R.B. Resnik (ed.), The Nature of Intelligence. Hillsdale, New Jersey: Lawrence Erlbaum.

Husserl, E. (1910-1911). Philosophie als strenge Wissenschaft. Logos, I, 289-341.

Hutten, E.H. (1956). The Language of Physics: An Introduction to the Philosophy of Science. London: Macmillan.

Isaacs, S. (1930). Intellectual Growth in Young Children. London: Routledge & Sons.

Jahoda, G. (1980). Theoretical and systematic approaches in cross-cultural psychology. In H. Triandis (ed.), Handbook of Cross-Cultural Psychology, vol. 1. Boston: Allyn & Bacon.

Jahoda, M. (1958). Current Concepts of Mental Health. New York: Basic Books.

Jahoda, M. (1977). Freud and the Dilemmas of Psychology. London: Hogarth Press.

Jahoda, M. (1979). The impact of unemployment in the 1930s and 1970s. Bulletin of The British Psychological Society, 32, 309-314.

James, W. (1889). The congress of physiological psychology at Paris. Mind, 14, 614-616.

James, W. (1890). The Principles of Psychology. New York: Holt.

James W. (1892). Psychology: The Briefer Course. New York: Holt.

Jemrich, R.I. & Sampson, P.F. (1966). Rotation for simple loading. Psychometrika, 31, 313-323.

Jessor, R. (1958). The problem of reductionism in psychology. Psychological Review, 57, 283-290.

Jones, E.E. & Kohler, R. (1958). The effects of plausibility on the learning of controversial statements. Journal of Abnormal and Social Psychology, 57, 315-320.

Jones, E.E. & Davis, K.E. (1965). From acts to dispositions: the attribution process in person perception. In L. Berkowitz (ed.), Advances in Experimental Social Psychology, vol. 2. New York: Academic Press.

Jones, G.V. (1976). A fragmentation hypothesis of memory: Cued recall of pictures and of sequential position. Journal of Experimental Psychology: General, 105, 277-293.

Joynson, R.B. (1970). The breakdown of modern psychology. Bulletin of The British Psychological Society, 23, 261-269.

Joynson, R.B. (1974). Psychology and Common Sense. London: Routledge & Kegan Paul.

Kamii, C. (1974). Pedagogical principles derived from Piaget's theory: relevance for educational practice. In M. Schwebel & J. Raph (eds), Piaget in the Classroom. London: Routledge & Kegan Paul.

Kantor, J.R. (1969). The Scientific Evolution of Psychology. Chicago: Principia Press.

Karnes, M.B., Teska, J.A. & Hodgins, A.S. (1970). The effects of four programs of classroom intervention on the intellectual and language development of four-year-old disadvantaged children. American Journal of Orthopsychiatry, 40, 58-76.

Karst, T.O. & Groutt, J.W. (1977). Inside mystical minds. In D. Bannister (ed.), New Perspectives in Personal Construct Theory. London: Academic Press.

Keehn, J.D. (1969). Consciousness, discrimination and the stimulus control of behaviour. In R.M. Gilbert & N.S. Sutherland (eds), Animal Discrimination Learning. London: Academic Press.

Kellaghan, T. (1977). The Evaluation of an Intervention Programme for Disadvantaged Children. Windsor: NFER.

Kelly, G.A. (1955). A Theory of Personality: The Psychology of Personal Constructs. New York: Norton.

Kelly, G.A. (1962). Europe's matrix of decision. In M.R. Jones (ed.), Nebraska Symposium on Motivation. Lincoln: Nebraska University Press.

Kelly, G.A. (1964). The language of hypothesis: Man's psychological instrument. Journal of Individual Psychology, 20, 137-152.

Kelly, G.A. (1969a). Ontological acceleration. In B.A. Maher (ed.), Clinical Psychology and Personality; The Selected Papers of George Kelly. New York: Wiley.

Kelly, G.A. (1969b). The strategy of psychological research. In B.A. Maher (ed.), Clinical Psychology and Personality; The Selected Papers of George Kelly. New York: Wiley.

Kelly, G.A. (1969c). Humanistic methodology in psychological research. In B.A. Maher (ed.), Clinical Psychology and Personality; The Selected Papers of George Kelly. New York: Wiley.

Kelly, G.A. (1969d). Psychotherapy and the nature of man. In B.A. Maher (ed.), Clinical Psychology and Personality; The Selected Papers of George Kelly. New York: Wiley.

Kelly, G.A. (1970). Behaviour is an experiment. In D. Bannister (ed.), Perspectives in Personal Construct Theory. London: Academic Press.

Kemp, W.B. (1971). The flow of energy in a hunting society. Scientific American, 225, 104-115.

Kendall, P.C. & Hollon, S.D. (eds) (in press). Cognitive Behavioural Interventions: Theory, Research and Procedures.

Kendler, H.H. (1968). Some specific reactions to general S-R theory. In T.R. Dixon & D.L. Horton (eds), Verbal Behavior and General Behavior Theory. Englewood Cliffs, New Jersey: Prentice-Hall.

Kenny, A. (1963). Action, Emotion and Will. London: Routledge & Kegan Paul.

Kinsey, A.C., Pomeroy, W.B. & Martin, C.E. (1948). Sexual Behavior of the Human Male. Philadelphia, Pennsylvania: Saunders.

Kinsey, A.C., Pomeroy, W.B., Martin, E.C. & Gebhard, P.M. (1953). Sexual Behavior in the Human Female. Philadelphia, Pennsylvania: Saunders.

Klahr, D. & Wallace, J.G. (1972). Class inclusion processes. In S. Farnham-Diggory (ed.), Information Processing in Children. New York: Academic Press.

Kline, P. (1979). Psychometrics and Psychology. London: Academic Press.

Kline, P. (1980). Fact and Fantasy in Freudian Theory, 2nd ed. London: Methuen.

Kline, P. & Storey, R. (1978). The dynamic personality inventory: What does it measure? British Journal of Psychology, 69, 375-383.

Koch, S. (1959). Epilogue. In S. Koch (ed.), Psychology: A Study of a Science, vol. 3. New York: McGraw-Hill.

Koch, S. (1961). Psychological science versus the science-humanism antinomy: Intimations of a significant science of man. American Psychologist, 16, 629-639.

Koch, S. (1964). Psychology and emerging conceptions of knowledge as unitary. In T.W. Wann (ed.), Behaviorism and Phenomenology. Chicago: University of Chicago Press.

Koch, S. (1974). Psychology as science. In S.C. Brown (ed.), Philosophy of Psychology. London: Macmillan.

Koestler, A. (1978). Janus: A Summing Up. London: Hutchinson; London: Picador, 1979.

Krasner, L. & Ullmann, L.P. (1965). Research in Behavior Modification: New Developments and Implications. New York: Holt, Rinehart & Winston.

Krech, D. (1950). Dynamic systems, psychological fields, and hypothetical constructs. Psychological Review, 57, 283-290.

Krechevski, I. (1932). The genesis of hypotheses in rats. California University Publications in Psychology, 6, 45-64.

Kroeber, A.L. & Kluckhohn, C. (1952). Culture: A Critical Review of Concepts and Definitions. Cambridge, Massachusetts: Peabody.

Kuhl, J. & Blankenship, V. (1979). The dynamic theory of achievement motivation: From episodic to dynamic thinking. Psychological Review, 86, 141-151.

Kuhn, T.S. (1962). The Structure of Scientific Revolutions. Chicago: University of Chicago Press.

Kuhn, T.S. (1977). Second thoughts on paradigms. In F. Suppe (ed.), The Structure of Scientific Theories, 2nd ed. Urbana, Illinois: University of Illinois Press.

Labov, W. (1970). The logic of non-standard English. In P. Williams (ed.), Language and Poverty: Perspectives of a Theme. Chicago: Markham.

Lader M. (1977). Psychiatry on Trial. Harmondsworth: Penguin.

Laing, R.D. (1971). Knots. Harmondsworth: Penguin.

Laird, J.D. (1974). Self-attribution of emotion: The effects of expressive behavior on the quality of emotional experience. Journal of Personality and Social Psychology, 29, 475-486.

Lakatos, I. (1970). Methodology of Scientific Research Programmes. In I. Lakatos & A. Musgrave (eds), Criticism and the Growth of Knowledge. Cambridge: Cambridge University Press.

Lakatos, I. (1974). The role of crucial experiments in science. Studies in History and Philosophy of Science, 4, 309-325.

Lakatos, I. & Musgrave, A. (1970). Criticism and the Growth of Knowledge. Cambridge: Cambridge University Press.

Lakoff, R. (1973). Language and woman's place. Language and Society, 2, 45-79. (Reprinted Harper & Row, 1975.)

Landfield, A.W. (1976). A personal construct approach to suicidal behaviour. In P. Slater (ed.), Explorations of Intrapersonal Space, vol. 1. Chichester: Wiley.

Landy, F.J. (1978). An opponent process theory of job satisfaction. Journal of Applied Psychology, 63, 533-547.

Lashley, W.S. (1929). Brain Mechanisms and Intelligence. Chicago: Chicago University Press.

Lawler, E.E. (1971). Pay and Organizational Effectiveness. New York: McGraw-Hill.

Lawler, E.E. & Suttle, J.L. (1973). Expectancy theory and job behavior. Organizational Behavior and Human Performance, 9, 482-503.

Leatherdale, W.H. (1974). The Role of Analogy, Model and Metaphor in Science. Amsterdam: North-Holland.

Lebowitz, F. (1979). Metropolitan Life. London: Sidgwick & Jackson.

Leighton, D. & Kluckhohn, C. (1947). Children of the People. Cambridge, Massachusetts: Harvard University Press.

Le Magnen, J. (1976). Interactions of glucostatic and lipostatic mechanisms in the regulatory control of feeding. In D. Novin, W. Wyrwicka & G. Bray (eds), Hunger: Basic Mechanisms and Clinical Implications. New York: Raven Press.

Levine, J.M. & Murphy, G. (1943). The learning and forgetting of controversial material. Journal of Abnormal and Social Psychology, 38, 507-517.

Lewin, K. (1935). A Dynamic Theory of Personality. New York: McGraw-Hill.

Lewin, K., Dembo, T., Festinger, L. & Sears, P.S. (1944). Level of aspiration. In J. McV. Hunt (ed.), Personality and the Behavior Disorders. New York: Ronald Press.

Lewin, R. (1977). 'Head start' pays off. New Scientist, March.
Lewis, C.S. (1943). The Abolition of Man. Oxford: Oxford University Press. (Reissued London: Collins, Fount Paperback, 1978.)
Lewis, M. & Brooks, J. (1975). Infants' social perception: A constructive view. In L. Cohen & P. Salapatek (eds), Perception in Infancy. New York: Academic Press.
Liddell, E.G.T. (1960). The Discovery of Reflexes. London, Oxford University Press.
Lienhardt, G. (1961). Divinity and Experience: The Religion of the Dinka. Oxford: Clarendon.
Lloyd, B. & Archer, J. (eds) (1976). Exploring Sex Differences. London: Academic Press.
Lock, A.J. (1980). The Guided Reinvention of Language. London: Academic Press.
Luborsky, L., Chandler, M., Averbach, A.H., Cohen, J. & Bachrach, H.M. (1971). Factors influencing the outcome of psychotherapy: A review of quantitative research. Psychological Bulletin, 78, 145-185.
Luce, R.D. & Raiffa, H. (1957). Games and Decisions. New York: Wiley.
Lukes, S. (1973). Emile Durkheim: His Life and Work: An Historical and Critical Study. London: Allen Lane.
Luria, A.R. (1966). Higher Cortical Functions in Man. London: Tavistock.
Luria, A.R. (1972). Aphasia reconsidered. Cortex, 8, 34-40.
Luria, A.R. & Yudovich, F.La. (1971). Speech and the Development of Mental Processes in the Child. Harmondsworth: Penguin.
Maccoby, E.E. & Jacklin, C.N. (1974). The Psychology of Sex Differences. California: Stanford University Press.
Mackenzie, B.D. (1977). Behaviourism and the Limits of Scientific Method. London: Routledge & Kegan Paul.
Mackie, J.L. (1974). The Cement of the Universe: A Study of Causation. Oxford: Oxford University Press.
Mackintosh, N.J. (1978). Conditioning. In B.M. Foss (ed.), Psychology Survey No. 1. London: Allen & Unwin.
MacMurray, J. (1961). Persons in Relation. London: Faber & Faber.
Magee, B. (1978). Men of Ideas. London: British Broadcasting Corporation.
Magnussen, D. & Endler, N.S. (1977). Personality at the Crossroads: Current Issues in Interactional Psychology. Hillsdale, New Jersey: Lawrence Erlbaum.
Mailer, N. (1957). The White Negro. New York: City Light Books.
Mair, J.M.M. (1970). Psychologists are human too. In D. Bannister (ed.), Perspectives in Personal Construct Theory. London: Academic Press.
Marcel, A.J. & Patterson, K.E. (1978). Word recognition and production: Reciprocity in clinical and normal studies. In J. Requin (ed.), Attention and Performance, vol 7. Hillsdale, New Jersey: Lawrence Erlbaum.
Marr, D. (1976). Early processing of visual information. Philosophical Transactions of the Royal Society, 275 (942), 483-524.
Marsh, P., Rosser, E. & Harré, R. (1978). The Rules of Disorder. London: Routledge & Kegan Paul.
Martin, I. & Levey, A.B. (1978). Evaluative conditioning. Advances in Behaviour Research and Therapy, 1, 57-101.
Maslow, A.H. (1970). Motivation and Personality, rev. ed. New York: Harper & Row.
Maslow, A.H. (1973). The Farther Reaches of Human Nature. Harmondsworth: Penguin.
Masterman, M. (1970). The nature of a paradigm. In I. Lakatos & A. Musgrave (eds), Criticism and the Growth of Knowledge. Cambridge: Cambridge University Press.
Mather, K. & Jinks, J.L. (1971). Biometrical Genetics. London: Chapman & Hall.

McClelland, D.C. (1971). Assessing Human Motivation. New York: General Learning Press.

McCoy, M. (1977). A reconstruction of emotion. In D. Bannister (ed.), New Perspectives in Personal Contruct Theory. London: Academic Press.

McDougall, W. (1932). The Energies of Men. London: Methuen.

McGinn, C. (1979). Action and its explanation. In N. Bolton (ed.), Philosophical Problems in Psychology. London: Methuen.

McGuire, W.J. (1973). The yin and yang of progress in social psychology. Journal of Personality and Social Psychology, 26, 446-456.

McLean, P.D. (1969). A triune concept of the brain and behavior. Toronto: University of Toronto Hincks Memorial Lecture.

McMahon, C.E. (1973). Images as motives and motivators: A historical perspective. American Journal of Psychology, 86, 465-490.

Mead, G. H. (1932). The Philosophy of the Present. Edited, with an introduction, by A.E. Murphy, with prefatory remarks by John Dewey. Chicago: Open Court.

Mead, G.H. (1934). Mind, Self, and Society: From the Standpoint of a Social Behaviorist. Edited, with an introduction, by C.W. Morris. Chicago: University of Chicago Press.

Mead, G.H. (1936). Movements of Thought in the Nineteenth Century. Edited and introduced by M.H. Moore. Chicago: University of Chicago Press.

Mead, G.H. (1938). The Philosophy of the Act. Edited and introduced by C.W. Morris. Chicago: University of Chicago Press.

Medawar, P.B. (1966). The Art of the Soluble. London: Methuen.

Medawar, P.B. (1974). A geometric model of reduction and emergence. In F.J. Ayala & T. Dhobzhansky (eds), Studies in the Philosophy of Biology. London: Macmillan.

Meehl, P.E. (1954). Clinical Versus Statistical Prediction: A Theoretical Analysis and a Review of the Evidence. Minneapolis: University of Minnesota Press.

Meehl, P.E. (1977). Specific etiology and other forms of strong inference: Some quantitative meanings. Journal of Medicine and Philosophy, 2, 33-53.

Meehl, P.E. (1978). Theoretical risks and tabular asterisks: Sir Karl, Sir Ronald and the slow progress of soft psychology. Journal of Consulting and Clinical Psychology, 46, 806-834.

Meichenbaum, D. & Asarnow, J. (in press). Cognitive-behavior modification and metacognitive development: Implications for the classroom. In P.C. Kendall & S.D. Hollon (eds), Cognitive-Behavioral Interventions. New York: Academic Press.

Meinong, A. (ed.) (1904). Untersuchungen zur Gegenstandstheorie und Psychologie. Leipzig: Barth.

Merleau-Ponty, M. (1962). Phenomenology of Perception. London: Routledge & Kegan Paul.

Merz, F. (1979). Geschlechterunterschiede und ihre Entwicklung. Zurich: Verlag fuer Psychologie.

Meyer, V. & Gelder, M.G. (1963). Behaviour therapy and phobic disorders. British Journal of Psychiatry, 109, 19-28.

Milgram, S. (1974). Obedience to Authority: An Experimental View. London: Tavistock.

Millar, K. (1979). Noise and the 'rehearsal-masking' hypothesis. British Journal of Psychology, 70, 565-577.

Miller, C. & Swift, K. (1976). Words and Women. London: Gallancy.

Miller, D.L. (1973). George Herbert Mead: Self, Language and the World. Austin: University of Texas Press.

Miller, E. (1972). Clinical Neuropsychology. Harmondsworth: Penguin.

Miller, G.A. (1969). Psychology as a means of promoting human welfare. American Psychologist, 24, 1063-1075.

Miller, G.A., Galanter, E. & Pribram, K.H. (1960). Plans and the Structure of Behavior. New York: Holt, Rinehart & Winston.

Mills, C.W. (1940). Situated actions and vocabularies of motive. American Sociological Review, 5, 904-913.

Milner, B. (1966). Amnesia following operations on the temporal lobes. In C.W.M. Whitty & O.L. Zangwill (eds), Amnesia. London: Butterworth.

Minsky, M. (1967). Computation: Finite and Infinite Machines. Englewood Cliffs, New Jersey: Prentice-Hall.

Minsky, M. & Papert, S. (1974). Artificial Intelligence. Eugene, Oregon: Condon Lectures.

Mischel, W. (1973). Towards a cognitive social learning reconceptualization of personality. Psychological Review, 80, 252-283.

Mischel, W. (1977). On the future of personality measurement. American Journal of Psychology, 32, 246-254.

Mitchell, T.R. (1974). Expectancy models of job satisfaction, occupational preference and effort: A theoretical, methodological and empirical appraisal. Psychological Bulletin, 81, 1053-1077.

Mitchell, T.R. & Biglan, A. (1971). Instrumentality theories: Current uses in psychology. Psychological Bulletin, 76, 432-454.

Mitroff, I.I. (1974). The Subjective Side of Science. Amsterdam: Elsevier.

Money, J. & Ehrhardt, A.A. (1972). Man and Woman, Boy and Girl. London: Johns Hopkins University Press.

Monod, J. (1972). Chance and Necessity. Glasgow: Collins.

Moos, R.H. (1976). The Human Context: Environmental Determinants of Behavior. New York: Wiley.

Morgan, M.J. (1977). Molyneux's Question: Vision, Touch and the Philosophy of Perception. Cambridge: Cambridge University Press.

Morris, C.W. (1946). Signs, Language and Behavior. Englewood Cliffs, New Jersey: Prentice-Hall.

Morris, D. (1967). The Naked Ape. London: Cape.

Moscovici, S. (1961). La Psychanalyse: Son Image et Son Public. Paris: Presses Universitaires de France (2nd ed., 1976).

Moscovici, S. (1972). Society and theory in social psychology. In J. Israel & H. Tajfel (eds), The Context of Social Psychology. London: Academic Press.

Moscovici, S. (1976). Social Influence and Social Change. London: Academic Press.

Murchison, C. (1936). A History of Psychology in Autobiography (John B. Watson, pp. 271-281). Worcester: Clark University Press.

Murray, H. (1938). Explorations in Personality. Oxford: Oxford University Press.

Nagel, E. (1965). Types of causal explanation in science. In D. Lerner (ed.), Cause and Effect. London: Collier-Macmillan.

Needham, J. (1954). Science and Civilisation in China. Cambridge: Cambridge University Press.

Neisser, U. (1967). Cognitive Psychology. New York: Appleton-Century-Crofts.

Neisser, U. (1976). Cognition and Reality. San Francisco: Freeman.

Newell, A. (1973). You can't play twenty questions with Nature and win. In W.G. Chase (ed.), Visual Information Processing. New York: Academic Press.

Newell, A. & Simon H. (1972). Human Problem Solving. Englewood Cliffs, New Jersey: Prentice-Hall.

Nicolis, G. & Prigogine, I. (1977). Self-Organization in Nonequilibrium Systems. New York: Wiley.

Nietzel, M.T., Winett, R.A., MacDonald, M.L. & Davidson, W.S. (1977). Behavioral Approaches to Community Psychology. New York: Pergamon Press.

Norman, D.A. & Rumelhart, D.E. (1975). Explorations in Cognition. San Francisco: Freeman.

Notterman, J.M. & Mintz, D.E. (1965). Dynamics of Response. New York: Wiley.

Nunnally, J.C. (1978). Psychometric Theory. New York: McGraw-Hill.

Olson, D. (1966). On conceptual strategies. In J.S. Bruner, R. Olver & P.M. Greenfield et al., Studies in Cognitive Growth. New York: Wiley.

Olson, D. (1970). Cognitive Development: The Child's Acquisition of Diagonality. New York: Academic Press.

Paillard, J. (1960). The patterning of skilled movement. In J. Field, H.W. Magoun & V.E. Hall (eds), Handbook of Physiology, vol. 2, pp. 1679-1708. Washington: American Physiological Society.

Parsons, T. & Shils, E.A. (eds) (1951). Toward a General Theory of Action. Cambridge, Massachusetts: Harvard University Press.

Passmore, J. (1978). Science and its Critics. London: Duckworth.

Penfield, W. (1958). The Excitable Cortex in Conscious Man. Liverpool: Liverpool University Press.

Peters, R.S. (1958). The Concept of Motivation. London: Routledge & Kegan Paul.

Peterson, K. & Wilson, J.J. (1978). Women Artists. London: The Women's Press.

Piaget, J. (1971). Structuralism. London: Routledge & Kegan Paul.

Pilbeam, D. (1972). The Ascent of Man. New York: Macmillan.

Platonov, K. (1959). The Word as a Physiological and Therapeutic Factor. Moscow: Foreign Languages Publishing House.

Pleck, J.H. & Sawyer, J. (eds) (1974). Men and Masculinity. London: Prentice-Hall.

Pollak, J.M. (1979). Obsessive-compulsive personality: A review. Psychological Bulletin, 86, 225-241.

Pompa, L. (1975). Vico: A Study of the 'New Science'. Cambridge: Cambridge University Press.

Popper, K.R. (1935). Logik der Forschung. Vienna.

Popper, K.R. (1959). The Logic of Scientific Discovery. London: Hutchinson.

Popper, K.R. (1963). Conjectures and Refutations. London: Routledge & Kegan Paul.

Popper, K.R. (1972). Objective Knowledge. Oxford: Clarendon Press.

Popper, K.R. (1977). Materialism transcends itself. In K.R. Popper & J.C. Eccles (eds), The Self and Its Brain. London: Springer International.

Porter, L.W. & Lawler, E.E. (1968). Managerial Attitudes and Performance. Homewood, Illinois: Irwin.

Power, R. (1976). A Model of Conversation. Unpublished working paper, University of Sussex, Department of Experimental Psychology.

Premack, D. (1977). Intelligence in Ape and Man. Hillsdale, New Jersey: Lawrence Erlbaum.

Prigogine, I, (1965). Steady states and entropy production. Physica, 31, 719-724.

Pylyshyn, Z.W. (1973). What the mind's eye tells the mind's brain: A critique of mental imagery. Psychological Bulletin, 80, 1-24.

Pylyshyn, Z.W. (1978). Computational models and empirical constraints. Behavioral and Brain Sciences, 1, 93.

Rachlin, H. (1976). Behavior and Learning. San Francisco: Freeman.

Radley, A. (1976). The student's use of personal constructs. Bulletin of The British Psychological Society, 28, 250 (abstract).

Rapoport, A. (1958). Various meanings of theory. American Sociological Review, 52, 927-988.

Rapoport, A. (1966). Conceptualization of a system as a mathematical model. In J.R. Lawrence (ed.), Operational Research and the Social Sciences. London: Tavistock.

Rappaport, R.A. (1971). The flow of energy in an agricultural society. Scientific American, 225, 116-132.

Rappoport, J., Davidson, W.S., Wilson, M.N. & Mitchell, A. (1975). Alternatives to blaming the victim or the environment: Our places to stand have not moved the earth. American Psychologist, 30, 525-528.

Razran, G. (1971). Mind in Evolution. Boston: Houghton Mifflin.

Reiche-Dolmatoff, G. (1976). Cosmology as ecological analysis: A view from the rain forest. Man, 11, 307-318.

Richards, A.I. (1970). Socialization and contemporary British anthropology. In P. Meyer (ed.), Socialization. London: Tavistock.

Richards, M.P.M. (1974). First steps in becoming social. In M.P.M. Richards (ed.), The Integration of a Child into a Social World. Cambridge: Cambridge University Press.

Robinson, W.P. & Arnold, J. (1975). The question-answer exchange between mothers and young children. European Journal of Social Psychology, 7, 151-164.

Romanes, G.J. (1887). Mental Evolution in Man. London: Murray.

Rose, J. (1978). The Perfect Gentleman. London: Hutchinson.

Rosenblueth, A., Wiener, N. & Bigelow, J. (1943). Behaviour, purpose and teleology. Philosophy of Science, 10, 18-24.

Rosenthal, R. (1967). Covert communication in the psychological experiment. Psychological Bulletin, 67, 356-367.

Rosenthal, R. (1978). How often are our numbers wrong? American Psychologist, 33, 1005-1008.

Rowan, J. (1973). Review of I.L. Child: Humanistic Psychology and the Research Tradition. British Journal of Psychology, 64, 647-648.

Rowe, D. (1971). Poor prognosis in a case of depression as predicted by the repertory grid. British Journal of Psychiatry, 118, 297-300.

Rozin, P. (1976). The evolution of intelligence and access to the cognitive unconscious. In J.M. Sprague (ed.), Progress in Psychobiology and Physiological Psychology, vol. 6. New York: Academic Press.

Rubinstein, D. (1977). The concept of action in the social sciences. Journal for the Theory of Social Behaviour, 7, 209-236.

Russell, B. (1926). On Education. London: Unwin.

Rutter, M. & Madge, N. (1976). Cycles of Disadvantage: A Review of Research. London: Heinemann.

Rutter, M., Maughan, B., Mortimore, P. & Ouston, J. (1979). Fifteen Thousand Hours: Secondary Schools and Their Effects on Children. London: Open Books.

Ryan, T.A. (1958). Drives, tasks and the initiation of behavior. American Journal of Psychology, 71, 74-93.

Ryan, T.A. (1970). Intentional Behavior, an Approach to Human Motivation. New York: Ronald Press.

Ryle, G. (1949). The Concept of Mind. London: Hutchinson.

Salmon, P. (1970). A psychology of personal growth. In D. Bannister (ed.), Perspectives in Personal Construct Theory. London: Academic Press.

Salmon, P. (1978). Doing psychological research. In F. Fransella (ed.), Personal Construct Psychology 1977. London: Academic Press.

Sanborn, D.A. (1971). The Language Process. The Hague: Mouton.

Savage-Rumbaugh, E.S., Rumbaugh, D.M. & Boysen, S. (1978). Linguistically-mediated tool use and exchange by chimpanzees. Behavioral and Brain Sciences, 1, 539-554.

Schachter, S. & Singer, J.E. (1962). Cognitive, social and physiological determinants of emotional state. Psychological Review, 69, 379-399.

Schaule, R.C. & Abelson, R.P. (1977). Scripts, Plans, Goals and Understanding. Hillsdale, New Jersey: Lawrence Erlbaum.

Schlegel, W.S. (1966). Die Sexualinstinkte des Menschen. Munich: Retten Verlag.

Schrödinger, E. (1948). What is Life? Cambridge: Cambridge University Press.

Schuman, H. & Johnson, M.P. (1976). Attitudes and behavior. Annual Review of Sociology, 2, 161-207.

Schutz, A. (1932). The Phenomenology of the Social World. London: Heinemann.

Schutz, A. (1964). The stranger: An essay in social psychology. In A.
    Brodersen (ed.), Studies in Social Theory (Collected Papers, II). The
    Hague: Nijhoff.
Schwab, D.P., Olian-Gottlieb, J.D. & Heneman, H.G. (1979). Between-subjects
    expectancy theory research: A statistical review of studies predicting
    effort and performance. Psychological Bulletin, 86, 139-147.
Schwebel, M. & Raph, J. (eds) (1974). Piaget in the Classroom. London:
    Routledge & Kegan Paul.
Schweitzer, S.O. & Smith, R.E. (1974). The persistence of the discouraged
    worker effects. Industrial and Labor Relations Review, 27, 249-260.
Scott, M. & Lyman, S.M. (1968). Accounts. American Sociological Review, 33,
    46-62.
Segal, H. (1964). Introduction to the Work of Melanie Klein. London: Hogarth
    Press.
Segal, H. (1979). Klein. London: Fontana-Collins.
Seligman, M.E.P. (1974). Helplessness. San Francisco: Freeman.
Sennett, R. (1974). The Fall of Public Man. Cambridge: Cambridge University
    Press.
Shallice, T. (1978). The dominant action system: An information-processing
    approach to consciousness. In K.S. Pope & J.L. Singer (eds), The Stream
    of Consciousness: Scientific Investigations into the Flow of Human
    Experience. New York: Plenum Press.
Shallice, T. & Warrington, E.K. (1970). Independent functioning of verbal
    memory stores: A neuropsychological study. Quarterly Journal of
    Experimental Psychology, 22, 261-273.
Shannon, C.E. & Weaver, W. (1949). The Mathematical Theory of Communication.
    Urbana: University of Illinois Press.
Shapere, D. (1964). The structure of scientific revolutions. Philosophical
    Review, 73, 383-394.
Sheppard, H.L. & Herrick, N.Q. (1972). Where Have All the Robots Gone? New
    York: Free Press.
Sherrington, C.S. (1906). The Integrative Action of the Nervous System. New
    Haven: Yale University Press.
Shotter, J. (1973). Acquired power: The transformation of natural into
    personal powers. Journal for the Theory of Social Behaviour, 3, 141-156.
Shotter, J. (1974). The development of personal powers. In M.P.M. Richards
    (ed.), The Integration of the Child into a Social World. Cambridge:
    Cambridge University Press.
Shotter, J. (1975). Images of Man in Psychological Research. London: Methuen.
Shotter, J. (in press a). Vico, moral worlds, accountability and personhood.
    In P. Heelas & A.J. Lock (eds), Indigenous Psychologies: Implicit Views of
    Mind and Human Nature. London: Academic Press.
Shotter, J. (in press b). Action, joint action and intentionality. In M.
    Brenner (ed.), The Structure of Action. Oxford: Blackwell.
Simon, H.A. (1957). Models of Man. New York: Wiley.
Simons, E.L. (1972). Primate Evolution. New York: Macmillan.
Simpson, G.C. (1949). The Meaning of Evolution. New Haven: Yale University
    Press.
Singh, J. (1966). Great Ideas in Information Theory, Language and Cybernetics.
    New York: Dover Publications.
Skinner, B.F. (1948). Walden Two. New York: Macmillan.
Skinner, B.F. (1968). The Technology of Teaching. New York: Appleton-
    Century-Crofts.
Skinner, B.F. (1969). Contingencies of Reinforcement: A Theoretical Analysis.
    New York: Appleton-Century-Crofts.
Skinner, B.F. (1971). Beyond Freedom and Dignity. New York: Knopf.
Skinner, B.F. (1972). Beyond Freedom and Dignity. London: Cape.

Skinner, B.F. (1973). Answers for my critics. In H. Wheeler (ed.), Beyond the Punitive Society. London: Wildwood House.

Skinner, B.F. (1974). About Behaviorism. New York: Knopf.

Sloman, A. (1978). The Computer Revolution in Philosophy: Philosophy, Science and Models of Mind. Hassocks, Sussex: Harvester Press.

Sloman, A. (1979). What about their internal languages? Behavioral and Brain Sciences, 1, 602-603.

Smail, D. (1977). Psychotherapy: A Personal Approach. London: Dent.

Smedslund, J. (1978). Bandura's theory of self-efficacy: A set of common sense theorems. Scandanavian Journal of Psychology, 19, 1-14.

Smedslund, J. (in press). Between the analytic and the arbitrary: A case study of psychological research. Scandanavian Journal of Psychology.

Smith, G. & James, T. (1975). The effects of pre-school education: Some American and British evidence. Oxford Review of Education, 1, 223-240.

Solomon, R.L. & Corbitt, J.D. (1974). An opponent-process theory of motivation. 1. Temporal dynamics of affect. Psychological Review, 81, 119-145.

Sonstroem, A.M. (1966). On the conservation of solids. In J.S. Bruner, R.R. Olver & P.M. Greenfield et al. (eds), Studies in Cognitive Growth. New York: Wiley.

Sorrentino, R.M. & Sheppard, B.H. (1978). Effects of affiliation-related motives on swimmers in individual versus group competition: A field experiment. Journal of Personality and Social Psychology, 36, 704-714.

Spiegelberg, H. (1960). The Phenomenological Movement: A Historical Introduction. The Hague: Nijhoff (2 vols).

Staddon, J.E. (1975). Learning as adaptation. In W.K. Estes (ed.), Handbook of Learning and Cognitive Processes, vol. 2. Hillsdale, New Jersey: Lawrence Erlbaum.

Staddon, J.E.R. & Simmelhag, V.L. (1971). The 'Superstition' experiment. A re-examination of its implications for the principles of adaptive behavior. Psychological Review, 78, 3-16.

Starr, C. (1971). Energy and Power. Scientific American, 225, 36-49.

Stokols, D. (1975). Toward a psychological theory of alienation. Psychological Review, 82, 26-44.

Stout, G.F. (1896). Analytic Psychology. London: Swan Sonnenschein.

Strasser, S. (1963). Phenomenology and the Human Sciences. Pittsburgh-Louvain: Duquesne University Press.

Strauss, A. (ed.) (1956). The Social Psychology of George Herbert Mead. Edited with an introduction by A. Strauss. Chicago: University of Chicago Press.

Strauss, A. (ed.) (1964). George Herbert Mead on Social Psychology: Selected Papers. Revised and enlarged edition. Chicago: Phoenix Books.

Suls, J.M. & Miller, R.L. (eds) (1977). Social Comparison Processes: Theoretical and Empirical Perspectives. New York: Wiley.

Suppe, F. (1977). The Structure of Scientific Theories, 2nd ed. Urbana: University of Illinois Press.

Susman, G.I. & Evered, R.D. (1978). An assessment of the scientific merits of action research. Administrative Science Quarterly, 23, 582-603.

Sussman, G.J. & McDermott, D.V. (1972). Why conniving is better than planning. AI Memo 255a. Cambridge, Massachusetts: MIT AI Laboratory.

Sutherland, N.S. (1970). Is the brain a physical system? In R. Borger & F. Cioffi (eds), Explanation in the Behavioural Sciences. Cambridge: Cambridge University Press.

Sutherland, N.S. (1975). Trapped in the box. British Association for Behavioural Psychotherapy Bulletin, 3, 54-57.

Swanson, J. (1966). On models. British Journal for the Philosophy of Science, 17, 297-311.

Tajfel, H. (1974). Social identity and intergroup behaviour. Social Science Information, 13, 65-93.

Tajfel, H. & Fraser, C. (1978). Introducing Social Psychology. Harmondsworth: Penguin.

Taylor, C. (1964). The Explanation of Behaviour. London: Routledge & Kegan Paul.

Taylor, R. (1966). Action and Purpose. Englewood Cliffs, New Jersey: Prentice-Hall.

Teuber, H.L. (1955). Physiological psychology. Annual Review of Psychology, 6, 267-294.

Thibaut, J.W. & Kelley, H.H. (1959). The Social Psychology of Groups. New York: Wiley.

Thomas, W.I. & Znaniecki, F.C. (1918). The Polish Peasant in Europe and America. Boston: Badger. (Five volumes: 1918-1920.)

Thorpe, W.H. (1969). Retrospect. In A. Koestler & J.R. Smythies (eds), Beyond Reductionism. London: Hutchinson.

Thurstone, L.L. (1947). Multiple factor analysis. A development and expansion of the vectors of the mind. Chicago: University of Chicago Press.

Tizard, B., Carmichael, H., Hughes, M. & Pinkerton, G. (in press). Four year olds talking to mothers and teachers. Monographs of the Journal of Child Psychiatry and Psychology.

Todd, N. (1977). Religious belief and personal construct theory. Unpublished PhD thesis, University of Nottingham.

Tolman, E.C. (1932). Purposive Behavior in Animals and Man. New York: Appleton-Century-Crofts.

Tolman, E.C. (1951). A psychological model. In T. Parsons & E.A. Shils (eds), Toward a General Theory of Action. Cambridge, Massachusetts: Harvard University Press.

Tolson, A. (1977). The Limits of Masculinity. London: Tavistock.

Toulmin, S. (1974). Rules and their relevance for understanding human behaviour. In T. Mischel (ed.), Understanding Other Persons. Oxford: Blackwell.

Toulmin, S. & Goodfield, J. (1965). The Discovery of Time. London: Hutchinson.

Tragesser, R.S. (1977). Phenomenology and Logic. Ithaca: Cornell University Press.

Tribus, M. & McIrvine, E.C. (1971). Energy and information. Scientific American, 225, 179-188.

Truax, C.B. & Carkhuff, R.R. (1964). Significant developments in psychotherapy research. In L.E. Abt & B.F. Reiss (eds), Progress in Clinical Psychology. New York: Grune & Stratton.

Turing, A.M. (1950). Computer machinery and intelligence. Mind, 59, 433-460.

Turner, M.B. (1967). Psychology and the Philosophy of Science. New York: Appleton-Century-Crofts.

Tyler, L. (1978). Individuality: Human Possibilities and Personal Choice in the Psychological Development of Men and Women. London: Jossey-Bass.

Underwood, G. (1978). Strategies of Information Processing. London: Academic Press.

Vaihinger, H. (1924). The Philosophy of 'As If': A System of the Theoretical, Practical and Religious Fictions of Mankind. Translated by C.K. Ogden. London: Routledge & Kegan Paul.

Van Lawick-Goodall, J. (1974). In the Shadow of Man. Glasgow: Collins.

Verplanck, W.S. (1955). Since learned behavior is innate, and vice versa, what now? Psychological Review, 52, 139-144.

Vickers, G. (1973). Motivational theory - a cybernetic contribution. Behavioral Science, 18, 242-249.

Von Bertalanffy, L. (1973). General System Theory. Harmondsworth: Penguin.

Von Cranach, M. (1980). Action in Interactive Situations. In M. von Cranach (ed.), Approaches to the Study of Goal Directed Action. Cambridge: Cambridge University Press.

Von Frisch, K. (1954). The Dancing Bees. London: Methuen.

Von Neumann, J. & Morgenstern, O. (1944). Theory of Games and Economic Behavior. Princeton: Princeton University Press.

Von Wright, G.H. (1971). Explanation and Understanding. London: Routledge & Kegan Paul.

Vroom, V.H. (1964). Work and Motivation. New York: Wiley.

Vygotsky, L.S. (1962). Thought and Language. Cambridge, Massachusetts: MIT Press.

Wahlsten, D. (1972). Phenotypic and genetic relations between initial response to shock and rate of avoidance learning in mice. Behavior Genetics, 2, 211-240.

Walker, E.L. (1973). Psychological complexity and preference: A hedgehog theory of behavior. In D.E. Berlyne & K.B. Madsen (eds), Pleasure, Reward, Preference. New York: Academic Press.

Walkerdine, V. & Sinha, C. (1978). The internal triangle: Language, reasoning and the social context. In I. Markova (ed.), The Social Context of Language. Chichester: Wiley.

Wallace, W.A. (1974). Causality and Scientific Explanation, vol. 2. Ann Arbor, Michigan: University of Michigan Press.

Walsh, K.W. (1978). Neuropsychology: A Clinical Approach. Edinburgh: Churchill Livingstone.

Walters, M. (1978). The Nude Male: A New Perspective. London: Paddington Press; Harmondsworth: Penguin, 1979.

Waly, P. & Cook, S.W. (1966). Attitude as a determinant of learning and memory: A failure to confirm. Journal of Personality and Social Psychology, 4, 280-288.

Ward, J. (1886). Psychology. Encyclopaedia Britannica, 9th ed.

Warnock, G.J. (ed.) (1962). Sense and Sensibilia (J.L. Austin). Oxford: Oxford University Press.

Warr, P.B. (1973). Towards a more human psychology. Bulletin of The British Psychological Society, 26, 1-8.

Warr, P.B. (1976). Theories of Motivation. In P.B. Warr (ed.), Personal Goals and Work Design. Chichester: Wiley.

Warr, P.B. (1977). Aided experiments in social psychology. Bulletin of The British Psychological Society, 30, 2-8.

Warr, P.B. (1978). Attitudes, actions and motives. In P.B. Warr (ed.), Psychology at Work. Harmondsworth: Penguin.

Warr, P.B. & Wall, T.D. (1975). Work and Well-being. Harmondsworth: Penguin.

Warren, N. (1978). Freudians and Laingians - The Naturalisation of False Consciousness. Encounter, March, 56-63.

Wason, P.C. (1968). Reasoning about a rule. Quarterly Journal of Experimental Psychology, 20, 273-281.

Watson, D.L. & Tharp, R.G. (1972). Self-Directed Behavior: Self-Modification for Personal Adjustment. Monterey, California: Brooks/Cole.

Weber, M. (1947). Theory of Social and Economic Organisation. (English translation.) London: Free Press.

Weiner, B. (1972). Theories of Motivation: From Mechanism to Cognition. New York: Markham.

Weinreich, H. & Chetwynd, J. (1976). Ideology and social change: The case of sex-role stereotyping. Paper read at the XXII International Congress of Psychology, Paris.

Weiskrantz, L. (1968). Treatments, inferences, and brain functions. In L. Weiskrantz (ed.), Analysis of Behavioral Change. New York: Harper & Row.

Weiss, P.A. (1969). The living system: Determinism stratified. In A. Koestler & J.R. Smythies (eds), Beyond Reductionism. London: Hutchinson.

Welford, A.T. (1968). Fundamentals of Skill. London: Methuen.

Welford, A.T. (1971). Christianity: A Psychologist's Translation. London: Hodder & Stoughton.

Wells, G. (1975). Language Development in Pre-School Children. Unpublished Report: University of Bristol.

Westland, G. (1978). Current Crises in Psychology. London: Heinemann.

Whitehead, A.N. (1932). The Aims of Education and Other Essays. London: Ernest Benn.

Whitehead, A.N. (1934). Written for the University of Chicago Press to help promote the publication of Mead's works.

Williams, J.D. (1954). The Compleat Strategist: Being a Primer in the Theory of Games of Strategy. New York: McGraw-Hill.

Williams, R. (1976). Keywords. London: Fontana.

Wilson, E.O. (1975). Sociobiology. Cambridge: Belknap Press.

Winch, P. (1958). The Idea of a Social Science and its Relation to Philosophy. London: Routledge & Kegan Paul.

Winograd, T. (1972). Understanding Natural Language. Edinburgh: Edinburgh University Press.

Witkin, H.A. & Goodenough, D.R. (1977). Field dependence and interpersonal behavior. Psychological Bulletin, 84, 661-689.

Wood, D.J. (in press). Teaching the young child - some relationships between social interaction, language and thought. In D. Olson (ed.), The Social Foundations of Language and Cognition. Essays in Honour of J.S. Bruner. New York: Norton.

Wood, D.J., Bruner J.S. & Ross, G. (1976). The role of tutoring in problem solving. Journal of Child Psychology and Psychiatry, 17, 89-100.

Wood, D.J. & Harris, M. (1977). An experiment in psychological intervention. Prospects, 7, 512-527. Paris: UNESCO.

Wood, D.J., Wood, H.A. & Middleton, D.J. (1978). An experimental evaluation of four face-to-face teaching strategies. International Journal of Behavioral Development, 1, 131-147.

Woodworth, R.S. (1931). Contemporary Schools of Psychology, 8th ed., 1949. London: Methuen.

Wright, C.J. & Nuthall, G. (1970). The relationships between teacher behaviors and pupil achievement in three elementary science lessons. American Education Research Journal, 7, 477-491.

Wright, M.C. (1940). Situated actions and vocabularies of motive. American Sociological Review, 5, 439-542.

Wundt, W. (1903). Grundzuege der Physiologischen Psychologie, 5th ed. Leipzig: Engelmann.

Wundt, W. (1916). Elements of Folk Psychology: Outlines of a Psychological History of the Development of Mankind. (Authorized translation by L. Schaub.) London: George Allen & Unwin.

Yankelovich, D. (1974). The meaning of work. In J.M. Rosow (ed.), The Worker and the Job. Englewood Cliffs, New Jersey: Prentice-Hall.

Zangwill, O.L. (1950). An Introduction to Modern Psychology. London: Methuen.

Author index

Note. Italic number indicates appearance of full reference in Bibliography.

Subject index